KT-177-651

Tower Hamlets College
Learning Centre

ES OF THE 2000

JÜRGEN MÜLLER (ED.)

MOVIES OF THE 2000s

IN COLLABORATION WITH
ddp images, HAMBURG

TASCHEN

ANYWHERE, EVERYWHERE
REFLECTIONS ON CONTEMPORARY CINEMA

A masterpiece – in black rubber and blood. A frenzied confusion of dark streaks, drawn by the boot heels of the man who now lies dead. Tracks without direction, without destination. Chaos. We are reminded, with some justification, of the works of Jackson Pollock, whose concept of "action painting" has been literally transposed by the Coen brothers. Furthermore, they show the creative process of the artist at work. His name is Anton Chigurh (Javier Bardem), who sets to work without warning: overpowering a policeman from behind, dragging him to the ground, and then strangling him with his own handcuffs. It is a fight to the death. Chigurh goes into an ecstatic trance as he works. He stares, wide-eyed, at the ceiling, enjoyment and effort reflected in his face. From its vantage point above, the camera observes this dance of the demon and his victim.

Notwithstanding the violence of his actions, Chigurh exhibits a high degree of concentration, using practiced hand movements. When the policeman's jugular vein bursts, he leans his head to one side to avoid the blood spurting into his eye. The work of art is only complete when his victim's final spasms have ceased. Chigurh lies on the floor, exhausted but satisfied. Afterward, he washes his own and the other man's blood from his wrists and cleans his blood-smeared sleeves, just as an artist might clean his utensils when his work is done.

The murder just described is one of the most powerful scenes in the film *No Country for Old Men* (2007); it catches the viewer completely off-guard. Joel and Ethan Coen's work was taken from the eponymous novel by Pulitzer Prize winner Cormac McCarthy and won no less than four Oscars: Best Film, Best Directing, Best Supporting Actor and Best Adapted Screenplay. *No Country for Old Men* and the artists involved also won numerous other awards, in both the United States and Europe.

Due to the demands of the medium, there are substantial differences between McCarthy's text and the Coen brothers' film. What links them fundamentally, however, is their laconic style. Acts of particular violence are presented in a manner so prosaic that they could be everyday activities. At the same time, we have to realize just how ambitious is the novel on which the film is based, whose title is taken from a verse in the 1928 William Butler Yeats poem, "Sailing to Byzantium." McCarthy's book uses literary history as a backdrop in a similar way to which the Coen film references the traditional western and its images. We are dealing with two instances of a spiritual journey, each of which involves a moral reckoning.

John Ford's country

The film *No Country for Old Men* tells the story of a brutal chase. In so doing, the thriller reveals a reality that is no longer being lived in harmony with its values and traditions. The movie is fundamentally critical of American society. And if its critique succeeds in giving us food for thought, it is down in no small measure to the character of the sheriff, Ed Tom Bell (Tommy Lee Jones). Ed Tom is a man of few words – which is precisely why he represents a moral authority. He is the real hero of the film, although this is not immediately obvious. Having said which, *No Country for Old Men* begins with his voice, before any images appear. We watch a black screen and listen to his narrative telling us how long he has been sheriff; how things used to be. He ends by grumbling about the changes through the generations and how he doesn't understand the world any more. All his familiarity with it has been lost. The conclusion of his speech is depressing: how can the law be enforced when people no longer have any concept of justice?

Even before the action has begun, it is clear the sheriff is powerless in the face of evil. From his perspective, the situation is paradoxical and absurd, but precisely for this reason he abdicates any moral responsibility, unable to offer any defense. This is why Ed Tom resigns his job at the end of the movie. When he recalls that he and his father were "pretty proud" of having held the same job at the same time, he is talking about the value of the office and the sheriff figure as a symbol of justice. He finds it hard to believe now that some of the old time lawmen never wore a gun.

From a formal point of view, the film's sketched beginning is important for the narrative, as it creates both proximity and distance. We hear a voice, without knowing who it belongs to, as if someone is speaking from the past. As the monologue proceeds, we see shots of the Texas desert as the sun slowly rises. As long as it is hidden behind the horizon, the images remain dark, giving only a hint of the landscape. Gradually, however, it gets light; we discover a sublime land in myriad shades of red and ochre and gain a sense of its vastness. We feel that we are witnessing a creation. If we initially thought we were seeing a world without people, windmills and fences show signs of civilization. The film *No Country for Old Men* begins slowly and poetically. It is as if time emerges together with the daylight, speeding everything up and setting the pace of life. Yet the images of landscape only serve to define the timeless space in which the story unfolds. The voiceover falls silent when the action proper begins.

The film's classic visual language and fluent narrative style captivate us from the start. Roger Deakins' photographic technique is so restrained that we are free to devote all our attention to the action. Moreover, *No Country for Old Men* has one special, processual feature: the camera appears to approach its subject, but this is then revealed as the forward movement of someone who eventually comes into shot. The aim is to render transparent the aesthetic boundary to the viewer, ostensibly dissolving the distance from the film's action; as such, it communicates both proximity and distance. The look of cars and clothes may also locate us in 1980, but the boundary separating past from present is removed through this clever device. The

film is happening in the here and now! Aside from that, the cinematography makes us aware of the pace of movement; of the slow progress made in the desert.

The use of lighting is just as stunning as the camera work. The contrast between inner and outer space is clearly articulated, reminiscent in some shots of the well-known opening and closing scenes of John Ford's *The Searchers*, a film made in 1956 and arguably the most famous western in film history. A relatively large number of scenes take place in dark interiors, thus requiring an artificial source of light. As a result, daylight takes on an abrasive quality. It dissolves the objective nature of the world. We find ourselves in the heat of Texas, one of the US states to which the country owes its most fundamental founding myths: that of the pioneers forging westward, bringing civilization and law to the inhospitable expanses of the Wild West.

Hunters and tracks

The shots of the scenery described here are reminiscent of western movies – apart from a sheriff arresting a man and taking him down to the jailhouse in his car. A ramrod-straight highway cuts through the landscape, marking out his route. The murder described above takes place in the sheriff's office. Film aficionados may be reminded of Hitchcock's *Torn Curtain* (1966), which stretches a murder scene out over four minutes in order to show how strenuous and time-consuming it is to kill a person. While Hitchcock films the murder as a gruesome event, the Coens surprise us with the sudden arrival and uncontrollable power of evil. This murderer knows his trade and his perfection of it gives him pleasure, as becomes obvious in the sequences that follow.

We see Chigurh after he has escaped from the sheriff's office, stopping a car with the police siren so that he can get hold of a vehicle that is not suspect. He kills the bewildered driver with a cattle gun. It is a technique that robs the victim of his humanity, dealing with him like a beast for slaughter. We then cut to a view through a telescopic sight at grazing antelopes. The hunter takes his time lining up the shot – "you hold still" he murmurs quietly to himself – and hits the target, though the wounded animal manages to escape. It becomes clear to the viewer that we are dealing with two hunters, neither of whom gives their prey a chance. But one of them is hunting – slaughtering – people.

The hunter with the 'scope is Llewelyn Moss (Josh Brolin), whom we initially take to be the real hero. When he follows the wounded antelope, he comes upon the scene of a drug deal gone wrong and finds a suitcase with two million dollars inside. The people involved in the drug deal are all dead, apart from a seriously wounded Mexican who begs Moss for water. The shots are cleverly constructed in such a way that a kind of cinematic palimpsest is created. When we look down with Moss onto the plain from a knoll, it is as if thousands of buffalo are moving across the prairie. And

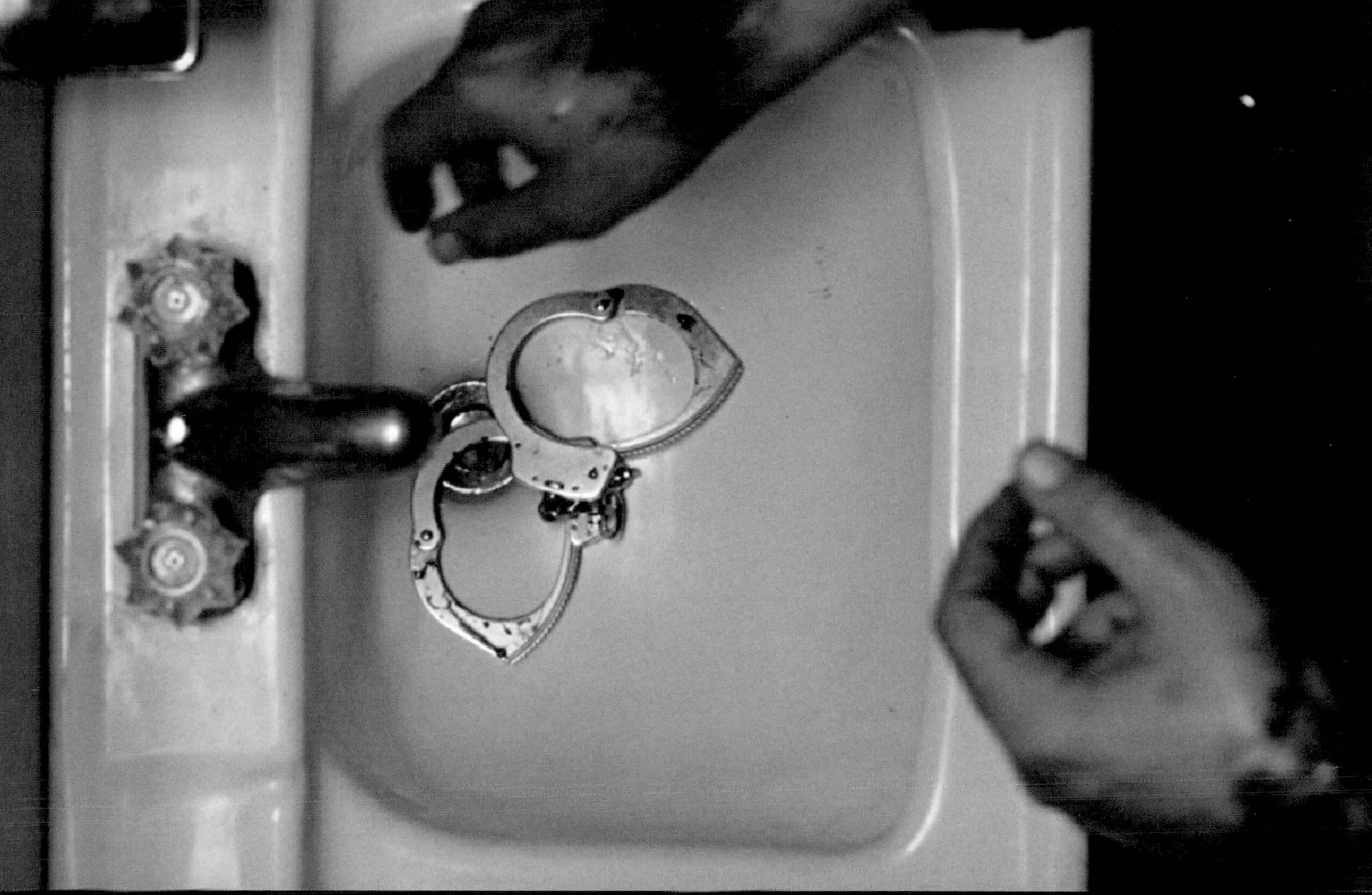

when he approaches the vehicles in the next shot, we get the impression of a wagon train that has been attacked by American Indians. Even the motif of the dying man who has survived seems familiar, reminding us of Ford's *3 Godfathers* (1948)

After going home to his wife Carla Jean (Kelly Macdonald), Llewelyn's guilty conscience pricks him into going back to the scene at nightfall. But just as he attempts to give the dying Mexican some water, he is discovered by the drug dealers and only narrowly manages to escape. The film steadily gathers pace, reaching its first climax in the chase. From now on, Moss finds himself confronted with contract killer Chigurh, who remains doggedly on his heels in order to get the money back for the Mafia. Following an exchange of gunfire, in which both men are badly injured, Moss manages to flee to Mexico. He is tracked down there by another bounty hunter called Wells (Woody Harrelson), who is however shot dead by Chigurh shortly afterward.

The pursuit engaged in by these two hunters, Moss and Chigurh, is stylized in the form of a duel. The Coen brothers draw parallels between the actions of both men, who could not be more different. The opponents keep searching for blood traces on the ground, looking for signs of the adversary's presence. It is as if hunting is the basic model of American culture that immediately emerges when a mere scratch is made in the surface of civilization. At one point, the contract killer is described in the film as a ghost: a direct pointer to perceiving him as an allegory of death. Anyone who meets and sees him is in extreme danger. Only an attendant at an isolated gas station in the desert and a trailer park employee survive an encounter with this sinister man.

Following Wells' death, Moss tells his wife to go to El Paso, but the Mexican gangsters find out about the meeting place and kill him. Carla Jean has revealed her husband's whereabouts to Sheriff Bell, but he arrives too late. Llewelyn Moss lies dead in his hotel room. In the evening, Ed Tom visits the cordoned-off crime scene, where Chigurh is also hiding. He senses the danger and is unwilling to die as another instance of collateral damage on the murderer's path. This sequence is extremely important. When Ed Tom opens the door to the room, we see his silhouette against the wall, in the outlined shape of a gunman holding a revolver in a duel. The camera shows the killer behind the door, its lock removed by the bolt gun. The sheriff searches the room, goes into the bathroom, and establishes that the window is closed. Finally, he sits down on the bed. Nothing happens! There is no showdown, although it should have taken place. This suggests that the two men are not operating on the same level of reality: they seem incapable of encountering each other. In the end, Chigurh kills Carla Jean Moss. As he makes his escape, he is involved in an automobile accident, in which he once again sustains serious injury. The film should really end at this point, but it has an epilogue – of sorts.

The last scene shows the sheriff at home, talking to his wife over the dining table. He tells her about two dreams he has had. He squirms slightly to begin with, as if he finds it unpleasant to talk about. But then he relates that he met his father twice. In the first dream, he meets him in town and

receives money that he then loses. In the second, he is in the mountains. It is wintertime and the ground is covered in snow. His father rides past him, snuggled up in a blanket. He keeps a taper burning so that he can light a camp fire later. Apparently, he knows that his father will be waiting for him.

The meaning of this dream is unclear. The image of fire in winter is central, as it serves to give direction in the dark as well as give out heat. It can be construed as a symbol of hope, but also of aspiration. Is it not worth being the guardian of this fire? Even if the plot can be recounted in simple terms, the film still remains rather enigmatic. It defies any single interpretation. What is its real theme?

Tracks

No Country contains a series of motifs, the frequency of which suggests their significance. The ability to read tracks connects characters as different as Llewelyn Moss, Chigurh, Wells and Sheriff Bell. They all recognize the symbolic nature of what is real, and are able to interpret it. The metaphor of hunting is complex. In contrast to Europe, hunting in the USA is not a privilege, but instead represents a right of the free man. The scene in which we meet Moss for the first time can be seen in this light. Hunting is part of the American identity.

The mise-en-scène of the sequence in which the contract killer breaks into his victim's trailer is especially powerful. As he goes inside and looks around, the camera imitates his analytical eye. When he sits on the sofa, we see who sat there before. The views of the bed and inside the refrigerator operate in a similar way. It is uncanny how close he seems to be to the people he is pursuing. He sees through Moss, and ends up taking the money away from him.

Finding and avoiding tracks are two sides of the same coin. Someone looking down at their own boots is an action mimicked by the camera several times. It is the look of a tracker who knows that every move can be read on the ground. For no obvious reason and apparently automatically, Moss picks up his bullet casing during the antelope hunt, so that he does not leave any tracks. Chigurh repeatedly avoids blood so that he does not leave any tracks himself; he throws his blood-stained socks away. His perfected avoidance of tracks is a recurrent theme: at the start of the film; during the hotel scene with Carson Wells when he puts his boots up on the bed; and at the end, when he checks outside the house whether there is any blood on the soles of his boots after killing Carla Jean.

The motif of money also plays a key role. Human aspirations are geared to this fetish. But it cuts a destructive path through society, and those who express an interest in it must pay with their lives. Money is a symbol of treachery. The transponder is hidden in the case, in the midst of some carefully arranged banknotes, leading the killer to Moss. Moss in turn offers the young men at the border five hundred dollars in the form of a blood-

stained banknote in exchange for a jacket to cover his wound. The musicians who take him to the hospital are rewarded just as generously for their help. By contrast, there are several scenes in the film showing the worthlessness of money. In studied vein, Chigurh opens the cover of the ventilation shaft with a coin in order to get the hidden money for himself.

The way the psychopathic killer is portrayed is central to the film's aesthetic power of persuasion. Javier Bardem's performance is a real tour de force. On the one hand his cruel, absolute nature makes him appear like an invincible, avenging angel. On the other hand, his precision and alertness mark him out as the perfect hunter. This man seems so superhuman that he might well have come straight from a nightmare or a horror movie, yet his depiction is not so exaggerated as to make him completely unrealistic. On the contrary: when he patches himself up again after exchanging shots with Llewelyn Moss, we marvel once more at his attention to detail, though now it also reveals his vulnerability. So it is not so much the killer's physical capabilities that are inhuman as his bizarre ethos. He does his job as if he were exacting revenge. The extreme form that his self-perception has taken in the process is demonstrated in the scene where he is crossing a bridge during the chase. He rolls down the window to shoot at a crow, which he misses. Every living thing has become his enemy.

If we consider once more the traditions of the western, we might imagine Chigurh as a half-caste. Throughout the film we keep seeing paintings showing American Indians in the interior shots, images of a lost civilization. Would it be excessive to read *No Country for Old Men* in this context as a pessimistic reflection on American history? Might Chigurh not be seen as the ghost of a repressed genocide that underlies the country's civilization? This would also explain his inhumane killing techniques. He indiscriminately slaughters his victims like cattle, robbing them of any identity, just as was done to the indigenous peoples. In this context, it is worth noting that he is the only central male figure who does not wear a cowboy hat. The theory that the past genocide has not been resolved is naturally a bold one. In this respect, the Coens have left a track. When the film has ostensibly finished and the credits start to roll, *No Country for Old Men* continues at the level of soundtrack: we hear a clock ticking, inextricably linked to the noise of a rattle, echoing the music of the American Indians.

Home of the brave

Nevertheless, the film seems in every respect a reflection of American identity. From this perspective, the year 1980 represents a time when America was completely at one with itself. On the surface, at least, everything in the world is OK. All the men wear cowboy hats and boots, and the automobiles are all American-made. Seen from this angle, we have here a period film with a meticulous approach to set design. Even the sheriff carries out his investigations on horseback. The TVs are the only things made by Hitachi, which seems an insignificant detail. Again and again, the film clearly

demonstrates that the people are part of American civilization, and defined by a collective identity. Moss is forced to get new clothes on several occasions. Every time he goes into a store, hats, boots and socks are presented to him in succession. To the salesman's question whether he would accept white socks, Moss replies that he *only* wears white! In the meeting between Wells and a senior Mafia representative, they are both wearing the same suit, but in different colors. The production detail clearly indicates a certain tendency to conform.

Two scenes also make reference to the Vietnam War. This effectively came to an end for American troops in 1973, although it was not until April 1975 and the fall of Saigon to the North Vietnamese that President Gerald R. Ford announced it as "a war that is finished as far as America is concerned." Moss, Wells and a guard at the Mexican border all make brief references to the war, though whether or not and how this is meant to connect them remains unclear. "So what does that make me, your buddy?" Llewelyn asks Carson Wells in the hospital, the latter apparently having made the effortless transition from colonel in the US army to bounty hunter.

The mise-en-scène of interiors could also be understood in the context of American collective psychology. The relationship between inside and outside space seems problematic in *No Country for Old Men.* They do not relate to each other but instead exist in a state of mutual independence. For this reason, the set design of rooms is significant, as the glorifying images and paintings of American history actually represent a distortion of the past. At any rate, it is noticeable how often the paintings show American Indians riding peacefully across valleys and prairies. Only at the end of the film, when Bell is visiting his uncle, do we sense that outdoor space is not being denied in this shabby dwelling, but literally represents part of the interior; in the same way that the portrayal of this man strikes us as particularly realistic as well. Confined to a wheelchair, he lives alone in the desert with his cats, attaching no importance to external approval. In *No Country for Old Men*, interior and external spaces pose the question of the inner and outer nature of human beings.

Parallels are drawn between the uniform styles of both motel architecture and clothing. On a related note, the Coens play with the motifs of doors and room numbers: we are constantly standing in front of and looking at doors, or seeing numbers that are designed to suggest a specific identity. Yet in reality it is far from clear what lies behind a number, as becomes evident in the course of the film.

The narrative style of *No Country for Old Men* is proof that we can no longer think of classic storytelling in terms of the western. Friendship and catharsis no longer exist as decisive motives. Money has corrupted co-operation between people. Instead of having a clear-cut hero and classic narrative, the killer and Moss are depicted with equal attention, just as if they were brothers. We may start off identifying with the latter, but in the end our hopes are dashed. He is characterized as homo faber, the constantly inventive craftsman who makes tools to help him escape. He represents a pragmatic world view based on purposeful rationality. The problem, however, is that his opponent behaves completely irrationally and thereby continues

to outclass him. He no longer distinguishes between people and utensils, the end justifying all means as far as he is concerned.

Perhaps we should even view Moss, Chigurh and Bell as facets of one and the same identity. The Coen brothers suggest as much with a processual hint. When Moss comes back from the desert, he finds his wife sitting in front of the TV and takes his place beside her. The sequence is filmed in such a way that it looks like a dialogue with the TV set. The reverse shot from the perspective of the TV shows the couple seated together on the sofa. We see the same sequence again, when Chigurh searches the trailer as part of his pursuit and takes a seat on the same piece of furniture. Once again, we see him from the TV's point of view, followed by his reflected view on the TV screen. We are presented with this visual sequence for a third time when the sheriff searches the trailer with his deputy.

In a formal sense, the scenes of Moss, Chigurh and Bell sitting in turn on the sofa in front of the TV suggest that they are more alike than we initially thought, which also implicates us as viewers in some way. Basically, they represent different aspects of a common identity. But what do these three protagonists epitomize? Moss might stand for the pursuit of happiness that will ultimately prove his downfall. Chigurh is a reminder to contemporary America of the massacre of Native Americans, by exacting an eye for an eye in his role as avenging angel. Ed Tom, on the other hand, is the most passive of the three characters. He embodies resignation and bewilderment in the face of circumstance. He is the only one who can to an extent counterbalance the present through values and role models.

Support for this reading of a multiple American identity comprised of the three men is found in the last fade in the film, which creates a contextual link between Chigurh's limping exit and the shot of the retired sheriff. They have both played their part. The dreams already described then follow. Yet while the first dream about losing money succinctly summarizes the entire plot of the film, the "father" in the second could be reminiscent of a figure from American Indian myth. This dream seems like an acknowledgement of original American roots – though not in the sense of glorifying folklore, as it appears in the many images of the indigenous peoples in the film – but as a memento to the dead. At any rate, what strikes us is how casual and yet emotional the sheriff's dream stories seem. Tommy Lee Jones is, without doubt, one of the most outstanding actors of our generation. His Texan origins may have played a part in casting him, and maybe also the fact that his grandmother came from the Cherokee tribe.

No Country for Old Men ends with Ed Tom Bell sitting in the dinette of his home. We see a profile of the prairie landscape through a window behind him, while the old man appears to be staring through a side opening into an imaginary place far away. The symmetrical composition of the image is immediately striking – it comes across as factitious and empty. On the right side of the wall there is a photo of a highway cutting through a barren mountainous landscape; beneath it, there is a lamp with an antique copper pot for a base. These objects could be interpreted as curious souvenirs of America's past.

The final sequence ostensibly represents both an ending and an anticipated new beginning. Values, however, cannot simply be conjured out of thin air. They are inextricably linked to an everyday life in which they are constantly tested and either assumed or rejected as part of a wider social consensus. If the Coen brothers' film is taken as a cultural statement, then it can also be seen as telling the story of an end to the exemplary status of western civilization, which has had its most powerful protagonist in the United States. The sense of mission and foreign policy initiatives of this country went hand in hand with its self-confidence as a freedom-loving nation whose role was to fight despotism and national chauvinism while bringing democracy and justice to the world. Yet this conviction seems somehow to have been lost during the second half of the twentieth century. Perhaps the most powerful symbol in this context is still the Vietnam War, which plays a significant role in *No Country for Old Men* even if mentioned only indirectly or as an apparent aside.

If the United States has increasingly lost its political authority since the Second World War, then this has also had repercussions for film production. The gradual decline in the aesthetic influence of American cinema is just one of the consequences. For decades, Hollywood was the most effective mouthpiece for the American way of life. Today, however, the naïve faith in the future and unshakeable optimism that was once disseminated by the Dream Factory now has a hollow ring to it. In the cold light of political reality, all the traditional indoctrination and ideological proselytizing of US cinema scarcely works any more. From today's perspective, the classic Western in particular looks very much like a propaganda instrument used to underpin the moral integrity of the American state.

Significantly, almost three years after *No Country for Old Men*, the Coen brothers directed *True Grit* (2010), a Western that just as unsparingly sweeps away American mythology. The story of young Mattie (Hailee Steinfeld) – who sets off into the wild with the decrepit US Marshal Rooster Cogburn (Jeff Bridges) and a vain Texas Ranger (Matt Damon) to bring her father's murderer to justice – is not a narrative about the establishment of a social order, but rather about its dissolution. The adaptation of Charles Portis' eponymous novel (already made into a film by Henry Hathaway in 1969, with John Wayne in the role of the Marshal) shows a country in which the state has by and large withdrawn, leaving greed and violence in charge. In the final analysis the real courage alluded to in the title lies less in proving oneself brave in a man-to-man fight than in breaking through the state of moral neglect and taking responsibility through one's actions.

The fact that the roughneck, hard-drinking US Marshal – played magnificently by Jeff Bridges – finally rises to the occasion by saving the girl's life is by no means a happy ending in which Cogburn is accepted into a community through his heroic deed. On the contrary, this is precisely what turns him into an exotic figure. In the epilogue, we discover that the old warhorse has spent the last 25 years of his life performing in a Wild West show, almost as a folklore exhibit. As Joel and Ethan Coen's movie is filmed from the perspective of reminiscence, an ever-present subtext to the images, Rooster Cogburn appears even more as a relic of the past. He

resembles Ed Tom Bell in this respect. Both are survivors of a bygone America, as well as the cinema of yesteryear.

The end of cinema

Media are finite too; and currently it does indeed seem as if the narrative and formal possibilities of cinema have been exhausted. It is hard to say at this time whether there can be a revival and, if so, how this would look. Whether 3-D technology can at least provide another economic boost will become clearer over the next few years. At this stage, the extent to which cross-media concepts have a future is equally impossible to predict – whether interactive computer games will continue the narrative potential of the feature film or whether interactivity can be successfully implemented in the cinema.

There is a good argument that the first decade of the 21st century will be the last in which cinema as a mass medium will continue in the form we have always known it. For a profound transformation is well under way. The mighty leaps in technology and media in recent years have already radically changed the way we receive film and our awareness of the cinematic image. This applies particularly to digitization, of course, which has shattered the moving image's photographic association with reality, though it retains the ability to convey an impression of it. On the one hand, this opens up unprecedented creative possibilities to film-makers; yet, as a direct result of the digital quantum leap, the feature film has now been replaced by video games – not just in terms of popularity with the younger generation, but also from an economic point of view. It would seem that it is hard to beat the attraction of interactivity combined with convincingly presented virtual reality.

Another factor equally as portentous for cinema is the steadily growing significance of "home cinema," which is increasingly marginalizing the traditional film theater as a place for experiencing media and making its mark on recent viewing habits. Thus, for example, television has had success with innovative series formats in harnessing a mass audience that has (to some extent, at least) deserted cinema. So, while the feature film is exposed in the public perception to growing competition from both computer games and TV series, cinema operators and film producers are faced with the added fact that, increasingly, large-screen TVs, video projectors and surround sound systems are ranking as standard in private households, considerably narrowing the gap between domestic film consumption and the big screen experience.

The replacement of VHS by digital technology has raised film viewing within our own four walls to a new level, and not just from a technical point of view. DVDs and Blu-ray discs also offer aficionados convenient access to specialized film knowledge. For some time now, versions have been available boasting the status of "classic editions" with extensive special extras menus, in a way that was previously familiar only in music

and literature. At the same time, vast quantities of movies have become available to a global public, or at least its affluent sections, pretty much on demand – whether as DVDs for rental or sale, or via downloads. Added to which, various internet portals have led to an explosion in the availability of moving images. Anyone with internet access has a massive store of film history at his or her fingertips. Paradoxically, however, this has not resulted in more canonization; rather, the canon has been eliminated. For the almost total availability of films – increasingly taken for granted – allows viewers to help themselves to precisely whatever they like. The result is that audiences are becoming progressively specialized and differentiated: in other words, fragmented.

While films used to be experienced collectively in a movie theater, this is becoming a rarer occurrence: the communal physical experience is gradually receding. With the help of digital social networks, a niche culture is also spreading within the sphere of film, in which even the smallest community has its own sample. As long as there remained a universally valid film canon, it was possible to perceive the history of cinema as a chronology of styles. Nowadays, cinema going back beyond the 1960s is virtually unknown to the younger generations. Using history as a classification system has given way to a coexistence of styles, genres and traditions – the chaotic synchronicity of the internet age. Admittedly, this brings with it considerable freedom of choice, but it also involves the danger of randomness. Whether you take a critical stance against these changes or grasp them as an opportunity, a collective film memory might soon belong to the past, given such developments. This does not mean that cinema will no longer exist, but its myth-creating power will have to be redefined; it will be transformed, become more multifaceted and will potentially disappear.

The digital revolution has not only led to the progressive perfecting of playback technology and made access to movies decidedly easier; it has also fundamentally changed recording options. Camcorders and handycams have to some extent led to a democratization of film-making that goes far beyond the vision of an anti-commercial cinema, as formulated pre-millennium by the well publicized Dogme 95 group. Film consumers nowadays are frequently amateur film-makers as well – and by no means just on a "primitive" level. This means that there are countless movies on the internet made by enthusiasts, in which cinematic role models are playfully associated and parodied.

Michel Gondry's *Be Kind Rewind* (2007/08) is a charming story about the world of these film fanatics who remake and replay their favorite movies, although in this film at least they use outmoded VHS technology. In the process, Gondry develops a poetry all his own, in which the possibility of fast forwarding and rewinding signifies both a condition and liberation of filmic images. It allows him to convey a sense of the creative potential and aesthetic heterogeneity of the constantly growing stream of amateur movies that are accessed on the internet in their millions across the globe each and every day. The success of these films is not measured by ticket sales or the storage media they use, but by the number of hits and user

ratings. In this way, a film scene has emerged in parallel with that of "industrialized" cinema: one that has its own unique rankings, stars and commercial strategies and now has a decisive influence on the daily media experiences of globalized youth.

Even if the various developments in film production outlined above have not left an equal mark, there is one definite outcome: cinema in the age of digitization and globalization has developed such diversity and so many possible variations that no one, in good conscience, can see the bigger picture any more. We are in the thick of it. Every statement we make already means taking sides and giving a perspective on an entity that can no longer be represented. Correspondingly, the following observations are not designed to cover all the developments in the past decade, but rather to sketch out some of the anomalies and trends. Simply by choosing *No Country for Old Men*, we have gone for an approach that attempts to describe the change that has taken place over the last ten years, with contemporary American cinema as its point of departure.

Anything goes

If we are to believe what Hollywood producers say, the cinema-going public has never been as unpredictable as it is today. In fact, unexpected box-office flops such as Frank Miller's star-studded comic adaptation *The Spirit* (2008) would seem to confirm this assessment, as do the disappointing returns realized by Nicole Kidman in a few films, despite her figuring among the most popular screen stars of today. As such, the constant trend of sequels, prequels and remakes can doubtless be seen as a sign of insecurity in a sector that lacks both good storylines and sure-fire recipes for success. While, on the one hand, the studios experienced difficulty in releasing formulaic hits, the maxim for the cinema during the past decade appeared on the other hand to be: anything goes. It could be a Western (*True Grit*), musical (*Chicago*, 2002), pirate movie (*Pirates of the Caribbean: The Curse of the Black Pearl*, 2003) or a chivalric film (*A Knight's Tale*, 2001) – just about every has-been genre was successfully updated, without any serious attempts being made to breathe fresh life into the forms.

Anything went. This already applied to star directors of the international auteur film which is, of course, only subject to a limited extent to the laws of the market. In this vein, Todd Haynes made the Douglas Sirk style melodrama (*Far from Heaven*, 2002) and Lars von Trier an experimental film with a star-studded cast (*Dogville*, 2003). Aleksandr Sokurov made a movie about Russian history (*Russian Ark / Russkiy kovcheg*, 2002) in a single tracking shot and Michael Haneke made a German tale of childhood without music and in black and white (*The White Ribbon / Das weiße Band*, 2009) – to name just four examples of the artistic diversity and formal perfection in film after the turn of the millennium. At the same time, these four films (one could also mention many others) led cinema to a logical conclusion: film-makers cannot actually go any further.

Even just these few examples give an insight into the way that a synchronicity of styles and genres (that hitherto existed in an historical context) has become a matter of course in the production of film as well as its viewing context. A director who films in black and white nowadays is therefore not automatically referencing film history. He or she is using a stylistic means that present-day cinema goers find neither particularly unconventional, nor radical, nor anachronistic. To an equally insignificant degree, a pirate movie does not necessarily imply a harking back to the costume film of the classic studio era. Since the turn of the new millennium, an historical or evolutionary consciousness seems, by and large, to have become increasingly alien to cinema. For this reason, too, it is extremely difficult to distinguish film waves, schools or fashions when compared with earlier decades.

Under attack

Anyone looking back on cinema in the first decade of the new millennium cannot but reflect on September 11, 2001: an event that gave a shocked global audience sitting in front of their TV sets the deeply disturbing sense of experiencing a disaster movie, live. For the terrorist attacks on New York and Washington signaled a particular turning point for US cinema as much as they did for the political arena.

Since the earliest days of Hollywood, one of its perfectly mastered disciplines has involved processing the American fear of an attack on home territory into entertainment – whether in the form of Westerns, thrillers, science fiction, war, disaster, fantasy or horror films. And, as at the peak of Cold War frenzy, threat scenarios were also extremely popular in the Dream Factory at the turn of the millennium: two such examples are Jerry Bruckheimer's naïve World War 2 epic *Pearl Harbor* (2001) and the thriller set in the present day, *The Sum of All Fears* (2002). The fact that the Al Qaeda attacks touched on a theme of US cinema seemed to trigger an even greater frenzy of activity among the players in Hollywood.

As an immediate response, film launches were postponed, while projects that seemed too sensitive in the context of the national state of shock were either shelved or re-written. For example, the cinema launch of Sam Raimi's *Spider-Man* (2002) was advertised in trailers before 9/11: these showed the superhero in action, in a large spider's web between the towers of the World Trade Center. When the film was eventually released in spring 2002, the Twin Towers only appeared for a second as a reflection in the protagonist's eyes. The producers did not want to ask any more of the audience. With a budget of around 140 million dollars, nerves were apparently raw.

The airplane attacks on the World Trade Center were acts of modern iconoclasm targeted at a major icon of western civilization. They also hit the most myth-laden landscape of American cinema alongside Monument Valley. Film-makers very quickly accommodated to the fact that the destruction of the Twin Towers was indelibly inscribed into the Manhattan skyline after

9/11. What was once such a self-conscious symbol of democratic America henceforth became an allegory for the crisis of western capitalism. Hence, in *Gangs of New York* (2002), Martin Scorsese showed the well known panorama in order to associate his blood-soaked epic about a 19th-century gang war with the American reality of the 21st century. The film draws to a close with a sequence reconstructing the transformation of the cityscape over the past 200 years in a stream of dissolves, ending with the image of the Twin Towers.

A few years later, Steven Spielberg chose the skyline with the Twin Towers as the background for a key scene in *Munich* (2005) – a suggestion that the thriller (about the Israeli secret service's relentless pursuit of the 1972 Olympic terrorists) should be understood as a reflection of the Bush administration's anti-terrorist policies. If nothing else, Spielberg's film tackles the issue of how far a society that is founded on respect for human rights can go in pursuit of terrorists. At the end of the day the violent deeds of the Mossad agents in *Munich* are barely distinguishable from those of the terrorists. If the 9/11 attacks challenged the USA as a political, as well as a cultural, leading power, it also meant that America's supremacy was brought into question by the images. Given the political climate fueled by conservative and reactionary forces in the country, many observers expected Hollywood to intervene in the war of images with a wave of patriotic war movies. But this did not happen. With an eye to the sensitized and anxious public worldwide, the studios probably shied away from the risk, on the one hand, of expensive flops, as war movies are big budget films; on the other hand, there was no mistaking the fact that large sections of the film industry were distancing themselves from the conservative administration.

Through the other person's eyes

Liberal Hollywood reacted to George W. Bush's war against terror by attempting to force open the "western" view of US cinema. This became particularly evident in a series of episode films that set out on a crusade against the ignorance, intolerance and lack of conscience of the West, ostensibly from an objective standpoint but actually with no less than holy rage – one of the few phenomena to take the form of a film wave in the decade. Paul Haggis' Oscar-winning drama *Crash* (2004) was one of the most successful of these multi-perspective films, linking several plot threads into a cross-section of Los Angeles, torn apart by ethnic conflicts, and ending in a fairytale finale. In a less emotionally charged way, Stephen Gaghan gave us the story about the global fight for oil in his political thriller *Syriana* (2005), in multiple perspectives verging on the chaotic.

What was surely the most ambitious episode film of the post 9/11 age was made, however, by Mexican director Alejandro González Iñárritu: in *Babel* (2006) he conveyed a fascinating impression of the tense cultural relations in the globalized world – not only in the expert way he set the diverse location scenes in California, Mexico, Morocco and Japan, but also

by allocating parts to lesser known actors and non-professionals of various nationalities on an almost equal footing to celebrities like Brad Pitt and Cate Blanchett. For all its formal complexity and elegant style, however, *Babel* suffered from a lack of analytical depth. It may be that this particular risk of the multi-perspective narrative was one reason why the euphoria about the episode film proved only a temporary phenomenon. More of a problem, at least from a commercial point of view, could well lie in the inability of this type of film to fulfill the need of the audience to identify with a story – certainly not to the extent that standard hero-centric narratives are able to do.

In the course of the decade, with questions being raised with increasing urgency about the success and legitimacy of Bush's war policy (even within the USA) and support for the government fading across the board, war made a comeback on US screens. Now, however, the films manifested a conspicuously skeptical and critical stance on the whole. They challenged the view of war as a reasonable political instrument and showed little interest in its ambiguous visual appeal. With his two-part film, *Flags of Our Fathers* (2006) and *Letters from Iwo Jima* (2006), Clint Eastwood – over 70 and still an outstanding American director – transposed the multi-perspective approach to the war movie genre, showing the notorious battle of Iwo Jima in the Pacific War firstly from the point of view of American, then Japanese, soldiers.

Kathryn Bigelow made a fantastic analysis of the psyche of male soldiers in her Oscar-winning masterpiece *The Hurt Locker* (2008), a war film that avoided any obvious taking of sides and moral judgment. The war seems to have become the sole reality for her protagonists: members of a special unit responsible for defusing bombs in Iraq. When the squad commander strides out in a weird, astronaut-style suit to defuse an explosive charge, there is nothing heroic about it any more. The camera sees a person completely alienated from civilian life, doing a Sisyphus job as ridiculous as it is deadly – a man who needs war like a drug. As in the post-Vietnam years, more and more movies reached the cinemas about men returning from war. Paul Haggis, a director and author involved in some of the decade's most memorable American films, successfully addressed the subject of the destruction of a young man's personality through the military intervention in a particularly powerful way in his army thriller *In the Valley of Elah* (2007). Remarkably enough, the plot concentrates wholly on the man's father, a retired military policeman played by Tommy Lee Jones, who sees his military-ethos-dominated world view completely shattered when he investigates the circumstances surrounding his son's death. At the end, this disillusioned old man with the strikingly furrowed face raises the Stars and Stripes – upside down – in front of his house: the symbol of a nation in crisis. Once again, Tommy Lee Jones embodies a man who stands for the values of old America. By putting him center stage, Haggis not only focuses on the inner sensibilities of America; this way, he also gets around the need to visualize the son's traumatic experiences in greater detail – a decision that was often evident in movies dealing with the wars in Iraq and Afghanistan. The horror of war was very rarely portrayed in concrete terms in the past decade, most likely also in the knowledge that the destructive effect of real-life videos posted

on the internet, showing hostage executions, torture or targeted killings of civilians, were far more disturbing than any fiction. The brutalization of images in the wake of 9/11 was achieved to the greatest extent without any input from cinema. It is noticeable just how fervently film-makers set about reflecting and questioning the myth of the soldier hero from unusual angles. This certainly applied to films dealing with the war against Hitler's Germany too – for this was the last legitimate war conducted by the nation in the eyes of many Americans. Hence in *Valkyrie* (2008) Tom Cruise slipped into a German army uniform to play Hitler's would-be assassin, von Stauffenberg. Despite this odd take on the genre, however, Bryan Singer's thriller failed to breathe fresh life into it – quite unlike Quentin Tarantino's movie-quoting battlefield, *Inglourious Basterds* (2009). Throwing historical accuracy and political correctness to the wind, Tarantino let loose an American-Jewish hit squad in German-occupied France, with the remit to collect as many Nazi scalps as possible: a tasteless, extremely gory (but also highly original and liberating) Gothic tale about the World War that provocatively inverted the customary perpetrator–victim axis. No doubt about it – seldom has a director been more entertaining than Tarantino in dispatching the myth of the soldier as the decent combatant fighting for good.

Paranoid

Recalling the past decade of cinema, it becomes blatantly obvious that a whole series of movies did evoke the events of September 11 to a greater or lesser extent – such as Peter Jackson's classic remake *King Kong* (2005) or the pseudo-documentary monster movie *Cloverfield* (2007), which were both located in Manhattan – but at the same time we are still to get the Big Hollywood Movie about the national trauma of 9/11. Oliver Stone had a go at it, and failed: in the final analysis, *World Trade Center* (2006) was no more than a melodramatic disaster movie that remained trapped formulaically in the genre. It did no justice to the impact of this unique event.

Paul Greengrass' *United 93* (2006) was a far more convincing attempt: it reconstructed the fate of the fourth hijacked passenger plane of 9/11 that crashed in the open in Pennsylvania in circumstances that have never been completely clarified. It is an extremely moving drama, filmed by Greengrass in semi-documentary style; a typical example of the visual realism that increasingly found its way into mainstream films after the turn of the millennium. One of the reasons why *United 93* worked so well could also lie in the fact that the film visualized a subsidiary location of 9/11 that had hardly been represented in the media at all due to a lack of documentary footage, unlike the events in New York. So, instead of competing directly with authentic images, Greengrass' film was in some way filling a visual vacuum. While American cinema struggled with a direct approach to the events of 9/11, film-makers grappled all the more intensely with the social and political

consequences of the attacks. In the face of wars in Afghanistan and Iraq, as well as Abu Ghraib, Guantanamo, Halliburton and Blackwater, liberal minds in Hollywood seemed to be increasingly reminded of the scandal-surrounded administration of Richard Nixon. So, as the new millennium dawned, the Dream Factory proved more politically energized than it had been since the 1970s, as New Hollywood film-makers portrayed the shock waves unleashed on home territory by Vietnam and Watergate. George Clooney became the symbolic figure of new American political cinema that settled accounts with the Bush administration, sometimes directly and sometimes through innuendo, depicting the deeply rooted unease in US society and calling for a moral regeneration in the land.

The second directorial work from the screen star was the black and white *Good Night, and Good Luck* (2005), paying homage to the famous journalist Ed Murrow in the form of an intimate play. During the communist witch-hunt of the early 1950s, Murrow defied the notorious senator, Joseph McCarthy, making Clooney's film an unequivocal challenge to a government that exploited the spreading fear of terrorism to restrict civil liberties.

Cinema of the 1970s found a new lease of life most clearly in paranoia thrillers that were filled with a deep mistrust of political leadership. Films like Tony Gilroy's *Michael Clayton* (2007) with Clooney in the title role, or Jonathan Demme's remake *The Manchurian Candidate* (2004) suggested that the country was threatened less by external enemies – by President Bush's sworn "axis of evil" – than from within, by unscrupulous politicians and state institutions that operate secretly as executive agents for powerful economic interests and big business. As in the 1970s' models for the genre, the investigative journalist was the archetypal hero in these thrillers: an incorruptible bloodhound with unerring instincts, like Russell Crowe's long-haired Cal McAffrey character, bloated from excessive whiskey consumption, in Kevin Macdonald's *State of Play* (2009). He is forced to work with a young online editor who plays it straight, making him seem even more like the last of a species becoming extinct, a representative of the old analogue world. In this way, the movie also deals *en passant* with the subject of the escalating competition between old and new media, an analogy with the position of cinema and the internet.

In *Zodiac* (2007) a reporter hooks up with a cartoonist and policeman in pursuit of a publicity-craving killer who puts coded ads about his murders in a daily newspaper. The intensity of David Fincher's creepy detective movie about a real-life series of murders in San Francisco and the Bay area in the 1960s and '70s is caused not least by the fact that the killer's identity remains vague, and seems to take shape only in the deliberations and utterances of the investigators; he is like a news phantom that only exists in the media, an even stronger manifestation of everyone's suppressed fear that the real threat originates in the midst of society.

Previously, Fincher had given us a claustrophobic thriller in *Panic Room* (2002), which raised the issue of the paranoia of middle-class America. Critics interpreted the film's title – the name of its main location, a bunker-like private secure room that turns out to be a trap – as an allegory about cinema. It could just as easily form the caption for the decade in cinema.

The faltering hero

As both writer and director, Tony Gilroy was one of the formative figures of new paranoia cinema. Based on Robert Ludlum's best-selling novels, he also created the protagonist who was to make his mark on the action movie after the turn of the millennium: Jason Bourne. And, like no other screen hero in the decade, Bourne gave form to America's identity crisis – the man with no memory, who gradually realizes that he has been trained by the CIA at some point to become the perfect killing machine.

With his all-American aspect, Matt Damon proved to be perfectly cast in the role of the agent who is forced to acknowledge that he has killed for an organization with totally obscure objectives – one that has been infiltrated by traitors, as is finally revealed. So, in the Bourne trilogy (2002, 2004, 2007), the CIA comes over as a threatening and anonymous power that strives for total control and has no scruples whatsoever in liquidating the agents who have outlived their usefulness. It is a negative, or at least ambivalent, portrait of the secret service, characteristic of the decade that is also reflected in Stephen Gaghan's *Syriana* (2005) or Robert De Niro's *The Good Shepherd* (2006).

The Bourne films set the benchmark above all through their breathtaking visual style, taken to extremes by Paul Greengrass who directed the second and third parts of the trilogy. In *The Bourne Supremacy* (2004) and *The Bourne Ultimatum* (2007), rapidly changing perspectives and locations and a constantly moving, documentary-style, hand-held camera created the nightmarish impression of an unstable, totally interconnected world; one without authoritative values, where the legitimacy of state action has been fundamentally shaken, and where there is virtually no chance of objective knowledge, with every semblance of safety turning out to be a mere illusion.

While the episode films attempted to describe the crisis of the globalized world objectively by incorporating different angles, an opposite approach was expressed in the films that made the hand-held camera their most important stylistic device. They showed the shattered American identity effectively from the inside. The view of the swaying camera corresponded to that of the faltering hero: the rug was visually pulled from under his feet, along with the legitimacy of his actions.

Faced with the crazy tempo of blockbuster films like *Bourne* with their emphasis on action, a whole series of minor US movies consciously slowed the pace, taking a more fundamental look at the life plans and lifestyles of perfectly normal American citizens. A charming example of this "slow cinema" is Jonathan Dayton's and Valerie Faris' *Little Miss Sunshine* (2005), a quaint family tale in the form of a satirical road movie with its critical sights set on the grotesque world of beauty pageants.

This indie movie's overwhelming popularity with audiences can undoubtedly be explained by its tongue-in-cheek humor and empathy with the quirky main characters. This does not, however, alter the film's essentially bleak conclusion, painting as it does a picture of a country that is economically depleted, morally bankrupt and yet driven by a clinical belief in success. Jason Reitman's

high-octane tragicomedy *Up in the Air* (2009) is also devoted to the absurd nature of the American Way of Life: George Clooney takes center stage as businessman Ryan Bingham, who travels across America by plane to conduct redundancy talks on behalf of a consultancy firm, though his real interest in doing so is to collect the highest number of air miles he can.

What is interesting is that even in *Up in the Air* – a film that basically conforms to the traditional hero story format – we find striking changes in perspective. For Reitman contrasts his amoral protagonist's (initially) vacuous existence with the situation of real US citizens affected by redundancy who are given a voice in the form of short statements. Reitman's film, developed before the actual start of the economic crisis, also reflects the flawlessly smooth surface of the traditional, star-based cinema that often seems as far removed from the real lives of ordinary people as his air-miles collector.

The interruptions in continuity referred to in the fictional story of *Up in the Air* were certainly nothing unusual in a cinema decade in which the demarcation between fiction and non-fiction film was generally becoming less fixed. This trend certainly became most evident in the use of the pseudo-documentary, hand-held camera already alluded to and which is now employed with monotonous regularity: it allowed even big budget films to approximate more closely to the documentary, something that was still a rarity in the 1990s.

On the other hand, documentary film-makers now use fairly standard elements of the feature film in order to boost the appeal and powers of persuasion of their productions.

Michael Moore's huge success, as a director whose polemical documentaries have made him a symbol of the anti-globalization movement and American counter-culture of the Bush era, can be explained at least in part by this trend.

Real fiction

Now, as we know, a tendency toward realism in times of political and economic crisis is nothing new, in certain areas of cinema at least. In the decade just ended, however, the way that many film-makers played around with reality and fiction, the authentic and the fake, was particularly noticeable. In this vein, comedian Sacha Baron Cohen took the investigative drive of a Michael Moore to absurd levels in his "mockumentary" *Borat: Cultural Learnings of America for Make Benefit Glorious Nation of Kazakhstan* (2006). The movie's hit-and-run style admittedly has a fresh, new look on-screen, but the film-makers resorted to a device that they had already tested extensively on TV. To this extent, *Borat* might also be taken as an indication that cinema is increasingly drawing on the successful formulae of its media competitor in order to appeal to a younger audience. Recent series formats like *Twilight* (2008–2012) are further evidence for this.

At a time when the computer has long been established as a multimedia unit, the transitions between the different media are, almost inevitably,

proving seamless. In this respect, the growing crossover of genres such as the documentary and feature film can also be explained by behavioral changes in media users. In fact, the mixed film form is altogether becoming the rule: in modern animation films, cartoon characters act quite naturally in front of real backgrounds and alongside "real" actors. A documentary animation film caused a major sensation for the first time with *Waltz with Bashir* (*Vals im Bashir*, 2008). And it is becoming almost a given that actors do not just move around on screen in locations that are computer-generated, but are themselves digitally reworked in post-production. The separation of real-life films and animation movies now seems almost ridiculous.

Digital reality

Despite the moral outrage and sense of reality in many films, the Dream Factory naturally fulfilled its primary purpose as well, first and foremost in the post 9/11 period: providing mass global audiences with escapist entertainment, a job that Hollywood always carried out reliably especially in times of war and crisis. Indeed, blockbuster cinema at the start of the 21st century ventured into completely new fantasy worlds – facilitated by the digital revolution. Hence, without the technological quantum leap, the overwhelming success of the *Lord of the Rings* trilogy (2001, 2002, 2003), the *Harry Potter* series (2001–2011) or even the *Chronicles of Narnia* (2005, 2008, 2010) would be inconceivable. The door to high fantasy literature could only be unlocked for the "live-action movie" through the use of digital effects on a truly grand scale, drawing millions of fans into the motion-picture theaters.

A key attraction of these films was, of course, that they filled the huge multiplex screens with fabulous visual appeal: breakneck flights through the Hogwarts School of Witchcraft and Wizardry, for example, or the stunning landscapes of Middle Earth. The crowning glory of digital illusion, however, and a decisive improvement on the fantasy films of old was that mythical creatures now evolved into believable characters in a visual sense as well, thanks to motion capture technology. The figure of the schizophrenic gnome Gollum in Peter Jackson's *Lord of the Rings* has to be the most outstanding example of this.

The push in technology that swept the cinema did not just encourage film-makers to adapt fantasy novels, however – manga and graphic novels increasingly served as source material for live-action movies. So Tobey Maguire put on his Spider-Man costume and was brilliant as the superhero of the series, despite his slight build.

Batman, too, enjoyed a screen comeback under Christopher Nolan's direction, sparking a real hype with the compulsive gloom of *The Dark Knight* (2007), though this was undoubtedly intensified by the untimely death of Heath Ledger, the star who played the "Joker."

The film adaptation by Robert Rodriguez and Frank Miller of the latter's graphic eponymous novel, *Sin City* (2005), faithfully transposed

the comic's expressive neo-noir look using digital animation, outdoing both the Batman and Spider-Man series in flamboyance. Miller also provided the source material for Zack Snyder's controversial hit *300* (2006), a gory, highly artificial "sword-and-sandal" epic that some critics accused of a fascist-style cult of the body and glorification of violence; criticisms that were also raised when Snyder's *Watchmen* (2008/2009) was released. At the same time, however, this dark movie (based on the eponymous comic cycle by Dave Gibbons and Alan Moore) proved emphatically that graphic novels, which were regarded as un-filmable for a long time, could now be suitably adapted as well. Given the ever-escalating crisis in ideas in mainstream cinema, this opened up a drastically needed pool of material for Hollywood.

The new digital possibilities not only unleashed creativity, however; they also did the opposite by encouraging the unimaginative regurgitation of successful formulae. An expensive end-of-the-world epic such as Roland Emmerich's *2012* (2009) is a sharp reminder that film-makers often use digital technology solely as a means of perfecting the cinematic illusion. And while fantasy figures like Gollum from *Lord of the Rings* come alive in their strange way, many digital disaster scenarios wind up as soulless, computerized trash. Motion pictures such as *300*, which actually try to create an original digital aesthetic, are still the exception rather than the rule. It is equally rare for film-makers to find a suitable narrative structure for this aesthetic; one example, however, is Christopher Nolan, who fascinates with different levels of consciousness and reality in *Inception* (2010). As only a handful of other movies have done, this sci-fi thriller shows how any fantasy has the potential to be realized onscreen. Limits to digital cinema are indeed a thing of the past; everything can be represented. Anything goes.

Leaving aside the issues of artistic quality and originality, a twofold development is associated with the increased use of digital image creation. On the one hand, the persuasive power of the image inheres in its ability to construct an alternative world; in other words, the opportunity it gives the viewer to perceive reality in a new, yet equally convincing, way. On the other hand, a raft of digital image generation processes has made the viewer skeptical of special effects that have no truck with reality. Cinematic images present themselves as real, but this can no longer be relied on. And so, the question arises: how does the viewer actually perceive disaster movies, *2012*-style? Can digital epics like these convey any sense at all of the true horror of apocalyptic events? Given its digital potential, cinema now finds itself to some extent facing the widespread suspicion of being inauthentic. And this does not just apply to feature films; with documentary makers such as Michael Moore making more and more appearances in their own films, an obvious explanation is their desire to reassure the viewer that the images are authentic.

Faced with the digital wasteland emerging from vast swathes of entertainment cinema, some film-makers have discovered the charm of the "real thing:" the genuine nature of analogue film. The *Bourne* movies, for instance, are distinguished from standard, off-the-shelf action movies

by their systematic reliance on classic stunts and an aura of original location. The same counter-tendencies were also apparent in the way the stars were filmed. While, on the one hand, a merciless pressure to be flawless prevailed – whether through asceticism, personal training, Botox, scalpel or, if all else fails, digital post-production – cinema at the same time showed a conspicuous interest in real physicality. Mickey Rourke's memorable performance in Darren Aronofsky's *The Wrestler* (2008) is an extreme example of this; and, indeed, Russell Crowe's films are vibrant not least because of the almost anachronistic physical presence of their star.

Off into the unknown

The introduction of digital projection at the end of the decade finally provided cinema with the route to a new dimension. Many saw the beginning of the three-dimensional age of cinema in James Cameron's *Avatar* (2009) – a kind of cinema promising a totally new spatial film experience by projecting the viewer as it were into the filmic space. The fall from dizzying heights in the final battle of Cameron's 3-D movie signaled an unprecedented thrill in cinema, even prompting comparisons with the legendary Lumière brothers' film *Arrival of a Train at La Ciotat* (*L'arrivée d'un train à La Ciotat*, 1895). Following this logic, *Avatar* completes the circle with its link back to early cinema.

The belief that the digital rebirth of 3-D cinema (which had already made a brief appearance in the 1950s) would trigger a fantastic boom was also stimulated by the fact that Cameron's science-fiction fable breached familiar cinematic boundaries from a financial point of view as well. Within a few weeks, *Avatar* had out-grossed his earlier blockbuster, *Titanic* (1997) – up to that point, the most successful movie of all time. In the period that followed, however, no other 3-D film came anywhere close to matching *Avatar*'s success; this was doubtless because the film goes beyond the mere three-dimensional to fully explore the potential of digital film technology, as well as presenting a critique of civilization that, even if rather naïve, absolutely captured the spirit of its time.

The story may also come over as simplistic and reminiscent of a computer game, but the implicit desire for a completely new beginning, which means leaving the previous life behind, represents an ideal for our morally bankrupt culture. *Avatar* makes it possible to escape to a world in which there is only good or evil and where morality is part of a natural, original state. The lanky inhabitants of the moon Pandora are superior to human beings; not just physically, but morally as well. In this way, *Avatar*'s faraway world is a vehicle for Cameron's modern allegory of cinema as a locus of our desires.

If we think back again to the final shot in *No Country for Old Men*, to the image of the sheriff grown old, sitting in his dinette as if waiting for what is to come, then we are justified in coming to a sad conclusion. Since its beginnings, cinema has oscillated between escapism and realism. While films like *Avatar* may be defined by their attempt to replace and transcend

reality, the Coen brothers' film reminds us that movies draw on the mundane: they reflect what is real and existing.

The future – the thing that is invisible but will surely come – cannot ultimately be represented. If we interpret the wide window behind Ed Tom as a reference to a cinema screen, then the view of the vast, empty and desolate landscape seems tantamount to a look into the future – albeit according to the interior space in which we find ourselves. In this way, the shot conveys to us an idea of the vastness that is inherent in the premonition of farewell and an end to the cinema of old. This finite nature is hard to bear.

Jürgen Müller / Jörn Hetebrügge

BRIDGET JONES'S DIARY

2001 – UK / USA – 97 MIN. – COMEDY
DIRECTOR SHARON MAGUIRE (*1960)
SCREENPLAY HELEN FIELDING, ANDREW DAVIES, RICHARD CURTIS from the novel by HELEN FIELDING DIRECTOR OF PHOTOGRAPHY STUART DRYBURGH EDITING MARTIN WALSH
MUSIC PATRICK DOYLE PRODUCTION TIM BEVAN, JONATHAN CAVENDISH, ERIC FELLNER for LITTLE BIRD, STUDIO CANAL, WORKING TITLE FILMS.
STARRING RENÉE ZELLWEGER (Bridget Jones), HUGH GRANT (Daniel Cleaver), COLIN FIRTH (Mark Darcy), GEMMA JONES (Bridget's Mother), JIM BROADBENT (Bridget's Father), SHIRLEY HENDERSON (Jude), SALLY PHILLIPS (Shazza), JAMES CALLIS (Tom), PAUL BROOKE (Mr. Fitzherbert), FELICITY MONTAGU (Perpetua).

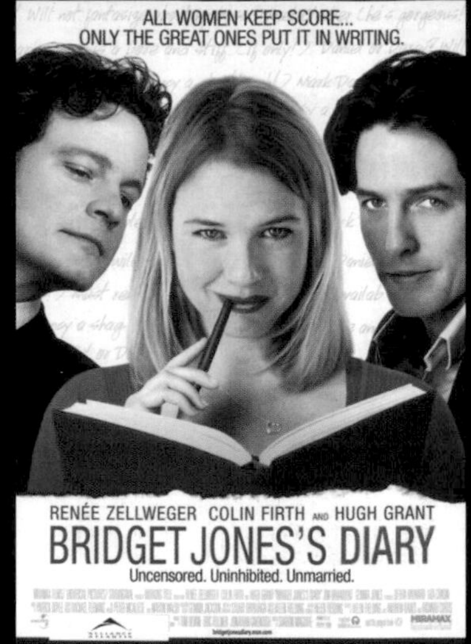

"To Bridget, who cannot cook, but who we love just as she is."

In an age when post-feminist singles literature was not yet stacked floor to ceiling in bookstores, a woman like Bridget Jones was still very much alone. This was someone who had had enough of the struggle and finally wanted a man – a disgrace to her sex. As millions of other females were going through a similar experience, however, Helen Fielding's collection of newspaper columns, "Bridget Jones's Diary," became a bestseller: the overweight cry-baby with massive ego problems became the darling of a whole generation of lonely hearts. Sharon Maguire's direction contributed in no small way to this success.

As the desperately unhappy, permanently single Bridget Jones, Renée Zellweger painted a wonderful portrait of misery. She cried her eyes out on the sofa, cuddling only a pillow and clutching her third glass, at least, of red wine. Bridget, who works for a small London publisher, is a woman with a big heart. But she is lonely, a victim of the metropolitan love economy with its inexorable rules of sexual selection. Other women are having their second child while her biological clock is still ticking. It's no wonder she smokes, drinks and eats too much. Her frustration gathers in the form of baby fat on her hips – at least in her own opinion of herself, which has plummeted as a result. Who on earth would want a wet blanket like her, who has lost her figure and has a butt "as big as Brazil?" Presumably not even the despicable Mark Darcy (Colin Firth), the arrogant lawyer her mother has chosen for her; and certainly not her boss, Daniel Cleaver (Hugh Grant), the repulsive womanizer who is shamelessly good looking. Bridget's pride would prohibit her anyway from falling for a creep like that. Instead, she prescribes herself a strict diet.

Unfortunately, embarrassing episodes are Bridget's specialty: after making a complete idiot of herself in front of Mark the first time they meet, she manages to repeat the process at a reception for the publisher's world-famous authors, including Salman Rushdie (playing himself). Her pride also leaves a lot to be desired. All Daniel needs are a few saucy emails to get her into bed. Ridiculous Bridget! In the end, both men actually end up fighting over her. The reason is obvious: Renée Zellweger, the plump girl with glowing cheeks and sweet double chin, is simply irresistible. Not in spite of, but because of, the 22 lb/10 kg the Hollywood star deliberately piled on in audacious method style. The

1

2

painfully skimpy outfits she squeezes into are just crying out to be ripped from her body – men are not complex creatures. Quite unlike the heroine of this movie, whose overall humor lies in the gulf between self-perception and actual appearance, Bridget also oozes that mixture of unmistakable British sarcasm and rank ignorance which also has its advantages on the marriage market. With her inimitable, pouting expression, Zellweger was perfect for bringing Bridget's complexes to life on the big screen, while also preserving the dignity of this ironic, fictional character. In 2001, she was diametrically opposed to Amélie – not elegantly French, but loud, coarse and undeniably sexual.

The fact that the sequel, *Bridget Jones: The Edge of Reason* (2004), did not have the same spark was mainly due to the absence of Hugh Grant as Daniel Cleaver. In *Notting Hill* (1999) he had played, as it were, the male

"Glory be, they didn't muck it up. *Bridget Jones's Diary*, a beloved book about a heroine both lovable and human, has been made against all odds into a funny and charming movie that understands the charm of the original, and preserves it." *Chicago Sun-Times*

3

1 Making a complete fool of herself: Bridget Jones (Renée Zellweger), the lowly publishing assistant with a big heart, is the queen of excruciating gaffes.

2 The one and only Darcy (Colin Firth): Mark's collection of horrendous knitted sweaters and lurid ties is a running gag in the film.

3 All by myself: Bridget wallows in self-pity on her lonely sofa. Will her single life never end?

4 Girl's fantasy: marrying her boss, Daniel, becomes Bridget's most cherished dream. Hugh Grant is brilliant as the notorious philanderer and heartbreaker.

counterpart to Bridget Jones: not as a wallflower, however, but as a dangerous charmer and heartbreaker. If he is the man for a night at the movies, then Colin Firth as the aloof Mark is the man for life. The audience may think him a bore, but his horrendous knitted jumpers are as much part of the running gags in the film as Daniel's unspeakably sexist jokes ("P.S. Like your tits in that top.") What's more, he is the one and only Darcy; the living proof of the reference's source. Fielding's book follows the long tradition of female confessional literature since the time of Jane Austen, with its eternal questions: why do women always have the choice between two evils in relation to men, and nothing else; and why do the chances of sex increase with the size and ugliness of the lingerie chosen for this purpose. Bridget's problems date back centuries, but seldom have they been expressed in such a frank and contemporary way. PB

5 Romance in the air: Bridget Jones, icon of a whole generation of lonely hearts, finally finds love with Mark.

6 Pouting and dieting: Renée Zellweger is perfectly cast as the weepy singleton in a big city. The actress put on over 20 lb / 9 kg for the part.

"Openhearted and girlish in some ways, canny and sophisticated in others, Bridget is entertaining even when in the deepest funk." *The New York Times*

COLIN FIRTH Actor Colin Firth (b. 1960) is a phenomenon of popular culture, for he can be seen to exist in two guises. Since the well-loved BBC mini-series *Pride and Prejudice* (1995), based on Jane Austen's classic novel, the whole world has come to identify him with the somewhat awkward, inexplicably lovable Fitzwilliam Darcy. Others have had a similar experience, but this Doppelganger developed a curious life of its own. Firth became the pin-up of literary female fantasy. So for the Mark Darcy role in the film version of *Bridget Jones's Diary* (2001), with its nod to the Jane Austen character, there could be only one candidate: Mr. Darcy, a.k.a. Colin Firth himself. As an ongoing in-joke, Bridget's unattainable, unattached heartthrob added his unique touch of irony to the film.

In his second identity, the national sex symbol leads a normal life as a respectable actor. Raised in an academic family in Nigeria, Firth had a successful debut in the critical film about a boarding school, *Another Country* (1984). His best-known roles include appearances in *Valmont* (1989), *The English Patient* (1996), *Fever Pitch* (1997), *Shakespeare in Love* (1998), *The Importance of Being Earnest* (2002), *Love Actually* (2003), *Girl with a Pearl Earring* (2003) and *Where the Truth Lies* (2005). He often plays the unlucky lover against rivals such as Rupert Everett, Hugh Grant, Ralph Fiennes and Joseph Fiennes. His moving performance in Tom Ford's stylistically breathtaking film adaptation *A Single Man* (2009) marked a break with this self-deprecating character. Colin Firth won an Oscar nomination for this role as a gay college professor mourning his dead lover.

AMÉLIE

LE FABULEUX DESTIN D'AMÉLIE POULAIN

2001 – FRANCE / GERMANY – 122 MIN. – COMEDY
DIRECTOR JEAN-PIERRE JEUNET (*1953)
SCREENPLAY GUILLAUME LAURANT, JEAN-PIERRE JEUNET
DIRECTOR OF PHOTOGRAPHY BRUNO DELBONNEL EDITING HERVÉ SCHNEID MUSIC YANN TIERSEN
PRODUCTION JEAN-MARC DESCHAMPS, CLAUDIE OSSARD for FRANCE 3 CINÉMA, STUDIOCANAL, TAPIOCA FILMS, VICTOIRES INTERNATIONAL, FILMSTIFTUNG, MMC INDEPENDENT GMBH, SOFICA SOFINERGIE 5.
STARRING AUDREY TAUTOU (Amélie Poulain), MATHIEU KASSOVITZ (Nino Quincampoix), RUFUS (Raphaël Poulain), LORELLA CRAVOTTA (Amandine Poulain), SERGE MERLIN (Dufayel), JAMEL DEBBOUZE (Lucien), CLOTILDE MOLLET (Gina), CLAIRE MAURIER (Suzanne), ISABELLE NANTY (Georgette), DOMINIQUE PINON (Joseph), URBAIN CANCELIER (Collignon), ARTUS DE PENGUERN (Hipolito), YOLANDE MOREAU (Madeleine Wallace).

"Maybe she is just different from the others."

Strange things happened in the spring of 2001: all over France, people flocked to the cinemas to be entranced by a funny little girl from the Paris district of Montmartre called Amélie Poulain (Audrey Tautou). She became the nation's darling overnight: her picture was plastered on every billboard and she even impressed the French President. The French had apparently gone mad, but Amélie marched on to further victories. Throughout the world, the sight of her awoke unprecedented feelings of happiness; no-one left the cinema without a smile on their face and, for a brief moment, everyone was French. Everyone, too, was infatuated with the previously unknown actress, Audrey Tautou. This French film increased the domestic share of the market to over 50 percent, while rents in Montmartre shot into the stratosphere.

The story of *Amélie*'s success can be told like the film itself – as a fabulous fairytale. Yet how does a film actually become the favorite of millions of cinemagoers? A dreamy leading actress with a sweet smile is certainly not enough. The other ingredients required are: suicidal goldfish; globetrotting garden gnomes; fake love letters; a secret casket; a whole album of useless passport photos; and all sorts of other whimsical notions. Whatever had been churning around in the head of the director, Jean-Pierre Jeunet, in the years leading up to his biggest success was worked through in this film. Ordinary things are transformed into pure magic when Amélie discovers them. When she returns the casket to the old man to whom it belonged as a child, she gives him back his youth; the love letters of someone presumed dead sweeten the memories for his widow and thus her whole life. But her greatest mission is to find the person who created the mysterious photo album: clearly a soulmate who collects peculiar things and loves coincidences like herself. Once she has found him (Mathieu Kassovitz), he has to take part in a complicated paper chase before getting his property back. Admittedly, this young woman wants to do the best for people, but for her the strategy is always closer to her heart than the objective, and the dream preferable to reality. One suspects that Amélie is a romantic, making her the loneliest person on earth until the happy ending.

Jeunet also pursues a similarly rigorous approach with the artificial look that characterizes his style. Using computer-generated, saturated colors, equally artificial cloudscapes and short focus, he created the postcard vision of Paris that so enchantingly illustrates the heroine's flight from reality: a postmodern nostalgia trip in crimson and apple green, from which all traces of the ugly and the ordinary have been erased. What Woody Allen did for Manhattan, Jeunet did for Montmartre. Nothing is real here, yet it is all "typically French." This also applies to the people who inhabit the artist's quarter, from the Impressionist painter with brittle bones who paints the same picture every

1
2

1 In Amélie's order of things, bed is only good for dreaming. This makes her the loneliest person in the world – until the happy ending.

2 Escaping reality to the dream world of cinema: and Amélie (Audrey Tatou) herself is the most beautiful projected image that cinema has to offer.

3 On the artificiality of images: each image was post-processed on computer for Jeunet's "postcard movie." The effect is both surreal and magical.

year, to the grouchy greengrocer, the jealous lover, the beggar with set working hours, the resolute bistro owner and the girl with strange preferences who works for her. There is no Pompidou Center, no McDonald's and no venal supermarket to disrupt the picturesque image of a Paris that is apparently immune to globalization. It was a stroke of paradoxical logic that Amélie herself became a global brand.

There was even a protest in Parliament against the flattering image of grim reality. By the same token, the Cannes Film Festival rejected the film on the grounds that it was "uninteresting." A classic error of judgment: Jeunet had simply undermined all expectations of what a "typically French" film should be. In fact, this was a Paris only known from the MGM Technicolor musicals; but, as Jeunet rightly pointed out, it was also taken from the poetic inter-war films of the likes of Marcel Carné or René Clair. By contrast, there was no end to the innovative way he transposed his countless ideas onto the screen: can anyone fail to empathize when the love-struck heroine deflates like a balloon after yet another missed opportunity? The skilled animator gives a grateful public what cinema has always excelled at – a little escapism, a slight elevation of everyday life and a shot of seductive sentimentalism. It would be difficult, moreover, to miss the irony in the last spoonful of sugar in this wonderful cupcake of a film. For what else can Amélie do? She takes the blind man by the hand and shows him the world in which she lives. PB

4 Grumpy greengrocer Collignon (Urbain Cancelier) is also part of the idealized world of Montmartre.

5 Even the trip round Paris with Nino (Mathieu Kassovitz) is just a dream. Amélie is too fond of her fantasies to face reality.

6 Pretty, cute and sassy: as Amélie, the previously unknown Audrey Tautou became the pin-up of a whole generation of filmgoers, and not just in France.

"*Amélie* is a fantastic jigsaw puzzle that dreams of being a real picture. The picture remains a copy, but the puzzle is an original." *Die Welt*

JEAN-PIERRE JEUNET Self-taught, Jean-Pierre Jeunet is one of the most visionary and innovative filmmakers of our time. There is no doubt whatsoever that Hollywood has benefited more from the Frenchman's ideas than the other way round. A genuine fantasist who started by making advertising and animated films, he creates magical parallel worlds – closed systems far removed from any realistic scenario – in movies like *Delicatessen* (1991) and, more recently, *Micmacs* (*Micmacs à tire-larigot*, 2009).

If he is occasionally accused of kitsch, then this kitsch is for the most part distinctly gloomy: his big break was *Delicatessen* (1991), a quirky nightmare vision of a post-apocalyptic world, in which a homicidal butcher supplies his tenants with human flesh. Its successor, *The City of Lost Children* (*La cité des enfants perdus*, 1995), also made with his regular collaborator Marc Caro, was even more bizarre and less amusing. His surrealist style is characterized by the use of extremely wide-angle lenses, as well as a cohort of actors that is underpinned by the unforgettably striking features of Dominique Pinon and Jean-Claude Dreyfus.

Most of his projects also share a remarkably long lead time. For *Amélie* (*Le fabuleux destin d'Amélie Poulain*, 2001), his most optimistic film to date, he apparently took 25 years. He had to delay it for the unpopular franchise sequel *Alien: Resurrection* (1997), an attention-grabbing debut for a Frenchman in Hollywood. The commercial success of both films made it possible for him to realize another pet project: *A Very Long Engagement* (*Un long dimanche de fiançailles*, 2004) is a tragic love story set in the trenches of World War I, unashamedly sentimental but with shocking images of actual war events. His protégée, Audrey Tautou, once again had the lead role.

MOULIN ROUGE!

2001 – AUSTRALIA / USA – 127 MIN. – MUSICAL
DIRECTOR BAZ LUHRMANN (*1962)
SCREENPLAY BAZ LUHRMANN, CRAIG PEARCE DIRECTOR OF PHOTOGRAPHY DONALD CALPINE
EDITING JILL BILCOCK MUSIC CRAIG ARMSTRONG PRODUCTION FRED BARON, MARTIN BROWN, BAZ LUHRMANN for 20TH CENTURY FOX, BAZMARK FILMS.
STARRING NICOLE KIDMAN (Satine), EWAN MCGREGOR (Christian), JOHN LEGUIZAMO (Toulouse-Lautrec), JIM BROADBENT (Harold Zidler), RICHARD ROXBURGH (The Duke), GARRY MCDONALD (The Doctor), JACEK KOMAN (The Unconscious Argentinian), MATTHEW WHITTET (Satie), CAROLINE O'CONNOR (Nini Legs-in-the-Air), KYLIE MINOGUE (The Green Fairy).
ACADEMY AWARDS 2002 OSCARS for BEST ART DIRECTION, Set Direction (CATHERINE MARTIN, BRIGITTE BROCH) and BEST COSTUME DESIGN (CATHERINE MARTIN, ANGUS STRATHIE).

"Here we are – now entertain us!"

Paris 1900; the camera is drawn as if by an irresistible force into the palace of sin, the Moulin Rouge, and the gates of Hell open onto the epitome of fin-de-siècle pleasure. The only question is, which century are we in? The cancan in this mythical venue is danced to a disco beat. Jacques Offenbach is no more, and the harsh riffs of Nirvana's "Smells Like Teen Spirit" penetrate the wickedly sensual harmonies of "Lady Marmalade." The paying customer recognizes the choreography of swirling dresses, camisoles, garters and legs, legs, legs, but its kinetic energy – amplified to dizzying effect by fast cutting – is like nothing we have ever seen before. Perhaps the turn of the century tends toward the decadent, but the real Moulin Rouge has never witnessed this level of escapism and excess.

Moulin Rouge! the movie with the exclamation mark, urging our utmost enjoyment of the experience. Dance, while you still can! A reference-crammed monster of a film, a pastiche of classical opera from "La Traviata" through "La Bohème" and countless contemporary pop songs, this musical crossover with elements of 2001 MTV appeared a little weird to many viewers. What was its point? With hindsight, Baz Luhrmann's ultimate homage seems like the last glittering vestige of a postmodern era that was not only enormously complicated, but also a lot of fun.

What is more, Luhrmann's anachronistic blend of pop culture and art nouveau makes absolute sense. *Moulin Rouge!* is the last part of his "Red Curtain Trilogy:" the audience already knows from *Strictly Ballroom* (1992) and *William Shakespeare's Romeo + Juliet* (1996) what to expect when the lights go down, and it is certainly not naturalism. We are meant to feel the way the Moulin Rouge presented itself to audiences in 1900 – as the latest thing, rather than a sedate nostalgia show, brought to us via the hits, popular tunes and dissolute morals of the present day. The celebrated rebirth of the musical, somewhat premature at that point, was indispensable for this purpose; but in the form of a completely artificial technical product – you rarely hear just one song at a time – Luhrmann's digital musical drama is above all a direct cinematic experience.

Does *Moulin Rouge!* have a heart? The story transports us into a magical underworld in which everything can be bought: the love of a courtesan, the paintings of Toulouse-Lautrec, or the rights to a hugely successful pop song. Penniless writer Christian (Ewan McGregor) becomes part of the Bohemian set in the Montmartre district of Paris, composing the musical within the musical ("Spectacular, Spectacular") with its denizens. The bohemian types around small-of-stature Henri de Toulouse-Lautrec (John Leguizamo) are the

1

"Images explode from the screen like corks from champagne bottles, working girls flirt with Jeans, and the dance halls are alive with the sound of music. You want innovation, look no further than this exercise in pop rock with its kitsch choreography, stunning camerawork and spastic editing. You want beef with your bearnaise, forget about it." *The Washington Post*

pop stars of their age; the link between the *demimonde* and high society. Naively, Christian falls in love with singer and courtesan Satine (Nicole Kidman), the glittering lucky star of Moulin Rouge impresario, Zidler (Jim Broadbent). They sing together – on the back of their bizarre elephant-house, which actually existed – a heart-rending medley of classics such as Elton John's "Your Song," "All You Need Is Love" by the Beatles and David Bowie's "Heroes." But Christian is forced to suffer. Zidler has promised (i.e., sold) Satine to another man long ago: the rich Duke (Richard Roxburgh). And she is dying: the consumptive courtesan and romantic poet are heroes, if only for a day. Satine dies, but Zidler's "Bohemian Rhapsody" knows no pity. The show must go on!

For Luhrmann does not take the classical love story of his bittersweet opera seriously, as love per se and the illusions we harbor about it. What, after all, are pop songs about? They are what move us to laugh or cry (culminating comically in Jim Broadbent's travesty of Madonna's "Like a Virgin.") And who

1 All you need is love: Satine (Nicole Kidman) the consumptive courtesan and Christian (Ewan McGregor) the romantic poet, in the longest MTV clip of all time.

2 The bohemian world laughs: art becomes pure pleasure – or simply the perfect show – in the eccentric group around the painter Toulouse-Lautrec (John Leguizamo).

3 Symbol of La Belle Époque: though the real Moulin Rouge arguably never witnessed the level of escapism and excess it does in Luhrmann's film.

4 Licentious activity: naive Christian realizes that Satine's love may be boundless but, more to the point, it can be bought. What's more, the star of the Moulin Rouge has long since been promised to someone else.

5 Up where we belong: the Moulin Rouge myth is alive and kicking through the film's wildly choreographed sequences. Nicole Kidman soars above it all as the terminally-ill singer.

"Another post-modern mix of myth, musical, comedy, romance and unfettered pastiche from the impressively inventive Luhrmann, here ransacking pop culture's iconographic archives – rather than the real Paris of 1900 – to mount a hyperkinetic update of the Orpheus myth." *Time Out Film Guide*

6

NICOLE KIDMAN In an age that is rich in celebrities and poor in stars, Kidman comes closest to the old ideal of the Hollywood icon. Flawless beauty, elegance and a height of almost 6 feet certainly did her no harm in her rise to become the highest paid female star in the film industry in 2006. Besides her good looks, however, Nicole Kidman was mainly convincing – for a time at least – through what appeared to be her uncanny feel for the right part. In saying that, the Australian actress with dual nationality struggled at first in Hollywood, appearing in half-baked movies like *Malice* (1993) and *Far and Away* (1992) alongside her husband Tom Cruise, in whose shadow she remained for a long time. She achieved initial artistic recognition in Gus Van Sant's extremely black media satire *To Die For* (1995). After Stanley Kubrick's thriller *Eyes Wide Shut* (1999), a film about a marriage in which he cast Cruise and Kidman as the couple, their relationship was at an end.

Their divorce unleashed undreamt-of energies: in breathless succession Kidman enjoyed artistic and commercial success with movies like *Moulin Rouge!* (2001), *The Others* (*Los otros*, 2001), *Dogville* (2003) and *Cold Mountain* (2003). Difficult projects like *The Human Stain* (2003) and *Birth* (2004) benefited from her credibility, which was often attributed to the open way in which she dealt with her unhappiness in love after separating from Cruise.

In other respects, Kidman gives the impression of being withdrawn and cool; yet she is a popular figure, as well as being an Oscar winner for the Virginia Woolf biopic *The Hours* (2002) in which she agreed to distort her looks with a fake nose. This was not enough to put the brakes on an ongoing rollercoaster of hits and flops, but more recently she has starred in Sidney Pollack's outstanding political thriller *The Interpreter* (2005) and Baz Luhrmann's sweeping national epic *Australia* (2008).

would ever have thought that Ewan McGregor and Nicole Kidman would not only harmonize beautifully, but actually be able to sing as well? Kidman was not just the star of the Moulin Rouge; the film turned her into an international movie star as well. Staggeringly beautiful, as remote as she was available, simultaneously ruined and lost, she was the perfect foil for this movie by her fellow Australian Luhrmann. Her red hair and red lips meld seamlessly with his lavishly applied color concept, reminiscent of the rich tones of Bollywood and old MGM movies. *Moulin Rouge!* is dangerous – less the rebirth than the unique reinvention of the musical, despite its enthusiastic successors like *Chicago* (2002). The movie transports us from reality as if on an absinthe high: rather like love, the "Green Witch" is addictive and renders us blind. PB

"*Moulin Rouge* the movie is more like the Moulin Rouge of my adolescent fantasies than the real Moulin Rouge ever could be. It isn't about tired, decadent people, but about glorious romantics, who believe in the glitz and the tinsel – who see the nightclub not as a shabby tourist trap but as a stage for their dreams." *Chicago Sun-Times*

6 Multicolor pop extravaganza and tragic operetta rolled into one: the dark Duke (Richard Roxburgh) intends to keep Satine in his clutches.

7 Homage to the moon: passing reference is made to the classic Méliès film *A Trip to the Moon* (1902) in a colorful kaleidoscope of art nouveau motifs.

8 Does *Moulin Rouge!* have a heart? The answer is as obvious as Luhrmann's good taste.

8

MULHOLLAND DRIVE

2001 – USA / FRANCE – 147 MIN. – DRAMA, PSYCHOLOGICAL THRILLER
DIRECTOR DAVID LYNCH (*1946)
SCREENPLAY DAVID LYNCH DIRECTOR OF PHOTOGRAPHY PETER DEMING EDITING MARY SWEENEY
MUSIC ANGELO BADALAMENTI PRODUCTION NEAL EDELSTEIN, TONY KRANTZ, MICHAEL POLAIRE, ALAIN SARDE, MARY SWEENEY for LES FILMS ALAIN SARDE, CANAL+, ASYMMETRICAL PRODUCTIONS, BABBO INC.
STARRING NAOMI WATTS (Betty Elms/Diane Selwyn), LAURA HARRING (Rita/Camilla), ANN MILLER (Coco Lenoix), JUSTIN THEROUX (Adam Kesher), DAN HEDAYA (Vincenzo Castigliane), ANGELO BADALAMENTI (Luigi Castigliani), PATRICK FISCHLER (Dan), MICHAEL COOKE (Herb), MARK PELLEGRINO (Joe Messing), MICHAEL J. ANDERSON (Mr. Roque), MELISSA GEORGE (Camilla Rhodes), MONTY MONTGOMERY (Cowboy).
IFF CANNES 2001 BEST DIRECTOR (David Lynch).

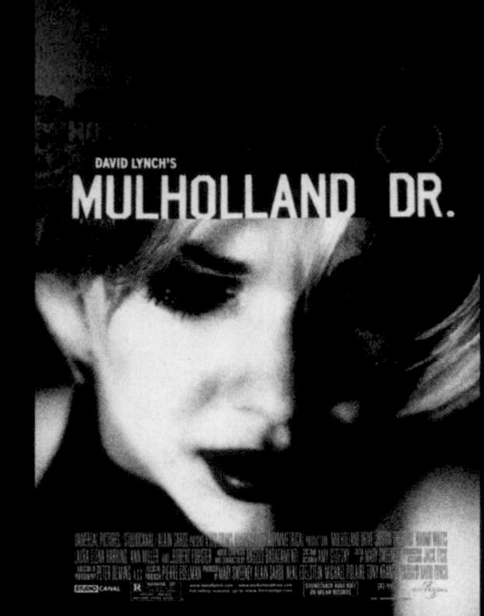

"Just like in the movies."

Mulholland Drive winds down from the hills into Los Angeles, the city of bright lights and angels. But David Lynch's streets, as already portrayed in *Lost Highway* (1997), lead straight to nowhere. Camilla (Laura Harring) must have forgotten this, along with everything else. A failed assassination attempt together with an accident followed by memory loss all result in her taking a shortcut through the bushes, down into the valley of glittering promise. But Mulholland Drive is to be her destiny. She will not find her identity; she is not even the leading lady.

The nascent star is Betty (Naomi Watts), a wide-eyed blonde who has just landed at the airport with the goal of taking Hollywood by storm. She finds the distraught Camilla in her aunt's apartment. Lacking a name, Camilla calls herself Rita, named for Rita Hayworth on a "Gilda" poster on the wall. In this movie, names are but smoke and mirrors; together with the roles played out, they change ownership at will. Yet Rita (suited to a cool brunette who is outwardly still a femme fatale) instinctively calls herself Betty in a film noir in which her first role is to uncover her true identity. But she never achieves her goal, while Betty's role in the film industry takes off as if in a dream: everyone loves the uncomplicated provincial beauty, while producers and casting agents hold their breath as she does her screen test. But the dream begins to dissolve. Why is there a sudden change of director during production?

How is it connected to the appearance of the "Cowboy," who urges the director to change the female lead at once? Evil omens begin to cloud the picture: another failed murder attempt, a monster behind the wall of a fast-food restaurant, a crazy theater somewhere in the underbelly of the city, and a blue key. Finally, the circumstances are reversed, with a look into the gaping depths of a box the same color of blue. Now Betty's name is Diane. She goes through hell, playing minor roles, working as a waitress in the fast-food restaurant, or as a prostitute. Camilla has the lead role and is now the director's lover instead. Death comes at the end. But what is a dream, and what is reality? And what do such concepts mean in a David Lynch movie?

The secret of *Mulholland Drive* lies, though only partly of course, in the history of its genesis. With its characters introduced at an infuriatingly slow pace and countless narrative strands that lead nowhere, the movie not only looks like a pilot for a TV series – that is precisely what it is. After the first run flopped – the series idea was similar to Lynch's groundbreaking production *Twin Peaks* (1990/91) – the TV company ABC pulled the production. Financed by a French company, a few sequences that had not been properly explained were re-shot. Since that time, no-one knows whether to mourn the lost series or whether to celebrate David Lynch's personal tragedy. For *Mulholland Drive* is a masterpiece.

1
2

3

1 Role-swapping: Naomi Watts and Laura Harring in David Lynch's enigmatic thriller about similarity, identity, and changing hair color.

2 Director's self-portrait: Adam Kesher (Justin Theroux) sees himself as the brilliant wheeler-dealer straddling art and commerce. The reality is somewhat different..

3 Humiliation Boulevard: director Adam faces unreasonable demands in the production meeting.

Nowhere has this darkest filmmaker of them all presented his themes in more glittering and cryptic fashion than here – the riddle of lost identity, Hollywood's surface beauty yet gloomy reality, the confusing play on similarities and role reversal. Two women with alternating hair color, two parts, and never-ending riddles: the pieces neither fit together, nor are meant to. Interpretations are still popping up on internet forums: the puzzle is put together in different ways, according to Freud's "dream logic" theory. But even dream logic is no more than a theory that founders in the face of Lynch's surreal worlds. It can suggest, but not explain. Furthermore, Freud didn't have a clue about Hollywood, unlike David Lynch who even reflected his own film's fate in the finished product: weird Hollywood moguls are enthroned behind glass panels, pulling or kick-starting projects as a result of Mafia conspiracies. The nightmarish distorted picture is not far removed from reality. No-one takes the expression "dream factory" more seriously than Lynch. Nevertheless, all is still "only an illusion." The audience has the same experience as Betty, who simply refuses to understand this lesson from the "Silencio" mystery theater. There, the illusion inheres in the mournful chants that are in fact just a recording. The wonderful plays of color and light, which make the film a real joy to watch, are also just an illusion: flickering, leaping, somnambulistic images – the morbidly glossy pipe dreams of a genius – dance out from the screen into the viewer's own head. "If you behave properly, you'll see me again; if you mess it up, you'll see me again twice," says the Cowboy to the director. Whatever thefilm David Lynch has made here, you want to revisit *Mulholland Drive* time after time.

PB

4

5

4 It begins at "Winkies": Camilla joins Betty (Naomi Watts) in the search for personal memories.

5 Disturbing game of deception: in the Hollywood Dream Factory, it has always been possible to swap names and roles. Camilla finds security in Rita Hayworth's glamour.

6 Nightmarish distortion of Hollywood reality: powerful movie moguls such as Mr. Roque (Michael J. Anderson) sit enthroned behind glass, pulling the strings.

7 Disturbing message: communications from the past fast become a nightmare.

"While watching *Mulholland Drive*, you might well wonder if any film maker has taken the cliché of Hollywood as 'the dream factory' more profoundly to heart than David Lynch. The newest film from the creator of *Blue Velvet* and *Twin Peaks* is a nervy full-scale nightmare of Tinseltown that seizes that concept by the throat and hurls it through the looking glass." *The New York Times*

NAOMI WATTS Apparently, she later said that she had come to Hollywood out of sheer naivety. So the dual role in David Lynch's *Mulholland Drive* (2001) seemed tailor-made for Naomi Watts. Yet she was convincing in it mainly because of her outstanding talent as an actor; no film fan will ever forget the screen test when she drives the whole of the casting crew to the brink of madness with her erotic intensity.
The Australian actress, born in England, had struggled along with a series of mediocre movies before this career breakthrough. She again reached a blockbuster audience with *The Ring* (2002), the remake of a Japanese horror classic. Since then, she has been part of the star elite who can choose high quality parts and improve their art in consequence. In Peter Jackson's remake *King Kong* (2005) she took over from the legendary Fay Wray, giving a convincing performance alongside the most masculine lead of all time. In her case the "Queen of Remakes" label should be regarded as an honorary title: the classic beauty of a Hitchcock blonde needs classic roles.
Yet it is preferable to see Naomi Watts in darker films. She was brilliant in, among others, Alejandro González Iñárritu's sensitive psychological drama *21 Grams* (2003),

Y TU MAMÁ TAMBIÉN
AND YOUR MOTHER TOO ...

2001 – MEXICO – 105 MIN. – TRAGICOMEDY
DIRECTOR ALFONSO CUARÓN (*1961)
SCREENPLAY ALFONSO CUARÓN, CARLOS CUARÓN DIRECTOR OF PHOTOGRAPHY EMMANUEL LUBEZKI
EDITING ALFONSO CUARÓN, ALEX RODRÍGUEZ PRODUCTION ALFONSO CUARÓN, JORGE VERGARA for ANHELO PRODUCCIONES.
STARRING DIEGO LUNA (Tenoch Iturbide), GAEL GARCÍA BERNAL (Julio Zapata), MARIBEL VERDÚ (Luisa Cortés), ANA LÓPEZ MERCADO (Ana Morelos), NATHAN GRINBERG (Manuel Huerta), VERÓNICA LANGER (María Eugenia Calles de Huerta), MARÍA AURA (Cecilia Huerta), JUAN CARLOS REMOLINA (Alejandro "Jano" Montes de Oca), SILVERIO PALACIOS (Jesús "Chuy" Carranza), DANIEL GIMÉNEZ CACHO (Narrator).
IFF VENICE 2001 Award for BEST SCREENPLAY (Alfonso Cuarón, Carlos Cuarón) and MARCELLO MASTROIANNI AWARD (Gael García Bernal, Diego Luna).

"The truth is cool, but unattainable."

Without any foreplay, the film begins with two sex scenes. This fits in with its young heroes, who think they're the greatest but still have a few things to learn. Tenoch (Diego Luna) is the pampered son of a corrupt Mexican politician; he leads a highly privileged life, which his middle-class friend Julio (Gael García Bernal) is only too happy to share. When their girlfriends leave on a European holiday, a horribly boring summer beckons. Until, that is, they get to know Luisa (Maribel Verdú) at a high society wedding: she is ten years older, and has a wonderful time with these loudmouths who have just turned seventeen. Recently betrayed by her husband, she accepts the two boys' fun offer of accompanying them on a spontaneous trip to the seaside. Her charms being very much in evidence, Tenoch and Julio are deliriously happy. So off they go, on a hot trip characterized by the cheerful interplay of youthful exuberance, female experience and, above all, three beautiful bodies. Adults are surprised at the explicit sexuality of *Y tu mamá también*, which gives adolescents just what they expect from American teen comedies: filthy jokes, acres of naked skin and an uninhibited tango of hormones. It is a summer road movie in the sun-drenched, dream landscape of Mexico with an excellent cast and stylish direction. There are plenty of poetic moments as well, like the exhilaratingly tender scene (done in one take) in which Luisa asks the bemused Tenoch to touch his penis before she seduces him using various stratagems. But all this is just half the story. As we are told by the omniscient narrator, the whole truth remains hidden. While the sound is cut and the image keeps running, this voice interrupts repeatedly to embellish what is on screen with additional information. Pretty soon we have learnt to distrust the images and pay more

1

2

attention to the free-roaming camera. In this way, cracks gradually appear in the romantic image of Mexico. We find out about a bricklayer in Mexico City who was knocked over on the highway because there was no pedestrian crossing anywhere on his way to work. Pictures of police brutality and terrible poverty fall in through the car window, but they seem invisible to the three happy occupants. The image and soundtrack confirm this ignorance, without turning it into an accusation. Director Alfonso Cuarón and his long-term cameraman Emmanuel Lubezki have simply found a totally convincing, artistic way of documenting social injustices without talking about them. By exposing the necessary gaps in cinematic narrative, they turn film into an impressive lesson in visualization. As one critic wrote, the wise narrator's voice in the midst of pubertal banter conveys the impression that Susan Sontag has voiced

"Last year's overlong, overwrought, and overpraised *Amores perros* refried the cold beans of Quentin Tarantino's *Pulp Fiction*. Funky and tender, *Y tu mamá también* is more thoughtful in redeeming a crass genre, evoking *Jules and Jim* as well as *Beavis and Butt-Head*." *The Village Voice*

3

1 Trip to paradise bay: director Alfonso Cuarón combines a feisty threesome with the lyrical elements of a summer road movie.

2 Casting an eye on youth: Julio (Gael García Bernal) and Tenoch (Diego Luna) mostly have adolescent mischief in mind.

3 Much is left unsaid. Luisa (Maribel Verdú) keeps her saddest secret to herself until the end.

4 The three have a destination, but do not keep their eyes on the road. It is left to the camera to register the schisms in real-life Mexico.

"Yes, it's about two teenage boys and an impulsive journey with an older woman that involves sexual discoveries. But it is also about the two Mexicos." *Chicago Sun-Times*

ALFONSO CUARÓN Born in Mexico City in 1961, Alfonso Cuarón resembles his fellow countryman, Guillermo del Toro, in combining magical and realistic worlds with modern production design – whether as a director, screenwriter or producer. While his teen dramas are not exactly realistic, an epicurean tendency to exaggerate differentiates his films from Hollywood's fast-food fantasy blockbusters. The son of a heart specialist, Cuarón began his career in Hollywood, however, after he caught Sydney Pollack's attention with his feature debut, an AIDS comedy entitled *Only with Your Partner* (*Sólo con tu pareja*, 1991). After a few teething troubles, two English language studio productions were assigned to him, the highly praised fantasy movie, *A Little Princess* (1995), and a modern film version of *Great Expectations* (1997).
Cuarón returned to his native Mexico with a burning desire to "get his hands dirty." He made an excellent job of this with his erotic road movie, *Y tu mamá también* (2001). Devoid of fantasy elements, but with a complex narrative structure and liberally sprinkled with sex, this minor picture became an international success. He wrote the screenplay, which was nominated for an Oscar, with his brother Carlos Cuarón. His sensational engagement for *Harry Potter and the Prisoner of Azkaban* (2004) saved the series about J.K. Rowling's apprentice magician from sinking into overly lightweight family entertainment. His dark take on magical realism was given a political dimension in the futuristic vision *Children of Men* (2006), starring Julianne Moore and Clive Owen. The special effects were as stunning as the pessimistic basic premise. Ten Mexicans competed overall for the various awards at the Oscar ceremony – alongside Cuarón's film were Guillermo del Toro's *Pan's Labyrinth* (*El laberinto del fauno*, 2006), which Cuarón produced, and Alejandro González Iñárritu's *Babel* (2006). Mexican cinema is now a world cinema, and the career of Alfonso Cuarón its epitome.

5 Poetic sex: Luisa is more mature than her young companions. Spoilt Tenoch can learn a lot from her.

6 Hormonal tangos sans foreplay: the young people's boisterous approach to sexuality is enthusiastically celebrated, yet not without thought.

7 A pool to oneself: Julio is only too happy to share Tenoch's lavish lifestyle; this also reveals the homoerotic aspects of their relationship.

"The movie, whose title translates as *'And Your Mama, Too,'* is another trumpet blast that there may be a New Mexican Cinema a-bornin'." *Chicago Sun-Times* a DVD commentary for the teen-flick *American Pie* (1999). The high spirited action then continues unfazed, following the same structure. Behind his or her laughter, each of the three young people is hiding unexpressed feelings, moods and personal secrets. For instance, Tenoch and Julio have slept with each other's girlfriend. When they confess, they spare the details in order to make the truth more palatable – life imitating art, and vice versa. The worst secret only comes to light at the end, when we discover what it has all been about for Cuarón: the close relationship between sex and death; the pervasive link in even the most innocent human sexual act between desire and pain, love and suffering. This is why *Y tu mamá también* – Cuarón's eventual big break as a director – is such a passionate celebration of life; because this life will inevitably end at some point. PB

6

"*Y tu mama* also echoes the unmistakable freshness and excitement of the Nouvelle Vague, the sense of joy in being alive and making movies, that made those works distinctive and unforgettable." *Los Angeles Times*

7

SPIRITED AWAY
SEN TO CHIHIRO NO KAMIKAKUSHI

2001 – JAPAN – 125 MIN. – ANIMATION, ADVENTURE MOVIE
DIRECTOR HAYAO MIYAZAKI (*1941)
SCREENPLAY HAYAO MIYAZAKI DIRECTOR OF PHOTOGRAPHY ATSUSHI OKUI EDITING TAKESHI SEYAMA
MUSIC JOE HISAISHI, YOUMI KIMURA (TITLE SONG) PRODUCTION TOSHIO SUZUKI FOR STUDIO GHIBLI, NTV, BUENA VISTA INTERNATIONAL.
VOICES DAVEIGH CHASE (Chihiro), JASON MARSDEN (Haku), SUZANNE PLESHETTE (Yubaba/Zeniba), MICHAEL CHIKLIS (Chihiro's Father), LAUREN HOLLY (Chihiro's Mother), JOHN RATZENBERGER (Aogaeru), TARA STRONG (Bôh), SUSAN EGAN (Lin), BOB BERGEN (Bandai-gaeru), RIVER SPIRIT (Kawa no Kami).
ACADEMY AWARDS 2003 OSCAR for BEST ANIMATED FEATURE (Hayao Miyazaki).
IFF BERLIN 2002 GOLDEN BEAR (Hayao Miyazaki).

"I smell something … a human!"

"Wake up, wake up!" Chihiro drums her head with both fists. For the 10-year-old heroine of Hayao Miyazaki's animated feature, *Spirited Away*, wrongly believes she is in a very bad dream. Just as she is en route to her new house with her parents, she is suddenly catapulted into a parallel world in which a witch called Yubaba runs a bath house for the gods. Her parents have been turned into pigs, the way back is cut off to Chihiro and, furthermore, her body is beginning to dissolve; the outlook is not exactly rosy for this little protagonist. She has only one option if she wants to survive in these circumstances – she must gather all her courage and ask Yubaba for a job, as useless creatures are turned into pigs by the witch and wind up sooner or later in the stomachs of hungry guests. Ultimately, the trip into this strange world is a personal journey for Chihiro; the anxious, spoiled child who moans all the time will become a confident and determined young girl.

Two climbing games are symptomatic of this transformation in the film: at the start of the story, Chihiro is scrambling down a steep wooden staircase; she scrabbles about hesitantly and in a panic on the stairs, before a rotten tread accelerates her descent in comical and dramatic fashion. Later, when she has to climb up the outside wall of the bath house to save a friend, her demeanor has changed completely: now utterly fearless, she throws herself onto a wobbly, fragile gutter in order to reach Yubaba's rooms beneath the roof. In a reference to Lewis Carroll's "Alice in Wonderland," the journey into the realm of fantasy – portrayed by Miyazaki as a positively exuberant, pyrotechnic display of visual ideas, rich in detail – begins with a passage through a tunnel. Yet for Chihiro it triggers the serious side of life; left to her own devices, she becomes part of a work process she can only survive by showing great tenacity and ingenuity. The little girl does, however, manage to keep her childlike innocence in the materialistic, profit-oriented world of the bath house, which is also a splendid reflection of Miyazaki's general interest in social and political subjects. Because the gold that Yubaba and her workers crave does not hold any value for her, Chihiro saves the workforce from the lonely god, "No-Face," who lures people with his alleged wealth and eventually threatens to devour everything.

Just how much work changes a person's nature is shown apart from that in the characters of the witch and her twin sister, Zeniba. Miyazaki is saying that Yubaba – strict, cunning and sometimes raving mad as well – stands for the working person, whereas the far more relaxed Zeniba, who lives far from the bath house turmoil in a little house on the moor, is the same person in her domestic setting.

"Miyazaki's magical world is filled with falling waterfalls; an airy place where time and space are fragile dimensions. It follows its own rules, which initially want to be fathomed – but then keep changing constantly. The film's narrative follows a slow rhythm, in which wonder and fear are allowed to balance one another." *Freitag*

1 Parable about capitalism for kids: in the materialistic realm of Yubaba the witch, Chihiro (voice: Daveigh Chase) has to prove her usefulness if she wants to survive.

2 Taking huge steps on the road to adulthood: Chihiro sticks fast to her goals.

3 Afternoon tea with gods and witches: Chihiro and "No-Face" visit Yubaba's twin sister, Zeniba (voice: Suzanne Pleshette).

4 The sad face of materialism: lonely god "No-Face" lures people with the promise of gold, but Chihiro's help is free of selfish motivation.

5 Chihiro's indispensable friend and mysterious helper: Haku (voice: Jason Marsden), ostensibly Yubaba's assistant, likes to assume different forms.

The fact that Miyazaki's films so often feature central female characters can be attributed to a theory of the auteur/director that is worth considering: according to this, adventure stories with male heroes tend to be livelier, with one-dimensional contrasts between good and evil, while female leads allow greater complexity in terms of character portrayal. For, in general, the separation of characters into good and evil in Miyazaki's movies never makes sense, as all the characters are always complex and motivated in equally complex ways. Hence, Zeniba has just the same skills as her sister and is capable of using them if she feels threatened, while Yubaba reveals herself to be an efficient businesswoman, a good organizer and an overly protective mother. For this reason, when Chihiro is leaving, she once again takes the witch completely by surprise: she gives her the pet name "Little Granny". LP

HAYAO MIYAZAKI Hayao Miyazaki is by far the most important and commercially successful animated film director in Japan, where his movies regularly pull in more than any Hollywood blockbuster. Since the 1960s, he has had many jobs in the animation sector, and in 1979 was able to direct his first feature film, *The Castle of Cagliostro* (*Rupan sansei: Kariosutoro no shiro*), an amusing story about the master thief, Lupin the Third, based on a manga by Monkey Punch. Miyazaki found his own personal style in 1984 with the post-apocalypse eco-thriller *Nausicaä of the Valley of the Wind* (*Kaze no tani no Naushika*). Its success in 1985 allowed him to set up the Ghibli studio, which must be the only animation studio to work in the style of the old Hollywood system: the staff are not hired for one-off projects but instead are employed full-time and receive a regular salary. Going back as far as "Nausicaä," Miyazaki's movies have mainly female leads, giving the director what he believes is greater diversity in characterization. Two masterpieces suitable for children, *My Neighbor Totoro* (*Tonari no Totoro*, 1988) and *Kiki's Delivery Service* (*Majo no takkyûbin*, 1989), tell the story of girls who win their own place in a world that is foreign to them, while *Princess Mononoke* (*Mononoke-hime*, 1997) is another take on the eco-subject of "Nausicaä," in which a young girl, San, desperately defends herself against the march of industrialization in a mythical Japan. A nice exception, and certainly Miyazaki's most personal work, is *Porco Rosso, a.k.a. The Crimson Pig* (*Kurenai no buta*, 1992), a complex and melancholy action comedy about the problems of middle-aged men. By way of example, he uses Marco, an Italian pilot who has been turned into a pig and works as a bounty hunter fighting pirates in the Adriatic in a rickety, red seaplane. Since *Spirited Away* (*Sen to Chihiro no kamikakushi*, 2001) was awarded the Oscar in 2003 for Best Animated Feature, if not before, Miyazaki has also been firmly established as a director of international repute. His most recent work, *Ponyo on the Cliff by the Sea* (*Gake no ue no Ponyo*, 2008), a kids' movie about the adventures of a five-year-old boy and a goldfish princess in a flooded coastal region, was released in 2010.

THE OTHERS

2001 – USA / SPAIN / FRANCE / ITALY – 104 MIN. – HORROR MOVIE
DIRECTOR ALEJANDRO AMENÁBAR (*1972)
SCREENPLAY ALEJANDRO AMENÁBAR **DIRECTOR OF PHOTOGRAPHY** JAVIER AGUIRRESAROBE
EDITING NACHO RUIZ CAPILLAS **MUSIC** ALEJANDRO AMENÁBAR **PRODUCTION** FERNANDO BOVAIRA, JOSÉ LUIS CUERDA, SUNMIN PARK for CRUISE/WAGNER/PRODUCTIONS, SOGECINE, LAS PRODUCCIONES DEL ESCORPION, DIMENSION FILMS, CANAL+ ESPAÑA.
STARRING NICOLE KIDMAN (Grace), CHRISTOPHER ECCLESTON (Charles), ALAKINA MANN (Anne), JAMES BENTLEY (Nicholas), FIONNULA FLANAGAN (Mrs. Mills), ERIC SYKES (Mr. Tuttle), ELAINE CASSIDY (Lydia), RENÉE ASHERSON (The Old Lady), KEITH ALLEN (Mr. Marlish), ALEXANDER VINCE (Victor).

"This house is ours."

The year is 1945; the setting, the island of Jersey in the English Channel. A house looms in the fog, cut off from the rest of the world: the classic haunted house. The Victorian era of great ghost stories seems closer in time than World War II. A strict mistress runs her home with military precision. Curtains must be closed at all times, for darkness is of paramount importance – Grace (Nicole Kidman) fears for the health of her children, Anne and Nicholas (Alakina Mann and James Bentley), who suffer from a rare photosensitive allergy. The new servants, led by kind-hearted nanny Mrs. Mills (Fionnula Flanagan), follow her instructions reluctantly. They know more about this house than Grace, who is Catholic and does not believe in ghosts. They worked here "before." The spirits refuse to be locked out. Perhaps they are already there. Doors open themselves; invisible hands play the piano. Little Anne has even seen the intruders. One awful day, the curtains disappear, and Grace is forced to realize that "sometimes the worlds of the living and the dead come together."

What is immediately striking about *The Others* is the dignified elegance of its mise-en-scène. The young Spanish-Chilean director Alejandro Amenábar not only takes his cue from the great models of the Gothic genre such as *Rebecca* (1940), *Gaslight* (1944) and *The Haunting* (1962), but actually directs like an old master. Avoiding any gory shock effects and in true Alfred Hitchcock style, the fear lurks within the mind of the viewer. Hardly innovative, you might think. But there is much in this quiet, elegant ghost film that turns out to be malicious deception. Imperceptibly, normal circumstances become reversed: it is not darkness but light that unleashes the horror, an effect that is carefully constructed by Amenábar, working with the lighting director. Then, of course, there is the final twist in the plot, a narrative device reminiscent of M. Night Shyamalan's *The Sixth Sense* (1999), and one that has become diluted in numerous subsequent movies to the point of becoming meaningless. In *The Others* this postmodern playing with increasingly heightened audience expectation

"We're already so deep in the brave new world of computerized special effects that we hardly notice any more that Hollywood is doing all the imagining for us. (...) In *The Others*, starring Nicole Kidman, we do the imagining, based on sounds that occur beyond the camera's eye, or by the looks on people's faces as they experience the supernatural."

The Washington Post

1 Ghostly presence: Nicole Kidman, modeled on Hitchcock's blondes, plays vigilant mother, Grace – the creepiest aspect of the entire film by far.

2 Servants Mrs. Mills, Lydia and Mr. Tuttle (Fionnula Flanagan, Elaine Cassidy, Eric Sykes) "worked here a long time ago." No reassurance whatsoever.

3 Grace resolutely protects her little family. But the ghosts cannot be locked out, and may even be here already.

4 Stricken souls of children: Grace's children Anne (Alakina Mann) and Nicholas (James Bentley) often have contact with the "others."

is firmly rooted in the narrative. There is a constant refusal to reveal who "the others" really are. In this way, the structure of the movie is not turned on its head by the breathtaking final act, but is rendered plausible from the outset. Completely different levels of meaning open up on repeated viewing – from an economic point of view, a function of the new narrative technique that is quite deliberate.

Seen in the cold light of day, *The Others* is located not so much within the tradition of the ghost or horror movie than as part of a whole series of recent films such as *The Truman Show* (1998) and *Eternal Sunshine of the Spotless Mind* (2004), which are underpinned by a profound identity crisis in the main character. It is the job of the stars to render such contradictions redundant. The scariest part of this movie by far is the sight of Nicole Kidman

ALEJANDRO AMENÁBAR Alejandro Amenábar was born in Santiago, Chile in 1972 to Spanish-Chilean parents. Just one year later the family fled Pinochet's military dictatorship and settled in Madrid. Amenábar later started a film studies course at Complutense University, though it was not enough to satisfy his penchant for occult and spiritual subjects. To relieve his boredom, he made his first feature film there, *Tesis* (1996): in this cheaply produced horror flick, some students are on the trail of a gang producing snuff films. The very next year came *Open Your Eyes* (*Abre los ojos*, 1997). His surreal treatment of male vanity and humiliation proved Amenábar as a great up-and-coming talent. After decades of Pedro Almodóvar's sole reign, Spanish cinema had a new star.

His next career boost, however, was externally driven. After seeing *Open Your Eyes*, Hollywood star Tom Cruise apparently took a great shine to the female lead, Penélope Cruz. In exchange for the rights to its remake, *Vanilla Sky* (2001), directed by Cameron Crowe and with Cruz reprising her leading role, Amenábar secured finance to film *The Others* (*Los otros*, 2001) as a big Hollywood production, with Cruise's then wife, Nicole Kidman, in the star role. Shortly after, Cruise separated from her.

It was not just this publicity, however, that helped to make this superior horror movie a resounding success. With supreme confidence, Amenábar had packed his themes of dreams, identity loss and the afterlife into a classic ghost story. In addition, as in all his films, he had also provided the music himself, as well as writing the screenplay and directing, thus radically increasing the number of personal awards he received at film festivals. For the rather more sedate film about assisted suicide, *The Sea Inside* (*Mar adentro*, 2004), with Javier Bardem playing a paraplegic sailor, he finally won the Oscar for Best Foreign Language Film. His most recent movie project is *Agora* (2009), an historical epic set in Ancient Egypt.

3
4

(looking like one of Hitchcock's blondes wandering ghost-like through an old-fashioned setting) with a look of terror on her face and holding a shotgun. As white as snow and as delicate as porcelain, she kick-started her second career as a respected actress and Hollywood's one and only diva with this film. Amenábar's movie itself became the forerunner of a new "Spanish Wave" that brought international acclaim to Latin American and Spanish horror specialists including Guillermo del Toro with *Pan's Labyrinth* (*El laberinto del fauno*, 2006) and Juan Antonio Bayona with *The Orphanage* (*El orfanato*, 2007). In its native country *The Others* (an English-language masterpiece filmed in Spain) won eight Goyas, including the awards for Best Film and Best Music; composed by young prodigy Amenábar himself, the score contributes significantly to the movie's spooky atmosphere. PB

"The most discomfiting thing in *The Others* isn't a human, a ghost, or even a place. It's the otherworldly light." *slate.com*

5 Mysterious light sensitivity: the children themselves are creatures of the night, strictly forbidden to leave the house.

6 Haunted house in the mist: director Amenábar skillfully draws us in with conventions of the genre, only to subvert them in a heart-stopping finale.

7 Dreams and madness: Grace's husband, Charles (Christopher Eccleston), who is believed dead, comes back from the war – but isn't there.

SEX AND LUCÍA
LUCÍA Y EL SEXO

2001 – SPAIN / FRANCE – 128 MIN. – EROTIC DRAMA
DIRECTOR JULIO MÉDEM (*1958)
SCREENPLAY JULIO MÉDEM DIRECTOR OF PHOTOGRAPHY KIKO DE LA RICA EDITING IVAN ALÉDO
MUSIC ALBERTO IGLESIAS PRODUCTION FERNANDO BOVAIRA, ENRIQUE LÓPEZ LAVIGNE for ALICIA PRODUCE, CANAL+ ESPAÑA, SOGECINE, SOGEPAQ, STUDIO CANAL, TELEVISIÓN ESPAÑOLA.
STARRING PAZ VEGA (Lucía), TRISTÁN ULLOA (Lorenzo), NAJWA NIMRI (Elena), DANIEL FREIRE (Carlos/Antonio), JAVIER CÁMARA (Pepe), ELENA ANAYA (Belén), SILVIA LLANOS (Luna), DIANA SUÁREZ (Belén's mother), JUAN FERNÁNDEZ (Jefe), CHARO ZAPARDIEL (Comadrona).

"I am lost forever."

Anyone going to the movies expecting a linear narrative with a beginning, middle and end is liable to find the work of Julio Médem rather problematic. Born in the Basque region, he studied psychiatry and then went on to a career in film directing; he is regarded as the most important Spanish *auteur* alongside Pedro Almodóvar. Critics are also fond of describing him as Europe's answer to David Lynch, and not without good reason: Médem and the American master of the mystery movie share an apparent interest in the subconscious and the darker side of life, which is reflected in labyrinthine narrative structures and a visual language rich in associations. In this way, *Sex and Lucía*, Médem's most commercially successful film to date, seems to follow more the logic of a dream than the laws of conventional cinema.

The film's heroine is Lucía (Paz Vega), a young waitress from Madrid who hurriedly leaves the capital in order to find peace on a barren sunny island after her psychologically frail boyfriend, Lorenzo, disappears in mysterious circumstances. Once there, however, she promptly loses her footing: when out walking, she fails to notice a deep hole, and falls into it. This plunge into darkness kick starts the plot once again, switching back six years. Cue full moon on a sea shore, with a couple making love in the water – two strangers in a magical, one-night stand. The woman, Elena (Najwa Nimri), becomes pregnant and hopes to find her lover once again. But the man, Lorenzo (Tristán Ulloa), knows nothing of all this. Instead, the young novelist meets Lucía, who approaches him in a bar and frankly admits how much she likes his work but, even more, how much she loves him. So, while Lorenzo and Lucía embark on a relationship filled with playful lovemaking, Elena gives birth to a daughter on her own. Back in the present day on the island, Lucía meets the mysterious diver Carlos (Daniel Freire). He introduces her to Elena, who is now running a

1 Paz Vega as sexy Lucía: the major discovery in Julio Médem's enigmatic love movie.

2 Fleeting happiness: suffering from writer's block, young author Lorenzo (Tristán Ulloa) finds peace with Lucía, but only for a short while.

3 Despite the somewhat racy title, *Sex and Lucía* handles sex and eroticism with an unusually light and authentic touch.

4 Lucía and Elena (Najwa Nimri) don't realize they both love the same man.

5 Elena, the beautiful stranger, spends a magical night of love with Lorenzo in the sea. One with consequences …

small boarding house on the island. It is here that Elena is trying to come to terms with the death of her child. She is distracted slightly from her pain by sleeping with Carlos, but she finds solace on the internet, chatting to a stranger. Lucía moves in with Elena and Carlos, gradually realizing that their lives are fatefully linked to each other through Lorenzo. Internal and external reality cannot be separated in *Sex and Lucía*. With its irritatingly dazzling light, a phallic lighthouse and strange holes that appear in the ground like gorges, the island becomes a sexualized landscape; a precarious terrain that is completely unconnected to the sea bed, according to Carlos. This means that, in stormy waters, the inhabitants are sent floundering, just like the protagonists whose lives are pitchforked into chaos by their desires. This applies to Lorenzo in particular, his story being pieced together like a jigsaw as the plot unfolds:

"Medem is one of the few directors who understands sensuality and knows how to make it happen on screen. *Sex and Lucía* specializes in pleasant eroticism, using nudity, Kiko de la Rica's dreamy cinematography and Alberto Iglesias' Goya-winning score to create episodes of voluptuous lovemaking." *Los Angeles Times*

thus we see how Lucía and Lorenzo's relationship gradually darkens when he gets writer's block but then, when Lorenzo learns about his little daughter, he is overcome by a writing fever; finally, worn out from paternal feelings and pornographic fantasies, he causes a terrible accident, driven to despair.

Through all this, it is still unclear in the final analysis whether the individual elements are actually about real events, Lorenzo's literary fantasies or, indeed, Lucía's memories and/or wild imaginings. Everything is presented on an equal basis, seamlessly interwoven. Médem skillfully blends levels of reality and time, distant places and different perspectives into a poetic cinematic language that beautifully expresses the chaos of human emotions, wishes and desires, while at the same time allowing us to catch a glimpse of the mysterious workings of artistic inspiration. In any event, the success of Médem's film at the box office was probably due less to its ambitious and original form than to its attractive title and a few explicit sex scenes – though they never run the sensationalist risk. Quite the opposite, in fact: sex and eroticism are dealt with in *Sex and Lucía* with a playfully light touch and genuine approach that are rarely found in the movies. JH

6 Fateful meeting: Belén's (Elena Anaya) aggressive eroticism casts a spell on Lorenzo.

7 Now and again, the weird, dream-like island to which Lucía escapes appears as a sexed-up landscape with phallic lighthouses …

8 … and deep holes that open up like abysses in front of her.

6

7

PAZ VEGA The reason why Paz Vega became indelibly imprinted in the minds of international audiences with *Sex and Lucía* (*Lucía y el sexo*, 2001), her first big feature film, is not just because she appears in a singularly naked way in Julio Médem's movie; born in Seville in 1976, the actress actually makes her first erotic appearance "dressed up to the nines" when she wraps male lead Tristán Ulloa around her finger in a bar – one of the most memorable seduction scenes in the movies of this decade. She attracted similar attention the following year in a weird, if brief, appearance in Pedro Almodóvar's *Talk to Her* (*Hable con ella*, 2002) in the context of a "faked" silent movie, playing the lover of a shrunken man who disappears into her vagina while she sleeps. Paz Vega then made the significant leap to Hollywood with a less daring role alongside Adam Sandler as a fiery Mexican housekeeper in James L. Brooks' rom-com *Spanglish* (2004). She also stuck to the Latino image in *10 Items or Less* (2006).
The Spanish actress once again revealed her more abandoned side in *The Lark Farm* (*La masseria delle allodole*, 2007) by Paolo and Vittorio Taviani, an oddly old-fashioned epic about the Armenian genocide that undermines its serious concerns with several eye-popping, sexy scenes. Paz Vega's appearance in Frank Miller's spectacular comic adaptation *The Spirit* (2008) was an alternative project: not exactly a masterpiece either, the film gave her scope to exploit her sex appeal to full effect in the role of the flamboyantly dangerous Plaster of Paris.

8

"One of the most inventive and erotic films you are likely to see this year." *BBC*

THE ROYAL TENENBAUMS

2001 – USA – 110 MIN. – COMEDY, DRAMA
DIRECTOR WES ANDERSON (*1969)
SCREENPLAY WES ANDERSON, OWEN WILSON DIRECTOR OF PHOTOGRAPHY ROBERT D. YEOMAN
EDITING DYLAN TICHENOR MUSIC MARK MOTHERSBAUGH PRODUCTION WES ANDERSON, BARRY MENDEL, SCOTT RUDIN for AMERICAN EMPIRICAL PICTURES, MORDECAI FILMS, TOUCHSTONE PICTURES.
STARRING GENE HACKMAN (Royal Tenenbaum), ANJELICA HUSTON (Etheline Tenenbaum), BEN STILLER (Chas Tenenbaum), GWYNETH PALTROW (Margot Tenenbaum), LUKE WILSON (Richie Tenenbaum), OWEN WILSON (Eli Cash), DANNY GLOVER (Henry Sherman), BILL MURRAY (Raleigh St. Clair), SEYMOUR CASSEL (Dusty), KUMAR PALLANA (Pagoda).

"I've always been considered an asshole for about as long as I can remember. That's just my style."

Somewhere in Manhattan stands the home of the Royal Tenenbaums, magnificent in its faded grandeur. It doesn't seem quite real. The best way to describe it is as a colorful comic strip from a daily newspaper or a "find-the-difference" picture from an old children's book lying forgotten in the attic. The characters sit as if framed in their rooms: Margot (Gwyneth Paltrow), who spends days on end smoking furtively in the bathroom; Chas (Ben Stiller), the paranoid safety fanatic in a flaming-red sweat suit, with his two look-alike sons Ari and Uzi; and Richie (Luke Wilson), who has been in love with his adoptive sister Margot since childhood and has set up a small tent to sleep in. These are the children of Etheline Tenenbaum (Anjelica Huston), who sadly follows the family's decline. All three, scowling glumly in their exquisite seclusion, are geniuses who have peaked early. Margot was a promising playwright, Chas a financial wizard, Richie a highly successful tennis pro before his career also took a dip. What else can we see? In front of the house is Eli Cash (Owen Wilson), a childhood friend of all three, who always wanted to be a Tenenbaum. But he can't get in. Just like Royal Tenenbaum (Gene Hackman), the outcast patriarch and flea-bag egocentric with the moral integrity of a five-year-old. Yet he is the one – the only one who isn't neurotic – to breathe life back into his prematurely senile clan. The characters are introduced in the elaborately interwoven opening credits, structured as a family chronicle to the incessant strains of "Hey Jude." Basically, the intro never stops: the picture simply acquires new aspects, décor and details. Wes Anderson plays like a child with the creative possibilities of the film medium, perfecting his own unique style in the process. Right from the start, the director found himself facing the accusation of putting "style over substance," of wallowing in middle-class nostalgia and not allowing his "flat" characters to develop in any way. But would anyone ever describe "Peanuts" as "flat"? And who wouldn't go to any lengths to be a Tenenbaum? These exceptionally gifted eccentrics wear the trappings of their failure like a crown: Margot, the elegant fur coat; Chas, the sweat suit; Richie, his Björn Borg headband. In a classier world, you would be

1

2

able to buy them as action figures in the Wes Anderson Merchandise Store, their outfits side by side with the red sailors' hats from *The Life Aquatic with Steve Zissou* (2004) and the Louis Vuitton suitcase from *The Darjeeling Limited* (2007). In the real world Anderson's films – especially *The Royal Tenenbaums* – struck a chord with the melancholic attitude to life of half a generation of 30-somethings, and made it hip.

There has never been an incarnation of New York like this, as the dream of a better childhood filled with memories of the Seventies and early Eighties. The basis of Anderson's inspiration for this colorful pastiche of numerous influences and references was an unhealthy consumption of movies and extensive reading of old editions of *New Yorker*, especially J.D. Salinger's short stories about the endearingly dysfunctional Glass family. The indulgent feel comes from the singer/songwriter gems of Bob Dylan, the Stones, Lou Reed and Nico in particular. Like Paul Thomas Anderson in *Magnolia* (1999), Wes Anderson also wrote many scenes specifically for the songs. When Margot sways to the sounds of "These Days" as she gets off the bus to greet Richie, it is a magical moment – every line fits perfectly, saying it all.

At the same time, its East-Coast humor makes *The Royal Tenenbaums* a very funny film, in which Royal Tenenbaum in particular personally thwarts the contrived sadness with some relish. Who else but a real rascal and hopeless bankrupt would come up with the idea of faking a terminal illness in order to be taken back by his compassionate family? The cover story is soon blown – no-one suffering from stomach cancer devours three cheeseburgers a day. Yet nobody can blame him for being hungry for the love of this family. PB

"Every single character in *The Royal Tenenbaums* is drawn with terrific wit and intelligence." *The Guardian*

1 No-one hates his father more than Chas Tenenbaum (Ben Stiller). Paranoid about safety, he raises his sons in a permanent state of high alert.

2 Neurosis as the norm: psychologist Raleigh (Bill Murray) has a number of dealings with the Tenenbaum family.

3

3 Margot Tenenbaum (Gwyneth Paltrow) spends her days in exquisite boredom. This *almost* bothers her mother, Etheline (Anjelica Huston).

4 Gene Hackman is outstanding as the selfish creep with dubious motives. His character even resorts to shameful trickery to implement his few good plans.

WES ANDERSON Influences such as Louis Malle, François Truffaut and Mike Nichols place Wes Anderson firmly within the tradition of the auteur film. At the same time, his unmistakable style makes him one of the most important figures in American independent cinema with his own loyal fan base. Anderson's films create a universe of their own, in which family ties and spiritual kinship play a leading role. An acting ensemble that barely changes – consisting mainly of Anjelica Huston, Bill Murray, Seymour Cassel, brothers Luke and Owen Wilson, and Jason Schwartzman – become embroiled in absurdly comical conflicts that are always the same, and that the director films with visual perfection. In each case the tone is playful, slightly quirky and profoundly melancholic.

You wouldn't guess the biography of this child prodigy from his films. Born in Houston, Texas in 1969, the philosophy student at Austin University became friends with the actor and screenwriter Owen Wilson. Their first film together, *Bottle Rocket* (1996), was well-received by the critics at least. However, it was *Rushmore* (1998) that made Anderson the darling of independent cinema. Its eccentric protagonist and ingenious underachiever, Max Fischer, drives the teaching staff crazy with meticulous theatre adaptations of film classics – a reminder of Anderson's own time in high school and an insight into his filmmaking style. In the family saga *The Royal Tenenbaums* (2001), too, he maintained his unorthodox treatment of conventions and references, only this time with a star cast. In terms of subject matter, father–son conflicts took center stage, while Anjelica Huston as the mother (like Anderson's own mother, Etheline Tenenbaum is an archaeologist) provided a firm footing. Gene Hackman's role as the father was reprised by Bill Murray in the sequel *The Life Aquatic with Steve Zissou* (2004), the latter already indebted to Anderson thanks to *Rushmore*, which gave him a second career in independent film. But the accusation of repetitiveness was articulated for the first time and even the affectionate reference to the underwater films of Jacques-Yves Cousteau could not bring success at the box-office.

Yet there can be no serious worries that Anderson, the sensitive and visionary filmmaker, will suffer the same fate as his fallen genius characters. The familiar pastel-colored trip to India, *The Darjeeling Limited* (2007), was convincing thanks to its considerably reduced cast and a more mature take on interpersonal relationships; and with the delightfully old-fashioned Roald Dahl adaptation *Fantastic Mr. Fox* (2009) he has even managed to reinvent himself once more – as a master of the animated movie.

HARRY POTTER 1–7

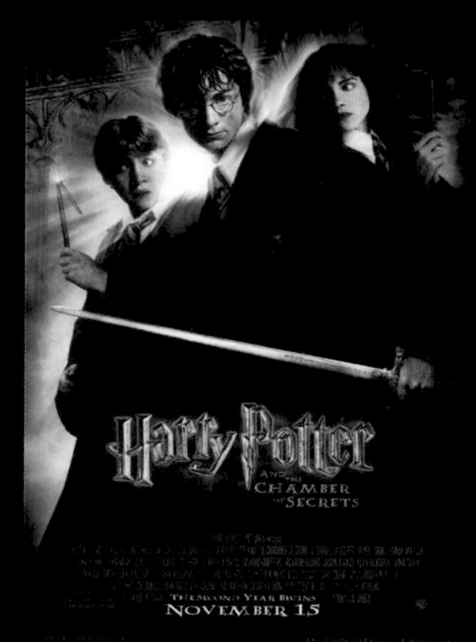

2001–2009 – UK / USA – 152 / 161 / 157 / 141 / 138 / 153 MIN. – FANTASY, LITERARY ADAPTATION
DIRECTOR CHRIS COLUMBUS (*1958; Parts 1, 2), ALFONSO CUARÓN (*1961; Part 3), MIKE NEWELL (*1942; Part 4), DAVID YATES (*1963; Parts 5, 6)
SCREENPLAY STEVE KLOVES (Parts 1–4, 6), MICHAEL GOLDENBERG (Part 5), from the novels by JOANNE K. ROWLING DIRECTOR OF PHOTOGRAPHY JOHN SEALE (Part 1), ROGER PRATT (Parts 2, 4), MICHAEL SERESIN (Part 3), SLAWOMIR IDZIAK (Part 5), BRUNO DELBONNEL (Part 6) EDITING RICHARD FRANCIS-BRUCE (Part 1), PETER HONESS (Part 2), STEVEN WEISBERG (Part 3), MICK AUDSLEY (Part 4), MARK DAY (Parts 5, 6)
MUSIC JOHN WILLIAMS (Parts 1–3), PATRICK DOYLE (Part 4), NICHOLAS HOOPER (Parts 5, 6) PRODUCTION DAVID HEYMAN (Parts 1–6), CHRIS COLUMBUS (Part 3), LORNE ORLEANS (Parts 3–5), MARK RADCLIFFE (Part 3), DAVID BARRON (Parts 5, 6) for HEYDAY FILMS (Parts 1–6), 1492 PICTURES (Parts 1–3), WARNER BROS. (Parts 1–6).
STARRING DANIEL RADCLIFFE (Harry Potter; Parts 1–6), EMMA WATSON (Hermione Granger; Parts 1–6), RUPERT GRINT (Ron Weasley; Parts 1–6), RICHARD HARRIS (Professor Albus Dumbledore; Parts 1, 2), MICHAEL GAMBON (Professor Albus Dumbledore, Parts 3–6), MAGGIE SMITH (Professor Minerva McGonagall; Parts 1–6), ROBBIE COLTRANE (Rubeus Hagrid; Parts 1–6), ALAN RICKMAN (Severus Snape; Parts 1–6), EMMA THOMPSON (Sybil Trelawney; Parts 3, 5), GARY OLDMAN (Sirius Black; Parts 3–5), DAVID THEWLIS (Remus Lupin; Parts 3, 5, 6), RALPH FIENNES (Lord Voldemort; Parts 4, 5), IMELDA STAUNTON (Dolores Umbridge; Part 5), HELENA BONHAM CARTER (Bellatrix Lestrange; Parts 5–7).

"You're a wizard, Harry." – "I'm a what?"

Magic and the movies make poor bedfellows. In the fantasy world of Joanne K. Rowling there are spells and potions, flying broomsticks, invisibility cloaks and even a reasonably credible place called London, but no cinema. Real magicians are presumably scornful of the mechanical trickery of moving images, in the same way that the full-blooded wizards of the *Harry Potter* novels look down on the world of the Muggles – poor little people like you and me. In transferring this fantasy world to the screen, however, the filmmakers could count on an audience that would have no trouble enthusing about the adventures of a bespectacled apprentice wizard, filmed using the simple magic of computer-generated special effects: an audience of innocent children.

A classic, and unprecedented, example of the modern event movie, the history of the *Harry Potter* film versions is a tale of superlatives. It begins with the worldwide consumption of over 400 million novels by a readership largely comprised of children and ends in the present day with the legendary box-office takings of over 4.4 billion dollars for the first five parts. The author, J.K. Rowling, sold the rights to her work to AOL Time Warner and was extra vigilant on behalf of her fans to ensure the films stayed true to the books; she also made sure that her much-loved characters were suitably cast with exclusively British and Irish actors. The project went through four directors and, at times in direct competition with Peter Jackson's *Lord of the Rings* trilogy (2001, 2002, 2003) unleashed an unparalleled surge in fantasy movies. The directors were not contracted to embellish Rowling's universe with their own ideas or conjure a little magic through their individual styles, which meant that everything ran smoothly.

Eagerly awaited by long queues of children, *Harry Potter and the Philosopher's Stone* (*Harry Potter and the Sorcerer's Stone*, 2001) established the blueprint for all the other parts, just like the novels. Unhappy orphan Harry Potter (Daniel Radcliffe) first becomes aware of his magical powers through the good-natured giant Hagrid (Robbie Coltrane) and thus escapes his beastly adoptive family. After a trip to Diagon Alley he takes the train from secret Platform 9¾ on King's

1 United against the forces of evil: Hermione (Emma Watson), Harry (Daniel Radcliffe) and Ron (Rupert Grint) form a secret society.

2 Flying broomsticks: the Hogwarts pupils measure their powers at the annual Quidditch championships. Unfortunately it's difficult to re-enact this particular sport.

3 Wise wizard: Professor Albus Dumbledore (Richard Harris) is Hogwarts' amiable and confident headmaster. Michael Gambon took over the role after Harris' death in October 2002.

"I went into the movie prejudiced by the hype. I left having enjoyed it immensely and admiring the skill which had gone into the making."

The Guardian

4 Robbie Coltrane is the perfect incarnation of Rubeus Hagrid, Hogwarts' mysterious gamekeeper. The giant often has useful information.

5 In praise of the British boarding school: at Hogwarts it's lifelong learning for the three magic students Harry, Hermione and Ron. The child actors became stars overnight.

Cross station to Hogwarts School of Witchcraft and Wizardry. His future companions make an appearance: his ever-helpful best friend, Ron Weasley (Rupert Grint), and the opinionated bookworm, Hermione Granger (Emma Watson).

Diagon Alley and the castle-like Hogwarts are part of an ostensibly Victorian parallel world that has its own laws and is hidden to the Muggles. At their elite boarding school, instead of spelling and algebra, the pupils learn the practice of magic and the effects of secret herbs and essences such as asphodel and wolfsbane. The venerable members of the teaching staff, led by wise old headmaster Professor Albus Dumbledore (Richard Harris), all wear magic hats. Each part covers the events of a school year, the highlight of which is a breathtakingly fantastic ball game called Quidditch, which is played on flying broomsticks. At the end of each school year, Harry like all the others must return to the disliked real world, where he is strictly forbidden from using any kind of magic.

ALAN RICKMAN No-one plays a villain quite like Alan Rickman. Hollywood in particular always hires him to play the comical bad guy – whether he is falling wide-eyed from a skyscraper or threatening to cut someone's heart out with a spoon. *Harry Potter* fans, however, know him as the sinister Severus Snape, the black magic teacher and shady character who fluctuates between good and evil. In fact, in his native UK he tends to play gentle characters – a clear-cut case of transcontinental split personality. Born in London in 1946, Rickman came to the movies at a late stage. After many years working in experimental theater and training as a graphic designer, the role of the seducer, the Vicomte de Valmont, in *Les liaisons dangereuses* made him, initially, a stage star. In 1987, the Royal Shakespeare Company's London production became a hit on Broadway as well. Shortly afterward, Rickman made his magnificent screen debut as the cool, suave villain Hans Gruber in the action movie classic *Die Hard* (1987/88).
His interpretation of the Sheriff of Nottingham in the mega-blockbuster *Robin Hood – Prince of Thieves* (1991) was another career highlight. His mad antics stole the show from the actual star, Kevin Costner. On the other hand, he showed his melancholic side in Ang Lee's film version of Jane Austen's *Sense and Sensibility* (1995) and in the wonderfully innocuous, London-based romance, *Love Actually* (2003). He has been a permanent feature of the Potter universe since Harry Potter and the Philosopher's Stone (2001). His appearances, often only brief, send ice-cold shivers down the back, the combination of incisive arrogance and veiled vulnerability revealing his excellent acting ability. Rickman has also appeared as the cruel landowner in *Quigley Down Under* (1990), the ridiculous Spock lookalike in *Galaxy Quest* (1999) and the guilt-ridden driver involved in an accident in *Snow Cake* (2005/06). In Tim Burton's film version of the Stephen Sondheim musical *Sweeney Todd – The Demon Barber of Fleet Street* (2007) he also shone as the sinister Judge Turpin. He is now also directing in the theater.

6 Dark nobility: the "pure-blood" wizard Draco Malfoy (Tom Felton) and his father Lucius Malfoy (Jason Isaacs) are some of Harry's arch enemies.

7 A headstrong achiever: smart-aleck Hermione was far more popular with audiences than with her less gifted fellow pupils.

8 Vision of the future: Headmaster Dumbledore (Michael Gambon) knows that Hogwarts faces dark times. He mostly keeps this knowledge to himself.

"More than anything the Harry Potter series is the most popular description of burgeoning adolescent consciousness that has ever been created." *The Village Voice*

Harry is among his own kind in the idyllic world of Hogwarts. Nevertheless, the fact that he also has to learn the difference between white and black magic sets him apart from his fellow pupils: he is the chosen one in the fight against the unspeakable Lord Voldemort, the Dark Lord who murdered Harry's parents and initially remains formless. The lightning-shaped scar on his forehead results from their early, nerve-wracking encounter and makes Harry the biggest celebrity in Hogwarts.

The film versions also created ubiquitous stars of the three young principal actors, especially Daniel Radcliffe. He was only 11 years old when he started out and the greatest attraction of the series by far was to watch him and the other characters growing up. It was also the first series to age along with its audience, with Harry, Ron and Hermione gradually experiencing all the (frequently painful) stages of adolescent development. This exploration of the inner self and the 'magical' powers inhabiting the body were always more fascinating than the major task (to halt the rise of evil) that concludes each part and is hinted at in the title: Harry meets his playmates (*Harry Potter and the Philosopher's Stone*, 2001); stands up to rivals his own age (*Harry Potter and the Chamber of Secrets*, 2002); becomes a teenager (*Harry Potter and the Prisoner of Azkaban*, 2004); discovers girls (*Harry Potter and the Goblet of Fire*, 2005); experiences his first kiss (*Harry Potter and the Order of the Phoenix*, 2007); and has his first major relationship problems (*Harry Potter and the Half-Blood Prince*, 2009).

It is the story of a boy whose faltering progress is observed pityingly at best by the naturally more mature Hermione: "Boys!" Everyone, however, even Muggle children, can relate to what is exemplified here by Rowling's characters:

“What’s developing here, it’s clear, is one of the most important franchises in movie history, a series of films that consolidate all of the advances in computer-aided animation, linked to the extraordinary creative work of J.K. Rowling, who has created a mythological world as grand as *Star Wars*, but filled with more wit and humanity.” *Chicago Sun-Times*

8

9 Magic and madness: Emma Thompson also makes a typical guest appearance as wacky soothsayer Sybil Trelawney.

10 Expecto Patronum: Remus Lupin (David Thewlis) teaches spells in Hogwarts as Defence Against the Dark Arts.

11 The twilight zone: surprisingly enough, devious black wizard Snape (Alan Rickman) often protects the children from danger.

12 Fantasy creature with a heart and soul: Dobby, the mournful house-elf, warns Harry against returning to Hogwarts.

"Harry Potter has not come of age, not by a long shot. But the Harry Potter film adaptations have." *die tageszeitung*

strengthening personality traits through sustained learning; the fight against internal and external demons as the mission of life; the acceptance of, yet resistance to, a fate that has partly been predetermined and must end in death. The evil Lord Voldemort embodies the latter, as well as the sexuality slowly awakening in Harry, which he has to accept as a part of himself.

Psychological detours like this are as much part of the *Potter* phenomenon as the knowledge that none of the films' directors were able to deviate from the book. Turning toward the 'dark side' is shown through the novels as it is in real life. In the third part, however, Alfonso Cuarón managed to develop a spectacular new direction: its subtle, Gothic romanticism is very different from the child-like imagination of the first films, which Chris Columbus made primarily as family entertainment. In the final parts, barely suitable for children any more, David Yates was able to continue this tradition. The characters increasingly matured in personality, with the young actors serving less and less as 'fillers' between appearances by great British actors – all of them outstanding – such as Richard Harris, Maggie Smith, David Thewlis and Alan Rickman.

Ultimately, however, it was precisely this stylistic continuity that paid off. For, taken together, the films constitute an original pictorial universe to which future generations will also be able to relate. Platform 9¾, Diagon Alley, the Forbidden Forest, Whomping Willow and, of course, the classic British boarding school, Hogwarts, with its moving stairs and literally living murals – it defies explanation that this unique fantasy world was advertised with just two-dimensional posters. The special effects could also be seen to mature through the series, but then such magic can only be found in the movies. PB

“No-one can argue against the fairy tale, the fantasy portal between childhood and adulthood, certainly not when its divinely-produced cinematic dream musters all that technology, star glamour and craftsmanship can bring to its material.” *Die Zeit*

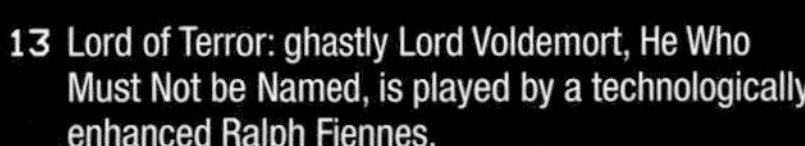

13 Lord of Terror: ghastly Lord Voldemort, He Who Must Not be Named, is played by a technologically enhanced Ralph Fiennes.

14 Enemy even in death: Voldemort penetrates Dumbledore's tomb in his search for the magic wand.

15 Beautiful witchcraft: Helena Bonham Carter appears as Bellatrix Lestrange, Voldemort's loyal servant.

16 Attack of the Death Eaters: storm clouds gather over Hogwarts. With every film, the series became more complex and somber.

16

THE LORD OF THE RINGS

2001–2003 – NEW ZEALAND / USA – 178 MIN. / 179 MIN. / 201 MIN. – FANTASY, LITERARY ADAPTATION
DIRECTOR PETER JACKSON (*1961)
SCREENPLAY FRAN WALSH, PHILIPPA BOYENS, PETER JACKSON from the novel by J. R. R. TOLKIEN DIRECTOR OF PHOTOGRAPHY ANDREW LESNIE EDITING JOHN GILBERT MUSIC HOWARD SHORE PRODUCTION PETER JACKSON, FRAN WALSH, BARRIE M. OSBORNE, TIM SANDERS for NEW LINE CINEMA, WINGNUT FILMS.
STARRING VIGGO MORTENSEN (Aragorn), IAN MCKELLEN (Gandalf), LIV TYLER (Arwen), ELIJAH WOOD (Frodo Baggins), IAN HOLM (Bilbo Baggins), SEAN ASTIN (Samwise "Sam" Gamgee), BILLY BOYD (Pippin), DOMINIC MONAGHAN (Merry), CATE BLANCHETT (Galadriel), SEAN BEAN (Boromir), ORLANDO BLOOM (Legolas), JOHN RHYS-DAVIES (Gimli), CHRISTOPHER LEE (Saruman), HUGO WEAVING (Elrond), ANDY SERKIS (Gollum).
ACADEMY AWARDS 2002 OSCARS for BEST CINEMATOGRAPHY (Andrew Lesnie), BEST VISUAL EFFECTS (Jim Rygiel, Randall William Cook, Richard Taylor, Mark Stetson), BEST MAKEUP (Peter Owen, Richard Taylor) and BEST MUSIC, Original Score (Howard Shore).
ACADEMY AWARDS 2003 OSCARS for BEST SOUND EDITING (Ethan Van der Ryn, Mike Hopkins) and BEST VISUAL EFFECTS (Jim Rygiel, Joe Letteri, Randall William Cook, Alex Funke).
ACADEMY AWARDS 2004 OSCARS for BEST PICTURE (Barrie M. Osborne, Peter Jackson, Fran Walsh), BEST DIRECTOR (Peter Jackson), BEST ADAPTED SCREENPLAY (Fran Walsh, Philippa Boyens, Peter Jackson), BEST ART DIRECTION – Set Decoration (Grant Major, Dan Hennah, Alan Lee), BEST COSTUME DESIGN (Ngila Dickson, Richard Taylor), BEST FILM EDITING (Jamie Selkirk), BEST MAKEUP (Richard Taylor, Peter King), BEST MUSIC, Original Score (Howard Shore), BEST MUSIC, Original Song (Fran Walsh, Howard Shore, Annie Lennox), BEST SOUND MIXING (Christopher Boyes, Michael Semanick, Michael Hedges, Hammond Peek) and BEST VISUAL EFFECTS (Jim Rygiel, Joe Letteri, Randall William Cook, Alex Funke).

"One Ring to rule them all ..."

The magic of cinema is like the Ring that everything revolves around: a sensitive commodity. The very people who think they own it are not very good at handling its seductive power. The more global "event" cinema lavishes on action-packed projects and special effects, the weaker the magic seems to be. So it is no bad thing that, from the outset, J.R.R. Tolkien developed his "Lord of the Rings" trilogy as a parallel world, within which different standards apply. What constitutes the myth of Middle-earth has little to do with fantasy per se. The land of hobbits, elves, wizards and orcs forms a closed universe that seems far removed even from human imagination, and certainly from the mundane workings of escapist, nostalgic filmmaking. This is not the case, of course, but the success of Peter Jackson's film adaptation is clearly based on more than just the eye-watering budget of 300 million dollars, the most spectacular computer effects in movie history, and a glittering array of superb actors. The story of the film's development – itself widely advertised at great expense – is too similar to the mystical tale

1

1 Tantalizing poetry of terror: Ring-bearer Frodo (Elijah Wood) develops superhuman powers on an unprecedented journey filled with trials of endurance.

2 Not so exciting, but reliable: infallible archer Legolas (Orlando Bloom), descended from the elves, joins the Fellowship.

3 Dwarf Gimli (John Rhys-Davies) has also sworn to protect the Ring-bearer. Like the Hobbits, he was digitally shrunk.

"It may seem churlish to remember how shallow *The Lord of the Rings* is, when the Peter Jackson movies have turned out to be such terrifically enjoyable escapism. I started the series an atheist and finished an agnostic." *The Guardian*

4 Aragorn (Viggo Mortensen) is the first of the Hobbits' companions, and initially the most mysterious. As the rightful King of Gondor, he takes back the throne.

5 Gandalf (Ian McKellen), the wise wizard, fights the forces of evil with his wits and magic. His early death is one of the emotional high points of the series, but the good-natured old man returns as Gandalf the White, a quasi-godlike super-wizard with new, and destructive, powers.

itself for us not to interpret Jackson's mammoth project as the equivalent of Frodo's onerous journey to the fateful mountain.

This project could never have been realized without Jackson's belief in a higher purpose and the reward that comes from risk-taking. From initial discussions with New Line through final edit, the New Zealand director was conscious of having to fulfill the expectations of millions of Tolkien fans. The unprecedented division of the story into three films of equal length followed on from the decision to represent Tolkien's world as consistently and realistically as possible. With this order of magnitude, it was also a case of committing even skeptics to this nine-hour marathon, convincing them with a somewhat crude – and utterly humorless – admixture of New Age esotericism and medieval romanticism. The ending is familiar: over a three-year period, millions of fans old and new would rather have missed Christmas than the latest installment of the *Lord of the Rings* trilogy.

Jackson brought the mythical world of Middle-earth to life with a huge cast of human characters and fabulous creatures, a multitude of even more

stunning locations, majestic panoramic panning shots and an eye for the tiniest detail. Tantalizingly orchestrated terror made the threat to this world believable: Sauron, the unseen Dark Lord of Mordor, covets the all-powerful Ring that finds itself after a 1000-year pre-history in the possession of a small hobbit, Frodo (Elijah Wood). Sauron's fearsome servants, the Nazgûl or Ringwraiths, are already riding across the Shire, the safe world of the peace-loving hobbits, where the first part – *The Fellowship* – begins. A grueling, David-and-Goliath style battle of good against evil sees the little hobbit taking the ring to Mount Doom in order to destroy it in the fires there. The population of Middle-earth forms an alliance to protect him. With nine companions, including the wise wizard Gandalf (Ian McKellen) and future king Aragorn (Viggo Mortensen), the Ring-bearer gets caught up in countless battles with the Uruk-hai orcs, evil spawn of the wizard Saruman (Christopher Lee). It is a tale of trials: all sorts of new experiences and sacrifices make its heroes wiser, yet also sadder. It is dark subject matter, exploring primeval instinct and the fatefulness of individual actions, as much as the rational desire for a personal happy-ever-after.

PETER JACKSON Self-taught movie enthusiast Peter Jackson already had a dedicated fan base before the worldwide success of his *Lord of the Rings* trilogy. Born in 1961 in a small New Zealand coastal resort near Wellington, he began experimenting with a Super 8 movie camera and ultra-cheap special effects when still a child. Originally intended as a short film, the alien horror flick *Bad Taste* (1987) had a cast of friends like its fore-runners, with Jackson himself in front of the camera for some of the time, making the alien masks in his mother's kitchen. The film became an unexpected cult classic. Jackson confirmed his reputation as a master of gore with *Braindead* (1992). In between came *Meet the Feebles* (1989), a nihilistic parody of The Muppets with group sex orgies, drugs and vomiting bunnies. In *Heavenly Creatures* (1994) a story about two female teenage killers told in dreamlike images, this new talent mixed fantastic and realistic elements for the first time. Thanks to the newly established company, Weta Digital, he was integrating digital effects as well. His first Hollywood movie followed, with Michael J. Fox in the lead role in the convoluted horror comedy *The Frighteners* (1996). As usual, however, it was filmed almost exclusively in New Zealand. This was also where Jackson realized the most expensive film project of all time: his adaptation of J.R.R. Tolkien's literary classic, "The Lord of the Rings." Using international stars and pioneering special effects, the mammoth trilogy grossed around 3 billion dollars from a budget of 300 million. Shot simultaneously over a two-year period, the three parts – *The Fellowship of the Ring* (2001), *The Two Towers* (2002) and *The Return of the King* (2003) – won a total of 17 Oscars, including the award for Best Director. *King Kong* (2005), with only a slightly smaller budget (200 million dollars), came next. For the independent director and producer, this lavish remake of the 1933 monster classic meant the realization of a childhood dream. Against all expectations, the highly ambitious movie was by no means a flop, but instead proved once again to be a hit at the box-office.
Since then, Jackson has made *The Lovely Bones* (2009) starring Rachel Weisz and Mark Wahlberg, from the eponymous bestselling novel by Alice Sebold. Jackson's production "*The Adventures of Tintin: The Secret of the Unicorn*," directed by Steven Spielberg, is scheduled for release in 2011, with his two-part adaptation of "The Hobbit" by J.R.R. Tolkien currently in pre-production.

6 Precise eye for detail: meticulous attention was also paid to physical attributes such as the elves' ears, seen here on archer Legolas.

7 Attack of the Oliphaunts: Sauron's army has gigantic mythical creatures at its disposal, which blindly obey the Dark Lord.

8 Spawn of evil: Sauron created the Orcs and Uruk-hai, giving him almost unlimited power.

9 Ethereal beauty: elf princess Arwen (Liv Tyler) must renounce her immortality to live as a human at Aragorn's side. A heartrending decision.

"In unveiling the Holy Grail for action-fantasy aficionados, director and co-writer Peter Jackson has begun a series to rival *Star Wars* in the pantheon." *Time Out Film Guide*

9

10 Fascinating character study: schizophrenic halfling Gollum, digitally animated from actor Andy Serkis' movements, steals the show from all those involved. He proves to be an indispensable guide on the way to Mordor. What he really craves, however, is the Ring that once belonged to him – "My precious!"

"One Ring to Rule Them All. One Ring to Find Them. One Ring to Bring Them All and In The Darkness Bind Them."

Inscription of the Ring

Jackson's triumph over the real world, however, would have been unthinkable without the latest computer technology. Normal-size actors were digitally reduced to hobbit proportions, while specially developed programs created breathtaking pixel battles between fearsome monsters and vast armies. An almost totally digital character – the schizophrenic halfling Gollum, animated from the movements of the actor Andy Serkis – steals the show in the second part of the trilogy. The strange aesthetics are not based solely on modern special effects, however, but on their mingling with ancient props. Years of preparation in the shooting location, New Zealand, saw the production of tons of cast-iron swords, battle-axes, armor and belt buckles. In each case they reflect the same attention to detail as the idyllic hill formations of the Shire, the enchanted elf kingdom of Rivendell and the massive, satanic mountains of Mordor. Stereotypical Celtic and Gothic language forms merge with the unreal and the uncanny, dramatically speeded up by computer.

This extremely polymorphous world is held together by skillful editing and exquisite camerawork. As with the companions separated by various battles, a complex cliff-hanger structure also keeps the audience in suspense as to the fate of the different groups. Wildly beautiful panning shots over mountain ranges give illusory relief; here, the camera is like the glowing red eye of Sauron, from whose searching look there is virtually no escape.

11

Movie-goers are left with the sense that the full scope and splendor of Middle-earth has been opened to them. This is one of the most important differences between *The Lord of the Rings* trilogy and the less inspired imitators spawned by its success or its oft-cited predecessor, *Star Wars* (1977, 1980, 1983, 1999, 2002, 2005, 2008). The world of J.R.R. Tolkien cannot simply be constructed at will, which in turn links Middle-earth with our own world. Critical comparisons – Jackson's trilogy was read as a reflection on contemporary wars and ecological crises with their racist elements – do not do complete justice to the special quality of the work. The mythological structure of the tale is more akin to a flight into an alternative historical narrative than a fairytale relevant to the present day. With its relentless sequence of great battles and intimate moments, "The Lord of the Rings" can be seen as the modern take on "The Iliad" of Homer or even the Bible. For some, it really is a substitute religion. In the hands of Peter Jackson, who won a total of 17 Oscars for his faithful adaptation of the book, the films quite simply became three of the all-time best.

PB

12

"It's mine.
My own.
My precious!"

Bilbo Baggins

13

14

11 Love between Arwen and Aragorn begins in Rivendell. This enchanted stronghold of the elves is one of the most beautiful and delicate creations in the film.

12 Gollum, Gollum! The creature is torn between self-pity, greed and hatred in his schizophrenic conversations with himself.

13 Riders of darkness: the Nazgûl are already riding through the Shire, searching for the Ring.

14 The Riders of Rohan: the humans have military strength as well, but Sauron's armies are superior in number.

15 Shot in Peter Jackson's homeland: the mountain ranges of New Zealand form a majestic backdrop.

"Jackson's flights of fantasy bow before Tolkien and are quite unlike anything you are likely to ever see on film. Or at least until next December." *slantmagazine.com*

15

ALI

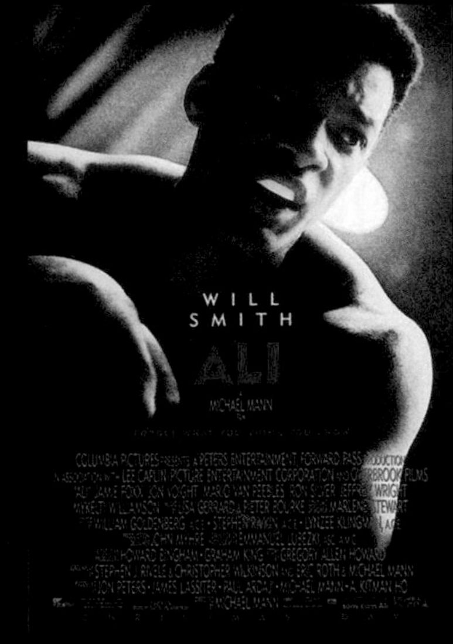

2001 – USA – 157 MIN. / 165 MIN. DIRECTOR'S CUT. – BIOPIC, BOXING MOVIE
DIRECTOR MICHAEL MANN (*1943)
SCREENPLAY GREGORY ALLEN HOWARD, STEPHEN J. RIVELE, CHRISTOPHER WILKINSON, ERIC ROTH, MICHAEL MANN DIRECTOR OF PHOTOGRAPHY EMMANUEL LUBEZKI
EDITING WILLIAM GOLDENBERG, LYNZEE KLINGMAN, STEPHEN E. RIVKIN STUART WAKS
MUSIC PIETER BOURKE, LISA GERRARD PRODUCTION PAUL ARDAJI, A. KITMAN HO, JAMES LASSITER, MICHAEL MANN, JON PETERS, MICHAEL WAXMAN, JOHN D. SCHOFIELD for COLUMBIA PICTURES, FORWARD PASS, INITIAL ENTERTAINMENT GROUP, MOONLIGHTING FILMS, OVERBROOK ENTERTAINMENT, PETERS ENTERTAINMENT, PICTURE ENTERTAINMENT CORPORATION.
STARRING WILL SMITH (Cassius Clay/Cassius X/Muhammad Ali), JAMIE FOXX (Drew "Bundini" Brown), JON VOIGHT (Howard Cosell), MARIO VAN PEEBLES (Malcolm X), GIANCARLO ESPOSITO (Cassius Clay, Sr.) RON SILVER (Angelo Dundee), JEFFREY WRIGHT (Howard Bingham), MYKELTI WILLIAMSON (Don King), JADA PINKETT SMITH (Sonji Roi), NONA GAYE (Belinda Ali), MICHAEL MICHELE (Veronica Porche), BARRY SHABAKA HENLEY (Manager).

"Float like a butterfly, sting like a bee."

He is young, fast, strong, sexy and provocatively self-confident. When Cassius Clay (Will Smith) beat Sonny Liston to win the World Heavyweight Championship in 1964, it was not only the boxing world that was turned on its head. For, unlike other black champions before him, Cassius Clay believed that his place in an American society divided by white people's racism was not just in the ring. He took the side of the Black Muslims very publicly and made a show of shedding his "slave name." From then on, he would be known as Muhammad Ali – and he rapidly danced his light-footed way from one win to the next.

Then, however, the establishment fought back. When Ali refused to do military service in 1967 at the peak of his career, denouncing the Vietnam War, he was stripped of his world title. Sentenced to five years' imprisonment and a hefty fine by the courts, he managed to stay out of prison on bail; without a passport and boxing license, however, he was forced to give up his career in the ring. Yet Ali came back to win another title fight: as a clear outsider he entered the ring against the young George Foreman in Zaire in 1974. And through winning the legendary "Rumble in the Jungle" he finally achieved mythical status. Not only is Ali regarded as the best boxer of all time, he was also the first true global star of the sport. While documentary filmmakers kept going back to his story, especially Leon Gast in his inspirational *When We Were Kings* (1996), for a long time Hollywood shied away from bringing the material to the big screen – probably out of concern that the images would have to compete with the real Ali. Michael Mann was the first to rise to the challenge. And the director of *Heat* (1995) and *The Insider* (1999) passed with flying colors. His film is a powerful homage to the unique personality of Ali.

Right from the brilliant opening sequence, Mann links his hero's story with the political events of the time. The course of Ali's life, as emphasized by the direction, does not run in some way parallel to the African-American liberation movement, but is part of it. Ali is more than just a protagonist of his own story; he is writing history. The film does not turn into an idealization of him, however, which makes it all the more remarkable. One reason for this is Emmanuel Lubezki's outstanding camerawork, which gives a fascinating directness and authenticity to even the most famous moments in Ali's life.

The fact that we are barely conscious of any comparison with the real Ali is naturally down to Will Smith, whose performance has been rated by some critics as on a par with Robert De Niro's in *Raging Bull* (1980). Indeed, Smith's portrayal is impressive in more than just the physical resemblance.

1

2

3

“It is a measure of Michael Mann’s imaginative virility as a director, and Will Smith’s status as one of Hollywood’s most charming and intelligent leading men, that this biopic fails as little as it does.” *The Guardian*

1 Story of a legend: Michael Mann’s film shows Ali (Will Smith) not as an underdog fighting his way to the top …

2 … but as a self-confident, single-minded man who knows from the outset that he is the champion.

3 Ali’s name was still Cassius Clay when he won his first World Championship title. Shortly after, he cast off his “slave name” and became Muhammad Ali, symbol of the Black Power movement.

4

4 *Ali*'s superb cast includes Will Smith's wife, Jada Pinkett Smith, as Ali's first wife; Giancarlo Esposito (l.) as his father; and Barry Shabaka Henley (r.) as his bulldog-faced manager.

5 The single, unswerving focus of the film is Will Smith, who brings Ali's charismatic appeal to the screen in an astonishingly convincing way and …

6 … oozes a sex appeal barely evident in his previous roles – seen here with Michael Michele as Veronica Porche.

"If awards still have anything to do with rewarding balls-out daring, then Michael Mann's *Ali* deserves a fistful." *Rolling Stone*

Surprisingly to many, the actor who rose to superstar status in action comedies like *Men in Black* (1997) is convincing due to a charismatic appeal astonishingly similar to that of his real-life model; an aura that is beautifully developed in cinemascope format.

Ali conspicuously flouts the dramatic dictates of mainstream cinema. The film naturally shows the eponymous hero as a ladies' man, but certainly does not focus on his private life or pass any moral judgment thereon. It is equally astonishing how little space is actually taken up by the grippingly staged boxing matches, the final fight against Foreman being the exception. And though Ali's career definitely gives us the classic suspense curve of rise, fall and comeback, the storyline is by no means presented in the usual pattern of a rollercoaster ride.

6

7 *Ali* certainly delivers some thrilling boxing sequences, but overall the fights take up surprisingly little running time.

8 Ali caused a media sensation with his irreverent humor. Here we see him reaching on camera for the hairpiece of famous sports journalist Howard Cosell (Jon Voight).

9 Black idol: Ali's famous fight in Zaire against George Foreman, "The Rumble in the Jungle," is the climax and conclusion of the movie.

"*Ali* is a bruiser, unwieldy in length and ambition. But Mann and Smith deliver this powerhouse with the urgency of a champ's left hook." *Rolling Stone*

10

10 Ali is hailed as a hero during his traveling show by ordinary people in the streets of Kinshasa. Their battle cry "Ali, bomaye!" (Ali, kill him!) spurs him on to victory against his opponent, who is deemed the superior.

11 Boxer as politician: the champ openly campaigned for the Black Muslims and their intellectual leader Malcolm X (Mario Van Peebles).

The film is not about an underdog fighting his way to the top, in search of catharsis. *Ali* follows the path of a courageous and single-minded man; a boxer who is confident in himself and knows that he is the champion. In fighting for the World Championship belt, Ali is not motivated first and foremost by wealth and status. For him, the title is above all the expression of his independence, a freedom that is not granted to him by other people, institutions or society. The World Championship title is not conferred on Ali – he takes it for himself, or so it seems. And it is this directness that determines the structure of the film. The key scene in the movie is set in Zaire. Ali walks the streets of Kinshasa, accompanied by his countless supporters: simple folk from the local population. And, when faced with their enthusiasm and the daubing on walls that celebrates him as a symbol of freedom and peace, he realizes that the impending fight against Foreman is actually a mission. When, at the end of the film, Ali climbs in triumph onto the ropes of the boxing ring, arms thrust into the night sky, it is the whole world that he is embracing. JH

EMMANUEL LUBEZKI The career of cameraman Emmanuel Lubezki, born in Mexico City in 1964, is closely linked with that of director Alfonso Cuarón. Friends since their student days, they both had their movie breakthrough with the romantic comedy *Sólo con tu pareja* (1991), the first of their five feature film collaborations to date. After Lubezki filmed Alfonso Arau's hit melodrama *Like Water for Chocolate* (*Como agua para chocolate*, 1992) the following year, he moved to America like Cuarón.
There, they made *A Little Princess* (1994), a film that earned Lubezki the first of what are now four Oscar nominations, and qualified the two filmmakers for "greater things" in the eyes of studio bosses: Cuarón's star-studded Dickens adaptation *Great Expectations* (1998) then established Lubezki's talent for sensuous, fairytale atmospheres, as did Martin Brest's *Meet Joe Black* (1998); he then went on to prove himself in the horror genre as well with Tim Burton's *Sleepy Hollow* (1999).
Since *Y tu mamá también* (*And Your Mother Too*, 2001), the Mexican low-budget road movie directed by Cuarón which became an unexpected international hit, Lubezki's trademark has increasingly been his expertise with the hand-held camera. The versatile way he uses this technique is demonstrated in his work for two directors regarded as the outstanding stylists of contemporary cinema: Lubezki shot Michael Mann's exciting, realistic biopic *Ali* (2001) as well as Terrence Malick's *The New World* (2005) and *The Tree of Life* (2011), two movies in which the cameraman proved himself the master of natural light. By contrast, Lubezki's tracking shots were impressive in a different way in Cuarón's dark futuristic vision, *Children of Men* (2006); seldom before have cinematic images conveyed with such intensity a sense of the horrors of war.

A BEAUTIFUL MIND

2001 – USA – 135 MIN. – BIOPIC, PSYCHOLOGICAL DRAMA
DIRECTOR RON HOWARD (*1954)
SCREENPLAY AKIVA GOLDSMAN from a biography by SYLVIA NASAR
DIRECTOR OF PHOTOGRAPHY ROGER DEAKINS EDITING DANIEL P. HANLEY, MIKE HILL MUSIC JAMES HORNER
PRODUCTION BRIAN GRAZER, RON HOWARD for UNIVERSAL, IMAGINE ENTERTAINMENT, DREAMWORKS SKG.
STARRING RUSSELL CROWE (John Nash), ED HARRIS (William Parcher), JENNIFER CONNELLY (Alicia Nash), CHRISTOPHER PLUMMER (Dr. Rosen), PAUL BETTANY (Charles), ADAM GOLDBERG (Sol), ANTHONY RAPP (Bender), JOSH LUCAS (Hansen), JASON GRAY-STANFORD (Ainsley), JUDD HIRSCH (Helinger), VIVIEN CARDONE (Marcee).
ACADEMY AWARDS 2002 OSCARS for BEST PICTURE (Brian Grazer, Ron Howard), BEST DIRECTOR (Ron Howard), BEST ADAPTED SCREENPLAY (Akiva Goldsman), and BEST SUPPORTING ACTRESS (Jennifer Connelly).

"There could be a mathematical explanation for how bad your tie is."

Five young women visit a bar. They are all beautiful, but the blonde in the middle of their group is attracting everyone's attention. So what happens when five young men, promising scientists every one, all make a pass at her at the same time? They obstruct one another, the four remaining girls are offended and every one of them spends the night alone. The only solution to the problem: a joint agreement in the best possible interests of all.

John Nash (Russell Crowe) is in the process of developing the game theory that will win him the Nobel Prize decades later. Adam Smith has had his day, and the future belongs to "governing dynamics." Meanwhile, the engineer of this scientific revolution is an oddball at the mathematics faculty of Princeton University – muttering under his breath, drawing circles in the air and generally giving the impression of being somewhere else. He considers academic papers and lessons a waste of time. For the numbers genius, social interaction is one of the theoretical words he likes to borrow, without understanding what it means in practice. To his fellow students, this eccentric outsider is an enigma, just as much as he is to himself.

It soon becomes apparent that John Nash is suffering from paranoid schizophrenia. The symptoms worsen, with his intellectual world becoming increasingly confused. He becomes a Pentagon spy, decoding the political enemy's secret messages from newspaper articles, and repeatedly prevents a threatened atomic bomb attack on the USA by Russia. His paranoia is that of the Cold War. Yet his handler, the sinister William Parcher (Ed Harris) in the floppy hat, is only a figment of his imagination – just like his room-mate Charles (Paul Bettany), whom he regards as his best friend. Hounded by his demons, John slips into madness under the eyes of the psychiatrists. It takes time, better medication and the love of his wife Alicia (Jennifer Connelly) to help

him recover, together with the award of the Nobel Prize in 1994, a late recognition of one of the most important mathematicians of the twentieth century.

Or did John Nash cure himself, through the power of his own logic? In *A Beautiful Mind*, two genres compete with each other – the biopic and science fiction. Director Ron Howard did not opt conclusively for one or the other, thereby attracting a great deal of criticism but also four Oscars. For Howard's tale of genius and madness has little to do with the life of the real John Nash (*1928). No mention is made of his homosexual tendencies, his illegitimacy or the intermittent separation from his wife, who was far less patient with the schizophrenic's suffering than her angelic counterpart in the film. Ron Howard, held in awe for his sentimental films "inspired" by real life (*Apollo 13*, 1995), had pulled it off once more. Yet here, of all places, his high-handed approach

"With insidious skill, the movie plays on our willing suspension of disbelief, our readiness in the shadowy cavern of the cinema to believe in the presence of aliens and elaborate conspiracies. In fact, *A Beautiful Mind* is pulling us into the mind of a paranoid schizophrenic." *The Observer*

3

1 Mathematics as abstract art: numerical genius John Nash (Russell Crowe) lives in his own world. For him, formulae are a substitute for human communication.

2 His employer, the sinister CIA agent William Parcher (Ed Harris), only exists in Nash's imagination.

3 Sheltered from the outside world: Alicia (Jennifer Connelly) senses that she is gradually losing her husband. They both have to live with his illness.

4 Nobel Prizewinner as a young man: Russell Crowe won an Oscar nomination for his humorous and moving portrait of a disabled genius.

"Mr Crowe, with his superhuman powers of concentration, shows us a man who dwells almost entirely in an inner world, and he dramatizes that inwardness as if nobody were watching." *The New York Times*

5

5 As a student, Alicia met and fell in love with the young John Nash at M.I.T. Jennifer Connelly is superb in the role, for which she won an Oscar.

6 Friends for life. Nash gets on surprisingly well with his laidback roommate, Charles (Paul Bettany); like little Marcee (Vivien Cardone) he, too, is a product of his imagination. He must learn to ignore them both.

had its own logic. Basically, Howard makes films the way Nash did math. The social world is reduced to recognizable patterns and relationships. This is what the thought experiment at the beginning means: Howard sets it out formulaically, fitting it neatly into the picture. If, like Nash, one sees math as abstract art, the mathematician himself becomes an abstract quantity. John Nash does not exist. He realizes himself through the wild collage of newspaper clippings with which he plasters his office and the columns of formulae painted on glass panels. His life amounts to nothing more than a "dead drop:" a mass of obscure information. Russell Crowe conveyed the pathos of Nash's situation to staggering effect, reducing entire audiences to tears. His acting follows the Hollywood template for portraying disability established in *Rain Man* (1988); it is devoid of overacting, however, and for this very reason is deeply moving. Never before has a Hollywood star been seen to smoke in such a geeky way. His Nash draws us into his illness with nervous gesticulations, searching looks and awkward smiles – and we find ourselves inside this mad mind far sooner than anticipated. Howard's game theory has worked: how do I reduce and change a true story in such a way that my colleagues and I win as many Oscars as possible? Mathematics for all – with maximum success. PB

RON HOWARD Many Americans have grown up with the films of Ron Howard and he is now one of the most influential and successful directors in Hollywood. At the tender age of 6, little, red-haired "Ronny Howard" had a part in the small-town series *The Andy Griffith Show* (1960–1968) and later played one of the teenagers in George Lucas' *American Graffiti* (1973). Encouraged by B-movie legend Roger Corman, he ventured into directing with an inoffensive debut, *Grand Theft Auto* (1977).
Blockbusters soon followed: *Splash* (1984), *Cocoon* (1985), *Willow* (1988), *Parenthood* (1989), *Backdraft* (1991) with Robert De Niro, *Far and Away* (1992) with Nicole Kidman and *Apollo 13* (1995) with Tom Hanks, all of which benefited from his considerable technical skills. Yet Howard wanted more. With *A Beautiful Mind* (2001) and *Cinderella Man* (2005), his picture about a boxer's failed life during the Depression, he turned increasingly to darker themes. He has become a specialist in exemplary biographical films distinguished by exquisitely nostalgic set designs, outstanding performances and a good dose of schmaltz – no one in Hollywood is better at softening hard subjects than Ron Howard. He has been rewarded with two Oscars to date, both for *A Beautiful Mind*. With the sensational conspiracy thriller *The Da Vinci Code* (2006) from the bestselling novel by Dan Brown, he went back to his original strengths; in spite of scathing criticism, it generated astronomical box-office returns, as did the sequel *Angels*

8 WOMEN
8 FEMMES

2001 – FRANCE – 103 MIN. – MUSICAL, COMEDY, THRILLER
DIRECTOR FRANÇOIS OZON (*1967)
SCREENPLAY FRANÇOIS OZON, MARINA DE VAN, from a play by ROBERT THOMAS
DIRECTOR OF PHOTOGRAPHY JEANNE LAPOIRIE EDITING LAWRENCE BAWEDIN MUSIC KRISHNA LEVY
PRODUCTION OLIVIER DELBOSC, MARC MISSONIER FOR BIM, CANAL+, CENTRE NATIONAL DE LA CINÉMATOGRAPHIE, FIDÉLITÉ PRODUCTIONS, FRANCE 2 CINÉMA, GIMAGES 5, LOCAL FILMS, MARS FILMS.
STARRING CATHERINE DENEUVE (Gaby), ISABELLE HUPPERT (Augustine), DANIELLE DARRIEUX (Mamy), FANNY ARDANT (Pierrette), EMMANUELLE BÉART (Louise), VIRGINIE LEDOYEN (Suzon), LUDIVINE SAGNIER (Catherine), FIRMINE RICHARD (Madame Chanel), DOMINIQUE LAMURE (Marcel, The Husband).
IFF BERLIN 2002 SILVER BEAR for "AN OUTSTANDING ARTISTIC CONTRIBUTION BY AN ENSEMBLE OF ACTRESSES" (Catherine Deneuve, Isabelle Huppert, Emmanuelle Béart, Fanny Ardant, Virginie Ledoyen, Danielle Darrieux, Firmine Richard, Ludivine Sagnier).

"Actually, it's like a detective novel: one of us isn't telling the truth, and she is the murderer."

Eight women, cut off from the outside world in a snow-bound country house. Plus a man, the head of the household. But he is lying face down on the bed – with a knife in his back. Suzon (Virginie Ledoyen) is home from college to spend Christmas in the bosom of her family: with "Papa" Marcel, a successful businessman; her mother, Gaby, as elegant as she is remote (Catherine Deneuve); and her little sister, Catherine (Ludivine Sagnier), who devours trashy novels in rapid succession and hates the fact that at 16 she is still treated as the baby of the family. Then there's the grandmother, "Mamy" (Danielle Darrieux), who may be stuck in a wheelchair but can still hold her liquor; she has sought refuge in her son-in-law's house with her haggard younger daughter, Augustine (Isabelle Huppert). And, of course, the house has its worthy soul: the cook, Madame Chanel (Firmine Richard). But now Papa is dead – murdered. So, instead of enjoying an idyllic family celebration, Suzon is suddenly confronted with a scene out of an Agatha Christie detective novel. For it goes without saying that the culprit, or rather the female culprit, must still be in the house. Suspicion quickly falls on Marcel's floozy sister, Pierrette (Fanny Ardant), who has turned up unexpectedly. It is clear, however, that even the mild-mannered maid Louise (Emmanuelle Béart) knows more than she is letting on. Indeed,

1

"Movies like *8 Women* are essentially made for movie-lovers. You have to have seen overdecorated studio musicals, and you have to know who Darrieux and Deneuve and Beart and Huppert and Ardant are, to get the full flavor." *Chicago Sun-Times*

it soon becomes apparent that all the women present are hiding a juicy secret. Yet the question of who killed Papa is not really what François Ozon's musical ensemble comedy is about. *8 Women* is actually a study of the very enigma of French cinema itself: the actresses. Indeed, Truffaut's comment that the job of a director is to get beautiful women to do beautiful things can surely not have been applied with as much evident pleasure since George Cukor's *The Women* (1939), as the murder plot of this lurid yet lightly comedic whodunit is merely a vehicle for letting eight fabulous actresses loose on one another.

Ozon does not even attempt to make the outrageous plot credible. He wants to provide the perfect stage for his stars, conveying this from the start through a kitschy aesthetic style with garish colors, theatrical sets and symmetrical shots reminiscent of Douglas Sirk's melodramas of the 1950s or a Jacques Demy musical such as *The Umbrellas of Cherbourg* (*Les parapluies de Cherbourg*, 1964). In this respect, it is no great surprise when Ludivine Sagnier suddenly breaks into song with "Papa, t'es plus dans l'coup" ("Daddy, you're not in it anymore") with Catherine Deneuve and Virginie Ledoyen dancing along, or when Isabelle Huppert seats herself at the piano and gives a stunning rendition of Françoise Hardy's "Message Personnel," or when Danielle Darrieux brings the preceding turmoil to a mature conclusion with her version of Georges Brassens's "Il n'y a pas d'amour heureux" ("There's no happiness in love").

Ozon makes an aesthetic link between *8 Women* and his film version of Fassbinder's *Water Drops on Burning Rocks* (*Gouttes d'eau sur pierres brûlantes*,

1 The enigma of French cinema per se: its female stars. François Ozon presents eight of them in a lurid comedy thriller that would simply be spoiled by the presence of men.

2 Catfight: Isabelle Huppert (left) as the haggard spinster and Emmanuelle Béart as the sexy maid are as diametrically opposed as …

3 … the two Truffaut muses, Catherine Deneuve (left) and Fanny Ardant. But Ozon's actress tribute has a few surprising twists in store.

2

FRANÇOIS OZON In French auteur cinema, which is currently experiencing a crisis, Ozon is the only new director in recent years to command a fairly large international fan base. One reason for this, no doubt, is that his films are in the tradition of the great French "women's directors" like Truffaut or Sautet, while their stridency, originality and liberal tendency has grabbed the attention of younger film buffs. Born in Paris in 1967 and a La Fémis film school graduate, Ozon revealed a personal signature even in his early short films while establishing his trademark themes – for example, the fetishism, homosexuality and dissolution of gender roles in *A Summer Dress* (*Une robe d'été*, 1996). Ozon caused more of a stir for the first time with the medium-length macabre thriller *See the Sea* (*Regarde la mer*, 1997), before directing his first full-length feature, the black comedy *Sitcom* (1998). *Criminal Lovers* (*Les amants criminels*, 1999), a disturbing mixture of didactic drama, gangster movie and fairytale, was followed by *Water Drops on Burning Rocks* (*Gouttes d'eau sur pierres brûlantes*, 1999), a theatrical psychodrama from a play by his hero, Rainer Werner Fassbinder. Ozon's preference for female leads was established in *Under the Sand* (*Sous le sable*, 2000), an intense psychodrama in which Charlotte Rampling made her first appearance in front of his camera. The musical comedy *8 Women* (*8 femmes*, 2002), Ozon's biggest success to date, confirmed his reputation as a woman's director, as did the excellent thriller *Swimming Pool* (2003). In *Five Times Two* (*5x2*, 2004), a love story told backwards, Ozon reflected without illusions on a failed marriage. With *Time to Leave* (*Le temps qui reste*, 2005) he produced a sensitive drama about cancer. Finally, *Angel* (2006), the story of the rise and fall of a woman writer from a poor background, once again showed Ozon to be

4

"In a cast where everybody has fun, Huppert has the most, as Augustine. She and her mother (Darrieux) have been living rent-free in Marcel's cottage with her sister (Deneuve), but that has not inspired Augustine to compromise in her fierce resentment and spinsterish isolation. She stalks around the set like Whistler's mother, frowning from behind her horn-rims and making disapproval into a lifestyle." *Chicago Sun-Times*

2000), which is admittedly a rather gloomy, highly artificial chamber play with musical elements. Yet, in other respects, the *enfant terrible* of French auteur cinema remains true to himself. At least it should come as no great surprise to his fans that he relishes the deconstruction of bourgeois respectability through his tongue-in-cheek thriller, staging the cozy, upper class home as a clinically clean façade behind which the burning depths of human passions are concealed. In Ozon's cinematic world, avarice, jealousy and sado-masochism are as natural as homosexuality and the dissolution of traditional gender roles. This adds a delightful piquancy to the divas' antics.

8 Women is the gift of a cineaste to movie lovers. Anyone who comes into this category and does not reject musicals out of hand will experience the film, with its countless references to cinema history, as a jam-packed lucky bag, a cabaret of magical moments. It's impossible not to think of Truffaut when his muses Fanny Ardant and Catherine Deneuve are rolling around the floor, hair flying, only to start cuddling the next minute. Does Ozon love women? When asked this question by a journalist, Deneuve replied suggestively that she could not possibly answer that. He definitely does love actresses, though. It speaks for itself.

JH

4 *8 Women* brings together four generations of French cinema's female stars. Their obvious delight in making this spoof is written all over their faces.

5 The divas' dancing and singing numbers are among the high points of the movie. Catherine Deneuve is seen here in a wonderful scene reminiscent of her performances in the musicals of Jacques Demy.

6 Isabelle Huppert has the courage to be ugly: but elderly spinster Augustine gets her moment in the spotlight …

7 Whodunit? Suzon (Virginie Ledoyen) with the alleged proof. But who cares about the truth, when the hunt for the perpetrator is as entertaining as it is in Ozon's tongue-in-cheek comedy?

"… all eight women are something to see and marvel at. Whatever you call this one-of-a-kind bonbon spiked with wit and malice, it's classic oo-la-la." *Rolling Stone*

7

ICE AGE

2001 – USA – 81 MIN. – ANIMATION, COMEDY
DIRECTOR CHRIS WEDGE (*1957), CARLOS SALDANHA (*1968)
SCREENPLAY MICHAEL J. WILSON, MICHAEL BERG, PETER ACKERMAN
EDITING JOHN CARNOCHAN MUSIC DAVID NEWMAN PRODUCTION JOHN C. DONKIN, LORI FORTE, CHRISTOPHER MELEDANDRI for 20TH CENTURY FOX, BLUE SKY STUDIOS.
VOICES RAY ROMANO (Manfred), JOHN LEGUIZAMO (Sid), DENIS LEARY (Diego), GORAN VISNJIC (Soto), JACK BLACK (Zeke), CEDRIC THE ENTERTAINER (Carl), STEPHEN ROOT (Frank/Start), DIEDRICH BADER (Saber-Toothed Tiger), ALAN TUDYK (Lenny/Oscar/Dab), LORRI BAGLEY (Jennifer), JANE KRAKOWSKI (Rachel), PETER ACKERMAN (Dodo/Macrauchenia), P.J. BENJAMIN (Dodo), JOSH HAMILTON (Dodo/Erdferkel), CHRIS WEDGE (Dodo/Scrat), TARA STRONG (Baby Roshan).

"Come on guys, stick together"

Although this movie is set in a dark period of Earth's history – an ice age 20,000 years ago – the subject matter could hardly be more topical: climate change forcing all living creatures to migrate to warmer zones. Furthermore, this ecological disaster is not a stroke of fate, but creature-made. A prehistoric saber-toothed squirrel called Scrat (Chris Wedge) tries desperately to bury his precious acorn in a time when food is short, but this apparently innocent operation triggers an avalanche that displaces entire mountains. In the process, *Ice Age* makes equal reference to the early and pre-history of moving images, for species extinction and evolution form the framework for a manic rollercoaster ride through a "cinema of attractions" packed with slapstick and humor.

Sid (John Leguizamo), a clumsy sloth that has abandoned his family, and eccentric mammoth Manfred (Ray Romano) meet up right at the start of the film. When a human settlement is attacked by saber-toothed tigers – seeking revenge for their fellow species members that have been killed – Stone Age woman Nadia dies in the torrential waters of a river. Her child Baby Roshan (Tara Strong), however, is saved by Manfred. Elective affinities and unnatural alliances seem to be central to the plot. In a narrative reminiscent of *Monsters, Inc.* (2001), the sloth and the mammoth decide to return the child to its own kind; they turn around, choosing to take the dangerous route over the glacier. Before long, saber-toothed tiger Diego (Denis Leary) joins the trio. His secret mission is to bring the baby back alive to his leader.

Thus begins the turbulent journey of four very different teammates who slowly find common ground. After Nadia's death, however, any female creatures are conspicuous by their absence: women are apparently superfluous for this type of evolutionary story. The arduous way leads eventually through a huge museum-like cave; alongside animals frozen in ice or already extinct there is

1

2

1 Scrat – a combination of the words "squirrel" and "rat" – is the most popular character in *Ice Age.*

2 As only becomes clear in the sequel *Ice Age: The Meltdown* (2006), saber-toothed tiger Diego suffers from aquaphobia.

3 Food may be scarce in the Ice Age, but this prehistoric squirrel has a real obsession with an acorn.

"... the ice age is dawning, thanks in part to the hyperactive antics of a prehistoric rodent – half squirrel, half rat, all nervous energy – named Scrat." *Variety*

5

4 Sid the sloth is by no means lazy: he does some pretty acrobatic ski moves to save Roshan.

5 Stoic woolly mammoth Manfred is slow to warm to the exuberant giant sloth.

6 The friends must overcome many dangers: avalanches, glacial caves and lava flows, as well as a pack of saber-toothed tigers.

also the UFO recovered by scientists from the ice in sci-fi movie *The Thing from Another World* (1951). In a key scene, the four friends inspect the cave paintings. And the philosophical question as to whether androids dream of electric sheep receives a clear answer – the subconscious of computer-animated characters is imagined as an early form of hand-drawn cartoon animation.

The audience also finds out why the mammoth is on his own: his family has fallen victim to the spears of human hunters. But now Manfred has found a substitute – when the group gets caught in a lava flow, he puts his own life on the line by saving Diego. As planned, the four friends are lured into an ambush by the saber-toothed tigers, but Diego finally stands up to his own pack: love, friendship and team spirit conquer bloodlust and the desire for revenge. Roshan is handed over to her father and both Manfred and Diego decide to make peace with the humans.

In *Ice Age*, survival is not assured by war and the physical ability to adapt. Instead, as the anarchist, geographer and writer Pjotr Kropotkin wrote back in 1900, evolutionary progress only happens through mutual support. According

"This digitally animated movie, filled with a cast of charming, funny critters from long ago, is family entertainment at its most bright-eyed and bushy-tailed." *The Washington Post*

7

8

7 The convincing representation of structures and textures like ice and fur is a challenge for digital animation.

8 Sid talks with a lisp, Manfred has a New York accent, and Diego rarely loses his cool.

9 Mastery of fire is fundamental to the development of civilization – but Sid turns even this into slapstick.

ANIMATION FILMS The first animation films developed in parallel with early cinema. This genre denotes techniques that are not filmed in real time. Instead, it involves editing separate images together in such a way that the audience perceives them as a motion picture. To do this, filmmakers need to use around 24 images per second; cartoons entail a huge amount of work. They were traditionally based on photos or drawings, but there were also experiments with silhouettes and boards of nails; the second of these methods involved a box containing over a hundred thousand adjustable nails, which were used to create light and shadow images.
Nowadays, many of the blockbusters are created using predominantly computer-based, specialist software; alternatively, traditionally captured material is digitized and processed. This raises the question as to whether films in which the characters' movements are produced by what is known as "motion capture" can be classified as marionette or hand-puppet movies – this process makes it possible to record the movements of living creatures and convert them into computer graphics. Animation films are found not only in cinema, television and advertising but also in art, architecture, design and the natural sciences.

to the film, however, this solidarity occurs exclusively in the bourgeois nuclear family, regardless of all the flocks, herds and packs. These traditional values – upheld by many American animation films and Walt Disney in particular – experience a fundamental revision in this movie through the idea of the multicultural patchwork. And, although it deals with ecological issues, the spheres of man and animal remain distinctly separate. That said, the delightful escapades of the hybrid creature Scrat in the opening and closing sequences focus on the central role of nature as a chaotic force in the development of species; and even the greatest cultural achievements like fire, for instance, are seen to occur by chance and as a result of teamwork, not through the efforts of individuals. The existence of every life form, no matter how stupid and irritating, is justified in this film. PLB

9

TALK TO HER

HABLE CON ELLA

2002 – SPAIN – 112 MIN. – MELODRAMA
DIRECTOR PEDRO ALMODÓVAR (*1951)
SCREENPLAY PEDRO ALMODÓVAR DIRECTOR OF PHOTOGRAPHY JAVIER AGUIRRESAROBE
EDITING JOSÉ SALCEDO MUSIC ALBERTO IGLESIAS PRODUCTION MICHEL RUBEN, AGUSTÍN ALMODÓVAR for EL DESEO S.A., ANTENA 3 TELEVISIÓN, GOOD MACHINE, VÍA DIGITAL.
STARRING JAVIER CÁMARA (Benigno Martín), DARÍO GRANDINETTI (Marco Zuluaga), LEONOR WATLING (Alicia), ROSARIO FLORES (Lydia González), MARIOLA FUENTES (Rosa), GERALDINE CHAPLIN (Katerina Bilova), ROBERTO ÁLVAREZ (Doctor), ELENA ANAYA (Ángela), LOLA DUEÑAS (Matilde), FELE MARTÍNEZ (Alfredo), PAZ VEGA (Amparo).
ACADEMY AWARDS 2003 OSCAR for BEST ORIGINAL SCREENPLAY (Pedro Almodóvar).

"Tell me everything!"

Benigno (Javier Cámara) and Marco (Darío Grandinetti) happen to sit next to each other in the theater. Soon after, their paths cross again – this time in the hospital, where Benigno works as a nurse. He dedicates himself to caring for Alicia (Leonor Watling), a young dancer who has been lying in a coma since an automobile crash and with whom he has been secretly in love since before the accident. Marco, who earns a living as a travel writer, shares a similar fate. His love is for Lydia (Rosario Flores), a bullfighter rendered unconscious by an injury in the arena. Unlike Benigno, however, who talks incessantly to Alicia, Marco sits silently at Lydia's bedside, as if she were already dead. Yet a friendship develops between the two men; one that endures even following Lydia's demise and the arrest of Benigno soon after, on the accusation of making Alicia pregnant.

It is rather unusual to find the surges of emotion of traditional "women's pictures" in contemporary cinema. In Pedro Almodóvar's films, they are the norm. *Women on the Verge of a Nervous Breakdown* (*Mujeres al borde de un ataque de nervios*, 1988), the title of his hit comedy, could well be used as a caption for the Spaniard's filmography: in the 1980s he achieved cult status with flamboyant farces and rose to become master of the modern movie melodrama with his Oscar-winning masterpiece *All About My Mother* (*Todo sobre mi madre*, 1999).

Almodóvar's career is remarkable, precisely because he has remained true to himself in his films, whether comedies or melodramas; and not only in his sympathy for eccentric figures and a penchant for a garish aesthetic style that does not shy away from kitsch. Even though the star of European auteur cinema (who openly admits to being homosexual and a "mummy's boy") has long since outgrown his role as *enfant terrible*, Almodóvar has retained his zest for provoking the macho culture of his native Spain with wonderfully vulgar jokes and by crossing all sorts of boundaries.

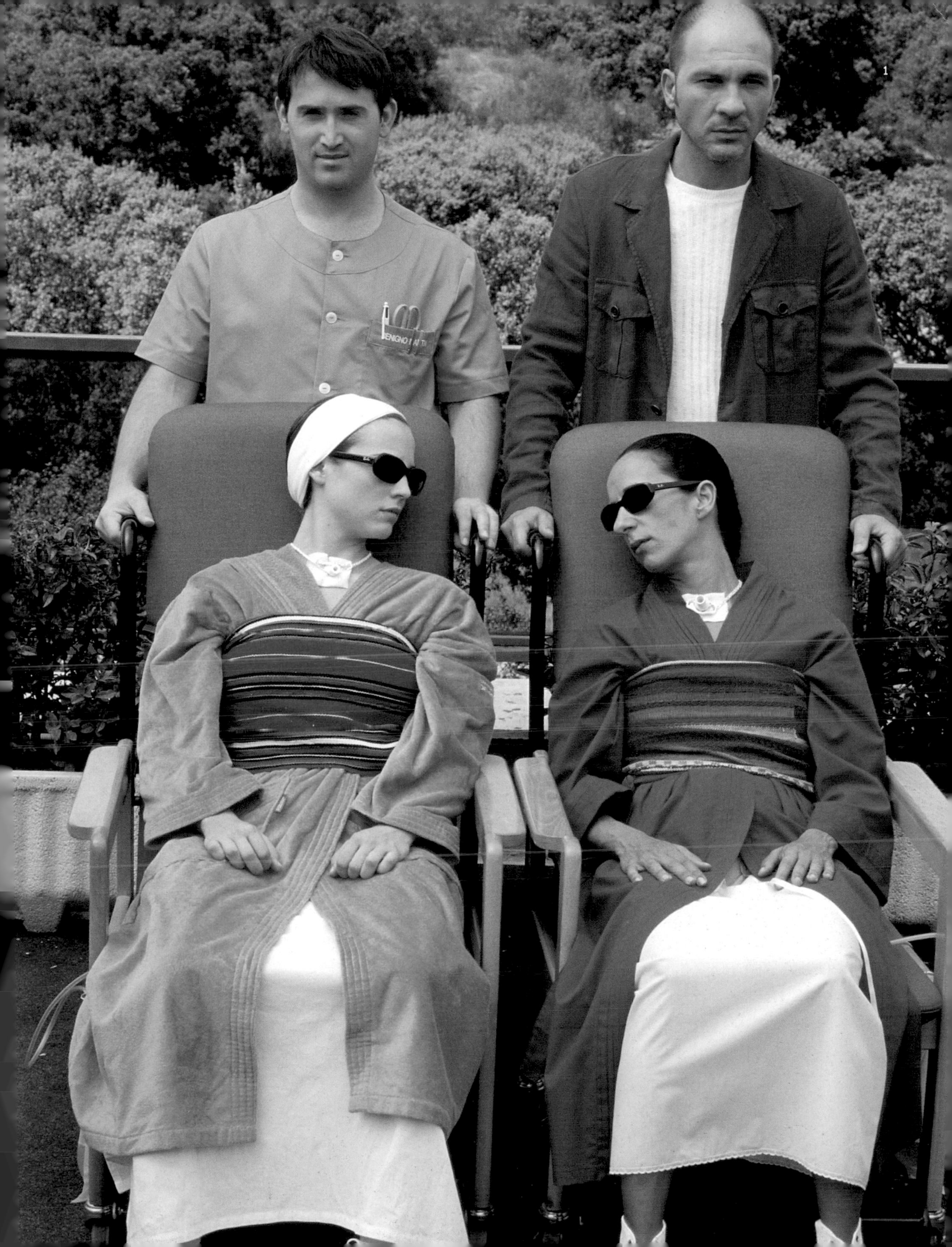

1

1 The cinema of Pedro Almodóvar, the great director of melodrama, is a combination of extreme artificiality and real feeling. This includes his masterpiece *Talk to Her*, the story of two men whose lovers are both in a coma.

2 Not a macho man: Marco (Darío Grandinetti), ruggedly handsome on the outside, turns out to be ultra sensitive.

3 Geraldine Chaplin, at one time Carlos Saura's favorite leading lady, plays ballet teacher Katerina Bilova – a classic role for Charlie Chaplin's daughter, who once wanted to become a dancer herself.

"*Talk to Her* combines improbable melodrama (gored bullfighters, comatose ballerinas) with subtly kinky bedside vigils and sensational denouements, and yet at the end, we are undeniably touched." *Chicago Sun-Times*

4

4 Compared to Almodóvar's earlier works, *Talk to Her* seems less flamboyant – probably because, for a change, men take center stage in this movie.

5 Almodóvar's bravura is also evident in his sensitive portrayal of Alicia, who is lying in a coma. The part of the "sleeping" dancer presented an unusual challenge for actress Leonor Watling.

So, in *Talk to Her* – which for a change shows two men on the edge of a nervous breakdown – the traditional gender roles are also suspended: the androgynous nature of Benigno, a gentle oddball whom his colleagues think is gay, makes him as typical an Almodóvar character as Lydia, the female bullfighter. And Marco, who is attractively masculine on the outside, reveals himself at the start as a "softie," when tears stream down his cheeks in the theater. In spite of these unusual characters, *Talk to Her* on the whole lacks the shrill tone so typical of Almodóvar. There is no strident outburst of temper, verging on hysteria, which is usually a distinctive feature in his films. The vulnerability of his protagonists is conspicuous and makes them appear withdrawn, with the film's color scheme similarly toned down to match. So by Almodóvar standards, at any rate, *Talk to Her* is a rather quiet melodrama that tells the story of the power of love and the value of friendship – but, above all, of the fear and inability of lovers to communicate and open up to one another. Almodóvar uses a device in order to convey the hidden desires and agonies of his introverted heroes: he externalizes their emotional lives to a degree by introducing artists such as Pina Bausch and her famous dance theater or Caetano Veloso, who sings a wonderfully melancholic version of the well-known Mexican song, "Cucurrucucu Paloma." But the (strange) highpoint of the film is a "fake" silent film in which a shrunken man disappears into his

ALBERTO IGLESIAS Pedro Almodóvar's recent films have an unmistakably melancholic, mysterious sound, produced by Spain's most famous and most honored film composer, Alberto Iglesias. Born in San Sebastian in 1955, he began to write film scores in the 1980s. This classically trained Basque musician, who also appears as a composer of electronic music, attracted considerable attention for the first time with Julio Medem's outstanding feature film debut, *Cows* (*Vacas*, 1991/1992), with a soundtrack that added considerably to its gloomy, magical mood. They continued their successful collaboration in the years that followed: Medem's *The Red Squirrel* (*La ardilla roja*, 1993), *Earth* (*Tierra*,1996), *The Lovers of the Arctic Circle* (*Los amantes del Círculo Polar*, 1998) and *Sex and Lucía* (*Lucía y el sexo*, 2001) each won Iglesias the Goya award for best Spanish film composer of the year. With *The Flower of My Secret* (*La flor de mi secreto*, 1995) he began his ongoing partnership with Almodóvar, which includes masterly melodramas such as *All About My Mother* (*Todo sobre mi madre*, 1999), *Talk to Her* (*Hable con ella*, 2002) and *To Return* (*Volver*, 2006), which likewise brought Iglesias the premier Spanish film award.

Although his subtle compositions have little in common with the prevalent manipulative Hollywood style, Iglesias has now also become established internationally: he composed the music for Oliver Stone's *Comandante* (2002) and Steven Soderbergh's two-parter, *Che: Part One* (2008) and *Che: Part Two* (2008), as well as the Oscar-nominated soundtracks for Fernando Meirelles' *The Constant Gardener* (2005) and Marc Forster's *The Kite Runner* (2007).

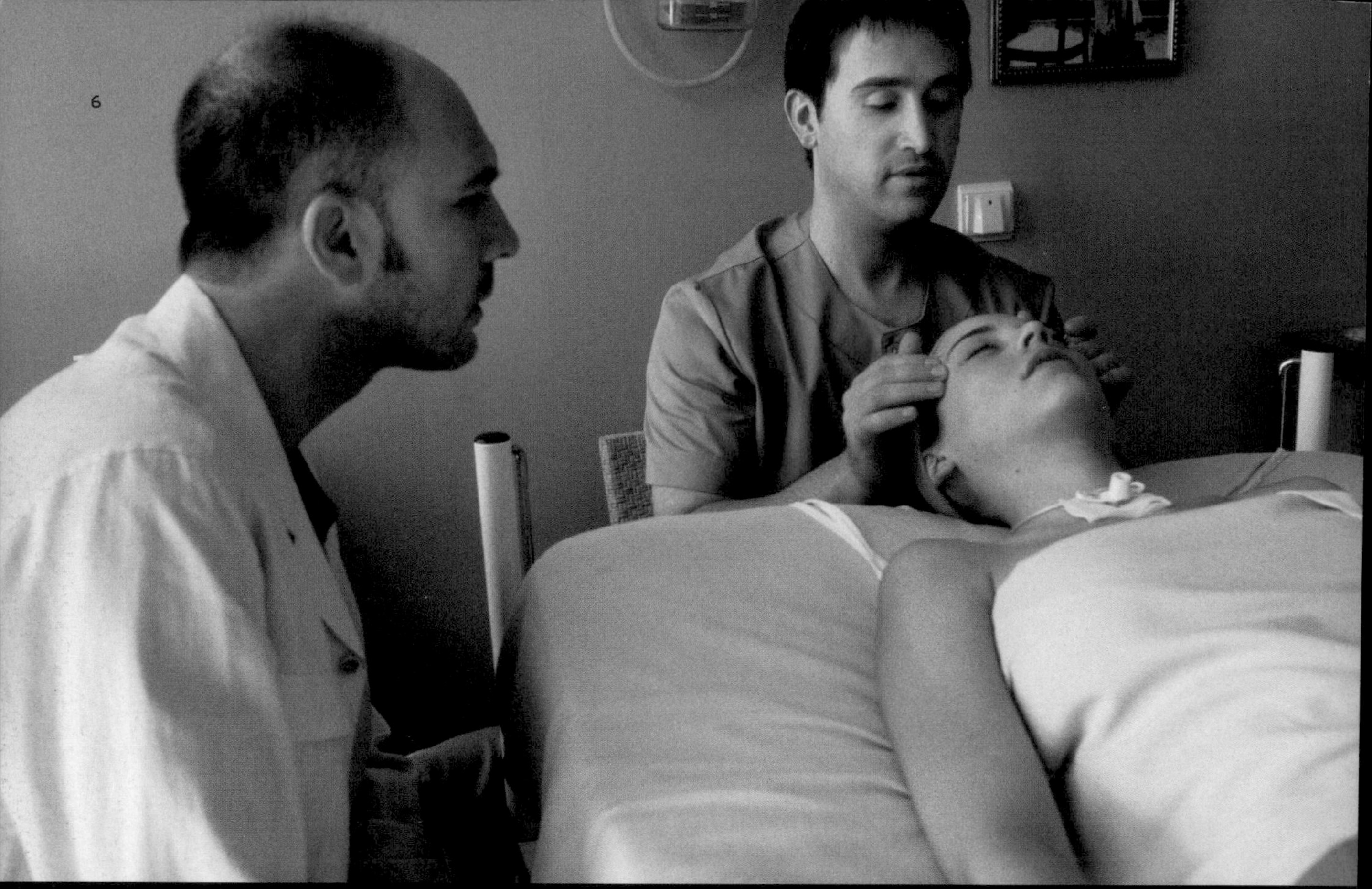

6 Unlike Marco, Benigno talks to Alicia incessantly. Javier Cámara won the Audience Award for Best Actor at the 2002 European Film Awards for his performance as the misfit.

7 Almodóvar has always loved to poke fun at Spanish macho culture. *Talk to Her* not only presents us with a female toreador (Rosario Flores), but also …

8 … a bizarre silent movie about a shrinking man who slips into his lover's enormous vagina, never to return.

lover's vagina, never to be seen again. It is an example of just how little Almodóvar's fantasy takes account of political correctness, and at the same time of how far he will go in subjecting the viewer to ambivalent experiences. For the scene that seems so amusing at first glance ultimately leads to Benigno's abuse of Alicia, suggested through the coalescing bubbles of a lava lamp in the film. Movie magician Pedro Almodóvar presents a conundrum: not only are his melodramas not thrown off balance by the most extreme and improbable twists and turns, they somehow gain in emotional intensity thereby. A high degree of artificiality and the utmost emotional authenticity always go hand-in-hand in his films. This is true of *Talk to Her*, in which the artificial, decidedly mysterious mise-en-scène corresponds perfectly to the outrageous leaps in the screenplay. In the cinema of Pedro Almodóvar, everything seems possible at any given moment – even the miracle of a woman who wakens from a coma in childbirth.

JH

"At the risk of sounding pretentious, I'd say that *Talk to Her* is like an exquisite Swiss watch powered by a Mediterranean heart." *The Observer*

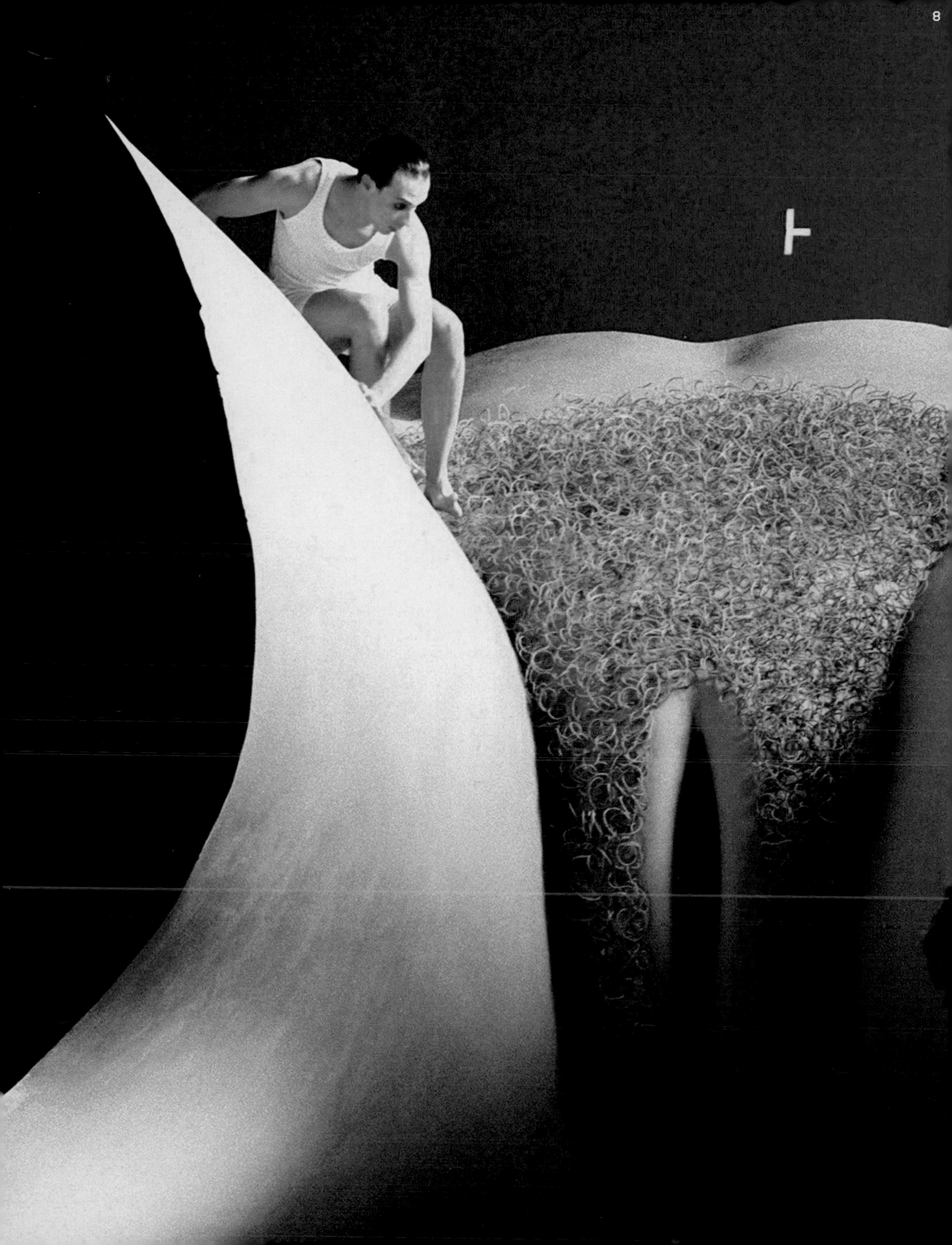

MY BIG FAT GREEK WEDDING

2002 – USA / CANADA – 95 MIN. – COMEDY
DIRECTOR JOEL ZWICK (*1942)
SCREENPLAY NIA VARDALOS DIRECTOR OF PHOTOGRAPHY JEFF JUR EDITING MIA GOLDMAN
MUSIC ALEXANDER JANKO, CHRIS WILSON PRODUCTION GARY GOETZMAN, TOM HANKS, RITA WILSON for HBO, MPH, GOLD CIRCLE, PLAYTONE, BIG WEDDING, ONTARIO FILM DEVELOPMENT CORPORATION.
STARRING NIA VARDALOS (Toula Portokalos), MICHAEL CONSTANTINE (Gus Portokalos), LAINIE KAZAN (Maria Portokalos), LOUIS MANDYLOR (Nick Portokalos), JOHN CORBETT (Ian Miller), FIONA REID (Harriet Miller), BRUCE GRAY (Rodney Miller), ANDREA MARTIN (Aunt Voula), GALE GARNETT (Aunt Lexy), STAVROULA LOGOTHETTIS (Athena), JOEY FATONE (Angelo).

"What do you mean he don't eat no meat? t Oh, that's okay. I make lamb."

Even now, no one is quite sure how a small, underfinanced ethno-comedy managed to become the most successful independent film of all time. If you were to ask Gus Portokalos (Michael Constantine), the proudest Greek man in all Chicago, however, the answer would be clear. Ethno-comedy? The origin of the word is Greek! The Greeks invented everything: astronomy, philosophy and democracy. Every word in the human language, even "kimono," has Greek roots. So it's only logical that, with a 5-million-dollar mini-budget, *My Big Fat Greek Wedding* was able to pull in over 368 million dollars worldwide, outstripping even the relative profit margin of *Titanic* (1997).

With the fiercely vocal pride of an immigrant, Gus makes the life of his daughter Toula (Nia Vardalos) even more difficult. Just turned 30, the ugly duckling has long since (wrongly) believed that she is past her "sell-by date." After all, the main purpose in life of Greek girls is "to marry Greek boys, make Greek babies and stuff everyone full of food till the end of their days." According to her, this is how her parents, and everyone else's, view the matter. Yet Toula cannot fulfill the desperate wishes of her huge family (she has 27 cousins alone). Her American dream is slightly different – she wants to be a travel agent. Working in her father Gus's restaurant, "Dancing Zorba's," causes her untold agonies. But when she finally does attract a man and visibly blossoms, total disaster looms. For Ian Miller (John Corbett) is not only a vegetarian but, as the name itself indicates – he is not Greek! Gus the patriarch is horrified. The word "patriarchy" is also Greek in origin, though it is understood across the globe. In fact, the source of the humor in *My Big Fat Greek Wedding* could be any minority group that clings on to its cultural traditions in the land of unlimited opportunity, whether out of pride or pure nostalgia. Perhaps everyone was sick of the sight of pasta; hence the camera pans to gyros – prepared in the yard at home, of course. Not much actually distinguishes the film from its forerunners and imitators. Experienced sitcom director Joel Zwick serves up clichés with varying levels of fat content, prepared with a generous dollop of warm-hearted humor that never offends. But the script of lead actress Nia Vardalos, who brought her own life experiences to the table, gives this harmless slapstick comedy its essential dose of spice.

Vardalos knows her compatriots. Her choice of cast provides a movie experience that has become a rarity – engaging with real people, whose virtues and vices are familiar. This applies to the father, Gus (who can warm to any idea in the end, as long as you convince him it's his own), and to Nia's mother, Maria (Lainie Kazan), the long-suffering matriarch who is the champion of such intrigues. And it applies not least to Toula herself, who succeeds in something all immigrant children have to manage: reconciling the traditions and rituals of their new homeland with those of their native country. Only Ian's thin-lipped parents seem over-exaggerated (or, as Gus says, "dry as a piece of toast") and find this balancing act more of a struggle. No problem, however

1

2

3

4

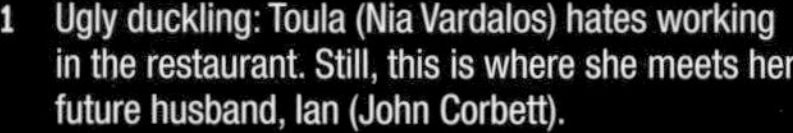

1 Ugly duckling: Toula (Nia Vardalos) hates working in the restaurant. Still, this is where she meets her future husband, Ian (John Corbett).

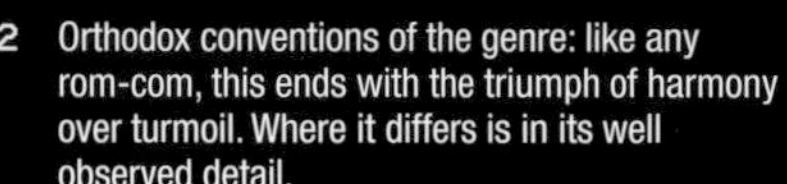

2 Orthodox conventions of the genre: like any rom-com, this ends with the triumph of harmony over turmoil. Where it differs is in its well observed detail.

3 Greek women are pretty good at self-help too: Toula's mother Maria (Lainie Kazan) is an expert improviser.

"It's delightful to see its original writer-performer Nia Vardalos play the lead on screen. She looks like a real person: an organic talent – very different from a possible genetically-modified casting of, say, Jennifer Aniston." *The Guardian*

5

6

7

4 Multicultural romance with an edge: actress Nia Vardalos wrote the screenplay for herself in this international hit. It is based on painful experience.

5 Toula's cousins are always up for a bit of fun, even with a non-Greek for a relative. Angelo (Joey Fatone), seen here on the right, makes many jokes at Ian's expense.

6 Dry as a bone: the strange customs make Ian's tight-lipped WASP parents (Fiona Reid, Bruce Gray) uncomfortable. Life is more sedate back home.

7 He is a Greek patriarch: Gus Portokalos (Michael Constantine), the proudest Greek in all Chicago, makes life difficult for his daughter.

– a little ouzo works wonders. By the end, the film has the audience in the palm of its hand, so much so that it can practically dispense with the punchlines sprinkled with so much Greek generosity before.

The engagement was a fiasco, and the Greek Orthodox baptism of the bridegroom a ludicrous scene. But the eventual wedding (and the film steers towards it as surely as Odysseus to Ithaca) is a spectacle that stands on its own merits, where harmony triumphs. It was precisely what audiences wanted to see. The real basis of the success, however, was Rita Wilson's discovery of the unknown Greek-Canadian Nia Vardalos on a cabaret stage one evening. Blessed with Greek roots as well, the actress recognized her own life and convinced her not-entirely-unknown husband, Tom Hanks, of the potential of a movie project. Vardalos wrote the screenplay and drummed up business at Greek associations and matchmaking events. The rest of the story involves huge profits for Hanks' company, Playtone, and co-financing broadcaster, HBO. The term "economy" is also famously Greek as well, of course. PB

LAINIE KAZAN Lainie Kazan can look back on a long career as an actress and singer that is marked by both highs and lows. Without any doubt, her role as the plump, loud and overbearingly affectionate Greek mama in the sleeper hit *My Big Fat Greek Wedding* (2002) belongs in the highlights category. Kazan is actually of Spanish and Russian-Jewish origin rather than Greek. Born in Brooklyn in 1940, she first found herself in the limelight when she stepped into the lead role for a day in the Broadway musical "Funny Girl," as Barbra Streisand was ill. This led to several record deals and an appearance in *Playboy* magazine. Alongside parts in obscure pulp movies like *Dayton's Devils* (1968) the attractive starlet then became a regular feature in Dean Martin's Las Vegas shows. The *Playboy* photos also inspired the legendary comic book artist Jack Kirby for his DC Comics' super-heroine Big Barda, a "valkyrie with a brain" in the reverent words of the novelist Michael Chabon.

A decade and many showbiz disappointments later, Kazan was only able to enjoy renewed success in maternal roles. In fact, to use her own words, up until now she has played "everyone's mother apart from Whoopi Goldberg." In Richard Benjamin's comedy *My Favorite Year* (1982) she produced alongside Peter O'Toole "one of the great Jewish mother scenes in cinema history," according to the *New York Times*. For the part as Bette Midler's mother in *Beaches* (1988) she made herself look about 30 years older. Following the remake of her greatest movie success in the TV series *My Big Fat Greek Life* (2003) she has appeared in, among others, the highly charged secret agent comedy *You Don't Mess with the Zohan* (2008) – as a Jewish mother, of course. Alongside appearances like this, the born entertainer also continues to devote herself to her great passion, singing.

SPIDER-MAN

2002 – USA – 121 MIN. – ACTION MOVIE, COMIC BOOK ADAPTATION
DIRECTOR SAM RAIMI (*1959)
SCREENPLAY DAVID KOEPP DIRECTOR OF PHOTOGRAPHY DON BURGESS EDITING ARTHUR COBURN, BOB MURAWSKI MUSIC DANNY ELFMAN PRODUCTION IAN BRYCE, LAURA ZISKIN for COLUMBIA PICTURES, MARVEL ENTERPRISES, LAURA ZISKIN ENTERPRISES.
STARRING TOBEY MAGUIRE (Peter Parker/Spider-Man), WILLEM DAFOE (Norman Osborn/Green Goblin), KIRSTEN DUNST (Mary Jane Watson), JAMES FRANCO (Harry Osborn), CLIFF ROBERTSON (Ben Parker), ROSEMARY HARRIS (May Parker), J.K. SIMMONS (J. Jonah Jameson), BRUCE CAMPBELL (Ring Announcer), STANLEY ANDERSON (General Slocum), MICHAEL PAPAJOHN (Carjacker).

"Who am I? – I'm Spider-Man!"

"You are now at the age when a man makes decisions that determine what kind of a person he will be for the rest of his life!" Uncle Ben (Cliff Robertson) gives this fatherly advice to his nephew Peter (Tobey Maguire), who is suddenly changing: he shuts himself in his room, he's becoming unreliable and he is attracting attention for getting into fights at school, where he has always been considered a goofy nerd. But since he visited a research unit at the university with his school class, where genetic experiments were being carried out on spiders, Peter has had a secret: one of the modified super-spiders escaped from its terrarium and bit his hand. Following a night filled with restless dreams and cramps, Peter has become a new person: he is super-strong, has lightning reflexes and doesn't even need his glasses any more. Even more significantly, tiny suction pads have grown out of his fingertips that allow him to climb walls of buildings, and he can shoot spider's threads as thick as fingers from glands on his wrists. Projecting these threads in front of him, he silently swings from one to the other, zipping between the urban canyons of New York with the darting movement that will become his trademark.

Fundamentally, Sam Raimi is telling a classic coming-of-age story, in which a young person faces some big questions: who am I, where am I going,

1

1 Being prepared: Peter Parker (Tobey Maguire) as Spider-Man, always around to lend a tenacious hand if required.

2 Transformed overnight: Peter is bursting with dynamism after being bitten by the spider.

3 Unlike Peter, weapons contractor Osborn (Willem Dafoe) submits himself voluntarily to his dangerous genetic experiments.

4 The age-old conflict between Good and Evil is reflected in the clash of the Titans.

"Raimi mixes his flair for the sensational (*The Evil Dead*) and the subtle (*A Simple Plan*) into one knockout package. Peter testing his new powers with small skips and jumps until he is leaping across rooftops is Raimi's style in a nutshell: slow build, huge payoff." *Rolling Stone*

where do I fit in? It is no coincidence that Peter meets his spider fate at the end of puberty, i.e. at that time of life when the latent potential in a person comes to fruition. But these developments (and this is the main message) do not absolve a person from making important decisions. He may have suddenly become super-strong, but "great strength brings great responsibility" – the last advice Uncle Ben is able to give his nephew before being shot soon afterward by a thief (Michael Papajohn) on the run.

It's a bitter lesson for Peter, for he had helped this selfsame thief to get away. His first impulse on discovering his superior powers was to get rich by winning 3,000 dollars in a wrestling competition. When the promoter swindles him out of the promised fee and is robbed a moment later, Peter allows the thief to escape; he does not realize that, in doing so, he will inadvertently cause his uncle's murder.

From then on, Peter works for justice and order, incognito of course. As "the friendly neighborhood spider" he is on the spot whenever there is a fire, whenever crooks are on the run or, even worse, whenever sleazy scoundrels seek to harm the love of his life, Mary Jane (Kirsten Dunst). Since meeting her at the age of six, he has been crazy about this girl, who is blissfully unaware of his love for her – and naturally must never know that her hitherto unassuming classmate leads a double life as a superhero.

For Spider-Man may be invincible, but the people Peter Parker loves are not. This is the masked blue-and-red superhero's weak spot. His most dangerous rival, the Green Goblin, knows it too. This mega-baddie leads a double life as well: behind the grotesque mask hides brilliant weapons developer Norman Osborn (Willem Dafoe), none other than the father of Harry (James Franco), Peter Parker's best friend. He, too, has superhuman powers after testing a prototype serum on himself. But in a modern variation on the Jekyll and Hyde theme, the potion unleashes uncontrollable urges. Only Spider-Man can stop his rise to absolute power. When Spider-Man rejects the Goblin's proposal to form a terrifying alliance of superpowers, the Goblin kidnaps Mary Jane; now

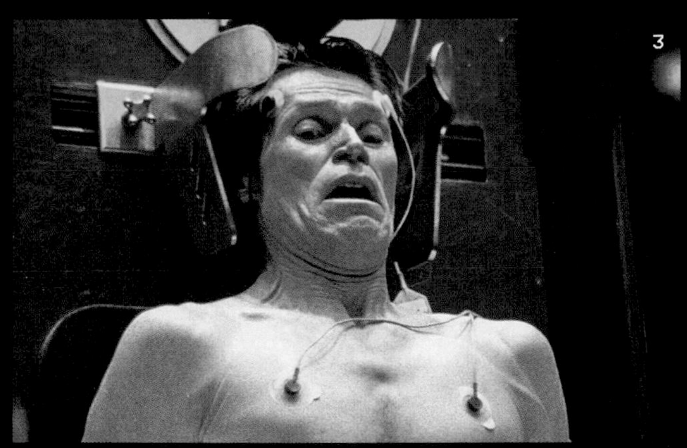

3

"It's the little things that float this $139 million balloon. That includes the upside-down kiss when Mary Jane slowly pulls down Spidey's mask for a smacker and nearly strips his face naked before he leaps away. Maguire and Dunst keep *Spider-Man* on a high with their sweet-sexy yearning, spinning a web of dazzle and delicacy that might just restore the good name of movie escapism." *Rolling Stone*

4

“It is all carried off with such gusto it’s impossible not to be swept along by the fun.” *The Guardian*

7

5 No-one suspects that ordinary student Peter Parker lurks inside the snazzy spider's costume.

6 Even though he would love to, Spider-Man must never reveal himself to the love of his life, Mary Jane (Kirsten Dunst).

7 So near and yet so far: since Peter Parker transformed into a superhero, he has inhabited a different world from Mary Jane. More than just a peck is out of the question.

8 His enemies have to conceal themselves well – Spider-Man is always ready to leap into action.

a final battle of the titans ensues, such as the metropolis has never seen before … The Green Goblin and Spider-Man have one thing in common, however, in that they owe their supernatural abilities to experimental science. Yet this similarity disappears when they are pitted against one another. What remains is the age-old battle between Good and Evil, which in the end can only be won by the person who is basically honorable and well intentioned. In this sense, the comic-book characters from the worlds of Marvel® (as well as Spider-Man, Blade, X-Men, the Hulk and Iron Man) and DC comics (Superman, Batman) will never go out of fashion; they have furnished international blockbuster cinema with a whole range of material for different movie series since the mid-1990s.

EP

SAM RAIMI Skimming the ground at breakneck speed, the camera glides over the forest floor, negotiating ponds and tree stumps in its effortless flight. This effective opening sequence was filmed with a camera attached to a simple board and carried by two assistants; the movie was *The Evil Dead* (1981), the infamous splatter movie that first established the reputation of Samuel Marshall Raimi.

Born in 1959 in Royal Oak, Michigan to a family of Eastern European origin, Raimi was fascinated by film and cinema from a very young age. From 1977, he followed up his first youthful experiments with a camera with several horror shorts. Back then, his friend and flat mate Bruce Campbell had parts in two of them – the star of the Evil Dead series who also made minor guest appearances in Raimi's movies on a number of occasions (priceless: the Maître d' in *Spider-Man 3*, 2007). While the 350,000 dollars he raised himself had to suffice for *The Evil Dead*, by the time of the second sequel the budgets had increased considerably – *Darkman* (1990) for instance, or the contemporary western *The Quick and the Dead* (1995) are some of the big-production B-movies that paved the way for the huge budgets of the three Spider-Man films (2002, 2004 and 2007). In terms of content, Raimi is extremely versatile: alongside the horror and fantasy of the *Evil Dead* and *Spider-Man* trilogies, the dark revenge epic *Darkman* and the story about a clairvoyant, *The Gift* (2000), he made the slightly tongue-in-cheek thrillers *Crimewave* (1985) and *A Simple Plan* (1998) as well as the sports drama *For Love of the Game* (1999). Raimi has a long-standing friendship with the Coen brothers, Joel and Ethan, with whom he co-wrote *Crimewave* and *The Hudsucker Proxy* (1994) and in whose movies he occasionally appears (e.g. *Miller's Crossing*, 1990). Raimi is married to Gillian Greene, daughter of the actor Lorne Greene, famous for his roles as Ben

BOWLING FOR COLUMBINE

BOWLING FOR COLUMBINE

2002 – CANADA / USA / GERMANY – 120 MIN. – SATIRE, DOCUMENTARY
DIRECTOR MICHAEL MOORE (*1954)
SCREENPLAY MICHAEL MOORE CAMERA OPERATORS BRIAN DANITZ, MICHAEL MCDONOUGH
EDITING KURT ENGFEHR MUSIC JEFF GIBBS PRODUCTION CHARLES BISCHOP, MICHAEL DONOVAN, KATHLEEN GLYNN, JIM CZARNECKI for ALLIANCE ATLANTIS COMMUNICATIONS, DOG EAT DOG FILMS, ICONOLATRY PRODUCTIONS, SALTER STREET FILMS.
ACADEMY AWARDS 2003 OSCAR for BEST DOCUMENTARY, Features (Michael Moore, Michael Donovan).
IFF CANNES 2002 55TH ANNIVERSARY PRIZE (Michael Moore).

BOWLING FOR
COLUMBINE
One nation under the gun.

"Well, here's my first question: Do you think it's kind of dangerous handing out guns at a bank?"

Glasses, belly, beard and baseball hat. This describes the most unusual star of recent American cinema: a heroic figure whose outward appearance challenges the current stereotypical concepts of screen attraction. Paradoxically, in fact, it holds the key to the astonishing success of documentary filmmaker Michael Moore. For this exceptionally gifted satirist wields his appearance – seemingly innocuous and totally lacking in glamour – like a weapon in his films. It is at its most effective in *Bowling for Columbine*, which won him an Oscar and turned him into the symbol of American counter culture during the Bush era.

In the film, Moore explores the question of why, year for year, more people in the USA lose their lives as a result of guns than in any other western industrialized nation. His starting point in this process was the high school massacre in Littleton on April 20, 1999, in which two youths ran amok, killing 13 fellow pupils and teachers. The ironic title itself, a reference to the allegation that the perpetrators had arranged to meet at a bowling alley before the carnage, gives a clear indication that the film is not going to be a painstaking reconstruction of, or even a sober reflection on, events. Instead, Moore uses the sensational bloodbath as an opportunity to evaluate his native land in a way that is both entertaining and polemical – a country which, in his eyes, is run by capital and ruled by fear, racism and social impoverishment.

The chaotic reality of America as claimed by Moore finds an effective equivalent in a cinematic form that is extremely heterogeneous. Montage sequences in a compressed collage style and accompanied by a trenchant commentary alternate with interviews with "ordinary" citizens and illustrious personalities such as shock-rocker Marilyn Manson, together with uncut footage of the CCTV cameras from the shooting spree at Columbine High School. It even includes a sick animation showing the paranoia of white people as the driving force of US history.

Moore relies on emotion and entertainment to spread his message. He disguises his moralizing with black humor and satirical snapshots of real life, like his own bizarre experiment in opening a bank account and receiving a gun as a bonus. This insane scene is also of note in that it gave his critics proof that Moore was constantly bending reality in order to achieve his desired results. For it seems that the firearm was not handed out instantly to the filmmaker by the bank, unlike the way the incident was portrayed on screen.

It is debatable how much, if any, fiction a documentary movie can contain. It is, therefore, hardly surprising that Moore's pointed attacks arouse vehement protest, as the filmmaker directs himself as his own protagonist. In the well-composed chaos, he alone can give the viewer guidance and perspective on

1

2

1 Camera as weapon: as an investigative documentary filmmaker, Michael Moore is confident in the role of political activist. During the Bush years, he was one of the leading opposition figures in the US.

2 In *Bowling for Columbine*, Moore satirizes the US arms lobby. Oddly enough, one of the director's hobbies as a young man was shooting guns.

"The questions that Moore asks are designed to spark debate. The answers are packaged in a way that will produce laughter, tears and anger. A film like this doesn't come along very often."

San Francisco Chronicle

MICHAEL MOORE Born on April 23, 1954 in Davison near Flint in the state of Michigan, Michael Moore's most sensational performance to date was at the Academy Awards in 2003, when he used his acceptance speech for the *Bowling for Columbine* Oscar to make a verbal attack on the US administration. Evidently, however, he had a sense of mission even before his career as a documentary filmmaker: he attended a seminary in his youth and was elected at the age of just 18 to the school board in his home town. When he turned 20, Moore moved on to journalism, before causing quite a stir in 1989 with his very first documentary film, *Roger & Me*. This critique of the closure of the General Motors factory in Flint, in the satirical tone now characteristic of Moore, put the first-time director on the map as an early opponent of globalization. It was a reputation he enhanced with *Canadian Bacon* (1995) – his only feature film to date – and his documentary *The Big One* (1995), which he followed with a range of TV work and publications. In 2002, he boosted his profile further with *Bowling for Columbine*, which replaced *Roger & Me* as the best documentary at the box-office. Moore's *Fahrenheit 9/11* (2004), a direct attack on George W. Bush and his War on Terror, won the Palme d'Or (Golden Palm) in Cannes and exceeded the box-office receipts of its predecessor, though it failed in its goal of preventing Bush's re-election.

Since then the left-wing film activist has found himself subjected, not just to the fierce hostility of his political opponents, but also increasingly to criticism of his working methods. The documentary movie *Manufacturing Dissent* (2007) fundamentally challenged Moore's credibility, pointing up what appeared to be deliberate manipulation in his films. Nevertheless, Moore has remained true to himself, and with *Sicko* (2007) has recently turned his attention to the ailing American health system.

3 A highlight of real-life satire: Moore opens a bank account – and the bank rewards him with a rifle. Critics accused the filmmaker of excessively distorting reality in scenes like this.

4 Famous supporters: shock-rocker Marilyn Manson shares Moore's critical view of contemporary America. His appearance in the film made it even more appealing to young viewers.

5 A man of the people: when directing himself, Moore always signalizes his empathy with ordinary folk.

issues. In his dual role as investigative reporter and activist with movie camera, Moore becomes a positive role model – as an intrepid and upstanding man of the people, who provides comfort and gives victims a voice through exposing injustices and making a stand. At the same time, Moore engages with an opponent who could scarcely be more appropriate in cinematic terms – Hollywood veteran, Charlton Heston, who was President of the National Rifle Association (NRA) in his lifetime and lent a prominent face to the powerful gun lobby. More specifically, a cold face, for Moore stylized Heston visually to create his counterpart: a gaunt old man and cynical hardliner who brandished a gun at an NRA convention a few days after Littleton, declaring the right to bear arms with the words: "From my cold dead hands."

The extent to which Moore's documentary follows the rules of popular cinema becomes very clear when it comes to a showdown between the antagonists: using his own membership of the NRA, dating back to his youth, as a cover, the filmmaker manages to inveigle his way into an interview with Heston. He catches the unsuspecting and visibly senile actor out with critical questions, so that Heston is not only exposed to allegations of racism but also ends up running away, despite being on his own property: a memorable scene that amounts to a demolition job on the screen icon. The vacuum left by the downfall of Heston is ultimately filled by Moore himself, though even this leaves a bitter aftertaste. JH

CITY OF GOD
CIDADE DE DEUS

2002 – BRAZIL / FRANCE – 130 MIN. – GANGSTER MOVIE, DRAMA
DIRECTOR FERNANDO MEIRELLES (*1955)
SCREENPLAY BRÁULIO MANTOVANI, based on the novel by PAULO LINS
DIRECTOR OF PHOTOGRAPHY CÉSAR CHARLONE EDITING DANIEL REZENDE MUSIC ED CORTÊS, ANTONIO PINTO PRODUCTION ANDREA BARATA RIBEIRO, MAURICIO ANDRADE RAMOS for O2 FILMES, VIDEOFILMES.
STARRING ALEXANDRE RODRIGUES (Buscapé), LEANDRO FIRMINO (Locke), PHELLIPE HAAGENSEN (Bené), JONATHAN HAAGENSEN (Cabeleira), MATHEUS NACHTERGAELE (Sandro Cenoura/Carrot), SEU JORGE (Mané), JEFECHANDER SUPLINO (Alicate), ALICE BRAGA (Angélica), ROBERTA RODRIGUES (Berenice), DOUGLAS SILVA (Dadinho/Li'l Dice).

"Ain't Li'l Dice no more, now I'm the boss Li'l Zé, you jerk, understand?"

In Cidade de Deus, the most god-forsaken district of Rio de Janeiro, killing is fun. More fun than living, that is. The chicken that the gangster Li'l Zé is trying to trap in the superb opening scene is blissfully unaware of this, however. It runs away, with a jeering crowd in hot pursuit. Samba blares out. A crazy chase ensues, but suddenly stops. The police have moved in; facing them, the inflamed gang of youths; in the middle, the chicken. In the breathless silence, all that can be heard is the click of guns being cocked. The bloodbath is inevitable, but it is postponed. The camera rotates 360 degrees, tumbling back into the past, to where it all began – the rise of Li'l Dice, alias Li'l Zé, to become the most feared gangster in the district; the daily battle for power and territory; and the vicious circle of violence and crime. At the end, we are back with the chicken, and frazzled to boot.

City of God, a work of art created out of the squalor of real life, tells an old story using the latest techniques. The story of the slums is packaged in the form of a great legend, using a frenzied combination of jump cuts, match frames, split screens, freeze frames and flashbacks, all organically interwoven in epic narrative loops. Whole biographies are played out through time-lapse and completed with the next scene, or next gunshot. Life expectancy is short in the City of God. And yet we remember the names: charismatic Bené, Li'l Zé's assistant, killed in the strobe light of his own going-away party; beautiful Cabeleira, gunned down by the police; "Knockout Ned" and "Carrot," Li'l Zé's only rivals in the drug war spanning decades – and Buscapé, the innocuous first-person narrator with a camera, in a place where no camera has dared go before. These characters, based to an extent on real life, are taken from a book by Paulo Lins, himself a child of Cidade de Deus. The film tells the story of their lives from the early 60s through the cynical 80s, using grainy, saturated colors to create a raw mix of documentary film and epic movie.

With a nod to both MTV and blaxploitation – funk, soul and gold-rim eyeglasses – the director Fernando Meirelles was naturally suspected of glorifying violence and whitewashing brutal content with aesthetic style. Several shattering scenes would, in fact, allay these suspicions. Although direct, graphic representation of violence is largely avoided, when Li'l Zé lets a member of the "dwarf gang" choose which of his two little companions he is going to shoot, the audience suffers a sense of paralysis. Killers – and their victims – have never been so young. Comparisons with gangster epics like Martin Scorsese's *Goodfellas* (1990) were actually more useful as evidence for classifying it as a film of outstanding cinematic quality. Along with Alejandro González Iñárritu's *Amores Perros* (2000), *City of God* put Latin America and its social reality on the map of world cinema, with a breathtaking mixture of visionary power and technical perfection.

1

2

1 Seeds of violence: Li'l Dice (Douglas Silva) aka Li'l Zé (later: Leandro Firmino) gave cinema one of the most terrifying hit men in its history.

2 Trash can existence: the "City of God" housing project was supposed to provide a home for the poorest in society. It became instead the feared stronghold of criminal activity and violence.

3 Documenting social reality: Buscapé / Rocket (Alexandre Rodrigues) goes where no other camera dares. He earns his first cash with the images.

The key to the film's disturbing proximity to real life lies in the fact that it was almost entirely cast with non-professional actors. Almost all of them were recruited from the Cidade de Deus area, the shanty town built overnight in the 60s by Brazilian town planners (Buscapé calls it a "garbage can") – an apology for shelter for the poor, homeless people who exist on the city's fringes. In such a place, where skillful gun handling improves a person's odds more than reading or writing, Meirelles' crew turned several hundred street kids into highly-gifted actors who would otherwise never have discovered their talents. In workshops that ran for months, they learnt how to improvise dialogue and express their own experiences through art: development aid as it should be.

The most impressive outcome of this work was the demonic performance of young Leandro Firmino (apparently very gentle in real life) as gangster boss, Li'l Zé. He has brought to the big screen a killer who easily rivals villains from Rico and Scarface to Joe Pesci. He laughs crazily as he kills, quickly and without a second thought. Great fun! PB

ALICE BRAGA The Hispanic community in the US is already hailing her as Hollywood's next screen goddess. In fact, Alice Braga is the only one in the huge cast of *City of God* (*Cidade de Deus*, 2002) who can point to an international career. In a fairly minor role, she plays the beach girl Angélica who guides gang leader Bené onto the straight and narrow. Born in São Paulo in 1983, this beautiful actress is the niece of Brazilian film star Sonia Braga (*Kiss of the Spider Woman*, 1985); she had previously appeared in commercials and worked on a short film. In her next movie *Lower City* (*Cidade Baixa*, 2005) she had another opportunity to prove her *fatale* effect on men – though this time as a feisty stripper who falls in love with two friends at the same time. The role was created for her by the big daddy of Brazilian cinema, producer Walter Salles. The *New York Times* instantly called the rather petite Braga "one of the most forthrightly and powerfully sexual screen actresses in the world." Hollywood has so far preferred to see her more as a good girl, casting her alongside big-name stars. In the apocalyptic vision *I am Legend* (2007) she saves the world with Will Smith, as religiously inspired survivors of an epidemic. Legendary screenwriter David Mamet cast her alongside Chiwetel Ejiofor in his martial arts drama *Redbelt* (2008). In Brazil, where she continues to live and work, Fernando Meirelles gave her another part after *City of God*, this time in his memorable literary adaptation *Blindness* (2008). Alice Braga plays a leading role in *Repo Men* (2010), a dark, futuristic vision of the trade in human organs, also starring Jude Law and Forest Whitaker.

4 Force of movement: director Meirelles tells the story of daily survival in the slums with stylistic panache and visionary zeal.

5 Mad decisions over life and death: as a test of courage, Li'l Zé (Leandro Firmino) forces a boy to kill his friend. Killers and their victims have never been so young.

6 Sensitive Buscapé is caught in the middle. Co-director Kátia Lund was mainly responsible for training the non-professional actors.

"*City of God* churns with furious energy as it plunges into the story of the slum gangs of Rio de Janeiro. Breathtaking and terrifying, urgently involved with its characters, it announces a new director of great gifts and passions: Fernando Meirelles." *Chicago Sun-Times*

THE PIANIST ♛♛♛

LE PIANISTE

2002 – FRANCE / GERMANY / UK / POLAND – 150 MIN. – DRAMA, LITERARY ADAPTATION
DIRECTOR ROMAN POLANSKI (*1933)
SCREENPLAY RONALD HARWOOD, from the book of the same name by WLADYSLAW SZPILMAN **DIRECTOR OF PHOTOGRAPHY** PAWEL EDELMAN **EDITING** HERVÉ DE LUZE **MUSIC** WOJCIECH KILAR **PRODUCTION** ROBERT BENMUSSA, ROMAN POLANSKI, ALAIN SARDE for HERITAGE FILMS, STUDIO BABELSBERG, R. P. PRODUCTIONS, RUNTEAM, CANAL+, STUDIO CANAL, TELEWIZJA POLSKA.
STARRING ADRIEN BRODY (Wladyslaw Szpilman), THOMAS KRETSCHMANN (Captain Wilm Hosenfeld), FRANK FINLAY (Father), MAUREEN LIPMAN (Mother), JESSICA KATE MEYER (Halina), EMILIA FOX (Dorota), ED STOPPARD (Henryk), RUTH PLATT (Janina Godlewska), ROY SMILES (Itzak Heller), PAUL BRADLEY (Yehuda), DANIEL CALTAGIRONE (Majorek), EUGENE BIRD (Wink).
ACADEMY AWARDS 2003 OSCARS for BEST DIRECTOR (Roman Polanski), BEST LEADING ACTOR (Adrien Brody) and BEST ADAPTED SCREENPLAY (Ronald Harwood).
IFF CANNES 2002 GOLDEN PALM (Roman Polanski).

"Go on, play."

Roman Polanski has made intensely personal films throughout his life, precisely as a way, or so it would appear, of keeping the real world at bay. The director of *Rosemary's Baby* (1968) and master of comedic horror wrapped himself in the protective cloak of the surreal. At the age of 68, he cast it off for his late masterpiece, *The Pianist*. The memoirs of the piano player and composer Wladyslaw Szpilman (1911–2000) bear a chilling resemblance to those of the man who fled the Kraków ghetto as a child and lost his mother in the gas chambers of Auschwitz.

The German attack on Warsaw in 1939 transformed the world of Polish Jew Szpilman (Adrien Brody) into a hell both real and surreal. A bomb explodes during a radio recording, life invading art. A sober, almost cold eye registers the series of steadily worsening horrors to which the 360,000 Jews of the city now find themselves subjected: being made to wear the Star of David, public humiliation, arbitrary executions and, finally, their forcible removal into a zoned area of the city – the Warsaw ghetto. Hunger, misery and yet more executions follow. By chance, Szpilman escapes the deportation, but he never sees his family again. The Nazis let him carry on working, but a pianist's hands are poorly suited to hauling bricks. Just before the uprising of the 60,000 remaining Jews, he manages to escape again. The self-confident, almost dandyish ladies' man of the start has become a hunted man. Like a ghost, he wanders from

1

1 Music in a time of fear: Adrien Brody won the Oscar for his moving performance as pianist Wladyslaw Szpilman.

2 Music lover Captain Wilm Hosenfeld (Thomas Kretschmann) allows Szpilman to escape. The event is said to have actually happened.

3 The artist and his instrument: music becomes the haunting reminder of a world beyond the barbarity.

4 Stylish and fearless: before the Germans invaded, Szpilman was a popular ladies' man. Admirer Dorota (Emilia Fox) later provides him with a hideout.

one hiding place to the next; more dead than alive, he suffers hunger, sickness, despair and the permanent fear of being discovered.

Adrien Brody shoulders the enormous burden of expressing all these feelings as precisely and unemotionally as possible. He has no one to support him. Szpilman's flight is the start of an indefatigable solo performance by Brody, which symbolizes the individual's isolation during the catastrophe and was rewarded for its intensity with the Oscar. Scurrying and ducking through ruins devoid of human beings, like an animal looking for food, he turns every movement into a master-class in acting. The extent to which human fear and the survival instinct are interdependent can be read in his eyes. And yet Szpilman's survival is down to sheer coincidence.

After almost half an hour without speaking, Szpilman has a hair-raising experience in the famous key scene of the film. A German regular army officer (Thomas Kretschmann) has found him, in an unpredictable manner. The sound

ADRIEN BRODY His appealing hangdog look masks the resolute way in which Adrien Brody forges a distinctive image for each of his parts. For a long time, he went virtually unnoticed, on account of an attractive exterior combined with a serious approach to acting that is often compared to that of Al Pacino. Son of the well known photojournalist, Sylvia Plachy, Brody was born in the New York district of Queens in 1973 and accumulated merely good reviews for films such as Steven Soderbergh's *King of the Hill* (1993) and *The Last Time I Committed Suicide* (1997). Most of the scenes that included him in Terrence Malick's war film *The Thin Red Line* (1998) ended up on the cutting room floor. In outsider roles, for instance as the bisexual punk in Spike Lee's *Summer of Sam* (1999) or as the Jewish teenager with a conscience in Barry Levinson's 50s drama *Liberty Heights* (1999), he was able gradually to boost his profile. For Ken Loach, he took the lead role as a labor union activist fighting capitalism in *Bread and Roses* (2000). The Oscar for his subtle portrayal in Roman Polański's Holocaust drama *The Pianist* (2002) was a huge surprise, though the road had been well paved. Brody, the youngest male Oscar award winner till then, had dropped 30 pounds for the part of the persecuted pianist Wladyslaw Szpilman; he also learned how to play the piano. If that wasn't enough, he gave one of the few acceptance speeches worth listening to at the Oscars: just before the start of the Iraq war, he appealed for peace between nations, making a direct link to the film.
Since then, things have calmed down a little for this highly gifted method actor. When he starred opposite a huge, hairy ape in Peter Jackson's remake of *King Kong* (2005), the cards were stacked against him. In Wes Anderson's nostalgic view of India, *The Darjeeling Limited* (2007), Brody joined with Owen Wilson and Jason Schwartzman in a wonderful trio of brothers on a journey of enlightenment.

his music playing may have given the pianist's hiding place away, but now he is asked to play. For a few minutes, Chopin's Ballade No. 1 in G minor reminds both artist and listener of a world beyond the barbarism. The expertly composed scene does not provide any easy answers, but the music may have saved Szpilman's life. The fact that it actually happened is nothing short of a miracle.

Szpilman's fate is a unique case, however. There is no hero in *The Pianist*. This is why Polanski's direction (which also earned him an Oscar) avoids the usual Hollywood dramatization. He had his reasons for turning down the opportunity to collaborate on Spielberg's *Schindler's List* (1993), a film with its own merits. The purpose of the relentless objectivity – no close-ups, with only sparing use of the music – is realism, and nothing else. The attention to

3

"Polanski ensures that viewers are guided, not by intellect or feeling, but by the spatial perception of their own bodies. The power of suggestion of his images and the spaces they occupy is so strong – for instance, when Szpilman yet again runs the high risk of leaving his hideout after months of being confined – that we experience each new freedom as both a personal and physical liberation." *Der Tagesspiegel*

4

Szpilman, brilliantly played by Adrien Brody, comes to resemble one of Samuel Beckett's gaunt existential clowns, shambling through a barren, bombed-out landscape clutching a jar of pickles. He is like the walking punchline to a cosmic jest of unfathomable cruelty." *The New York Times*

5

5 The only one left in the ghetto: Polanski's images are shocking – a landmark in the way art portrays the Holocaust.

6 Szpilman's journey through Hell begins with his removal to the ghetto. The director bears witness to the terrible events he saw with his own eyes.

7 Masterly mise-en-scène: from a window, Szpilman watches the start of the uprising in the Warsaw ghetto.

8 Public humiliation: German soldiers force some Jews to play a final serenade. This is only the start of the horrors; there is far, far worse to come.

detail of the shots (partly filmed in Warsaw itself) produces a documentary effect: many were reconstructed from famous archive material. Yet another factor ensures the impression of utmost authenticity: Polanski knows what it looks like when people are shot. They do not collapse into heroic poses.

There are, however, subtleties within the classic montage style as well. Like Brody, the viewer sees many of the disturbing scenes only from a window. The mise-en-scène creates distance, making us merely observers. Polanski has not lost his artistry, but is simply applying it differently – creating a landmark in his dramatic treatment of the Holocaust.

Art triumphs in the end and, along with it, life. The pianist's hands glide over the keys as if nothing has happened. It is an image of hope, which lasts like all the others in a film that moves through its avoidance of pathos. PB

FAR FROM HEAVEN

2002 – USA – 107 MIN. – MELODRAMA
DIRECTOR TODD HAYNES (*1961)
SCREENPLAY TODD HAYNES **DIRECTOR OF PHOTOGRAPHY** EDWARD LACHMAN **EDITING** JAMES LYONS **MUSIC** ELMER BERNSTEIN **PRODUCTION** JODY ALLEN, CHRISTINE VACHON for FOCUS FEATURES, KILLER FILMS, JOHN WELLS PRODUCTIONS, SECTION EIGHT.
STARRING JULIANNE MOORE (Cathy Whitaker), DENNIS QUAID (Frank Whitaker), DENNIS HAYSBERT (Raymond Deagan), PATRICIA CLARKSON (Eleanor Fine), VIOLA DAVIS (Sybil), RYAN WARD (David Whitaker), LINDSEY ANDRETTA (Janice Whitaker), JORDAN PURYEAR (Sarah Deagan), J. B. ADAMS (Morris Farnsworth).

"I've learned my lesson about mixing in other worlds. I've seen the sparks fly ... all kinds."

Rays of sunshine piercing through brightly colored leaves; gleaming cars on pristine streets; women in radiant dresses: the idealized image of an American small town in the 1950s. Cathy Whitaker (Julianne Moore) is a respected woman in Hartford, Connecticut, and husband Frank (Dennis Quaid) is a successful sales director for a TV manufacturer; they live with their two delightful children in an imposing house, and employ a housekeeper of color. But cracks appear in the seemingly perfect family idyll. Frank pretends to work late, so that he can secretly indulge his homosexual tendencies. When Cathy makes a surprise visit to his office one evening, she catches him with another man. Frank is ashamed of his desires, and tries to overcome them with the help of a psychiatrist. The subject is too great a taboo for them to tell their friends about, of course, so their marital problems stay firmly within the family. By contrast, Cathy causes an even bigger public sensation: her friendly dealings with Raymond Deagan (Dennis Haysbert), the black son of her late gardener, are noted with suspicion. No sooner have they been seen together, than the rumors spread through the small town like wildfire.

Far from Heaven pays homage to the Hollywood melodramas of the 50s: the "weepies" we associate mainly with one director, Douglas Sirk. Director Todd Haynes modeled his movie on the Sirk's classic, *All That Heaven Allows* (1955), though he also references other films of that period. *Far from Heaven* looks like a perfect imitation in cinematic terms: camera shots over treetops, showing the changing seasons; the use of mirrors in the mise-en-scène; the gorgeous Technicolor; and lighting that has a surreal quality in parts. In order faithfully to reproduce this "Sirk look," cameraman Edward Lachman used traditional lighting techniques and camera filters from the 1950s. The illusion is completed by the music of Elmer Bernstein (1922–2004), whose last soundtrack allowed him to return to the start of his long career: to the days of classical movie scores, Hollywood-style. It quickly becomes evident that, for Todd Haynes, it was not a question of realistically portraying life in the 1950s, but about the glossy veneer applied by Hollywood to avoid any kind of social embarrassment.

According to Todd Haynes, he wanted *Far from Heaven* to be the "Sirk" film that the German director was never able to make in '50s Hollywood

1
2

1 Cathy (Julianne Moore) expresses sympathy to Raymond (Dennis Haysbert) for his father's death. Later, the newspaper will say she is "nice to niggers."

2 Silent farewell: Cathy watches as the train leaves town with Raymond and his daughter.

3 No Technicolor dream: Todd Haynes' subtle homage to 1950s Hollywood received four Oscar nominations.

Admittedly, his melodramas did contain hints about Rock Hudson's closet homosexuality, which only became public after the actor died from AIDS in 1985; dealing openly with same-sex love was, however, a taboo subject in classical Hollywood cinema. Nevertheless, the more obviously camp actors were occasionally included as exaggerated, comical, minor characters: Clifton Webb as Waldo Lydecker in *Laura* (1944), for example, and George Sanders as Addison DeWitt in *All About Eve* (1950). In *Far from Heaven*, this old stereotype is represented – fortunately only briefly – in art dealer Morris Farnsworth (J.B. Adams), whose strange ways may be sneered at, but are tolerated.

In his own interpretation of the "Sirk film" (*Fear Eats the Soul/Angst essen Seele auf*, 1974) Rainer Werner Fassbinder not only transfers the plot to West Germany, but also replaces the issue of difference (class adherence) with that of skin color. Haynes also puts racial conflict at the center of the film. The basic principle remains the same in all three films, however: society is the insurmountable obstacle standing in the way of the main characters' happiness. Distrust of anything different, the fear of deviating from the norm – in this sense, this paranoid attitude of the McCarthy era is ever-present in *Far from Heaven*; at one point, the name of the anti-communist senator is

4 Frank Whitaker (Dennis Quaid) makes contact with other men in a backstreet bar.

5 Surrounded by suspicion: in a restaurant for black people, Cathy is the stranger eyed with distrust.

6 Cathy has an animated conversation with Raymond about abstract painting at an art exhibition.

"It rediscovers the aching, desiring humanity in a genre – and a period – too often subjected to easy parody or ironic appropriation. In a word, it's divine." *The New York Times*

dropped into the conversation in passing, when Cathy's friends are joking about her red hair. Apparently, Haynes also wanted his film to be seen as a statement about the neo-conservative values of the Bush era.

Frank is the only one for whom the film holds the hope of a conciliatory ending. As he continues to live out his sexuality in secret, he avoids any public conflict. He gets a divorce and lives with his lover. Cathy, on the other hand, is left all alone with the children. For Raymond is intent on leaving town with his daughter, as he sees plenty of hostility in store for him in Hartford, and not just from white folk. Cathy wants to see him one last time. Their silent farewell at the station is a deliberate reminder of what must be the best known unfulfilled love story in cinema, David Lean's *Brief Encounter* (1945). CZ

“Rather than imitating Sirk, I wanted to apply his methods: treating social criticism as an emotional experience that is not blatant, but calls for interpretation” *Todd Haynes*

7 All that heaven allows: Douglas Sirk’s interpretation of his film title was far less positive than that of his studio bosses. What he meant was “heaven is stingy.” Todd Haynes, by contrast, gave his movie a pretty unambiguous title.

8 Cathy is still happy at the New Year’s Eve dinner. But she will see a lot of changes in the year to come.

9 Good-looking, successful and happy. To the outside world, the Whitakers seem the ideal couple.

10 Like Douglas Sirk, Todd Haynes also occasionally uses mirrors to create interesting perspectives onscreen.

11 In the evening, Frank wanders through Hartford to meet men. His wife thinks he is working long hours.

12 Secrets behind doors: Cathy is stunned to find Frank in an intimate embrace with another man.

"This brilliantly and comprehensively captures the look, feel, and sound of glamorous 50s tearjerkers like *All That Heaven Allows*, not to mock or feel superior to them but to say new things with their vocabulary." *Chicago Reader*

JULIANNE MOORE Born Julie Anne Smith in Fayetteville, North Carolina in 1960, the actress began her career with off-Broadway plays in New York. For three years from 1985 she had a part in the soap opera *As the World Turns* (1956–2010), for which she won an Emmy award.
The flame-haired actress had her first major film roles in Robert Altman's *Short Cuts* (1993) and Louis Malle's *Vanya on 42nd Street* (1994). She had already worked with Todd Haynes in *Safe* (1995), in which she plays a housewife whose allergies cause her to retreat completely from the outside world. But her breakthrough really only came in the complex role of drug-addicted porn star and caring mother Amber Waves in *Boogie Nights* (1997), which earned her a first Oscar nomination; the second came in 2000 for the Graham Greene adaptation *The End of the Affair* (1999). In 2003, she was nominated not only for her leading role in *Far from Heaven* (2002) but also for Best Supporting Actress in *The Hours* (2002), though she once again came away empty-handed. Afterward, she had starring roles in several stage productions, while in cinema she came to notice once again in Tom Ford's *A Single Man* (2009). She was brilliant with Annette Bening in *The Kids Are All Right* (2010), in which they play a lesbian couple meeting the biological father of their children for the first time.

8 MILE

2002 – USA – 110 MIN. – BIOPIC
DIRECTOR CURTIS HANSON (*1945)
SCREENPLAY SCOTT SILVER DIRECTOR OF PHOTOGRAPHY RODRIGO PRIETO EDITING CRAIG KITSON, JAY RABINOWITZ MUSIC PROOF PRODUCTION BRIAN GRAZER, CURTIS HANSON, JIMMY IOVINE for IMAGINE ENTERTAINMENT, MIKONA PRODUCTIONS.
STARRING EMINEM (Jimmy "B-Rabbit" Smith), KIM BASINGER (Stephanie), MEKHI PHIFER (Future), BRITTANY MURPHY (Alex), EVAN JONES (Cheddar Bob), OMAR BENSON MILLER (Sol George), DE'ANGELO WILSON (DJ Iz).
ACADEMY AWARDS 2003 OSCAR for BEST MUSIC, Original Song "Lose Yourself" (Jeff Bass, Eminem, Luis Resto).

"I'm a piece of fucking white shit, I say it proudly."

His hood pulled down over his face, feet tapping as if in time to jumping ropes and fists jabbing forward alternately; not a boxer preparing for a bout, but a rapper. White man Jimmy "B-Rabbit" Smith (Eminem) is getting ready for a "battle" – a rap competition where rappers "diss" each other in a popular form of hip-hop. Rabbit goes on stage and makes a complete hash of it, choking up. There isn't another "battle" until the end of the movie. Then Rabbit not only has the courage to let rip, he actually out-raps everyone else. His rhymes also tell of how miserable his life really is, shattering the hip-hop cliché of the loudmouthed, macho guy. Rabbit's life is set out for the viewer between these two appearances. He works in an automobile plant and has to put up with his boss's bullying. He and his younger sister live with their mother (Kim Basinger) and her lover, who is no older than Rabbit. They live in a trailer park, which they will soon have to leave because they haven't paid the rent. They are "white trash," no doubt about it: the white underclass of America.

1

1 Jimmy "Rabbit" Smith (Eminem) tries to make it as a white man in the black-dominated hip-hop business.

2 Talking about it: Jimmy's new girlfriend, Alex (Brittany Murphy), slept with producer Wink to further her modeling career.

3 The "battle" won: from left, DJ Iz (De'Angelo Wilson), Sol George (Omar Benson Miller), Jimmy, Cheddar Bob (Evan Jones), and Future (Mekhi Phifer) go home.

4 Jimmy cruising the hood with his buddies Future, Sol George, Cheddar Bob and DJ Iz.

"Hanson (abetted by cinematographer Rodrigo Prieto) evokes the oppressive atmosphere of rundown neighborhoods like Detroit's 8 Mile, as well as the day-to-day experience of being nickled and dimed in America." *TV Guide*

CURTIS HANSON Alongside *8 Mile*, another two movie vehicles for pop stars were produced in 2001/2002: *Glitter* with Mariah Carey, and *Crossroads* with Britney Spears. Of them, only *8 Mile* went beyond this role, due mainly to director Curtis Hanson who since the 1980s has distinguished himself as a man with a sure hand for intelligent entertainment movies. His career reads almost like that of a French New Wave director: cineaste, film critic and Hitchcock fan.

Born in Reno, Nevada on March 24, 1945, Curtis Hanson knows the film business inside out. One of his first jobs was writing the screenplay for *White Dog* (1982) by cult director Samuel Fuller. His directorial debut came with teen flick *Losin' It* (1983) with Tom Cruise. Its success brought him offers of more teen movies. But Hanson turned them down and went on to tackle various other genres, such as thrillers (*The Bedroom Window*, 1986), action movies (*The River Wild*, 1994) and comedies (*In Her Shoes*, 2005). His directorial masterpieces include the dark corruption thriller *L.A. Confidential* (1997) from the novel by James Ellroy (for which Hanson won the Oscar for Best Adapted Screenplay jointly with Brian Helgeland) and the subtle comedy, *Wonder Boys* (2000).

“Eminem holds the camera by natural right. His screen presence is electric.” *Rolling Stone*

3

8 Mile is Rabbit’s story and, to a certain extent, that of Eminem as well. He carved out a career as a white man in the black hip-hop business and, also like Rabbit, comes from Detroit. So it is hardly surprising that the rapper acquits himself well as an actor here, though his task was made all the more difficult by world-class actress Kim Basinger playing his mother. Eminem’s powerful soundtrack won him the Oscar for the song “Lose Yourself.” Moreover, the movie also manages to give us some sense of hip-hop’s fascination: for example, when the workers rap in front of the factory gates about their economic situation or when Rabbit and his buddy, Future (Mekhi Phifer), invest the words of the timeless rock song “Sweet Home Alabama” with some pizzazz, giving it contemporary relevance.

8 Mile is more than just a music biopic, however; it is a piece of socially committed cinema (we actually see Eminem rapping for the first time 30 minutes into the film). The protagonists are representative of a young generation facing social and economic decline. Rabbit and the others in his crowd all want just one thing – to get out of Detroit. Their hope is to find careers that will allow them to move away: Cheddar Bob (Evan Jones), the other white member of the group besides Rabbit, also wants to be a rapper; Future stages the “battles;” and Wink (Eugene Byrd) has connections to a local production company. Rabbit’s new girlfriend, Alex (Brittany Murphy), dreams of eventually becoming a model and she even becomes involved with Wink as a way of advancing her chosen career.

5

5

6

5 Jimmy lives in a trailer with his mother Stephanie (Kim Basinger) and little sister Lily (Chloe Greenfield).

6 Jimmy writes his lyrics on the bus, on his way to work at the auto plant.

7 Sense of achievement: Jimmy wins the rap battle against Lotto (Nashawn "Ox" Breedlove).

"Here Eminem plays, if not himself, a version of himself, and we understand why he has been accepted as a star in a genre mostly owned by blacks." *Chicago Sun-Times*

The movie's other great headliner is the city of Detroit. The once flourishing industrial city and headquarters of General Motors is suffering acutely from the downturn in the automobile industry. One of the main occupations of Rabbit and his friends is driving around the neighborhood, which gives us a glimpse of a city in decline with its empty stores and dilapidated houses. Mexican cinematographer Rodrigo Prieto (*Brokeback Mountain*, 2005) captures this urban decay in compelling images.

The title *8 Mile* refers to 8 Mile Road, which separates the nicer parts of the city from the not so nice ones. The number code used by the rappers in the final battle – the 3-1-3s against the 8-1-0s – is likewise rooted in fact. The actual city zone (with telephone code 313) is set against that of the suburbs, "phony Detroit" (code 810). HJK

7

THE RING

BEFORE YOU DIE,
YOU SEE
the
ring

2002 – USA / JAPAN – 115 MIN. – HORROR MOVIE
DIRECTOR GORE VERBINSKI (*1964)
SCREENPLAY EHREN KRUGER, based on the novel by KÔJI SUZUKI
DIRECTOR OF PHOTOGRAPHY BOJAN BAZELLI EDITING CRAIG WOOD MUSIC HANS ZIMMER
PRODUCTION LAURIE MACDONALD, WALTER F. PARKES for DREAMWORKS SKG, MACDONALD/PARKES PRODUCTIONS, BENDERSPINK.
STARRING NAOMI WATTS (Rachel Keller), MARTIN HENDERSON (Noah Clay), DAVID DORFMAN (Aidan Keller), BRIAN COX (Richard Morgan), JANE ALEXANDER (Dr. Grasnik), RACHAEL BELLA (Becca Kotler), AMBER TAMBLYN (Katie Embry), LINDSAY FROST (Ruth Embry), DAVEIGH CHASE (Samara Morgan), SHANNON COCHRAN (Anna Morgan).

"Seven days!"

A strange video is circulating among young people in the city: they watch it as a test of courage when they are partying away from parental supervision on weekends. Everyone who watches the video – a kind of dream sequence of black and white symbolic images that ends with a shot of an old well – receives a phone call, with a voice saying the person has seven days to live. What begins as a joke ends in gruesome death, as fun-loving Katie (Amber Tamblyn) dies exactly seven days after seeing the video.

Her aunt, journalist and single parent Rachel Keller (Naomi Watts), scents a story and begins an investigation. In fact, she finds the secret VHS cassette and she, too, gets the call after viewing it. What is also disturbing afterward is that her face on photos seems blurred, just as had happened with Katie and her friends. When her son Aidan (David Dorfman) also watches the video when no-one is supervising him, and receives the death threat by phone, Rachel becomes seriously concerned; she has to solve the mystery, and there's not much time left …

The ingredients of this horror scenario are relatively old-fashioned: it is about an undead spirit and an evil curse, along with omens of its fulfillment to varying degrees. Verbinski's adaptation is based on the classic spine-chiller repertoire: isolated locations, dark nights, creaking doors and the obligatory double ending all combine in this story about a beautiful woman who goes in search of the truth behind a modern urban legend. Yet it is precisely this collision of modern environments with ancient fears that makes *The Ring* so effective (and which is fairly typical of many US remakes of original Japanese material that have penetrated the market since the late 1990s). On the one hand, there is modern man's sphere of existence, which acquires knowledge of the world through a plethora of technical appliances (the cell phone and

1

> **"The final payoff shocker will have you talking when you leave the theater. Especially when someone in your group remembers that you saw the video, too – when you watched the movie."**
>
> *San Francisco Chronicle*

1 Rachel (Naomi Watts) must delve deep into the Morgan family's secrets – encountering resistance in the process.

2 All Rachel cares about is her son, Aidan (David Dorfman). But Samara's curse affects him, too.

3 The secret of every good horror movie lies in the fascination with terror. Samara's accursed video also has a hypnotic appeal.

4 Media critique, 2002-style: the gateway to Hell is in every living room.

television are the main props here) in order to influence temporal events; on the other, there is a zone of supernatural, deadly phenomena. And this other, unknown and irrational dimension penetrates directly into our everyday lives through the channels of modern media.

This is exactly what happens in the case of the victims of the cursed video. With the help of her ex-boyfriend and son's father, Noah (Martin Henderson), Rachel's investigation leads her to Moesko Island. There, many years before, childless horse breeders Anna and Richard Morgan (Shannon Cochran and Brian Cox) adopted a daughter, Samara (Daveigh Chase). When Samara began to display abnormal abilities, however – one of the things she could do was force others to have bad dreams – the Morgans immediately exiled the child to the hayloft in the barn. Anna ended up pushing Samara into a well, where she suffered a horrible death through starvation a week later. The VHS video that has now appeared is, in a sense, little Samara's accusation in pictures. And she haunts anyone watching it after seven days – the TV switches itself on, the final sequence of the video appears, and Samara climbs out of the well, coming closer to shot level and clambering through the screen into the present day, where she kills her victims by electrocuting them.

When Rachel and Noah find the aforementioned well and Samara's mortal remains, the curse seems to be dissipated. Yet Noah is killed a day later. And

THE WORLD OF THE RING Gore Verbinski's film adaptation is not a prelude to a world of novels and films with many branches, but to a degree it marks the point at which the material finally became a phenomenon of the international entertainment industry. It started with the Japanese best-seller "The Ring" (1991) by Kôji Suzuki, which the author followed up in 1995 with the novel "The Spiral – Ring II" and "Loop – Ring III" in 1998. Unlike the later film adaptations, the protagonist in the first novel is male, while the evil girl, Sadako, is an hermaphrodite who has been raped and killed by the doctor treating her.
In 1995, the material was initially adapted for TV in Takigawa Chisui's *Ring: Kanzenban* (*Ringu: Kanzen-ban*). After its first incarnation as a manga (1996, by Kôji Suzuki and Nagai Koujirou) *Ring* (*Ringu*) reached the big screen for the first time in a movie directed by Hideo Nakata. A year later it was followed by a two-volume manga version by Hiroshi Takahashi and Misao Inagaki. At the same time as the publication of the follow-up novels, the film sequel *Rasen – The Spiral* (directed by Jôji Iida) appeared in Japan, and in 1999 Hideo Nakata produced another film sequel in *Ring 2*. In 2000, Norio Tsuruta gave us the prequel *Ringu 0: Bâsudei* from Kôji Suzuki's short story "Ring: Birthday." Dreamworks followed Verbinski's American remake in 2005 with another sequel, *The Ring 2*, with Hideo Nakata once again stepping into the director's shoes.

3
4

now Rachel realizes that she herself has not been spared because she salvaged Samara's corpse, but because she made a copy of the video for Noah, and thus spread the curse. To save her son, there is only one option: Aidan must distribute the tape. The curse can no longer be stopped …

When Samara comes out of the TV set during the film's gruesome climax, turning a character from a world existing only on celluloid suddenly into "fact," it can be understood not least as a metaphor for a reality that is increasingly constructed by the media. The world of images gains in importance at the expense of actuality, as more and more people are subjected to its law. In this sense, *The Ring* does not just tell a ghost story – it is also the story of a world that is in danger of losing any sense of reality. EP

"Atmosphere is a key factor in creating the experience that is *The Ring*. Almost every scene is shot in a washed-out, drab style that casts an effective pall of fear, dread, and foreboding over the entire film." *Best-Horror-Movies.com*

5 Samara (Daveigh Chase) encodes her accusation in beautiful, dream-like picture puzzles.

6 Becca (Rachael Bella) witnessed her friend Katie being killed by Samara; it has left her a psychological wreck.

7 Samara's motive is revenge: for her parents' lack of love and for the torture she had to endure at the hands of doctors.

“Though *The Ring* abuses the loud-noise scare, it successfully rachets up the tension and never goes slack, meaning you keep having to find new edges on your seat.” *Philadelphia City Paper*

IN THIS WORLD

2002 – UK – 88 MIN. – SOCIAL DRAMA
DIRECTOR MICHAEL WINTERBOTTOM (*1961)
SCREENPLAY TONY GRISONI DIRECTOR OF PHOTOGRAPHY MARCEL ZYSKIND EDITING PETER CHRISTELIS
MUSIC DARIO MARIANELLI PRODUCTION ANDREW EATON, ANITA OVERLAND for FILM CONSORTIUM, BBC, FILM COUNCIL, THE WORKS, REVOLUTION FILMS.
STARRING JAMAL UDIN TORABI (Jamal), ENAYATULLAH (Enayat), IMRAN PARACHA (Travel Agent), HIDDAYATULLAH (Enayat's Brother), JAMAU (Enayat's Father), WAKEEL KHAN (Enayat's Uncle 1), LAL ZARIN (Enayat's Uncle 2), AHSAN RAZA (Money Changer), MIRWAIS TORABI (Jamal's Older Brother), ABDUL AHMAD (Groom).
IFF BERLIN 2003 GOLDEN BEAR (Michael Winterbottom).

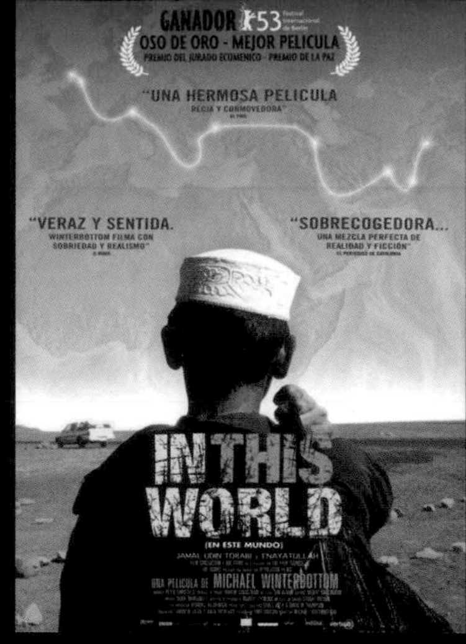

"He is not in this world"

Pakistan, February 2002. Over 50,000 people, most of them Afghans, are living in the Shamshatoo refugee camp in the north-west of the country – in miserable conditions and with little prospect of improvement. Among them is orphaned youth Jamal (Jamal Udin Torabi). When his uncle, a market trader from nearby Peshawar, enlists the help of people smugglers to arrange a better life for his son Enayat (Enayatullah), Jamal is allowed to accompany his older cousin because he speaks a little English. So the two boys set out on a long and dangerous journey that will take them through Iran, Turkey, Italy and France to the UK.

Like some of his fellow filmmakers, British director Michael Winterbottom did not need the terrorist attacks on September 11, 2001 to make him politically aware. Yet, although the idea for *In This World* had developed before President Bush declared the "war on terror," the outbreak of the war in Afghanistan had a considerable impact on both the production and the public perception of this low-budget project, shot in original locations with non-professional actors, a digital camera and minimal crew. While the latter found themselves subjected to growing bureaucratic obstacles and an increasingly precarious security situation because of events (which forced them to improvise all the more) the conflict also meant that the movie enjoyed huge media coverage at the Berlin International Film Festival in 2003. Everyone was moved by the global political situation, with the film quite deservedly winning the Golden Bear award.

Winterbottom himself described *In This World* as the document of a journey his team organized for the two protagonists. Jamal and Enayat, who kept their real names and had never left home before, thus had few terms of reference, like all the other people appearing in the film: they all either played themselves or a similar character. This goes a long way to giving the movie its extraordinary authenticity and power. Jamal and Enayat's curiosity and uncertainty seem completely natural, whatever the situation: whether they are crossing seemingly endless desert landscapes in packed long-distance buses or in the cargo areas of trucks or pick-ups; whether their journey through nowhere is interrupted by controls; or whether they are forced to wait for days on end in provisional shelters for the people smugglers who are supposed to take them on to the next stage. And even when these two extraordinary movie heroes lose all confidence in what to do for a time, and find themselves unexpectedly propelled back to the journey's starting point, they never once lose heart.

1

"In this case it is not about propaganda – about something holy or even something along the lines of the criminal foreigner. No, Jamal and Enayat are human beings with needs who find themselves in life-or-death situations, and portrayed as such, acquire a human face and dignity." *Jump Cut*

At a time when even the remotest corner of the earth is only the much-quoted "mouse click" away for the world's more affluent populations, or perhaps a day's travel via jet plane, *In This World* powerfully conveys the efforts and risks that migrants take in order to flee the poverty of their native lands. Winterbottom's film gives a face to these hundreds of thousands of migrants. He shows at close quarters what it means to be a so-called "economic migrant:" to be far from home and handed over to strangers speaking a language you do not understand; and to entrust your savings to them – as well as, ultimately, your life. When Jamal and Enayat cross the border between Iran and Turkey at night, on foot and over high, snow-covered mountains (the camera shows this in dark, coarsely pixellated images that give a sketchy picture of the action), they witness smugglers being shot by border guards. While they both

1 Two among millions: seldom has the theme of global migration been so powerfully visualized by cinema as in Michael Winterbottom's semi-documentary film about two young Afghans on their long journey to Europe.

2 *In This World* owes its strength not least to the non-professional actors, Jamal Udin Torabi and Enayatullah, who more or less play themselves.

3 Winterbottom's film is not just engaging political cinema, but also a poignant road movie …

4 … with two very different heroes: the more time we spend with the gentle, if sometimes rather inept, Enayat and his funny younger cousin Jamal, the more we become attached to them.

"Though the film looks like a documentary, it isn't. Instead, without an ounce of phony Hollywood uplift, Winterbottom's film cuts right to the heart." *Rolling Stone*

5

MICHAEL WINTERBOTTOM He is one of the most productive, versatile, and thought-provoking directors in European cinema. Born on March 29, 1961 in the English town of Blackburn, Michael Winterbottom initially studied English literature and then film, before beginning his career as an editor at Thames Television. He made his debut as a director with two documentaries about Ingmar Bergman.

The pilot for the TV crime series "Cracker" (1993–1996) proved his talent for popular formats, while *Butterfly Kiss* (1995) – a harsh road movie made for cinema, with Amanda Plummer as a lesbian psychopath who carves a bloody trail across northern England – proved his penchant for extreme subjects. In the years that followed, Winterbottom turned out a varied program of work as a director, including movies worth seeing like the underrated Thomas Hardy adaptation *Jude* (1996) with the subsequent *Titanic* star, Kate Winslet; the dark love story *I Want You* (1997) with Rachel Weisz, who was virtually unknown at that time; the Bosnian war drama *Welcome to Sarajevo* (1997); the French-style tale of a love triangle *With or Without You* (1999); and the British socio-realist, urban drama *Wonderland* (1999).

Winterbottom's second Hardy adaptation and his most expensive project to date – the star-studded western in a snow-covered epic setting, *The Claim* (2000) – was not well-received. This may have been the reason he went on to direct fairly small-scale productions, such as *24 Hour Party People* (2002), a lively portrait of the music scene in Manchester; the award-winning, quasi-documentary refugee drama *In This World* (2002); and the formally experimental romantic movie about music and sex, *9 Songs* (2004). With the docu-drama *The Road to Guantanamo* (2006) and *A Mighty Heart* (2007), Winterbottom confirmed his reputation as one of the leading political minds in world cinema.

5 When shooting had finished, 16-year-old lead actor Jamal Udin Torabi applied for asylum in the UK – an indication of just how close to reality this extraordinary film is.

6 Agonizing uncertainty: on their perilous journey into the unknown, Enayat and Jamal often have to endure seemingly endless periods of waiting in places that are utterly strange to them. Winterbottom filmed exclusively in original locations.

7 Homeless, and at the mercy of everything. Enayat and Jamal have no choice but to put their fate in the hands of strangers. This will ultimately have fatal consequences for one of them.

"*In This World* reveals a situation and involves us in an experience. No one seeing it will fail to be moved or to gain an understanding of what millions of people today are going through." *The Observer*

survive this danger unharmed, Enayat dies a few weeks later on the ship's passage from Istanbul to Trieste. Closed in a freight container with other refugees, he suffers a horrible death by suffocation. Jamal survives, however, and manages to make it through to London.

In This World caused considerable controversy: some critics found fault with it, saying that the complex conditions of global migration had largely been glossed over. Others complained that the movie's documentary style masked its manipulative techniques and the fictional nature of the story. The extent to which Winterbottom's refugee drama approximated to reality became evident after filming was completed, however, when Jamal applied for asylum in the UK instead of returning home. JH

25TH HOUR

2002 – USA – 134 MIN. – PSYCHOLOGICAL DRAMA
DIRECTOR SPIKE LEE (*1957)
SCREENPLAY DAVID BENIOFF, from the novel of the same name
DIRECTOR OF PHOTOGRAPHY RODRIGO PRIETO EDITING BARRY ALEXANDER BROWN
MUSIC TERENCE BLANCHARD PRODUCTION SPIKE LEE, JON KILIK, TOBEY MAGUIRE, JULIA CHASMAN for TOUCHSTONE PICTURES, 40 ACRES & A MULE FILMWORKS, INDUSTRY ENTERTAINMENT, GAMUT FILMS.
STARRING EDWARD NORTON (Monty Brogan), PHILIP SEYMOUR HOFFMAN (Jacob Elinsky), BARRY PEPPER (Francis Slaughtery), ROSARIO DAWSON (Naturelle Riviera), ANNA PAQUIN (Mary D'Annunzio), BRIAN COX (James Brogan), TONY SIRAGUSA (Kostya Novotny).

"Fuck you, Monty Brogan!"

"Fuck you!" He curses everyone: black, white, Jew, and Muslim through to Pakistani taxi drivers. Drug dealer Monty Brogan (Edward Norton) flips out in the restroom of his father's bar, screaming hatred to all and sundry at his reflection. There are just 24 hours to go before he starts a 7-year prison sentence. But then he realizes who got him into all this trouble – he did. "Fuck you, Monty Brogan!"

Monty still has a few things to sort out in these few remaining hours. Firstly, he visits his father James (Brian Cox), a widower and former firefighter who now runs a bar. Then he meets two old friends he has known since childhood: Jacob (Philip Seymour Hoffman), an awkward and insecure teacher who is on the point of starting a relationship with his student, Mary (Anna Paquin); and broker Frank (Barry Pepper), who juggles ostentatiously with fistfuls of dollars. Monty goes to an exclusive club with them and bumps into his girlfriend, Naturelle (Rosario Dawson). He wants to clear up something with her as well: Monty is nagged by the sense that it was she who grassed him up to the cops. He is smart, cool and charismatic – but then Monty, as played by the wonderful Edward Norton, is nothing like the dealers found in gangster movies. Basically, he is nothing like a criminal. "How on earth did it come to this?" he asks himself. And his father, girlfriend and friends ask themselves why they did nothing to stop him. *25th Hour* is the melancholic portrait of a man who once had so many choices open to him; now, however, he must leave his stunning girlfriend, chic apartment and beloved dog, and submit to harsh prison life. At one point, Monty remarks that the best thing he ever did was to take a badly injured dog off the street to a veterinarian, and then give it a home. It's a bitter stock-take of his life. Director Spike Lee (*Inside Man*, 2006) had already focused on one day in New York City – in his highly-charged racial drama *Do The Right Thing* in 1989, a title that could apply equally well to the theme of *25th Hour*.

1

1 A free man for one more day, then dealer Monty Brogan (Edward Norton) has to go to jail.

2 Monty enjoys a farewell party in a disco with his friends Jacob (Philip Seymour Hoffman, 2nd from left) and Francis (Barry Pepper, right): the booze is flowing, but they're not letting their hair down.

3 Monty's Irish father, James (Brian Cox), owns the bar and is an ex-firefighter: he insists on driving his son to jail.

4 We'll wait for you! Francis reassures Monty that their old life will carry on when he has finished his seven-year stretch. But Monty has doubts.

"New York in the wake of 9/11 is more than just a distinctive location. It defines the movie's underlying mood like a kind of cipher." *film-dienst*

Monty only notices how often he has *not* done the right thing when it is too late. Just as he tells one man's story, Spike Lee also tells the story of the city in which Monty (and the filmmaker) live – New York, post-9/11. Back in the opening credits we see a bitterly elegiac celebration of the Big Apple's skyline, featuring the two blue "Tribute in Light" sculptures marking the spot of the Twin Towers. There is a memorial plaque to the firefighters who died in the bar owned by Monty's father. A scene with a powerful musical soundtrack shows Monty's friends looking down from Frank's apartment onto Ground Zero, that gaping wound in the heart of the city. And the end credits are accompanied by "The Fuse," Bruce Springsteen's hymn to 9/11.

David Benioff's novel was written before 2001, and the screenplay was already complete when the attacks on the World Trade Center took place. 9/11

“Norton penetrates the mindset of a guy with an expiration date on his freedom, creating a character that has existed comfortably on dubious moral ground but is neither a bad person nor entirely unsympathetic.” *Variety*

4

5

5 Monty suspects his girlfriend Naturelle (Rosario Dawson) of informing on him to the police.

6 Francis also wonders whether Naturelle is Monty's girlfriend for purely altruistic reasons.

7 Naturelle: is she really a nice, natural girl – as her name suggests?

EDWARD NORTON He was determined to act in a Spike Lee movie, and apparently asked for only a tenth of his usual fee. Actor Edward Norton (*1969) can afford to be choosy. His very first film *Primal Fear* (1996) earned him a Golden Globe, thus distinguishing him as a character actor alongside Richard Gere. An attorney's son, he took acting classes while studying history at Yale. He received an Oscar nomination for his second film, the neo-Nazi drama *American History X* (1998), and in 1999 had his breakthrough with *Fight Club* directed by David Fincher. Then, just a year later, he made his directorial debut with *Keeping the Faith*, a comedy featuring Jenna Elfman and Ben Stiller. Norton seems to enjoy change and fresh challenges, as witnessed by his filmography: it lists a wide range of productions, from a horror flick about cannibalism *Red Dragon* (2002) through to an historical epic, *Kingdom of Heaven* (2005). In *The Incredible Hulk* (2008) he played the green monster; the following year, he took on the dual role of two very different twin brothers in the black comedy, *Leaves of Grass* (2009). In his private life he has had relationships with singer Courtney Love, appearing as a guitarist in her band, Hole, and with fellow actor Salma Hayek, with whom he appeared in the artist biopic *Frida* (2002). Norton lives in New York.

6

was incorporated at a later stage, making *25th Hour* the first feature film about New York in the wake of the attacks. The result is the story of a bungled life and a wounded city that fit together remarkably well. The 25th hour of the title refers to a fairly long, imaginary sequence at the end of the movie: James is driving his son Monty to the prison. And he tells the story of how Monty's life could continue if he were to run away now. He could travel West, without ever stopping or turning back. He could take a job and work for a living, somewhere where no questions would be asked, and one day Naturelle would follow him and they could start a family. So a fictitious hour is added to the 24 actual hours of Monty's last day of freedom. But it will remain a fiction, because he doesn't run away, but instead atones for all the bad things he has done in his life.

HJK

GOOD BYE, LENIN!

2002 – GERMANY – 121 MIN. – TRAGICOMEDY
DIRECTOR WOLFGANG BECKER (*1954)
SCREENPLAY BERND LICHTENBERG, WOLFGANG BECKER DIRECTOR OF PHOTOGRAPHY MARTIN KUKULA
EDITING PETER R. ADAM MUSIC YANN TIERSEN PRODUCTION STEFAN ARNDT for X FILME CREATIVE POOL, WESTDEUTSCHER RUNDFUNK, ARTE.
STARRING DANIEL BRÜHL (Alex Kerner), KATRIN SASS (Christiane Kerner), MARIA SIMON (Ariane Kerner), CHULPAN KHAMATOVA (Lara), FLORIAN LUKAS (Denis), ALEXANDER BEYER (Rainer), BURGHART KLAUSSNER (Robert Kerner), MICHAEL GWISDEK (Director Klapprath), CHRISTINE SCHORN (Mrs Schäfer), STEFAN WALZ (Sigmund Jähn).

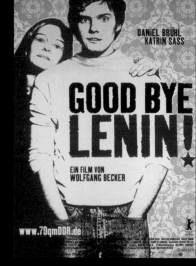

DANIEL BRÜHL
KATRIN SASS
GOOD BYE LENIN!
EIN FILM VON WOLFGANG BECKER
www.79qmDDR.de

"Coca-Cola is a socialist drink?"

It is the fall of 1989 and the world is looking on spellbound at the demise of East Germany. The joyous events take their historic course, but in the midst of everything Alex (Daniel Brühl) has other concerns in East Berlin. His mother Christiane (Katrin Sass) is lying in a coma. By the time she awakens, she has missed everything: the resignation of Erich Honecker, the fall of the Berlin Wall and the victory of capitalism in the former socialist paradise. Big BMWs are parked between the dreary concrete apartment blocks and Alex's sister Ariane (Maria Simon) has a job at Burger King. Alex is now at a loss. For, since his father ran off to the West, his mother has been an inveterate communist. How will she endure the shattering of her lifelong dream? The doctors say that any excitement could kill her. So, while East and West are getting chummy, Alex's imagination – fuelled by his love for his mother – goes into overdrive. The East lives on in the 850 ft² / 79 m² of their little apartment. Their old plywood furniture is rapidly reclaimed from the street, and Alex fills old East German packaging (long since gone from the supermarket shelves) with new products from the West. It's a labeling scam on a massive scale, just so mom doesn't suspect anything. And when the bedridden patient asks for her old TV and spots a huge Coca-Cola banner on the apartment block opposite, Alex goes to even greater lengths. Enthusiastically assisted by his friend Denis (Florian Lukas) he films bogus news broadcasts – "Focus on Today" – and plays them

1
2
40 Jahre DDR
mein
Staat
Qualität

"A softhearted tribute to – of all things – Communism, *Good Bye, Lenin!*, the German director Wolfgang Becker's social satire, has a knobby tone that somewhat mutes its crowd-pleasing ambitions and keeps it from becoming, 'My Big, Fat Life Is Beautiful.'" *The New York Times*

to her from a hidden video recorder. These news items report that the socialist East has taken over the Coca-Cola Company and is allowing thousands of West Germans, suffering under capitalism, to enter the East. A brilliant propaganda trick: the direction of the elated East Germans tumbling over the border is simply reversed.

Wolfgang Becker's *Good Bye, Lenin!* is the definitive movie of German reunification, made at a safe distance from actual events. As Marx used to say, history is repeating itself, in this case as farce. Yet there is a great deal of truth in the farce, in that many East Germans applied a massive displacement process to console themselves as they mourned the loss of their past lives – "Eastalgia" was a remarkable phenomenon in the post-reunification period that was even appropriated by many West Germans. The less attractive sides of the dictatorship were as skillfully edited out as the consequences of reunification, from loss of identity to mass unemployment. The young hero's surreal game of deception is actually plausible, as pretending all was well in the world had to a large extent been part of the political raison d'être of the fallen republic. Criticism of this process was kept within limits. It was all too clear that the film had struck a chord with many in both East and West. With audiences of seven and a half million in Germany, the movie was then sold in over seventy countries, triggering a minor renaissance in German cinema, which had gone unnoticed for years. It even surpassed the figures achieved by *Run, Lola, Run* (1998).

What determines the experiment's success (besides the loving portrayal of "real socialist" details) is its tragicomic tone, which stops short of boisterous

3

4

1 On the West's streets, paved with gold: the joys of capitalism still seem alien to East Berliner Alex (Daniel Brühl).

2 Tinkering with the GDR matrix: State Council head, Erich Honecker, long since removed, is re-hung for the staging exercise.

3 Commercials in paradise: confused, the mother Christiane (Katrin Sass) clocks the changes in the "worker's and peasant's state" – which no longer exists.

4 From comedy to tragedy: Alex would do anything for his sick mother. He finds comfort in the arms of a nurse, Lara (Chulpan Khamatova).

"Was East Germany really still alive in 1990? It seems almost incredible watching this clever, poignant little movie from director Wolfgang Becker, that delivers the shock of the new and the shock of the old." *The Guardian*

5

6

"Wolfgang Becker's terrific film fantasy *Good Bye, Lenin!* deploys plenty of irony to resist the relentless march of history." *Der Spiegel*

7

8

5 Welcome to Burger King: Alex's sister Ariane (Maria Simon) starts on the bottom rung in the new world of work – the experience of many East Germans.

6 Old-style "Focus on Today": even the antiquated news program makes a comeback in the hands of techno-freak Denis (Florian Lukas).

7 Fade to a better past: in the GDR, Christiane was a dyed-in-the-wool Communist.

8 Tragicomic hero: the fallen GDR wasn't paradise for Alex, just home. And it leads to a painful break in his personal life.

slapstick on the one hand and political provocation on the other; instead, it softens the drama of profound social upheaval with subtle black humor. Under the direction of Wolfgang Becker (a West German, incidentally) the young star Daniel Brühl and seasoned East German actress Katrin Saß give us a sense of the mother–son relationship that is nothing less than magical. Many viewers do not realize that the mother plays along with her son's selfless game herself toward the end, as she wants to preserve his own childhood dreams of a better socialism. The most moving and poetic image in the movie, however, takes the form of a stone statue: when the mother actually manages to walk out of the house and is forced to confront all the changes, she comes face to face with Lenin. Hauled away by a helicopter, his raised hand signals goodbye, while at the same time pointing to a different future. PB

DANIEL BRÜHL Daniel Brühl is the best-known face of new German cinema. Son of director Hanno Brühl, he was born in Barcelona in 1978 and brought up bilingual; he regards himself as a European actor. Repeatedly cast in the role of young romantic and sensitive idealist, he often tries to accentuate his gritty masculine side in interviews, so far unconvincingly.

In saying that, he first attracted attention with his convincing performance as a schizophrenic in Hans Weingartner's *The White Sound* (*Das weiße Rauschen*, 1999/2001). The breakthrough, however, came with *Good Bye, Lenin!* (2002). He became an international star in the role of Alex, an East Berliner with his head in the clouds who fakes the triumph of socialism for his mother. Brühl played a similar part in Weingartner's *The Edukators* (*Die fetten Jahre sind vorbei*, 2003/2004), as an anti-capitalist "spontaneous activist" whose clever protests unexpectedly degenerate into terrorism. Another German film of his worth seeing is Achim von Borries' drama *Love in Thoughts* (*Was nützt die Liebe in Gedanken*, 2002/2004). Two hopelessly romantic school pupils make a suicide pact against the atmospheric background of the Weimar Republic, with Brühl's co-star in the movie, August Diehl, revealing another example of the new, softer male image in German film.

Brühl mainly works with historical material on the international scene. In period movie *Ladies in Lavender* (2004) he even stole the hearts of Judi Dench and Maggie Smith. He seems, however, to attach greater importance to political subjects. In the European co-production *Merry Christmas* (*Joyeux Noël*, 2004/2005) he played a German officer who organizes a Christmas ceasefire between enemy troops in World War I. In *Salvador* (Puig Antich) (2006), one of several Spanish language movies he has made, he was cast in the role of an anarchist executed under Franco's rule. Brühl won widespread acclaim, of course, for his role as the lovestruck German army hero, Fredrick Zoller, in Quentin Tarantino's Nazi farce *Inglourious Basterds* (2009); this came after fairly minor roles in Julie Delpy's directorial debut *2 Days in Paris* (*Deux jours à Paris*, 2006/2007) and the Hollywood thriller *The Bourne Ultimatum* (2007).

ELEPHANT

2003 – USA – 78 MIN. – DRAMA
DIRECTOR GUS VAN SANT (*1952)
SCREENPLAY GUS VAN SANT DIRECTOR OF PHOTOGRAPHY HARRIS SAVIDES EDITING GUS VAN SANT
PRODUCTION DANY WOLF for HBO FILMS/MENO FILMS/BLUE RELIEF PRODUCTIONS.
STARRING ALEX FROST (Alex), ERIC DEULEN (Eric), JOHN ROBINSON (John), ELIAS MCCONNELL (Elias), CARRIE FINKLEA (Carrie), NATHAN TYSON (Nathan), NICOLE GEORGE (Nicole), BRITTANY MOUNTAIN (Brittany), KRISTEN HICKS (Michelle), ALICIA MILES (Acadia), BENNIE DIXON (Benny), TIMOTHY BOTTOMS (John's Father), MATT MALLOY (Mr. Luce).
IFF CANNES 2003 GOLDEN PALM (Gus Van Sant).

"Most importantly – have fun, man!"

They say that films have their own language. *Elephant*, a testament to absent words, has an architecture. A school building is measured, step by step, room by room, in uncut camera shots lasting minutes, which are sensational to say the least. The camera fixes itself on boys, girls and individual groups on their way along endless corridors, following them into the gym, cafeteria, offices and dark room. We all remember these places, though the memories of their unreal atmosphere have long since been suppressed. Everything seems muffled: the movements, the voices, the echo of steps and conversation snatches from the nooks and crannies of a school building that seems to have no beginning and no end. The figures in it walk slowly, or rather they float through the corridors as if they were not really alive, but the living dead. Wait a minute, though – even here the eerie reality is getting confused with our prior knowledge. The eye of the camera is innocent, unlike the viewer's.

The film is the nightmarish reconstruction of an "ordinary" school day like the one when 12 pupils and a teacher in Columbine High School in Littleton, Colorado fell victim to the killing spree perpetrated by two fellow students – the survey of a massacre. No one knew what would happen that day. But the audience knows it from the start and searches feverishly for indications, clues and ways of explaining the impending disaster. Who is the boy in the yellow T-shirt who seems popular with everyone? Will he survive the horror? What does the cross on another boy's red jacket mean? Will he be saved, or is he a target? The building becomes a trap. Where are the possible exits and escape routes? More than anything, of course, the eye looks for reasons for the deed; for answers to the powerless question "why?"

Director Gus Van Sant was heavily criticized for his refusal to load his mind-blowing study with a meaning. Criticism only increased after it was awarded the Golden Palm at Cannes, the art house Mecca. In a mood of uncertainty after Columbine and 9/11, a film without a convenient message was the ultimate provocation. Yet he who looks will find. Everything that is generally believed to motivate future killers is there, from the insensitive teaching staff to teasing fellow pupils and, of course, brutalizing video games. Alex (Alex Frost) and Eric (Eric Deulen) order the weapons on the internet without any problem, as if Van Sant's intention is to support Michael Moore's identical critique in *Bowling for Columbine* (2002). After all, doesn't the Steadicam – apparently taking an impartial view – simulate the perspective of a first-person shooter as it walks through the corridors hunting for victims? But the usual

1

2

1 School of perception: the perspective keeps changing, bringing people in and out of focus.

2 Discharging violence: the perpetrators are viewed with the same empathy as their victims. Certainty has proved false; only perplexity remains.

3 Eric (Eric Deulen) and Alex (Alex Frost) order weapons on the internet. Most of the actors kept their real names.

"By making the camera an observer, we get a perspective that often comes out of horror movies, a choice that whips the ordinary with the terrifying, an unforgettable mix." *The New York Times*

context is absent from these images: there is no music, and no explanatory dialogue to guide our thoughts. It is not the film but the viewer alone who makes the connections, at his or her own risk. On the evening before the deed, taciturn Alex plays "Für Elise" on the piano, the haunting leitmotif of the film. So is Beethoven also guilty of causing school massacres?

The possible reasons lie deeper, hidden within the fabric of the film, in its eerie silence that seems so peaceful yet expresses the sense of being lost that young people have – the proverbial elephant in the room. The one thing no one dares talk about. No one is happy at this school, and everyone has something to hide: John, who prefers detention to talking about his alcoholic father; the envied school couple, threatened by a pregnancy; ugly duckling Michelle, who hides all her fat cells with long track bottoms, flouting all the rules; the three anorexic school beauties, who go straight from lunch to the rest room, as if operated by remote control. Less responsible filmmakers make high school comedies from the same characters. Van Sant gives these eventual victims, and the perpetrators, back their dignity with his empathetic eye verging on glorification. *Elephant* exerts a hypnotic, irresistible pull on the viewer. The excellent non-professional cast, who virtually play themselves, are as responsible for this as the movie's avant-garde style. Where horror tries to take hold, Van Sant finds delicate beauty, and sets art against violence. Instead of explaining the inexplicable, he celebrates life and thus creates space for grief. PB

4 Adolescent problem areas: taunted Michelle (Kristen Hicks) hides not only her unloved body, but her feelings as well.

5 A sympathetic eye: director Gus Van Sant tells the story of his young protagonists' vulnerability in an understanding and affectionate way.

6 Asking "Why?": Alex, who commits the crime, is a sensitive loner and accomplished pianist.

7 A testament to silence: like all his fellow students, John (John Robinson) has problems he would rather keep from the others.

GUS VAN SANT The career of this pioneering indie director is unique from both an artistic and a commercial point of view. As the legitimate heir of John Cassavetes, Gus Van Sant managed to achieve the aesthetic and textual regeneration of independent film, returning to his roots after what has become the almost standard slide into mainstream production. The early films *Mala Noche* (1985), *Drugstore Cowboy* (1989) and *My Own Private Idaho* (1991) already contain his central themes. He portrays young people sensitively and unsparingly, showing disturbed teenagers, dropouts and junkies in all their beauty and despair. Success followed as well: *My Own Private Idaho*, a dynamic mixture of hustler romance and Shakespeare quotes, made him as famous as his leading actors, River Phoenix and Keanu Reeves.
What followed was an intriguing flirtation with the mainstream. The black media satire *To Die For* (1995) with Nicole Kidman was followed by the Oscar-winning story of a genius, *Good Will Hunting* (1997), produced from a screenplay by its main stars Matt Damon and Ben Affleck. The theme of the problem child recurs in this film, though in a form suitable for the masses, an idea that was then repeated in *Finding Forrester* (2000). In between, however, came the experiment that got everyone's dander up – *Psycho* (1998), an almost identical visual remake of the eponymous Hitchcock classic.
Now financially independent, Van Sant revisited his strengths with the relatively ambitious avant-garde films *Gerry* (2002), *Elephant* (2003) and *Last Days* (2005), the last of which was a free reconstruction of Kurt Cobain's final days, and the skateboard drama *Paranoid Park* (2008): bittersweet portraits of youth, which the openly homosexual filmmaker imbues with his own hint of eroticism. He then returned to conventional film-making with his double Oscar-winning biopic *Milk* (2008), a moving portrayal of the eponymous Harvey Milk, the first openly gay mayor in America. Gus Van Sant continues to elude categorization.

DOGVILLE

2003 – DENMARK / SWEDEN / UK / FRANCE / GERMANY / NETHERLANDS – 178 MIN. – DRAMA
DIRECTOR LARS VON TRIER (*1956)
SCREENPLAY LARS VON TRIER DIRECTOR OF PHOTOGRAPHY ANTHONY DOD MANTLE
EDITING MOLLY MARLENE STENSGÅRD MUSIC JOACHIM HOLBEK, ANDERS VALBRO
PRODUCTION VIBEKE WINDELØV for ZENTROPA, ISABELLA FILMS, SOMETHING ELSE, MEMPHIS FILMS, TROLLHÄTTAN FILM.
STARRING NICOLE KIDMAN (Grace), PAUL BETTANY (Tom Edison), STELLAN SKARSGÅRD (Chuck), LAUREN BACALL (Ma Ginger), HARRIET ANDERSSON (Gloria), BLAIR BROWN (Mrs. Henson), BILL RAYMOND (Mr. Henson), CHLOË SEVIGNY (Liz Henson), JEREMY DAVIES (Bill Henson), PATRICIA CLARKSON (Vera), BEN GAZZARA (Jack McKay), PHILIP BAKER HALL (Tom Edison Sr.), JAMES CAAN (The Big Man), JEAN-MARC BARR (The Man with the Big Hat), UDO KIER (The Man in the Coat).

"This town is rotten from the inside out."

Two roads lead to Dogville, but none leads out. According to one reading of this, director Lars von Trier reveals himself in his most uncompromising film to date as the person he may always have been: a destroyer of cinema and its illusions. He has ruthlessly reduced his setting, the god-forsaken town of Dogville in the Rocky Mountains, to a bare stage. Chalk marks indicate street names and houses, residents knock on invisible doors, and even the village dog is only painted in. The only indications of the time period – the Great Depression – are the sparse sets and the costumes worn by the actors. The characters busy themselves in a desultory manner as glass cutters or apple farmers, while awaiting their cue. It is pure theater, unbearable for movie fans. But cinema is not far removed from the place where Lauren Bacall picks invisible gooseberries. If you look at it another way, and in this film you have to do this all the time, the radical abandonment of everything external itself reveals the power of the cinematic illusion, still intact. Enter Nicole Kidman.

As in a Brechtian *Lehrstück* ("teaching play"), the Danish master introduces the angelic innocence of Kidman's character into the village community in order to test these lost souls. Pursued by gangsters, Grace needs shelter, and finds it. The village poet, Tom Edison (Paul Bettany), who has not yet written a single line, manages to persuade his suspicious neighbors to help. In dark times he sees the act of compassion as the way to the moral high ground. The fragile and beautiful woman earns respect through her incredible humility and help with minor tasks. Yet her firm belief in man's goodness leads to disaster. When the sheriff arrives with the promise of a reward, the tide turns. After trying to escape, the woman they are looking for is chained up in an iron collar, exploited more and more shamelessly by the women, and raped by the men. In Dogville, where goodness will always be a stranger, a human being has become a captive animal.

With his trademark cinematic tools – disturbing close-ups and innovative editing – Lars von Trier realizes his concept of the theater-film in *Dogville.* At the same time he tells a story of female passion, as he had before in *Breaking the Waves* (1996) and *Dancer in the Dark* (2000). Once again, he countered the now familiar accusations of sadism with the assertion that a part of himself

1

2

1 The good person of Dogville: Grace (Nicole Kidman) is a gangster's daughter with a naive and reckless faith in people. This will lead to disaster.

2 The perfect theater-film: a minimal set confirms the enduring power of cinematic illusion.

3 Selfless empathy: Grace will live to regret her help for troubled family man Chuck (Stellan Skarsgård).

4 A woman's passion: Grace wins the villagers' favor by performing menial tasks. But her humility is cruelly rewarded.

"While you watch the movie, it can seem ridiculously long-winded. But once it's over, its characters' miserable faces remain etched in your memory, and its cynical message lingers." *The New York Times*

3

is also in each one of his characters: it applies to Grace as well as Tom, the sentimental artist who cannot think of a more inspired description than "illustration." *Dogville* is a parable and its director unscrupulously exploits its consciously anti-realist precursors in the theater – from Bertolt Brecht's *The Good Person of Szechwan* to Thornton Wilder's *Our Town*. Their didactic style is preserved, but the associated existential questions are updated in a way that is less than faithful. In this work, von Trier pushes his moral and philosophical nightmares to unprecedented extremes. It is not just a question of human depravity and weakness; it is also about the vanity of tolerance, the ultimate contempt for the sinner through eternal grace, as embodied in Grace. A diabolical chalk circle, with no way out – unless like Grace you proceed to gruesome revenge and cast aside every hard-won insight.

"The austere, stripped-down set, which seemed mere affectation, is really a foreshadowing of the way von Trier intends to strip the townsfolk of their social decorums and reveal their true animal selves." *The Independent*

4

5

“If there is any town this world would be better without, this is it.”

5 A star-studded cast: movie icons such as Lauren Bacall (Ma Ginger), James Caan (The Big Man) and Ben Gazzara as blind widower Jack reference the traditions of American cinema.

6 Tribunal of the righteous: Dogville is a nightmare town where liars and hypocrites sit in judgment over the good guys. Grace is punished for her defiance.

7 Portrait of the artist: village poet Tom Edison (Paul Bettany) is plagued by the same doubts as director Lars von Trier. But his self-pity just seems ridiculous.

Dogville was interpreted by many US critics as a sweeping blow against America. Von Trier had already earned the same criticism for *Dancer in the Dark*. It was in fact the initial inspiration for the film, the first part of his announced “America trilogy,” which he unapologetically pursued with *Manderlay* (2005). The Dane had never been to the country himself because of his fear of flying: he asked his outstanding cast – Lauren Bacall, Ben Gazzara, James Caan and Chloë Sevigny are all linked to the great traditions of American cinema – to come to the film shoot in a bare hangar near Göteborg. His reasonable statement on the matter was that no one from Hollywood had ever been to Casablanca. Furthermore, Dogville is of course anywhere. It should equally be borne in mind that the ascetic, stylist and provoker is also hot on self-irony. The idea of introducing images showing the misery of the Depression into the end credits, overlaid with the satirical track of David Bowie’s hymn “Young Americans,” is as banal as it is inspired. Lars von Trier, the epitome of the sublime and lucid in directing, still makes essential viewing. PB

6

7

PAUL BETTANY Born in London in 1971, Paul Bettany is one of the most conspicuous newcomers in the first decade of the millennium. With his first major role as the aspiring criminal in the neo-noir movie *Gangster No. 1* (2000) he became indelibly imprinted in the minds of the public. Bettany played the young Malcolm McDowell character, whose coldly calculating, evil look was not actually seen again after his early appearances. Cynically elegant and with the pallor of a gravedigger, he embodies the most decadent (and attractive) features of the English aristocrat.

He then appeared in the postmodern chivalric parody, *A Knight's Tale* (2001), as the pleasure loving poet Chaucer, in a rare display of his comic side. As the imaginary roommate of the schizophrenic mathematics genius John Nash, he once again sent shivers down the audience's spine in *A Beautiful Mind* (2001). Constantly referred to, wrongly, as the successor to Ewan McGregor and Jude Law, Bettany proved in Lars von Trier's dynamic theater experiment *Dogville* (2003) that he does not play difficult parts just for a change: his feeble, wannabe philosopher Tom Edison turns from benefactor to traitor under pressure from the community.

Following a moving appearance as the ship's doctor in the seafaring epic *Master and Commander: The Far Side of the World* (2003) he finally went over to the dark side in another Hollywood film: Paul Bettany's murderous albino monk Silas is one of the few things we remember from the blockbusting film adaptation *The Da Vinci Code* (2006).

FINDING NEMO

2003 – USA – 100 MIN. – ANIMATION MOVIE, COMEDY
DIRECTOR ANDREW STANTON (*1965)
SCREENPLAY ANDREW STANTON, BOB PETERSON, DAVID REYNOLDS
DIRECTOR OF PHOTOGRAPHY SHARON CALAHAN, JEREMY LASKY EDITING DAVID IAN SALTER
MUSIC THOMAS NEWMAN PRODUCTION GRAHAM WALTERS for PIXAR ANIMATION STUDIOS, WALT DISNEY PICTURES.
VOICES ALBERT BROOKS (Marlin), ELLEN DEGENERES (Dory), ALEXANDER GOULD (Nemo), WILLEM DAFOE (Gill), BRAD GARRETT (Bloat), ALLISON JANNEY (Peach), AUSTIN PENDLETON (Gurgle), STEPHEN ROOT (Bubbles), VICKI LEWIS (Deb/Flo), JOE RANFT (Jacques).
ACADEMY AWARDS 2004 OSCAR for BEST ANIMATED FEATURE (Andrew Stanton).

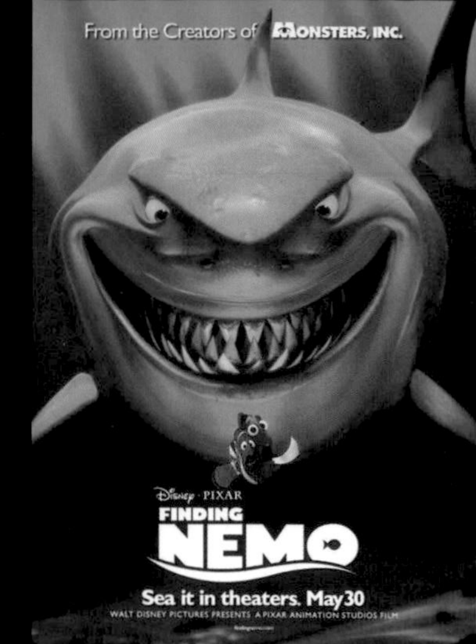

"Just keep swimming"

Some things are easily forgotten. When *Finding Nemo* was released in 2003 (with worldwide revenues of over 800 million dollars) it was not just the audiences that made it what was then one of the greatest animated cartoons of all time; the critics raved about it as well. Not least because they in particular could appreciate the technical achievement of Andrew Stanton's animation team (and computers): portraying the movement of water is one of the most difficult tasks for an animator, due to light refraction among other things, and a cartoon movie in which just about every scene is set either in the ocean or in an aquarium had never been made until then.

As such, nearly every journalist insisted on providing lengthy and enthusiastic descriptions of this animated underwater world: from the colorful coral reef with its sea anemones (which represents the home of the clownfish Nemo and his father Marlin) to the "forest" of jellyfish and the fake exoticism of the aquarium in a Sydney dental practice, where Nemo is held in captivity. The publicity gave all the relevant figures: 99,079 fish, 74,472 jellyfish and 111,998 aquarium pebbles are said to have been programmed into the computer for this movie.

A few years down the line, computers and software have already advanced by generations, and for some time now CGI movies have been opening up new worlds; what once seemed progressive, we now take for granted. Yet what, beyond the technical innovations of that time, was so appealing about *Finding Nemo* that made it one of Pixar's most commercially successful films? Perhaps it was the relatively conventional narrative structure, in this case a subtle variation on the standard formula of its affiliate Disney, which gives it a very familiar look.

1

“The view from the fish tank to the dentist’s chair and the window overlooking the harbor is just one of the visual wonders of a film that rewrites the book on animating water, which experts say is the hardest element to achieve.” *Rolling Stone*

1 The ocean is big and wide, but clownfish are rather small. What Nemo finds exciting, his father Marlin often regards with distrust.

2 Almost made it: Marlin has traveled all the way to Sydney to save Nemo.

3 Finally reunited: Nemo and Marlin at home in the imaginatively designed reef landscape.

For decades, Disney's stories had consistently involved single fathers and their sons, which latter seemed different from the rest and had to prove in the course of the plot that they somehow measured up to paternal standards. *Finding Nemo* inverts this standard format: here, it is not captured Nemo who has to prove something, but his excessively anxious and overprotective father Marlin, who eventually regains his son's respect by crossing the wide ocean in search of his offspring – though he has never had the courage to venture out of his coral reef before.

Parallel storylines in the movie involve, on the one hand, Marlin's search (with the help of Dory, a female blue doctor fish with short-term memory loss) and, on the other, the efforts of Nemo and his fellow captives to escape from the aquarium.

Throughout the movie, the points of comedy and danger are held in subtle balance. Just about every sequence ends in action and terrible threats faced by the main characters, yet the story still retains its humor. The horrible lantern fish from the deep ocean tries to kill Marlin and Dory, yet simultaneously its "lantern" provides enough light for Dory to identify the name and address on the diving goggles and lead the searchers in the right direction. The jellyfish, with their poisonous stings, are also such a beautiful sight that Dory begins to hop around boisterously on top of them. In the scene where Nemo finally

ANDREW STANTON Born in Rockport, Massachusetts in 1965, Andrew Stanton is now one of the most successful animators in the world. He directed three films for Pixar studios between 1998 and 2008, of which *Finding Nemo* (2003) and *WALL•E* (2008) each won the Oscar for Best Animated Feature in their respective years. With worldwide box office takings of over 800 million dollars, *Finding Nemo* is the second most successful film after *Toy Story 3* (2010)". Stanton originally studied animation at the California Institute of the Arts (CalArts), graduating in 1987.
He has worked for Pixar since 1990 (he was the company's ninth employee) in various capacities as animator, producer or director in nearly every Pixar production. For instance, he co-wrote the screenplay for the first feature-length Pixar film *Toy Story* (1995), directed by John Lasseter. Stanton made his first appearance as co-director with *A Bug's Life* (1998) alongside John Lasseter: this was the story of an ant that tries to protect its species from horrible grasshoppers.
Following the huge hit of his fish comedy *Finding Nemo*, Stanton gave us the equally impressive WALL•E, his most recent work as a director to date: a movie inspired by silent comedy stars such as Chaplin and Keaton, which tells (with long periods of practically no speech) the story of a little robot that cleans up abandoned, garbage-filled land. Stanton's latest project is an adaptation of Edgar Rice Burroughs' science fiction novels from the Barsoom series: *John Carter of Mars* will be a combination of computer animation and live action, and is due for release in 2012.

4 In the aquarium, with a view of the sea – and a dental practice. Let's get the heck out of here!

5 Marlin meets some interesting guys on his journey: cool turtles surfing the ocean currents.

6 Vegetarian? Marlin and Dory are right to be a bit skeptical.

"Pixar's creatures have humanity that most flesh-and-blood movies can't touch." *Philadelphia City Paper*

manages to escape from the dental practice, things are deadly serious: his life is at stake. Yet, at the same time, it is a totally absurd and macabre slapstick number that ends in a leap into the sink of the treatment room.

While the feelings of fear, danger and loss can be easily understood by younger viewers, the movie's humor is more directed at adults. There are sharks that have set up a self-help group for secret vegetarians; aquarium fish that provide sarcastic commentaries on root canal treatments and X-rays; and the fear-inducing appearance of the dentist's niece, Darla, a notorious "fish killer" with glaring dental braces who is characterized by Bernard Herrmann's music for the classic shower scene in Alfred Hitchcock's *Psycho* (1960). The fun is always serious, and vice-versa. *Finding Nemo* quite rightly won the Oscar for Best Animated Feature in February 2004. LP

PIRATES OF THE CARIBBEAN: THE CURSE OF THE BLACK PEARL

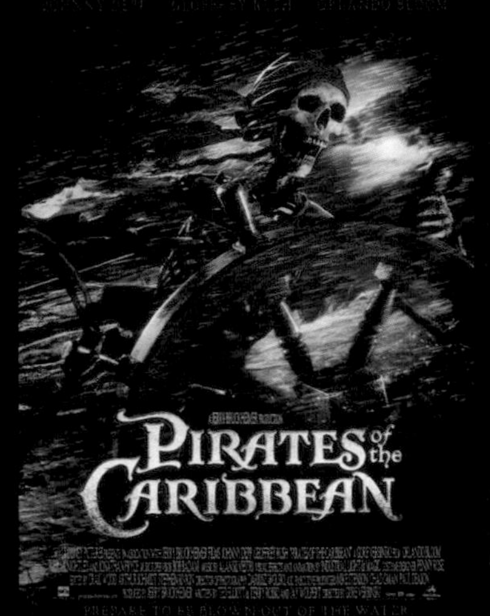

2003 – USA – 143 MIN. – PIRATE MOVIE
DIRECTOR GORE VERBINSKI (*1964)
SCREENPLAY TED ELLIOTT, TERRY ROSSIO, STUART BEATTIE, JAY WOLPERT
DIRECTOR OF PHOTOGRAPHY DARIUSZ WOLSKI EDITING STEPHEN E. RIVKIN, ARTHUR SCHMIDT, CRAIG WOOD MUSIC KLAUS BADELT PRODUCTION JERRY BRUCKHEIMER for JERRY BRUCKHEIMER FILMS, WALT DISNEY PICTURES.
STARRING JOHNNY DEPP (Captain Jack Sparrow), GEOFFREY RUSH (Barbossa), ORLANDO BLOOM (Will Turner), KEIRA KNIGHTLEY (Elizabeth Swann), JACK DAVENPORT (Norrington), JONATHAN PRYCE (Governor Swann), LEE ARENBERG (Pintel), MACKENZIE CROOK (Ragetti), DAMIAN O'HARE (Lieutenant Gillette), GILES NEW (Murtogg).

"That is, without doubt, the worst pirate I've ever seen."

It was a mixture of brazen, buccaneering spirit and economic acuity that made *Pirates of the Caribbean* an unprecedented success. From the very start, Disney has processed its biggest blockbusters into Disneyland rides of varying levels of amusement – not the other way round. Breaking the pop-cultural exploitation chain, its inversion points up the precedence given to merchandising at the expense of all claims to creativity. The audience was captivated by its irony, rather than the burden of hype: this seems appropriate for a film in which avaricious cutthroats have all the sympathy and a fly-by-night buccaneer with a weird demeanor throws all ideas of good and evil into disarray. As Captain Jack Sparrow, Johnny Depp was in marvelous form – the most tongue-in-cheek pirate of all time.

Just as the film managed to synthesize very effectively the well-known clichés of a genre deemed passé, the actor (who up until then was mainly regarded as a quirky oddball) created a postmodern action hero with iconic status. With a spectacular disregard for events – and probably for Gore Verbinski's direction as well – Captain Jack performs for no one but himself. He swaggers around with a perplexed air and lurching gait, muttering pearls of wisdom mainly for his own benefit. He is a boozy pirate without a ship, who cannot do

“The action comedy *Pirates of the Caribbean – The Curse of the Black Pearl* raises one of the most overlooked and important cinematic questions of our time: Can a movie maintain the dramatic integrity of a theme park ride? In this case the answer is – sure.” *The New York Times*

anything right and yet makes everything right; the anarchic element amid the calculated extravagance. His very first appearance is a class act: prancing along, he reaches the shores of Port Royal and safety, fleeing from a boat’s mast as it silently sinks in the harbor. He goes on to free the Governor’s beautiful daughter, Elizabeth (Keira Knightley), on several occasions and eventually leads her to the brave blacksmith and pirate’s son, Will Turner (Orlando Bloom). This is the action, such as it is. But all that counts is the attitude, the sweeping gestures and the attractive figure – and the right garb, of course. Matted dreadlocks, braided goatee, pearls through his hair and lucky charms make Jack Sparrow the rock star of pirates – no wonder, if like Depp your own personal style is modeled on the Keith Richards look and attitude. On top of this, his flamboyant travesty of the traditional pirate character and effeminate habits permit all sorts of associations for anyone who does not simply take a child’s delight in his terrific comedy act. So is Jack Sparrow bi- or asexual, or just perverse in a polymorphous kind of way? The question is definitely appropriate in terms of the triangular relationship of the main characters. Elizabeth can’t

1 Nautical yarn: eccentric pirate captain Jack Sparrow (Johnny Depp) and governor's daughter Elizabeth (Keira Knightley) have a somewhat tense relationship.

2 Under false colors: producer Jerry Bruckheimer successfully revived a moribund genre with this ironic take on the pirate movie and its well known motifs.

3 Rock star among buccaneers: alongside Jack Sparrow, Will (Orlando Bloom) is bound to be a bland, if pretty, hero. He gains in stature as the series progresses.

figure it out. Captain Jack's desire, however, seems to be centered on winning back his beloved *Black Pearl*. This digitally-enhanced sea epic made lavish use of the usual elements of the genre, as one might expect from Jerry Bruckheimer. For the pyromaniac among Hollywood's successful producers, a film set in an age before the invention of dynamite did not actually make much sense, but the various acrobatics in the rigging, sword fights, cannon-firing and, of course, Caribbean locations provided a more than effective substitute. A spine-tingling surprise came halfway through the film for the uninitiated: the *Black Pearl* mutineers, Sparrow's arch rivals, are revealed as a bunch of undead ghouls – walking corpses, covered in scurvy and eternally damned. The fact that Captain Jack and the British Governor's redcoats get involved in swashbuckling swordfights with them makes as little sense as this temporary alliance – but it is good fun. Visitors to the Disneyland theme park in Anaheim were, of course, already familiar with the ghoulish storyline from the ghost train there. Likewise with the grouchy Captain Barbossa (Geoffrey Rush): both in the film and in Disneyland, he drinks red wine that flows visibly

JERRY BRUCKHEIMER For three decades, the name Jerry Bruckheimer has stood in Hollywood for lurid popcorn movies, fun action and sheer unlimited power. As a producer of blockbusters, he understands his audience and seems to know better than anyone what it wants: explosions, speed, cars crashing in slow motion, and still more explosions. His unmistakable style is characterized by incredibly dynamic momentum, slick editing, speeding camera shots, straightforward storylines and noisy soundtracks. It doesn't attract much praise from the critics, just millions of dollars at the box office instead.

A psychology graduate and former advertising filmmaker and photographer, he entered the movie business in 1972, his first experiences as a producer being in the neo-noir *Farewell, My Lovely* (1975) and the cult movie *American Gigolo* (1980). His big break came with the crew arranged by Michael Eisner with party animal Don Simpson and their first film together, *Flashdance* (1982). Since then his way has been paved with box-office hits like *Beverly Hills Cop* (1984), *Top Gun* (1985/86), *Bad Boys* (1995), *Crimson Tide* (1995), *The Rock* (1996), *Con Air* (1997), *Armageddon* (1998) and *Pirates of the Caribbean: The Curse of the Black Pearl* (2003). In 2001 Bruckheimer managed to create the successful patriotic war tearjerker *Pearl Harbor* (2001) in the same year as the grittily authentic battle movie, *Black Hawk Down*. While his directors, led by Tony Scott and Michael Bay, contented themselves on the whole with being his sidekicks, Bruckheimer hauled a whole bunch of underpaid character actors out of independent cinema and made them into action stars worth millions, like Nicolas Cage. As a sideline, Jerry Bruckheimer owns his own TV production company, and has been the executive producer on the globally successful series *CSI: Crime Scene Investigation* since 2000.

4 Flamboyant and dashing: in fabulous garb, actor Johnny Depp has created a postmodern icon in Captain Jack, who is rarely focused and frequently drunk.

5 The crew around Barbossa (Geoffrey Rush) reveals itself as a gruesome gang of the undead. Even before that he was a bit creepy.

6 Fair winds! Dry, but ship-less, Johnny Depp manages to deliver one of the coolest performances in film history.

7 Smooth sailing: this movie proved the springboard to an international career for British actress Keira Knightley.

down his throat through his ribs. Jack Sparrow is pitched against further adversaries in the two sequels that followed the unanticipated success of the original film (every previous pirate film had flopped in an equally spectacular fashion) in what was now a quite traditional and reasonably economical way. A new strand in the mystic supernatural storyline is embodied in the grim figure of Davy Jones, the tentacled pirate of the "Flying Dutchman" legend, magnificently played by Bill Nighy. Filmed back-to-back, *Pirates of the Caribbean: Dead Man's Chest* (2006) and *Pirates of the Caribbean: At World's End* (2007) could not recapture the freshness and carefree spirit of the first part, but on the other hand the box-office takings were even higher. Film piracy continued to cause Hollywood fear and alarm, but Disney had captured its plunder. PB

5

6

"You thought Brando's Fletcher Christian was bizarre? Check out Depp's swarthy pancake makeup and heavy mascara and jazzercising gestures – every line accompanied by a jiggly little dance. Depp is now squarely in the camp of Nicolas Cage and Crispin Glover. He is no mere actor. He is a role stylist." *Slate Magazine*

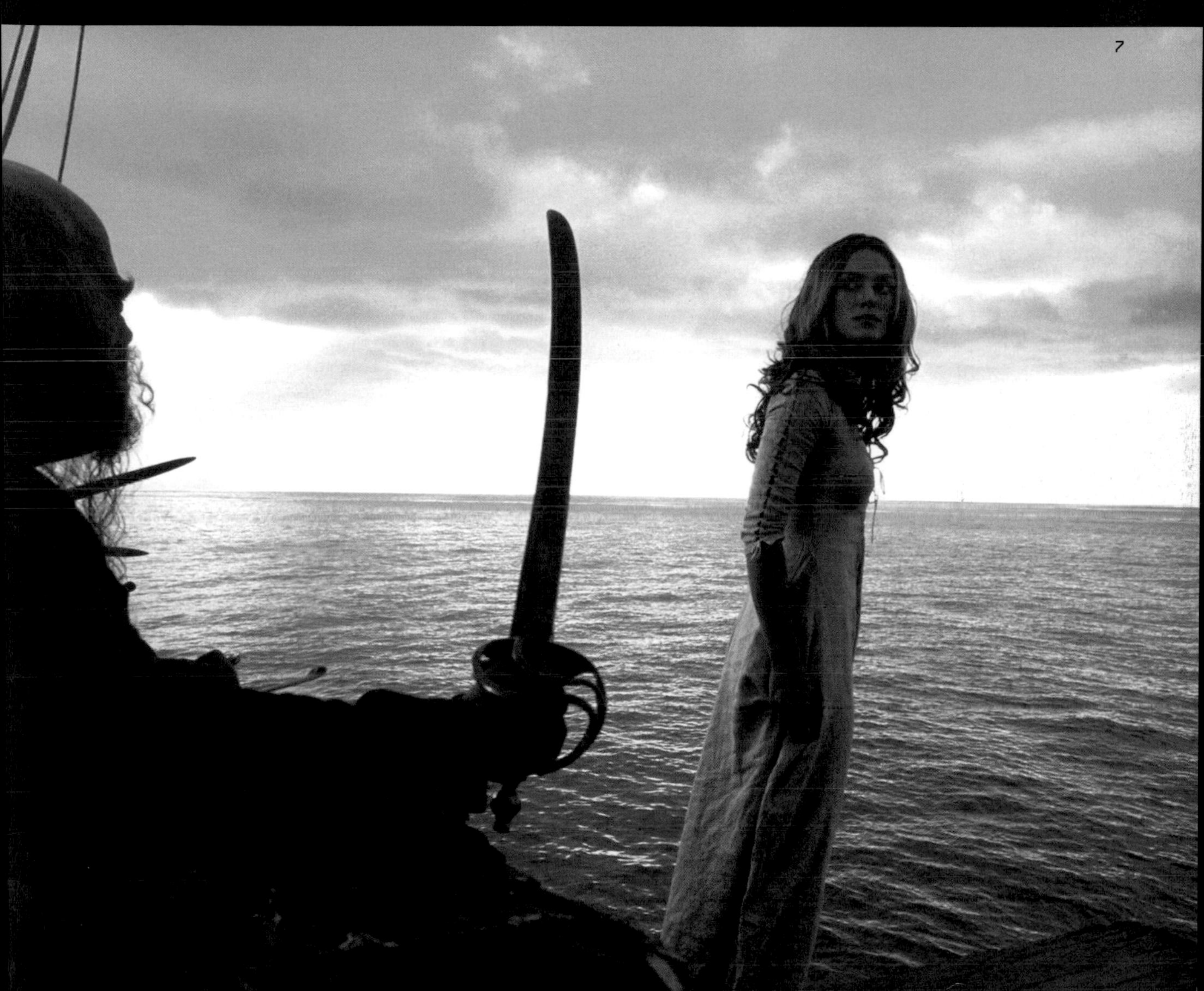

SPRING, SUMMER, FALL, WINTER ... AND SPRING

BOM YEOREUM GAEUL GYEOWOOL GEURIGO BOM

2003– SOUTH KOREA / GERMANY – 103 MIN. – DRAMA
IRECTOR KIM KI-DUK (*1960)
CREENPLAY KIM KI-DUK DIRECTOR OF PHOTOGRAPHY BAEK DONG-HYUN EDITING KIM KI-DUK
USIC BARK JI-WOONG PRODUCTION LEE SEUNG-JAE, KIM SO-HEE, KARL BAUMGARTNER, RAIMOND GOEBEL for LJ FILM, PANDORA FILM, KOREA PICTURES.
TARRING OH YOUNG-SU (Old Monk), KIM JONG-HO (Child Monk), SEO JAE-KYUNG Boy Monk), KIM YOUNG-MIN (Young Adult Monk), KIM KI-DUK (Adult Monk), HA YEO-JIN Girl), KIM JUNG-YOUNG (Girl's Mother).

"There are times when you have to let go what you possess."

An idyllic lake surrounded by steep, densely-forested mountains. A small temple on a wooden platform floats in the middle of the lake. The action in *Spring, Summer, Fall, Winter ... and Spring* takes place within the space of a few square yards. There, South Korean director Kim Ki-duk tells the story of a Buddhist monk and his pupil who live and pray in the temple. The temporal scope is as broad as the spatial context is narrow in this film, which is divided into five parts covering several decades of the pupil's life. In the first episode, the pupil (Kim Jong-ho), who is about 6 years old, takes the boat to the mainland and plays on the flat banks of the lake. With the curiosity and ignorance of a child, he begins to torture animals. He first ties a string with a stone attached around a fish, then a frog, and afterward a snake. The Master (Oh Young-soo) watches him and forces him to set the creatures free, with a stone tied around his own back.

In part 2 – set in a summer several years later – a sick young girl (Ha Yeo-jin) arrives on the island. The pupil, now a teenager (Seo Jae-kyung), falls in love with her and together they discover their sexuality. When his Master sends the girl away, it breaks the boy's heart and he leaves the temple. The remaining episodes are set in turn over the course of several years. Now a grown man (Kim Young-min), the former pupil has killed his wife in a jealous rage. He flees to his Master on the island but is found there by the police and arrested. In the concluding spring episode he has served his sentence and is now the Master (Kim Ki-duk) himself, instructing a pupil on the wooden island.

Sea, sun and morning mist: Kim Ki-duk develops his story using calm, almost contemplative, images that invariably feature the motifs of nature. It is about the different stages in a human life and how a person should approach his or her fellow humans and all the other living things on Earth. And, as much

1

2

3

“Though deeply rooted in Buddhist symbolism, which is not immediately obvious to everyone, the spiritualism in Kim Ki-duk’s film has universal relevance” *film-dienst*

4

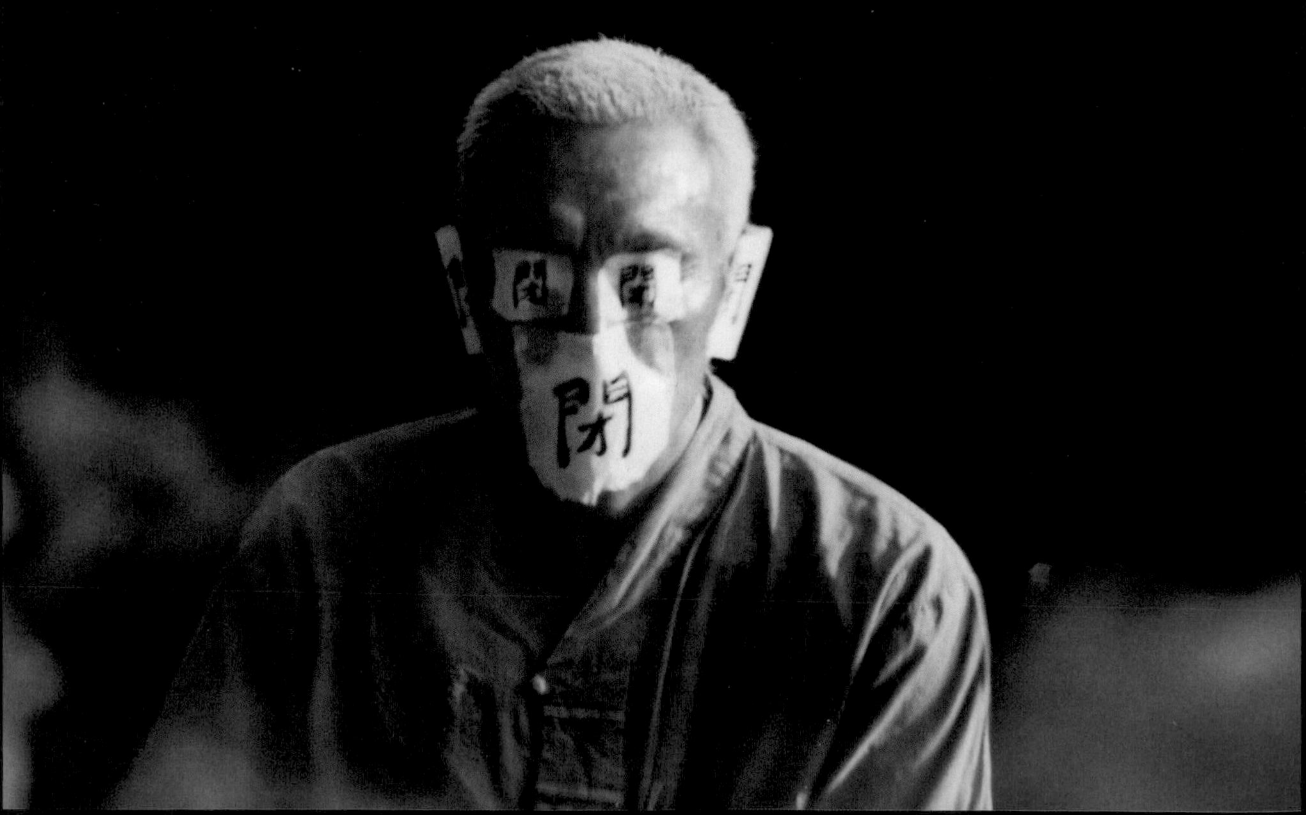

1 The pupil (Seo Jae-kyung) has his first sexual experiences with the girl (Ha Yeo-jin).

2 Catharsis: monk-turned-murderer (Kim Ki-duk, left) must carve characters in the wooden boards.

3 The pupil falls in love with the girl who has come to him and his Master to become well again.

4 See no evil, hear no evil, speak no evil: the Master (Oh Young-soo) performs a ritual – an expression of his guilt in helping a murderer?

5 The pupil as a boy (Kim Jong-ho): his torture of animals sets an endless train of guilt in motion.

"The seasons dictate the rhythm of this film. They are both reality and metaphor, in the same way that everything in the movie is both real and metaphorical – the sea, the nearby waterfall, the mountains, the animals, the hut and the boat."

Frankfurter Allgemeine Zeitung

KIM KI-DUK When his film *The Isle* (*Seom*, 2000) was screened at the Venice Film Festival, South Korean director Kim Ki-duk (*1960) made a sensational entrance onto the stage of international cinema: it was a movie featuring both moments of peace and a level of brutality rarely seen before, a combination that many found disturbing.

Kim has never attended film school. He moved with his parents to the capital, Seoul, when he was nine years old and, as a young man, worked as a farmer and factory worker, served in the marines, considered the priesthood, began to paint and finally taught himself how to make movies. The son of a Korean War veteran, he worked through his difficult childhood and adolescence in the drama *Address Unknown* (*Suchwiin bulmyeong*, 2001).

He won his first major award for *Samaritan Girl* (*Samaria*, 2004), which took the Silver Bear at the Berlin International Film Festival. Yet this drama about two casual prostitutes also met with a mixed response. It took *Spring, Summer, Fall, Winter … and Spring* (*Bom yeoreum gaeul gyeoul geurigo bom*, 2003) – in which he appears himself as the pupil in the last two episodes – for him to enjoy almost universal acclaim. "Guilt fascinates me," he told a German newspaper, "for it makes its mark on all religions. I was brought up a Christian and even spent two years at a Catholic school. Now I am attracted by Buddhism and its pursuit of universal harmony." Kim's documentary *Arirang* (2011) about his work as a filmmaker won the prestigious "Un Certain Regard" award at the Cannes Film Festival that year.

6

as it addresses the themes of a simple existence, concentration and meditation, it ignores neither the civilized world on the other side of the mountains nor the issues of evil. Stimuli from cell phones and newspapers constantly penetrate the isolation of the Buddhist retreat. And the way the pupil has to deal with this is also the object of the lesson imparted to him by the Master.

The film is absorbing, with its tight structure and quiet, condensed narrative style that proceeds with minimal dialogue. Each episode starts off the same way but with its own characteristics, including the changing seasons and the various domestic animals on the island. Kim Ki-duk strikes an astonishing balance between different moods; the film is for the most part focused and serious, but also has its funny moments.

The sequences containing symbols and metaphors are strangely fascinating.

"Everything develops quite naturally out of something else: violence from naivety, desire from innocence and from desire, death; atonement follows death, then punishment, and ultimately there is contemplation and redemption." *Frankfurter Allgemeine Zeitung*

7

8

6 The mother (Kim Jung-young) leaves her sick daughter with the Master and his pupil.

7 The pupil has become the Master: in the last two episodes, director Kim Ki-duk plays the main role himself.

8 An idyllic setting: the Master's small temple on a floating wooden platform in the middle of a lake.

For instance, the Master gets to the mainland from the island on a number of occasions without a boat, yet his feet stay dry. Another easily overlooked symbol is the special doorways: a door in the temple and the gateway at the landing stage that are seen at the beginning of each episode and are simply there, not enclosed by any wall, inside or out. So it is possible to go round them. But no one usually does, for they are part of the prescribed order, representing the rules that people must adhere to.

The calligraphy is also highly significant. When the Master writes on a scroll using a brush and water, the moment he has finished at the bottom he must begin again at the top because the characters have dried out: this is a symbol of the cyclical nature of life and its transience. And the characters that are carved into the platform's wooden decking involving enormous physical effort are finally able to heal even the soul of the pupil who became a murderer.

HJK

LOST IN TRANSLATION

2003 – USA / JAPAN – 102 MIN. – TRAGICOMEDY
DIRECTOR SOFIA COPPOLA (*1971)
SCREENPLAY SOFIA COPPOLA DIRECTOR OF PHOTOGRAPHY LANCE ACORD EDITING SARAH FLACK
MUSIC KEVIN SHIELDS PRODUCTION SOFIA COPPOLA, ROSS KATZ for AMERICAN ZOETROPE, ELEMENTAL FILMS, TOHOKASHINSHA FILM COMPANY, FOCUS FEATURES.
STARRING SCARLETT JOHANSSON (Charlotte), BILL MURRAY (Bob Harris), GIOVANNI RIBISI (John), AKIKO TAKESHITA (Ms. Kawasaki), DIAMOND YUKAI (Commercial Director), NAO ASUKA (Premium Fantasy Woman), ANNA FARIS (Kelly), CATHERINE LAMBERT (Jazz Singer), FUMIHIRO HAYASHI (Charlie), HIROKO KAWASAKI (Hiroko), TAKASHI FUJII (TV presenter).
ACADEMY AWARDS 2004 OSCAR for BEST ORIGINAL SCREENPLAY (Sofia Coppola).

"Let's never come here again, because it would never be as much fun."

An entire movie in jetlag, constantly weaving between waking and dreaming; why didn't anyone think of it before? Tokyo is the location for the hotel – a waiting room for lost souls – and jetlag is the feeling of transition that unites them. This is where Harris (Bill Murray) and Charlotte (Scarlett Johansson) experience a chaste, insomniac love between hotel bedroom and elevator, in limbo between not-yet-being-there and gone-once-more.

Appropriately enough, it was a befuddling drink that brought Bob here. This has-been Hollywood star is filming a commercial for a Japanese whiskey brand. Easy money, plus no one back home will ever see it. He has been married for 20 years to a woman who bombards him with calls from the US asking anxiously about things like carpet patterns; to an extent, the frustrated cynic is also running away from his own existence. Charlotte is accompanying her husband, a famous photographer, who does not have time for her. She is a philosophy graduate and does not have a clue about the man to whom she is married. Or, for that matter, about who she is and what she really wants. This is why she seeks out Bill, a considerably older man who, though he doesn't have any answers either, has the calm demeanor born of profound resignation. This gives her strength; with someone, you are not so alone.

Lost in Translation has often been reduced, somewhat unfairly, to the cultural collisions that to a large extent create the movie's comic potential. Bob's verbal clashes with the Japanese promo director, whose brutal directions always sound far more elaborate than the clipped translation "more intensity," underscore the title of the film. The alien nature of the different culture is never hidden, whether it is Bob and Charlotte having a Japanese meal or when he

1

2

3

"His crumpled face and her luscious loneliness are a match made in modern limbo. But they footle around like a couple from an E. M. Forster novel in search of a plug." *The Times*

4

5

1 Sleepless in Tokyo: Bob (Bill Murray) and Charlotte (Scarlett Johansson) are kindred spirits in the vacuum of globalized anonymity.

2 Land of smiles: Bob stoically appears on the show of a famous TV host (Takashi Fujii).

3 The dissatisfied actor is a star in Japan, his whiskey commercial a badge of sophisticated elegance.

4 Night owls with jetlag: Coppola's images seem wrapped in cotton wool, floating like the characters in a state halfway between waking and dreaming.

5 An insecure companion: Charlotte seeks meaning and direction, but more than anything she wants to find herself.

"A comedy of dislocation framing a love story bound up in an expression of existential melancholy, Sofia Coppola's film is a deft, manifold delight." *Time Out Film Guide*

is the guest star on a TV game show and finds himself subjected to the ravings of an overzealous presenter. Image and sound fail to provide the usual filter for understanding: huge advertising screens block the view and information is rendered unintelligible in the cacophony of the gambling dens. Then it all becomes quiet again, in an image that is as terrific as it is baffling: Bob is standing silently holding a golf club in front of the majestic background of Mount Fuji. Is it a huge backdrop to a Japanese golf course, or is it reality? In the land of empty symbols (for a Westerner) everything is possible, while every resolution is both confusing and sobering.

Yet this strangeness is simply an innocuous reflection of the existential alienation from themselves that the two are trying to overcome. The central part of the film is a night journey they embark on with Charlotte's Japanese friends; an expedition lasting about seven minutes taking them through restaurants, nightclubs and karaoke bars. The feeling of disorientation is overwhelming. The space and acoustics do not provide any kind of security. Where are they? Who are these people? And why on earth is Bob wearing this outrageous yellow T-shirt? But it is precisely in this sequence that the profound spiritual affinity between the two characters is revealed, probably only possible in this strange space. Bob struggles passionately through a karaoke rendition of "More Than This" by Roxy Music and everything is then OK.

Sofia Coppola produced her masterpiece with *Lost in Translation*, a bittersweet rom-com and charming portrait of an impossible love. The role of

6

6 A man in the crowd: occasionally provocative, the film plays with cultural differences, but uses them more as an expression of existential alienation.

7 Girl with a pearl earring: Scarlett Johansson won several awards for her role as the lonely globetrotting Charlotte. The independent film paved her way to stardom.

8 Whiskey time: director Sofia Coppola wrote the part of the washed-out actor for Bill Murray, and it won her an Oscar.

"Coppola is a confident, cool, detached filmmaker in a manner reminiscent of the European cinema of the Sixties, with suggestions also of classical Japanese film." *The Observer*

7

the jaded star was tailor-made for Bill Murray, whose phlegmatic facial expressions effortlessly dissolve the boundaries between comedy and tragedy. It may have made Scarlett Johansson famous, but the film belongs to him. It was shot on location, often without permission, a factor that gives some images an almost documentary quality. It doesn't bear thinking about, however, that Coppola might have followed the advice of her father, Francis Ford, who told her to use the medium of the future – a digital camera. She decided on what she felt, quite rightly, was the more "romantic" 35-mm format. Nothing could have been more appropriate for Bob and Charlotte's story. It ends with a final, hesitant kiss. Their parting words are lost in the street noise, remaining just between the two of them – it doesn't get any more romantic than this. PB

SOFIA COPPOLA It's not easy having one of the most famous directors in the world as a father. Born in 1971, Sofia Coppola is the daughter of Francis Ford Coppola, making her one of the Coppola clan that also includes Nicolas Cage and Jason Schwartzman. Yet she found it to her advantage to be underestimated from the outset; people hardly expected anything from the young woman who practically ended her own career as an actor with her unfortunate appearance in *The Godfather: Part III* (1990).
Today, Sofia Coppola is one of the most promising female directors in Hollywood. Fundamentally different from her father's epic films, her movies reveal her love of small details in relationships and, above all, style. A very feminine type of indie sensitivity was already evident in her debut *The Virgin Suicides* (1999), the tragic portrait of a strictly puritanical couple's five daughters from the bestseller by Jeffrey Eugenides. She even won the Oscar for Best Original Screenplay for *Lost in Translation* (2003). Coppola's images always seem to be shrouded in cotton wool, a unique atmosphere created by the lighting and sets. The perfect mise-en-scène is complemented by her choice of music: as well as having her own fashion label in Japan, she has become a musical trendsetter comparable only to Quentin Tarantino in her use of soundtracks – the punk and alternative music tracks integral to every student party.
This mix reached a provocative climax in *Marie Antoinette* (2006), a portrait of a queen that barely still rates as a historical film. The court at Versailles dances to scratchy guitar sounds, while the Rococo ostentation is wickedly glammed up. Her choice of a more elegiac, serious tone in *Somewhere* (2010) produced a superb result: chaired by Quentin Tarantino, the Venice Film Festival jury awarded the Golden Lion to this study of the loneliness of a famous actor, played by Stephen Dorff.

THE DREAMERS

2003 – ITALY / FRANCE / UK – 115 MIN. – EROTIC DRAMA, COMING-OF-AGE MOVIE
DIRECTOR BERNARDO BERTOLUCCI (*1940)
SCREENPLAY GILBERT ADAIR DIRECTOR OF PHOTOGRAPHY FABIO CIANCHETTI EDITING JACOPO QUADRI
MUSIC JANICE GINSBERG PRODUCTION JEREMY THOMAS for RECORDED PICTURE COMPANY, PENINSULA FILMS, FICTION FILMS.
STARRING MICHAEL PITT (Matthew), EVA GREEN (Isabelle), LOUIS GARREL (Theo), ANNA CHANCELLOR (Mother), ROBIN RENUCCI (Father), FLORIAN CADIOU (Patrick), JEAN-PIERRE LÉAUD (as himself), JEAN-PIERRE KALFON (as himself).

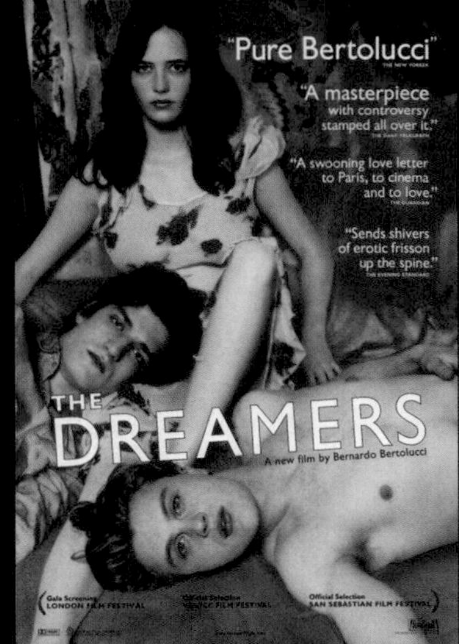

"We accept him, one of us!"

Paris, February 1968. The atmosphere is euphoric, a sign of the upheaval to come. Matthew (Michael Pitt), an American student, is new to the city. At a demonstration outside the Cinémathèque Française he meets brother and sister Isabelle and Theo (Eva Green and Louis Garrel), who are the same age as him and likewise have the movie bug. The three soon become inseparable. When Isabelle and Theo's parents go away on vacation, Matthew moves in with them. Cut off from the outside world, a ménage à trois develops, characterized by a passion for cinema, pleasure in arguments and sexual experimentation, burgeoning love, and jealousy. The trio only breaks out of its self-imposed isolation when a piece of paving smashes through a window in the apartment: the May revolution is kicking off on the streets of the Latin Quarter. Yet while Theo and Isabelle enthusiastically join the students' revolt, protesting against the power of the state, Matthew remains behind, disenchanted.

Sex, drugs and rock and roll are as much part of May '68 as the "Little Red Book" of Chairman Mao. *The Dreamers* extends this list to include the cinema. Of course, it would be an exaggeration to claim that seasoned director Bernardo Bertolucci attributed the birth of the revolt to the spirit of the cinéphile. But he impresses on us retrospectively how movies played a significant role in defining the ideas and feelings of the '68 generation. Cinema is a ubiquitous presence in Bertolucci's Paris. The city seems literally filled with the spirit of the Nouvelle Vague (French New Wave) and the anarchic charm of Jean-Luc Godard's first films. And in showing the famous cinéastes' protest against the firing of Cinémathèque founder Henri Langlois at the start of his film about 1968, he is making a direct link between the film revolution of the early 1960s and the great student revolt.

Inspired by Godard's *Breathless* (*À bout de soufflé*, 1959), Bertolucci had by 1968 become one of the leading left-wing members of European auteur cinema. He enjoys an almost personal relationship with his film material, as evidenced by the skillful way he weaves cinematic references through his later work. The best example of this is the scene in which his protagonists charge through the Louvre, just as Anna Karina, Claude Brasseur and Sami Frey had previously done in Godard's *Bande à part* (1964). Bertolucci edits sequences from Godard's movie into the three heroes' race, thus aligning himself effectively with the "freaks," as Theo and Isabelle call their exclusive cinéaste club in a reference to Tod Browning's eponymous horror classic.

Yet in his love of referencing, Bertolucci is far removed from the postmodern ironic cinema of quotation that so often falls flat with sterile in-jokes. Right from the start, his film radiates a thrilling vitality; we sense a euphoric attitude to life and desire for sensual experience, discovery and experimentation that seems actually to be inspired by the enthusiasm for cinema. *The Dreamers*

1
2

1 Three cinéphiles: Matthew, Isabelle and Theo (from left: Michael Pitt, Eva Green and Louis Garrel) re-enacting the race through the Louvre from Jean-Luc Godard's *Band of Outsiders* (1964).

2 *The Dreamers* contains numerous references to film history. The three-sided mirror can be read as an allusion to the famous polyvision sequences in Abel Gance's *Napoléon* (1927).

3 Friends and rivals: Theo (in background) is jealous because Matthew is getting closer to his sister.

is, then, more than just a declaration of love for cinema; the movie is an act of love by a cinéaste for whom cinema and eroticism are inseparable.

Almost inevitably, *The Dreamers* evokes another great Bertolucci film set in Paris. As in *Last Tango in Paris* (*Ultimo tango a Parigi*, 1972), the protagonists complete their erotic journey of self-discovery in a cavernous apartment of an old building, though it turns out to be a far from gloomy psychological landscape: there's no hint of the pessimism of the legendary, scandalous movie. Despite the incestuous impulses and weird sex games, the intercourse between the three characters appears relatively innocent. There may be disappointments and wounds, but the shared apartment proves ultimately to be a playground for Matthew, Theo and Isabelle. Before the actual revolt breaks out, the three heroes try out their own (sexual) revolution in advance. The fact that the parents are willing to leave the field open for them sheds light on the wider context of May '68 in Paris.

Critics were divided in their reception of *The Dreamers*. Some accused Bertolucci of lasciviousness, given the beautiful young stars (who were frequently naked) and permissive sex scenes; it is a reproach that has been leveled against his career since *Last Tango*. Others saw the revolution as besmirched, portrayed as a romp of narcissistic, middle-class kids. Yet given the playful ease of his directing and the unrestrained sensuality, originality and non-dogmatic view of 1968, the prevailing judgment was that a master of cinema had finally rediscovered his old form. JH

EVA GREEN She strikes Greta Garbo and Marlene Dietrich poses in *The Dreamers* and, at one point, even imitates Rita Hayworth's famous striptease from *Gilda* (1946). The fact that Eva Green's screen debut also proved to be her breakthrough is no doubt less to do with these tongue-in-cheek (self) orchestrations than with the sensitivity and confidence of her overall performance – especially in the uninhibited way the daughter of French actress Marlène Jobert, born in 1980, displays her beautiful young body in front of Bertolucci's camera.

Green's exceptionally good looks were then turned to further advantage in two expensive, if less revealing, costume movies: Jean-Paul Salomé's rollicking film about thieves *Adventures of Arsene Lupin* (*Arsène Lupin*, 2004) and Ridley Scott's lavish Crusades epic, *Kingdom of Heaven* (2005), which captured her rather dark and exotic aura but failed to exploit her talents as an actor. The French actress reached a mass international audience in the James Bond movie *Casino Royale* (2006), albeit as the first Bond girl that the super-agent (till now hardly a romantic) falls in love with. Her next movie, the 180-million-dollar fantasy epic *The Golden Compass* (2007), showed her in a fairytale setting but did not reveal any hidden sides of the actress. This may all change with the eagerly-awaited US thriller *Mona Lisa* (planned for 2011) in which Eva Green is due to appear alongside notorious bad boy Mickey Rourke. It is to be directed by the no less controversial, independent filmmaker Larry Clark.

4 Erotic shenanigans: the trio passes the time in the parental home playing risqué movie quiz games. Here, Isabelle imitates Rita Hayworth in *Gilda* (1946).

5 Matthew meets Isabelle and Theo at the famous demonstration in front of the Cinémathèque Française in February 1968. When May '68 erupts in Paris a few months later …

6 … the trio is torn apart. Matthew does not share the siblings' sudden revolutionary zeal. Bertolucci's view of the '68 generation was seen as provocative by some of his former fellow campaigners.

"The film is extraordinarily beautiful. Bertolucci is one of the great painters of the screen. He has a voluptuous way here of bathing his characters in scenes from great movies, and referring to others." *Chicago Sun-Times*

KILL BILL – VOLS. 1 & 2

2003/04 – USA – 111 MIN. / 136 MIN. – MARTIAL ARTS MOVIE, THRILLER
DIRECTOR QUENTIN TARANTINO (*1963)
SCREENPLAY QUENTIN TARANTINO, UMA THURMAN DIRECTOR OF PHOTOGRAPHY ROBERT RICHARDSON
EDITING SALLY MENKE MUSIC RZA/ROBERT RODRIGUEZ PRODUCTION LAWRENCE BENDER for MIRAMAX FILMS, A BAND APART, SUPER COOL MANCHU.
STARRING UMA THURMAN (Beatrix Kiddo/The Bride/Black Mamba), LUCY LIU (O-Ren Ishii/Cottonmouth), VIVICA A. FOX (Vernita Green/Copperhead), DARYL HANNAH (Elle Driver/California Mountain Snake), DAVID CARRADINE (Bill/Snake Charmer), MICHAEL MADSEN (Budd/Sidewinder), JULIE DREYFUS (Sofie Fatale), CHIAKI KURIYAMA (Gogo Yubari), SONNY CHIBA (Hattori Hanzo), MICHAEL PARKS (Earl McGraw, Esteban Vihaio), MICHAEL BOWEN (Buck), CHIA HUI LIU (Johnny Mo, Pai Mei), PERLA HANEY-JARDINE (B. B. Kiddo), SAMUEL L. JACKSON (Rufus).

"Revenge is never a straight line."

The first part of what was originally planned as a single movie begins with an old Klingon saying from *Star Trek II: The Wrath of Khan* (1982): i.e., a reference to the civilization in the Star Trek universe in which all moral concepts are geared to the strict rules of engagement of its warriors. The story begins in El Paso, however, rather than faraway galaxies. A heavily pregnant bride (Uma Thurman) lies on the ground, covered in blood; the sadistic leader of the "Deadly Viper Assassination Squad" responsible for this deed is her former lover, Bill (David Carradine), who is not only devoid of pity but has brutally sought to execute her with a shot to the head. Despite all odds Beatrix Kiddo survives, and after lying in a coma for almost five years sets off on a campaign of revenge that involves killing, one after another, the members of the gang she once belonged to as a professional assassin. It transpires, however, that her child had been saved by the doctors: B. B. (Perla Haney-Jardine) is now being raised by her father. Eventually the bride wins through – she kills Bill

Tarantino skillfully references the prototypes of the revenge movie in *Kill Bill* – the first part blends the audiovisual worlds of North American ghetto fights with bloodthirsty anime and Japanese samurai, while the second part combines superhero mythologies with the spaghetti western and Chinese kung-fu. In addition, cult figures such as actor David Carradine are enjoying something of a revival. Surprisingly the main concern is to extract strong female characters from the reference point of '70s exploitation movies while deleting the frequent sexism to be found there.

It goes without saying that Beatrix Kiddo's revenge campaign – rationally planned and morally justified by the wrong done to her – will be successful. An added complication is that, on another level, the bride has to fight her convoluted way through the referenced genres and the roles assigned within them. The rapist who exploits Beatrix's comatose condition does not constitute a serious opponent. More difficult is the almost tangible battle against stereotypes

1

1 "The deadliest woman in the world" (Uma Thurman as Beatrix Kiddo) – with the best sword that Hattori Hanzo ever made.

2 Beatrix Kiddo trains with her kung fu master, the legendary Pai Mei (Chia Hui Liu), who has also taught other members of the "Deadly Viper Assassination Squad" including Bill.

3 En route to the bloody showdown in the House of Blue Leaves in Tokyo where leader of the Yakuza, O-Ren Ishii (Lucy Liu), is waiting with The Crazy 88 gang.

4 Tarantino filmed parts of both movies in the famous Shaw Brothers Studios (1925–1985) in Hong Kong, which was instrumental in popularizing martial arts films.

"It's mercy, compassion and forgiveness I lack, not rationality." *The Bride*

3

psychotic female assassin in schoolgirl's dress; and, of course, the replica o the deadly geisha *Lady Snowblood* (*Shurayuki-hime*, 1973). All of these mus be defeated to enable the emergence of a positively cast female revenge fighter, the heroine of a vendetta. Lacking any alternatives, the bride relies initially on the samurai sword made by Hattori Hanzo, played by well-known actor Sonny Chiba from *The Streetfighter* (*Gekitotsu! Satsujin ken*, 1974).

It is great fun watching Thurman (who was involved in developing the part) as she hacks gangs of attackers to bits, or gives young boys a good thrashing. Yet, at the same time, critics were justified in saying that, as is so often the case, male clichés are only given new symbolic form: the bride sees red like Charles Bronson in *Death Wish* (1974); she wears Bruce Lee's yellow suit from *The Game of Death* (1978); and she is trained by the monk Pai Me

“David Carradine has thanked director Quentin Tarantino for reviving his career in the *Kill Bill* movies. He says: ‘Quentin’s famous for finding an actor who’s an outsider at the time, catapulting him back into the center of the industry.’” *WENN*

5 David Carradine (playing Bill here) became world famous through the TV series "Kung Fu" (1972–1975). He played Kwai Chang Caine, a Shaolin monk who travels the Wild West.

6 With her eye-patch, Elle Driver (Daryl Hannah) is reminiscent of Patch in the movie *Switchblade Sisters* (1975) and, even more so, of the lead actress in *Hooker's Revenge* (1974).

7 The character Pai Mei (or Bak Mei) is found in many Shaw Brothers kung fu films of the 1970s and '80s, e.g. *Clan of the White Lotus* (1980).

8 After the sword fight between Beatrix and O-Ren, we hear the title song of *Lady Snowblood* (1973), sung by its female star Meiko Kaji.

RAPE REVENGE MOVIES Before *Kill Bill*, the female vendetta was mainly found in a subgenre of the exploitation film: the so-called "rape revenge movie," such as *Coffy* (1973) with Pam Grier. As the cliché goes, a woman is raped and almost killed, followed by a showdown in which the torturers are brutally executed.
This genre is problematic, with its production of female characters that are in no way emancipated. Instead, the rape scenes and half-naked female killers satisfy a voyeuristic curiosity. The part of Elle Driver played by Daryl Hannah, for instance, is borrowed from the protagonist in the Swedish film *Hooker's Revenge* (*Thriller – en grym film*, 1974) – a rape revenge movie which principally involves hard-core porn.
The main inspiration for Quentin Tarantino's *Kill Bill*, however, was a famous classic of revenge cinema that breaks with this pattern: the Japanese film *Lady Snowblood* (*Shurayuki-hime*, 1973). Its female star Meiko Kaji plays Yuki, whose sole purpose in life is to avenge her mother. In terms of its structure, this movie is more reminiscent of a Western like *Once Upon a Time in the West* (*C'era una volta il West*, 1968).

(Chia Hui Liu, known for his role in *The 36th Chamber of Shaolin / Shao Lin san shi liu fang*, 1977). Yet this phase is a necessary interim stage. For, once Beatrix is reunited with her daughter B.B., she can finally break from paternal mentors and build her own genealogy. So no more swords need to be crossed in order to kill Bill. Instead, the most lethal woman in the world uses the mysterious "Five Point Pressure on the Heart Explosion Technique" to literally break Bill's heart. Unlike her arch enemy, Vernita Green, who lives as a housewife in a Pasadena suburb, Beatrix is no longer forced to decide between being cool or living in a middle-class idyll for her role as a mother. It remains to be seen which road B.B. will take; her destiny is now unimpeded, free from both obligation and a vocation determined by fate. PLB

and was hailed as "*Blair Witch* on water." There are no jittery, grainy images in this film, however. The well-composed shots have a direct, documentary feel as they were filmed using a digital camera, which allows a more dynamic way of shooting. It's not difficult to see Dogma cinema as its guiding principle. *Open Water* was marketed as a horror flick, though many viewers may have

straight from a travel ad. But this relaxing regime isn't really working for them, so the chance of a scuba-diving trip appeals. Early in the morning, they set out with other vacationers and crew. The sea is calm and the dive is well organized, apart from one small detail: two divers are counted twice, so that the boat leaves before Susan and Daniel resurface. When they do, all they can

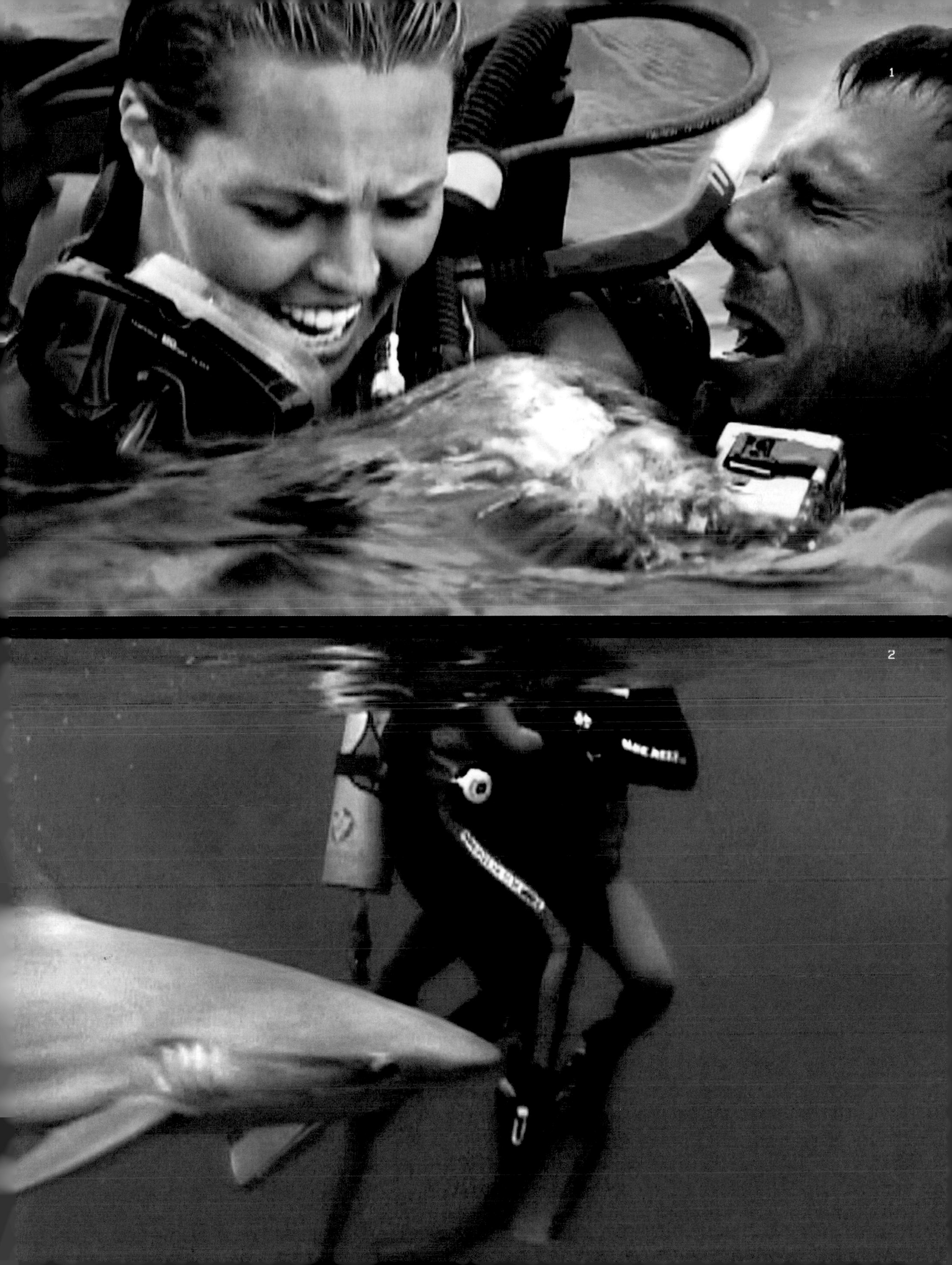
1
2

see is the open sea. They simply cannot believe they have been left on their own. They ask themselves if they are in the right place. The question soon becomes redundant, however, for they are being dragged away by the current, making any orientation impossible. So they begin to concentrate on what is beneath them. The sea becomes increasingly threatening. Gone is any fascination with the underwater world. When they come into contact with poisonous jellyfish, they realize how dangerous the water can be and how little they really know. Daniel picked up from a History Channel documentary that you mustn't drink salt water because it dehydrates the body even more. Hunger, thirst and cold set in. They play little games in an attempt to take their minds off things. Then the first shark fin appears. They are anxious, but do not panic. After all, they know that sharks keep their distance from humans. The shark disappears

1 The worst nightmare comes true: a shark attacks Susan (Blanchard Ryan) and Daniel (Daniel Travis).

2 The divers don't know what's going on under them. They cling to one another.

3 A shark circles the divers. The actors filmed their scenes with real sharks, and no cage.

"The nagging desire to help these people underscores the involvement of the audience in this superbly told story. You can almost taste the saltwater, and the fear." *San Francisco Chronicle*

4

4 Susan and Daniel had wanted to relax on a diving trip, like other tourists.

5 Susan and Daniel cling to one another. It is imperative they stay together in the face of danger.

again. But when more sharks pop up, circling ever closer, they become increasingly frightened. Previous certainties are questioned. They blame each other for their plight, only to cling to one another the next minute, declaring their mutual love. The fact that they are being driven apart seems a greater threat than the circling sharks. Swimming all alone at sea is the really horrific idea that is developed in the film.

Open Water closely scrutinizes the nuances of psychological reactions: the pleasure of finding candy, the mutual reassurances, the fear, the anger at the others and, finally, the panic. For the sharks are getting closer. They come into contact with them, and end up biting Daniel's leg. A line has been crossed. They both know they are vulnerable. Night falls. The next morning Susan is floating in the water with Daniel, who is dead, surrounded by countless sharks. The final long shot is quiet and unspectacular, making it all the more poignant. Susan takes off her diving gear and dives under. All that is visible now is the open sea. The camera in *Open Water* is positioned mostly just above the water's surface, hinting at what might be underneath, showing it for a few seconds and then coming up again. It does this repeatedly, in seeming fascination with the idea of the surface and what lurks beneath it. In this sense, *Open Water* picks up on a classic horror movie theme, only to give it a fresh take. The sea's surface as the border between two worlds is explored in its structure. The play of the waves and the graphic patterns they form, the delicate shades of color, the reflections of the sun – the film brings all of this together in an aesthetic composition that at times presents images as if in an abstract painting. What lies beneath we can only guess.

KK

CHRIS KENTIS *Open Water* is Chris Kentis' second film, and his most successful to date. A graduate of the Tisch School of the Arts at New York University, he was fascinated by the new digital technology that allowed films to be made to a tight budget. This meant that he could finance *Open Water* himself while ensuring maximum creative freedom. Kentis wrote the screenplay as well as directing and editing the movie; his wife, Laura Lau, handled the production side. They are both amateur divers, and had already done a lot of underwater filming before *Open Water*. A first cut of the film was shown at the Sundance Film Festival in 2004 and shortly afterward Lionsgate picked up the distribution. Chris Kentis made his first film *Grind* (1997) on 35mm, with a young Billy Crudup in the leading role. His most recent work, the horror movie *Silent House*, was released in 2011; it is a remake of the successful Uruguayan film *La casa muda* (2010) by Gustavo Hernández. The unusual thing about both films is that they were each shot in a single take. But Chris Kentis and Laura Lau can't get away from sharks. As far back as 2006, "Variety" announced that the couple was developing the screenplay for a thriller with the working title *Indianapolis* for Warner Bros. The eponymous US warship was sunk off the Philippines by a Japanese submarine in 1945. For days, the survivors floated in the sea among sharks. The film has not yet been made.

OLDBOY
OLDEUBOI

2003 – SOUTH KOREA – 120 MIN. – THRILLER
DIRECTOR PARK CHAN-WOOK (*1963)
SCREENPLAY HWANG JO-YUN, LIM JOON-HYUNG, PARK CHAN-WOOK, from a manga series by GARON TSUCHIYA and NOBUAKI MINEGISHI DIRECTOR OF PHOTOGRAPHY CHUNG CHUNG-HOON
EDITING KIM SANG-BEOM MUSIC CHOI SEUNG-HYUN, LEE JI-SOO, CHO YOUNG-WUK
PRODUCTION LIM SEUNG-YONG for EGG FILMS, SHOW EAST.
STARRING CHOI MIN-SIK (Oh Dae-su), YU JI-TAE (Lee Woo-jin), KANG HYE-JEONG (Mi-do), JI DAE-HAN (No Joo-hwan), OH DAL-SU (Park Cheol-woong), KIM BYEONG-OK (Mr. Han), LEE SEUNG-SHIN (Yoo Hyung-ja), YUN JIN-SEO (Lee Soo-ah).
IFF CANNES 2004 GRAND PRIZE OF THE JURY (Park Chan-wook).

"Laugh and the world laughs with you. Weep and you weep alone."

Oh Dae-su (Choi Min-sik) does not know why he was locked up for 15 years. Nor does he know why he was released again. When he goes into a sushi bar, he asks for a starter that is "something living." Yet the scene in which he eats an octopus, then collapses with its tentacles twitching in his mouth, is actually one of the more innocuous ones in *Oldboy*. In a previous life, Oh Dae-su was an average Seoul businessman, but he has just come straight from Hell. It had no windows, only a food hatch, a bed, a TV and hideous, brown-patterned wallpaper. He has aged prematurely in this solitary cell and almost lost his mind in the process. Throughout this time, the TV was his only friend; from it, he learned about his wife's death, for which he was blamed, and everything else going on in the world. He never found out how much longer his ordeal

Now his only thought is of revenge. What could he have done? Who could hate him that much? Who served him the same deep-fried dumplings every day for 15 years? He becomes a food tester, munching his way through every restaurant in the city, and finally finding the clue he needs. It triggers the carnage of bloody retribution. Teeth are smashed with a hammer, screwdrivers are rammed into skulls and an overly loquacious victim ends up cutting out his own tongue. Physical violence is ever-present, but even worse are the mental agonies that director Park Chan-wook forces his audience to witness.

Even in the Asian cinema of extremes, this Korean film claims a special place. Park Cheol-woong is its excellent protagonist. His primary motive is revenge. In *Oldboy*, elements of Greek mythology combine with Elizabethan

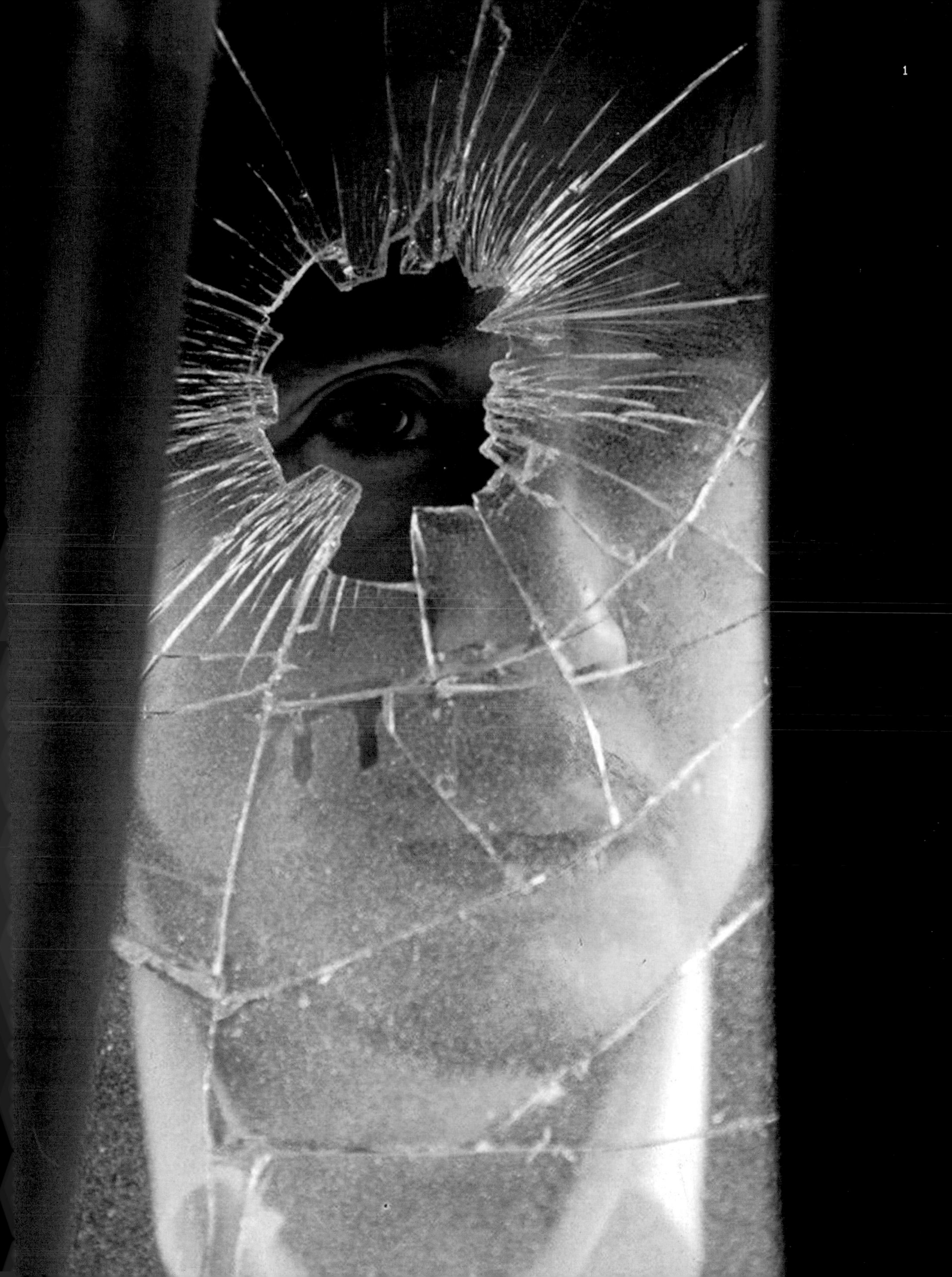
1

2

1 Revisiting the past: as a young man Oh Dae-su (Choi Min-sik) took the blame on himself. Was it curiosity? At any rate, the punishment was brutal.

2 Tooth for a tooth: no holds are barred in a bloody fight to get even. Oh Dae-su is blinded by revenge.

3 The prisoner gets his food through a small hatch. But he never gets to see his tormentors.

4 Asian cinema of extremes: in a bizarre escalation of physical and mental pain, Oh Dae-su finally succumbs to madness.

5 Top choreography: the released prisoner deals with 20 or so opponents in a brilliant fight sequence.

"Full of insanely grand passions, bloodthirsty violence and jet black comedy, it's a sadistic masterpiece that confirms Korea's current status as producer of some of the world's most exciting cinema." *BBC*

PARK CHAN-WOOK Along with Kim Ki-duk, Park Chan-wook ranks among the influential figures of new Korean cinema. After studying philosophy he became one of the most popular film critics in the country. Seeing Alfred Hitchcock's *Vertigo* (1958) however made such an impression on him that a career as a director became inevitable. That said, his first two feature films did not attract much of an audience. On the other hand, the third broke all records: *JSA: Joint Security Area* (*Gongdong gyeongbi guyeok JSA*, 2000), a convoluted thriller about an incident on the border between North and South Korea, touched on a taboo subject in the country and expressed exactly what many of his compatriots were feeling. Park then became the most popular film director, with 6 million followers.
Sympathy for Mr. Vengeance (*Boksuneun naui geot*, 2001/2002) began his "revenge trilogy," although this was not planned as such initially. The disturbing story of blackmail, an illegal kidney transplant and a father's revenge caught the audience by surprise with its exaggerated style and extreme violence, as well as its empathy with all the protagonists. Suppressed feelings of revenge and hatred are, for Park, the logical product of modern civilization based on the renunciation of drives. His aim is to create a cathartic effect through violent films: to this end, he made a significant contribution with *Oldboy* (*Oldeuboi*, 2003). The hallucinatory revenge fantasy also brought the Korean director international fame: Quentin Tarantino became his biggest fan, and he was awarded the Grand Prize of the Jury at Cannes. The trilogy was concluded with *Lady Vengeance* (*Chinjeolhan Geumjassi*, 2005). A female variation on the theme, this film also has a sequence that slowly fades to monochrome. He then proved that his high aesthetic aspirations were not devoid of humor with the strange rom-com *I'm a Cyborg* (*Saibogujiman kwenchana*, 2006) and the vampire farce *Thirst* (*Bakjwi*, 2009).

3

4

and punishment. It is about an eye for an eye and, literally, a tooth for a tooth. But, as in *Sympathy for Mr. Vengeance* (*Boksuneun naui geot*, 2001/2002) before it, the revenge motifs are spread across several factions as a consequence of reciprocal entanglements. No one is blameless, and everyone has a reason. The slightest transgression sets hellish processes in motion. Or, as expressed in the encoded poetry of *Oldboy*: a grain of sand sinks in the water in just the same way as a stone. For Park, it is less about violence per se than its causes; even more so, it is about its consequences.

While the double-dealing plot may be reminiscent of the Hollywood mind-games of a director like David Fincher, its intellectual weight and visual brilliance render this film, conceived from a manga series, strictly Asian. The bloodiest images are painful in their beauty, while the heavily contrasting colors and wonderful lighting effects create tableaux linked by the most astonishing editing. Seamlessly flowing into each other, flashbacks, dream sequences and real-time events together illustrate Oh Dae-su's descent into madness. A sequence in which the avenger, moving backward, wrestles about 20 adversaries and escapes is a unique display of choreographic virtuosity. It seems neither inappropriate nor cynical for these scenes to be accompanied by the sumptuous music directed by Jo Yeong-wook and based on classical arrangements. The comparison with Quentin Tarantino – who as jury president at the Cannes Film

5

Festival wanted to award the main prize to *Oldboy* – is a clumsy one. For Park, it is about making pain an emotional experience rather than an aesthetic one.

In the gleaming, metallic green world of his adversary Lee Woo-jin (Yu Ji-tae), the hero Oh Dae-su discovers the whole truth. The protagonists in *Oldboy* seek out their fate; they want it to find them. They want to savor revenge and, in that moment, comprehend its destructive effect. There are only losers in Park's grisly game of thoughtlessness, bad conscience, hypnosis, hallucination and incest, with its horrible "happy ending." Oh Dae-su's pain-distorted grimace, symptomatic of the whole film, lingers in the memory. For its examination of aesthetic extremes, the ultimate ending of *Oldboy* was the Grand Prize of the Jury at Cannes. PB

"The movie is put together with brutally uncompromising style and has the cold-steel edge of a knife against your throat. A dark and thrillingly horrible adventure into the realms of the unthinkable." *The Guardian*

6 Oh Dae-su begins an affair with sushi waitress Mi-do (Kang Hye-jeong). Though he doesn't know it, she is also a part of his past.

7 The emotional side of pain: in Mi-do's care, Oh Dae-su slowly recovers, but the trauma of years in prison stays with him.

8 No one is guiltless: cynical opponent Woo-jin (Yu Ji-tae) suffers even more than his worst enemy. He is destroyed by his own revenge.

BIG FISH

2003 – USA – 125 MIN. – FANTASY MOVIE, LITERARY ADAPTATION
DIRECTOR TIM BURTON (*1958)
SCREENPLAY JOHN AUGUST from the novel of the same name by DANIEL WALLACE
DIRECTOR OF PHOTOGRAPHY PHILIPPE ROUSSELOT EDITING CHRIS LEBENZON MUSIC DANNY ELFMAN
PRODUCTION RICHARD D. ZANUCK, BRUCE COHEN, DAN JINKS for COLUMBIA PICTURES, JINKS/COHEN COMPANY, ZANUCK COMPANY.
STARRING EWAN MCGREGOR (Edward Bloom as a Young Man), ALBERT FINNEY (Edward Bloom as an Old Man), BILLY CRUDUP (Will Bloom), JESSICA LANGE (Sandra Bloom as an Old Woman), HELENA BONHAM CARTER (Jenny/Witch), STEVE BUSCEMI (Norther Winslow), DANNY DEVITO (Amos Calloway), ALISON LOHMAN (Sandra Bloom as a Young Woman), ROBERT GUILLAUME (Dr. Bennett as an Old Man), MARION COTILLARD (Josephine Bloom), MATTHEW MCGRORY (Karl), ADA and ARIENE TAI (Ping and Jing).

Thanksgiving

"I've been no one but myself since the day I was born and if you can't see that, it's your failing and not mine."

Is it possible to tell what kind of person is being laid to rest from those attending a funeral service? Perhaps. Though if a circus ringmaster, a giant, a poet, a bank robber and Siamese twins pay a man their last respects, then he must have been a special person. Edward Bloom (Albert Finney) was indeed a unique individual – a traveling salesman, parachute jumper, circus worker, city owner, loving husband and father – and, more importantly, a gifted storyteller.

Edward's favorite story is how his son, Will (Billy Crudup), came into the world – while Edward (played as a young man by Ewan McGregor) struggles in a river with a gigantic catfish that has swallowed his wedding ring, Will's mother, Sandra (played as a young woman by Alison Lohman) delivers the baby in hospital. And with some force: the newborn baby is hurled into the world, sliding along the corridor like greased lightning. Is it all made up? Will is convinced it is. He refuses to listen any more to the apparent lies his father has been telling for decades. And when he rushes to the dying Edward's bedside, he finally wants to know the truth about his father. But Edward – physically weak but still mentally alert – keeps on telling his stories: the one about him leaving his hometown, meeting his wife, going to war, working as a salesman, getting caught up in a bank robbery, etc.

1

“Because Burton is the director, *Big Fish* of course is a great-looking film, with a fantastical visual style that could be called Felliniesque if Burton had not by now earned the right to the adjective Burtonesque.” *Chicago Sun-Times*

4

1 A romantic: Edward (Ewan McGregor) demonstrates his love to Sandra with a huge, heart-shaped flower bed.

2 Edward ends up in China as a soldier and discovers Siamese twins Ping and Jing (Ada and Arlene Tai) in the Red Army's entertainment unit.

3 After much hesitation, Sandra (Alison Lohman) responds to love-struck Edward's wooing.

4 As a sales agent traveling through Kansas, Edward dreams of amazing worlds: the road becomes a mysterious sea …

5 … and after the water has abated, his car is found in a tree

Big Fish recalls stages of Edward's life, visualizing the fantastic anecdotes of the old storyteller: we see mermaids swimming along flooded highways, cars parked in trees, and branches snatching at people. The somewhat gloomy context of the southern states serves only to emphasize the old man's exuberant delight in spinning yarns and his cheerfully laid-back, mischievous tone.

Truth, invention, lie … What does it all mean? Are people characterized by their deeds or the stories they tell? The film asks these questions, and the answers provided by the great fantasy filmmaker Tim Burton are clear. We only have to think of his other work – from the wacky suburban fairytale *Edward Scissorhands* (1990) through the magnificent 3-D fable *Alice in Wonderland* (2010): anyone who makes films like this puts their faith in the boundless inventiveness of the human imagination. Simply look into the eyes of the old Edward Bloom – an enchanting performance by British screen legend Albert Finney (*Tom Jones*, 1963) – and the roguish twinkle says it all.

Big Fish is a seminal Tim Burton film, combining all the precepts of his narrative film style. All his movies are characterized by an affirmation of storytelling, trust in the imagination, the creation of completely autonomous worlds, surreal and playfully dark visual concepts, and stunning pictorial

EWAN MCGREGOR He gave up drama school to take on his first major role, and shared an apartment in London with future fellow actors Jude Law and Jonny Lee Miller. The story of Ewan McGregor (*1971) reads as if lucky breaks have fast-tracked him to the top. But his success has less to do with luck than ability and hard work. Over 50 movies in just 20 years – not many actors manage to achieve such an output. Having said that, the Scottish-born actor has demonstrated such a level of flexibility and versatility that he can be cast in pretty much any role, from a junkie in *Trainspotting* (1996) to the Jedi knight Obi-Wan Kenobi in George Lucas' second *Star Wars* trilogy (1999–2005). He became well known through British comedies including *Shallow Grave* (1994) and *Brassed Off* (1996), but *Star Wars* eventually made him an international star, followed by big Hollywood productions such as *The Island* (2005) and *Angels & Demons* (2009). He won Best Actor at the European Film Awards for Roman Polanski's French/English/German co-production *The Ghost* (*The Ghost Writer*, 2010).
Not only can Ewan McGregor act, he can also sing, as proved by his performances in such films as *Velvet Goldmine* (1998) and the musical *Moulin Rouge!* (2001). He has also managed to incorporate another hobby into his professional life – motorcycling. He has been on two major motorcycle journeys for a TV documentary series: from England through Europe and Russia to the USA; and from Scotland to South Africa.

6 Edward meets Karl the Giant at a circus. At 7½ feet / 2.29 meters, Matthew McGrory (1973–2005) appeared in the Guinness Book of Records as the tallest actor in the world.

7 Edward (Albert Finney) and Sandra (Jessica Lange) have a long and happy life together.

8 Ghost stories from childhood: in the forest as a boy, Edward meets the witch (Helena Bonham Carter), who can allegedly read from a person's eyes how he is going to die.

9 In the idyllic little village of Spectre, Edward comes across the multi-talented Norther Winslow (Steve Buscemi): poet, inventor – and bank robber.

language. There are also numerous references to his other works: protagonist Edward Bloom is the spiritual brother and namesake of both Edward Scissorhands and the eponymous hero of *Ed Wood* (1994). And familiar faces from the director's universe are there, too, in the form of Danny DeVito (*Batman Returns*, 1992) and Burton's long-term partner Helena Bonham Carter (*Sweeney Todd: The Demon Barber of Fleet Street*, 2007). Burton's particular visual language is sometimes compared to that of Italian maestro Federico Fellini (1920–1993). The latter directed *8½* (1963), a definitive movie about the filmmaker's craft, calling it "8½" because, although it was the ninth film in his career as a director, he – somewhat coyly – did not want to count it as a complete film in its own right. In a way, *Big Fish* can be seen as director Tim Burton's own, personal *8½* – and not just because it is his ninth full-length feature film. HJK

HEAD-ON
GEGEN DIE WAND

2003/04 – GERMANY – 121 MIN. – DRAMA
DIRECTOR FATIH AKIN (*1973)
SCREENPLAY FATIH AKIN DIRECTOR OF PHOTOGRAPHY RAINER KLAUSMANN EDITING ANDREW BIRD
MUSIC KLAUS MAECK PRODUCTION RALPH SCHWINGEL, STEFAN SCHUBERT for WÜSTE FILMPRODUKTION, CORAZÓN INTERNATIONAL, NORDDEUTSCHER RUNDFUNK, ARTE.
STARRING BIROL ÜNEL (Cahit), SIBEL KEKILLI (Sibel), DEMIR GÖKGÖL (Father), AYSEL ISCAN (Mother), CEM AKIN (Brother), CATRIN STRIEBECK (Maren), STEFAN GEBELHOFF (Nico), HERMANN LAUSE (Dr. Schiller), MELTEM CUMBUL (Selma), GÜVEN KIRAÇ (Seref).
IFF BERLIN 2004 GOLDEN BEAR (Fatih Akin).

"Your Turkish is really crap. What happened to your Turkish?" "Dumped it."

Two people who have nothing to lose – where would cinema be without them? When Sibel (Sibel Kekilli) and Cahit (Birol Ünel) first meet, they are both undergoing psychiatric treatment. She is a young, vibrant woman who has slit her wrists as a way of escaping the constraints of her Turkish parents' home. He has been dead inside for a long time, and has driven his car into a wall in spectacular fashion. Cahit – a down-and-out jerk, an alcoholic who collects glasses in a run-down Hamburg rock club – is not the man for Sibel, but he *is* Turkish. Her traditionally-minded parents would find him acceptable. So Sibel decides to marry him, perceiving this as her only route to an independent life. She makes no bones about why she needs him and this sham marriage: "I want to live, Cahit. I want to live, I want to dance, I want to screw – and not just with one guy, get it?" He doesn't get it. So she slits her wrists again, with a broken beer bottle, spraying blood all over the place.

Head-On is a raw, excessive movie taken straight from real life, with all the features of an exorcism. The editing is fast; the blood deep-red. Born in Hamburg, director Fatih Akin tells a story about third generation Turks, their desires and zest for life, with a self-destructive power that has not been seen in German cinema since Rainer Werner Fassbinder. His characters seek to cast off the shackles of their mothers and fathers, finally achieving the freedom they deserve. To achieve this, they will accept anything, even the paradox of an "arranged" marriage that follows the rules of Oriental patriarchy and Western laws for migrants, while simultaneously subverting them. And, lo and behold, a love story of epic proportions grows out of this partnership of convenience. Naturally, Cahit will fall in love with Sibel after his reluctant agreement to the marriage. He will be thrown into a jealous rage when she begins to exercise her new-won freedom. Until she wants to sleep with him, too, but abstains; otherwise, she says, it would no longer be simply the legal bond of man and wife. Both are incurable romantics and, in this case, it is never going to lead to a happy ending, but inevitably to disaster. The way Akin always manages to strike just the right tone in this overblown love story leaves a lasting impression.

1 Lust for life without boundaries: Sibel (Sibel Kekilli) has nothing left to lose. The force of her rebellion is breathtaking.

2 A wedding, Turkish style: Sibel and Cahit (Birol Ünel) follow traditional rules for the sham marriage, even though their motives are quite different.

3 Image of modern woman: cast out, Sibel is taken in by Selma (Meltem Cumbul), who runs a hotel in Istanbul.

4 Turkish punk and beer cans: Cahit is an outsider who is sick of life. He could tidy up a bit, though.

5 Over-the-top love opera minus kitsch: the real drama begins when their feelings emerge.

"A heartfelt shout of rage from Turkish-German filmmaker Fatih Akin, positioning *Head-On* as the German answer to *La Haine*." *The Guardian*

FATIH AKIN Born in Hamburg in 1973, Fatih Akin is one of the youngest and most important German directors to have also achieved international recognition. After small roles in theater and short films, this son of Turkish immigrants first attracted attention with his debut *Short Sharp Shock* (*Kurz und schmerzlos*, 1997/1998). This tale of petty gangsters, about three friends of different nationalities in Hamburg's red light district, was a surprising mixture of fast cuts and multilayered characters. Using directors like Martin Scorsese as role models, Akin found his own unique language combining genre conventions and realistic observation. He next showed his ability to switch genres with the upbeat road movie *In July* (*Im Juli*, 1999/2000). His meeting of cultures theme was once again explored, this time in the form of an eventful journey of love from Germany to Turkey. *Head-On* (*Gegen die Wand*, 2003/2004), the first part of a planned trilogy called "Love, Death and the Devil," became a huge hit. For the first time ever, a director of Turkish origin won the top German film award, the Golden Bear, at the Berlin Film Festival. The powerful drama about a marriage of convenience in a multicultural German context was a convincing portrait that avoided any false moralizing and handled the formal language of cinema with renewed confidence.
After *Crossing the Bridge: The Sound of Istanbul* (2004/2005), a documentary about the music scene in his beloved city, Akin produced another masterpiece with *The Edge of Heaven* (*Auf der anderen Seite*, 2006/2007), albeit a much quieter work. The second part of the trilogy (starring Fassbinder's muse Hanna Schygulla) weaves three plot lines and two deaths into a complex portrait of the relationships between two countries. His recent popular success, *Soul Kitchen* (2009) – a culinary multicultural comedy from his home town of Hamburg – is proof that Fatih Akin knows no boundaries.

Beyond the kitsch social setting, he describes the strangeness between two cultures without pitting one against the other. The appearance of a Turkish folk group against the picture-postcard backdrop of Istanbul – where the second half of the film is set – divides the drama into three acts. In his own words, Cahit has "dumped" his Turkish roots; but when Sibel cooks her mother's dishes for him, he starts to relent. In this way, the Turkish aspects give the movie its melancholic, exotic atmosphere. It derives its raw power from the hard life in Germany that for decades has denied its migrants acceptance on an equal basis. Among the alcohol and drugs, surrounded by the harsh sounds of Goth-punk and Turkish rhythms, Sibel and Cahit find a small corner of Hamburg's red light district in which to live their lives. The blend of everyday realism and metaphorical exaggeration is well-nigh perfect, making this a universal tale: love as intoxicating happiness and destructive demon. Everyone on the planet understands this language.

Fatih Akin was in fact convinced that this film would be an act of suicide on his part. Instead, he won the Golden Bear at the Berlin Film Festival. This award (the first time it had been given to a director of Turkish origin) marked not only a key turning point in German-Turkish relations and the achievement of a shared reality, but was also an important form of recognition for ever-cynical Turks in the old homeland. Upstanding patriots rejoiced in the cafés of Berlin and Istanbul at what was in every respect a provocative film. *Head-On* is a leading example of cinema that builds bridges without glossing over the foundations. PB

5

ETERNAL SUNSHINE OF THE SPOTLESS MIND

2004 – USA – 108 MIN. – LOVE STORY, PSYCHOLOGICAL DRAMA
DIRECTOR MICHEL GONDRY (*1963)
SCREENPLAY CHARLIE KAUFMAN, from a story by MICHEL GONDRY, PIERRE BISMUTH and CHARLIE KAUFMAN DIRECTOR OF PHOTOGRAPHY ELLEN KURAS EDITING VALDÍS ÓSKARSDÓTTIR
MUSIC JON BRION PRODUCTION ANTHONY BREGMAN, STEVE GOLIN for ANONYMOUS CONTENT, FOCUS FEATURES, THIS IS THAT PRODUCTIONS.
STARRING JIM CARREY (Joel Barish), KATE WINSLET (Clementine Kruczynski), TOM WILKINSON (Doctor Howard Mierzwiak), ELIJAH WOOD (Patrick), MARK RUFFALO (Stan), KIRSTEN DUNST (Mary), THOMAS JAY RYAN (Frank), JANE ADAMS (Carrie), DAVID CROSS (Rob), DEIRDRE O'CONNELL (Hollis).
ACADEMY AWARDS 2005 OSCAR for BEST ORIGINAL SCREENPLAY (Charlie Kaufman, Michel Gondry, Pierre Bismuth).

– *"Is there any risk of brain damage?"*
– *"Well, technically speaking, the procedure is brain damage."*

Love is blind, but not forever, unfortunately. When it is gone, memories remain. When Joel (Jim Carrey) and Clementine (Kate Winslet) meet on a beach on a cold St. Valentine's Day, this predestined road still seems a long one. They complement each other: he is an introvert and she is more than just a little eccentric. But neither their playful flirting nor Clem's wildly dyed blue hair prepare us at all for what *Eternal Sunshine* has in store for the audience. The background to the impending craziness is that they have actually known each other for a long time, and were even a couple. But Clem has had the memory of Joel erased from her mind. Dumped in such a ridiculous way, he finds out about it and takes his revenge by getting the same procedure. Naturally, they no longer remember any of this. Screenwriter Charlie Kaufman had already made a name for himself with *Being John Malkovich* (1999) and *Adaptation* (2002) as an expert in the nether regions of the brain. We live in cerebral times anyway: films as varied as *The Bourne Identity* (2002) or *50 First Dates* (2003/04) make memory loss a feature of the narrative. *Eternal Sunshine* gives it a further twist. Not only are large sections of the movie located in the heads of his protagonists, like Christopher Nolan's *Memento* (2000) and François Ozon's *5x2* (2004) before it, the film tells a love story (a pretty disastrous one) backward, at least in part. The initial meeting of the lovers on the beach basically belongs to the end of the story – anyone dreaming, or remembering traumatic events during a serious brain operation, for example, seldom does so chronologically. And, in the process, concepts like dreams, hallucinations or the suspension of time and space do not convey the complexity of the matter. This neurological extension of cinematic expression is made possible by a crazy innovation by

1

1 A comedy of repetitions: Clementine (Kate Winslet) and Joel (Jim Carrey) were once a couple, but have forgotten this. Clem's hair color changes with movements in time as well. The brilliant script concept earned the film an Oscar.

2 Detective work inside his head: his memory of Clementine, almost completely erased, drives Joel to search painstakingly for clues.

"The formidable Gondry/Kaufman/Carrey axis works marvel after marvel in expressing the bewildering beauty and existential horror of being trapped inside one's own addled mind, and in allegorising the self-preserving amnesia of a broken but hopeful heart." *Time Out Film Guide*

CHARLIE KAUFMAN Since his breakthrough with *Being John Malkovich* (1999) Charlie Kaufman has been regularly transporting his audience into the depths of the human psyche. Critics say that it is really only about his own mind. It is nothing short of miraculous that the most original and complex screenwriter of his generation ever made it in Hollywood with his ideas. Born in New York in 1958, Kaufman moved to Los Angeles after completing his film studies in 1991, and struggled along after a fashion as a writer for television. The screenplay for *Being John Malkovich* read like professional suicide: a hapless puppeteer finds a way into the head of the famous actor John Malkovich and sells the bizarre trip as a tourist attraction. Directed by Spike Jonze, well-known for his music videos, the film won several Oscar nominations. Kaufman first worked with Michel Gondry (like Jonze, a director of legendary music videos) on *Human Nature* (2001). The story about the taming of a man who has grown up in the wild was a flop, but has now achieved cult status. *Adaptation* (2002), also directed by Jonze, confirmed Kaufman's reputation as a self-reflexive screwball: a screenwriter with writer's block, played by Nicolas Cage, forms an alliance with a less scrupulous, presumably imaginary, twin.

In *Confessions of a Dangerous Mind* (2002) it became very clear that Kaufman was taking his bearings less from a successful mentor like Syd Field than from Franz Kafka or Samuel Beckett. On this one occasion, however, the individualist removed himself from the production process, as he was dissatisfied with the way George Clooney was directing the pipe dreams of game show impresario and imaginary CIA hitman, Chuck Barris. After a whole year without him, Gondry celebrated his greatest hit to date with Charlie Kaufman, one of his favorite screenwriters, with *Eternal Sunshine of the Spotless Mind* (2004). The sentimental sci-fi romance about love and erased memories won its three writers the Oscar for Best Original Screenplay. The way was then clear for Kaufman's most radical project yet: in *Synecdoche, New York* (2008) a theater director decides to stage his own life in real-time. For the first time, and in a consistent manner, Kaufman himself took on the role of director.

3 Mr. Potato Man from Hell: Joel has a lot of trouble finding his way through Michel Gondry's madcap patchwork style.

4 Eraserhead: Stan (Mark Ruffalo) is one of the shady memory-wiping staff of Lacuna Inc. He floats aimlessly through Joel's memory.

5 Dr. Mierzwiak (Tom Wilkinson) becomes the confused hero's worst enemy. Joel wants to call off the treatment.

a company called Lacuna Inc. A kind of thought helmet allows Dr. Howard Mierzwiak (Tom Wilkinson) to erase specific areas of the mind according to the client's specifications. Unfortunately, the appliance does not appear to be fully developed. During the operation Joel manages to leave his anesthetized body and watch the doctor's assistant, who is out of his depth, at work. For their part drugged up, Stan (Mark Ruffalo), Patrick (Elijah Wood) and Mary (Kirsten Dunst) don't just trash his memory, but his apartment as well. The Lacuna Inc. gang is partying in his head! Meanwhile, he has already decided that he will force himself to keep the memory of Clementine: he tries desperately to hide her from the assault on his mind and take her to a safe haven for inviolable memory fields like childhood.

Michel Gondry feels visibly at home in this chaotic mixture of consciousness levels. An acclaimed music video director, he flicks all the switches in his second feature film. Characters are arbitrarily teleported here and there, while image and sound tracks are divorced from one another. Joel changes spaces and times at will, wandering like Alice in Wonderland through the twists and

6

"The hiccups and eccentricities that define a Kaufman script – the anguished neuroses, the narrative kinks – are firmly in the service of a touching love story, not the other way around." *Los Angeles Times*

turns of his memory, which seem to have been created by the famous graphic artist M.C. Escher. Faces turn visibly pale; babies Joel and Clem take a foam bath in the kitchen sink. At this point, if not earlier, surprised viewers realize the difference between a normal flashback and a memory, and have to reorientate their orthodox ways of seeing. Gondry often uses traditional rewind techniques or stop-motion as technical aids instead of computer effects. The inventory of Joel's mind bends – Clem's potato men, lovingly crafted collages, and love letters – are an early indication of the bricolage-style aesthetic of his later films. Dr. Mierzwiak's thought helmet would pop up again as a toy gimmick in *The Science of Sleep* (*La science des rêves*, 2005/06). Gondry and Kaufman return cinema to its original Utopia: the representation of dream structures. It is also successful because, for the first time, Kaufman subordinates his intellectual capabilities to the subject matter. The melancholic heart of the story is always evident – Freud talks of habit; the romantic of spiritual kinship. In order to begin again, the lovers, portrayed with abandon by Carrey and Winslet, have to learn to accept their memories, the good along with the bad. In their dreams, they have the painful conversations they were never able to before. *Eternal Sunshine*, one of the craziest and saddest comedies ever, goes around in our heads while striking directly at our hearts. PB

7

8

9

6 It is hard to imagine more different characters. Clem's hair color is the first sign of the relationship ending.

7 Memory loss in an endless loop: Mary (Kirsten Dunst) was also in love with her boss at one time. She would have been better off getting a new job.

8 Sea of feelings: surreal, dreamlike images are part of the film's aesthetic vocabulary.

9 Happier days of a love lost: Kate Winslet received an Oscar nomination for her high-octane, wide-ranging performance.

"If films about coping with memory loss and/or reverse-order storytelling now constitute a mini-genre, then *Eternal Sunshine of the Spotless Mind* is arguably the best of the lot." *Variety*

BAD EDUCATION
LA MALA EDUCACIÓN

2004 – SPAIN – 106 MIN. – DRAMA
DIRECTOR PEDRO ALMODÓVAR (*1951)
SCREENPLAY PEDRO ALMODÓVAR DIRECTOR OF PHOTOGRAPHY JOSÉ LUIS ALCAINE EDITING JOSÉ SALCEDO
MUSIC ALBERTO IGLESIAS PRODUCTION AGUSTÍN ALMODÓVAR, PEDRO ALMODÓVAR, ESTHER GARCÍA for EL DESEO, CANAL+ ESPAÑA, TELEVISIÓN ESPAÑOLA (TVE).
STARRING GAEL GARCÍA BERNAL (Ángel/Juan/Zahara), FELE MARTÍNEZ (Enrique Goded), DANIEL GIMÉNEZ CACHO (Padre Manolo), LLUÍS HOMAR (Manuel Berenguer), FRANCISCO MAESTRE (Padre José), FRANCISCO BOIRA (Ignacio), JUAN FERNÁNDEZ (Martín), NACHO PÉREZ (Ignacio as a Child), RAÚL GARCÍA FORNEIRO (Enrique as a Child), JAVIER CÁMARA (Paca/Paquito), ALBERTO FERREIRO (Enrique Serrano).

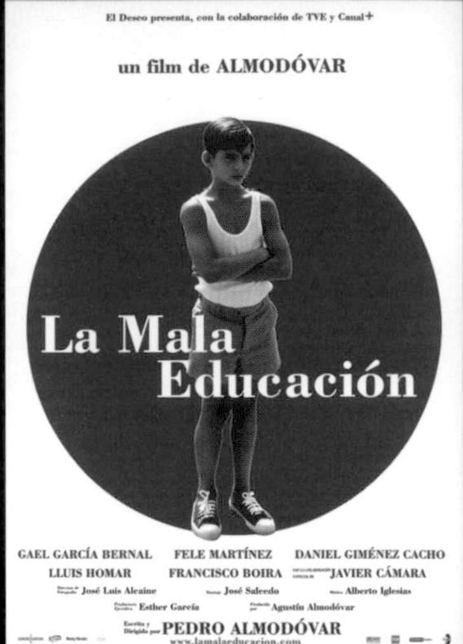

"It's as if all the films were talking about us."

Searching around for a new idea for a movie, successful young director Enrique (Fele Martínez) finds inspiration from an unexpected source when an actor (Gael García Bernal) calls on him, introducing himself as the love of his youth, Ignacio. Hoping for a film role, the good-looking visitor, who insists on being called "Ángel," entrusts Enrique with the story he has written himself: entitled "The Visit," it is ostensibly based on the experiences of children in a strict Catholic monastery school. In fact, Enrique does not recognize his purported ex-lover, but he takes the script nevertheless and becomes absorbed in it.

"The Visit" is the story of Ignacio (Gael García Bernal), a transsexual who makes a guest appearance as a singer called Zahara in his old home town; there, he meets his first great love Enrique (Alberto Ferreiro) again, after a gap of almost 13 years. He seduces him, though Enrique does not remember him. The next morning, Zahara calls on Padre Manolo (Daniel Giménez Cacho), his former teacher who abused him as a boy and threw Enrique out of the boarding school through jealousy – and who will now finally pay for his deeds if Zahara has anything to do with it.

Gripped by the story, Enrique tries to find out more about the mysterious Ángel. He tracks down his mother and learns that the attractive young man is not actually Ignacio, who died three years before, but his younger brother Juan. But that is far from being the only secret surrounding Ángel. All the same, Enrique becomes his lover. Furthermore, he even decides to make "The Visit," with Ángel in the starring role.

An Almodóvar film without a female lead – it sounds a bit strange, to begin with. But it becomes clear after little more than 15 minutes, when Gael García Bernal in a skintight Gaultier dress lip-synchs a thrilling recording of Sara Montiel's version of "Quizás, quizás, quizás" (Perhaps, Perhaps, Perhaps), that the great Spanish director also inhabits his own private, cinematic universe in *Bad Education*. It is a magnificently flamboyant world populated with drag queens, gays and obsessive characters from the worlds of church and cinema, in which everything seems to be dictated by the "law of desire," the title of an earlier film by Almodóvar (*La ley del deseo*, 1987).

Almodóvar himself called *Bad Education* a very personal, though not autobiographical, movie. And, naturally, we find it easy to see in the gay filmmaker Enrique his alter ego, the former monastery pupil from Castile. Yet it would be quite wrong to read *Bad Education* as personal revenge on the church on the part of the confessed agnostic. The real issue in the film is not

1

2

1 Male and female heartthrob from Mexico: in Pedro Almodóvar's dark melodrama *Bad Education*, Gael García Bernal plays a *homme fatal*.

2 The maestro's alter ego: Fele Martínez as gay director Enrique, who is unexpectedly confronted with his adolescent past.

3 In the monastery, Ignacio and Enrique (Nacho Pérez, l., and Raúl García Forneiro) are forced to keep their feelings for each other secret, but …

"Pedro Almodovar's new movie is like an ingenious toy that is a joy to behold, until you take it apart to see what makes it work, and then it never works again. While you're watching it, you don't realize how confused you are, because it either makes sense from moment to moment or, when it doesn't, you're distracted by the sex. Life is like that." *Chicago Sun-Times*

4 … Padre Manolo (Daniel Giménez Cacho) finds out about them. The jealous teacher, who has designs on Ignacio, destroys the boys' happiness by expelling Enrique from the boarding school.

5 A gentle boy, Ignacio is at the mercy of the priest's sexual advances in the monastery school. Almodóvar shows the man of the cloth as a tragic figure, despite his criminal acts.

6 The artist and his muse: Enrique guesses that "Ángel" is lying to him, but casts him in his movie anyway. Almodóvar portrays the director–actor relationship as a power struggle between two shrewd manipulators.

so much the child abuse by a priest, or condemnation of a monastic education, but rather the power of erotic desire as a force that defies all other compulsions and strives for gratification – and which goes beyond any moral judgment. No matter how destructive and violent its expression, Almodóvar shows it as profoundly human. Thus, even Padre Manolo is far from being a monster. The way the film makes us feel his tragedy without downplaying his deeds is further proof of the considerable sensitivity of Almodóvar, the great melodramatist of cinema. More than anything, however, *Bad Education* demonstrates the director's boundless love of filmmaking and cinema per se, which he presents as an alternative model to the Catholic educational institution. Almodóvar skillfully connects three different time levels, creating a complex film noir saturated with film references that playfully dissolves the borders between reality and fiction and the insider's and outsider's view, revealing identities as role play. The more he unfolds his dark, bewilderingly sensual melodrama,

6

7

GAEL GARCÍA BERNAL He is the face of New Mexican cinema that caused a sensation around the turn of the millennium: Gael García Bernal, born in Guadalajara in 1978 the son of an acting couple, made TV appearances in his teens. He went on to study in London at the famous Central School of Speech and Drama, before finally being catapulted into the minds of the international film-going public as the youthful underdog in Alejandro González Iñárritu's brilliant episode film *Amores perros* (2000). The following year, he consolidated his popularity as one of the three protagonists in Alfonso Cuarón's (homo-)erotic coming-of-age road movie *And Your Mother Too* (*Y tu mamá también*, 2001). From the outset, Bernal's choice of parts has revealed his critical awareness and interest in political themes: he played the title roles in *The Crime of Father Amaro* (*El crimen del padre Amaro*, 2002), which brought the wrath of the Catholic church down on him in no uncertain manner, and in *The Motorcyle Diaries* (*Diarios de motocicleta*, 2004). At the same time Bernal also broke into the English-speaking independent film market, helped along the way no doubt by his striking good looks. Pedro Almodóvar used the actor's physical attraction to full effect by casting him as the "homme fatal" in his black melodrama *Bad Education* (2004). Since then, Bernal has established his star status as well as his predilection for critiquing globalization and society in international productions starring prominent actors, including Iñárritu's *Babel* (2006), Fernando Meirelles' *Blindness* (2008) and Lukas Moodysson's *Mammoth* (2009).

7 Almodóvar also attended a Catholic boarding school as a child. The film title alludes not just to the educational methods in the monastery, however, but also ironically to cinema as a unique school of life.

8 A classic Almodóvar moment: Gael García Bernal's seductive vocal turn in a skintight Gaultier dress.

9 Sleeping Adonis: Enrique (Alberto Ferreiro) lies in bed, exhausted by sex and alcohol. He will only find out that it is the love of his youth, Ignacio, who seduced him when he reads the letter, for …

10 … Ignacio is now called Zahara, and is touring the country as a lascivious blonde female singer.

11 Zahara is accompanied by her "friend" Paca, a star role for Javier Cámara, who was brilliant as the sympathetic male nurse in Almodóvar's earlier film *Talk to Her* (*Hable con ella*, 2002).

12 Lluís Homar's performance is equally memorable. He went on to play the leading role in Almodóvarts *Broken Embraces* (*Los abrazos rotos*, 2009); seen here as Señor Berenguer, formerly Father Manolo, who remains a prisoner of his desires even after leaving the priesthood.

"Almodovar wants to intrigue and entertain us, and he certainly does, proving along the way that Gael Garcia Bernal has the same kind of screen presence that Antonio Banderas brought to Almodovar's earlier movies. For that matter, as Zahara, he also has the kind of presence that Carmen Maura brought." *Chicago Sun-Times*

evoking role models such as Billy Wilder's *Double Indemnity* (1944) and Hitchcock in the process, the more Almodóvar provides us with an insight into his filmic imagination and the sources of his inspiration. At one point we see an old movie theater whose wall is covered with countless scraps of posters from past film adventures – a wonderful and colorful collage of overlapping moving picture dreams that can be read as a symbolic representation of Almodóvar's cinema. But Almodóvar would not be who he is without visualizing more directly and provocatively the erotic fascination emanating from cinema; and so it is that the monastery pupils Ignacio and Enrique (Nacho Pérez and Raúl García Forneiro) are shown secretly attending the matinee of a Sara Montiel movie. Their gazes fixed on the sultry icon of Spanish cinema of the 1950s and '60s, the two boys sit in the dark hall and masturbate each other. A defining visit, as it turns out.

JH

2046

2004 – HONG KONG / CHINA / FRANCE / ITALY / GERMANY – 129 MIN. – MELODRAMA
DIRECTOR WONG KAR-WAI (*1958)
SCREENPLAY WONG KAR-WAI **CAMERA** CHRISTOPHER DOYLE, LAI YIU-FAI, KWAN PUN-LEUNG
EDITING WILLIAM CHANG **MUSIC** PEER RABEN, SHIGERU UMEBAYASHI
PRODUCTION WONG KAR-WAI, AMEDEO PAGANI, ERIC HEUMANN, MARC SILLAM for BLOCK 2, PARADIS FILMS, ORLY FILMS, JET TONE FILMS, SHANGHAI FILM GROUP, CLASSIC, ARTE FRANCE CINÉMA, FRANCE 3 CINÉMA, ZDF/ARTE.
STARRING TONY LEUNG (Chow Mo-wan), GONG LI (Su Li-zhen), TAKUYA KIMURA (Tak), FAYE WONG (Wang Jing-wen/Android), ZHANG ZIYI (Bai Ling), CARINA LAU (Lulu/Mimi/Android), MAGGIE CHEUNG (Su Li-zhen), WANG SUM (Mr. Wang/Train Captain).

"All memories are traces of tears."

Forward and backward. Even the opening credits are searching, groping, in flux … the Chinese characters move in and out of the screen, toward and away from the audience. We see a black marble sphere, but cannot tell from the reflections of light and color whether it is a convex or concave shape; if we are looking into a hole, or if the object is curving out toward us. The beginning of *2046* is intriguing and peculiar – just like the rest of the film: its storyline, its style and the history of how it came about. The story of journalist and man-about-town Chow Mo-wan (Tony Leung) also jumps back and forward. In 1966, he is sitting in a hotel in Hong Kong, remembering the great love of his life Su Li-zhen (Maggie Cheung) who left him four years previously in Singapore. He meets three women: dancer Ling (Zhang Ziyi), who falls in love with him; Wang Jing-wen (Faye Wong) the hotel owner's daughter; and a professional gambler (Gong Li), called Su Li-zhen like his lost love. He works in a hotel room, writing a science-fiction novel set in a city called 2046. Futuristic images – reminiscent of the German sci-fi classic *Metropolis* (1927) – are intercut on a regular basis.

1

"*2046* is basically a Proustian film. A desperate race against the fleeting moments of a life, the attempt to recall a lost past, conjuring it up as a magical instant, and capturing it in the image." *Die Zeit*

4

1 Dancer Bai Ling (Zhang Ziyi) moves into Room 2046 in the somewhat sleazy Oriental Hotel in Hong Kong.

2 Su Li-zhen (Gong Li), the great love of Chow Mo-wan's life, stays behind in Singapore, while he goes to Hong Kong.

3 Off to some start: the first thing Bai Ling hears from Chow Mo-wan in the next room is extremely noisy sex.

4 Bai Ling falls in love with Chow Mo-wan (Tony Leung), but he can't admit his true feelings.

5 Chow Mo-wan commutes between Room 2047 where he lives and Room 2046, where he has passionate sex with Bai Ling.

Does Chow the writer really meet the women, or do they only exist in his memory? And when exactly does the action take place? Top Chinese director Wong Kar-wai narrates the story in a stylishly erratic way. The cinematography and score, which alternates between *bel canto* arias and rumba, together create a surreal and intangible dream atmosphere that disorientates the viewer. As becomes clear, however, the story is about love: great, unfulfilled love and missed opportunity. "You don't recognize a kindred spirit if you meet it too late or too early," the film tells us. The protagonist Chow cannot forget one woman, and is therefore incapable of loving the others. Wong "illustrates" this idea of missing the right moment not least by continually interjecting time references such as "1000 hours later" and repeating "December 24" in respect of different years.

Added to which, Wong weaves together a network of references, allusions and parallels that his fans can quickly interpret for themselves. *2046* is a kind of sequel to *In the Mood for Love* (*Fa yeung nin wa*, 2000). Originally, Wong intended to film them both in parallel, but ended up finishing *2046* almost five years later due to financial problems. *In the Mood for Love* also features Tony Leung as a man who is unlucky in love. He writes kung-fu stories with his love

WONG KAR-WAI "My favorite comparison is that of a jazz band: we're jamming together," says director Wong Kar-wai in reference to his regular collaboration with certain colleagues. The "family" that works with Wong includes, most notably, cameraman Christopher Doyle, who has shot his films since his second work *Days of Being Wild* (*A Fei Zhengzhuan*, 1990) – apart from *My Blueberry Nights* (2007), Wong's first Hollywood movie – as well as production designer and editor William Chang and composer Shigeru Umebayashi.
Born in Shanghai in 1958, Wong moved to Hong Kong with his parents in 1963 and grew up in the tourist quarter of Tsimshatsui. The nostalgia-soaked Hong Kong of *2046* (2004) is that of his childhood. He began his career with *As Tears Go By* (*Wang jiao ka men*, 1988), then enjoyed his international breakthrough with *Chungking Express* (*Chongqing senlin*, 1994). While Wong's films are often love stories, he cannot be pinned down to one genre. In the case of *Ashes of Time* (*Dong xie xi du*, 1994), for instance, he has even made a historical martial arts movie.
The director's trademark has become a stylistic device, one that he perhaps overindulges in *Chungking Express* and which he also uses in *2046*: the juxtaposition of time-lapse and slow motion, with speeded-up and slowed-down action in one image.

6

7

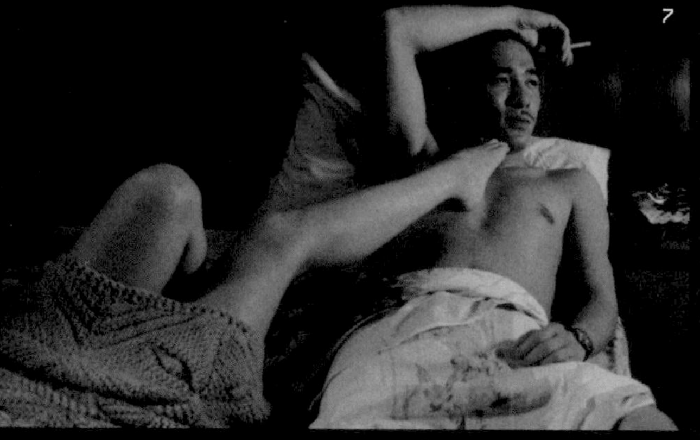

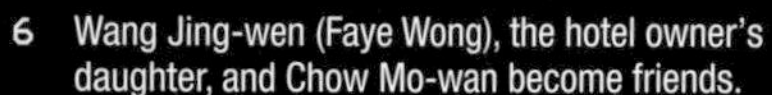

6 Wang Jing-wen (Faye Wong), the hotel owner's daughter, and Chow Mo-wan become friends.

7 Chow Mo-wan and Bai Ling end up back in bed together, after much hesitation and rejection.

8 Bored with his work as a journalist: Chow Mo-wan drifts around the restaurants and bars of Hong Kong, a boozer and gambler, and heartbreaker to boot.

9 The female android in Chow Mo-wan's science fiction story looks like Wang Jing-wen.

"Like Hitchcock, Mr Wong is at once a voyeur and fetishist par excellence. His actresses, who also include Gong Li and Maggie Cheung, dazzle like Olympian goddesses." *New York Times*

8

“The passage of time is marked not by the hands of a clock, but by the women who pass through one man’s life.” *New York Times*

interest in a hotel room bearing the number 2046. This year also has particular significance in the history of Hong Kong: the special status (conceded by China to the city in 1997 when it was handed over by the British) ends in 2046.

We can, of course, try to figure out all of these references – and become exasperated in the process. Alternatively, we can abandon ourselves to the intoxicating flow of ethereally beautiful images created by Wong’s favorite cameraman Christopher Doyle with the help of Lai Yiu-fai and Kwan Pun-leung: fabulous, saturated compositions in extra-wide cinemascope format that constantly play a game of hide-and-seek with the viewer as parts of the picture are obscured by objects, walls and frames. We can also plunge into the captivating atmosphere of beautiful melancholy and sad, sweet pain, abandoning ourselves to a film – more akin to painting than genre cinema – which somehow manages to convey feeling through images. HJK

ANCHORMAN: THE LEGEND OF RON BURGUNDY

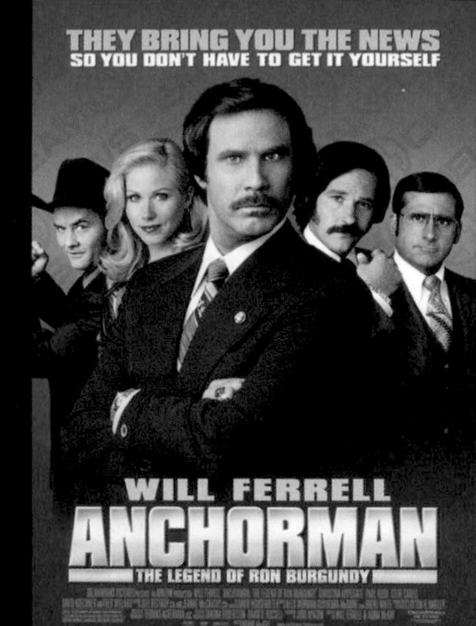

2004 – USA – 94 MIN. – COMEDY
DIRECTOR ADAM MCKAY (*1968)
SCREENPLAY WILL FERRELL, ADAM MCKAY DIRECTOR OF PHOTOGRAPHY THOMAS E. ACKERMAN
EDITING BRENT WHITE MUSIC ALEX WURMAN PRODUCTION JUDD APATOW, DAVID B. HOUSEHOLTER, SHAUNA ROBERTSON, DAVID O. RUSSELL for DREAMWORKS SKG, APATOW PRODUCTIONS, HERZOG-COWEN ENTERTAINMENT.
STARRING WILL FERRELL (Ron Burgundy), CHRISTINA APPLEGATE (Veronica Corningstone), PAUL RUDD (Brian Fantana), STEVE CARELL (Brick Tamland), DAVID KOECHNER (Champ Kind), FRED WILLARD (Ed Harken), CHRIS PARNELL (Garth Holliday), KATHRYN HAHN (Helen), FRED ARMISEN (Tino), SETH ROGEN (Cameraman), PAUL F. TOMPKINS (MC), DANNY TREJO (Bartender), BEN STILLER (Arturo Mendes).

"The times they are changing."

There was a time before cable TV, as this Hollywood movie reminds us, when it was the sole prerogative of men to read the news. The year is 1975, and Ron Burgundy (Will Ferrell) is top dog in his profession, working on the evening news program of broadcaster KVWN in San Diego. His assumption that "diversity" is the name of an ancient wooden ship from the days of the Civil War poses no problem. Together with his team – sex-mad reporter Brian Fantana (Paul Rudd), balding sports commentator Champ Kind (David Koechner) and a moronic weatherman by the name of Brick Tamland (Steve Carell) – Burgundy embodies the routine chauvinism of the times with his sideburns and prominent chest hair. Yet this is a comedy and, with guest appearances by Vince Vaughn, Luke Wilson and Jack Black, the Neanderthal masculinity of early tabloid journalism is exposed with all the crazy means at the movie's disposal. In his maroon jacket (which matches his shorts) Ron is completely obsessed with his looks; Brian owns a collection of scents that would be the envy of any teenage girl; and Brick even puts mayonnaise into a toaster. And the greatest mystery in this adolescent world is the meaning of true love.

1

BURGUNDY
SAN DIEGO'S BEST ANCHORMAN
CHANNEL 4
NEWS TEAM

“Amazingly, and here’s where the story gets too silly, even by its own standards, Veronica finds herself attracted to Ron.” *The Washington Post*

So the times are changing fundamentally when Veronica Corningstone (Christina Applegate) is hired as the token woman; not only does she wear Barbie pink and then purple – the color of the second-generation women’s movement – she is also smart and ambitious. And, despite all signs to the contrary, Ron and Christina fall in love. But when a biker throws Ron’s dog Baxter off a bridge, the traumatized anchorman misses the evening news and Veronica takes his place. She manages to assert herself in spite of diversionary tactics and ends up being promoted as the first female newsreader. Things come to a head: Veronica resorts to the power of the media, manipulating the teleprompter, while Burgundy is fired and runs to seed.

1 Veronica Corningstone (Christina Applegate) replaces burgundy-red machismo with sugar-sweet Barbie pink.

2 Ron (Will Ferrell) and his team use every means to fight their rivals in other TV stations – just like *Gangs of New York* (2002).

3 Splashing around like adolescents …

4 … and all Ron and his buddies seem to think about are cocktails, chest hair, and shorts to match their bathrobes.

5 What the audience doesn't realize: this anchorman reads everything – literally – from the teleprompter, without giving it a moment's thought.

CHRISTINA APPLEGATE (*1971), who was also a founder member of the girl group "Pussycat Dolls," originally became famous through her TV appearances: as Jesse Warner in the series *Jesse* (1998–2000) and, more particularly, as Kelly Bundy in the sitcom *Married with Children* (1987–1997). This lower-middle-class family of four from the Chicago suburbs is dominated by its grouchy father, Al, who sells ladies shoes, and his wife, Peggy, the laziest housewife in the world. In this series, Kelly is the opposite of an emancipated woman: this "featherbrain," as Al often refers to her, is pretty but naive and mainly interested in sex. It is, however, a role that Applegate has now managed to put behind her. She played the lead role in the comedy series *Samantha Who?* (2007–2009), for which she received several Emmy and Golden Globe nominations, and has also starred in feature films such as *Mars Attacks!* (1996) and *The Sweetest Thing* (2002). The actress, who is a vegetarian, is also an active supporter of the animal rights organization PETA.

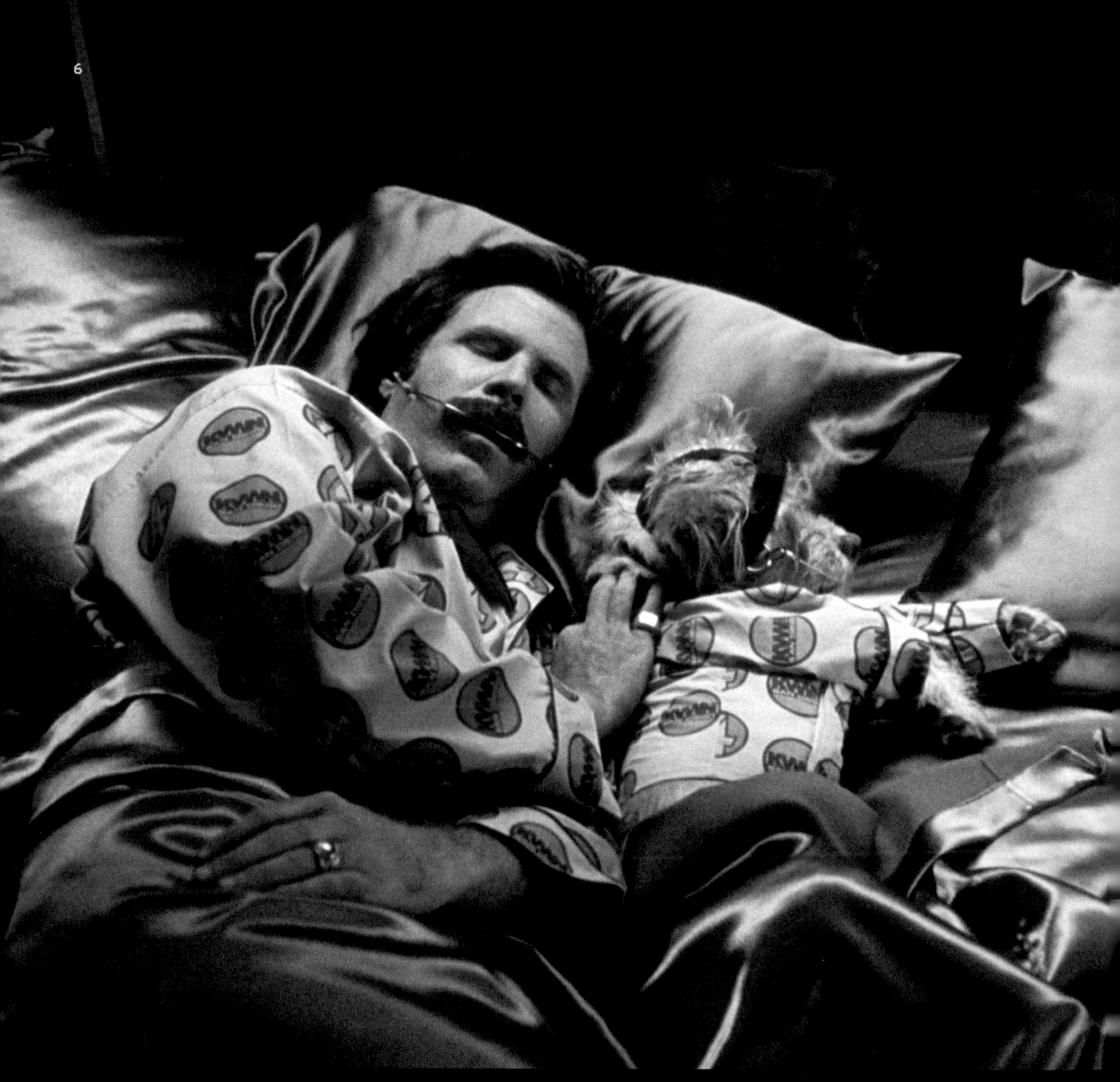

It is not too late for a traditional romantic ending, however. The birth of a baby panda is the hot story of the day and Veronica, dressed in innocent white, is meant to report it, but instead ends up in the bear pit. Ron is called on but it is his alter ego, Baxter, who winds up calming the wild beasts: the dog is indeed man's best friend. And, while Brick becomes an advisor to George W. Bush, Brian fronts a reality TV show called "Intercourse Island" and Champ is charged with sexual harassment, Veronica and Ron get on with presenting the news together.

The film is based on a true story. As "action news" – a bulletin format now adopted in many countries – became more prominent in 1970s America, Diana Robinson and Jacqui Mullen managed to make a major breakthrough as the first women news anchors. Despite the many references to this period, including an outtake featuring Burt Reynolds in *Smokey and the Bandit II* (1980) in which the notorious macho-man – who was not averse to self-parody – forgets his lines, the film alludes to the present day: the end credits thank several journalists for their insights into the world of television.

Almost 40 years later, many women are still fighting sexual harassment, bullying and prejudice in the workplace. Yet *Anchorman* is silent on the fact that Diana Robinson is an African-American: the concept of "diversity" rapidly pushed to its limits. So it is hardly surprising the humor of this movie has all the bite of a lapdog and that it is romantic love rather than work or politics that ultimately saves the lives of the protagonists. PLB

7

6 When corporate identity gets as far as the bedroom, it's too late for personal relationships.

7 Baxter not only saves Veronica and Ron from wild Kodiak bears, he also speaks their dialect fluently.

8 On their first date, Ron impresses Veronica with a flute solo worthy of Ian Anderson from the band Jethro Tull.

9 Big mustaches, sideburns and loud jackets are surefire recipes for success.

"Diversity comes in the form of the ambitious Veronica Corningstone". *USA Today*

8

9

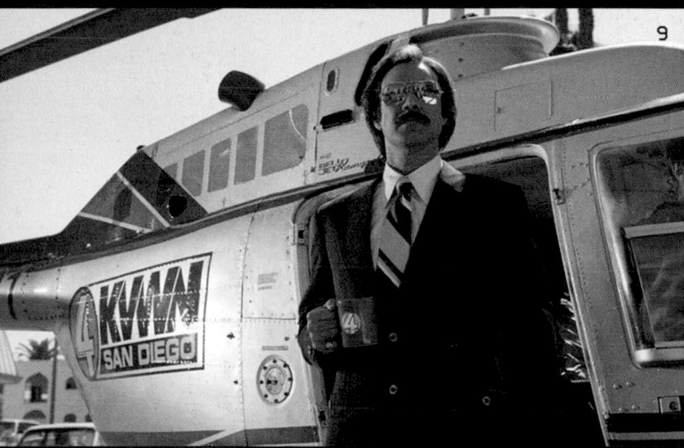

TURTLES CAN FLY
LAKPOSHTHA HÂM PARVAZ MIKONAND

2004 – IRAN / IRAQ – 98 MIN. – DRAMA, WAR MOVIE
DIRECTOR BAHMAN GHOBADI (*1969)
SCREENPLAY BAHMAN GHOBADI DIRECTOR OF PHOTOGRAPHY SHAHRIAR ASSADI
EDITING MOSTAFA KHERGHEPOOSH, HAYDEH SAFIYARI MUSIC HOSSEIN ALIZADEH
PRODUCTION BABAK AMINI, HAMID KARIM BATIN GHOBADI, HAMID GHAVAMI, BAHMAN GHOBADI for MIJ FILM CO.
STARRING SORAN EBRAHIM (Satellite), AVAZ LATIF (Agrin), SADDAM HOSSEIN FEYSAL (Pashow), HIRESH FEYSAL RAHMAN (Hengov), ABDOL RAHMAN KARIM (Riga), AJIL ZIBARI (Shirkooh).

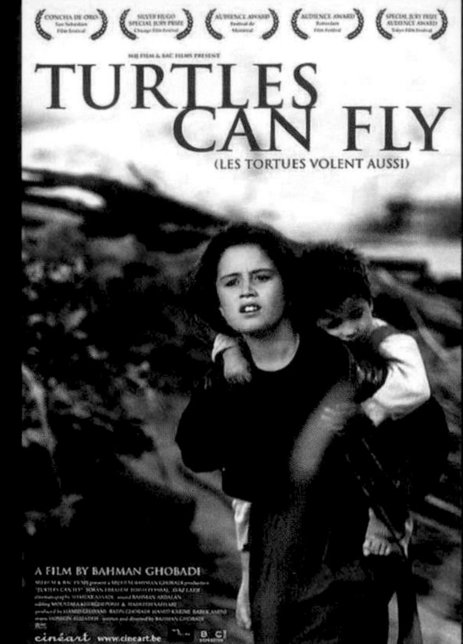

"You kept saying USA, USA until you fell on a USA mine."

A Kurdish refugee camp on the border of Iraq and Turkey, a few weeks before the start of the third Gulf War. The film centers on orphan children who make their living by gathering landmines – clearly a hazardous occupation. Their leader is the confident 13-year-old Satellite (Soran Ebrahim), whose nickname comes from his technical skills and somewhat tenuous command of English. His belief in the USA is seemingly unshakeable. To keep up to date with the approaching war, he acquires a satellite dish and tries to translate the English news for the villagers. Satellite falls in love with a quiet girl, Agrin (Avaz Latif); she and her brother Hengov (Hiresh Feysal Rahman) take care of a two-year-old blind boy, Riga (Abdol Rahman Karim). Rumor has it that Hengov, who has lost his arms, is a mysterious boy who can predict the future.

Turtles Can Fly was the first film to be made in Iraq after the fall of Saddam Hussein. Bahman Ghobadi gives a starkly realistic portrayal of the life of Kurdish refugee children; the main roles are all played by young non-professionals who have personally grown up through war and hardship. The term "children's movie" is only partially applicable, however, as these orphans have never had a childhood. They live in a region ravaged by the atrocities committed under Saddam's regime and the consequences of the two previous Iraq wars. In the film, Agrin and Hengov come from Halabja, the city where 5,000 Kurds were killed by a poison gas attack in 1988. Such indirect references are enough to spell out the horrors of war. Ghobadi does not show any violence directly, though the children's mutilations make the war an ever-present reality.

No one trusts the radio any more. People want to see pictures, believing only what they see in independent foreign broadcasts. Satellite swaps 15 radios and 500 dinar for a satellite dish. There is a problem, however, in that reports on Western TV on the impending Iraq offensive are infrequent, and in English; the young boy actually understands about as much of it as the village elders. He seems to confuse the word "reign" with "rain," translating George W. Bush's message as: "He says it will rain tomorrow." The villagers do not discover anything about their own local situation, so the technical progress turns out to be useless. By contrast, Hengov's predictions are far more accurate. They are also more important, especially when he warns the children about a planned explosion. By incorporating real news footage of the imminent Iraq war, Ghobadi underlines the semi-documentary nature of this film.

At the start of the narrative, Hengov has a premonition about the death of his sister, Agrin, who throws herself off a cliff. We only find out her reasons for doing so later in the film: she was raped by several Iraqi soldiers when her village was attacked. Riga is, in fact, her son; he is a daily reminder of what happened to her, so she wants to be rid of him. She ends up drowning him and taking her own life. This disturbing scene is Ghobadi's reference to a classic of the Italian Neorealist cinema he so admires: in Roberto Rossellini's *Germany Year Zero* (*Germania anno zero*, 1948) the young boy, Edmund, throws himself from a rooftop among the ruins of post-war Berlin because he cannot live with his shame.

1

2

"I despise violence, and have no desire to show it in my films either. I am not trying to glorify violence. You don't have to point the camera directly and show even more blood. I think the viewer also understands what is happening through small, symbolic elements."

Bahman Ghobadi on website critic.de

1 A world without adults: Bahman Ghobadi cast Kurdish orphans for his film. Avaz Latif plays the sad main character, Agrin.

2 War is everywhere: the children collect landmines to survive. And, instead of learning math, the young boys prefer rifle practice.

3 Advance notice from the air: a helicopter distributes flyers advising of the US military operation.

4 The faith of Satellite (Soran Ebrahim) in America seems unswerving. But when the US troops actually arrive, even he is too disillusioned to celebrate.

5 Ghobadi thinks the world of his actors. He put Avaz Latif in touch with a TV broadcaster. Riga, the little blind boy, was able to have a successful operation.

6 Agrin is incapable of maternal feelings for her blind son, because he is a constant reminder of her rape. She leaves Riga (Abdul Rahman Karim) to his fate in a minefield.

7 Children who are scarred by the war.

BAHMAN GHOBADI Bahman Ghobadi, born in north-west Iran in 1969, is now considered the most important representative of Kurdish cinema. His artistic endeavors began in photography, after which he studied as a film director; soon, however, he turned his hand to more practical projects. During the 1990s, he made several documentary shorts and worked as assistant director on Abbas Kiarostami's *The Wind Will Carry Us* (*Bad ma ra khahad bord*, 1999). He worked his own childhood memories and experiences of the first Gulf conflict into his feature debut, *A Time for Drunken Horses* (*Zamani barayé masti asbha*, 2000). The film is set in his birthplace, Baneh, and concerns five orphaned brothers and sisters fighting for an operation for their disabled brother. Ghobadi's films are characterized by a semi-documentary style and are invariably about the Kurds, who at 40-million-strong are the largest ethnic group in the world lacking their own state. Their problematic existence on the borders between Iran, Iraq and Turkey is also central to *Marooned in Iraq* (*Gomgashtei dar Aragh*, 2002) and *Half Moon* (*Niwemang*, 2006). Ghobadi is, however, also seen as a representative of New Iranian Cinema. In *No One Knows About Persian Cats* (*Kasi az gorbehaye irani khabar nadareh*, 2009) he gives an insight into the alternative music scene in Tehran, showing the attempts of young Iranians to defy the official ban on popular world music.

Turtles Can Fly draws an interesting parallel between historical events and local traditions, as the invasion of US troops in March 2003 coincided with the Persian New Year celebration of Nowruz. According to Kurdish myth, the folk hero Kaveh defeated tyrant Dehak on the same day in March. The festival's traditional red fish, the symbol of new life and hope, also play a key role in the film. At the end, Satellite receives a present of two red fish from Shirkooh (Ajil Zibari), whose uncle bought them from the Americans. But when the boy shakes the water bag containing the fish, he notices that they have only been painted red, and are losing their color. The anticipated new beginning and hope for a better future will not be fulfilled quite so easily. In the final scenes, when the Americans pass by in front of Satellite, he turns away; already disappointed. CZ

CRASH ııı

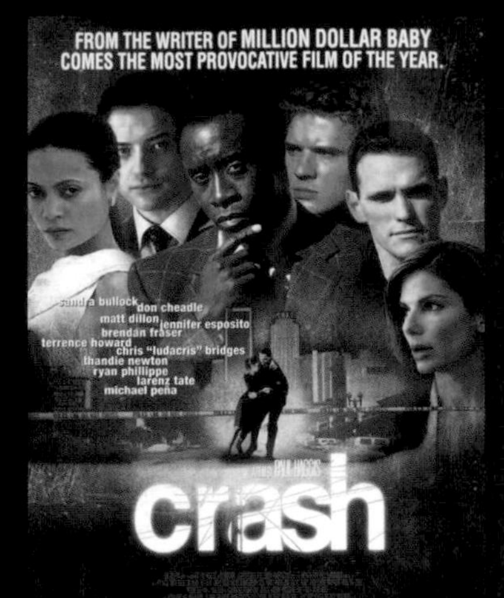

2004 – USA / GERMANY – 112 MIN. – SOCIAL DRAMA
DIRECTOR PAUL HAGGIS (*1953)
SCREENPLAY PAUL HAGGIS, ROBERT MORESCO **DIRECTOR OF PHOTOGRAPHY** J. MICHAEL MURO **EDITING** HUGHES WINBORNE **MUSIC** MARK ISHAM **PRODUCTION** DON CHEADLE, PAUL HAGGIS, MARK R. HARRIS, ROBERT MORESCO, CATHY SCHULMAN, BOB YARI for BOB YARI PRODUCTIONS, DEJ PRODUCTIONS, BLACKFRIARS BRIDGE FILMS, HARRIS COMPANY, APOLLOPROSCREEN FILMPRODUKTION, BULL'S EYE ENTERTAINMENT.
STARRING DON CHEADLE (Detective Graham Waters), MATT DILLON (Officer John Ryan), RYAN PHILLIPPE (Officer Tom Hansen), JENNIFER ESPOSITO (Ria), BRUCE KIRBY (Pop Ryan), LUDACRIS (Anthony), BRENDAN FRASER (Rick Cabot), SANDRA BULLOCK (Jean Cabot), TERRENCE HOWARD (Cameron Thayer), THANDIE NEWTON (Christine Thayer), LORETTA DEVINE (Shaniqua Johnson), SHAUN TOUB (Farhad), BAHAR SOOMEKH (Dorri), MICHAEL PEÑA (Daniel Ruiz), PETER WATERS (Larenz Tate).
ACADEMY AWARDS 2006 OSCARS for BEST PICTURE (Paul Haggis, Cathy Schulman), BEST ORIGINAL SCREENPLAY (Paul Haggis, Robert Moresco) and BEST FILM EDITING (Hughes Winborne).

"I am angry all the time ... and I don't know why."

Los Angeles – a city without a center, shapeless, devoid of visible landmarks apart from the Hollywood sign. For as long as we can remember, this is how movie-makers have portrayed this city of film. The architecture cries out for an episodic structure, while its emblematic quality is conveyed through parables – the city, not as a real place, but as metaphor. Paul Haggis approaches it in this way too. Within a 36-hour time-frame, he tells stories of people's lives and what divides them: a life behind metal and glass, in automobiles built as rolling fortresses, among the highways that isolate skin colors and ethnic groups from each other. Prejudices and stereotypes poison all forms of communication. If people manage to get together at all, it happens through sheer chance. The destructive metaphor for all this is the crash.

Crash begins and ends with an automobile accident. In the interim, other no less drastic encounters take place, characterized by the everyday racism of a metropolis that despairs of itself. A white policeman uses a traffic check to humiliate a black TV producer by sexually harassing his wife. An Iranian storekeeper has to put up with being called "Osama" by an arms dealer. A black detective thinks his partner is Mexican, because he has hardly registered anything during their nights together other than her skin color. The staggering

1

consequence of this is that Iranians become Arabs, Koreans become Chinese, and the racist abuse of the victims is passed down to those lower in the system. Some prejudices are promptly refuted, while others are confirmed in a sometimes fatal, if not comic, way. Two black friends complain eloquently about the hidden discrimination in white nightlife areas, where people like them are automatically thought to be gangsters, so they draw their guns and hijack a car on the open street.

With a complex episodic movie that skillfully weaves together disparate plot strands, Haggis rescues the long-discredited "message movie," though his exact message is as difficult to grasp as his unpleasant subject. Haggis tends to find the gray areas between black and white. Racism infects people like a short-term identity virus and can afflict anyone, even the viewer. When

"*Crash* is a film about racism and class conflict – and also a study of isolation. The distance fueled by resentments is the cause of loneliness in Haggis's protagonists." *Der Tagesspiegel*

3

4

1 A patchwork of minorities: in a sophisticated episodic structure, even locksmith Daniel Ruiz (Michael Peña) becomes a victim of racist attitudes.

2 Cut-throat logic of violence: among people of all skin colors, discrimination is practiced in the form of desperate acts.

3 TV producer's wife Christine Thayer (Thandie Newton) was the victim of a sexual assault.

4 Poignant mini-dramas: the cry for justice erupts in spiritually charged images.

"*Crash* is like a very good multi-strand TV show, the kind that America does so much better than us." *The Guardian*

PAUL HAGGIS Paul Haggis is by far the most sought-after screenwriter in Hollywood. His name guarantees quality and his participation almost automatically makes films "Oscar material." A reason for his flawless work may lie in his responsibility for a heap of trashy TV programs in the preceding years. For almost three decades Haggis, a Canadian born in 1953, worked for a living in the hard school of TV series production. His fear of going down in history as the creator of "Walker, Texas Ranger" (1993–2001) proved unfounded, however. Apart from somewhat compromising projects like that, he made several contributions to brilliant series like "L.A. Law" (1993–1994) and "thirtysomething" (1987–1988). Revolutionary in its complex plot structure, his own creation "EZ Streets" (1996–1997) was regarded as the legitimate precursor to "The Sopranos," which aired for the first time in 1999.

The breakthrough came with *Million Dollar Baby* (2004). Haggis had secured the film rights to two short stories by F.X. Toole; he wrote a screenplay for them, but passed the direction over to Clint Eastwood. This drama dealing with the assisted suicide of a young female boxer was controversial and won among other awards the Oscar for Best Motion Picture. The same honor was bestowed on his second feature film just a year later (after a first attempt that is best kept quiet): the long-term project *Crash* (2004) which also brought Haggis the Oscar for Best Original Screenplay. This episodic movie about the ugly theme of racism proved his profound feeling for real characters and a refusal to compromise, a rare art in Hollywood. He was then heavily involved in the fresh conceptual start for the popular James Bond series with his screenplay for *Casino Royale* (2006). The new prodigy then went back to work with Eastwood, writing and developing the screenplays for Eastwood's two-part World War II movies *Flags of Our Fathers* (2006) and *Letters from Iwo Jima* (2006), which similarly won an Oscar and several nominations. Another role in directing followed with *In the Valley of Elah* (2007). An elegiac drama about a father's search for his son who disappeared after returning from the Iraq war, this film cemented Haggis' reputation as one of the leading exponents of liberal Hollywood cinema.

5

Matt Dillon's policeman and his sick father portray themselves to a black hospital attendant as victims of government minority programs, his fury seems almost reasonable for a horrible moment. And the director does not draw the line at his own profession: the TV producer has to sack an actor because he does not talk "black" enough. An unforgivable act, but that is how films are made in Hollywood and elsewhere.

The redemption that is granted to the offenders, however, is in Hollywood's hands. In the car crash on the highway the policeman saves the very woman he had sexually humiliated the night before. His innocent colleague, on the other hand, who had been forced to look on helplessly, shoots dead a black petty criminal as a result of a misunderstanding – it turns out he is the detective's brother. The way their destinies intersect reminds us mostly of models like

"Insolent, incorrect, intelligent. Delighting in irony, both dialogue and plot constantly challenge the received ideas of a society in which an anti-racist attitude can conceal political manipulation." *Positif*

6

5 Verging on comedy: the dialogue between petty gangster Anthony (rapper Ludacris) and Peter (Larenz Tate) is an eloquent complaint about prejudice.

6 Racism as an everyday hazard: Detective Waters (Don Cheadle) and colleague Ria (Jennifer Esposito, left) investigate, but are not free from conflict themselves.

7 Delivered from evil: the desire for closure brings together culprits and victims – in the film, at least. Matt Dillon is outstanding in the complex role of racist cop Ryan.

Short Cuts (1993) or *Magnolia* (1999): loosely structured ensemble movies set – not by coincidence – in Los Angeles, in which the longing for stability within a state of existential isolation is articulated in powerful, spiritually laden images. While frogs fall from the sky in *Magnolia*, here it is purifying snow that makes the characters pause for a brief moment of regret. The award of the Oscar for Best Motion Picture to *Crash* was unusually controversial: Ang Lee's "gay western" *Brokeback Mountain* (2005) was passed over in its favor; never before had a winner of the best film award triumphed in only two other categories. But Haggis' low budget production, for which many of the stars worked without payment, is anything but a well-intentioned consensus movie. The honesty and incisiveness of its line of argument still has the power to surprise. And the way gifted actors like Matt Dillon, Don Cheadle, Terrence Howard and Sandra Bullock create poignant mini-dramas out of what are sometimes the most minor roles deserves the highest praise. PB

HOTEL RWANDA

2004 – UK / USA / ITALY / SOUTH AFRICA – 121 MIN. – DRAMA
IRECTOR TERRY GEORGE (*1952)
CREENPLAY KEIR PEARSON, TERRY GEORGE DIRECTOR OF PHOTOGRAPHY ROBERT FRAISSE
DITING NAOMI GERAGHTY MUSIC AFRO CELT SOUND SYSTEM, RUPERT GREGSON-WILLIAMS, ANDREA GUERRA PRODUCTION TERRY GEORGE, A. KITMAN HO for UNITED ARTISTS, LIONS GATE FILMS, INDUSTRIAL DEVELOPMENT CORPORATION OF SOUTH AFRICA, MIRACLE PICTURES, MIKADO FILM, ENDGAME ENTERTAINMENT.
TARRING DON CHEADLE (Paul Rusesabagina), SOPHIE OKONEDO (Tatiana Rusesabagina), HAKEEM KAE-KAZIM (George Rutaganda), TONY KGOROGE (Gregoire), NICK NOLTE (Colonel Oliver), FANA MOKOENA (General Bizimungu), CARA SEYMOUR (Pat Archer), ANTONIO DAVID LYONS (Thomas Mirama), DAVID O'HARA (David), JOAQUIN PHOENIX (Jack Daglish), JEAN RENO (Mr. Tillens).

"You're black. You're not even a nigger. You're an African."

Hotel Rwanda is a film that is full of unimaginable horrors and admirable rescue operations. Yet the scene that characterizes the movie, and is at the same time its most moving, shows something different. We see the hero of the story, hotel manager Paul Rusesabagina (Don Cheadle), wearing an immaculate suit and daintily holding an umbrella in the midst of the chaos. The rain is incessant, as befitting the context. The black man quietly and soothingly explains the inconceivable to a white missionary priest: "These men are not here to help us." He knows from personal experience. The French soldiers who have just arrived are not going to evacuate the Tutsis who have sought refuge in Hôtel des Mille Collines. The only people who will be flown out are the last remaining whites in the war zone – tourists, journalists and humanitarian aid workers. You can see the shame on their faces. And the quiet horror in the eyes of the ones left behind, left to their fate by the international community.

As a result of Paul's tireless interventions, 1,200 Tutsis will have survived which claimed the lives of almost a million members of the persecuted minority in spring 1994, the Milles Collines was the last refuge of human decency, a refugee camp disguised as a luxury hotel. What *Hotel Rwanda* tries, among other things, to show is how the real Paul Rusesabagina (a Hutu) carried out his task, with the mediating skills and calm approach of a hotel manager ameliorating every problem. Paul keeps up appearances while all around a machete-wielding mob vents its bloodlust. Every morning, he puts on his tie. He treats a general and war criminal like an old friend: a man he supplies, as in peacetime, with whiskey and Cuban cigars that are difficult to get. This means he can improve the refugees' conditions, allocating them to rooms like normal guests. In the most absurd scene, he presents one of them with a bill. It is not just about the semblance of normality, but about normality itself: by maintaining the hotel's standards, Paul is upholding the standards of civilized society. Until, out of sheer despair one morning, he cannot knot his tie and

1

1 Living through genocide: more than anything, Paul Rusesabagina (Don Cheadle) wants to get his wife Tatiana (Sophie Okonedo) and children to safety.

2 A soldier with no order to kill: Colonel Oliver's view of the situation is relentlessly matter-of-fact. As a UN forces representative, he cannot protect hotel owner Paul. The helplessness of the international community is apparent in the character of this seasoned fighter: cynical and tragic in equal measure, he is played by Nick Nolte with his usual gruffness.

"The film turns into a triumph for Don Cheadle, who never steps outside the character for emotional grandstanding or easy moralism. In all, I can hardly think of another movie in which sheer intelligence and decency have been made to seem so attractive or effective." *The New Yorker*

In a perilously gripping development, the international community pulls back ever further as the militia advance. Oliver, a UN colonel who is the most positive representative of the wider world, is a soldier with no mandate to kill; he is played by Nick Nolte in an even more gnarled and disillusioned way than usual. He ends up defending the hotel on his own initiative, just like Paul, whose calls to his employers in Brussels are far more effective than the useless UN negotiations in New York.

Comparisons with Steven Spielberg's *Schindler's List* (1993) are as pertinent as the recent question of legitimacy. How can a movie about genocide be presented in an entertainment context, if indeed it should be made at all? The Belfast-born director of *Hotel Rwanda*, Terry George (co-writer and co-producer, *In the Name of the Father*, 1993), films the massacre scenes only from a distance, or shrouded in mist; he refrains from filming what cannot be represented, but instead portrays the slightly idealized heroism of one man

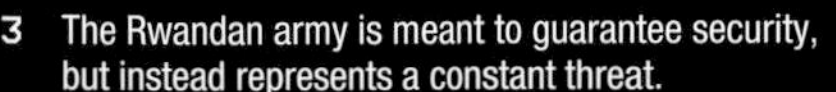

3 The Rwandan army is meant to guarantee security, but instead represents a constant threat.

4 Not much solidarity from the staff: the hotel workers comply with Paul's orders, but only reluctantly. Most are Hutus, like him.

5 Abandoned in the rain by the rest of the world: Paul and his refugees. Surrounded by killing, a just man desperately sticks to his principles.

who fears for his family more than anything. This is not the film that Michael Winterbottom (*Welcome to Sarajevo*, 1997) would have made. Political contexts are merely touched on. This was the only way George could confront a mass audience with the subject of mass murder, as authentically as possible. *Hotel Rwanda* performed well at the box office and was nominated for several Oscars. This level of success was not enjoyed by indie movie *Shooting Dogs* (2005), a more hard-edged attempt by Scottish director Michael Caton-Jones, using identically constructed scenes. It is worth seeing both films together.

The sustained focus in *Hotel Rwanda* is on the outstanding Don Cheadle in the role of Paul – a man who saves lives when he does not have to; a humble hero in the most desperate of times. All the statements in this deeply moving film – from horror at man's capacity for hatred to bitter criticism of a world averting its eyes – are filtered through the character of the man with the umbrella. It is not his fault that movies like this cannot prevent further slaughter and sustained inertia. PB

6

6 In the face of horror: as the Hutu militia edge closer, all Paul can do is get his family to safety – and hope for a miracle.

7 Putting a brave face on it: Paul cannot choose who he negotiates with.

8 Fleeing for their lives: the film constantly projects powerful images of human beings in a state of chaos.

9 Giving a face to responsibility and dignity: Don Cheadle as courageous hotel boss Paul Rusesabagina. The role earned him an Oscar nomination.

"The great strength of *Hotel Rwanda* is that it's not about superhuman heroism but simply about human decency. Surprisingly, George makes the latter every bit as gripping and entertaining as the former." *The Washington Post*

DON CHEADLE If Hollywood ever needs a really serious actor, there is none to match Don Cheadle. Even in mediocre movies, his appearance guarantees subtle understatement, strength of character and the highest degree of authenticity. Born in Kansas City in 1964, he had to be content with supporting roles for a long time, though he did become increasingly well known as a result.

Cheadle gained his first experience with TV series like *Fame* (1986) and *L.A. Law* (1986); his feature films include *Hamburger Hill* (1987), *Colors* (1988) and *Devil in a Blue Dress* (1995), with American film critics heaping praise on him for his (uncharacteristic) role as a trigger-happy petty gangster in the latter, a neo-noir movie by Carl Franklin. Don Cheadle became the actor of choice for prestigious ensemble movies. In Paul Thomas Anderson's *Boogie Nights* (1997) he played a minor porn star with big dreams of owning his own hi-fi business; though only a small part, his drug cop in Steven Soderbergh's *Traffic* (2000) represented the moral core of the whole film. Around this time, Soderbergh (who also cast him in *Ocean's Eleven*, 2001) commented that Don Cheadle would have been a big star a long time ago – had he not been black. After Paul Haggis' Oscar-winning parable about racism, *Crash* (2004), in which he once again played a policeman, this "actor's actor" appeared in his first lead role as Paul Rusesabagina in *Hotel Rwanda* (2004). No-one was better suited to the part of the modest hotel manager who behaves almost obsequiously while saving lives; it won him an Oscar nomination. Since then, Cheadle (who campaigns personally for victims of the civil war in Darfur) has been trying to escape the stigma of always being the good guy, in his professional life at least. In *Talk to Me* (2007) he paints a sensitive portrait of the scurrilous radio presenter and ex-con Petey Greene; in *Traitor* (2008) he slips completely into the role of a terrorist – though one with impeccable manners.

SIDEWAYS

2004 – USA – 126 MIN. GENRE TRAGICOMEDY
DIRECTOR ALEXANDER PAYNE (*1961)
SCREENPLAY ALEXANDER PAYNE, JIM TAYLOR, from the novel of the same name by REX PICKETT DIRECTOR OF PHOTOGRAPHY PHEDON PAPAMICHAEL EDITING KEVIN TENT
MUSIC ROLFE KENT PRODUCTION MICHAEL LONDON for MICHAEL LONDON PRODUCTIONS, FOX SEARCHLIGHT PICTURES.
STARRING PAUL GIAMATTI (Miles), THOMAS HADEN CHURCH (Jack), VIRGINIA MADSEN (Maya), SANDRA OH (Stephanie), MARYLOUISE BURKE (Miles' Mother), JESSICA HECHT (Victoria), ALYSIA REINER (Christine), SHAUN DUKE (Mike), MISSY DOTY (Cammi), M.C. GAINEY (Cammi's Husband), PATRICK GALLAGHER (Gary).
ACADEMY AWARDS 2005 OSCAR for BEST ADAPTED SCREENPLAY (Alexander Payne, Jim Taylor).

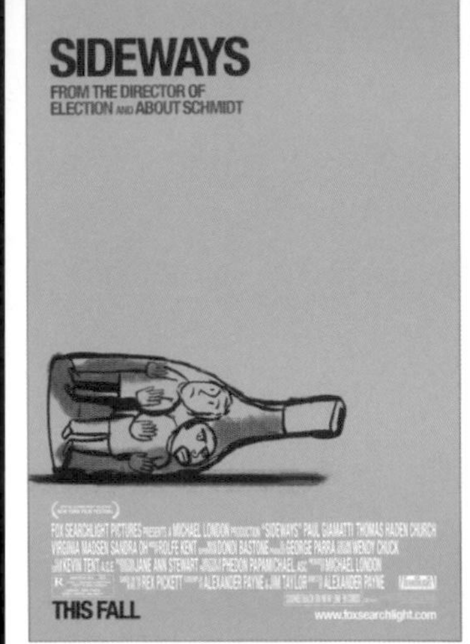

"If anybody orders Merlot, I'm leaving."

Wine-tinted eyeglasses don't make the facts any more palatable: life-affirming hedonism had a problematic status in the first decade of the new millennium. Cinema, too, became a locus of endless moral admonition: cigarette-smoking on film was severely curtailed and drinking treated like an addiction with serious consequences. *Sideways* is the refreshing exception to the rule. Showered with praise, this road movie does not try to downplay the dangers of alcoholism – in fact, its merrily tipsy atmosphere threatens to evaporate at any given moment. Yet the issue of morality is clearly restricted to asking: "Pinot Noir or Merlot?"

Miles (Paul Giamatti) is very clear on this point: "If anybody orders Merlot, I'm leaving." This somewhat thickset, junior high school teacher exudes a healthy self-confidence, at least as a connoisseur of a fine drop of wine. Nothing else signifies in this trip through the Californian vineyards in the company of his friend Jack (Thomas Haden Church); the stag vacation for groom-to-be Jack is the perfect excuse for a really good "booze cruise." They do, however, have very different attitudes. Jack (a bit dumb and a has-been TV actor) not only fails to appreciate the flowery sommelier vocabulary of his bibulous buddy, he thinks all wines taste equally good.

1

2

3

4

1 Two men, one opinion: Miles (Paul Giamatti) and Jack (Thomas Haden Church) at the wine tasting.

2 Pinot noir or merlot? It's a question of morality for the expert. Maybe Jack will get that one day. Miles gives it his best shot.

3 No penny for his thoughts: Jack uses his engagement trip to flirt illicitly with Stephanie (Sandra Oh).

"The emergence of Mr. Payne into the front ranks of American filmmakers isn't just cause for celebration; it's a reason for hope." *The New York Times*

5

4 Similar tastes: Maya (Virginia Madsen) shares Miles' taste for fine wines, but she knows where to stop.

5 Medium-budget buddy movie for grown-ups: Payne's feel for situation comedy is evident in his insights into a male friendship.

6 Cheers! Pleasant times are not forgotten in this witty tour through the tragedy and comedy of human existence.

"New classics of American cinema don't come along that often, so grab this one with both hands. It's an occasion for the singing of hosannas from the roof of every cinema." *The Guardian*

Blessed with a similar relationship to the opposite sex, the notorious philanderer mainly wants to party one last time – and in doing so touches a nerve in Miles. This sensitive soul, failed in a book project and just about everything else, is still in love with his ex-wife. His travelling companion's *joie de vivre* is a painful reminder of why he first sought refuge in alcohol. So gradually the façade of the cultivated connoisseur, who can hold his keen nose in a wine glass for minutes on end without as much as a sip, begins to disintegrate. In what is without doubt the most powerful scene, the desperate chap slugs back the unappetizing contents of a slop bucket at a wine-tasting – and demands more. Before that, we witness his reserved flirting with the wine waitress, Maya (Virginia Madsen), Jack's less restrained activities with her friend Stephanie (Sandra Oh) and the inevitable complications that follow. NB: in certain circumstances, it can perhaps be understood that a bachelor might yield to his erotic desires one last time. But he should not keep his wedding plans quiet if he does. And he certainly should not put his best buddy in the position of having to explain things afterward.

Sideways is a classic friends' comedy, though one with unforeseen ramifications. Initially, it was the critics who became intoxicated with this mid-budget independent film for grown-ups. What followed were five Oscar nominations and huge success at the box office. *Sideways* brought a bit of European *savoir-vivre* to Hollywood; sales of Pinot Noir rose, while those of Merlot sank into the cellar. This particular bottle more or less contains what

7

"Jack and Miles are male archetypes, as well as the two most fully realized comic creations in recent American movies." *The Village Voice*

PAUL GIAMATTI Born in Connecticut in 1967, Paul Giamatti only played supporting roles for a long time, turning them into an art form. Not much could be changed on the outside. So this Mr. Average with thinning hair used his fool's license and, from the thankless role of the comic sidekick, created complex characters that were not always likeable but had recognition value. As the mean station manager in the brilliant radio biopic *Private Parts* (1997) he infuriated radio legend Howard Stern. He played a nicer version of the same type in *Man on the Moon* (1999). As the neurotic oddball who loses his cool as he fluctuates between self-hate and self-love, Giamatti was naturally the man for Woody Allen, who cast him twice in succession in *Mighty Aphrodite* (1995) and *Deconstructing Harry* (1997). With his depressive charisma, the Yale graduate finally won two highly respected major roles. In the biopic *American Splendor* (2003) he played the eccentric comic book artist Harvey Pekar. He finally became famous in the role of permanently contrite wine expert Miles in Alexander Payne's tragicomedy *Sideways* (2004), which also brought him a display cabinet of film awards.
Meanwhile, Paul Giamatti is now in full control, moving between small independent productions and Hollywood blockbusters. Most recently he headed a wonderful ensemble cast in *Barney's Version* (2010): in this Canadian literary adaptation he plays a cynical TV producer looking back on a completely botched-up life. Among his best known supporting roles are his appearances in *My Best Friend's Wedding* (1997), *The Truman Show* (1998), *Saving Private Ryan* (1998), *Planet of the Apes* (2001) and *Cinderella Man* (2005).

8

7 The sommelier's nose: Jack's misfortunes at least give Miles something to laugh about.

8 More wine – it's enough to make you weep: Miles' capacity for self pity is matched only by his connoisseur's knowledge. There are certainly plenty of opportunities for both.

9 Just deserts: Thomas Haden Church was nominated for an Oscar for his mesmerizing portrayal of Jack.

it says on the label: soaring camera shots through sunny California, rattling comedy linked with life's tragedies, rounded off with the finely nuanced dialogue typical of the films of director Alexander Payne (*About Schmidt*, 2002). In a truly moving scene, Miles describes the qualities of Pinot Noir to the sharp-witted Maya as an extremely sensitive plant that needs care and attention – he is talking about himself, of course. The fact that such precious moments do not descend into the banal is mainly down to the performances of four great actors. Paul Giamatti, who has always been well known as a supporting actor, moves us to tears in the role of Miles – a real piece of casting genius. Filled to overflowing with self pity and other unpleasant qualities, Miles is a person we can love because of his faults.No-one describes the special quality of *Sideways* better than Miles, when he appraises a decent wine as "quaffable, but by no means transcendental." The film has a clear message, but does not browbeat the audience. It is an apologist for the desirable measure, enjoyment for its own sake, and a little inebriation without regret. This makes for a film you want to return to again and again. But, be careful – too much will be addictive. PB

THE INCREDIBLES

2004 – USA – 115 MIN. – ANIMATION, ACTION MOVIE
DIRECTOR BRAD BIRD (*1957)
SCREENPLAY BRAD BIRD DIRECTOR OF PHOTOGRAPHY ANDREW JIMENEZ, PATRICK LIN, JANET LUCROY
EDITING STEPHEN SCHAFFER MUSIC MICHAEL GIACCHINO PRODUCTION JOHN WALKER for PIXAR ANIMATION STUDIOS, WALT DISNEY PICTURES.
VOICES CRAIG T. NELSON (Bob Parr / Mr. Incredible), HOLLY HUNTER (Helen Parr/Elastigirl), SAMUEL L. JACKSON (Lucius Best/Frozone), JASON LEE (Buddy Pine/Syndrome), DOMINIQUE LOUIS (Bomb Voyage), WALLACE SHAWN (Gilbert Huph), SARAH VOWELL (Violet Parr), JEAN SINCERE (Mrs. Hogenson), BRAD BIRD (Edna "E" Mode), ELI FUCILE (Jack-Jack Parr).
ACADEMY AWARDS 2005 OSCARS for BEST ANIMATED FEATURE FILM (Brad Bird) and BEST SOUND EDITING (Michael Silvers, Randy Thom).

"No matter how many times you save the world, it always manages to get back in jeopardy again."

Bob Parr sits at a desk that is far too small for him. Just about everything in his workplace seems too small for this big, bulky man who is still "in his prime:" his tiny cubicle in the huge open-plan office of an insurance company, the seats and the computer. Bob's demeanor, the look on his face and the tone of his voice all express his profound resignation: this man is clearly fed up, for his life is closing in on him in every way imaginable. Bob can't be bothered with the routine worries of his wife and kids, preferring instead to retreat to his workshop that is stuffed full of memorabilia from his glorious past. In the evening, he meets his best pal, Lucius: they tell their wives they're going bowling, when in fact they secretly listen in to police radio and chase after arcane adventures. The guys are firmly in the grip of a midlife crisis.

In the meantime, amid all the troubles, Bob's wife Helen tries to manage the household and problems with the kids. Baby Jack-Jack is still relatively manageable, but adolescent teenager Violet and her younger brother Dash are permanently at loggerheads. To cap everything, Violet is unlucky in love and just wants to disappear, while Dash causes trouble at school and doesn't know where to channel his energy. So they all have their crosses to bear: the whole Parr family squabbles, moans and talks over one another.

But what's this we've gotten into here? An Ingmar Bergman drama? In fact, the Parrs are computer-animated cartoon characters in a movie made by Pixar studios, in which people are the main characters for the first time – after toys (*Toy Story*, 1995; *Toy Story 2*, 1999; *Toy Story 3*, 2010), endearing monsters (*Monsters, Inc.*, 2001), and fish (*Finding Nemo*, 2003). Yet, as *The Incredibles* writer and director Brad Bird explained, Pixar was initially skeptical about the proposal, which seemed a bit too grown-up; it was felt that children might have difficulty identifying with Bob's midlife crisis.

In fact, the domestic drama is portrayed in a comic rather than dramatic way, and is only one strand of the story: for Bob, Helen and Lucius turn out to be the superheroes Mr. Incredible (very strong), Elastigirl (very flexible) and Frozone (very frosty). The only thing is, the glory days of these full-time saviors

1
2

“The setup may try the patience of the very young, but Bird’s insistence on getting us into the heads of this family pays off when the action starts up. Suddenly it’s *James Bond*, *Indiana Jones* and the *X-Men* all rolled into one kick-out-the-jams spectacle.” *Rolling Stone*

1 Action is his middle name, but sadly Mr. Incredible (voiced by Craig T. Nelson) is now forced to scrape a living as an insurance agent.

2 After her husband manages to get himself into an apparently desperate situation, it falls to Helen aka Elastigirl (voiced by Holly Hunter) to bail him out again.

3 Boredom leads to problems: Mr. Incredible embarks on a series of wacky adventures.

3

4 Bob and his buddy Lucius (voiced by Samuel L. Jackson) find themselves facing a new assignment: evil bad guy Syndrome (voiced by Jason Lee) casts his shadow over them.

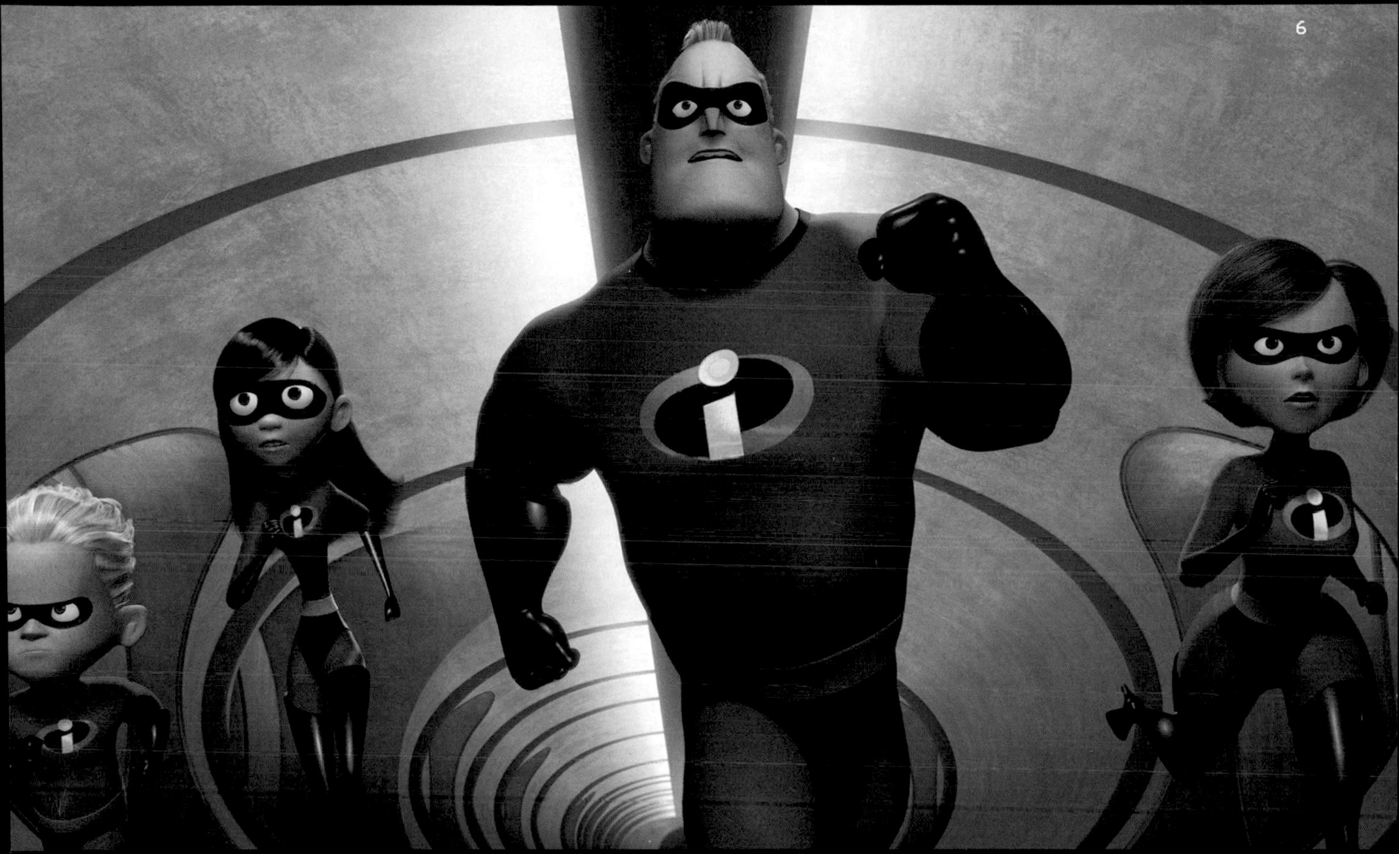

5 It's good to have friends: Frozone's "icy" skills help to repel Syndrome's attacks.

6 Back in action: the Parr family remembers its strength – sticking together.

of humanity were 15 years ago; they were forced back into "normal" lives in society by the government of the time, due to the number of compensation claims being made by people who didn't actually want to be saved. When a new arch-villain comes on the scene, however, the Parr family has to reactivate its superpowers – or, in the children's case, try them out for the first time. The result is that the second half of the movie is packed with whiz-bang action scenes. The idea of a mix of strong action and jokes with a serious foundation actually worked, as proved by the movie's immediate success. In the three days following release, *The Incredibles* took over 70 million dollars at the US box-office. In terms of representing human characters in computer-animated movies, *The Incredibles* was based on a completely different concept to Robert Zemeckis' *The Polar Express* (2004), which appeared at the same time. Using motion capture technology, the latter film creates characters that move realistically and look just like real people, yet which also seem rather soulless. *The Incredibles*, on the other hand, introduces stylized figures with whose all-too-human problems we can immediately identify, despite their ironic exaggeration.

7

8

Alongside this successful graphic realization, *The Incredibles* gives us an admirable retro-modern design from the 1950s and 60s, which had already characterized Bird's first feature film *The Iron Giant* (1999); here, it is beautifully reflected in the car design, the rows of suburban houses and Helen's modern kitchen. In the case of the island hideout of megalomaniac villain Syndrome, we find especially resonant echoes of Ken Adam's sets for James Bond movies. Another Bond reference is the hilarious appearance of the incredibly self-assured designer Edna Mode, known as "E," who tailors the super-outfits for the superheroes and, among other things, gives a very clear explanation as to why heroes should on no account wear a cape.

Bird's tale was probably also inspired to a degree by the parody *The Return of Captain Invincible* (1983); like *The Incredibles*, this film begins with newsreel shots of the Captain's heroic deeds, continues with the story of his decline and ends with his comeback. There are equally obvious influences from movies like *Spy Kids* (2001) and *X-Men* (2000), the "Captain Marvel" comics and Alan Moore's graphic novel for grown-ups, "Watchmen," in which the masked adventurers are represented as pretty average folk with pretty average problems. In the final analysis, it is precisely this paradox of the normal that contributes so much to the enormous enjoyment we derive from *The Incredibles* as well. LP

"We knew it would be a challenge. Creating a believable human is pretty much the hardest thing you can do with a computer, much harder than creating believable special effects."

(John Lasseter in: Mark Cotta Vaz: The Art of The Incredibles. San Francisco 2004, p. 6)

7 Is that what superpowers are good for, after all? The Parr family does the housework.

8 Sometimes, even superpowers do not help: Helen Parr certainly has her work cut out with her children.

9 Everyday life visibly boxes him in: Bob Parr is frustrated by the pressure to behave like an average person.

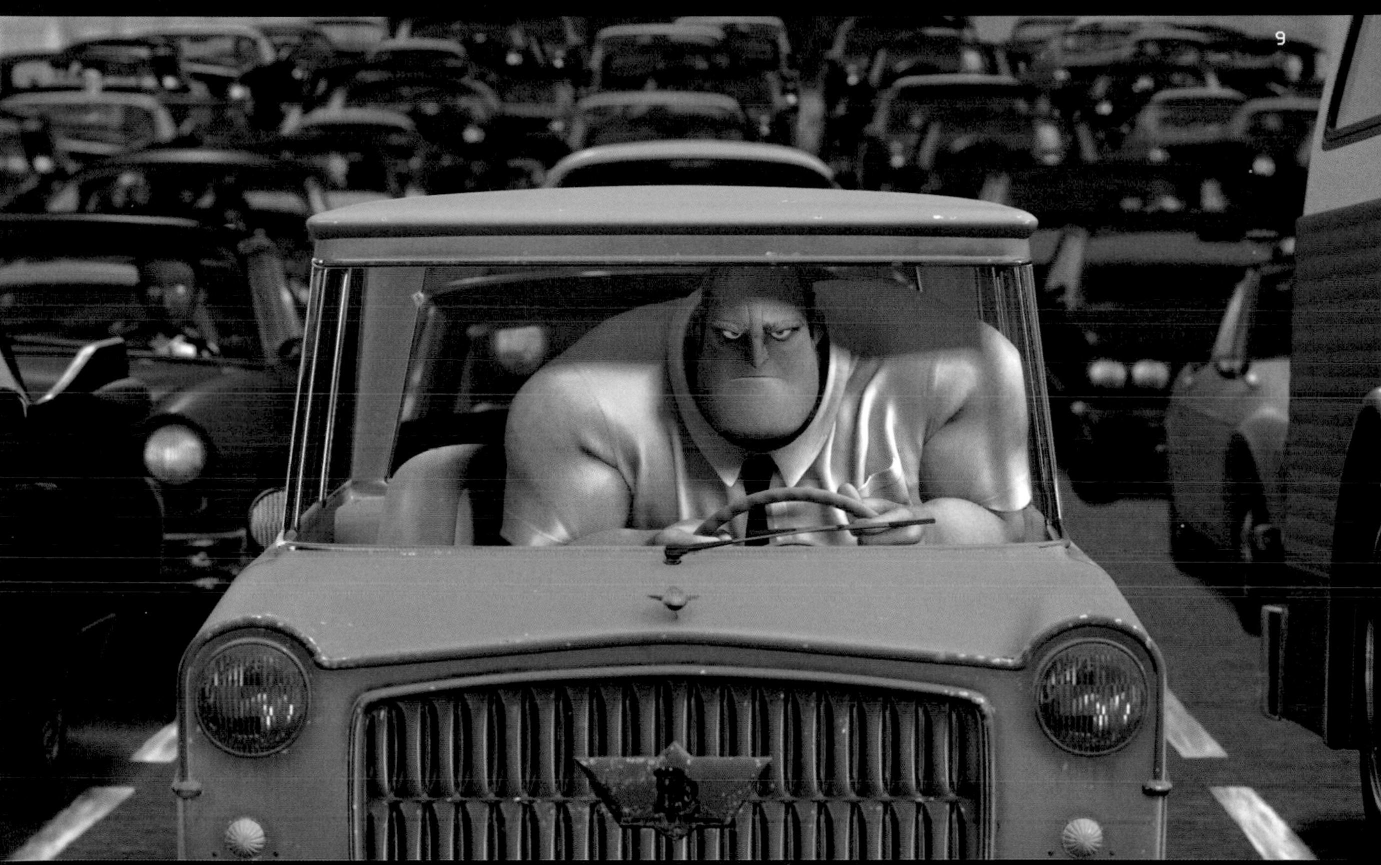

9

BRAD BIRD With just three completed feature films to his credit so far, Brad Bird (Phillip Bradley Bird) is nevertheless one of the most famous animation directors in the world – and one of the most creative. It is not only that the films he has made with Pixar – *The Incredibles* (2004) and *Ratatouille* (2007) – each won the Oscar for Best Animated Film in their respective years and took over 600 million dollars at the box-office, but also that the movies of this writer and director, born in Kalispell, Montana in 1957, have always been impressive on an artistic level too. Believable characters with human problems, ideas that are as original as they are surprising, plus a belief in animation as an art form are combined in Bird's movies to create sophisticated entertainment far beyond the usual children's movie.

Trained as an illustrator in his youth, Bird began building his experience as an animation director and producer on the TV series "Amazing Stories" (1985–1987). He produced the episode entitled "Family Dog" (1987), before working in the 1990s as an executive consultant for the popular cartoon series "The Simpsons," directing the follow-ups, "Krusty Gets Busted" (1990) and "Like Father, Like Clown" (1991). For his first own feature length movie, *The Iron Giant*, Bird adapted the eponymous children's book by Ted Hughes, a rite-of-passage story about a lonely boy who finds a huge, iron robot in the woods. In introducing the truly horrific wonder weapon from space to the world of human emotions, the boy learns something himself about life, death, friendship and betrayal.

Bird parodied super-hero movies and comics in an amusing way with his first computer-animated film, *The Incredibles*; equally successfully, he then went on in 2007 to tell the problem-ridden story of Remy the rat, determined to make it as a master chef in Paris. Bird is currently working on an adaptation of James Dalessandro's novel "1906," set during the famous earthquake in San Francisco.

MILLION DOLLAR BABY

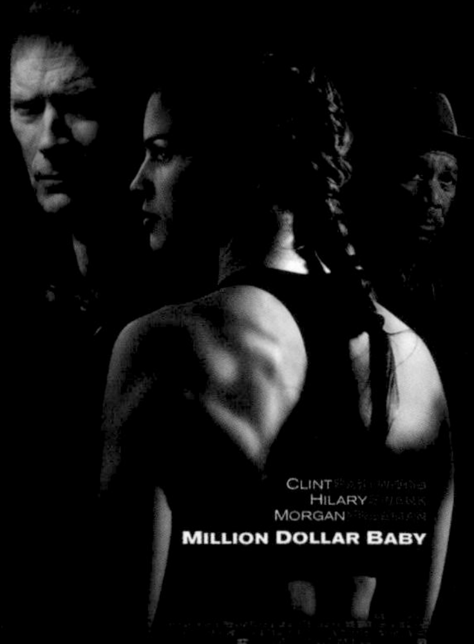

2004 – USA – 132 MIN. – BOXING FILM, DRAMA
DIRECTOR CLINT EASTWOOD (*1930)
SCREENPLAY PAUL HAGGIS, from the short story collection "ROPE BURNS: STORIES FROM THE CORNER" by F. X. TOOLE DIRECTOR OF PHOTOGRAPHY TOM STERN EDITING JOEL COX
MUSIC CLINT EASTWOOD PRODUCTION CLINT EASTWOOD, PAUL HAGGIS, TOM ROSENBERG, ALBERT S. RUDDY for WARNER BROS., LAKESHORE ENTERTAINMENT, MALPASO PRODUCTIONS, ALBERT S. RUDDY PRODUCTIONS, EPSILON MOTION PICTURES.
STARRING CLINT EASTWOOD (Frankie Dunn), HILARY SWANK (Maggie Fitzgerald), MORGAN FREEMAN (Eddie "Scrap-Iron" Dupris), JAY BARUCHEL (Danger Barch), MIKE COLTER (Big Willie Little), BRIAN F. O'BYRNE (Priester Horvak), BRUCE MACVITTIE (Mickey Mack), LUCIA RIJKER (Billie "The Blue Bear"), ANTHONY MACKIE (Shawrelle Berry), MARGO MARTINDALE (Earline Fitzgerald).
ACADEMY AWARDS 2005 OSCARS for BEST PICTURE (Clint Eastwood, Albert S. Ruddy, Tom Rosenberg), BEST DIRECTOR (Clint Eastwood), BEST LEADING ACTRESS (Hilary Swank) BEST SUPPORTING ACTOR (Morgan Freeman).

"Girly, tough ain't enough!"

Sergio Leone once said of Clint Eastwood that he only knew two facial expressions: one with, and one without, a hat. The expressive range of his films as a director is not much bigger. In his 25 years behind the camera, the lone rider has continued to tread his path of old, with gritted teeth and a steely stare. Or are we confusing the actor with the director? For, in actual fact, things are not what they used to be. Eastwood's films deal with self-doubt, his characters plagued with bad consciences, as if the point is to bury the ruthless "Dirty Harry" of the past forever. And nowhere else has he taken remorse to its ultimate conclusion as tenaciously and brilliantly as in *Million Dollar Baby* – as both actor and director.

His characters emerge from the partial shadows of the studio run by Frankie (Eastwood) with the help of former boxer Scrap (Morgan Freeman). They have a past that cannot be discussed, in order for them to exist in the present. Maggie (Hilary Swank) sees boxing as her last chance of escaping a meaningless, white trash existence. Frankie has good reasons for stonewalling her wish, one of which being Scrap's missing eye; the best cut man in the business, he knows all about the dangers of the sport. A young boxer has just left him to try his luck with a less cautious manager. Frankie tries to give excuses: that he doesn't coach women; that she is too old. But she refuses to accept any other trainer. Every evening, Maggie is there in the studio, working the punch bag until late into the night. What finally brings them together is spiritual kinship. She finds a father and he finds a daughter (his real daughter has returned his letters unopened for years). Frankie sets aside his fear of risk and accepts responsibility. Maggie will put him to a test far beyond anything he has ever experienced.

For Eastwood's films never go just one round. They do not end with the final knock-out that Maggie is soon administering to successive opponents. Until his dying days, Frankie will not forgive himself for the broken neck she suffers in an unfair fight. The fact that he must bring about her death himself in order to free this dynamic woman from her useless body does away with all the myths about winning that are associated with boxing films and the American dream itself – just as superior boxing movies have always done.

1

"Clint Eastwood's *Million Dollar Baby* is a masterpiece, pure and simple, deep and true ... *Million Dollar Baby* is Eastwood's 25th film as a director, and his best." *Chicago Sun-Times*

3

1 All or nothing: boxing becomes the ultimate blow for freedom for Maggie. Hilary Swank won the second Oscar in her career for her performance.

2 A father/daughter relationship develops between Maggie and her trainer, Frankie (Clint Eastwood). She is put to a grueling test.

3 Too fast for this sport: Maggie's fights seldom go more than one round. She wants a knock-out.

4 Eddie (Morgan Freeman) is over the hill. The former boxer spends his time thinking in his closet. He narrates the story.

5 Eastwood is in complete control of every move, both as director and actor. Swank's energy, however, can barely be contained.

Despite the irony of the tacky title, Million Dollar Baby is a positively classic film of its genre, but with the unmistakable Eastwood touch.

The compelling nature of the narrative and focus on the absolute essentials in simple, crystal-clear images earns our unqualified admiration. Morgan Freeman's familiar voice-over recites the only too well-known boxing rules, yet each one – the step back, the cover punch – is part of the storyline. The movie circles round its subject for a long time, only to catch us by surprise. Paul Haggis put together the screenplay from several short stories by F.X. Toole, bringing him an Oscar nomination. Hilary Swank and Morgan Freeman won their categories. With his quiet humanity, Freeman exudes a sense of calm that renders him the hidden heart of the film. Even in her crippled state, Swank demonstrates the sheer willpower that defined her powerful fights.

4

5

Eastwood earned two Oscars, as both director and producer, plus the wrath of disabled groups besides, who accused him of advocating mercy killing. The film's profundity makes this charge difficult to sustain. Unacceptable low blows are more like the demonic imported "former whore from East Berlin" who decks Maggie; or her mother in a Mickey Mouse T-shirt who is portrayed as a despicable welfare scrounger. The charm of Eastwood's films lies in the dialectic of the wisdom of old age and its mulish stubbornness. He is conservative, but allows himself to struggle for answers when faced with last requests. Even the priest, who from the start is besieged by Frankie's questions, cannot help him with this. At the end, the lone stranger who does not recognize himself anymore chooses the road back into the darkness. PB

6

"Maggie needs Frankie because she is looking for a father figure who believes in her. Frankie needs Maggie because his real daughter has sent back all his letters unopened for years. Each needs the other because the world is a drafty boxing hall. They need one another so much it is almost unbearable." *Die Zeit*

7

6 For Maggie, boxing rules apply to life as well. This gives Eddie, a quiet man, some cause for concern.

7 A quiet drama about regret and redemption: Frankie doesn't want to repeat past mistakes. He agrees to help, but very reluctantly.

8 Shadows on the soul: under Eastwood's skilful direction, boxing becomes a fateful world of stark contrasts.

HILARY SWANK (*1974) She has been nominated for a Best Leading Actress Oscar twice, and won it twice; born in 1974, she is the third youngest woman to have achieved this honor, and for leading roles far outside the traditional spectrum. The small, independent movie, *Boys Don't Cry* (1999) catapulted Hilary Swank overnight into the limelight. In this retelling of a true story, she took on the part of the transsexual Brandon Teena, born in the wrong body, who decides to go through life as a boy – with tragic consequences. In her trademark style, combining equal measures of forcefulness and sensitivity, she portrayed a budding professional boxer in *Million Dollar Baby* (2004). Her comments on her steep career curve when she was awarded the second Oscar were as appropriate as they befitted Hollywood: "I'm just a girl from a trailer park who had a dream." She did, in fact, come from a poor background, and her rise from humble beginnings to million dollar baby does seem like a fairy tale.
It all began with undemanding roles in movies like *Buffy the Vampire Slayer* (1992) and *The Next Karate Kid* (1994). When she was approached to do Boys Don't Cry, she was coasting along in the teen TV series "Beverly Hills, 90210" (1997–1998). She has not, however, managed to add much to her two major successes. Films like *Insomnia* (2002), *The Black Dahlia* (2006) and *Freedom Writers* (2007) benefited from her good performances without being convincing overall. Swank was also involved as a producer in the latter, a tearjerker about a high-school teacher.

GRIZZLY MAN

2004 – USA – 103 MIN. – DOCUMENTARY
DIRECTOR WERNER HERZOG (*1942)
SCREENPLAY WERNER HERZOG DIRECTOR OF PHOTOGRAPHY PETER ZEITLINGER EDITING JOE BINI
MUSIC RICHARD THOMPSON PRODUCTION ERIK NELSON for LIONS GATE.
FEATURING WERNER HERZOG (Narrator, Interviewer), TIMOTHY TREADWELL (Archive Images), JEWEL PALOVAK, CAROL DEXTER, VAL DEXTER, WARREN QUEENEY, AMIE HUGUENARD.

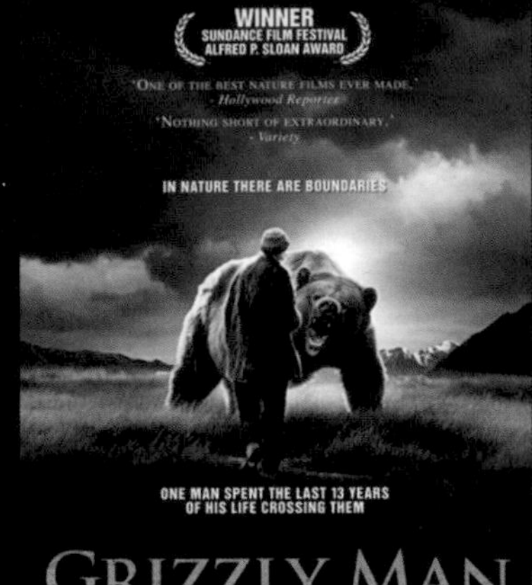

"If I show weakness, if I retreat, I may be hurt, I may be killed."

Imagine a huge bear coming up to you, weighing over 220 lb /100 kg, and snuffling at your hand. Imagine a hungry bear attacking you, threatening the lives of you and your partner.

Timothy Treadwell (1957–2003) experienced both scenarios. The self-appointed American animal welfare activist spent 13 consecutive summers with grizzly bears in a nature reserve in Alaska, beginning in 1991. In the fall of what was to be his final year with them, a bear killed Treadwell and his girlfriend Amie Huguenard. Treadwell shot 100 hours of video footage about himself and the bears in the last five years of his life. Director Werner Herzog – once a fellow exponent of the "New German Cinema" along with Rainer Werner Fassbinder and Wim Wenders – saw the material and used parts of it for *Grizzly Man*, a documentary like no other we are likely to have seen before. Treadwell in the foreground, bears in the background – this is the dominant camera shot in the film. The animal lover sets up the video camera in a prominent position and talks to the lens. The bears in the background are unconcerned, looking for something to eat in a field, trying to catch salmon in the river or simply lumbering around in the vicinity; at one point, two young males engage in a bitter fight, such that the viewer senses almost physically the power and the violence of the scene. Again and again, Treadwell plays quietly with some foxes that have become his pets. These nature shots have a fascinating beauty about them. Treadwell and his camera are trusted by the animals, apparently invisible to them – this way the predators present themselves openly in their natural state. The knowledgeable way a man untrained in biology handles the animals, cautious in spite of the fact that they have tolerated him in their living space for over a decade, is astonishing. Yet *Grizzly Man* is not primarily a film about animals, but the moving and even disturbing portrait of

1
2

1 One-man-show: Timothy Treadwell often filmed himself complacently in front of the camera, with the bears in the background.

2 A 28-year-old grizzly bear, tattooed with US Park Service number 141, attacked Treadwell and his girlfriend Amie Huguenard, killing them both.

3 Walk on the wild side: Treadwell surrounded himself with grizzlies, as if they were domestic pets. At night in his tent, he cuddled his childhood teddy bear.

4 A fox was reclusive Timothy Treadwell's pet for ten years.

5 Treadwell's girlfriend Amie Huguenard was with him during his last years in the wild.

6 Treadwell left behind 100 hours of documentary material; when he viewed it, Werner Herzog learned a great deal about bears, as well as gaining deep insight into the Grizzly Man's soul.

"Taking up one of his recurrent themes, Werner Herzog calls nature a place of 'chaos and murder'." *San Francisco Chronicle*

a man. In this sense, it slots easily into the series of Herzog's studies of the male psyche such as *Aguirre, Wrath of God* (*Aguirre, der Zorn Gottes*, 1972) and *Fitzcarraldo* (1982), with Treadwell standing shoulder to shoulder with those extreme fanatics that Klaus Kinski played for the director. There are not many shots in which Treadwell does not feature. By contrast, he hardly ever filmed his girlfriend, who was with him for the last two years. It is clear from his footage that Treadwell wanted to present a stylized image of himself as a lone fighter; an animal lover who has turned his back on human beings. Having said that, he comes over in quite different ways in front of the camera: sometimes egotistical and sometimes ironic; sometimes brooding; and sometimes almost drunk from the feeling of his own uniqueness and the task he has set himself. He rails against park rangers and tourists, continually stressing that he must protect the bears. And the word "love" crops up again and again: he loves the bears and foxes, and his life in the wild. Yet the cruelty of nature does not fit Treadwell's image of harmony. He refuses to accept that a wolf has killed one of his foxes, or that the bears eat their young in times of drought when no salmon come upriver. Yet he takes action as a result: he deepens the river for the salmon and begs the gods for rain. What kind of man was Timothy Treadwell? From Herzog's interviews with his friends and parents, and from what he said about himself, a picture emerges of a man searching for an elusive something, against the background of a middle-class upbringing, alcohol and drugs. He tried without success to become an actor and concocted wild fantasies about his origins. He hung out with life-threatening predators while sleeping in a tent with the cuddly teddy he had from his childhood. There is no coherent picture. Herzog viewed 100 hours' material in which Treadwell allows us to look deep into his soul. But the picture that emerges begs the question in the final analysis: is Treadwell an admirable individualist who is living his dream? Or a being who is extreme, crazy or even sick? HJK

PETER ZEITLINGER Cameraman Peter Zeitlinger has worked with Werner Herzog since the documentary *Death for Five Voices* (*Tod für fünf Stimmen*) in 1995. The collaboration has also produced documentaries such as *Little Dieter Needs to Fly* (1997) and *My Best Fiend* (*Mein liebster Feind*, 1999) as well as feature films including *Bad Lieutenant* (2009) with Nicolas Cage. He also shot Herzog's 3-D documentary *Cave of Forgotten Dreams* (2010).
Zeitlinger was born in Prague in 1960. In the wake of the Prague Spring, he left Czechoslovakia with his parents for Austria when he was barely ten years old. He used his experiences in making the Erhard Riedlsperger film *Tunnelkind* (1989), for which he was responsible for cinematography and screenplay. He studied at the Vienna Film School with experimental filmmakers Michael Snow and Peter Kubelka. Zeitlinger's extraordinary visual design in Ulrich Seidl's highly stylized documentary *Loss Is to Be Expected* (*Mit Verlust ist zu rechnen*, 1992) eventually brought the cameraman to the attention of Werner Herzog, marking the start of an enduring and creative partnership.

5

6

SIN CITY

2005 – USA – 124 MIN. – COMIC ADAPTATION, ACTION MOVIE
DIRECTORS ROBERT RODRIGUEZ (*1968), FRANK MILLER (*1957), QUENTIN TARANTINO (*1963)
SCREENPLAY FRANK MILLER, from his comic series of the same name
DIRECTOR OF PHOTOGRAPHY ROBERT RODRIGUEZ EDITING ROBERT RODRIGUEZ MUSIC JOHN DEBNEY, GRAEME REVELL, ROBERT RODRIGUEZ PRODUCTION ELISABETH AVELLAN for DIMENSION FILMS, TROUBLEMAKER STUDIOS.
STARRING BRUCE WILLIS (Hartigan), NICK STAHL (Roark Jr./Yellow Bastard), JESSICA ALBA (Nancy Callahan), MICKEY ROURKE (Marv), JAIME KING (Goldie/Wendy), ELIJAH WOOD (Kevin), CLIVE OWEN (Dwight), BENICIO DEL TORO (Jackie Boy), ROSARIO DAWSON (Gail), DEVON AOKI (Miho), BRITTANY MURPHY (Shellie), MAKENZIE VEGA (Young Nancy).
IFF CANNES 2006 VULCAIN PRIZE (Robert Rodriguez).

"Turn the right corner in Sin City and you can find anything."

Sin City is a wicked place, marked by violence, crime, corruption and prostitution. It is a product of Frank Miller's fertile imagination. The influential artist created 13 comic books between 1991 and 1992 about life in the dark alleys of Sin City, in stories that more or less interweave. Inspired by film noir, his drawing style relies on strong black and white contrasts and dispenses almost totally with color. Robert Rodriguez managed to transpose this striking signature style to celluloid in an empathetic way. According to him, it was not so easy to get Miller to join the project; the artist was not convinced it would be possible to convey the visual qualities of his comics to the filmic medium. But a test screening featuring the opening scene of *Sin City* persuaded him, and he came on board as co-director. The result is a visually stunning movie that really does look like a comic that's been brought to life. *Sin City* tells three of the thirteen stories from Miller's books: "The Hard Goodbye;" "The Big Fat Kill;" and "That Yellow Bastard." We see hulk-like Marv (Mickey Rourke) embarking on a bloody personal campaign to avenge the murder of Goldie (Jaime King), the woman he loved. In the process, he comes up against serial killer Kevin (Elijah Wood), who murders silently and with feline speed; and, in spite of Marv's immeasurable physical strength, it is only with great difficulty that he overcomes Kevin. We see Dwight (Clive Owen), a killer with his heart in the right place, going into battle for the prostitutes of Old Town. This is the only way that a long, bloody feud can be averted. For the truce between prostitutes, police and mafia is under threat, after notorious police officer Jackie Boy (Benicio del Toro) is

2

1 Sin City in the background – with nasty surprises lurking everywhere. But Becky (Alexis Bledel) is not as naive and alone as she first appears.

2 The movie opens with a seductive woman (Marley Shelton) and a view over the city. What is she running from? We never find out.

3 Dwight (Clive Owen) is around when there's trouble. He especially takes care of dirty work, without batting an eyelid.

4 The Roarks' run-down farm – angel of death Kevin (Elijah Wood) reads the Bible while Hartigan tries to free Nancy.

5 Partner Bob (Michael Madsen) behind him: aging cop Hartigan (Bruce Willis) suspects they are playing with marked cards.

"Other comic adaptations should really cease to exist after this movie, for *Sin City* gives a whole new meaning to the term 'comic adaptation'." *filmszene.de*

3

tricked and killed in the city's autonomous red-light district. The third storyline is a tale in two parts. Bruce Willis plays aging cop Hartigan, who manages to save young Nancy (Makenzie Vega) from the clutches of a child molester who turns out to be the Senator's son, Roark Jr. (Nick Stahl). Although Hartigan shoots him down, he survives badly wounded, and Hartigan ends up in the joint instead. The second part of the story takes place eight years later. Hartigan has been released from jail. Nancy Callahan is now a grown woman (Jessica Alba). A love story begins to unfold, but his old adversary Roark Jr. is lying in wait. The life-saving medical treatment has mutated him into a foul yellow monster intent on revenge. But Hartigan manages to save Nancy a second time and on this occasion he kills Roark Jr.

What is striking is that all three stories feature male heroes who have to fight, not only against their adversaries, but also their own shortcomings. Marv is violent and erratic: he is on medication to keep his fantasies under control. Pugnacious Dwight may act cool, but he starts to hallucinate in stressful situations: dead Jackie Boy talks to him when he is trying to dispose of the corpse. Hartigan, on the other hand, has an age-related heart condition and is fighting as much against his own body as against crime. Miller uses a simple narrative device: during long sequences, we hear what the protagonists are thinking as voice-overs. So we see the world through their eyes while simultaneously being privy to their emotional instability, which opens the door to the larger-than-life world of sex and crime.

9 Roark Jr. (Nick Stahl) has mutated into a foul yellow monster. Now he wants to avenge himself on Nancy and Hartigan.

10 Marv is framed for Goldie's murder but just manages to elude the police. His parole officer, Lucille (Carla Gugino), treats his wounds. They help each other, but do not become romantically involved. She is a lesbian and Marv only has thoughts for his lover.

FRANK MILLER Frank Miller became famous in the 1970s and 1980s for finding new ways of telling comic stories. Born in 1957, the graphic artist was influenced by film noir. His stories of murky heroes are told in high-contrast, black and white images. While he gave a new look to the icons of the big comic publishers like Marvel or DC, as in the case of Batman, he created a universe of its own with the "Sin City" stories. The film industry soon paid attention to his characters as well. He also made a name for himself as a screenwriter for *RoboCop 2* (1990) and *RoboCop 3* (1993).
Though his stories were used for a whole series of movies, for a long time Miller was reluctant to agree to a film version of "Sin City." It only happened in 2005, when Robert Rodriguez persuaded him that it could be done and involved him as co-director. This in turn led to Miller trying his own hand at directing in *The Spirit* (2008), working with similar effects to those previously used in Sin City. Zack Snyder's surprise hit movie *300* (2006) was also based on one of Frank Miller's comic books.

MATCH POINT

2005 UK / USA – 124 MIN. – THRILLER
DIRECTOR WOODY ALLEN (*1935)
SCREENPLAY WOODY ALLEN DIRECTOR OF PHOTOGRAPHY REMI ADEFARASIN EDITING ALISA LEPSELTER
PRODUCTION LETTY ARONSON, LUCY DARWIN, GARETH WILEY for BBC FILMS, THEMA PRODUCTIONS, JADA PRODUCTIONS.
STARRING JONATHAN RHYS MEYERS (Chris Wilton), SCARLETT JOHANSSON (Nola Rice), MATTHEW GOODE (Tom Hewett), EMILY MORTIMER (Chloe Hewett Wilton), BRIAN COX (Alec Hewett), PENELOPE WILTON (Eleanor Hewett), JAMES NESBITT (Detective Banner), EWEN BREMNER (Inspector Dowd), RUPERT PENRY-JONES (Henry), MIRANDA RAISON (Heather).

"I'd rather be lucky than good."

A tennis ball wobbles on the edge of the net in slow motion. It will fall on one side of it. Why not the other? What determines our lives – chance or fate? A director like Woody Allen does not deal with the great questions of world literature, and certainly not in *Match Point*. So how did this pitch-black thriller become his most successful film in a long time, heralding a return to his old form? Was it down to his astonishing decision to leave his familiar Manhattan and shift the action to London? The film was originally going to be shot in The Hamptons, the local hotspot for rich New Yorkers. At the end of the day, however, *Match Point* is simply a brilliant movie – with tennis courts in both locations.

Coach Chris Wilton (Jonathan Rhys Meyers) literally plays his way into the upper echelons of English society. He meets rich boy Tom Hewett (Matthew Goode) at the tennis club and, before long, is sitting next to his sister Chloe (Emily Mortimer) at the opera. His marriage to her is the winning match point in his life; his father-in-law even arranges a suitable job for him, while a loft apartment on the River Thames is suddenly within his reach. His reading matter – Dostoyevsky's "Crime and Punishment" – alerts us, however, to the approaching tragedy. Tom's American friend Nola Rice (Scarlett Johansson) is considerably more exciting than Chloe. Chris and Nola have a lot in common: the failed

1 An amoral hero: smooth operator Chris Wilton (Jonathan Rhys Meyers) marries unsuspecting Chloe (Emily Mortimer) for money and status.

2 For this failed tennis pro, the industrialist's daughter is the match point of his life. Woody Allen moves effortlessly across the court of English class differences.

3 Luxury home with view over the Thames: suddenly all Chris's dreams are fulfilled. But his happiness is short-lived. He has to decide – money or love.

"*Match Point*, which deserves to be ranked with Allen's *Annie Hall*, *Hannah and Her Sisters*, *Manhattan*, *Crimes and Misdemeanors* and *Everyone Says I Love You*, has a terrible fascination that lasts all the way through. We can see a little way ahead, we can anticipate some of the mistakes and hazards, but the movie is too clever for us, too cynical." *Chicago Sun-Times*

4 The talented Mr. Wilton nearly has it made: Tom (Matthew Goode) has the lifestyle that Chris craves. Sport is what brings them together.

5 The love triangle begins: privileged Tom (Matthew Goode) introduces his friend to his fiancée. Nola (Scarlett Johansson), attractive and just as ambitious, takes him on a road to perdition – but it's only temporary. The sparks fairly fly in Allen's movie, but his pessimism ultimately wins out over his faith in love.

tennis pro and the attractive drama student both long for the luxurious life that the Hewetts lead so effortlessly. Unfortunately, however, only Chris is a good actor. While Nola blows one audition after another and is eventually replaced by another woman more befitting Tom's status, the smooth nouveau-riche upstart hosts dinner parties as confidently as he fulfils his executive functions in the firm. By sheer chance, they meet up again months later in the Tate, when Chris solves the problem of the pregnancy resulting from their affair in chilling, calculated fashion. He comes to a cold-blooded decision in what is still a classic conflict between love and money. Crime has always fascinated Woody Allen, whether in *Take the Money and Run* (1969) or the thematically related *Crimes and Misdemeanors* (1989). Man's evil nature cannot be overlooked in his films; there is nothing of the altruist in the Holocaust jokes and agreeably neurotic behavior. There is no longer a Woody in this movie, though, loudly bemoaning the gloomy outcomes and neutralizing them with a snappy line or cheerful aphorism. To the musical strains of Enrico Caruso's resonant bel canto, *Match Point* is without doubt one of Allen's most pessimistic movies. At the same time, though, his bitter satire – modeled on Dostoyevsky, Strindberg, Dreiser and a touch of the English author, Jane Austen – is indescribably sophisticated, smart and even sexy.

There can be no question that setting the action in the context of a traditional European social hierarchy gives the film its necessary, additional edge. The protagonists are mercilessly crushed by 70-year-old Allen between the cold glass architecture of the business world and the elegantly paneled wealth of a heritage-conscious upper class. They think they know how to play the game, see themselves as best equipped in the fight for social recognition and encounter each other at the first match at the Ping-Pong table with nothing less than sexual aggression. Woody Allen was the first to discover the vamp in rising star Scarlett Johansson. Yet she is even more impressive in her downward plunge. From being an exotic adventure for Chris, Nola becomes a burden because of the baby she is carrying and, even worse, because of her feelings for him. She threatens to blow his cover. She interrupts his meetings. She has to go. The ball drops on the wrong side of the net. Yet this development is not inevitable; neither is the link between crime and punishment. To the very last twist in the plot, Woody Allen plays cat-and-mouse with the audience's expectations, even as he is allowing his characters a human dimension. They are just like us in their aspirations and fear of failure. This may also have been a contributing factor to the first box-office success enjoyed by the New York movie icon since *Hannah and Her Sisters* (1985). Not that Allen should rest on his laurels just yet. PB

9

6 Fatal attraction: they have far more in common with each other than with their respective partners. Chris, however, is the better actor.

7 Eleanor (Penelope Wilton), Tom and Chloe's mother, has reason to be worried. She is particularly unhappy about Tom's relationship with Nola.

8 Chris, however, is warmly welcomed into the family. Father-in-law (Brian Cox) even arranges a job for him.

9 Woody Allen was the first director to recognize Scarlett Johansson's potential as a sensual vamp. She went on to star in two of his next movies.

"The gloom of random, meaningless existence has rarely been so much fun, and Mr Allen's bite has never been so sharp, or so deep. A movie this good is no laughing matter."

The New York Times

SCARLETT JOHANSSON Virtually no other Hollywood star combines glamour with professional seriousness, a laid-back attitude with personal credibility, in the way Scarlett Johansson does. The daughter of Polish-Danish parents, she began working in movies as a child and, right from the start, seemed a good deal more mature than her (mostly older) male partners. "She is 13, but going on 30" was how Robert Redford described her in the role she played in her big break, *The Horse Whisperer* (1998). She had fairly minor parts in the Coen brothers' film *The Man Who Wasn't There* (2001) and in the cult film version of the comic book *Ghost World* (2001), yet afterward everyone was talking about Scarlett Johansson. As the junior sidekick to a superbly crumpled Bill Murray in Sofia Coppola's tantalizing story set in Tokyo, *Lost in Translation* (2003), she was catapulted into the grown-up sector and has remained there ever since. Her good looks have not done her any harm, of course. As the *Girl with a Pearl Earring* (2003) she allowed herself to be painted into the fictional biography of the famous Dutch painter Jan Vermeer and his unknown model. Completely enthralled by her natural charisma and beauty, and taking what might have been his last chance, Woody Allen hired her for three films outright: *Match Point* (2005), *Scoop* (2006) and *Vicky Cristina Barcelona* (2008) all contributed to his impressive comeback. Nowadays, however, the small-scale, unusual productions favored by Johansson can barely afford her. With films like *The Island* (2005), *The Prestige* (2006), *The Other Boleyn Girl* (2008) and *The Spirit* (2008), she has long since made it in blockbuster movies.

HIDDEN
CACHÉ

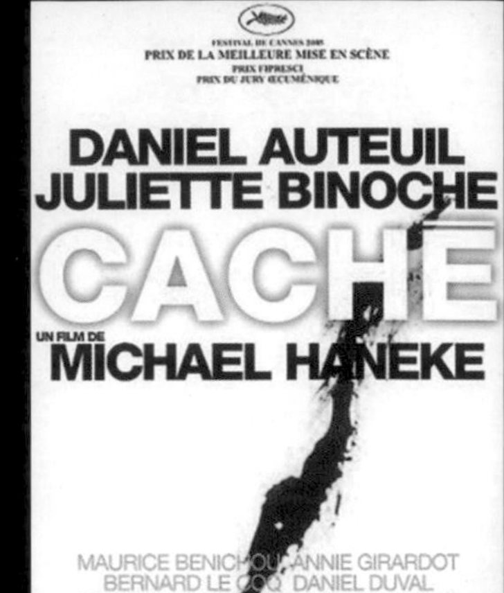

2005 – GERMANY / AUSTRIA / FRANCE / ITALY – 119 MIN. – DRAMA, THRILLER
DIRECTOR MICHAEL HANEKE (*1942)
SCREENPLAY MICHAEL HANEKE DIRECTOR OF PHOTOGRAPHY CHRISTIAN BERGER
EDITING MICHAEL HUDECEK, NADINE MUSE PRODUCTION VEIT HEIDUSCHKA, MARGARET MÉNÉGOZ for WEGA FILM, LES FILMS DU LOSANGE, BAVARIA FILM, BIM DISTRIBUZIONE.
STARRING DANIEL AUTEUIL (Georges Laurent), JULIETTE BINOCHE (Anne Laurent), MAURICE BÉNICHOU (Majid), ANNIE GIRARDOT (Georges' Mom), BERNARD LE COQ (Georges' Boss), WALID AFKIR (Majid's Son), LESTER MAKEDONSKY (Pierrot Laurent), DANIEL DUVAL (Pierre), NATHALIE RICHARD (Mathilde), DENIS PODALYDÈS (Yvon), AÏSSA MAÏGA (Chantal).
IFF CANNES 2005 BEST DIRECTOR (Michael Haneke).

"I've nothing to hide" / "Je n'ai rien à cacher"

The world of Georges Laurent (Daniel Auteuil) appears perfect: his job as presenter of a popular TV book show has brought him prosperity and recognition, while his private life would also seem as good as it gets. Georges is happily married to Anne (Juliette Binoche), an attractive publishing assistant. Their son, Pierrot (Lester Makedonsky), attends high school and is a talented swimmer. And their comfortable house in a quiet Paris suburb is the focal point of a cultured, broadminded circle of friends. But this middle-class idyll is abruptly invaded when the Laurents find a mysterious videotape on their doorstep: someone has filmed the exterior of their house, for two hours, without moving. Almost like a surveillance camera.

To begin with, Anne assumes it is a joke. But when another tape appears, along with a child's drawing showing a person with a bleeding mouth, and anonymous phone calls start to be received, Georges in particular becomes visibly upset. He dreams about a dark-skinned young boy with a blood-streaked face standing in front of him and threatening him with an axe. As a result, he gradually becomes convinced that an event from his childhood has caught up

1 Man with a past: director Michael Haneke says he always gets the impression that Daniel Auteuil is hiding something. As Georges Laurent, the top French actor plays a master of repression.

2 In *Hidden*, Auteuil plays the presenter of a popular TV book program – a model citizen whose home is a place where liberal, cultured friends come and go (here, Daniel Duval and Nathalie Richard) and …

3 … whose marriage to Anne (Juliette Binoche) is based on mutual trust and candor. Or so it seems …

"Michael Haneke's masterpiece: a compelling politico-psychological essay about the denial and guilt mixed into the foundations of western prosperity." *The Guardian*

4 … but does this impression actually correspond to reality? Georges becomes increasingly agitated when an anonymous video appears, showing the outside of the Laurents' house – shot on a fixed camera without any commentary.

5 Haneke subjects his audience to the frozen shot of the mysterious "surveillance video" for minutes on end, thereby raising the question: could there be a secret behind this squeaky clean façade?

with him. Back then, his parents had taken in an Algerian orphan boy; out of jealousy, Georges told lies about him, with the result that the planned adoption fell through. The boy, Majid, disappeared from Georges' life; is he now taking his revenge on him, 40 years down the line?

Whenever Michael Haneke tells a story about adults in his disturbing films, he always incorporates their childhood into the narrative. This is the case in *The Piano Teacher* (*La Pianiste*, 2001), in which Isabelle Huppert gives a fantastic performance as the neurotic heroine of the title; it also applies to his consummate thriller *Hidden* (*Caché*, 2005), in which another superstar of French cinema – Daniel Auteuil – takes center stage. And, as in *The Piano Teacher*, the TV presenter who seems so sophisticated reveals himself to be an emotionally warped character, displaying increasingly repellent traits as the past raises its ugly head within him.

According to Haneke, the starting point of *Hidden* is the issue of how a grown-up deals with a burden of guilt assumed as a child. Auteuil (who in the view of this German-born Austrian director always has an air of concealment in films) is outstanding in the role of the master of repression. Unwilling and incapable in equal measure of reflecting on his own wrongdoing or communicating

THE ALGERIAN WAR AND FRENCH CINEMA The difficulty with which the French public and state dealt (and are still dealing) with the Algerian War (1954–1962) is also reflected in its cinema. Thus, films that addressed the brutal war for Algerian independence were for a long time subjected to censorship. For instance, Jean-Luc Godard's *Le petit soldat* (1960/1963) about the bloody clashes between the French Secret Army Organization (OAS) and the Algerian National Liberation Front (FLN) in Switzerland could not be premiered in France until 1963. The *Battle of Algiers* (*La battaglia di Algeri*, 1966), Gillo Pontecorvo's stark portrayal of the Algerian guerrilla war and the French strategy that did not shrink from torture and terror methods, was banned until 1971 and has only been shown regularly since its re-release in 2004.
Even into the 1970s it was conspicuous how seldom French cinema dealt with the subject of the Algerian War. Critical feature films like René Vautier's *To Be Twenty in the Aures* (*Avoir 20 ans dans les Aurès*, 1972) or Yves Boisset's *Nothing to Report* (*R.A.S.*,1973) were exceptions – and subject to state control. Even the "beur cinema" – films by young directors of Maghrebi immigrant origin – that emerged in the 1980s directed its attention more to the reality of everyday life of the Arab-born population than to the past. A change has only gradually begun to take place since the turn of the millennium.
For the first time ever with Michael Haneke's *Hidden* (2005), a major French co-production dealt with the taboo massacre of October 17, 1961 in Paris, while genre cinema has also discovered the Algerian War as a subject. Rachid Bouchareb's *Outside the Law* (*Hors la loi*, 2010) – the story of the Algerian War of Independence from the point of view of three Arab brothers – was in competition at the Cannes Film Festival. The fact that the film was premiered there under tightened security measures is a clear indication of just how sensitive the subject continues to be.

6 Haneke contrasts the Laurents' educated middle-class milieu with the dreary existence of Majid (Maurice Bénichou), a Frenchman of Algerian origin. Georges goes to see him in his bare flat in the projects, because he thinks he is blackmailing him. But what is the connection between the two men?

7 Elite circle: among his guests, and sheltered from reality by a wall of books, the presenter is in his element.

8 A disturbing child's drawing arouses Georges' suspicion that the anonymous messages might be linked to an event from his childhood.

9 Latent racism: the more cornered Georges feels, the more it appears that his ostensibly ultra-cosmopolitan lifestyle is a tissue of lies.

"Nothing gets under the skin quite as effectively as the eye of a camera, as Haneke shows in his film." *Der Tagesspiegel*

“*Hidden* is a thriller, but one that takes the liberty of focusing, not just on the mechanics of suspense, but also politics, social issues and the sudden power shifts between people. As thrilling as this movie is, it could equally well be called a melodrama or political allegory.” *Profil*

openly, the self-image of the cosmopolitan, educated individual he has projected in his private and professional life is exposed increasingly as a tissue of lies. Thus, the irritatingly sustained, static view of the Laurents' house that opens *Hidden* becomes to a certain extent a symbol of Georges' existence: when fast forwarded, the image suddenly becomes identifiable as a video recording, at which point the peaceful façade also appears as a delusion, or stage set.

Hidden has been compared by critics to the nightmarish vision of a David Lynch movie. Like a typically Lynchian hero, Georges does in fact display increasingly paranoid behavior. And when the protagonist sets out in search of Majid, finally finding him in a dreary community apartment, the levels of reality in the movie become increasingly blurred. Is Majid behind the mysterious tapes? Or is it his son? Or is the film actually showing us the psyche of its haunted main character? Viewers are constantly forced to consider their individual perspectives, qualifying or discarding their findings. Haneke's film resists any clear-cut reading and calls for an audience to be actively involved.

What is also remarkable about *Hidden* is that it addresses a subject that has been taboo in France for decades. It is clear that Majid's parents fell victim to the notorious “Paris massacre” in October 1961, when French security forces killed up to 200 Algerian demonstrators. In a painful and occasionally shocking way, Haneke suggests that the wounds of this slaughter have by no means healed, but have instead been buried ever deeper in the psyche of those involved as a result of the event being hushed up for decades. This has contributed directly to divisions in society; indeed, the merciless eye that Haneke focuses on Georges is ultimately targeted on French society itself. JH

A HISTORY OF VIOLENCE

2005 – USA – 96 MIN. – THRILLER, DRAMA
DIRECTOR DAVID CRONENBERG (*1943)
SCREENPLAY JOSH OLSON, from a graphic novel by JOHN WAGNER and VINCE LOCKE
DIRECTOR OF PHOTOGRAPHY PETER SUSCHITZKY EDITING RONALD SANDERS MUSIC HOWARD SHORE
PRODUCTION CHRIS BENDER, J. C. SPINK for NEW LINE PRODUCTIONS, BENDERSPINK.
STARRING VIGGO MORTENSEN (Tom Stall), MARIA BELLO (Edie Stall), ASHTON HOLMES (Jack Stall), ED HARRIS (Carl Fogarty), WILLIAM HURT (Richie Cusack), PETER MACNEILL (Sheriff Sam Carney), HEIDI HAYES (Sarah Stall), STEPHEN MCHATTIE (Leland Jones), GREG BRYK (William "Billy" Orser), KYLE SCHMIDT (Bobby).

"I saw you turn into Joey right before my eyes. I saw a killer."

Tom Stall (Viggo Mortensen) is a man satisfied with life. He owns a modest, thriving diner in Millbrook, a small town in the US state of Indiana. His marriage to pretty lawyer Edie (Maria Bello) still has the spark of the early years. Even their two children, 15-year-old Jack (Ashton Holmes) and little Sarah (Heidi Hayes), have turned out well. A picture-perfect family. Yet a shadow falls over it when one day two sinister figures appear in Tom's fast-food restaurant and pull out their weapons. Tom actually manages to kill them, and becomes a local hero in the process, attracting national media coverage. But his peaceful life is over. Soon afterward, Carl Fogarty (Ed Harris), an East Coast gangster, shows up at Tom's place to settle an old score. For what neither his family nor anyone else in Millbrook realizes is that Tom, whose real name is Joey Cusack, used to be a mafia hit man himself in Philadelphia.

David Cronenberg was never a man for a relaxed night at the movies. For four decades, the Canadian director has been shattering audiences with weird, nightmarish movies in which he visualizes physical deformations, transformations and mutations with arcane pleasure. This is one of the main reasons why his films have acquired cult status, especially *Videodrome* (1983) and *The Fly* (1986). The fact that they are by no means appreciated only by devoted horror fans, and that critics regard Cronenberg as a film artist ranking alongside David Lynch, can be explained by both the brilliant and original

2

3

"Other films this year will have to sweat bullets to match the explosive power and subversive wit of David Cronenberg's *A History of Violence*. It slams you like a body punch and then starts messing with your head."

Rolling Stone

1 Faced with the unexpected (male) violence threatening her family, Edie (Maria Bello) also reaches for a gun.

2 The killer inside: a brutal side lies dormant within loving family man Tom (Viggo Mortensen) that …

3 … seems to match that of ruthless gangster Fogarty (Ed Harris).

4 Home becomes a prison: Maria Bello was nominated for a Golden Globe for her outstanding performance as Edie.

craftsmanship in his work and its subversive nature. *A History of Violence*, a detour into the genre movie for Cronenberg, combines all these qualities, though at first glance there seems very little to indicate the maestro's trademark signature in this straightforward thriller based on a graphic novel – except for Fogarty's deformed left eye. Even the violent climaxes are more reminiscent of Tarantino with their stylized elegance and subtle comedy. The storyline, too, has an ultra-stateside feel to it: the hero whose past catches up with him; the family man who defends his home against threat; the pastoral idyll threatened by big cities – these are all archetypal patterns in American cinema. Cronenberg, however, who described his movie as an example of "americana," uses the classic tale in order to rupture and reflect it in a subtle way.

For what primarily distinguishes Tom Stall from popular Hollywood heroes is that his capacity for violent conflict resolution takes on pathological features – all the more because, for so long and in so convincing a way, he has managed to hide his past from the family as well as the audience. When Fogarty and Tom's mafioso brother Richie (William Hurt) – who enters the plot later –

VIGGO MORTENSEN Hardly any other figure in the international movie business is as multi-talented as Viggo Mortensen. Born in New York City in 1958 to an American mother and Danish father, he spent his childhood in different European and South American countries, which explains his fluency in English, Spanish, Italian and Danish. From school, the strikingly handsome athlete – who is also an excellent horseman – went on to study politics and Spanish. In the early 1980s, he embarked on his acting career, but this did not stop him simultaneously emerging as a musician, writer, painter, photographer and publisher. If Mortensen only rose to stardom in his mid-40s, this was no doubt primarily down to his wide-ranging aptitudes and a career plan that was not overly driven by commercial considerations.
The story goes that his son persuaded him to accept the part of Aragorn in Peter Jackson's *The Lord of the Rings* trilogy (2001–2003), which made him internationally famous. Mortensen's name, however, had been familiar to a smaller circle of movie buffs, if not since his screen debut in Peter Weir's *Witness* (1985) then at the very latest after his excellent performance in Sean Penn's tense family drama *The Indian Runner* (1991). In the years that followed he gave convincing performances in films as varied as *Carlito's Way* (1993), *The Portrait of a Lady* (1996), *G.I. Jane* (1997) and even *Psycho* (1998). Of course, he rarely had top billing, but that has all changed now. David Cronenberg has cast him in a leading role twice in succession: firstly in *A History of Violence* (2005) and then in the gripping Russian mafia thriller *Eastern Promises* (2007), in which he was outstanding as an undercover go-between, a role that earned Mortensen an Oscar nomination.

describe Tom as being a natural at killing, it is merely confirmed by the automatic way in which he wipes out his opponents. No matter how much Tom reassures Edie that he has changed, he cannot shake off his past. Joey is part of him: his dark side.

Yet Cronenberg is, ostensibly at least, less concerned about revealing his hero's essentially violent nature than with providing the audience with an intensely unsettling movie experience. For, in the final analysis, it is the killer in Tom that makes him so attractive to us. This is demonstrated in a particularly extreme way by a disturbingly erotic scene. When Edie realizes she has married a violent criminal, her reaction is one of disgust, and she shrinks away from Tom's tender approaches. He pursues her, however, overpowers her on the stairs, and forces her to have sex. And she succumbs, visibly aroused by his aggressiveness, only to withdraw again after the raw act, she is nauseated, but this time by herself as well. Tom's violence, as appalling as it may seem, not only arouses Edie's desire, but also makes us as viewers receptive to it as well. Cronenberg knows that our secret wishes have nothing to do with morality. Joey is part of us too.

So do bloodthirsty pictures have an inherently cathartic effect? In the end, Tom kills his brother Richie, eliminating to an extent his evil alter ego. He then washes off the blood in a lake and returns to his family. The intense finale shows Edie and the children sitting at the table. Tom appears; he hesitates in the doorway, an anxious look on his face. Eventually, the daughter sets out a plate for him and the son passes the meat to his father. Edie and Tom, however, observe each other in silence. A fresh start? Perhaps. JH

6

5 He was a brilliant hero as Aragorn in Peter Jackson's *Lord of the Rings* (2001/2002/2003) trilogy, whereas David Cronenberg here casts Viggo Mortensen as a good citizen with a murderous past.

6 *A History of Violence* gives us excellent actors even in supporting roles: whether it is William Hurt as Tom's older brother …

7 … Ed Harris as a cold-blooded killer, or …

8 … Ashton Holmes as Tom's son – all of them represent male characters with a violent streak that is manifested to varying degrees.

"*A History of Violence* finds Mr. Cronenberg at the top of his form. Few directors working today know more about the erotics of screen violence than this filmmaker, who can make your head spin and your pulse quicken with a single edit." *The New York Times*

7

8

THE CHILD
L'ENFANT

2005 – BELGIUM / FRANCE – 100 MIN. – DRAMA
DIRECTORS JEAN-PIERRE (*1951), LUC DARDENNE (*1954)
SCREENPLAY JEAN-PIERRE, LUC DARDENNE **DIRECTOR OF PHOTOGRAPHY** ALAIN MARCOEN
EDITING MARIE-HÉLÈNE DOZO **PRODUCTION** JEAN-PIERRE and LUC DARDENNE, DENIS FREYD for LES FILMS DU FLEUVE, ARCHIPEL 35, RTBF, SCOPE INVEST, ARTE FRANCE CINEMA.
STARRING JÉRÉMIE RENIER (Bruno), DÉBORAH FRANÇOIS (Sonia), JÉRÉMIE SEGARD (Steve), FABRIZIO RONGIONE (Young Gangster), OLIVIER GOURMET (Policeman), ANNE GÉRARD (Fence), BERNARD MARBAIX (Fence), JEAN-CLAUDE BONIVERD (Policeman), FRÉDÉRIC BODSON (Older Gangster), MARIE-ROSE ROLAND (Pregnant Woman).
IFF CANNES 2005 GOLDEN PALM (Jean-Pierre and Luc Dardenne).

"Bruno, where is Jimmy?" – "I've sold him."

A young man goes into an empty apartment, carrying a newborn baby. In a darkened room, he takes off his jacket, spreads it on the floor and carefully lays the baby on top of it. He then goes next door and waits. The silence is broken by the tone of a cell phone: "Yes?" A brief instruction. The man shuts the room door from inside. Shortly afterward, there are muffled noises from the apartment, ending with a door clicking shut, and another cell phone message. The man goes back into the first room, lifts the brown envelope lying on his jacket, opens it, and takes out a bundle of banknotes – Bruno has just sold Jimmy, his nine-day-old son.

Bruno (Jérémie Renier) is a drifter. A deadbeat crook for whom moral categories apparently do not exist. Barely an adult himself, he incites adolescents to commit thefts. And when his girlfriend Sonia (Déborah François) leaves the baby with him for a short period while she attends an appointment with the authorities, he takes the opportunity to earn a fast buck. For Bruno, everything has sales value, whether it's a cell phone, a digital camera – or even his own son. "We'll have another one," he says to Sonia when he goes back to her without Jimmy; he doesn't understand her horror at what he has done.

Bruno's home, or rather his patch, is the suburbs of the Belgian city, Seraing. It is a miserable environment, where idle factories and coal dumps bear witness to the decline of the Belgian steel industry, and freeways and discount supermarkets signal the progressive break-up of society. Brothers Jean-Pierre and Luc Dardenne also grew up in Seraing. These award-winning filmmakers keep on going back there, to tell the stories of people whom they once described as "survivors of a great tragedy."

Although the tragedy – the disintegration of an industrial community – is ever-present in *The Child* by virtue of the location itself, it is never dealt with superficially in the plot. The film is completely focused on the present-day lives of the protagonists, which are captured with documentary-style objectivity: using a hand-held camera, no background music, and apparently no directorial constraints. This means that Bruno's behavior is neither explained in depth, nor excused. The Dardenne brothers do not judge or apply psychology – they document. And they do so with a care and attention that avoids any emotion or gesture. Unlike British director, Ken Loach, with whom they are often compared due to the similarities in their subject matter, the two Belgians do not openly

1

2

indict the system. Their films do not invite the viewer to identify or take sides. For this very reason, they may initially appear brusque and inaccessible. At the same time, however, they exude a sense of authenticity and proximity to real life that is rarely found in the movies. Hence *The Child* unexpectedly acquires the weight of an existential drama when Bruno's life goes off the rails, transcending specific destinies to revolve around the question of individual guilt and the possibility of forgiveness.

Admittedly, Bruno manages to buy Jimmy back, but it does not wipe the slate clean: Sonia rejects him and reports him to the police. Even the gangsters he has become involved with do not forgive him; they force him with violence to pay for the lost business. Bruno, who had previously coped with his life of crime with the greatest of ease, now becomes a hunted man. To square his

1 The petty thief and the baby: everything has a market value for young drifter Bruno (Jérémie Renier) – even his own child.

2 Families without a future? The films of Jean-Pierre and Luc Dardenne show people whose lives are a battle for survival in places ravaged by industrial decline.

3 Jérémie Renier (*1981) is one of the Dardenne brothers' favorite actors. He plays the small-time criminal hero in a remarkably natural and sensitive way.

"Here is a film where God does not intervene and the directors do not mistake themselves for God. It makes the solutions at the ends of other pictures seem like child's play." *Chicago Sun-Times*

4

4 The viewer feels ambivalent about Bruno's behavior. On the one hand, it is irresponsible and criminal, but we also sense a deep tenderness in his relationship with Sonia (Déborah François).

5 Barely an adult himself, Bruno encourages younger children to commit crime. His own childhood seems to be reflected in the figure of young Steve (Jérémie Segard).

debts, he and an underage partner in crime commit a dangerous mugging, resulting in a breakneck getaway. They both end up having to leap into the ice-cold water of a canal in order to save their skins, and stay there for several agonizingly long moments. But it is to no avail; when the boy is caught, Bruno hands himself in to the police and shoulders the blame.

In a painfully direct way, *The Child* visualizes the consequences that Bruno must suffer for his actions. In doing so, the film also conveys an idea of the icy implacability of a society that made Bruno's moral bankruptcy possible in the first place. Whether the hardships he has suffered have had a cathartic effect in the meantime, and whether he truly acknowledges his guilt or is merely resigned to it, remains open in the final analysis. There is still hope, however: the film ends with Sonia visiting Bruno in prison. Sobbing, he clasps her hands; the final scene shows the couple crying as they sit together at the table. A fresh start? Perhaps. But the very fact that Bruno is capable of shedding tears seems like a minor miracle in this moving film. JH

JEAN-PIERRE AND LUC DARDENNE Their movies, which evoke comparisons with Robert Bresson's by virtue of their artistic clarity and philosophical depth, are lacking in glamour to say the least. Furthermore, they always seem a little out of place in the parade of stars at Cannes. All the same, Jean-Pierre and Luc Dardenne now rank as the unofficial kings of the French festival, for the Belgian brothers are among the few directors who have won the main award twice, the Golden Palm (Palme d'Or), at the most important film festival in the world.

Raised in the Belgian province of Liège, the brothers began their career as producers and directors of politically engaged documentaries in the 1970s. They made the leap to feature films with *Falsch* (1986), yet remained committed to representing the social reality of their native region. The Dardennes had their breakthrough ten years later with *La Promesse* (1996), a crushingly intense movie about illegal immigration, in the course of which they worked for the first time with Olivier Gourmet and Jérémie Renier, who was then only 15 years old: they would become established as their favorite actors.

Rosetta (1999), the story of a girl's fight for survival with an alcoholic mother, brought the filmmakers their first major success in Cannes. With their next movie, *The Son* (*Le fils*, 2002), a complex drama about a carpentry teacher who takes on his own son's murderer in his workshop, the directing team turned in another masterpiece that brought Olivier Gourmet the Best Actor award at Cannes.

The Child (*L'enfant*, 2005), in which their minimalist cinematic technique reached full maturity, won the Dardenne brothers a second Golden Palm. Their success story in Cannes then reached its conclusion (for the time being) with the Best Screenplay award for their movie *Lorna's Silence* (*Le silence de Lorna*, 2008), which once again deals with the theme of immigration.

THE CONSTANT GARDENER

2005 – UK / GERMANY – 129 MIN. – POLITICAL THRILLER
DIRECTOR FERNANDO MEIRELLES (*1955)
SCREENPLAY JEFFREY CAINE, from the novel of the same name by JOHN LE CARRÉ
DIRECTOR OF PHOTOGRAPHY CÉSAR CHARLONE EDITING CLAIRE SIMPSON MUSIC ALBERTO IGLESIAS
PRODUCTION SIMON CHANNING WILLIAMS for POTBOILER PRODUCTIONS, EPSILON MOTION PICTURES, SCION FILMS, UK FILM COUNCIL AND VIERTE BABELSBERG FILM.
STARRING RALPH FIENNES (Justin Quayle), RACHEL WEISZ (Tessa Quayle), HUBERT KOUNDÉ (Dr. Arnold Bluhm), DANNY HUSTON (Sandy Woodrow), BILL NIGHY (Sir Bernard Pellegrin), RICHARD MCCABE (Arthur "Ham" Hammond), ARCHIE PANJABI (Ghita Pearson), PETE POSTLETHWAITE (Dr. Lorbeer), ANNEKE KIM SARNAU (Birgit).
ACADEMY AWARDS 2006 OSCAR for BEST SUPPORTING ACTRESS (Rachel Weisz).

"Yeah, but these are three people that we can help."

The colors of this film are burned into our memory. Turquoise and rust-red blend together in the images of Lake Turkana in Kenya, as if in a psychedelic mise-en-scène, while the slums of Nairobi glisten under the African sun in shades of strong red, blue and dirty orange. By contrast, London and Berlin lie under a gray veil, any color in the images virtually washed out. The difference could not be greater, but it strikes at the heart of the conflict addressed by this film: the exploitation of the black continent by the Western world. In this movie, Africa is not an object of desire that takes Europeans back to the essentials of life with its romantic sunsets and spectacular nature. No, here Africa is the backyard of our civilization, and Africans are its guinea pigs, who suffer and die for our prosperity. Hence Africa's colors burn themselves into the viewer's vision like a shrill accusation, while the grayness of Europe indicates a combination of threat, misery and guilt. Brazilian director Fernando Meirelles (*Cidade de Deus / City of God*, 2002) successfully uses color to reflect the psychological profile of the main character, a man caught between geography and politics. Justin Quayle (Ralph Fiennes) is a quiet diplomat with no interest in carving out a career for himself. He is posted to Africa to coordinate aid for the British High Commission. The audience, however, only discovers this some time later.

The film begins with a death. Tessa (Rachel Weisz), Justin's beautiful young wife, is killed at Lake Turkana: viciously murdered by unknown parties. The story behind this unfolds in a series of flashbacks. Tessa and Justin meet at a lecture, where she makes a passionate attack on the policies of the British government; he is captivated by her spirit. When he is posted to Africa, she asks him to take her with him. Together with a Kenyan doctor (Hubert Koundé) she is investigating a pharmaceutical scandal, which it later transpires has penetrated the highest government circles. The only response she gets to a written report she sends to London about Justin's boss is a prejudiced letter.

1

"There is more to the film than a twisting plot and a topical hook, and also more than visual bravura, colorful locations and fine, mostly British, acting. [...] This is a supremely well-executed piece of popular entertainment that is likely to linger in your mind and may even trouble your conscience." *The New York Times*

1 Justin Quayle (Ralph Fiennes) loves his garden more than anything. But he is forced to face the painful fact that the world is not a garden in bloom.

2 His wife's death hits Justin hard. He begins to think seriously about her work in Kenya.

3 In the slums of Nairobi: Tessa (Rachel Weisz) is a passionate activist, campaigning for people in Africa.

A few days later, Tessa is dead. As he mourns her death, Justin begins to ask questions about Tessa's work. His only pleasure had been tending to his garden, but he now takes up Tessa's research and, in doing so, feels closer to her than he had when she was alive. Suspended from his job and without a diplomatic passport (which has been taken away from him) he throws himself into a frantic odyssey across Europe and Africa to find out what really happened. He is soon privy to what Tessa had discovered: on the orders of a global pharmaceutical company, a British firm called ThreeBees is testing an as yet unlicensed medicine for treating tuberculosis on the slum dwellers of Nairobi. People are dying of it, but anyone who refuses to take the medicine is denied any further healthcare. But he unearths even more: not only do the British government and his bosses know about the trials, they actually support them. "We're not killing anyone who wouldn't die anyway" is the cynical excuse given by Justin's diplomatic colleague, Sandy (Danny Huston). The noose around Justin's neck is becoming ever tighter. Hit men are targeting him as well, yet it almost seems as if he is seeking death himself. Like his wife, he dies on the shores of Lake Turkana, a mystical non-place that reunites him with Tessa.

The Constant Gardener is an extraordinary movie with a cast of outstanding actors, even in the most minor roles. With his restrained yet expressive performance, Ralph Fiennes placed controversial, topical themes under the

FERNANDO MEIRELLES Cinema in Brazil may not be as famous as its football, but in the last few years movies from this South American country have become increasingly well known. This is due not least to Fernando Meirelles, whose masterpiece *City of God* (*Cidade de Deus*, 2002) received four Oscar nominations and reached an audience of millions. Shot in the *favelas* of Rio de Janeiro, he cast nearly all the parts with non-professional actors, his innovative camera direction and fast editing technique totally convincing. As he says himself, he acquired his craft mainly by shooting ads and music videos: "In advertising I learned how to film, how to be concise, and how to convey what you mean – that is a fantastic school" (planetinterview.de).

Fernando Meirelles was born in 1955 in São Paulo, Brazil. After qualifying as an architect, he made experimental films and worked in television during the 1980s, where he made a name for himself with popular children's programs. His first material for grown-ups was *Maids* (*Domésticas*, 2001), the movie he made about the daily lives of female domestics in São Paulo. His big international break then came with *City of God*, from a screenplay by Paulo Lins. The film's success in Brazil even spawned a TV series entitled "City of Men" ("Cidade dos Homens," 2002–2005), which was also shot in the *favelas*. Three years after his surprise hit, Meirelles made another international movie. The book by seasoned political thriller writer John Le Carré gave us *The Constant Gardener* (2005), a poetic film about a controversial subject: the entanglements of politics and business in Africa. Meirelles' latest movie, *Blindness* (2008), from a novel by the Nobel prizewinning Portuguese writer José Saramago, opened the 61st Cannes Film Festival. Despite his international success, Fernando Meirelles lives and works in Brazil, where he also made the series for television "Som e Fúria" (Sound and Fury) in 2009; he also keeps busy as a producer.

"There is a terrific pulse of energy in this film, a voltage which drives it over two hours. It is not just an intricate, despairing meditation on the shabby compromises involved in maintaining Britain's interests and waning foreign prestige. There is real anger here, and a real sense that it is worthwhile striking back against wrongdoing." *The Guardian*

6

4 Justin's colleague Sandy Woodrow (Danny Huston) knows more than he lets on.

5 Dr. Lorbeer (Pete Postlethwaite) has already penetrated deep into the "dark heart of Africa."

6 A *tour de force* across the continent: Justin is determined to find out who killed his wife, thereby putting his own life in danger.

7 The film ends with an imaginary meeting between the two lovers. Justin's murderers are already right behind him.

ens of a microscope. For Justin, the sophisticated European, this political awakening becomes a *tour de force* through his own mind. Fernando Meirelles finds coherent images for both the political and the psychological levels. As n his first big hit *City of God* (*Cidade de Deus*, 2002), which is set in the *favelas* of Rio de Janeiro, here too he films the slum quarters with a cinematic excess that interrupts the narrative flow. Above all, the rhythm created by the camerawork and editing, together with the highly reflexive and poetic use of cinematic devices, prevent the movie from becoming a political device. Fernando Meirelles is not primarily concerned with such messages in his films: "I certainly don't see myself as an activist or political filmmaker," he said in an interview for the Swiss movie website OutNow.CH. "They are simply things I find interesting. The next one I make could be a romantic comedy." KK

GOOD NIGHT, AND GOOD LUCK

2005 – USA / UK / FRANCE / JAPAN – 93 MIN. – B/W – POLITICAL THRILLER
DIRECTOR GEORGE CLOONEY (*1961)
SCREENPLAY GEORGE CLOONEY, GRANT HESLOV DIRECTOR OF PHOTOGRAPHY ROBERT ELSWIT
EDITING STEPHEN MIRRIONE MUSIC ALLEN SVIRIDOFF, DIANNE REEVES
PRODUCTION GRANT HESLOV for WARNER INDEPENDENT PICTURES, 2929 PRODUCTIONS, PARTICIPANT PRODUCTIONS, DAVIS-FILMS, REDBUS PICTURES, TOHOKUSHINSHA FILM, SECTION EIGHT.
STARRING DAVID STRATHAIRN (Edward R. Murrow), GEORGE CLOONEY (Fred Friendly), JEFF DANIELS (Sig Mickelson), FRANK LANGELLA (William Paley), ROBERT DOWNEY JR. (Joe Wershba), PATRICIA CLARKSON (Shirley Wershba), RAY WISE (Don Hollenbeck), MATT ROSS (Eddie Scott), THOMAS MCCARTHY (Palmer Williams), REED DIAMOND (John Aaron).
IFF VENICE 2005 VOLPI CUP for BEST ACTOR (David Strathairn), GOLDEN OSELLA for BEST SCREENPLAY (George Clooney, Grant Heslov).

"We're going to do this story now, because the terror is right here in this room!"

The film begins as a tribute to its protagonists and actors. Sweeping across a banqueting hall, the camera captures in soft black-and-white images all those involved in "See It Now" – the legendary news broadcast from Columbia Broadcasting System in the 1950s. A group photo is brought to life. It is also a picture of the film crew: Fred Friendly, played by the movie's writer and director, George Clooney, stands alongside Don Hewitt, played by Grant Heslov, co-writer and producer of the film. They are flanked on either side by some of Hollywood's major B-listers: Robert Downey Jr., Matt Ross and Tom McCarthy. The only woman on the editorial staff (Patricia Clarkson as Shirley Wershba) is taking the photo. Only one man is missing – the movie's hero and lead actor.

Edward R. Murrow, played by David Strathairn, stands backstage, inhaling one of his countless cigarettes. It is October 8, 1958. The respected TV journalist is about to give a speech before the assembled hierarchy of the American media association. He begins, but, after a few moments, the smiles freeze on the faces of everyone present. Murrow tells them straight that, if things continue the way they are, television can safely abdicate its role as an informative medium. His words are eloquent, linguistically honed warnings about a questionable system. The viewer immediately senses that, in this film, precision of speech and thought are far more important than epic breadth and passion. Where a nation no longer has the courage to believe in itself, the heart will yet beat

1

2

1 David Strathairn as Edward R. Murrow. He has a cigarette in his mouth in practically every scene. Committed to the truth, and nothing but the truth, Murrow had no regard for his own health in his crusade to tell people the facts.

2 Director George Clooney and producer Grant Heslov turned back the clock for their CBS News biopic with its meticulous attention to detail. Don Hollenbeck, played by Ray Wise, reads the latest news.

3 George Clooney excelled: not only as the director, but also in a supporting role. As Fred Friendly, the resourceful and courageous executive producer of CBS News, he was at his best.

– this is the theme of the movie, and a fundamentally American one at that. George Clooney, who found himself exposed to considerable public censure because of his misgivings about the US invasion of Iraq, took a piece of contemporary American history and journalistic moral courage and made it his own. The present day was reflected in the historic instance of CBS versus McCarthy. Just as Senator McCarthy busied himself in the early 50s with what he perceived as widespread "Reds under the bed," President George W. Bush claimed the existence of nuclear weapons in Iraq. In each case, and the movie shows this in a wonderfully intelligent and precise way, civil rights and liberal values are the first victims of political caprice and collective hysteria.

The movie achieves an impressive balance between cinematic effect and contemporary historical authenticity. Real documentary footage is artistically edited into the film. Apart from two scenes, the action never leaves the editorial rooms of the CBS studio; this gives the movie a claustrophobic atmosphere

SENATOR JOSEPH MCCARTHY VS. EDWARD R. MURROW "The good old senator from Wisconsin always played himself best" – as Grant Heslov and George Clooney established when preparing for *Good Night, and Good Luck*. So they deliberately avoided casting the part of Joseph McCarthy. His TV appearance on the CBS broadcast "See It Now" in 1954 was a milestone on the road to his political self-demolition. In hindsight, his performance was so grotesque that it is hard to believe the power and influence that this politician once exercised on American society. But things that seem crazy in retrospect are usually the ordinary moments in contemporary history.

McCarthy not only fuelled fears of Communist infiltration, he burned himself on their flames in the end. In the long run, no enlightened, liberal society can endure the stream of discourse and accusations that McCarthy disgorged on the nation. In a cheap attempt at self-defence, he accused one of the least corruptible left-wing supporters imaginable – the publicly respected journalist Edward R. Murrow – and corrupted himself in the process. He was no longer pursuing an educational goal, but instead a witch-hunt. Murrow did not even have to attack the senator personally to arouse his wrath; all he did was expose his denunciation techniques. McCarthy behaved like a bull on the TV program, swaggeringly clawing the ground with his hoof, steam snorting from his nostrils, and then charging wildly at Murrow. The latter did not even pull aside the proverbial red cloth, but simply let the senator run right into it. Behind it was nothing but a wall of generally known facts and public trust.

When McCarthy tried yet again to denounce someone in a commission set up against him at the end of 1954, a lawyer hurled the question furiously at him: "Have you no sense of decency, sir, at long last? Have you left no sense of decency?" The hearing, which like many others was transmitted on TV, finally tipped public opinion against the senator from Wisconsin. McCarthy would no longer be tolerated. He died three years later of cirrhosis of the liver.

“Clooney’s point will not please everybody. Clooney is suggesting that the fear McCarthy was trading in, the fear people have of getting blown up, is pervasive today; that the spirit of McCarthy, an authoritarianism disguised in patriotic language, lives on; and that TV news is no longer a match for it.” *Der Tagesspiegel*

4

while simultaneously creating the sense of a close-knit, intimate workplace. The tension is counterbalanced with cool jazz inserts that are recorded live and reflect the spirit of hand-crafted, analogue TV. Clouds of silver smoke unfurl steadily in the light. Clooney joked about the filming, saying it was the only set where people went outside *not* to smoke. The heightened atmosphere is sustained most effectively through deliberate pauses in actions and words. In the three or four seconds before Murrow goes on air, the whole weight of journalistic responsibility is expressed in his face. The entire film is shot with telephoto lenses that capture even the slightest movement. When David Strathairn raises an eyebrow or forcefully exhales cigarette smoke, it speaks volumes. With a brief, contemptuous, sidelong glance, he exposes all the shallowness of an interview with a celebrity that he has to conduct in order to bring in viewers and advertising revenue for the broadcaster. We feast on these angry, disdainful, tense and uncompromising looks from Strathairn that permeate the movie. The film reflects the ambivalent role of television as a medium of information and entertainment. Yet when the plug is finally pulled by network boss William Paley (an impressive performance by Frank Langella) on the heroes and "See It Now," this does not signal the end of their principled journalistic approach. It is, however, the beginning of a change in direction toward commercialism. When their program is dropped, Fred Friendly and Ed Murrow react with composure and black humor; probably the only irrevocable way of countering all forms of power and political narrow-mindedness. SR

"Clooney's excellent film uses the past to make today's media and their audiences address their responsibilities." *The Guardian*

5

"Clooney made this film because he was furious: furious that the American media had described him as a 'traitor,' because he took part in a demonstration in 2003; and furious about a political system that was blatantly defended by the media. For this reason, *Good Night* became a film about the political responsibility of the media." *Frankfurter Allgemeine Sonntagszeitung*

4 Still a distinctly male domain in the 1950s: planning the editorial strategy against Senator Joseph McCarthy. Also in league: Joe Wershba, played by Robert Downey Jr.

5 Even the cigarette cloud cannot darken the light of truth. A news item is read through first, and then broadcast. The broadcast station ends up firing its own heroes.

6 David Strathairn gives a powerful performance as Edward R. Murrow. Murrow's famous "Good night, and good luck" at the end of each presentation provided the title for the film.

BROKEBACK MOUNTAIN

2005 – USA / CANADA – 134 MIN. – MELODRAMA
DIRECTOR ANG LEE (*1954)
SCREENPLAY LARRY MCMURTRY, DIANA OSSANA, from a short story by ANNIE PROULX
DIRECTOR OF PHOTOGRAPHY RODRIGO PRIETO EDITING GERALDINE PERONI, DYLAN TICHENOR
MUSIC GUSTAVO SANTAOLALLA PRODUCTION DIANA OSSANA, JAMES SCHAMUS for GOOD MACHINE, ALBERTA FILM ENTERTAINMENT, FOCUS FEATURES, RIVER ROAD ENTERTAINMENT, PARAMOUNT PICTURES.
STARRING HEATH LEDGER (Ennis Del Mar), JAKE GYLLENHAAL (Jack Twist), RANDY QUAID (Joe Aguirre), MICHELLE WILLIAMS (Alma), ANNE HATHAWAY (Lureen Newsome), LINDA CARDELLINI (Cassie), KATE MARA (Alma Jr.), MARY LIBOIRON (Fayette Newsome), GRAHAM BECKEL (L. D. Newsome), ANNA FARIS (Lashawn Malone), DAVID HARBOUR (Randall Malone).
ACADEMY AWARDS 2006 OSCARS for BEST DIRECTING (Ang Lee), BEST ADAPTED SCREENPLAY (Larry McMurtry, Diana Ossana) and BEST MUSIC (Gustavo Santaolalla).
IFF VENICE 2005 GOLDEN LION (Ang Lee).

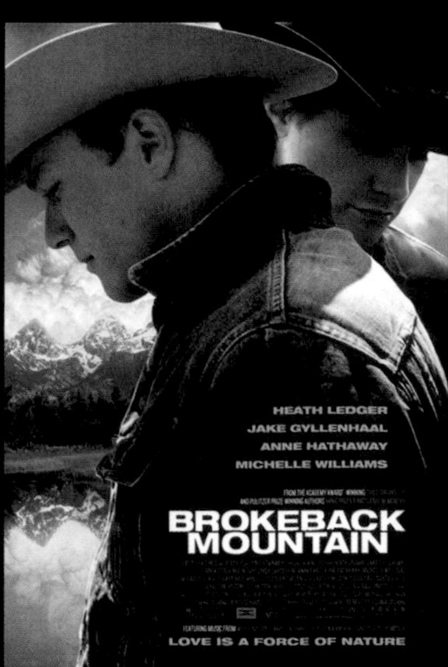

"I don't get you, Ennis Del Mar."

Two men are cooling their heels in a parking lot in Signal, Wyoming. They size each other up with brief, furtive glances, their cowboy hats pulled down over their faces and fingers tucked into their jeans pockets. If this was a Sergio Leone western, they would promptly draw their pistols and shoot each other. But these two are waiting for work. It's hard to believe that in 1963 there were actually cowboys plying their trade. Jack Twist (Jake Gyllenhaal) and Ennis Del Mar (Heath Ledger) are off to herd sheep up on Brokeback Mountain. They will eat beans and get extremely bored in the wilderness; until, that is, they do something that cowboys have never done in films before.

The now famous love scene in the tent, which appears more like a wrestling match, is a short one. Yet it was enough to turn *Brokeback Mountain* into a political football. Seldom has a film been awaited with such anticipation as Ang Lee's "gay western," especially after it won the Golden Lion award in Venice. Conservative elements were thrown into disarray, to the delight of their liberal opponents. The Taiwanese director was accused of bringing complete disgrace to this male genre. Or was it not more that he had "deconstructed" it, turning it on its head? Suddenly, everyone realized what had really happened back then in *Red River* (1948) between John Wayne and Montgomery Clift; the subtext became the text. Yet Lee's film is far more complex than this and, even after several viewings, remains so full of questions and ambiguities that it defies any categorization. It positively shies away from commitment, apparently uncertain of its message – just like its central character, the lone rancher Ennis Del Mar, heart-achingly played by the late Heath Ledger.

When their work is done, Ennis leaves a disappointed Jack with a curt "see you around." Shortly afterward, Jack throws up. On the morning after their experience together in the tent, he had come across a sheep torn to

1

pieces in the herd: punishment for his transgression and a reminder of a brutal trauma in childhood. He knows from his father what happens to gay men in these parts. In fact, however, it is his inner limitations alone that stand in the way of true love. He is the one who hides behind the clichéd image of the lonesome ranger, who represses his feelings, and who maintains the façade of the hard man. This will eventually destroy Jack, as well as Ennis' wife Alma (Michelle Williams), whom he later marries and has children with, ignoring his own feelings. Two decades of hippie culture and gay rights activism pass in the time period covered by this film, which has imperceptibly attained the status of American epic.

Lee's heroes, however, are always prisoners of their own rules and beliefs. Once or twice a year, Ennis and Jack meet for a "fishing trip" on Brokeback

"Both Mr Ledger and Mr Gyllenhaal make this anguished love story physically palpable. Mr Ledger magically and mysteriously disappears beneath the skin of his lean, sinewy character. It is a great screen performance, as good as the best of Marlon Brando and Sean Penn." *The New York Times*

3

1 Seasoned cowboys: Ennis (Heath Ledger) and Jack (Jake Gyllenhaal) meet when looking for work. Real cowboys were unemployed in 1963.

2 Gay or straight? Ledger and Gyllenhaal play with the visual vocabulary of the Western genre. Their love must remain a secret.

3 Faraway, so close: the two men can only express their love in the isolation of Brokeback Mountain.

4 A milestone in gay cinema: the love between two cowboys, sensitively filmed by director Ang Lee, lit a longstanding fuse.

Mountain (Alma alone knows in her heart what is really happening). But Brokeback Mountain is not enough. As in John Ford's Monument Valley, the vast plains of Wyoming – stunningly filmed by Rodrigo Prieto in Alberta – provide space, but do not suffice. The trips there (which have become tortuous for Jack, who despairs of his lover) are as inadequate for life as the beans were back then. Tragedy strikes Ennis in the end, along with the realization that he has done everything wrong: the victim of his own self-denial and shame, but also of his ingrained conservatism.

Deep down, *Brokeback Mountain* is pure melodrama about forbidden love; a series of painful scenes that are more Douglas Sirk than John Ford. It is certainly not the film that Gus Van Sant would have made although, along with Joel Schumacher, he had expressed an interest in this short story by

ANG LEE Ang Lee is one of the most prominent and, above all, most versatile filmmakers of our time. In nearly every film, he dips into another culture, in a way that always reveals more commonalities than differences. For, while he works through his personal themes time after time, with the unique capacity for empathy that is all his own, Ang Lee produces a film from every culture, whether it is ancient China or England circa 1800; the focus for him is the conflict between modernity and tradition, between the individual and society.

This migrant's take on different cultural environments has a solid autobiographical base. Born to Taiwanese parents, who moved back to their homeland in the wake of the Cultural Revolution, he spent time in China as a child; Lee then immigrated to the USA in 1978 after completing his film studies at the age of 24. His first three films – *Pushing Hands / Tui shou* (1991/92), *The Wedding Banquet / Xi yan*, (1992/1993) and *Eat Drink Man Woman / Yin shi nan nu* (1994) – were made as Taiwan/US co-productions. These humorous stories of Taiwanese migrants living in American exile soon made him an international favorite at festivals. The elegiac film version of the Jane Austen novel *Sense and Sensibility* (1995) – the label fits just about all of his films – also gave him his big commercial break. He went on to demonstrate that emotional tension between the sexes was not restricted to the English landed gentry with *The Ice Storm* (1997), a painful satire about the promises of freedom of 70s America. With *Crouching Tiger, Hidden Dragon / Wo hu cang long* (2000), an Oscar-winning homage to Hong Kong cinema with positively lyrical fight scenes, Lee moved over effortlessly to the blockbuster business; however, his follow-up film adaptation *Hulk* (2003) backfired. So the outstanding success of *Brokeback Mountain* (2005) was all the more surprising: a pretty small-scale production that was nonetheless controversial. He promptly reprised his Golden Lion success in Venice with the Chinese resistance thriller *Lust, Caution / Se, jie* (2007). The complete list of film awards won by Ang Lee is immense.

6

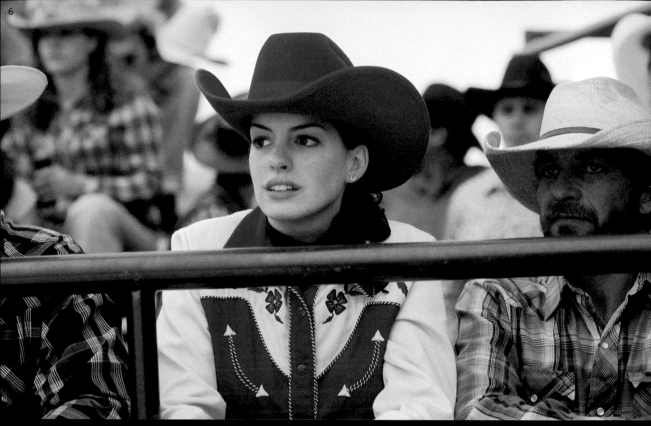

5 Obvious symbolism: while Jack looks ahead bravely, Ennis is still plagued with doubts. Heath Ledger's performance ranks as the best of his career.

6 Self-confident rodeo queen Lureen marries Jack. For the first time, Anne Hathaway became a candidate for serious roles.

7 Ennis gets married, too but his union with Alma (Michelle Williams) turns out even unhappier than Jack's. She really loves him.

8 The role did no harm to Jake Gyllenhaal. Quite the reverse: the young nerd became an action star and sex symbol after *Brokeback Mountain.*

"This slow and stoic movie, hailed as a gay Western, feels neither gay nor especially Western: it is a study of love under siege." *The New Yorker*

Annie Proulx. You don't make "queer cinema" with two heterosexual lead actors who are established favorites with the ladies and who maintain both on- and off-screen they are "not gay." Perhaps it was simply Ang Lee's unmitigated gall in making his lovers wear cowboy hats, or directing them with the same discretion and empathy as he always does, whether in *Sense and Sensibility* (1995) or *The Ice Storm* (1997). And when the film lost out to *Crash* (2004) in the Academy Award for Best Motion Picture, it was immediately interpreted by a disappointed fan base as a backlash. Yet Ang Lee's courageous plea against intolerance, for which he won the Oscar for Best Directing, had clearly increased awareness. Brokeback Mountain represented a milestone for Hollywood: one that remains unique to date. PB

7

CAPOTE

2005 – CANADA / USA – 114 MIN. – DRAMA, BIOPIC
DIRECTOR BENNETT MILLER (*1966)
SCREENPLAY DAN FUTTERMAN from the book "CAPOTE: A BIOGRAPHY" by GERALD CLARKE
DIRECTOR OF PHOTOGRAPHY ADAM KIMMEL EDITING CHRISTOPHER TELLEFSEN MUSIC MYCHAEL DANNA
PRODUCTION CAROLINE BARON, MICHAEL OHOVEN, WILLIAM VINCE for A-LINE PICTURES, COOPER'S TOWN PRODUCTIONS, INFINITY MEDIA.

STARRING PHILIP SEYMOUR HOFFMAN (Truman Capote), CATHERINE KEENER (Nelle Harper Lee), CLIFTON COLLINS JR. (Perry Smith), CHRIS COOPER (Alvin Dewey), BOB BALABAN (William Shawn), BRUCE GREENWOOD (Jack Dunphy), AMY RYAN (Marie Dewey), MARK PELLEGRINO (Richard Hickock), ALLIE MICKELSON (Laura Kinney), ADAM KIMMEL (Richard Avedon).
ACADEMY AWARDS 2006 OSCAR for BEST ACTOR IN A LEADING ROLE (Philip Seymour Hoffman).

"If I leave here without understanding you, the world will see you as a monster. I don't want that."

A subject seeks out its author – the romantic concept of a writer's creative process. According to this biopic's narrative, this is actually how Truman Capote's novel "In Cold Blood" came about. A small news item in the "New York Times" in November 1959 leapt off the page for writer Truman Capote (Philip Seymour Hoffman): a farmer's family – father, mother, 16-year-old daughter and 15-year-old son – had been shot dead in Holcomb, a sleepy little town of 2000 inhabitants in Kansas in the Midwest. On the spur of the moment, Capote traveled to Kansas to write an article about the case. His planned short research trip became three years in all, during which time Capote researched the case. And, instead of the article, he wrote a book that made him world famous and founded a new literary genre – the factual novel.

Capote is a great and very moving film – astonishingly enough, the work of two novices. Bennett Miller (*Moneyball*, 2011) had never directed before, while Dan Futterman was originally an actor (*The Birdcage*, 1996) now writing his first screenplay. Using Gerald Clarke's biography of Capote as source material, they tell the story of the genesis of "In Cold Blood," starting from the moment when Capote spots the news item and ending with the publication of the book.

A celebrated star of New York's bohemian society since the success of his novel "Breakfast at Tiffany's" (1958), Capote meets with suspicion at first in the little town of Holcomb. The town is in shock, its inhabitants disturbed by a stranger, especially someone like Capote, with his camp demeanor and falsetto voice. He arrives with his dear friend and assistant Harper Lee (Catherine Keener); an author herself, she would go on to win the Pulitzer Prize two years later with "To Kill a Mockingbird." Together, they gradually manage to make a connection with the small town's community. Sheriff Alvin Dewey (Chris Cooper) invites them to his home, and they even end up spending Thanksgiving with him and his family.

1

“What makes Bennett Miller’s film so interesting is its determination to cast Capote not as the hero of his own endeavour, but as its Shakespearean villain: a vampiric opportunist seeking literary laurels amid a wreckage of lives, and literally opening the coffin lids on a quadruple murder that would inspire the best book he never deserved to write.” *Sight and Sound*

1 Truman Capote: the darling of New York bohemian society sets out on a journey into the realm of evil.

2 Capote and his confidante Harper Lee (Catherine Keener) go to great lengths to investigate the background to the horrific crime and give a voice to the two suspects.

3 Tough sheriff Alvin Dewey (Chris Cooper) – convinced by the sincerity and seriousness of Capote's intentions – cooperates with him.

4 A successful hunt: the suspects picked up, Sheriff Dewey delivers Perry Smith (Clifton Collins Jr.) …

5 … and Richard Hickock (Mark Pellegrino, right) to prison in Lansing (Kansas), where they are hanged four-and-a-half years later.

The case takes a new turn when the culprits – Perry Smith (Clifton Collins Jr.) and Richard "Dick" Hickock (Mark Pellegrino) – are captured in Las Vegas. Capote interviews them both, trying to find out about their life stories, motives and how the crime happened. Through endless hours of conversation, Capote and Smith become closer, and a trust verging on sympathy develops. Capote also becomes an active participant rather than a mere observer: he helps them both, arranging lawyers for them. "I also want them to stay alive" he says at one point. "I still need their story after all." *Capote* is the fascinating and disturbing story about how a work of art originates. More than anything, it is about a clash between different worlds. The dark world of crime meets the good, decent world of respectable Americans. It results in six deaths: the four family members and the two perpetrators who are eventually executed. The monstrous nature of this clash becomes especially noticeable in the contrast between the beautiful, almost contemplative images of rural Kansas captured by cameraman Adam Kimmel, and the mental image of the crime committed there. The flamboyant world of the famous gay writer and darling of the moment, Truman Capote, also came face to face with that of Perry Smith, a violent criminal with a record. What remained was an emotionally damaged author who would not write another novel in his lifetime. Surprisingly, Capote found things in common with Smith in the process: he was also creative – gifted at drawing – and, like him, grew up without parents. The relationship between these two men becomes the definitive duel in the film: the novelist finally uses lies and emotional blackmail to extract from the murderer the detailed account of the night of the crime. Although Capote feels sympathy for the man charged

"Adam Kimmel's controlled camera work creates a textured, grainy visual field, its retro flavor enhanced by a desaturated color palette and a painterly eye for the empty, wintry landscapes." *Variety*

6

7

6 Torn between pity – love, even – for Smith and the desire to complete the novel "In Cold Blood," Capote becomes a lonely man.

7 Another real writer: Harper Lee wrote the novel "To Kill a Mockingbird", which won the Pulitzer Prize in 1961 and was made into a movie with Gregory Peck a year later.

8 In the course of many interview hours, Capote discovers a spiritual affinity with the murderer Perry Smith.

CATHERINE KEENER Born in 1959, Catherine Keener's first major role was in Tom DiCillo's comedy *Johnny Suede* (1991). She also collaborated on the indie director's next three movies (including *The Real Blonde*, 1997). In *Johnny Suede* she played the girlfriend of Brad Pitt, no less. Yet while his career soon launched to superstardom, Catherine Keener made her name mainly through distinctive minor roles in small, but beautifully crafted, films.
Her filmography reads like a "best-of" list of independent films: she starred in *Out of Sight* (1998) and *Full Frontal* (2002) by Steven Soderbergh and in Spike Jonze's *Being John Malkovich* (1999). For the last in this list, as well as for *Capote*, she received an Oscar nomination for Best Supporting Actress. She portrayed Nelle Harper Lee in *Capote* as a fascinating, strong-willed woman. And it took an actress of Catherine Keener's caliber to make us notice her character at all alongside Philip Seymour Hoffman's brilliant, one-man show.

with murder, he is forced to watch as he gradually heads toward the gallows. And, almost schizophrenically, he even wants it to happen, so that he can put the story behind him and finish his novel.

Leading actor Philip Seymour Hoffman – who deservedly won the Oscar for his virtuoso performance – succeeds in making this conflict visible and tangible. He manages to make his Capote, who initially comes over as a high-pitched caricature, into a well-rounded, vibrant character, fostering understanding and empathy in the viewer. His performance will surely earn him a place of honor in the cinematic history of artist biopics. Truman Capote (1924–84) was a fascinating writer and colorful personality. Thanks to this film, he will long be associated with the face of Seymour Hoffman. HJK

8

WALK THE LINE

2005 – USA / GERMANY – 136 MIN. – BIOPIC, MUSIC FILM
DIRECTOR JAMES MANGOLD (*1963)
SCREENPLAY GILL DENNIS, JAMES MANGOLD DIRECTOR OF PHOTOGRAPHY PHEDON PAPAMICHAEL
EDITING MICHAEL MCCUSKER MUSIC T-BONE BURNETT PRODUCTION CATHY KONRAD, JAMES KEACH for FOX 2000 PICTURES, TREE LINE FILMS, KONRAD PICTURES.
STARRING JOAQUIN PHOENIX (Johnny Cash), REESE WITHERSPOON (June Carter), GINNIFER GOODWIN (Vivian Cash), ROBERT PATRICK (Ray Cash), SHELBY LYNNE (Cary Cash), DAN JOHN MILLER (Luther Perkins), LARRY BAGBY (Marshall Grant), TYLER HILTON (Elvis Presley), WAYLON PAYNE (Jerry Lee Lewis), JOHNATHAN RICE (Roy Orbison), DALLAS ROBERTS (Sam Phillips), SANDRA ELLIS LAFFERTY (Maybelle Carter), DAN BEENE (Ezra Carter), RIDGE CANIPE (Johnny Cash as a Boy).
ACADEMY AWARDS 2006 OSCAR for BEST LEADING ACTRESS (Reese Witherspoon).

"Love is a burning thing, and it makes a fiery ring."

At his first audition, Johnny Cash (Joaquin Phoenix) is asked by the owner of the Sun Record Company in Memphis, Sam Phillips (Dallas Roberts), what song he would sing before he died: his answer is one that people would remember; one that is honest and unique. Slowly, the first notes of "Folsom Prison Blues" emanate from the guitar – a song written by Johnny Cash when he was in the air force. Cash begins, tentatively, to sing, defiantly staring down the recording studio boss. The bass kicks in, and then the electric guitar. The classic Johnny Cash sound is born: a sound that is "thundering like a train, sharp as a razor" as country singer June Carter (Reese Witherspoon) would later describe it after being introduced to this black-garbed newcomer. The audiences loved the mixture of rockabilly and country, and Cash's somewhat languid singing style. Cash was just as sexy as his tour mates, Jerry Lee Lewis (Waylon Payne) and Elvis (Tyler Hilton). Girls wrote him sacks-full of letters; they threw themselves at him. All of this is shown in *Walk the Line*, bringing alive for a brief time the atmosphere of the rock-and-roll days of Memphis, when numerous small labels sprang up and white teenagers stormed the charts. These young men, influenced by the blues, sang about sex or crime things that had no place in the white mainstream music of Doris Day.

Walk the Line is a conventional, if understated, biopic. The film explores the myth of Johnny Cash (1932–2003), who was involved in the making of the film before he died, recounting the time before he became a legend. We see Cash as the eternally insecure rough diamond, trying to find his place as a musician and a man. The film spans the period from his poor childhood in Arkansas up to the peak of his career in 1968. The result is a story of loss and

complicated love, success and guilt, fall and salvation. The premature death of his brother in an accident, for which the strict father (Robert Patrick) blamed Johnny, has left a void in his life. In this sense, director James Mangold had Elia Kazan's *East of Eden* (1955) with James Dean in mind. The mother, played by singer Shelby Lynne, brought him up with music in the form of religious songs. Before embarking on his musical career, he struggles to make a living as a sales rep for household goods. His first marriage suffers from his constant absences and dependency on drugs and alcohol and, when he meets June Carter, whom he first admired as a child star on the radio, he falls in love with her. But they do not have a relationship as they are both committed to other people. Torn between religious moral attitudes and the musician's life of excess, he sinks into addiction, spending a short time in prison for smuggling amphetamines

"Even though the real-life Johnny Cash had far more breakdowns and contradictions than the main character in *Walk the Line*, and even though there are controversial subjects in this man's life and songs that are barely touched upon onscreen, Mangold still manages to sneak ambiguous images into a straightforward story time and again." *Stuttgarter Zeitung*

1 A man filled with dark, melancholic thoughts: the young Johnny Cash as played by Joaquin Phoenix.

2 Musician Johnathan Rice as Roy Orbison, bringing the rockabilly days of the '50s to life.

3 The famous concert in Folsom Prison in 1968: Johnny Cash projects himself as outlaw.

4 Country singer June Carter (Reese Witherspoon) was the great love of Cash's life, though it took many years for them to get together.

rom Mexico into the USA in his guitar, and collapsing drunk onstage. He only nanages to overcome his alcohol and drug addiction with the support of June Carter and her family. The problematic relationship between Johnny and June s a continuous thread running through the movie. When June gets caught up n Johnny's band at their first encounter, we sense that she will not be able o break free from him for the rest of the film; as it happens, she becomes bound to him for the rest of her life. They circle one another, getting closer together before pushing each other away, until June finally accepts the marriage proposal Johnny makes to her onstage. The way they both define their relationship with looks and gestures makes for great acting. What is more, Joaquin Phoenix and Reese Witherspoon – who won an Oscar for her role – perform the songs themselves, unlike the music biopic *Ray* (2004) about the life of Ray Charles

5

5 Grand sentiments on the concert stage: June finally accepts Johnny's marriage proposal.

6 Man with a guitar: Johnny Cash had a long way to go before becoming a country legend.

7 Johnny Cash is torn between his family and the demands of life as a musician.

that appeared the year before. The result is a quite distinctive film sound, in which the music hits us as real and immediate. Even though Phoenix replicated the typical Cash movements to perfection and even lowered the pitch of his voice for filming, he is still totally himself.

The camera is always located on stage, right next to the singers, so that it captures their perspective. The concert scenes reflect Johnny Cash's development, showing his insecurities, his collapses and his successes. By 1968 he is clean, and at the peak of his career. The film's narrative is framed by the legendary concert in Folsom Prison that year, the live recording of which would become one of his most successful albums. In the opening shots, the camera roams through the empty prison. We hear the rhythmic stomping of the basses and footfall getting louder and louder. The prison inmates wait for Johnny Cash to appear. He is sitting in a side room, looking at a circular saw: his brother Jack was killed by one just like it. The flashback to his life so far then begins. Toward the end of the film, Cash stands finally on the prison stage; he gives a thrilling concert, powerful and self-assured. KK

JOAQUIN PHOENIX Joaquin Phoenix is a no-holds-barred kind of actor. For his role in *Walk the Line* he learned to play the guitar and move and sing like Johnny Cash. During filming, he made reckless use of his body, falling off chairs and crashing around so realistically that James Mangold was afraid he might seriously injure himself. The part of the screwed-up, drug dependent singer Johnny Cash was to become his best performance. Born in 1974 in Puerto Rico, he became an actor like his four brothers and sisters. He began his career with appearances in TV shows and commercials. His first hit was the TV series "Seven Brides for Seven Brothers" (1982–1983), playing alongside his older brother River Phoenix, who died of a heroin overdose in Joaquin's arms in 1993. After this traumatic experience, the 19-year-old initially turned his back on acting. He did not appear before the camera again until 1995, in Gus Van Sant's media satire *To Die For*. In the years that followed, his screen work included a part alongside Liv Tyler in *Inventing the Abbots* [illegible] and with Sean Penn in Oliver Stone's psycho-thriller *U Turn* [illegible]. He was brilliant with Nicolas Cage in *8MM* (1999) as the sex trade expert. He created chances for himself, firstly with an Oscar nomination for Best Supporting Actor for his role as Roman emperor Commodus in *Gladiator* (2000), and then for Best Leading Actor with *Walk the Line*. His performance as a journalist in *Hotel Rwanda* (2004) met with widespread critical acclaim. He not only appeared before the camera in *We Own the Night* (2007) but also had a producer's role. In 2008 he announced he was giving up acting to become a rap musician. It turned out to be a set-up, however: a bit of performance art for Casey Affleck's "mockumentary" *I'm Still Here* (2010). Joaquin Phoenix went back to Hollywood. His most recent project is *The Master*, a film by Paul Thomas Anderson about the founding of a sect with overtones of Scientology. It is due for cinema release in 2013.

RIDING ALONE FOR THOUSANDS OF MILES
QIAN LI ZOU DAN QI

2005 – HONG KONG / CHINA / JAPAN – 107 MIN. – DRAMA
DIRECTOR ZHANG YIMOU (*1951)
SCREENPLAY ZOU JINGZHI from a story by ZHANG YIMOU, ZOU JINGZHI, WANG BIN
DIRECTOR OF PHOTOGRAPHY ZHAO XIAODING EDITING CHENG LONG MUSIC GUO WENJING
PRODUCTION ZHANG WEIPING, BILL KONG, ZHANG YIMOU, XIU JIAN for BEIJING NEW PICTURES, EDKO FILM, CHINA FILM CO-PRODUCTION CORPORATION, TOHO COMPANY.
STARRING KEN TAKAKURA (Gou-ichi Takata), SHINOBU TERAJIMA (Rie Takata), KIICHI NAKAI (Ken-ichi Takata), KEN NAKAMOTO (Electrician), LI JIAMIN (Li Jiamin), WEN JIANG (Jasmine), QIU LIN (Lingo), BIN LI (Director Li), CHEN ZILIANG (Chen), YANG ZHENBO (Yang Yang).

"I'm not very good with people."

Gou-ichi Takata (Ken Takakura) is a taciturn man. So taciturn, that we wonder at the beginning of Zhang Yimou's quiet drama *Riding Alone for Thousands of Miles* if he is ever going to utter a sound at all, beyond a few throw-away thoughts in voice-over.

At any rate, this is how he briefly introduces us to the plot of the film, only to fall silent again: Mr. Takata and his son Ken-ichi (Kiichi Nakai) have not spoken to each other for ten years, since an argument. But now Ken-ichi is in hospital and his wife Rie (Shinobu Terajima) has begged her father-in-law to come to Tokyo in the hope of effecting reconciliation between the two men. But what might have become the starting point for a story seems to lead just as quickly up a blind alley: Ken-ichi refuses to see his father. Mr Takata is forced to retreat, although he accepts this too without a word.

The film was specially written for legendary actor Ken Takakura, who became famous in the West as "Japan's Clint Eastwood" primarily for his roles as an aging Yakuza boss. He also plays Mr. Takata with an inscrutable poker face: a man who will always withdraw into himself when burdened with emotional stress. The images that Zhang and his cameraman find for Takata in his self-imposed isolation are clear, cool and tightly composed. The dominant color pervading the whole film is a greenish-blue, yet at some point it disappears from the Japanese world of things and re-emerges in the expansive Chinese landscapes of Yunnan that Takata immediately seeks out, corresponding to the transformation of the man who finds no expression for his feelings. For when saying goodbye, Rie gives him a video tape with a report filmed by Ken-ichi in China about the Beijing opera and actor Li Jiamin, which ends with Ken-ichi promising to return again the following year to film Li's interpretation of the famous opera "Riding Alone for Thousands of Miles."

And this is where the story proper actually begins: mindful that seriously ill Ken-ichi will not be able to fulfill his promise, Mr Takata sets out for China himself on the spur of the moment, in order to find Li and make a film, though more than anything it is a way of re-establishing a link with his son. Yet it will

1

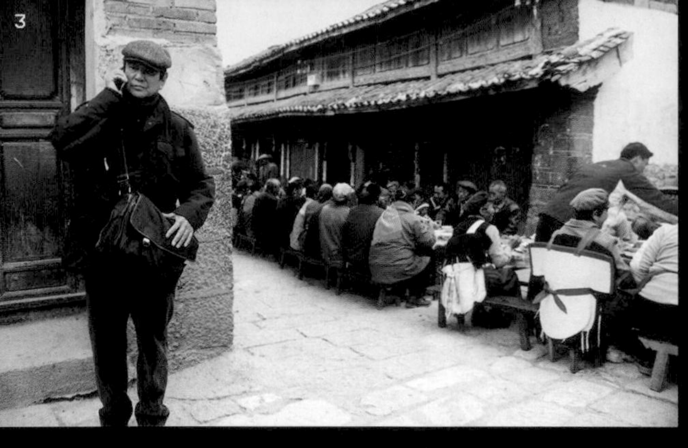

not be easy, as a whole series of unexpected events begins to unfold. *Riding Alone for Thousands of Miles* has sometimes been criticized for Zhang's portrayal of a rather flattering and slightly nostalgic view of China. The real theme of the film is, however, something different: after his global success with the martial arts dramas *Hero* (2002) and *House of Flying Daggers* (2004), Zhang presents us here with a small drama that includes some rather comical scenes about the different forms communication can take: it is about the lack of it, as much as the multifarious options for somehow reaching an understanding with each other.

For as the journey begins, the film suddenly introduces an excess of communication: interpreters with varying language skills appear, or are present on the telephone; a video request message is designed to melt the hearts of

"Known as the Clint Eastwood of Japan, Takakura's dominant performance deserves such comparison. It further stands up to the film's more melodramatic tendencies, creating a buffer against the story's inclination to go soft." *The Austin Chronicle*

1 After his wife's death, Gou-Ichi Takata (Ken Takakura) retreats to a remote fishing village.

2 Man of few words: all Mr. Takata wants is peace and quiet. Only when his son becomes seriously ill does he decide on a course of action that will take him to China.

3 Residents of the rural province where Beijing Opera star Li Jiamin was born throw a great banquet for Mr. Takata. He has to take a call, but slowly begins to relax thanks to the kindness of his hosts.

4 It may seem like a duel, but is actually a meeting: the villagers introduce Mr. Takata to Li Jiamin's son Yang Yang (Yang Zhenbo), who is to travel to see his father in prison.

5 The trip to China and meeting little Yang Yang melt Mr. Takata's frozen heart.

Chinese bureaucrats; and Takata finally ends up receiving phone messages from his dying son, conveyed through his daughter-in-law. But Takata's learning process begins as the story literally takes him further away from the verbal communication that is becoming increasingly complicated. When he eventually has to spend a night in the mountains of Yunnan province with Li Jiamin's son, Yang Yang (Yang Zhenbo), the Japanese man and the little Chinese boy can only become closer emotionally, as no linguistic communication is possible. It ends with tears finally flowing, but not in a sentimental sense – just as the logical conclusion. LP

ZHANG YIMOU Born in Xi'an in China's Shaanxi province in 1951, Zhang Yimou suffered harassment during what became known as the Cultural Revolution as the son of a former officer of the Kuomintang; like millions of other Chinese, he was sent to work in the countryside for the purpose of re-education. After buying himself a camera in 1974, however, Zhang became a successful photographer and used it to apply to the Beijing film academy in 1978. One of Zhang's fellow students at the academy was Chen Kaige, who also went on to become internationally famous; together with Tian Zhuangzhuang and Wu Ziniu they would go down in history as the so-called "Fifth Generation" that radically modernized Chinese cinema.

After completing his studies in 1982, Zhang began working as a cameraman on films including Chen Kaige's *Yellow Earth* (*Huang tu di*, 1985) and *The Big Parade* (*Da yue bing*, 1986); he also appeared in an acting role in *Old Well* (*Lao jing*, 1986, directed by Wu Tianming). Zhang's directorial debut was the drama *Red Sorghum* (*Hong gao liang*, 1987), which won the Golden Bear at the Berlin Film Festival in 1988 and also introduced him to the leading actress and new global star Gong Li, who plays a self-assured woman in China under Japanese occupation. Many of Zhang's ensuing films with Gong Li, including *Ju Dou* (1990), *Raise the Red Lantern* (*Da hong deng long gao gao gua*, 1991), *The Story of Qiu Ju* (*Qiu Ju da guan si*, 1992) and *To Live* (*Huozhe*, 1994), became successful in the West, not least due to their outstanding photography and ingenious use of color, while films like *Red Lantern* and *To Live* were banned in China.

Since the late 1990s, however, Zhang has attracted increasing criticism in the West on the grounds that he has been cozying up to the Chinese leadership with noticeably less political movies; his grandiose opening ceremony for the Olympic Games in Beijing in 2008 met with a similar reproach. Zhang's most recent global hits to date have been the martial arts dramas *Hero* (2002) and *House of Flying Daggers* (2004). In 2006 he directed the costume drama *Curse of the Golden Flower* (*Man cheng jin dai huang*

MUNICH

2005 – USA / CANADA / FRANCE – 164 MIN. – POLITICAL THRILLER
DIRECTOR STEVEN SPIELBERG (*1946)
SCREENPLAY TONY KUSHNER, ERIC ROTH from the book "VENGEANCE" by GEORGE JONAS
DIRECTOR OF PHOTOGRAPHY JANUSZ KAMINSKI EDITING MICHAEL KAHN MUSIC JOHN WILLIAMS
PRODUCTION KATHLEEN KENNEDY, BARRY MENDEL, STEVEN SPIELBERG, COLIN WILSON for UNIVERSAL, AMBLIN ENTERTAINMENT, DREAMWORKS PICTURES, THE KENNEDY/MARSHALL COMPANY, BARRY MENDEL PRODUCTIONS.
STARRING ERIC BANA (Avner), DANIEL CRAIG (Steve), GEOFFREY RUSH (Ephraim), MATHIEU KASSOVITZ (Robert), HANNS ZISCHLER (Hans), CIARÁN HINDS (Carl), AYELET ZURER (Daphna), MICHAEL LONSDALE (Papa), MATHIEU AMALRIC (Louis), GILA ALMAGOR (Avner's Mother), MORITZ BLEIBTREU (Andreas), VALERIA BRUNI TEDESCHI (Sylvie), MARIE-JOSÉE CROZE (Jeanette), MERET BECKER (Yvonne), YVAN ATTAL (Tony), LYNN COHEN (Golda Meir), SHARON ALEXANDER (General Nadev), BIJAN DANESHMAND (Kamal Nasser), OMAR METWALLY (Ali), AMI WEINBERG (General Zamir).

"There's no peace at the end of this, no matter what you believe."

The Olympic Games in Munich, which up to this point had been characterized by their exuberance, were abruptly halted on September 5, 1972. Palestinian terrorists from the "Black September" group penetrated the Olympic village, killing two Israeli athletes and taking nine others hostage. During a botched attempt to free them at an airport near Munich the following day, all the hostages were killed. Steven Spielberg tells the story of these actions and their consequences in his film that was "inspired by real events," as indicated in a caption inserted after the movie title in the opening credits. Three decades after the Holocaust, Jews are dying again on German soil, and the state of Israel is pierced to its heart by it. "Forget peace for now, we have to show them we're strong," states Prime Minister Golda Meir in Spielberg's script. She dispatches a five-man special team under the command of her former bodyguard Avner Kaufman (Eric Bana). Its generously funded mission is to kill the eleven masterminds of the attack, without the official knowledge of the government. Together with his team – Robert (Mathieu Kassovitz), who actually deactivates bombs but now has to build some; document forger Hans (Hanns Zischler); hitman Steve (Daniel Craig); and "cleaner" Carl (Ciarán Hinds), who removes incriminating evidence from crime scenes – Avner works his way

1
OTEL
2
מוזיאון ישראל ירושלים
the israel museum, jerusalem

“The thorny heart of *Munich* is the knowledge that vengeance is a self-perpetuating murder machine that drags successive generations into a mire of tit-for-tat bloodshed.” *TV Guide*

1 Bombing in Cyprus: Hans (Hanns Zischler) and Robert (Mathieu Kassovitz) disappear; “cleaner” Carl (Ciarán Hinds) goes into the hotel and removes all traces.

2 In shock: Avner (Eric Bana) and his pregnant wife Daphna (Ayelet Zurer) watch a TV report showing the bodies of the dead athletes being brought home.

3 Avner and Daphna celebrate the birth of their first child, a daughter.

5

6

4 "Now we have to show strength." Israeli Prime Minister Golda Meir (Lynn Cohen) is determined to exact revenge for the Munich attack.

5 Assassinate 11 people; area of operations, Europe: liaison officer Ephraim (Geoffrey Rush) explains the mission to Avner.

6 General Zamir (Ami Weinberg) brings Avner to Jerusalem to meet Golda Meir.

across Europe, and occasionally the Lebanon, killing six of the men on the list. Avner is not a cold-blooded state assassin; none of his commandos is. This leads to a few foul-ups that end in either high tension or bizarre situations. While the five men are hardly killing machines, their mission at some point develops its own momentum and the agents begin to feel something akin to "sporting ambition." They set their sights on assassinating outside Europe, their designated sphere of activity, and also kill their actual targets' successors at the same time.

Spielberg portrays the Munich assault as a media event, with TV journalists broadcasting live from the Olympic village across the world. Avner and his crew are involved in image cultivation of a sort, as their job is to present Israel to global audiences as a country capable of defending itself. For Israel wants to counterbalance the images of dead athletes with something else and, for this reason, Avner's commando unit is supposed to kill primarily with bombs, as they have greater impact in the media.

Looked at from a purely technical point of view, Spielberg has produced a great, fast-paced thriller. A running time of almost three hours and over seventy speaking parts makes for a compelling movie and heavyweight protagonists. The story of *Munich* is told in a gripping way, and beautifully filmed; the big cities with their 70s look are magnificent to behold. But, of course, the director of *Schindler's List* and the founder of the internationally renowned Shoah Foundation wanted more than that. He combines the brilliant

ERIC BANA A Mossad agent; the green monster, Hulk; and Hector, a Trojan prince: though he does not yet have a particularly extensive filmography, Eric Bana can already look back on some colorful roles. Bana, who was born in Melbourne, Australia on August 9, 1968 to a Croatian father and German mother, had parts in TV series and films in his native country. Hollywood took notice of the up-and-coming star with *Chopper* (2000), the portrait of the Australian criminal "Chopper" Read. "He has a quality no acting school can teach. You cannot look away from him," wrote influential US critic Roger Ebert about Bana's performance. He made his US debut in Ridley Scott's war movie *Black Hawk Down* (2001) and followed this in 2003 with his first leading role, in Ang Lee's comic book adaptation *Hulk*; then, in 2005, he landed a part with Hollywood's most influential director, Steven Spielberg.

Motorsport fan Bana has an imposing physique in front of the camera, which makes him ideal for roles requiring physical strength. He thus played Hector alongside Brad Pitt in Wolfgang Petersen's *Troy* (2004), and was briefly considered to succeed Pierce Brosnan as James Bond. The part was snatched away from him, however, by his colleague in *Munich*, Daniel Craig.

7

7 Eye for an eye: the 11 perpetrators of the deadly Munich attack are identified.

8 His job is actually to defuse bombs, but now he must build them: Robert (Mathieu Kassovitz, with Eric Bana).

9 Murdered: Avner and Steve (Daniel Craig) discover their colleague's body, document forger Hans.

"This mournful masterpiece is Steven Spielberg's harshest film yet, which is saying something, given *Schindler's List* and *Saving Private Ryan*." *Rolling Stone*

8

9

“As a thriller *Munich* is efficient, absorbing, effective. As an ethical argument, it is haunting.”

Chicago Sun-Times

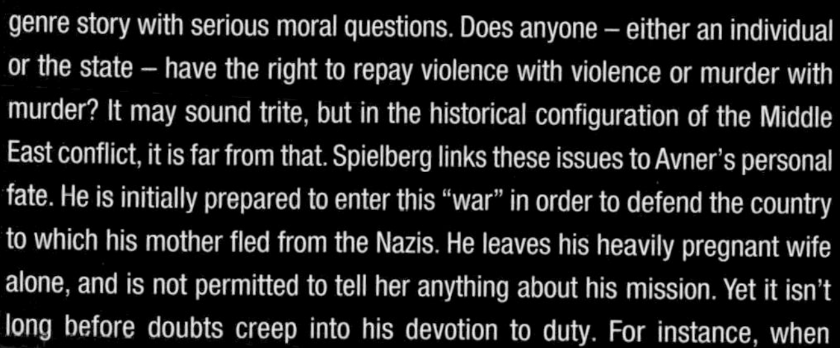

genre story with serious moral questions. Does anyone – either an individual or the state – have the right to repay violence with violence or murder with murder? It may sound trite, but in the historical configuration of the Middle East conflict, it is far from that. Spielberg links these issues to Avner’s personal fate. He is initially prepared to enter this “war” in order to defend the country to which his mother fled from the Nazis. He leaves his heavily pregnant wife alone, and is not permitted to tell her anything about his mission. Yet it isn’t long before doubts creep into his devotion to duty. For instance, when he is congratulated on both the birth of his daughter and a successful murder at the same time; and when he sees one of their victims as a civilized gentleman and loving father. Avner only begins to ask questions about his victims’ guilt after he has killed them. What this “war” wreaks on his mind are feelings of guilt and paranoia, together with the fear that he will never be able to live in peace with his wife and little daughter again. By the end, Avner is a broken man.

HJK

10 Team briefing: Avner with Steve, Hans, Robert, and Carl.

11 Avner and the others travel to Amsterdam to avenge Carl’s murder. Robert is starting to have doubts.

LITTLE MISS SUNSHINE

2006 – USA – 101 MIN. – TRAGICOMEDY
DIRECTORS JONATHAN DAYTON (*1957), VALERIE FARIS (*1958)
SCREENPLAY MICHAEL ARNDT DIRECTOR OF PHOTOGRAPHY TIM SUHRSTEDT EDITING PAMELA MARTIN
MUSIC MYCHAEL DANNA, DEVOTCHKA PRODUCTION ALBERT BERGER, DAVID T. FRIENDLY, PETER SARAF, MARC TURTLETAUB, RON YERXA for BIG BEACH, THIRD GEAR, DEEP RIVER, BONA FIDE.
STARRING ABIGAIL BRESLIN (Olive Hoover), GREG KINNEAR (Richard Hoover), TONI COLLETTE (Sheryl Hoover), ALAN ARKIN (Grandpa Edwin Hoover), PAUL DANO (Dwayne), STEVE CARELL (Frank Ginsberg), JUSTIN SHILTON (Josh), BRYAN CRANSTON (Stan Grossman), MARC TURTLETAUB (Doctor), JULIO OSCAR MECHOSO (Mechanic).
ACADEMY AWARDS 2007 OSCARS for BEST ORIGINAL SCREENPLAY (Michael Arndt) and BEST SUPPORTING ACTOR (Alan Arkin).

"Everybody just ... pretend to be normal, okay?"

Striving for happiness is written into the American constitution, and the Hoovers are definitely an American family. But what happens if your personal concept of happiness makes someone else miserable? This way of thinking is alien to the father, Richard (Greg Kinnear): this embarrassingly unsuccessful life coach divides the world into winners and losers, and still thinks he is on the right side. He believes that happiness can be made to happen. This is why, one sunny day, he bundles his whole crazy family into a bright yellow VW minibus and drives them to California. Does his seven-year-old daughter Olive (Abigail Breslin) dream of taking part in a children's beauty contest called "Little Miss Sunshine"? Well, she should just go there and win it. He refuses to believe that humiliation awaits the chubby child.

The worn-out vehicle symbolizes the state of the family, which is barely holding it together: an overworked mother; her intellectual, suicidal brother; a grandpa addicted to sex; and a son who has kept a resolute silence for months. The clutch is shot, and the driver oblivious to the real world. But when the Hoovers get into third gear at one point – a hair-raisingly dangerous maneuver – there's no holding them back.

Little Miss Sunshine's journey proved just as successful. Sold at the Sundance Film Festival for over 10 million dollars to the giant Fox Searchlight company, this caustic comedy about losers became one of the most successful independent films of all time, despite a faltering start. Michael Arndt won the Oscar for Best Original Screenplay although, following the movie's own logic,

1

2

1 Waiting for the bus: child star Abigail Breslin puts heart and soul into her performance as seven-year-old Olive.

2 Family in action: when their bright yellow VW bus goes into third gear, the Hoovers are unstoppable.

3 Primal scream therapy, Hoover-style: Olive is pleased about taking part in the "Little Miss Sunshine" competition.

a more modest result might have been more appropriate. The writer, Arndt, and director-couple Jonathan Dayton and Valerie Faris are careful not to make winners out of losers. What matters is the delicate balance between irony and sensitivity with which they handle the indie cliché of the dysfunctional family. There is also an element of anarchy: who wants to be functional anyway? But the main thing is that, en route from Arizona to California, no one is abandoned. This feel-good movie does not poke fun at its suffering protagonists. All the characters are lovingly acted and portrayed; they discover their weaknesses, as well as their strengths.

They have their fair share of disasters, of course. Richard finally learns that his handbook for success will never be published. His homosexual brother-in-law, Frank (Steve Carell) – in the latter's own opinion the most important Proust researcher in the country – meets the attractive student on whose account he tried to commit suicide, and who is the lover of the second-best Proust expert. All life is a competition. And it must ultimately come to an end: the Hoovers reach their destination in the nick of time, exhausted – and with a corpse in the trunk. The film is paradoxically brought to life by the melancholic expressions of its completely different characters, together with their tension-

STEVE CARELL Born in 1962, Steve Carell is not a comedian to laugh at his own jokes. In fact, he never laughs at all. He has the dry humor of a newsman who is used to delivering a load of nonsense with a straight, statesmanlike expression. It is hardly surprising: he first became known between 1999 and 2005 in the famous American TV news spoof *The Daily Show*. Before that, however, he experienced a difficult time in the television industry that might well have crushed those of a less optimistic disposition. Then, with his 30th birthday approaching, Carell landed a fairly small part in the sentimental family movie *Curly Sue* (1991).

Things began to look up. He again played a newsman as Jim Carrey's rival Evan in *Bruce Almighty* (2003). In *Anchorman: The Legend of Ron Burgundy* (2004), Carell was brilliant as the somewhat dim-witted weatherman. He then collaborated with this comedy's producer, Judd Apatow, in developing what became the biggest success for them both until then: *The 40 Year Old Virgin* (2005). His lead role as a frustrated wallflower was a perfect vehicle for the typical Apatow blend of dry humor and affection.

Carell proved that behind the pained expression was a real actor in his interpretation of the lovesick, homosexual Frank in the sleeper *Little Miss Sunshine* (2006). After that came the less than brilliant spin-off *Evan Almighty* (2007), a resurrection in the gentle love comedy *Dan in Real Life* (2007) alongside Juliette Binoche, and a well-judged performance as the "not completely incompetent" secret agent Maxwell Smart in *Get Smart* (2008). Since 2005 he has also played the exceptionally unfunny office manager Michael Scott in the sitcom *The Office* (2005 to date). The Steve Carell factor made sure the original British format made it in the States as well.

“Told as a picaresque road trip, *Little Miss Sunshine* employs razor-sharp humor and a deceptively realistic style to satirize a corrupt society that heroes of low status must navigate by their wits alone.” *Los Angeles Times*

4

4 Live and let live: Grandpa Edwin (Alan Arkin) explains his hedonistic life philosophy to Olive.

5 A real winner: at the age of 72, Alan Arkin won the Oscar for Best Supporting Actor.

6 Overworked mother Sheryl (Toni Collette) does her best to keep her dysfunctional family together.

7 Who is suicidal here? Frank (Steve Carell) of all people is supposed to watch over his problematic nephew Dwayne (Paul Dano).

“All six actors are excellent, working together impressively and gradually winning our respect and sympathy.” *The Guardian*

fueled interaction in the tightest of spaces. Richard and Frank are obviously separated by more than just the back seat; they inhabit different planets. Fifteen-year-old Dwayne (Paul Dano) is given advice on sex and drugs by his hedonistic grandpa, though he is far less interested than his shocked parents. Little Olive beams through her gigantic horn-rimmed eyeglasses, her beloved Discman in her lap, and thankfully doesn’t hear a word. They are condemned to sit glued to the seats, playing this strange game called “family.” They make the best of it, as does the expert camerawork of MTV and commercial directors Dayton and Faris. The contrast between mobility and immobility drives the film – and, like the elusive leading actor from a happier hippie era, sometimes unpredictably. In the end, all hell breaks loose in the questionable freedom of a ghastly beauty pageant. Next to the other competitors, who are all presented like little hookers, Olive (whose cheerful character Abigail Breslin plays with all her heart and soul) does not really have a chance. Yet she seizes the day with both hands. In a daring burlesque routine her grandpa has taught her, she unmasks not only the phony way in which the whole event is sexualized, but also the appalling, winning-is-everything mentality of her father, Richard. By now, he is fidgeting beside her on the stage with the whole family: they have finally understood what really matters. It is an incredible, truly feel-good moment in cinema. PB

5

6

7

THE LIVES OF OTHERS

DAS LEBEN DER ANDEREN

2005/06 – GERMANY – 137 MIN. – POLITICAL DRAMA
DIRECTOR FLORIAN HENCKEL VON DONNERSMARCK (*1973)
SCREENPLAY FLORIAN HENCKEL VON DONNERSMARCK DIRECTOR OF PHOTOGRAPHY HAGEN BOGDANSKI
EDITING PATRICIA ROMMEL MUSIC STÉPHANE MOUCHA, GABRIEL YARED
PRODUCTION QUIRIN BERG, MAX WIEDEMANN FOR WIEDEMANN & BERG FILMPRODUKTION, ARTE, BAYERISCHER RUNDFUNK/CREADO.
STARRING SEBASTIAN KOCH (Georg Dreymann), MARTINA GEDECK (Christa-Maria Sieland), ULRICH MÜHE (Captain Gerd Wiesler), ULRICH TUKUR (Lieutenant-Colonel Anton Grubitz), THOMAS THIEME (Minister Bruno Hempf), HANS-UWE BAUER (Paul Hauser), MATTHIAS BRENNER (Karl Wallner), VOLKMAR KLEINERT (Albert Jerska), CHARLY HÜBNER (Udo), HERBERT KNAUP (Gregor Hessenstein).
ACADEMY AWARDS 2007 OSCAR for BEST FOREIGN LANGUAGE FILM.

"Are you still on the right side?"

The Lives of Others takes place in the Orwellian year of 1984. In a state that will not survive to see the digital age, the nightmare of total surveillance is already a reality. The East German secret police, known as the "Stasi," deploy analogue technology, including audio recorders and typewriters, but they also use people – the only possible flaw in the system. A small man becomes the defining image of the film: he sits in an attic with two huge headphones clamped to his head, listening to and noting down the lives of other people with ruthless efficiency.

Stasi captain Gerd Wiesler (Ulrich Mühe) is assigned to writer Georg Dreymann (Sebastian Koch) and stage actress Christa Sieland (Martina Gedeck), the artistic couple in the flat below him. The police have nothing on Dreymann. While colleagues suffer under employment bans, he is no oppositionist, nor even an opportunist. Neither the unsuspecting author nor Wiesler know the real reason for this "operational procedure," which is that the Minister of Culture wants rid of his rival so that he can win the beautiful actress for himself. But Wiesler does not need a reason. Introduced as a brutally efficient interrogation expert, he is the ideal weapon of a spy apparatus that relies on suspicion alone to exist. Anything at all – a wrong opinion, a stupid joke – will be discovered in the end. And in actual fact Dreymann, shocked by the suicide of a proscribed colleague, soon develops a spirit of opposition. Wiesler seems to be fulfilling his mission.

1
2

3

4

"Ulrich Mühe plays the secret agent with gravitas and a degree of humor, which also accounts for the screenplay's charm. It contains some odd scenes, yet is painfully researched down to the last detail. The story makes plenty of significant points, impressing us with its relentlessly sober analysis." *Die Zeit*

5

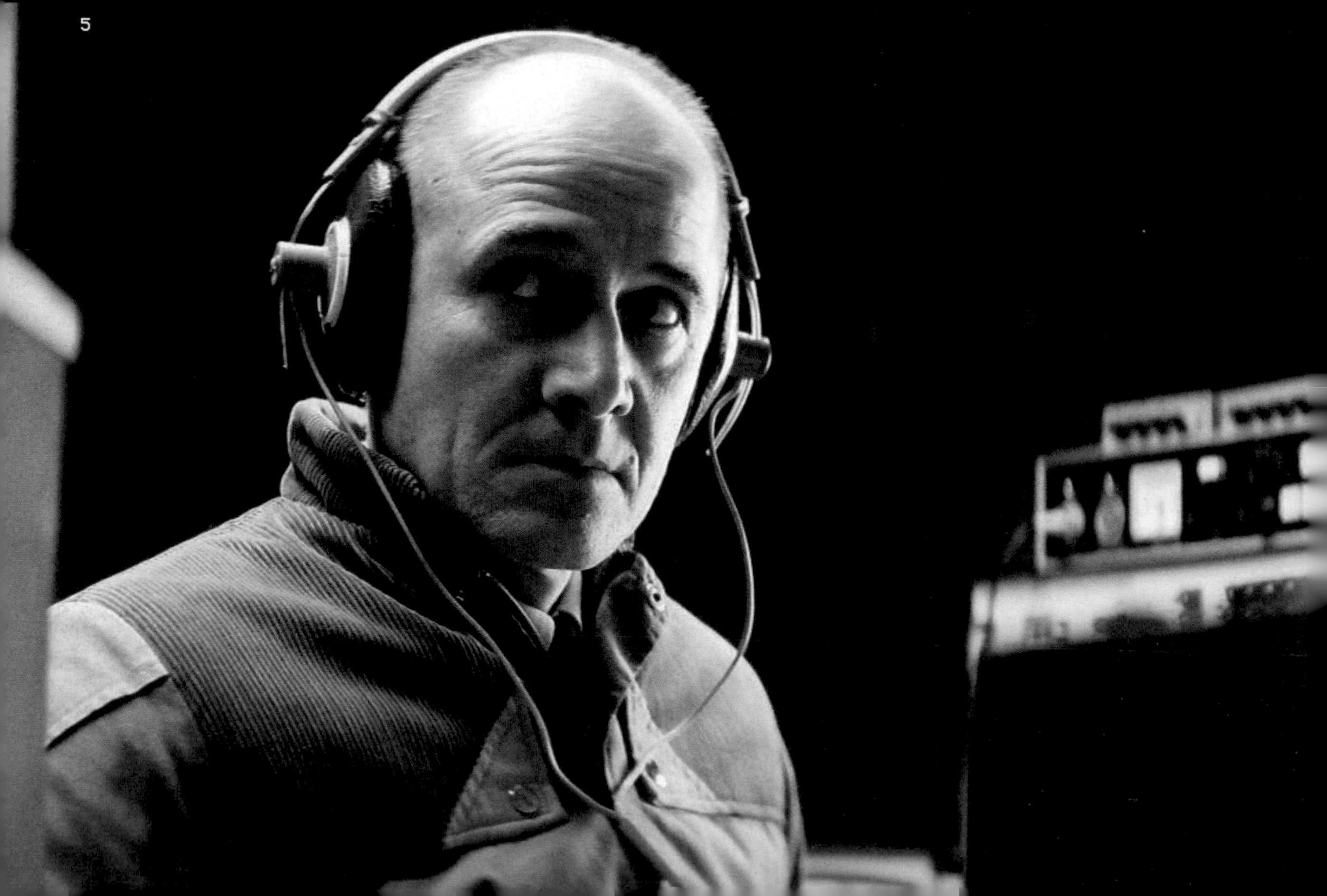

1 Bureaucratic puppet master in uniform: Stasi captain Wiesler (Ulrich Mühe) serves the system without hesitation.

2 Actress Christa Sieland (Martina Gedeck) becomes the target of male interests. She is threatened with a professional ban.

3 Higher authority: Wiesler's Stasi boss Grubitz (Ulrich Tukur) puts pressure on the spy who has doubts.

4 Epilogue: the man at the center of power becomes one of the many gray specters on the margins of society after the Wall comes down.

5 The surveillance state and its victims: Ulrich Mühe, himself persecuted by the Stasi, is brilliant as its opponent.

6 Georg Dreymann (Sebastian Koch) accesses the official files. Like many East German citizens, he cannot believe what he is reading.

But suddenly, even the spy isn't what he used to be. The lovers' generosity, the open intellectual debates over red wine and beautiful music, the bohemian lives of the artists, and life itself – all of this has changed the captain. He feeds false reports into his typewriter and starts to protect his victims.

The man in the attic is one of the saddest figures in movie history. Wiesler does not have a life. The spy in the gray polyester jacket belongs to the gray drabness of everyday life under socialism, which the film effectively contrasts with the cozy world of the life-affirming artists, which is painted in light shades of brown. And he will return to this grayness. His transformation may seem improbable and it also fails to provide redemption. With incredible empathy, the great Ulrich Mühe plays a man who discovers life and dies inside in the process. He realizes what he has subconsciously known for a long time: the "good person" that the writer (who is true to party principles) describes is not the product of the system, but its enemy. He has not only destroyed the lives of others, but also wasted his own. Outstanding performances, incredibly lucid imagery, and minimal mise-en-scène are the key features of the movie, which won the West German novice director Florian Henckel von Donnersmarck the Oscar for Best Foreign Film. The phenomenal success of this directorial newcomer in the USA – the low budget production took over 75 million dollars worldwide – can be explained by the sentiments of a nation that gives new currency to surveillance scenarios in the time of the Patriot Act. In addition, Hollywood's narrative models shine through the German theme: history is individualized, taking the form of parable rather than realistic reproduction. There were only a few Wieslers, and personal or even erotic motifs played a somewhat subordinate

"... an elegant blend of political thriller, romantic melodrama, drama about conscience, and social portrait." *Süddeutsche Zeitung*

7

7 Watched from above: the lovers have no idea that they are under surveillance. Every movement they make is meticulously recorded and transcribed by Wiesler.

8 Writer Dreymann is neither an opportunist nor a dissident. The turn of events makes his apartment into a meeting place for conspirators.

9 Contradictions in the lives of Christa and Georg begin to pile up. The state leaves them no options.

10 The bohemian life: bearable in the art circles of "real-life socialism." No-one suspects the whole apartment has long been bugged.

"Wiesler is a fascinating character. His face is a mask, trained by his life to reflect no emotion. Sometimes not even his eyes move. As played in Mühe's performance of infinite subtlety, he watches Dreymann as a cat awaits a mouse." *Chicago Sun-Times*

8

role in the musty atmosphere of East German socialism. But von Donnersmarck also knows about the unshakeable limits of a dictatorship. The transformation of the individual does not bring down the system. The perpetrator's debts are not written off. On the contrary, Wiesler's maneuvers lead directly to disaster.

After relaxed comedies such as *Good Bye Lenin!* (2002), von Donnersmarck's masterpiece forms an important counterpoint in the German discourse on the past, characterized as it is by idealization. In addition, *The Lives of Others*, filmed in original locations, is above all a gripping spy thriller with all the ingredients of the genre: infamous surveillance methods, conspiratorial meetings, lethal bartering and secret stashes under the floorboards. When the writer discovers the audio cables behind his wallpaper after the fall of the Berlin Wall, he realizes quite a few things. He never meets his guardian angel. PB

“Like the omnipresent tentacles of East Germany’s onetime secret police, *The Lives of Others* grips like a boa constrictor.” *Variety*

ULRICH MÜHE Born in 1953 in Grimma, Saxony, Ulrich Mühe certainly embodied the reunification of East and West Germany in terms of his biography, but more than anything his top-rate professional work before and after the Wall came down earned him a reputation as one of the few “all-German” actors. He is remembered for his quiet, insistent and often clinical interpretation of roles. After his military service as a border soldier and theatrical training in Leipzig, Mühe began acting on the main East Berlin stages in 1982, under the direction of Heiner Müller, among others. In fall 1989 he was involved in organizing the demonstration on Berliner Alexanderplatz. After reunification he became well-known to an international audience for his films with Michael Haneke, and especially for his part in *The Lives of Others*. In East Germany, Mühe and his future wife Jenny Gröllmann soon became known as the “DEFA dream couple,” through films such as *Hälfte des Lebens* (*Half of Life*, 1984) that were produced by the state-owned company Deutsche Film-Aktiengesellschaft. As early as 1986, however, Bernhard Wicki cast him in the West German film version of *Das Spinnennetz* (*Spider’s Web*), as a careerist and “human chameleon.” When he starred as a Hamburg publisher in Helmut Dietl’s Oscar-nominated political and media satire *Schtonk!* in 1991, he had long since been regarded as a West German by the uninformed. In this film version about the scandal surrounding the fake Hitler diaries, he was also to prove his talent for comedy. That changed dramatically with Michael Haneke’s oppressive studies of power. The intense Austrian director cast the quiet actor in movies like *Benny’s Video* (1992) and *Funny Games* (1996/1997). Some of his films for cinema and TV, such as *Nikolaikirche* (1995), *Der Blaue* (1997) and *Hunger auf Leben* (2004), dealt with the process of coming to terms with East Germany’s past. Yet the “role of his life,” personally as well, was to be the Stasi captain Gerd Wiesler in Florian Henckel von Donnersmarck’s *The Lives of Others* (2005/2006). Mühe, who won the European Film award for Best Actor, saw himself as a victim of the Stasi. The controversy surrounding the film opened up old wounds. Ulrich Mühe, one of the most popular German film and television actors, died far too prematurely of cancer a few months after the film’s Oscar win.

10

THE WIND THAT SHAKES THE BARLEY

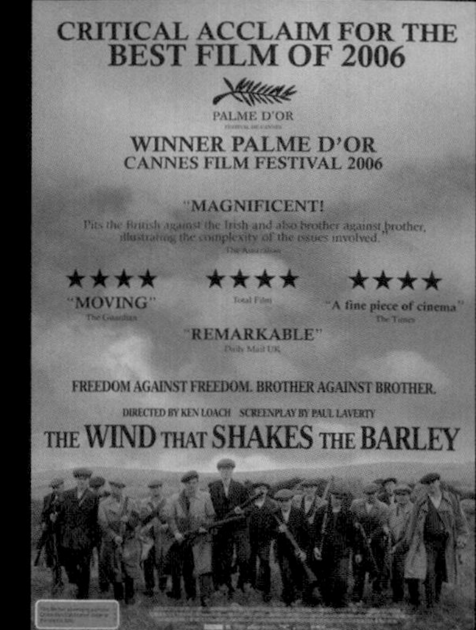

2006 – UK / IRELAND / GERMANY / ITALY / SPAIN / FRANCE – 127 MIN. – HISTORICAL FILM, POLITICAL DRAMA
DIRECTOR KEN LOACH (*1936)
SCREENPLAY PAUL LAVERTY DIRECTOR OF PHOTOGRAPHY BARRY ACKROYD EDITING JONATHAN MORRIS
MUSIC GEORGE FENTON PRODUCTION REBECCA O'BRIEN for BÓRD SCANNÁN NA HÉIREANN, UK FILM COUNCIL, PATHÉ, SIXTEEN FILMS, ELEMENT FILMS, EMC PRODUKTION, BIM DISTRIBUZIONE, TORNASOL FILMS, MATADOR PICTURES.
STARRING CILLIAN MURPHY (Damien), PÁDRAIC DELANEY (Teddy), LIAM CUNNINGHAM (Dan), ORLA FITZGERALD (Sinead), MARY O'RIORDAN (Peggy), MARY MURPHY (Bernadette), LAURENCE BARRY (Micheail), DAMIEN KEARNEY (Finbar), FRANK BOURKE (Leo), MYLES HORGAN (Rory), ROGER ALLAM (Sir John Hamilton).
IFF CANNES 2006 GOLDEN PALM (Ken Loach).

"I hope this Ireland we're fighting for is worth it."

A thatched cottage in a forest settlement; armed men threaten the inhabitants at gunpoint, all of whom are forced to line up on the stoop, children and old women included. This is the opening scene of *The Wind That Shakes the Barley*. It is repeated half way through the film: the house, armed men, women, children … Only it was English soldiers persecuting the Irish in the first scene, and now it is Irishmen fighting their own people.

Director Ken Loach tells the story of the Anglo-Irish War (1919–1921) in *The Wind That Shakes the Barley*, which takes its title from a folk song. The Irish Republican Army (IRA) fought a guerilla war against the British occupation force, the notorious "Black and Tans," most of whom were veterans of the First World War. This background is no doubt one reason why English-born Loach has often been accused of taking an anti-British stance. This claim can at best be made, however, by someone who has only seen the first half of the film, which deals with the politicization and radicalization of the Irish population. Loach describes this through the experiences of two brothers: Damien O'Sullivan (Cillian Murphy), a young doctor who is about to take up a job in London, and his brother Teddy (Pádraic Delaney). But British soldiers then murder 17-year-old Micheail in front of Damien because he can only say his name in Gaelic, not in English. And when Damien is forced to watch at the railroad station as Englishmen beat up the train conductor, he changes his plans and decides to

1

2

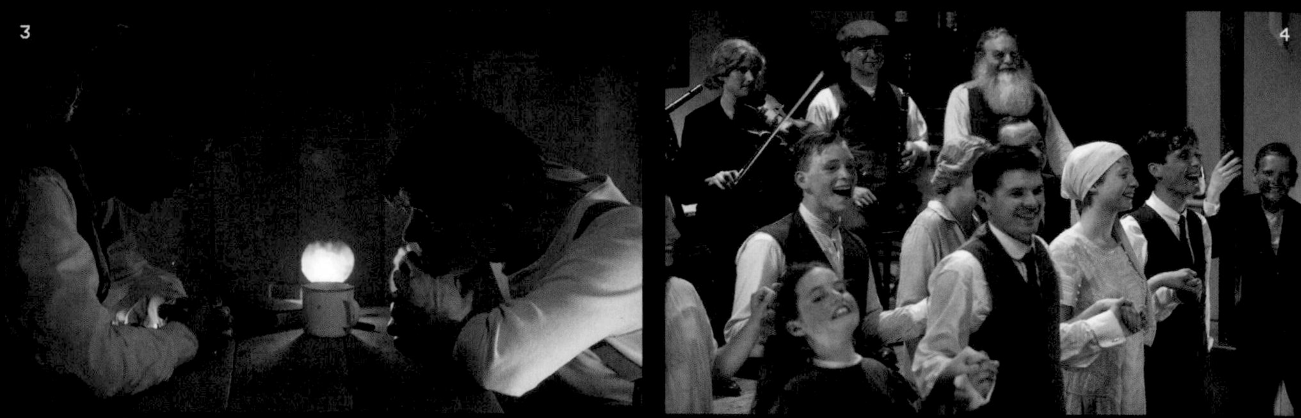

"The history presented in *The Wind That Shakes the Barley* hardly feels like a closed book or a museum display. It is as alive and as troubling as anything on the evening news, though far more thoughtful and beautiful."

The New York Times

5

1 Train conductor Dan (Liam Cunningham) leads the IRA's guerilla war against the English occupiers.

2 Damien (Cillian Murphy, far right) and the other IRA fighters take landowner Sir John Hamilton (Roger Allam, third from left) to be executed after he betrayed his young employee Chris and, with him, the whole section.

3 Two brothers on different sides of the law: "Free Stater" Teddy (Pádraic Delaney) has had IRA man Damien thrown into prison.

4 Damien, his girlfriend Sinead (Orla Fitzgerald), who has just had her head shaved by the English, and the rest of the group celebrate the ceasefire.

5 Damien, Teddy and their group set a trap for the English soldiers, attacking them with rifles and hand grenades.

6 Almost idyllic: Damien and his friends play the Irish sport hurling – a variation of hockey that the English tried to ban, frequently and unsuccessfully.

join his brother's local IRA cell; Teddy has been part of the armed struggle for some time. They attack British duty stations, kill the soldiers and steal their guns. They drill men in hats and coats, some with wooden guns, training them up in the lush green fields and woods of Ireland.

In two sequences, the Irish are involved in the most harmless of pursuits – playing the Irish version of hockey called hurling on one occasion, and billiards the second time – when the English arrive and harass them. Damien's IRA cell falls into the hands of the English, and Teddy is tortured appallingly. Anyone looking for proof of Loach's black-and-white approach is most likely to find it at the beginning of the movie. Yet gradually the image of the guerilla war becomes clouded by bitterness, no matter how much it may be justified from the point of view of the oppressed. Damien, the doctor who is supposed to save lives, has to shoot firstly a traitorous landowner and then the young lad, Chris, who betrayed the group under pressure.

KEN LOACH A blue-collar filmmaker born on June 17, 1936, the son of a factory worker, Ken Loach has always been conscious of his background, which he incorporates into the privileged setting of his films. In dramas and bittersweet comedies like *Raining Stones* (1993), *My Name is Joe* (1998) and *Ae Fond Kiss* (2004) he deals with themes like poverty, unemployment, and xenophobia. His TV drama *Cathy Come Home* (1966) about the social decline of a middle-class family even triggered a parliamentary debate about poverty in England.

Loach began his career at the BBC, where he was a pioneer of the docudrama format. He carried this documentary-style approach into his cinematic projects as well; his films are characterized by socially relevant themes, a meticulously portrayed social environment, and involvement with non-professionals. They are always underpinned by his great empathy for the protagonists.

Although he mainly deals with contemporary subjects, *The Wind That Shakes the Barley* is not his only historical movie: *Land and Freedom* (1995) is set during the Spanish Civil War, while in the four-part TV series "Days of Hope" (1975) he tells the story of the English working-class movement. Loach has made over 40 films since his movie debut with *Poor Cow* in 1967, garnering many awards and distinctions at the three main European film festivals in Berlin, Cannes and Venice.

7

7 Damien and Dan await execution. But a young guard helps them to escape.

8 Sinead, Damien's lover and the sister of murdered Micheail, secretly supplies the IRA men with cigarettes.

9 Teddy (Pádraic Delaney) protests: an independent Irish court has imprisoned, of all people, the man who funds weapons for the IRA.

10 Duty weighs heavily: Damien has shot dead the young traitor Chris Riley, whom he has known since childhood.

"Director of photography Barry Ackroyd captures the beauty of a landscape that seems to confer a stilled dignity to the nationalist struggle." *Sight & Sound*

Micheail and Chris, who are both murdered; the recurrent image of the cottage; the two O'Sullivan brothers; England and Ireland – the movie uses several examples of mirror images and creates partner relationships as well as pairs of opposites. Ireland's natural beauty (captured beautifully by cameraman Barry Ackroyd) on the one hand and the shots of the brutality of this war on the other ultimately form precisely this type of opposition. Brothers Damien and Teddy O'Sullivan finally end up as enemies instead of allies. Consistent with the perverse logic of this war, the ceasefire does not bring peace to the Irish, but instead brings the war to their own people. The prospect of their own government, albeit under the control of the British crown, creates two factions among the Irish: the so-called "Free Staters," who approved of the peace treaty, and the IRA, who wanted to fight on for a completely independent state Damien and Teddy stand on opposite sides of this conflict. And when the cottage in the woods reappears for the third and last time, one of the brothers comes to announce that he has had the other one executed. HJK

"Like the folk song from which it draws its title (and which laments 'the foreign chains that bind us'), the tone is more melancholic than defiant, with a twang of bitterness underlying its themes of discord and discontent." *The Observer*

10

BABEL

2006 – FRANCE / USA / MEXICO – 143 MIN. – EPISODE MOVIE, POLITICAL DRAMA
DIRECTOR ALEJANDRO GONZÁLEZ IÑÁRRITU (1963)
SCREENPLAY GUILLERMO ARRIAGA DIRECTOR OF PHOTOGRAPHY RODRIGO PRIETO EDITING DOUGLAS CRISE, STEPHEN MIRRIONE MUSIC GUSTAVO SANTAOLALLA PRODUCTION STEVE GOLIN, ALEJANDRO GONZÁLEZ IÑÁRRITU, JON KILIK for PARAMOUNT PICTURES, ANONYMOUS CONTENT, ZETA FILM, CENTRAL FILMS, MEDIA RIGHTS CAPITAL.
STARRING BRAD PITT (Richard Jones), CATE BLANCHETT (Susan Jones), BOUBKER AIT EL CAID (Yussef), SAID TARCHANI (Ahmed), ADRIANA BARRAZA (Amelia), GAEL GARCÍA BERNAL (Santiago), ELLE FANNING (Debbie Jones), NATHAN GAMBLE (Mike Jones), RINKO KIKUCHI (Chieko Wataya), KÔJI YAKUSHO (Yasujiro Wataya), SATOSHI NIKAIDO (Inspector Kenji Mamiya).
ACADEMY AWARDS 2007 OSCAR for BEST MUSIC (Gustavo Santaolalla).
IFF CANNES 2006 AWARD for BEST DIRECTOR (Alejandro González Iñárritu), PRIZE OF THE ECUMENICAL JURY (Alejandro González Iñárritu), VULCAIN PRIZE (Stephen Mirrione).

"It's all over the news. Everybody is paying attention!"

The movie begins with a black screen. Sounds are heard: footsteps, someone breathing, and a whistling wind. It then becomes light, and we see a desert nomad walking toward his neighbor. He plans to sell him a modern hunting rifle that a Japanese amateur hunter has given him as a gift for loyal service. The neighbor is a goat farmer, so the weapon could be useful in protecting his herd from jackals. A price is quickly negotiated. The farmer's sons head off with the rifle and the herd – an ill-fated transaction, as it unleashes a chain of dramatic, ultimately fatal events.

From his first two films onward, *Amores Perros* (2000) and *21 Grams* (2003), Mexican director Alejandro González Iñárritu has made clear his fascination for fateful, coincidental encounters between strangers. He believes that everything is interconnected, and anyone can meet anyone else. An accident or bad luck is always pivotal: the trigger for a non-linear narrative with multiple meanings. Interwoven to varying degrees, several narrative strands run through the films, which constitute a trilogy. While Amores Perros and 21 Grams are still tightly restricted in geographical terms, the plot in Babel has gone global in its worldwide distribution. When American tourist Susan (Cate Blanchett) is hit by a rifle bullet on a coach trip across the Moroccan desert, her husband Richard (Brad Pitt) finds out just how powerless the international diplomatic system really is. He fights to save his wife in a simple hut, while a heavily armed media industry talks prematurely of a terrorist incident. Neither they, nor the police who are feverishly investigating, have any idea that the perpetrators are actually the two hapless shepherd boys, who were practicing shots with the rifle. In the meantime, Amelia (Adriana Barraza), the Mexican nanny to the couple's children who stayed behind in San Diego, takes them with her to her son's wedding in Mexico. Amelia has been really looking forward to this day for some time, but it turns into a disaster for her. On the return journey, her nephew Santiago (Gael García Bernal) bursts through the border in a shoot-out and

"As a film director, Iñárritu has good reason to distrust words; he eschews them, allowing the texture of surfaces to speak instead. His cameraman, Rodrigo Prieto, captured these images with different film stock in each country: the sensuality in a handshake, a look, a kiss, or a gesture used to pass a hash pipe to calm nerves; and in the longing of a deaf-mute girl for physical contact." *Süddeutsche Zeitung*

2

flees from the police. He leaves Amelia and the children entrusted to her care in the middle of the desert in the dark. The next day, half dying of thirst, she is picked up by the police and expelled from the country.

The third strand of the film is about the deaf Japanese girl Chieko (Rinko Kikuchi), who is suffering a serious identity crisis following her mother's suicide. She feels unloved. Her father (Kôji Yakusho) is the amateur hunter who presented the rifle as a gift to the Moroccan farmer.

The theme of the movie's title runs through each of the narrative strands: failure to communicate and catastrophic misunderstandings. At one point, Richard says to Susan: "We have to talk more!" Tokyo's urban landscape also offers a counter-image rich in contrast to the shots of the desert and the Mexican suburbs. Many of the scenes are connected to each other either by association or thematically. Susan's bone-chilling scream in the hut follows the silent voice-over of a dental practice, where the deaf girl Chieko is sitting. Another scene cuts from a beheaded chicken with blood spurting from its neck to Susan, just after she has been shot in the bus. Like the children's game "grapevine", individual messages are passed on to the next scene and given new interpretations.

According to the Bible, God is furious at man's dream of omnipotence and destroys its symbol, the Tower of Babel. He scatters human beings across the world in a confusion of languages. At the end of the movie, when the camera slowly pulls back from the balcony of a huge apartment block into the Tokyo night, the viewer senses that the dream of the Tower of Babel lives on. The film's opening and closing scenes refer to ancient and modern ways of

1 The two shepherd boys Yussef (Boubker Ait El Caid) and Ahmed (Said Tarchani) still do not realize that the shooting at a tourist bus in the desert has had dramatic consequences. Are they guilty or innocent?

2 Far from home and all alone, his emotions spill out after the crisis has been successfully resolved: Brad Pitt as Richard Jones.

3 A desolate landscape, two shepherd boys, and the latest hunting rifle – fate in all its guises takes its course.

4 Intense pain for a lost child: leaning against the tour bus window, Susan Jones (Cate Blanchett) ponders on her life.

"Alongside countless non-professional actors, who give it their all, stars are the main protagonists – celebrities who forgo their star image for Iñárritu." *Frankfurter Rundschau*

5

“Besides all the communication problems, there is a universal grammar of gestures and facial expressions in Iñárritu’s work that become eloquent when language is no longer an option. In fear or in joy, in panic or through a sense of loss, the faces become equal. Then, it doesn’t matter whether someone is from the American middle class, a Muslim shepherd, or a Japanese teenager.” *Der Tagesspiegel*

5 On a relaxed high, Chieko (Rinko Kikuchi) forgets her troubles for a few hours. But the effect of the drugs she has taken does not last long.

6 Now sober, Chieko leaves the disco. Gone is the stimulating vibration of the beat; only melancholy remains.

7 Yasujiro Wataya (Kôji Yakusho) has been lonely since his wife died. He also has problems with his daughter Chieko.

8 Chieko is deaf. But the sadness around her makes her life far more depressing.

9 In despair, Chieko throws herself into her father's arms. Finally, he understands her. They look for a new way ahead together.

life. What comes between them and connects them are love, pain, happiness, hope, life and death. The movie compresses these universal human features into a kaleidoscopic, artistic representation of our time. And it is not afraid to make an ambivalent judgment: the world may keep on networking and using boundless means of communication, but cultural and emotional differences will continue to cause disaster for human beings. The smallest misunderstandings become the driving force of destiny in people's lives. Yet, at the same time, the chance of an important experience or the possibility of renewal is inherent in every disaster. The winners in the movie are the American couple who overcome their marriage crisis. The Moroccan goat farmer, on the other hand, loses a son and the Mexican nanny her livelihood. SR

6

7

8
9

ADRIANA BARRAZA In a red velvet evening dress and ripped nylon stockings, her dark hair matted with dust and sweat, Adriana Barraza plays a Mexican nanny to two American children, wandering through the bleak borderland between the USA and Mexico. Her desperate attempt to get help is like a surreal dance in daytime. The sun beats down relentlessly on her, as she struggles with bushes and stones: even the soft, sandy soil under her feet is trying to drag her down. But she does not give up, staggering on and dragging her red silk shawl behind her like a magician's cape.

She is like a character from an ancient Greek tragedy, cast into the American desert by a cruel director-god. Her steadfast maternal care and willingness to make sacrifices are totally alien to this barren soil. She will conquer the desert and yet lose everything, for the border official who deals with her case in the days that follow only regards her as a criminal and not a Joan of Arc figure, providing care and assistance. Director Alejandro González Iñárritu had already entrusted this extremely popular actress, born in Mexico in 1956, with an important supporting role in *Amores Perros* (2000). In it, she plays the stern mother of Octavio (Gael García Bernal) who is always on the go. In *Babel*, the two actors once again form a perfect contrast in terms of age and gender. Warm, gentle and self-contained, she makes her wired nephew appear somewhat chaotic. But she owed her Oscar nomination for Best Supporting Actress to more than just her naturalness and inner serenity: it was her terrific, complex and emotional performance at the end, winning the hearts of her audience as the self-sacrificing Amelia.

10 Frantically seeking help: Amelia (Adriana Barraza) wanders around the border zone between Mexico and the USA. Her nephew has simply abandoned her and the two children in the desert, following a wild car chase.

11 She loves them like her own children. But the US authorities still end up treating Amelia like a criminal and deporting her.

12 Harassed by border guards: under provocation, Santiago (Gael García Bernal) suddenly snaps.

13 Amelia does not want to miss her son's wedding in Mexico. So she takes the Jones' children, entrusted to her care, over the border – a trip that will have dire consequences.

"Because González Iñárritu is a romantic vis-à-vis cinema, he sees the power of images taking over where discourse fails, and builds on this universal language of film." *Frankfurter Allgemeine Zeitung*

13

PAN'S LABYRINTH !!!

EL LABERINTO DEL FAUNO

2006 – SPAIN / MEXICO / USA – 119 MIN. – FANTASY MOVIE
DIRECTOR GUILLERMO DEL TORO (*1964)
SCREENPLAY GUILLERMO DEL TORO DIRECTOR OF PHOTOGRAPHY GUILLERMO NAVARRO
EDITING BERNAT VILAPLANA MUSIC JAVIER NAVARRETE PRODUCTION ÁLVARO AUGUSTÍN, FRIDA TORRESBLANCO, ALFONSO CUARÓN, GUILLERMO DEL TORO, BERTHA NAVARRO for TEQUILA GANG, ESPERANTO FILMOJ, ESTUDIOS PICASSO, TELECINCO.
STARRING IVANA BAQUERO (Ofelia), ARIADNA GIL (Carmen), ÁLEX ANGULO (Doctor), SERGI LÓPEZ (Vidal), MARIBEL VERDÚ (Mercedes), CÉSAR VEA (Serrano), ROGER CASAMAJOR (Pedro), DOUG JONES (Pan / Pale Man), MANOLO SOLO (Garcés), GONZALO URIARTE (Francés).
ACADEMY AWARDS 2007 OSCARS for BEST CINEMATOGRAPHY (Guillermo Navarro), BEST ART DIRECTION (Eugenio Caballero, Pilar Revuelta) and BEST MAKEUP (David Martí, Montse Ribé).

"The world is a cruel place."

Twelve-year-old Ofelia (Ivana Baquero) is one of the countless children for whom no provision has been made in the adult world. After her father's death, she moves with her mother Carmen (Ariadna Gil) to live with her new husband, fascist Captain Vidal (Sergi López). Her mother brings her up with tough love, but it quickly becomes obvious that this woman has long since lost her way in life as well. On General Franco's orders, Vidal has set up in a former mill in the middle of an inhospitable forest and is ruthlessly pursuing a group of resistance fighters. Furthermore, he is only interested in his son, who will soon be brought into the world by heavily pregnant Carmen. Yet the fate of the unborn child is uncertain, not least because of the arduous journey the captain has expected his wife to take. Meanwhile, her daughter takes refuge in the fantasy dream world of her fairytale books. Under the guidance of a faun (Doug Jones), who lives in a nearby fossilized labyrinth, Ofelia must undertake three tasks in order to prove that she is the rightful princess of her imaginary kingdom.

Pan's Labyrinth deals with the clash of reality and fantasy. The gruesome reality is opposed to a dream world that arouses equal terror; one that is exclusively perceived by the young heroine. It will always be hidden from the limited outlook of the fascist Vidal, just like the humanity and moral superiority of his servant Mercedes, Ofelia's only ally on the other side of her dream kingdom. It is significant that the tyrant cannot for a moment imagine that Mercedes is on the side of the partisans. When her double-crossing is finally exposed, he says: "No disrespect, but it's only a woman after all."

2

"In *Pan's Labyrinth*, Del Toro has perhaps his strongest cast ever, beginning with the protean Sergi López, most familiar as the hotel manager in Stephen Frears' *Dirty Pretty Things*, and including Maribel Verdú, almost unrecognizable (she was the heartthrob of *Y Tu Mamá También*) and young Ivana Baquero as Ofelia." Los Angeles Times

“Transcendent, passionate, full of beauty and endlessly affecting, this is without question the movie of the year.”

BBC

For director Guillermo del Toro, the plot’s locations are at least as important as the actors. Each individual place for the action in *Pan’s Labyrinth* reflects the inner nature of one of the characters. It is the mill in Vidal’s case, characterized by straight lines and a Spartan order that borders on the obsessive. The huge, redundant mill wheel on the back wall of his room picks up the motif of the watch that no longer works; he inherited the timepiece from his father, a general killed in action. This preserved the exact moment of his death, having been thrown to the ground when he fell. In this way, del Toro reveals the sadistic Vidal to be a prisoner of his own past, only capable of passing on the questionable inheritance of his father to his own children. This beast in human form was himself once a child who has been destroyed by the pressures of the grown-up world. Besides the theme of civil war, the suffering of a child’s soul within a reality governed by constraints and fears is the main motif in the film. Ofelia’s fantasy world should in no way be seen as an alternative creation to the disillusioning reality. Instead, it represents the level of consciousness that can control life experiences through a child’s imagination. This possibility has long since been lost to adults. At one point, Carmen remarks that she used to believe in fairy tales; but when Ofelia asks her to sing a soothing lullaby she remembers the tune, but not the words.

Del Toro’s demons – the child-eating “pale man” (also played by Doug Jones) but also the faun, a creature almost fossilized by countless years and impossible to imagine ever having been young – are all incarnations of the fact that even dreamy Ofelia cannot straddle the borders between the worlds indefinitely. So in the end the heroine has to decide whether she wants to go on living, paying the price of her innocence, or retreat to the existence beyond reality for ever. SH

1 Ofelia (Ivana Baquero) in the Underworld: the semi-orphan’s battle with the unfeeling world of adults shifts increasingly into a fairytale shadow realm, full of mythical creatures and demons.

2 The lord of the Labyrinth, an ancient faun (Doug Jones), is Ofelia’s only guide through the tests she must pass in order to prove she is the looked-for princess.

3 The tests push Ofelia to her limits. The task is made all the more difficult, as her expeditions also bring the adults’ wrath down upon her.

3

4

4 When the future princess throws his warnings to the wind, her paternal friend seems finally to abandon her too.

5 There are a few decent folk, even among the grown-ups. For instance, the resistance fighter Mercedes (Maribel Verdú), who has secretly infiltrated the lion's den, and has to pay a high price for doing so.

6 Dinner for one – the Pale Man sleeps in front of his sumptuous table. Woe betide anyone who is tempted by the delicacies.

7 The monster has woken. One of the most exciting aspects of *Pan's Labyrinth* is the fantastic sets and costumes. For actor Doug Jones, the transformation involved hours of torture, a real tour de force by the makeup artists.

"Del Toro's masterful direction shifts from fantasy to reality and back again with remarkable fluidity."

Variety

5

6

GUILLERMO DEL TORO The Mexican director born in Guadalajara in 1964 learned about the subject of the Spanish Civil War, a central motif in *Pan's Labyrinth* (*El laberinto del fauno*, 2006), from film historian Emilio García Herrera, whom del Toro describes as a father figure and his cinematic mentor. He had already dealt with this theme in *The Devil's Backbone* (*El espinazo del diablo*, 2001): del Toro calls it his second most important movie after *Pan's Labyrinth* and it has many parallels to the later work, especially the theme of children at the mercy of a world dominated by war and horror. Alongside such social and political subjects, fairytale elements always predominate in del Toro's films, and the director knows how to link these very disparate narrative levels together with the utmost skill. From an aesthetic point of view all of his works are distinguished by a meticulous use of color, as well as extremely fluid camerawork which nonetheless follows strict patterns of movement that constantly seem to be mapping out the topography of locations right into every nook and cranny. Del Toro is a director who asserts his right to fully control visible reality, as this seems to be the only way he can create a sustainable projection surface for his fantastic subjects straight from comic books. These characteristics are found in highly personal works such as *Hellboy* (2004), which the director took ten years to make, as well as in commissioned movies such as *Blade II* (2002). Del Toro is devoting himself to a fairytale theme in his most recent project as well: the film version of J.R.R. Tolkien's "The Hobbit."

TALLADEGA NIGHTS: THE BALLAD OF RICKY BOBBY

2006 – USA – 108 MIN. – ACTION, COMEDY, SPORTS MOVIE
DIRECTOR ADAM MCKAY (*1968)
SCREENPLAY WILL FERRELL, ADAM MCKAY DIRECTOR OF PHOTOGRAPHY OLIVER WOOD
EDITING BRENT WHITE MUSIC ALEX WURMAN PRODUCTION JUDD APATOW, JIMMY MILLER for COLUMBIA PICTURES, SONY COMPUTER ENTERTAINMENT, APATOW PRODUCTIONS, GH ONE, HIGH, WIDE AND HANDSOME, MOSAIC MEDIA, RELATIVITY MEDIA.
STARRING WILL FERRELL (Ricky Bobby), JOHN C. REILLY (Cal Naughton, Jr.), SACHA BARON COHEN (Jean Girard), GARY COLE (Reese Bobby), JANE LYNCH (Lucy Bobby), LESLIE BIBB (Carley Bobby), AMY ADAMS (Susan), HOUSTON TUMLIN (Walker), GRAYSON RUSSELL (Texas Ranger), GREG GERMANN (Larry Dennit).

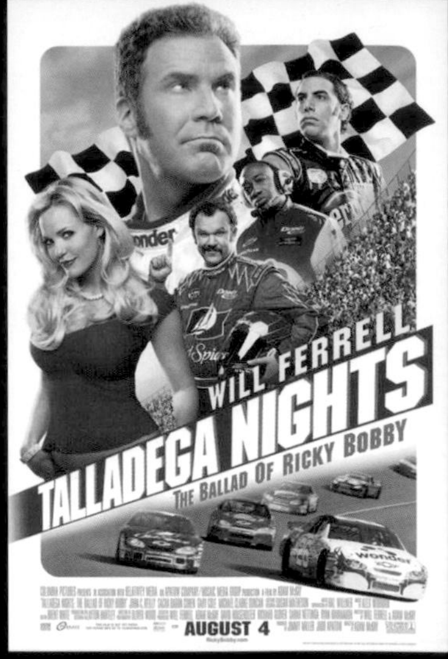

"You don't need to think. You need to drive. You need speed."

"If you're not first, you're last." Anyone who has to think about a dictum like this has already lost. Ricky Bobby (Will Ferrell) never thinks. That's what makes him the hottest shot in NASCAR racing, the ultimate sport for adrenalin junkie dummies; and that's what happens when you live your life according to your pothead father's pearls of wisdom. All he left his son was this slogan and a real trauma when he shamefully abandoned the family – in a car of course – shortly after the birth. Ricky must win, and he always does. In no time at all, this nobody has become a racing idol covered in advertising logos, with the classic pit chick for a wife and two spoiled sons. He is also completely cracked. What he lacks in intelligence, he makes up for in ignorance. His victories would be unthinkable without the weaving skills of his racing mate and constant second, Cal (John C. Reilly), yet the very idea of letting this faithful friend win just once would never occur to him.

Talladega Nights: The Ballad of Ricky Bobby is about the addiction to winning and what this can do to people like Ricky – it makes them easy prey for gay Frenchmen. Smug and sophisticated, Jean Girard (Sacha Baron Cohen) is a man who enjoys existential literature even when overtaking; he is also Ricky's nemesis. The latter's career is brought to an abrupt halt, as this arrogant high-flyer literally kisses the tarmac. After his exit from motor racing, he loses not just his wife and home to his "best friend" Cal, but the accident has left him with such an injury that he even fails as a pizza delivery driver.

Lead actor Will Ferrell and his director, Adam McKay, with whom he co-wrote the screenplay, did not in fact set out to negate the rules of the sports movie; with his father's help, Ricky makes a brilliant comeback. But NASCAR racing has its own rules and following them leads straight to a frenzy of rage. In this garish test lab that puts corporate America under the microscope, reality and satire are inseparable and, like every TV broadcast, every outcome is inevitably comedic. Is it really such an exaggeration when Ricky includes his sponsors along with his beloved "baby Jesus" when saying Grace? Which TV consumer of average sophistication would not follow Ricky's example after a racing accident by ripping his clothes off, roaring loudly, then hopping around naked over the track, consumed by invisible flames? The two *Saturday Night*

1

Live veterans just love indulging in these surreal techniques, pushing an explosive mixture of hyped-up, witty dialogue and crazy computer action to the limit.

And yet, just like motor racing, the movie would be nothing without its protagonists. Exceptionally gifted comic Will Ferrell has two very rare talents: the ability to combine every kind of dopiness in a single facial expression, as well as to cede to an even better alternative if necessary: for example, when Jean Girard (Sacha Baron "Ali G" Cohen) – his arch rival sent as if by fate – steals the show from under his feet. The man with the craziest French accent since Peter Sellers' Inspector Clouseau embodies everything in this movie that is feared by the Homer Simpsons of society, including Ricky: homosexuality, intellect and sophistication. The subversive punch line of their pseudo-political mini-war is, of course, their reconciliation in the form of a passionate kiss,

"As a cultural artifact, *Talladega Nights* is both completely phony and, therefore, utterly authentic. Or, to put it differently: this movie is the real thing. It's finger lickin' good. It's eatin' good in the neighborhood. It's the King of Beers. It's Wonder Bread." *The New York Times*

1 Ricky Bobby (Will Ferrell), the fastest hotshot in the NASCAR series, has just one problem: he cannot lose.

2 Career in plaster: after his accident, the traumatized Ricky stinks even as a pizza delivery man, and becomes increasingly desperate.

3 His wife Carley (Leslie Bibb) sticks faithfully by him. The characters are as subtle as a product placement.

4 Will Ferrell is the king of fiendish facial expressions. As Ricky Bobby, this gifted comedian demonstrates the full extent of his skills – and at full throttle, too!

broadcast live to the furthest reaches of the network. There are many reasons why the film shot to the number one slot in the US movie charts. For one, it is the type of popcorn movie that is always a hit. Above all, however, it is because its humor works on a number of levels. At its most basic, it corresponds to the ingeniously dopey slapstick of the Farrelly brothers. Yet its abundant imagery is not just loaded with shameless product placement. The amount of information increases apace – whether about pop knowledge or sports fanaticism or simply through repetition – the engine fires up and slapstick, irony and biting social satire race neck-and-neck for pole position. And, as if by some miracle, they all reach the line at the same time. What sets this movie above other comparable spoofs is the love of its subject – motor racing – and of its heroes. The reformed Ricky Bobby knows that it is OK to lose sometimes as well. The main thing is to do it at full throttle! PB

WILL FERRELL Born in California in 1967, Ferrell is one of the most popular and highly paid comic actors in US cinema alongside Ben Stiller and Adam Sandler. The rest of the world gradually got to know him through minor roles, such as the crazy fashion mogul Jacobim Mugatu in the futuristic comedy *Zoolander* (2001). Home audiences were his long-term fans thanks to his appearances from 1995 through 2002 in the TV talent spoof "Saturday Night Live." His stock turns included daring improvisations and parodies of famous personalities such as George W. Bush. For better or worse, his breakthrough came with the campus romp *Old School* (2003). Through these and other appearances he became part of what became known as the "frat pack," together with Ben Stiller, Jack Black, Vince Vaughn and brothers Owen and Luke Wilson.
He also had lead roles in the TV spoof *Anchorman: The Legend of Ron Burgundy* (2004) and motor racing satire *Talladega Nights: The Ballad of Ricky Bobby* (2006). Ferrell, whose characters are mostly distinguished by a complete lack of self-consciousness, can provoke gales of laughter just by making a sheepish face.
He proved his talent for serious acting, too, in Woody Allen's *Melinda and Melinda* (2004) – the fact that the movie bombed was in no way down to him – as well as in *Stranger Than Fiction* (2006), in which he unexpectedly found himself the fictional protagonist of a female novelist fighting writer's block. In real life, Will Ferrell has no intentions of allowing his comic talents to fade away: he was a hit as one of the same-sex pair in the totally bonkers ice-skating movie *Blades of Glory* (2007).

BORAT:
CULTURAL LEARNINGS OF AMERICA FOR MAKE BENEFIT GLORIOUS NATION OF KAZAKHSTAN

2006 – USA – 84 MIN. – COMEDY, POLITICAL SATIRE
DIRECTOR LARRY CHARLES (*1956)
SCREENPLAY SACHA BARON COHEN, ANTHONY HINES, PETER BAYNHAM, DAN MAZER, from a story by SACHA BARON COHEN, ANTHONY HINES, PETER BAYNHAM and TODD PHILLIPS
DIRECTOR OF PHOTOGRAPHY LUKE GEISSBUHLER, ANTHONY HARDWICK EDITING CRAIG ALPERT, PETER TESCHNER, JAMES THOMAS MUSIC ERRAN BARON COHEN
PRODUCTION SACHA BARON COHEN, JAY ROACH for FOUR BY TWO, EVERYMAN PICTURES, ONE AMERICA, 20TH CENTURY FOX.
STARRING SACHA BARON COHEN (Borat Sagdiyev), KEN DAVITIAN (Azamat Bagatov), LUENELL (as herself), PAMELA ANDERSON (as herself).

"We support your war of terror!"

The global citizen of 2006 was a comical TV reporter from Kazakhstan with an engaging smile and rather eccentric opinions. Everyone knew Borat – the nice, big man in the shabby, gray suit. Audiences went in droves to see the new "moviefilm" of British comedian Sacha Baron Cohen that was as funny as it was controversial. A year earlier, only a few people had encountered him, and it might have been better for them if they hadn't.

In the guise of an amateur video documentary of the Kazakh Information Ministry, *Borat* is a blend of documentary and fiction – a "mockumentary" from the heart of darkness. At the start, Borat (Cohen's linguistically challenged alter ego) leaves his impoverished home village for America, with the aim of acquiring valuable experiences for his country. Before he goes, he says goodbye to his sister – the "fourth best prostitute in all Kazakhstan" – with a French kiss and a wink, and warns the "village rapist" to exercise restraint. The highlight of his report is the annual "Jew race," in which papier-mâché caricatures of Jewish figures are chased through the village; Borat, like all the other inhabitants apparently, is a dyed-in-the-wool anti-Semite, not to mention a racist and chauvinist – all in all, an unreconstructed barbarian. Charming! In the land of his dreams, Borat's outlandish ways are not met with reciprocal affection. He talks to women as if they were prostitutes and thinks all blacks look like Michael Jackson. In New York he carries a live chicken on the subway, washes his underwear in Central Park and masturbates in front of the "Victoria's Secret" window display. Yet, even though not all men want to be greeted with a kiss, Americans are above all polite people. And some even agree with a few of his homophobic and sexist utterances. A rodeo audience applauds him enthusiastically when the strange guest gives a bloodthirsty speech praising George W. Bush's "war on terror" against Iraqi men, women and children: there is only widespread horror when he makes a botch of singing the American national anthem. Borat then finds himself on an insightful road trip to California, where he thinks of hiding Pamela Anderson in the wedding sack typical of his country and taking her home with him. He avoids flying because he is afraid that "the Jews" could repeat "their September 11 attack."

1

1 Very nice! As Kazakh TV reporter Borat, Sacha Baron Cohen travels across the land of endless opportunities, never failing to provoke.

2 Borat – temporarily – wins over the rodeo audience with his own version of *The Land of the Free*.

3 Three men in an ice cream van, very hairy and highly dangerous. What Borat really wanted was a Hummer.

"*Borat* wasn't just the funniest movie of the year, but the most controversial, fudging the divide between comedy, documentary and faux-documentary." *Newsweek*

4 On the road: globetrotting Borat is a world leader in mastering the art of local customs and codes of conduct.

5 Give me five! The precise role of his “manager” Azamat (Ken Davitian) is a well kept secret.

6 Cultural exchanges: for an avowed racist, Borat isn’t the least bit prejudiced in practice.

Borat was bombarded with complaints from several directions. Cohen’s audacious performance, an acting *tour de force* that involved staying in role minute by minute, proved very effective. The film crew led the village (actually in Romania) to believe they were making a documentary about living conditions there, so the residents felt as duped as the many Americans who had been fooled by Borat’s alleged naivety into making “thoughtless comments;” not to mention the Kazakh government, which sparked a diplomatic crisis through concerns about its country’s reputation.

As a social experiment wickedly overstepping the boundaries of taste, morality and political correctness, *Borat* is second to none. As was the case with his earlier bogus character, “Ali G,” Cohen’s most powerful weapon is uncertainty. What is staged, and what isn’t? How do you respond to the question: “What’s the best weapon to defend yourself against Jews?” Can we laugh at the arms dealer who unapologetically recommends “a 9mm or Glock automatic?” Cohen’s guerrilla tactics reveal systemic prejudices that would otherwise remain hidden. He makes as much fun of dangerous ignorance as the excessive

7 Few have mastered Cohen's art of staying in role, even in the most awkward situations. Like this brave driving instructor, for example.

8 Sexy time again! Cohen set new standards in terms of humor, intercultural tolerance and exciting swimwear in his "moviefilm," disguised as a documentary.

9 Amazed observers in cosmopolitan USA: sophisticated ladies instruct the interesting guest in table manners and the use of toilet paper.

"This year you are not going to find a more appalling, tasteless, grotesque, politically incorrect or slanderous film than *Borat*." *The Hollywood Reporter*

8

"A film so funny, so breathtakingly offensive, so suicidally discourteous, that strictly speaking it shouldn't be legal at all."

The Guardian

tolerance that lets a stranger get away with the most extreme forms of behavior because of their assumed cultural identity (the real madness proves to be the belief of all involved that such a barbaric Kazakhstan actually exists). The sting in the tail is that anyone mocking uneducated Midwest Americans has already fallen into the trap of prejudice. The success of this experimental format relies not least on an artistic contradiction. The movie's clip structure is based on the exhibitionist formats of the YouTube era, the internet and reality TV, hidden cameras, *Jackass* (2000–2002) and especially Cohen's own TV series, *Da Ali G Show* (2000, 2003–2004). These modern means are used by a man from a village where no-one has even heard of MTV or Sacha Baron Cohen. And in a global setting, the backwoodsman becomes the ultimate *agent provocateur.*

PB

SACHA BARON COHEN London-born in 1971 into a Jewish family with Welsh-Israeli roots, Sacha Baron Cohen is virtually unknown as a public figure. This TV comic, who is loved and feared in equal measure, makes his appearances almost exclusively in his various characters. These include, in particular, the impudent, would-be rapper Ali G with his TV series *Da Ali G Show*, broadcast between 2000 and 2004. In this guise he drew out unsuspecting, mostly high-profile interviewees with his foul-mouthed, provocative presentational style. Recurrent themes were already in evidence in the character's trademark homophobia and racism ("Is it because I is black?"). Cohen has such a perfect command of postmodern engagement with ethnic and sexual stereotypes that he constantly finds himself embroiled in controversies of his own making. With *Ali G Indahouse* (2002) the character also acquired his own feature film.

Meanwhile, his audience was also becoming familiar with the character of the Kazakh TV reporter Borat Sagdiyev through his appearances in *Da Ali G Show*. The film *Borat: Cultural Learnings of America for Make Benefit Glorious Nation of Kazakhstan* (2006) went on to become an international media phenomenon. Another character is gay Austrian fashion journalist, Brüno, who confronts clueless photographic models and minor celebrities on the world's catwalks on the subject of, among other things, the Holocaust. He also made his appearance on the big screen in 2009 in *Brüno*. Cohen claims that his working methods serve to highlight existing stereotypes and prejudices. He admits, however, that his increasing fame is making it more difficult to keep up the deception. Ali G and Borat have now been pronounced dead. Sacha Baron Cohen has made mainstream acting appearances in *Talladega Nights: The Ballad of Ricky Bobby* (2006) and *Sweeney Todd: The Demon Barber of Fleet Street* (2007).

BLACK BOOK
ZWARTBOEK

2006 – NETHERLANDS / GERMANY / BELGIUM – 145 MIN. – HISTORICAL DRAMA, THRILLER
DIRECTOR PAUL VERHOEVEN (*1938)
SCREENPLAY GERARD SOETEMAN, PAUL VERHOEVEN DIRECTOR OF PHOTOGRAPHY KARL WALTER LINDENLAUB EDITING JOB TER BURG, JAMES HERBERT MUSIC ANNE DUDLEY
PRODUCTION JEROEN BEKER, TEUN HILTE, SAN FU MALTHA, JENS MEURER, JOS VAN DER LINDEN, FRANS VAN GESTEL for FU WORKS, CONTENTFILM INTERNATIONAL, VIP 4 MEDIENFONDS, AVRO TELEVISION, HOCUS FOCUS FILMS.
STARRING CARICE VAN HOUTEN (Rachel Stein/Ellis de Vries), SEBASTIAN KOCH (Ludwig Müntze), THOM HOFFMAN (Hans Akkermans), HALINA REIJN (Ronnie), WALDEMAR KOBUS (Günther Franken), DEREK DE LINT (Gerben Kuipers), CHRISTIAN BERKEL (General Käutner), DOLF DE VRIES (Notar Wim Smaal), PETER BLOK (Van Gein), MICHIEL HUISMAN (Rob).
IFF VENICE 2006 YOUNG CINEMA AWARD (Paul Verhoeven).

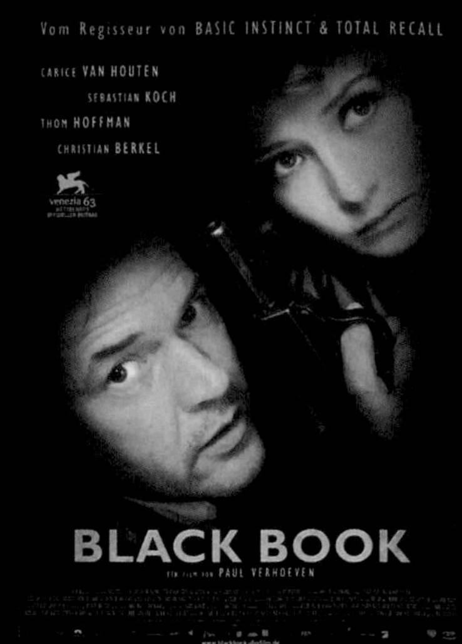

"I never knew this would happen. To fear the liberation ..."

Paul Verhoeven's movies are all about sex and violence. Vehicles for these themes include wicked satire (*Starship Troopers*, 1997), unremitting scandal (*Basic Instinct*, 1992) and a spectacular flop (*Showgirls*, 1995). When Hollywood had nothing more to offer him, he went back home to the Netherlands and made *Black Book*. It is the story of Jewish singer Rachel Stein (Carice van Houten), who goes into hiding in Holland, joins a resistance group, becomes a spy and falls in love with a Nazi. A sensitive theme is not enough for Verhoeven, however; without the slightest qualm, he turns history into an adventure playground for his obsessions, telling the story in a provocative, emotional and sensual way – an unusual type of filmmaking that is now quite rare. Verhoeven's weapon is a trashy style. The plot hurtles breathlessly from one event to the next. Gory action and abandoned eroticism go hand in hand in an abysmal thriller about deception and betrayal. A particularly juicy scene shows Rachel, under her code name Ellis de Vries, as a singer at an SS party. The obese Nazi who had murdered her parents a few scenes earlier is sitting at the piano. After throwing up in private, she sings the Marlene Dietrich song "Ich bin die fesche Lola" with all the boldness and sensuality of the original.

Rachel is assigned as a "honey trap" blonde to the stamp collector and Gestapo head Müntze (Sebastian Koch). Her confident appearance and carefully dyed pubic hair – a scene that Verhoeven naturally does not pass up – cannot deceive the urbane Nazi for long. Yet in this movie the main female character holds all the cards. Carice van Houten has not only been compared to Jean

1
2

1 Good and bad Nazis: chilling General Käutner (Christian Berkel) is one of the most evil of them. He heads operations against the Resistance.

2 Their escape was betrayed. Rachel (Carice van Houten) watches in horror as her parents are murdered. Her only option is to go underground.

3 The elegant 40s look: as Ellis de Vries, Rachel becomes the blonde honey trap for an officer of the Gestapo, Ludwig Müntze (Sebastian Koch).

Harlow and Greta Garbo, but also lives up to them with her mix of acute survival instinct and devastating sex appeal. No other actress since Hanna Schygulla has been fortunate enough to win such a role.

Not all the characters are as consistent: Müntze's transformation into a secret resistance member is hardly plausible. For Verhoeven, "thriller" means that the plot drives the characters, not the other way around. But for him the moral ambiguity is a political statement as well. The Dutch resistance is comprised of upstanding patriots, anti-Semites and wealthy characters whose money comes from Jews murdered out of sheer greed; we find ridiculous caricatures of evil among the Nazis as well as the sensitive Müntze, for whom the bewildered viewer is forced to grieve at the end. The Dutch already knew from Verhoeven's earlier movie *Soldiers* (*Soldaat van Oranje*, 1977) that an ambivalent history of resistance and collaboration is little cause for national self-congratulation. Yet this breaking of taboos is only of secondary interest to the director. In his view, human behavior in wartime does not follow the rules of political correctness – and especially not those of the Hollywood script department. *Black Book* is, it could be said, a crass movie for crass times. It makes sense, therefore, that the Nazi generals are waging their war on "terrorism;" and that the collaborators, including Rachel aka Ellis de Vries, are covered in liquid manure after the war is over.

CARICE VAN HOUTEN In her native Netherlands, Carice van Houten has been a well known star for a long time, receiving numerous awards for her roles in film and television. At the age of 22, she played a teenager who is hopelessly in love with Mick Jagger in Martin Koolhoven's *Suzy Q* (1999). Van Houten then starred as a cat who transforms into a woman in the children's film *Undercover Kitty* (*Minoes*, 2001) which was well received throughout Europe. Other movies include the drama *Father's Affair* (*De passievrucht*, 2003) and the love story *Black Swans* (*Zwarte zwanen*, 2004/2005). An actress trained at the Amsterdam Kleinkunstacademie, she has also made regular stage appearances.

But it was not until *Black Book*, following Paul Verhoeven's return to his old homeland after 20 years in Hollywood, that van Houten gained international recognition beyond the traditionally small-scale Dutch film industry. She plays the attractive Jewish singer, Rachel Stein, who knows how to use her sexuality as a weapon of resistance against the German occupiers. She talks and sings in the movie in Dutch, German and Hebrew. The daring way in which she occupied the role, proving both her comic and dramatic capabilities in the process, was received with resounding enthusiasm by the media. Since then, this charismatic actress has been the darling of glossy magazines and is on the verge of a great Hollywood career, albeit rather reluctantly, as she herself has said. In Bryan Singer's *Valkyrie* (2008), Carice van Houten starred as the wife of von Stauffenberg, the would-be Hitler assassin played by Tom Cruise. More recently, she has acted alongside Jude Law in the sci-fi movie *Repo Men* (2009/2010).

"Written by Mr. Verhoeven and his sometime screenwriter, Gerard Soeteman, *Black Book* encompasses the best and very worst of its director's signature pulp brutalism, which means it's pretty much a hoot."

The New York Times

4

4 A ruthless war rages between the Dutch resistance and the German occupying forces. Who can Rachel trust?

5 A real Verhoeven movie: Rachel fights with every means at her disposal. The director makes no allowances for national taboos in his trademark blend of sex and violence.

6 The end of the war brings blind revenge rather than salvation: Rachel is publicly humiliated as an alleged collaborator.

7 "Winner takes all:" Rachel's friend Ronnie (Halina Reijn) clearly has no problem with the German occupiers. She does, however, help her to escape.

Such shock effects form an effective contrast to the classical appearance of what at that point was the most expensive Dutch production of all time. Elegant composition and lavish sets are reminiscent of Hollywood's "Golden Age" in the 1930s and early 1940s. The prioritization of plot over psychology appears as a relic from this bygone era. Hitchcock defined film as "life with all the dull bits cut out." Verhoeven, who lived through the Occupation in Amsterdam and The Hague, sticks to this principle, in addition giving us the scenes that were censored back then. Steven Soderbergh attempted a similar mismatch between modern content and traditional form in *The Good German* (2006), but was unsuccessful. *Black Book* is powerful and intelligent entertainment cinema, European-style, and a real visual treat from beginning to end. PB

"Moral relativism reigns, but blessed with a resourceful and attractive protagonist, Black Book doesn't dwell on it."

The Village Voice

"*Black Book* is as subversive as it is traditional, both enamored of conventional notions of heroism and frankly contemptuous of them." *Los Angeles Times*

THE LAST KING OF SCOTLAND

2006 – UK / USA / GERMANY – 121 MIN. – BIOPIC, POLITICAL THRILLER
DIRECTOR KEVIN MACDONALD (*1967)
SCREENPLAY PETER MORGAN, JEREMY BROCK from the book of the same name by GILES FODEN DIRECTOR OF PHOTOGRAPHY ANTHONY DOD MANTLE EDITING JUSTINE WRIGHT
MUSIC ALEX HEFFES PRODUCTION LISA BRYER, ANDREA CALDERWOOD, ANDREW MACDONALD, ALLON REICH, TESSA ROSS, CHRISTINE RUPPERT, CHARLES STEEL for FOX SEARCHLIGHT PICTURES, DNA FILMS, FILM4.
STARRING FOREST WHITAKER (Idi Amin), JAMES MCAVOY (Nicholas Garrigan), KERRY WASHINGTON (Kay Amin), GILLIAN ANDERSON (Sarah Merrit), SIMON MCBURNEY (Nigel Stone), DAVID OYELOWO (Dr. Junju).
ACADEMY AWARDS 2007 OSCAR for BEST LEADING ACTOR (Forest Whitaker).

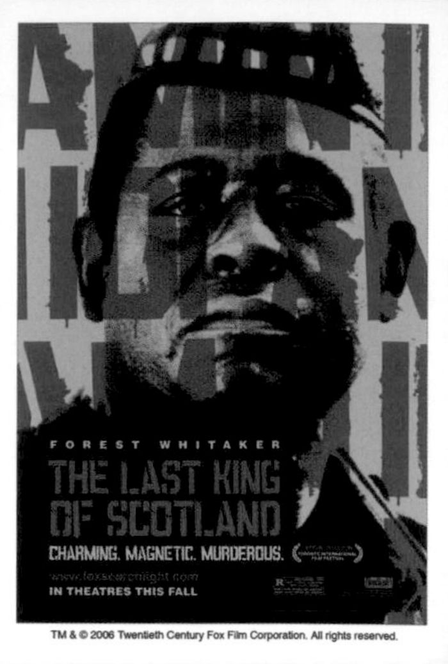

"I think your death will be the first real thing that has happened to you."

The film tells the story of keen young doctor Nicholas Garrigan (James McAvoy), who becomes the personal physician and advisor to the Ugandan dictator, Idi Amin (Forest Whitaker); his youthful exuberance seems to cloud his judgment, however, blinding him to the monstrous actions of the irrational despot. Like the insouciant Garrigan, the states that brought the real Idi Amin to power in 1971 and continued to support him also turned a blind eye, unwilling to acknowledge what was happening in Uganda: the mass persecution and murder of political opponents and "undesirables." Garrigan, too, sees, hears and says nothing as long as Amin is favoring him, the naive beneficiary of his brutal ruling clique, and entrusting him with setting up a health system. Thus, just as the political clown Idi Amin was himself an erratic puppet of Great Britain, Garrigan ends up as Amin's court jester, as becomes evident in the gruesome depiction of torture toward the end of the film.

Forest Whitaker plays the violent ruler with disturbing intensity. Whitaker's Amin reminds us of Marlon Brando in *Apocalypse Now* (1979) as butcher Walter E. Kurtz, who conducted a reign of terror in the Cambodian jungle. But the film does not attempt to denounce Amin, painting him rather as a man of contradictions: mostly moody, often extremely generous to Nicholas, in turns

1

1 African dictator Idi Amin as he has never yet been seen in a film – thanks to Forest Whitaker's brilliantly terrifying performance.

2 Guest at court: the misfortunes of Nicholas Garrigan (James McAvoy) take their bloody course after this meeting with attractive Kay Amin (Kerry Washington).

3 Uganda's popular oppressor: voluble and unpredictable.

"Forest Whitaker's bravura performance can be described by a rather unfashionable word: he plays the mass murderer Idi Amin with a bonhomie that sends a cold shiver down the spine." *Die Zeit*

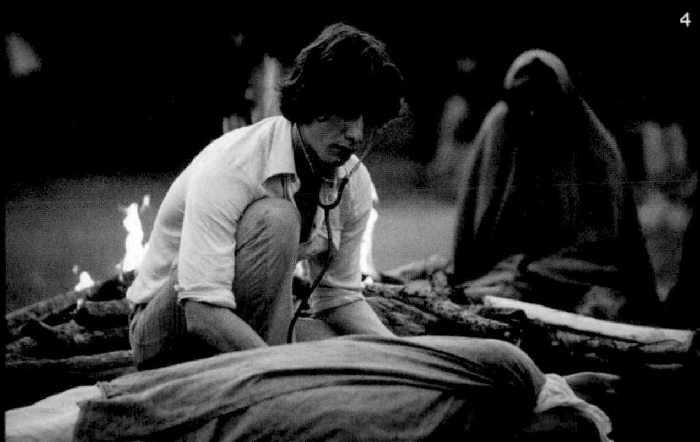

4 His face speaks volumes – suffering in silence, surrounded by misery.

5 Boyish Dr Garrigan succumbs increasingly to the illusion of power, until he nearly pays for it with his life.

paternally punitive, or childish, even intellectual on occasion; vulnerable, constantly distrustful and paranoid but also lonely, surrounded by armed mercenaries. Amin, who owed his career to intensive training in the British army, dominates the action, and not just by his sheer physical presence and unpredictability. From the outset, the often anxious faces reveal that something is not right, that all the wild parties are hiding something; the story initially hints at this secret then turns to exposing it, with increasing urgency.

Right from the start, the beautiful smoke and mirrors of carefree, feel-good music and sun-drenched images reveal unsettling gaps on closer inspection, through which we catch glimpses of the other, darker side. Thus, amid the relaxed, light-hearted mood of the opening scenes, men in uniform patrol in the background, as bafflingly gaunt figures run around the night streets; residents seem to trust the medicine men more than doctors, apparently struck by a strange oppression even though they ostensibly cheer Amin; and young men are brutally dragged away by the militia in broad daylight. And finally we see a dying cow, knocked down and fatally injured by the dictator's car.

The pitiful animal not only brings Amin and Garrigan together but its haunting death cries become the allegory of the sorely afflicted population:

6 The cheerful façade doesn't last long.

7 Political buffoonery or calculated madness? Amin's clique adopts a heroic pose.

Uganda is on its deathbed, with Amin its executioner rather than savior. But it is Garrigan who unceremoniously puts the cow out of its misery with a gunshot, impressing Amin and sealing an unequal friendship between the two men that will end so terribly after Garrigan impregnates one of Amin's four wives at one of the raucous parties – Uganda, a wild beauty, torture chamber and slaughterhouse.

The Last King of Scotland develops this story almost deceptively: we always see things through Garrigan's eyes, knowing only as much or as little as he does. At some point, much too late, he turns against Amin and even tries to kill him, but he fails and his plot is thwarted. Anthony Dod Mantle's cinematography effectively draws us emotionally into the cycle of corruption through the use of intoxicating images and ecstatic action sequences. Sharp contrasts, grainy resolution and saturated colors give the film a remarkable period atmosphere. Mantle's wild images authenticate the fictional story in an extremely sensual way, seamlessly connecting them to real-life events. This painfully beautiful film ends with Nicholas managing to escape from the dictator – just in the nick of time. BR

FOREST WHITAKER Born in 1961, the African-American actor, film producer and director began studying music, before making his debut in 1982 with a bit part in the thriller *Tag: The Assassination Game*. Whitaker may often have only attracted attention in supporting roles, but he has gone on to develop as a versatile character actor.
His skillful acting combined with an impressive physical presence have resulted in numerous awards, including Best Actor at Cannes in 1988 for his role as jazz musician Charlie "Bird" Parker in Clint Eastwood's biopic *Bird* (1988). As well as numerous critics' awards, Whitaker won the Golden Globe and Oscar for Best Actor at the ceremonies in 2007 for his leading role in *The Last King of Scotland*.
Whitaker has acted alongside famous Hollywood greats in many successful movies by well-known directors, for example *Platoon* (1986), *The Color of Money* (1986), *Good Morning, Vietnam* (1987), *The Crying Game* (1992) and *Prêt-à-Porter* (1994); he has also appeared in independent films such as *Smoke* (1995) and as the eponymous lead in Jim Jarmusch's *Ghost Dog: The Way of the Samurai* (1999).

THE QUEEN

2006 – UK / FRANCE / ITALY – 97 MIN. – BIOPIC, HISTORICAL DRAMA
DIRECTOR STEPHEN FREARS (*1941)
SCREENPLAY PETER MORGAN DIRECTOR OF PHOTOGRAPHY AFFONSO BEATO EDITING LUCIA ZUCCHETTI
MUSIC ALEXANDRE DESPLAT PRODUCTION ANDY HARRIES, CHRISTINE LANGAN, TRACEY SEAWARD for CANAL+, FRANCE 3 CINÉMA, PATHÉ, FUTURE FILMS, SCOTT RUDIN PRODUCTIONS, GRANADA, BIM DISTRIBUZIONE.
STARRING HELEN MIRREN (Queen Elizabeth II), MICHAEL SHEEN (Tony Blair), JAMES CROMWELL (Prince Philip), ALEX JENNINGS (Prince Charles), HELEN MCCRORY (Cherie Blair), SYLVIA SYMS (Queen Mother), ROGER ALLAM (Sir Robin Janvrin), TIM MCMULLAN (Stephen Lamport), DOUGLAS REITH (Lord Airlie).
ACADEMY AWARDS 2007 OSCAR for BEST LEADING ACTRESS (Helen Mirren).

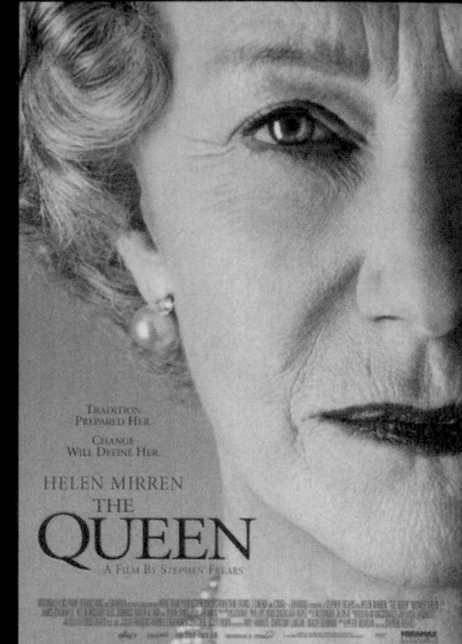

"This is a private matter."

The insidious transition from star to celebrity cult in our time has gripped not just the cinema but a far older institution – the British monarchy. Its head, HM Queen Elizabeth II, is its last surviving star; at least, she is the way Helen Mirren plays her. In the opening scene of *The Queen*, she is posing for the court artist and presenting herself as she wants to be seen, with the corners of her mouth majestically drawn down and the stern gaze of tradition. This star does not show her feelings; she is representative. Yet, as if it had been painted by Velázquez himself, the symbolic order of the scene is far more complex. The monarch's eye is trained anxiously on the television; a new breed of politician, a populist and media darling called Tony Blair (Michael Sheen), has just been elected Prime Minister. He is the tenth PM in Elizabeth's reign; the first was Winston Churchill and she will survive him as well. The real storm is yet to come, the TV event of 1997: the death in a car accident of Diana, Princess of Wales, the former Lady Diana Spencer and pin-up girl of the celebrity age.

As a semi-fictional reconstruction of this time, *The Queen* shows more than the biggest crisis to face the Windsor monarchy. A whole world view was shattered on an underpass pillar in Paris. The late "queen of hearts" forces the genuine article, the real Queen, into a battle of traditional versus modern. Diana secured a high media profile and the love of an entire people through scandalous revelations about her emotional life, thus destroying what the royal house had built up over the centuries: respect for the institution. How could the Queen forgive this? Yet now she is even supposed to show her feelings, because that is what her deeply affected people want. As a symbol of "genuine" mourning, the flag is meant to fly at half-mast over Buckingham Palace. Elizabeth refuses, which is formally correct, as Diana was no longer a member of the Royal Family following her divorce from Charles. But the protocols of a media society, the tabloid press and television, see it differently. Her apparent coldness is jeopardizing the state's raison d'être. At the end of a tortuous process, the Queen has to capitulate to save the throne. The person helping her is none other than the man whose curtsy on being sworn into office became a slapstick parody: Tony Blair.

Stephen Frears brings the course of events to life with a stunning montage of archive material and authentic-looking fiction. In keeping with the subject matter, he reconciles contradictions – great cinema and reality TV, sitcom and soap, the sublime and the ridiculous – in a glittering symbiosis. When the Windsors follow events on their TV set wearing dressing gowns, they look a bit like that normal and terribly nice TV family – with Prince Philip (James

1

Cromwell) as Al Bundy, always ready with a misplaced judgment. All he sees in the grieving masses who have transformed the palace entrance into a sea of flowers is a load of crazies holding candles. Paradoxically, however, they are the ones who represent the inner cohesion of a nation, not the royals who are in residence far away in the Scottish Highlands. It takes countless phone calls with Blair to mend what already seems in tatters. Amid all the hysteria he keeps a cool head – entirely to his own advantage.

In line with good old British tradition, Frears puts the two representatives of monarchist and democratic principles on an equal footing. For an avowed Leftie, it is astonishing how sympathetic his portraits turn out. What is even more surprising is the way he keeps everyone happy, both critics and admirers of the Establishment he epitomizes. You do not have to like Tony Blair to admire

"Where many would have expected dry, straight drama, Frears boldly asks us to accept these people as humans: flawed and ill-advised but ultimately with good reasons." *filmcritic.com*

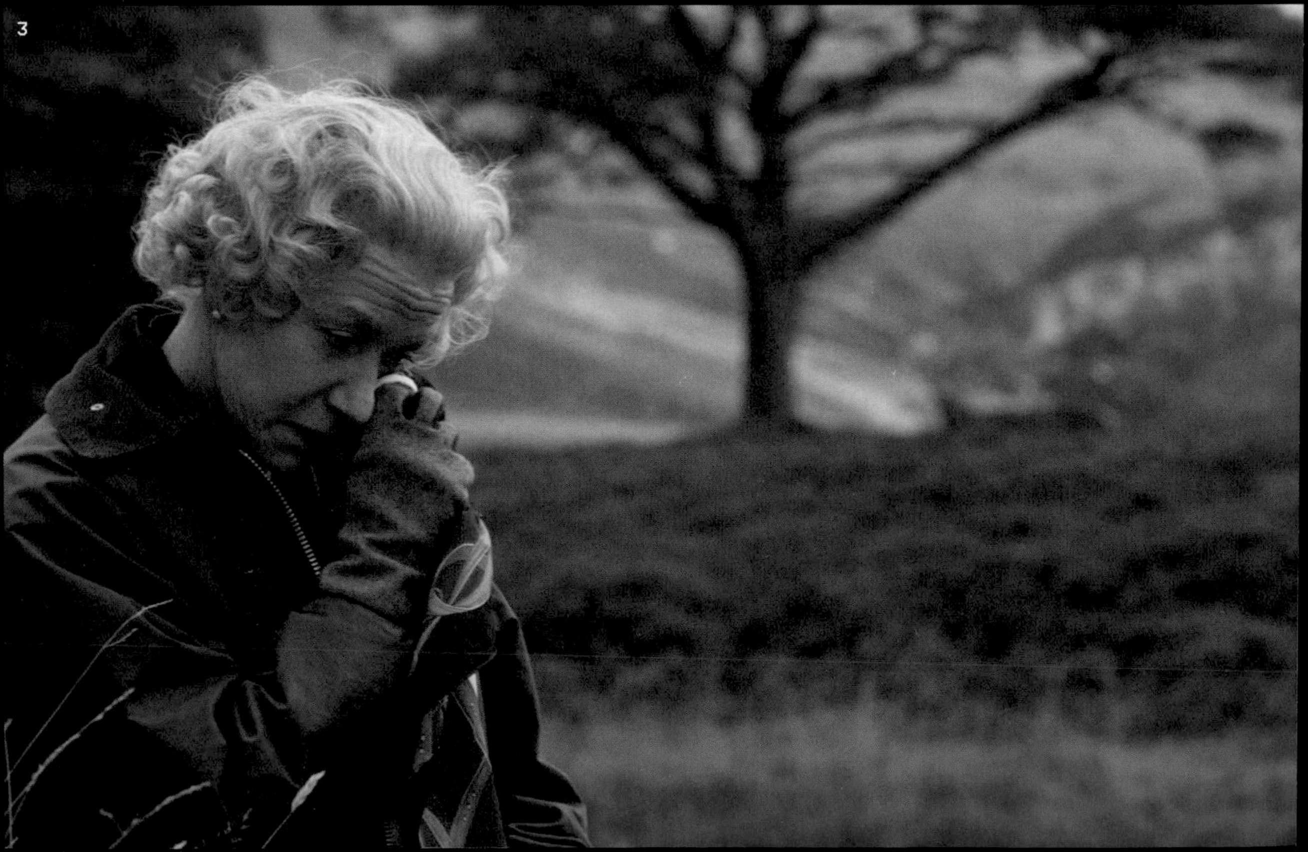

1 Stern look of tradition: Helen Mirren is convincing in her Oscar-winning role as Queen Elizabeth II, and not just on account of the physical similarity.

2 The royal family looks at the sea of flowers in front of Buckingham Palace, in a late gesture of sympathy with the people.

3 Key scene: Elizabeth bows to the pressure in the wilds of the Scottish Highlands.

4 A frightfully nice family: the mood of the public gives even Prince Philip, brilliantly played by James Cromwell, food for thought.

Michael Sheen's brilliant portrayal of a true political strategist; and you can despise the royals, yet love Mirren's Queen all the more for it. Of course, she has much more to offer than just astonishing similarity to the real person. With ironic gravity, amusement and dismay, she embodies at one and the same time the sense and non-sense of an authority that is self-legitimized. She does not understand the world any more, but has to conform to it because without it she does not exist. *The Queen* is an intellectual delight, as only real life can provide; at the same time it is a lesson in humility that is awe-inspiring. Only half joking, Mirren dedicated her well-deserved Oscar to the Queen, which has a certain logic. PB

STEPHEN FREARS Born in Leicester in 1941, Stephen Frears is the heavyweight of British cinema. He avoids being restricted to one genre and follows other people's screenplays for the most part in terms of style, which makes him a craftsman. But Frears decides on the themes. His first success was *My Beautiful Laundrette* (1985), a controversial didactic movie about racism and homophobia in Thatcher's England whose screenplay was written by Hanif Kureishi. They continued their successful partnership with the anarchic tale about interracial relationships, *Sammy and Rosie Get Laid* (1987). Frears portrayed quite different social outsiders in the film adaptation of *Dangerous Liaisons* (1988). This costume drama about the erotic intrigues of the aristocracy, brilliantly cast with John Malkovich and Glenn Close, paved the way to Hollywood. Yet films like *The Grifters* (1990) and *Accidental Hero* (1992) encouraged him to return to safe ground at home.
As if to prove the point, the small budget yet heart-warming comedy drama *The Snapper* (1993) became an international hit. From the novel by Roddy Doyle about the problems of a pregnant girl in Catholic Ireland, Frears showed once again his feel for working class sensitivities. Similarly, he told the famous story of "Dr. Jekyll and Mr. Hyde" from the perspective of a servant girl in *Mary Reilly* (1996), though this interesting genre crossover flopped. The long-winded postmodern western *The Hi-Lo Country* (1998) turned out to be another career low, though it now seems like a thematic forerunner of Ang Lee's *Brokeback Mountain* (2005). With *High Fidelity* (2000) the British director played it safe commercially, though he shifted the action of Nick Hornby's British cult novel to Chicago – maybe just to annoy his fellow Brits.
The man who learned his craft with legendary filmmakers such as Karel Reisz and Lindsay Anderson finally struck gold with *The Queen* (2006). This complex docudrama about the British monarchy's reaction to Diana's death earned him an Oscar nomination and a BAFTA Best Film Award.

THE DEPARTED

2006 – USA – 151 MIN. – GANGSTER MOVIE
DIRECTOR MARTIN SCORSESE (*1942)
SCREENPLAY WILLIAM MONAHAN DIRECTOR OF PHOTOGRAPHY MICHAEL BALLHAUS
EDITING THELMA SHOONMAKER MUSIC HOWARD SHORE
PRODUCTION GRAHAM KING, BRAD GREY, GIANNI NUNNARI, BRAD PITT for WARNER BROS., PLAN B ENTERTAINMENT, INITIAL ENTERTAINMENT GROUP, VERTIGO ENTERTAINMENT, MEDIA ASIA FILMS.
STARRING LEONARDO DICAPRIO (William M. Costigan), MATT DAMON (Colin Sullivan), JACK NICHOLSON (Frank Costello), MARK WAHLBERG (Dignam), MARTIN SHEEN (Queenan), ALEC BALDWIN (Ellerby), RAY WINSTONE (Mr. French), VERA FARMIGA (Dr. Madolyn Madden), ANTHONY ANDERSON (Brown), DAVID O'HARA (Fitzy).
ACADEMY AWARDS 2007 OSCARS for BEST PICTURE (Graham King), BEST DIRECTOR (Martin Scorsese), BEST ADAPTED SCREENPLAY (William Monahan) and BEST FILM EDITING (Thelma Shoonmaker).

"I don't want to be a product of my environment. I want my environment to be a product of me."

A typical Hollywood irony: Martin Scorsese, one of Hollywood's pioneering filmmakers, finally won his first Oscar after years of failed attempts – for a remake. But anyone who has influenced world cinema like Scorsese – who was 64 at the time of filming *The Departed* – must be allowed to take something back from it. It is even logical in a sense that the film has a sibling in the highly praised Hong Kong original version, *Infernal Affairs* (*Mou gaan dou*, 2002); some would even say a twin. The structure of this violent drama – half gangster movie, half spy thriller – follows the laws of symmetry to the letter.

Two police cadets enter the service. Billy Costigan (Leonardo DiCaprio) is sent undercover to infiltrate Boston's Irish mafia. Like almost every character, he has a doppelganger: ambitious Colin Sullivan (Matt Damon) was raised from childhood by powerful mob boss Frank Costello (Jack Nicholson), for the purpose in turn of penetrating the Boston Police Special Unit. Costello assumes the role of father figure to both, but neither knows of the other's existence. The dominant dialectic is one of loyalty and betrayal. It leads inexorably to disaster, when each is assigned to find the other: it is not only Costello but also gruff police chief, Captain Ellerby (Alec Baldwin), who wants to know who has infiltrated their hermetically sealed system. Costigan and Sullivan are looking for the mole or, in the parlance of both systems, the "rat." They are looking for the other and for themselves at the same time.

Such a fiendish set-up requires a diabolical center, and Jack Nicholson is the right man for the job. As the underworld boss, an Irish monster with apparently limitless access to babes and dough, Nicholson's Frank Costello gives his two protégés a hellishly hard time. To its credit, the movie's balance

is never tipped by his flamboyantly hammed-up performance (complete with broad grin and bloody shirt). On the other hand, who else could get away with imitating a nibbling rat or brandishing severed limbs and dildos as if it were the most natural thing in the world? It was the first time Scorsese had worked with the acting giant and it was to be an unforgettable experience all round: cameraman Michael Ballhaus later recounted many an anecdote about Nicholson's bright ideas on directing, which drove Scorsese to distraction and mostly wound up on the cutting-room floor.

The outstanding performances by the two famous young actors were another matter. In this movie, Matt Damon perfected the role of the passive careerist who demonstrates a boundless capacity for assimilation, even in an evil system. The physical resemblance to his doppelganger is deceptive. As

2

"Scorsese has hit his stride again, and he has produced something with as much gusto as his best films of 20 or 30 years back; it grips and shocks and entertains – all with the help of first-class writing from Monahan, firing off dialogue of which Mamet would be proud. Scorsese, that American movie giant, has never been asleep exactly, but now he is very much awake." *The Guardian*

3

1 Leonardo DiCaprio, the greatest method actor of his generation, experiences an identity crisis as undercover policeman Billy Costigan.

2 Sergeant Dignam (Mark Wahlberg) swears more profusely than is normal for a Scorsese film.

3 Similarly gifted police boss Ellerby (Alec Baldwin) searches for a rat in his own ranks.

4 Mistake in the system: police mole Colin Sullivan (Matt Damon) deletes his rival's identity.

ALEC BALDWIN Alec Baldwin, the oldest and best known of the four acting brothers (the others are Stephen, William and Daniel) was for a long time a victim of the modern cult of the celebrity. Headlines tended to be made less by his movies than his marriage to fellow actor Kim Basinger, their espousal of animal rights and vegetarianism, and the nerve-racking battle for custody of their daughter Ireland. He got his breakthrough playing alongside Sean Connery in *The Hunt for Red October* (1990) and had a leading role in the comic book adaptation *The Shadow* (1994), but Baldwin continued to be the popular target of ridicule and parody. After taking refuge in the theater, he turned things around impressively with outstanding performances as a "tough guy." In an earlier role as a real estate boss in James Foley's *Glengarry Glen Ross* (1992) he had put the fear of God in his underlings, Jack Lemmon, Al Pacino and Kevin Spacey; he was also well-suited to the role of cynical power seeker as the casino boss in *The Cooler* (2003) and as the voluble police chief in Martin Scorsese's *The Departed* (2006). Incidentally, the man with the husky voice is a regular commentator on political life: his verbal attacks on former US President, George W. Bush, and his Vice President Dick Cheney are legendary. A move into the political arena is not out of the question.

5

"The dialogue crackles wittily and obscenely, and the set-pieces are superbly staged, whether in dockland shoot-outs or in an ironic confrontation in a porn cinema. And the violence is casual, matter of fact, part of a way of life." *The Observer*

the undercover cop, Costigan, Leonardo DiCaprio is tormented precisely because of his loss of identity. He not only has to do the groundwork for Costello's homicidal activities, his whole personality along with his personal data has been erased from police records as a precautionary measure. DiCaprio's struggle with his split identity renders plausible his visits to the police psychologist. The latter's professional assessment will resonate with anyone who admires classical method acting: "I find your vulnerability rather disconcerting."

Crime and betrayal: after the worthy epics *Gangs of New York* (2002) and *The Aviator* (2004), Scorsese was back on his home territory of "mean streets" with *The Departed* – and back to his old form. It was no great leap for him to move from the New York Mafia to the Irish mobsters of south Boston. The same rules are applied for killing, even if communication is more effectiv due to the significant part played by cell phones. He even manages to heighte the destructive energy of his style with clunky excesses of violence and grotesqu tirades of swearing. The movie actually relates to the classic original like it evil, sordid twin. At the same time, the old master exhibits a new composure and not just in the final scene, which is more chaotic than inevitable. Ballhaus camera avoids the grand gesture in favor of greater intimacy, while edito Thelma Schoonmaker blurs the boundaries between the systems wit precise, seamless editing that earned her one of the film's four well deserve Oscars. *The Departed* has proved Martin Scorsese's most successful movi to date.

P

5 Job interview: Billy starts to throw his weight about, to catch the attention of his new colleagues and win their trust.

6 Job interview: Billy draws attention to himself and wins the trust of his new colleagues with an unexpected show of strength.

7 They play hardball in the Irish underworld. But Costigan has already learned to take it on the chin.

8 Even introvert Colin resorts to ruthless tactics when necessary. There is a danger of his cover being blown.

"*The Departed* is Scorsese's most purely enjoyable movie in years. But it's not for the faint of heart. It's rude, bleak, violent and defiantly un-PC." *Newsweek*

CASINO ROYALE

2006 – UK / USA / CZECH REPUBLIC / GERMANY – 144 MIN. – SPY FILM, ACTION MOVIE
DIRECTOR MARTIN CAMPBELL (*1940)
SCREENPLAY NEAL PURVIS, ROBERT WADE, PAUL HAGGIS, from the novel by IAN FLEMING
DIRECTOR OF PHOTOGRAPHY PHIL MEHEUX EDITING STUART BAIRD MUSIC DAVID ARNOLD
PRODUCTION BARBARA BROCCOLI, MICHAEL G. WILSON for METRO-GOLDWYN-MAYER, EON PRODUCTIONS, COLUMBIA PICTURES, DANJAG, BABELSBERG FILM, CASINO ROYALE PRODUCTIONS, STILLKING FILMS, UNITED ARTISTS.
STARRING DANIEL CRAIG (James Bond), EVA GREEN (Vesper Lynd), JUDI DENCH (M), MADS MIKKELSEN (Le Chiffre), JEFFREY WRIGHT (Felix Leiter), GIANCARLO GIANNINI (Mathis), CATERINA MURINO (Solange), SIMON ABKARIAN (Alex Dimitrios), ISAACH DE BANKOLÉ (Steven Obanno), LUDGER PISTOR (Mendel).

"Christ, I miss the Cold War."

When Ursula Andress rose like Venus from the foaming waves in *Dr. No* (1962), it was the dawn of a new age: the Cold War had become hot, and only one man could win it. The scene is repeated in *Casino Royale*. Only this time the pearly drops of water are running down the steely-muscled body of James Bond himself, though once again the appearance marks a new beginning. In his 21st adventure (according to the official count of Bond films) the most irresistible secret agent in the world experiences a rebirth. This applies not only to the new Bond, Daniel Craig, who is now the sixth in the role, but to this much-loved concept.

Quite a lot is expected of die-hard aficionados. On the orders of the British Secret Service, Bond must eliminate a dangerous opponent: the card-playing Le Chiffre (Mads Mikkelsen), who bleeds from one eye and funds international terrorism with swindles worth millions. But the spy does this without any help from Moneypenny, without the brilliant inventions of Q, without exploding boxes, laser watches or sexist quips at the expense of the usual "Bond girls." In fact, there are no Bond girls. Nor does the megalomaniac arch villain have any in his fiendish HQ, which Bond blows up in a final battle 30 minutes before the end (the laser watch was set after this). The Bond formula, once style-defining with its dependably recurrent glamorous and violent elements, has been unceremoniously swept aside.

Instead of endlessly innovative extravagances, the audience gets a modern, more Spartan look, real stunts in place of special effects – and Daniel Craig. It's no coincidence that the best Bond since Sean Connery is closer to his creator Ian Fleming's original than all his predecessors. *Casino Royale* is the film version of the first book in the series: Fleming's family had withheld the rights to it for decades. True to the source material, Bond must first earn his license to kill here and is, like Craig, as yet an unknown quantity. He cannot allow himself the sophisticated snobbery of Pierce Brosnan, who would no

1

"Yes, Daniel Craig makes a superb Bond: Leaner, more taciturn, less sex-obsessed, able to be hurt in body and soul, not giving a damn if his martini is shaken or stirred." *Chicago Sun-Times*

2

3

1 A new Bond and fresh approach: Daniel Craig as 007 is harder, but also more vulnerable, than his predecessors.

2 The first Bond girl is a woman. The secret agent will never recover from meeting Vesper Lynd (Eva Green).

3 Brilliantly brought to life by Eva Green, the brainy Vesper has a sure-fire wit and plays her own game.

doubt have avoided the first action sequence of note (a breathtaking pursuit, on foot no less, across a filthy construction site in Madagascar) at all costs. Even at this stage, the scene reveals everything about the new, masculine, physical profile of the movie. Craig's Bond is no urbane gentleman, but a proletarian fighter who gets his hands dirty. His boss, M (Judi Dench), somewhat disparagingly though accurately, describes him as a "weapon on legs." Yet the killing machine is also vulnerable, as proved in a torture scene when Le Chiffre chains him naked to a chair with the intention of robbing him of his crown jewels. In what is perhaps the strangest of all Bond scenes to date, he does not prevent a bomb exploding, but instead his own heart attack. In this way, the canonical scenes of the series are cleverly deconstructed again and again, and presented in a new form. Bond's favorite drink is still a vodka martini, but the question of whether it should be shaken or stirred is put decisively into perspective: "Do I look like I give a damn?"

As a real man, however, the new Bond is not completely closed off to his emotions. Love enters his life for the first time since *On Her Majesty's Secret Service* (1969) in the form of Vesper Lynd (Eva Green). She has the looks of a classic Bond girl. As an equal partner, the female agent is in a position to provide a flawless analysis of Bond's character in a brilliant argument during a short train journey. Vesper is conveying the money for Le Chiffre's million-stake poker game in Montenegro, which Bond naturally wins. But he will lose her in the end. The tragic outcome of the affair explains (apropos of nothing)

JUDI DENCH Judi Dench was born in the English town of York in 1934 and appointed DBE (Dame Commander of the Order of the British Empire) by HM Queen Elizabeth II in 1988. The intervening years saw an awe-inspiring stage career. As an ensemble member of the Royal Shakespeare Company among others she regularly delighted audiences, winning seven Laurence Olivier Theatre Awards in the process. Cinema did without her services for far too long. It was said that she did not have "the face for movies" – a monstrous error of judgment. Dench shot to fame in an 8-minute appearance as Queen Elizabeth I in *Shakespeare in Love* (1998), which won her the Oscar for Best Supporting Actress. Before that, we saw her alongside her good friend Maggie Smith in the Merchant-Ivory literary adaptation of *A Room with a View* (1985). Since *GoldenEye* (1995), she has also been a firm feature of the James Bond series, playing the Secret Service boss M who does not tolerate any gaffs on the part of pleasure-loving "00s." Her serious presence even enabled her to weather the planned Bond re-launch with *Casino Royale* (2006). Judi Dench never fails to be splendidly ironic as the domineering old lady in literary adaptations such as *The Importance of Being Earnest* (2002) and *Pride & Prejudice* (2005). Yet her performances become no less than harrowingly good in parts that break from such "safe" characterizations. Hence, she received an Oscar nomination for her performance as Iris Murdoch, the writer with Alzheimer's, in *Iris* (2001) as well as for the teacher consumed by jealousy in *Notes on a Scandal* (2006). Even now, however, showered as she is on all sides with honors, Dame Judi Dench will drop any movie role for even a minor acting job on stage.

many of Bond's subsequent foibles, including his troubled relationship to women. *Casino Royale* was a huge hit at the box office, after much skepticism about Daniel Craig in particular. His bold reinterpretation, coupled with his considerable charisma, convinced the critics. In retrospect, the rejuvenation therapy appears to have given a last-gasp kiss-of-life to Bond, as the concept of the franchise series fizzles out. Parodies like *Austin Powers: International Man of Mystery* (1997) appeared far more inventive than the original. While the real James Bond had to be content with self-reference, a certain Jason Bourne stole his initials and provided us with a higher quality, more contemporaneous action movie with every film. With *Casino Royale*, Bond has come bang up to date in artistic terms, ready for a high-octane race with his competitor. PB

4

4 Sometimes Bond's boss "M" (Judi Dench) wishes she was back in the Cold War. At least then the rules were clear.

5 Playing poker on Her Majesty's Service: Bond must ruin his opponent in order to make him play ball. He survives several attempts on his life in the process.

6 Evil eye: Danish actor Mads Mikkelsen as Le Chiffre gives us one of the most unusual Bond villains.

"It is all ridiculously enjoyable, because the smirking and the quips and the gadgets have been cut back – and the emotion and wholesome sado-masochism have been pumped up." *The Guardian*

5

CURSE OF THE GOLDEN FLOWER

MAN CHENG JIN DAI HUANG JIN JIA

2006 – HONG KONG / CHINA – 114 MIN. – COSTUME DRAMA
DIRECTOR ZHANG YIMOU (*1951)
SCREENPLAY ZHANG YIMOU from the play "LEI YU" (THUNDERSTORM) by CAO YU
DIRECTOR OF PHOTOGRAPHY ZHAO XIAODING EDITING CHENG LONG MUSIC SHIGERU UMEBAYASHI
PRODUCTION ZHANG WEIPING, WILLIAM KONG, ZHANG YIMOU for BEIJING NEW PICTURES, EDKO FILM, ELITE GROUP.
STARRING CHOW YUN-FAT (Emperor), GONG LI (Empress), JAY CHOU (Prince Jie), LIU YE (Crown Prince), NI DAHONG (Imperial Physician Jiang), CHEN YIN (Mrs. Jiang), LI MAN (Chan), QIN JUNJIE (Prince Cheng).

"Is resistance worth it?"

When *Curse of the Golden Flower* was released in cinemas in 2007 the critics were divided, as with just about every recent film by Zhang Yimou. While some continued to enthuse about the director's visual creativity and his painstakingly detailed mise-en-scène, others felt that they, and the dramatic story about the fall of an emperor's family during the Tang Dynasty in 928 AD, had been overwhelmed by the lavish gloss of golden sets and costumes. And for those who had previously regarded Zhang as a dissident who had defended the rights of the individual against violence, bureaucracy and state power in films like *Red Sorghum* (*Hong gao liang*, 1987) and *The Story of Qiu Ju* (*Qiu Ju da guan si*, 1992), all the ornamental pomp and splendor and the elaborate mass scenes were merely further proof that Zhang had become an official filmmaker of the Chinese state, who now indulged in meaningless choreography, having long since been taken in by the decadence of power that is on show here.

To see Zhang as a political filmmaker and his works as direct parables of social and political development in China has always been a projection on the part of the West, however, and falls short of the mark. How then should *The Curse of the Golden Flower* be interpreted? As being, quite simply, supportive of the state, because in the end the emperor and along with him the social order triumphs at any price? This illusion might just be sustainable when thousands of anonymous hands whisk away the dead, blood-soaked warriors from the battle zone in the palace, lay down new carpets and replace the broken chrysanthemum vases. But the emperor's entire family is dead and his victory is, in reality, his most bitter defeat. So perhaps we should instead see the film as an analogy of capitalism, of the decadence and depths that lurk behind the glittering façades?

It could also be that *Curse of the Golden Flower* is "just" a story with two oppressed women in a patriarchal society at its center, who are either claiming their rights or seeking revenge. It is a tale Zhang has always been interested in and one that is not too far removed from other films he has made with Gong Li, who brings her dramatic talents to the role of the empress in this movie. As the daughter of the old emperor, she is of true noble blood, but is now under the rule of her husband, a former provincial governor who has been administering medicine to her every two hours for the past ten years, although she is not ill. This is simply a form of bullying; an act of oppression that would have consequences if she were to refuse. It becomes intolerable when she realizes that the emperor has recently been replacing the "medicine" with poison designed to drive her insane and finally kill her. For a long time, however, she has been planning a coup that will put her son Prince Jie (Jay Chou) on the throne on the day of the Chrysanthemum Festival, which is traditionally dedicated to the wellbeing of the family.

Another spouse also has reasons for seeking revenge: the emperor's first wife (Chen Yin) is presumed dead, but was actually denounced and thrown in prison when the then provincial governor saw the emperor's daughter as a better option. But she has reappeared, as the imperial physician's wife of

1

2

1 Medicine? As the Empress (Gong Li) well knows, every sip her husband gives her contains a dose of poison.

2 Pageantry of power: the imperial family in front of their palace.

3 A strong woman, she weaves intrigues to free herself from dependency on the emperor. But he has already seen through the empress.

"For some years now Zhang Yimou has been operating in a league all of his own. He seems to redefine his own standards with every film, with ever-increasing energy – it keeps getting a bit more magnificent and faster, and higher and wider ..." *Süddeutsche Zeitung*

3

4

4 Without realizing it, the Crown Prince (Liu Ye) is involved in an incestuous relationship with his half-sister Chan (Li Man).

5 Pageantry in red and gold: Zhang Yimou's *Curse of the Golden Flower* was one of the most expensive Chinese films ever made.

all people, who mixes the poison for the empress. In reality, the personal relationships between the various characters are even more complicated, not least because the princes are also vying for power. Only the Crown Prince (Liu Ye) is not involved; instead, he is maintaining two incestuous relationships, one with his stepmother, the empress, and the other (unaware of the family relationship) with Chan (Li Man), the imperial physician's daughter whose mother, of course, is also his own. Just about everyone in this scenario has something to hide, but there are no real secrets – hardly surprising in a palace with thousands of "invisible" servants. The only one in this morass of intrigue, divided loyalties and vengeful activity who has any sort of overview is the emperor: a man who entrenches himself behind an inscrutable patriarchal smile while being prepared for every eventuality – his warriors always seem to appear from nowhere. As such, it remains unclear as to whether he also has a human side; but, even if he does, he is always prepared to sacrifice it in his drive to maintain power. Thus, the imperial drama runs its course, its intimate and melodramatic aspects clearly of more interest to Zhang than the

CHOW YUN-FAT was the biggest star in Hong Kong action cinema in the late 1980s through early 1990s. Through hails of bullets choreographed by director John Woo, as in *The Killer* (*Dip huet seung hung*, 1989) and *Hard Boiled* (*Lat sau san taam*, 1992), he became internationally famous as the supercool hero with trench coat and guns – slightly melancholic, but always the last man standing amidst the carnage.

Born in 1955 on Lamma Island in Hong Kong (then a British colony) Chow took an acting course at the age of 17 and went on to carve a meteoric career in various TV series, where he made regular appearances until the mid-1980s. The films of John Woo, however, were the key to his greater success in cinema, and eventually ensured his career in Hollywood, where he made his debut in 1998 in the action movie *The Replacement Killers*, co-produced by Woo.

Since then, he has appeared in many films, including *Anna and the King* (1999) alongside Jodie Foster, and Ang Lee's international success *Crouching Tiger, Hidden Dragon* (*Wo hu cang long*, 2000) in which he starred as the legendary swordsman; he also had a minor role as a pirate captain in *Pirates of the Caribbean: At World's End* (2007). He even impressed on the big screen in China as the famous philosopher *Confucius* (*Kong zi*, 2010). Chow's trademark is the massive screen presence he exudes through his calm demeanor and somewhat minimalist expression. Off-screen, the star is said to be extremely friendly and modest. His most recent feature film is the comedy Western set in 1920s China, *Let the Bullets Fly* (2010), in which he plays a brutal gangster.

6 The emperor (Chow Yun-Fat) is always one step ahead of his rivals for power. He must act alone to win.

7 Prince Jie (Jay Chou) stands faithfully by his mother, but there's nothing he or his troops can do against the well prepared emperor.

8 As if from nowhere: the emperor's guards appear out of the blue in sensationally choreographed fight scenes.

9 A woman humiliated: the emperor's first wife, presumed dead, suddenly appears in the palace as an ally of the present empress.

mass choreography of the battle everything hinges on – which was staged by Ching Siu-Tung, whose *Chinese Ghost Story* trilogy (*Sien nui yau wan*, 1987/1990/1991) won him international acclaim and who for more than two decades has been regarded as one of Hong Kong's most important action directors and fight choreographers. This becomes particularly evident in the scenes where the imperial guard attacks the mansion of the physician and his wife, followed by a chase during which black-garbed warriors swing through narrow gorges on ropes. The fight scenes are, of course, spectacular; yet nothing is as moving in this film as the face of Gong Li, fighting back tears of fury and despair beneath the layers of golden clothes and make-up she wears in this world of ritual and ceremony.

IP

YELLA

2006/07 – GERMANY – 88 MIN. – DRAMA
DIRECTOR CHRISTIAN PETZOLD (*1960)
SCREENPLAY CHRISTIAN PETZOLD DIRECTOR OF PHOTOGRAPHY HANS FROMM EDITING BETTINA BÖHLER
MUSIC STEFAN WILL PRODUCTION FLORIAN KOERNER VON GUSTORF, MICHAEL WEBER for SCHRAMM FILM KOERNER & WEBER, ZDF, ARTE.
STARRING NINA HOSS (Yella), DEVID STRIESOW (Philipp), HINNERK SCHÖNEMANN (Ben), BURGHART KLAUSSNER (Dr. Gunthen), BARBARA AUER (Barbara Gunthen), CHRISTIAN REDL (Yella's Father), WANJA MUES (Sprenger), MICHAEL WITTENBORN (Dr. Schmidt-Ott), MARTIN BRAMBACH (Dr. Fritz), JOACHIM NIMTZ (Prietzel).
IFF BERLIN 2007 SILVER BEAR for BEST ACTRESS (Nina Hoss).

"Do you know about broker posing? Like young lawyers in crappy Grisham movies?"

Yella (Nina Hoss) wants to get away. Away from the small East German town in which the specters of blandly renovated houses already bear witness to emptiness and despair; away from her father, who may look after her but cannot offer her a future; and away from a marriage to bankrupt building contractor Ben (Hinnerk Schönemann), who lives in hope of getting the big contract for the airport even though this has long since proved an investment disaster. She won't be put off by either the ideas or reactions of the man who is still her husband, who oscillates between being seductive and threatening, and certainly not by fate. Yet her escape looks like grinding to a halt on her very first day when her new company goes bust. Then she happens to meet Philipp (Devid Striesow) – a crafty businessman like her husband but, unlike him, successful and smart. She soon sets herself up as his assistant, workin on negotiations with companies dependent on venture capital.

What starts out as a social drama about young women moving out o East Germany turns into an engaging observation of work in the context o globalization and finally reveals itself as a kind of "scary movie" about th individual in an age of hyper-capitalism. Like the capital that dominate conversations and occasionally manifests itself in bundles of banknotes tha are exchanged by hand (but mostly flit through space in numbers and abstrac property relations), this odd couple are like ghosts wandering through a dream like German reality that seems to consist of hotel and conference rooms an company cars – inhospitable non-places of a transitory nature. So when Yell

orders a taxi in the dreary industrial estate of the Hannover expo site to go to the "corner of Rue de Paris and Sydney Garden," it says more about notional concepts of place than many sociological studies.

Like no other German director in the last 15 years, Christian Petzold has created memorable images of German society: in *The State I Am In* (*Die innere Sicherheit*, 2000), the nomadic and monadic existence of ex-terrorists living underground who try in vain to maintain the veneer of the petit bourgeois family; in *Gespenster* (2005), the fairytale forest of Berlin's Tiergarten nestling alongside the genteel jewel in the city's crown, Potsdamer Platz; and in *Wolfsburg* (2003), the misery of medium-size towns where work and narrow-mindedness destroy any dream of another life. Petzold always avoids the superficially

"Yella easily reduces those around her to ghosts. Her perceptions are not accompanied by thoughts. Her intellectual side has already been erased, and now she only has the strength to feel. She is aware of movement ..." *Süddeutsche Zeitung*

3

1 Love in a time of venture capitalism: Yella (Nina Hoss).

2 The corporate raider who loves me: Philipp (Devid Striesow) as the incarnation of capitalist enterprise.

3 Gestures and poses: Christian Petzold's films are a vibrant mix of real presence and dense symbolism.

4 Having escaped from the waters of the Elbe, Yella leaves her old life behind and dives into the world of risk management.

striking and metaphorically exaggerated in favor of what might be called a pathological unease that seems to shimmer in and behind things but never takes a distinctive form. Petzold's movies are fairytales and sentimental regional films at one and the same time, telling of a desire for security and happiness. But they also relentlessly reveal that, behind the prosperous façades and average family appearances, it is not desperation that prevails but a rupture that strikes right to the core. Petzold inherited an attention to place and things from New German cinema, which avoids any look of studio and sets, while his eye for plot and character has been influenced by American movies. The way someone drives, peels an orange or folds his arms behind his head says more about that character's relationship to the world than beautifully written or spoken words, which inevitably sound like a screenplay, or elaborate groupings of characters from a bourgeois tragedy. So *Yella* may seem alienating at first glance, because genre clichés (thriller, melodrama) and echoes of auteurist cinema create expectations that the film has no intention of fulfilling. If we allow ourselves to become involved in the movie's own enclosed empirical world and its cognitive processes, however, we will be richly rewarded by the best that German cinema has produced since reunification. MH

BERLIN SCHOOL In the first half of the 1990s, Angela Schanelec, Thomas Arslan and Christian Petzold studied together at the Berlin Film School: three directors who only ten years later would be generally identified as representatives of a common artistic direction.
Their films are distinguished by a tendency to deal with contemporary, everyday subjects, using quiet visual language with frequently lengthy, static shots and deliberately dispassionate mise-en-scène: a film score that does not stir the emotions, no great empathy for the characters and no dramatic cathartic effects. Their role models were Robert Bresson, Michelangelo Antonioni and Yasujiro Ozu, while their rejection of movie-making that directly manipulated feelings often brought the accusation of being un-cinematic.
The label "Berlin School" only appeared after they had attracted attention at festivals and the influential French film magazine "Cahiers du cinéma" had bestowed the epithet "German New Wave" on the group. Yet there was still no unified program, nor any self-labeling as a school. A second and third generation developed as quickly as it had been proclaimed, including both male and female directors such as Henner Winckler, Christoph Hochhäusler, Maren Ade, Benjamin Heisenberg, Valeska Grisebach and Ulrich Köhler. Meanwhile, even a magazine – "Revolver" – has become associated with this artistic school, with the result that Germany now has an actual film movement with its own name as well as a journal.

ZODIAC

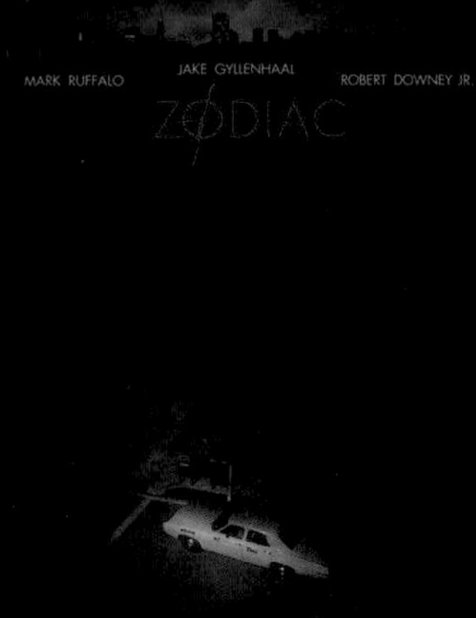

2007 – USA – 157 MIN. / 162 MIN. DIRECTOR'S CUT – THRILLER
DIRECTOR DAVID FINCHER (*1962)
SCREENPLAY JAMES VANDERBILT, from the novel of the same name by ROBERT GRAYSMITH
DIRECTOR OF PHOTOGRAPHY HARRIS SAVIDES **EDITING** ANGUS WALL **MUSIC** DAVID SHIRE
PRODUCTION CEÁN CHAFFIN, BRAD FISCHER, MIKE MEDAVOY, ARNOLD MESSER, JAMES VANDERBILT for PHOENIX PICTURES, ROAD REBEL, PARAMOUNT PICTURES, WARNER BROS.
STARRING JAKE GYLLENHAAL (Robert Graysmith), MARK RUFFALO (Inspector David Toschi), ANTHONY EDWARDS (Inspector William Armstrong), ROBERT DOWNEY JR. (Paul Avery), CHLOË SEVIGNY (Melanie), ELIAS KOTEAS (Sgt. Jack Mulanax), JOHN CARROLL LYNCH (Arthur Leigh Allen), PHILIP BAKER HALL (Sherwood Morrill), BRIAN COX (Melvin Belli), JIMMI SIMPSON (Mike Mageau).

"Just because you can't prove it doesn't mean it's not true."

Two lovers are brutally shot dead in a park. Four weeks later, an anonymous letter arrives at the "San Francisco Chronicle." It passes through many hands before arriving in the editorial team's mailbox, eventually reaching the desk of the editor-in-chief in a camera shot that is fairly typical of David Fincher's movies. *Zodiac* is a film about a serial killer: a police procedural movie like Fincher's biggest success beforehand, *Se7en* (1995). Yet this excellent depiction of a period in history and its monstrosities is also primarily a movie about newspapers. No one had heard of computers in 1969. Chain-smoking journalists hammer away on their typewriters, sleeves rolled up. It's not entirely coincidental that the yellow tones of the hallowed premises call to mind the colors of whiskey and nicotine. As far as the letter is concerned, it is of course the first time the Zodiac killer has claimed responsibility. Director David Fincher deliberately picked this true case so that he could break some of the rules of the genre. Five murders in the San Francisco area between 1968 and 1969 are still attributed to the Zodiac killer, who was never identified. This guarantees from the outset that *Zodiac* will be a frustrating thriller. Instead of satisfying the desire to find the culprit, Fincher shifts attention to his pursuers: the phlegmatic cop David Toschi (Mark Ruffalo), who looks very like Inspector Columbo and was a role model for Steve McQueen in *Bullitt* (1968); Paul Avery (Robert Downey Jr.), the newshound of the "Chronicle" who is arrogant and drunken in equal measures; and finally Robert Graysmith (Jake Gyllenhaal), whose book provides source material for the case. The action is set when he is

1

1 Inspector David Toschi (Mark Ruffalo), clearly based on Peter Falk's "Columbo" character, searches for the Zodiac.

2 Letters to the editor: the killer spreads his threats through claims of responsibility, radio interviews and well placed clues.

3 Death in the rear view mirror: the Zodiac finds his victims in deserted parking lots and anywhere that lovers meet.

4 The search becomes a self-destructive obsession for insignificant cartoonist Robert Graysmith (Jake Gyllenhaal).

5 When night falls in San Francisco: Inspector Toschi can't do much more than wait in agony for the next murder.

"*Zodiac* is the *All the President's Men* of serial killer movies, with Woodward and Bernstein played by a cop and a cartoonist."

Chicago Sun-Times

working as a cartoonist for the newspaper, the smallest cog in its wheel. But just like the professionals, hunting down the Zodiac becomes a self-destructive obsession for him as well.

The killer does what is expected in such a movie: he entices those hunting him down with coded messages that ostensibly reveal his identity, leaving handwriting samples, fingerprints, and scraps of clothing. But departing from the rules of the genre, the pieces of the puzzle do not fit together. Not even the murders – two different couples and a taxi driver – betray a pattern. When Zodiac even incriminates himself in other murders, the movie is in danger of falling apart; the tension is almost unbearable when he disappears without a trace for five years. Fear is not what sustains the dynamic over the movie's two-and-a-half hours. Fincher is a master of that emotion, but the tension is actually created by his depiction of the more disturbing sense of cluelessness, executed with a compelling eye for detail. The gruesome murders take place at the start of the film. What follows is an overwhelming feeling of sheer impotence. With full cooperation of the media – radio, television and of course the "Chronicle," hungry for a scoop – Zodiac broadcasts on all channels, taking control of an entire city over the incessant murmur of the soundtrack. In terms of content, *Zodiac* has less of a similarity to *Se7en* than to Fritz Lang's *M* (*M – Eine Stadt sucht einen Mörder*, 1931), one of the earliest movies about a serial killer. As in that film, the metaphorical dovetailing of state, media and morality illustrates a new information society as yet without rules – nowadays no TV station would grant a telephone interview to a wanted murderer. Fincher models his style on the classics of that time, especially Alan J. Pakula's Watergate thriller *All the President's Men* (1976).

JAKE GYLLENHAAL Jake Gyllenhaal was born in 1980 in Los Angeles, the heart of the movie industry. His father, Stephen Gyllenhaal, is a director and his mother a screenwriter. He had his first driving lesson courtesy of Paul Newman. Some people are just lucky. His first part at age 11 was in *City Slickers* (1991). After appearing in some of his father's films and breaking off his studies in New York, the young actor attracted quite widespread attention in *October Sky* (1998) as a young rocket maker with big dreams. He then had his breakthrough with *Donnie Darko* (2000/2001), an offbeat fantasy movie about a schizophrenic adolescent and his best friend, a large, imaginary rabbit with criminal intent; it went on to become a cult movie on DVD. Gyllenhaal perpetuated the image of the disturbed teenager in *Moonlight Mile* (2002). In this intelligent tragicomedy, Gyllenhaal becomes involved with Susan Sarandon and Dustin Hoffman, parents of his murdered girlfriend who smother him with love.
Since 2005, Jake Gyllenhaal has enjoyed the unchallenged status of leading man, even in more mature roles. That year, he appeared firstly as a frustrated Iraq war soldier in Sam Mendes' dry-as-dust desert movie, *Jarhead*. Shortly after that his performance in Ang Lee's celebrated melodrama *Brokeback Mountain* (2005) won him an Oscar nomination for Best Supporting Actor. The part of Jack Twist, a cowboy who falls in love with his workmate (played by Heath Ledger), was a brave career move that paid off. In David Fincher's *Zodiac* (2007), Gyllenhaal brings his usual blend of sensitivity and naivety to the role of newspaper cartoonist Robert Graysmith, whose pursuit of a serial killer becomes a dangerous obsession.

6

6 Men at work: Steve McQueen's character in *Bullitt* was based on tough investigator Toschi.

7 Robert's wife Melanie (Chloë Sevigny) leaves her husband, unable to take any more of the heat.

8 Jake Gyllenhaal's sensitive performance takes him one step closer to maturity as a character actor.

9 Nicotine and whiskey: as seasoned journalist Paul Avery, Robert Downey Jr. reasserts his outstanding talents as an actor.

Once again we see men involved in frantic phone calls, in the throes of a sinister threat. Their environment is gray and functional. The city looks like San Francisco in the seventies, not the frequently glorified birthplace of the flower-power movement. Precisely by avoiding any aesthetic effects, *Zodiac* actually looks like a film from that problematic period in American history. Under the direction of Harris Savides, the HD digital camera gives this exquisitely filmed movie a suitably documentary feel as well.

David Fincher, born in 1962 and raised in California, knew about the Zodiac murders from his childhood. While he was not able to clearly identify a culprit, he manages to create an important piece of work about memory. With unexpected restraint, a perfect fusion of form and content and an outstanding group of actors, *Zodiac* is his most uncharacteristic film to date, as well as the most personal – and his best. PB

7

"It is impossible not to enjoy *Zodiac*: if enjoy is the word for a picture so often scary and stomach-turning." *The Guardian*

8
9

4 MONTHS, 3 WEEKS & 2 DAYS
4 LUNI, 3 SĂPTĂMÂNI ŞI 2 ZILE

2007 – ROMANIA – 113 MIN. – DRAMA
DIRECTOR CRISTIAN MUNGIU (*1968)
SCREENPLAY CRISTIAN MUNGIU DIRECTOR OF PHOTOGRAPHY OLEG MUTU EDITING DANA BUNESCU
PRODUCTION CRISTIAN MUNGIU, OLEG MUTU for MOBRA FILMS, Saga Film.
STARRING ANAMARIA MARINCA (Otilia), LAURA VASILIU (Gabita), VLAD IVANOV (Mr Bebe), ALEXANDRU POTOCEAN (Adi Radu), ION SAPDARU (Dr. Rusu), TEODOR CORBAN (Hotel Receptionist), TANIA POPA (Night Receptionist), DORU ANA (Benzanirul), EUGENIA BOSÂNCEANU (Bebe's Mother), MARIOARA STERIAN (Adela Racoviceanu), MIHAELA ALEXANDRU (Daniela).
IFF CANNES 2007 GOLDEN PALM (Christian Mungiu).

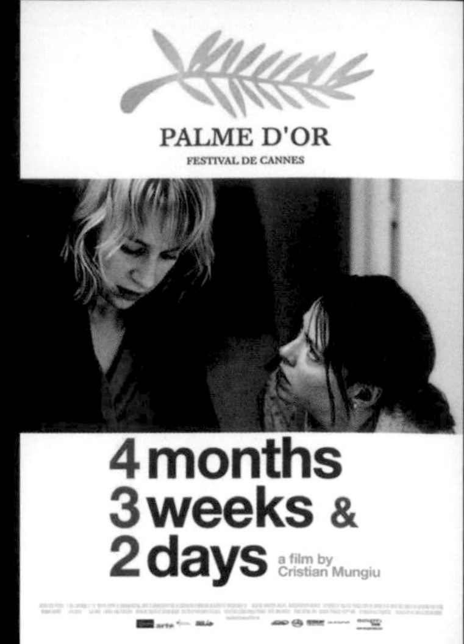

"This isn't a game. You get put in prison for this."

Romania in the winter of 1987: student Otilia (Anamaria Marinca) is taking a bus across the city to organize an illegal abortion for her fellow student, Gabita (Laura Vasiliu). The Ceauşescu regime has only two more years to go, yet there is no sign of the impending collapse. The streets covered in gray slush are dimly lit, while worn-out cars and long queues in front of shops paint a bleak picture of the socialist society that then existed. It is what a banned documentary film might look like, retrieved by someone from a sealed archive after 20 years.

Cristian Mungiu tells the story of *4 Months, 3 Weeks & 2 Days* in long shots, with sparse dialogue and no music. This less-than-enthralling narrative style is of course familiar in films from the socialist era, but unbearable tension runs through the images that appear as if they have been filmed in real time. For what the women are about to do is not just illegal; the dictatorship's harsh policy punishes the potentially life-threatening procedure in the same way as murder. The threat lurks in the background of every scene. Even booking a hotel room turns into an interrogation. The abortionist Mr Bebe (Vlad Ivanov), who is picked up a short while later in a desolate suburb by Otilia, is just how we imagine an informer for the all-powerful security service in his greasy leather jacket.

The situation rapidly deteriorates in the bare hotel room. The camera lingers for several minutes on Bebe as he explains the impending procedure in minute detail. This transfers the young women's fear directly to the viewer. Bebe is annoyed: Otilia booked the wrong hotel, so he had to hand over his ID. What's more, Gabita is way over two months pregnant. But in the drab world on the other side of the Iron Curtain, here too everything has its price. And Bebe's price suddenly rises drastically. In the first of several unbelievable twists and turns, he shamelessly exploits the situation.

1

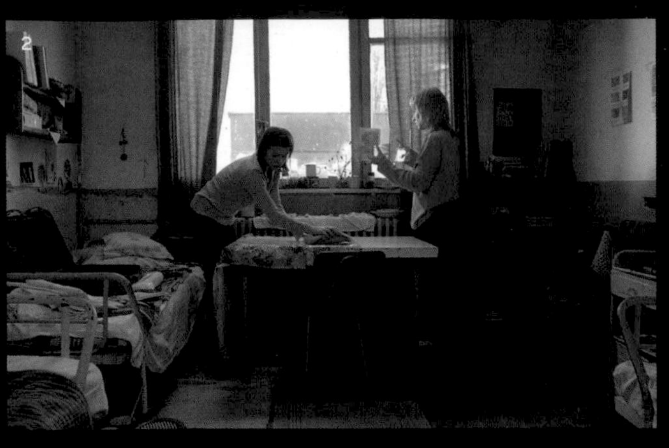

4 Months, 3 Weeks & 2 Days combines the sharp observation of social realism with the precision of a thriller and the physicality of a horror movie. Oleg Mutu's camerawork is remarkable: in another scene, when Otilia has to go to a birthday party – almost fainting with tension while her friend remains on the hotel bed with a probe inserted – his hand-held camera is not static, but quietly composed. Mungiu uses everyday scenes to show the reality of a totalitarian surveillance state that is never visible, but becomes tangible through the actions of the protagonists. We sense the fear in Anamaria Marinca's marvelous portrayal of Otilia in particular, but also an uncontrollable rage that drives her on to resolve the crisis. This even extends to getting rid of the fetus, in a night that could not be any darker. Mungiu's film won the Golden Palm in Cannes to the unanimous acclaim of the world press, praising its radical

"Cristian Mungiu's film is a nightmare of social-realist suspense, a jewel of what is now considered the Romanian new wave." *The Guardian*

3

1 Otilia (Anamaria Marinca) becomes a resolute crisis manager to organize an abortion for her friend, Gabita.

2 Sharp observation of social realism: organizing everyday items – food, soap, cigarettes – requires considerable skill in the student dorm.

3 Gabita (Laura Vasiliu) is as pregnant as the title suggests – and can't cope with the situation. Without Otilia, she would be lost.

4 Powerless rage: Otilia pushes herself to the limits of exhaustion for her friend, risking everything.

5 "Doctor" Bebe (Vlad Ivanov), the attending physician, shamefully exploits the young women's situation. He demands far more than just money.

6 Unbearable tension: conversations with Bebe are like an interrogation. No one trusts anyone else in the totalitarian surveillance state.

"*4 Months* is a shockingly matter-of-fact horror film."

Village Voice

7
8

"4 Months, 3 Weeks and 2 Days is not just about holding to account a failed ideology and past age. It is a film that haunts us because its images take root in our memory."

Die Tageszeitung

7 In the bathroom: Gabita doesn't have to see what's happening in the hotel room. The horror is subtly conveyed to the viewer.

8 Anywhere but here: Oleg Mutu's camera continually finds shocking images for the sense of shame and powerlessness.

9 Silent mourning for a ruined life: the film is not a drama about abortion, but a furious protest against an inhuman system.

approach that is conspicuously absent in movies such as *The Lives of Others* (2006). It combines hatred for an inhumane system with mourning for a wasted life. The additional title "Memories from a Golden Age" – the film was envisaged as the first part of a planned trilogy of the same name – reads like a ghastly irony. Stories of women like Otilia and Gabita gave Mungiu the material for the film: women who accepted cruel treatment to terminate a pregnancy, but often saw the procedure as an act of opposition as well. On the other hand, *4 Months, 3 Weeks & 2 Days* lends itself even less as a stance for or against abortion than *Juno* (2007). It is a movie about existential themes such as freedom and fear, life and death and, if nothing else, taking responsibility. Presumably, its ruthless radicalism can be explained by the fact that such a brilliantly made film came from a country without a cinema tradition of any note. Mungiu shows images that had to be shown, as did the French – and Polish, Czech and Yugoslavian – New Wave before him. The only really significant New Wave in recent years is Romanian.

PB

CRISTIAN MUNGIU Cristian Mungiu was born in Iaşi in the far north-east of Romania in 1968. After studying film in the capital, Bucharest, he gained his first experience as assistant director on the Canadian co-production shot in Romania, *Teen Knight* (1998), and the Holocaust farce *Train of Life* (*Train de vie*, 1998), an international co-production by his fellow Romanian, Radu Mihaileanu. The mainstream industry held less attraction for him, however, than being able to fulfill his own vision of realism.
Even his first feature film, *Occident* (2002), was shown at the Cannes Film Festival in the "Directors' Fortnight" section. This was a quiet tragicomedy about the desire of young Romanians to emigrate to the West. Mungiu was also one of the young Romanian film directors who each contributed an episode for the omnibus film *Lost and Found* (2005). His second feature, *4 Months, 3 Weeks & 2 Days* (2007), took Cannes by storm. The story of an illegal abortion in Romania under the Ceauşescu regime won everyone over with its straightforward realism, passionate storytelling and outstanding performances. The director of photography, Oleg Mutu, was also responsible for Cristi Puiu's moving film about dying, *The Death of Mr. Lazarescu* (*Moartea domnului Lăzărescu*, 2005), which had attracted a great deal of attention two years earlier. It was impossible to ignore the "Romanian New Wave" any longer, which also included Catalin Mitulescu and Corneliu Porumboiu.
4 Months, 3 Weeks & 2 Days won Mungiu the Golden Palm award, the first Romanian director ever to receive it; the European Film Awards for Best Film and Best Director later joined it on the shelf. Instead of resting on his laurels, Mungiu made a dramatic statement to raise awareness of the cultural crisis in his country: as Romanian cinema at that time had a mere 35 cinemas, the director traveled around towns and villages with rented projection equipment to show his compatriots his award-winning movie.

CONTROL

2007 – UK / USA / AUSTRALIA / JAPAN – 122 MIN. – DRAMA, BIOGRAPHY
DIRECTOR ANTON CORBIJN (*1955)
SCREENPLAY MATT GREENHALGH, from the autobiography "TOUCHING FROM A DISTANCE" by DEBORAH CURTIS **DIRECTOR OF PHOTOGRAPHY** MARTIN RUHE **EDITING** ANDREW HULME
MUSIC JOY DIVISION, NEW ORDER **PRODUCTION** ANTON CORBIJN, TODD ECKERT, ORIAN WILLIAMS for 3 DOGS AND A PONY, NORTHSEA, BECKER FILMS, CLARAFLORA, WARNER MUSIC.
STARRING SAM RILEY (Ian Curtis), SAMANTHA MORTON (Deborah Curtis), ALEXANDRA MARIA LARA (Annik Honoré), JOE ANDERSON (Peter Hook), JAMES ANTHONY PEARSON (Bernard Summer), HARRY TREADAWAY (Stephen Morris), CRAIG PARKINSON (Tony Wilson), TOBY KEBELL (Rob Gretton), HERBERT GRÖNEMEYER (Local GP), ROBERT SHELLY (Twinny), ANDREW SHERIDAN (Terry Mason).

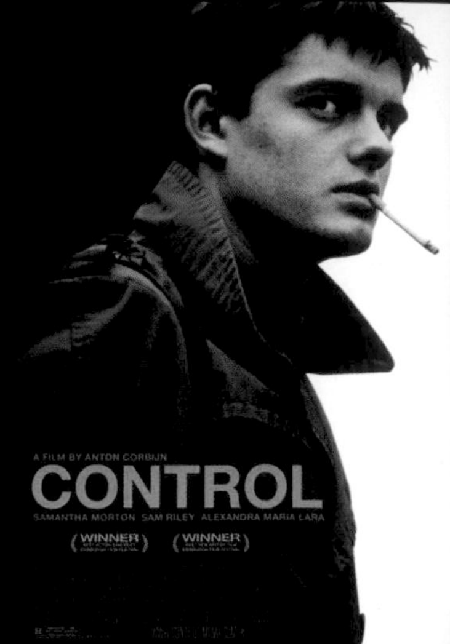

"Man. City blue"

The story goes that the Sex Pistols played a Manchester club in the 1970s to an audience of just 40 people. Yet everyone who was there is said to have formed a band after that gig. One of them called itself "Joy Division" after a Nazi brothel in World War II. Made up of four young Mancunians, the band only became really famous when its lead singer, Ian Curtis, committed suicide in May 1980.

The movie, based on the autobiography by Curtis' widow Deborah "Touching from a distance," is an account of the psychological trauma suffered by Ian Curtis contextualized by the story of the band. Although focusing on his suicide and the events that led up to it, however, the film is also about Curtis' life.

Anton Corbijn knew Ian Curtis personally, having photographed the band o more than one occasion in late 1979 and early 1980; Joy Division had motivate him to leave Holland for London in the 70s. One of his images is indelibl imprinted in the collective cultural psyche: it shows the band at the entranc to Lancaster Gate subway station in London. The film does not follow up thi scene, however, retrospective hero worship not being its theme; instead, i shows the fate of one individual against the backdrop of a particular atmospher of the time. "Anyone thinking of Joy Division remembers it all in black an white," according to Corbijn. "Everything was black and white: the photos, th mood, all of it." As such, the movie was shot in monochrome as well. Filmin

1

"In his directorial debut, *Control*, which profiles the life and suicide of Ian Curtis, Dutch photographer and music historian Anton Corbijn fills the screen with powerful black-and-white images that resonate with the lingering, ultra-cool sounds of Joy Division." *taz*

ANTON CORBIJN According to this top Dutch photographer born in 1955, music has always been a vital part of his life. Even before he picked up a camera and took his first photos of bands at open air concerts, he would lie on the floor of the TV-free parental vicarage in the village of Strijen in southern Netherlands and lose himself in listening to music. For him, a record was more than just a vehicle for sound; cover, design, track list, A and B sides – all of these are lacking in modern discs, as he comments on a scene in the movie in which Ian Curtis listens half-naked in his sister's fur coat to a new David Bowie record. As far as he is concerned, you cannot fall in love with a CD.
In the 1980s, Anton Corbijn rose rapidly to fame for his unusual portraits of bands and musicians such as Joy Division, Miles Davis, U2 and David Bowie, and soon became successful at making music videos as well. He always felt that "rock photographer" was a derogatory description of his work. From the outset, his images were far more than just poster compositions of striking or hagiographic band poses. Throughout the decade, according to one critic, he "renovated" star after star. He unmasked them by revealing their human side in a new, artistic way. In the process, he also set new mainstream standards, treading "a fine line verging on phoniness" (Ulf Poschardt).
Sincerity in his work became a new kind of fetishism, but he could not be pinned down. Since the 1990s, his portraits of musicians and actors have been characterized increasingly by their conscious, almost ironic, staging in the style of film stills. Nowadays, he very rarely accepts music video commissions. His first feature film direction points to a return to the realism elaborated in the aesthetic and poetic style of his early photographs. The fact that he picked the fate of the short-lived, New Wave idol Ian Curtis – for whose star portrayal he was largely responsible – is surprising, in so far as the Ian Curtis in the film is never seen as the Ian Curtis from the old photos. It is as if Anton Corbijn is beginning his work again from scratch.

1 Portrait of a reluctant icon: Sam Riley as Ian Curtis, the charismatic lead singer of Joy Division.

2 The band in the movie cut new versions of Joy Division's original songs. It created a completely new soundtrack, which was perfect for the film.

3 Fans believed Ian Curtis' singing and dancing style could not be replicated. Actor Sam Riley defied all expectations.

4 A global career begins right at home. Curtis' living room was painted in Man. City blue, the color of one of the two great football clubs of Manchester.

"Riley is excellent as Curtis, and not just because of his physical similarities to the icon. Riley captures the singer's personal struggles and later his depression brought on by epilepsy." *epd-Film*

in England took place during the hottest summer for years, giving the outside shots an uncharacteristic and completely unanticipated freshness.

What the film implies, Corbijn takes to its logical conclusion. And the story he tells unfolds without being sidetracked; avoiding cheap sensationalism, he approaches his subject with quiet composure and a total commitment to accuracy. Every shot is there for a reason; nothing is unintentional. The art direction conjures up the spirit of the 1970s and the British post-punk era. Then, besides the lovingly crafted set detail, Corbijn sought to introduce a little piece of Holland into the film as well. In the first shot, for instance, when we see Ian Curtis going home with a new David Bowie album under his arm, it is a reference to the young Anton Corbijn who became totally self-absorbed and inaccessible in anticipation of a newly released record.

The original material was cut from three to two hours, strengthening the narrative in the process. What at first appeared problematic in terms of finance turned out to be a bonus: an ambitious first-time director (and top photographer to boot); an unknown cameraman (Martin Ruhe), who captured the film's fabulous imagery; and a young musician without acting experience, Sam Riley, in the lead role. The money men looked skeptically on all of this. Corbijn's close friends supported the project and helped out: people such as Herbert Grönemeyer, who also had a minor part, while Samantha Morton and the German actress Alexandra Maria Lara ensured top-notch acting performances.

With filming under way, it soon became obvious that the team was a godsend – especially Sam Riley, who replicated Curtis's unique style of dancing so closely that even die-hard Joy Division fans approved of the stage scenes.

"Music was the trigger in just about everything I did; the reason I took up photography and moved to England. Music is an extremely important part of my life." *Anton Corbijn in: epd-Film*

6

5 A life split between band and family, stage and home becomes unbearable for Ian Curtis. When epilepsy threatens to control him, he feels trapped.

6 Deciding to get married young: Ian and Deborah Curtis. Samantha Morton coped brilliantly with the complex, difficult role of the singer's wife.

7 Alexandra Maria Lara as Annik Honoré. The casting of the film turned out highly opportune, and not just from a cinematic point of view. Sam Riley and Alexandra Maria Lara became an item in real life.

Almost all the movie's songs were recorded live by the four actors who played the band members, the soundtrack thus becoming an integral part of the narrative. The musical elements fit seamlessly with the action, like a background monochrome color that cannot be seen, but is vividly felt. This gives the scenes a heightened and tangible sense of anguish. At one point, Annik Honoré (Alexandra Maria Lara) asks Ian Curtis (Sam Riley) what his favorite color is. "Man. City blue," he replies, referring to the light blue colors of Manchester City football team. The room Curtis shut himself in to write his songs was painted this shade. In the film, it becomes a muted gray.

Of one thing in the movie, there is no doubt. Ian Curtis is inwardly conflicted, enduring the terrible psychological strain of a man who cannot choose between the two women he loves, and suffers increasingly from epileptic fits. Just as the band's prospects peak, he reaches the end of his tether. The movie portrays him as a tragic figure, always striving to be true to himself and others, but simultaneously wanting to be someone else. "Young people are homesick for the future," as Jean-Paul Sartre once said. Judging by this film, Ian Curtis abandoned his future much too soon. At the age of just 23, he left behind a remarkably mature body of work. SR

NO COUNTRY FOR OLD MEN ♂♂♂♂

2007 – USA – 122 MIN. – CRIME THRILLER, DRAMA
DIRECTORS ETHAN COEN (*1957), JOEL COEN (*1954)
SCREENPLAY JOEL AND ETHAN COEN, from the novel by the same name by CORMAC MCCARTHY **DIRECTOR OF PHOTOGRAPHY** ROGER DEAKINS **EDITING** RODERICK JAYNES (PSEUDONYM for JOEL AND ETHAN COEN) **MUSIC** CARTER BURWELL **PRODUCTION** JOEL and ETHAN COEN, SCOTT RUDIN for PARAMOUNT VANTAGE, MIRAMAX FILMS, SCOTT RUDIN PRODUCTIONS, MIKE ZOSS PRODUCTIONS.
STARRING TOMMY LEE JONES (Sheriff Ed Tom Bell), JAVIER BARDEM (Anton Chigurh), JOSH BROLIN (Llewelyn Moss), WOODY HARRELSON (Carson Wells), KELLY MACDONALD (Carla Jean Moss), GARRET DILLAHUNT (Deputy Wendell), RODGER BOYCE (Sheriff Roscoe Giddens), TESS HARPER (Loretta Bell), BARRY CORBIN (Ellis), BETH GRANT (Carla Jean's Mother).
ACADEMY AWARDS 2008 OSCARS for BEST PICTURE (Joel and Ethan Coen, Scott Rudin), BEST DIRECTOR (Joel and Ethan Coen), BEST ADAPTED SCREENPLAY (Joel and Ethan Coen) and BEST ACTOR IN A SUPPORTING ROLE (Javier Bardem).

"Do you have any idea how crazy you are?"

In the gruesome world of *No Country for Old Men*, anyone leaving a trace is lost. Close to the Mexican border, Vietnam veteran Llewelyn Moss (Josh Brolin) shoots an antelope and its bloody tracks lead him to the scene of a drug deal gone wrong. He takes a bag of money, which contains a tracking device. At the same time, contract serial killer Chigurh (Javier Bardem) strangles a policeman, leaving marks of the brutal fight on the police station floor that are reminiscent of an avant-garde painting. It is not just the camera that registers these violations of normalcy with a clinical eye: Sheriff Ed Tom Bell (Tommy Lee Jones) follows the tracks of both fugitives, mainly to protect the harmless Moss from madman Chigurh, who is now pursuing the fortunate finder on the desert highways of Texas. Moss demonstrates both ingenuity and caution in stashing the money in the air vent of a motel room; but there, too, scratches are left on the sheet metal behind the grille. And Chigurh's receiver is emitting increasingly frantic signals.

The icy killer with the peculiar name and the most ridiculous haircut in cinema history never leaves any traces. Chigurh comes from nowhere and will disappear back there. Even in the wacky world of director brothers Joel and Ethan Coen, he is a weird creation: a devil / angel of destiny who kills using a gas canister gun, after allowing his victims to toss a coin – and

when he does spare someone's life, it is somehow even creepier. With Javier Bardem's sardonic poker face, tight-fitting clothes and striking coiffure, the *New York Times* dubbed him a "Beatle from Hell." The Coens ventured into their first literary adaptation with *No Country for Old Men*. They won an Oscar for this process, as well as for Best Direction and Best Film. Cormac McCarthy's novel, which they adapted virtually word for word, allowed them to revisit their dark movies like *Blood Simple* (1984) and *Miller's Crossing* (1990). McCarthy turns the desert into a primordial site of violence, weaving a new myth of killing and dying into American legend. Here, all human emotion is punished, while every hope of security turns to sand. It is a new world, which gives Sheriff Bell nightmares. The Coens set the stage for this anxious state in majestic fashion, with menacingly quiet shots of the landscape. Before,

1 Chigurh, the most enigmatic killer in film history, hasn't finished yet. Javier Bardem won an Oscar for his performance.

2 Sheriff Ed Tom Bell (Tommy Lee Jones) doesn't understand the world any more. This is no country for old men – if it ever was.

3 Clues in the sand: the aftermath of a drug deal gone wrong sets Bell on the right track. But he always gets there too late.

4 Beatle from Hell: with his ridiculous haircut and an even more absurd weapon, Chigurh turns the desert into a battlefield.

"The Coens are back with a vengeance, showing their various imitators and detractors what great American film-making looks like." *The Guardian*

5 The loot doesn't bring Llewelyn Moss (Josh Brolin) any luck. After a shootout in the hotel, he flees over the Mexican border.

6 Looking the devil in the eye: Llewelyn's wife, Carla Jean (Kelly Macdonald), is one of the few people to see Chigurh's face.

7 Myth of eternal life and death: the western desert becomes the poisoned, primordial seedbed of violence in the Coens' tale.

"*No Country for Old Men* is purgatory for the squeamish and the easily spooked. For formalists – those moviegoers sent into raptures by tight editing, nimble camera work and faultless sound design – it's pure heaven." *The New York Times*

JOEL AND ETHAN COEN Brothers Joel and Ethan Coen are famous for their unmistakably eccentric style, wild plays on genre and unconventional division of labor; they do everything together, or so they say. Just for form's sake Joel, born in 1954, appears as director, while Ethan, who is three years his junior, is credited as producer. They use a pseudonym when it comes to editing, for legal reasons. The brothers from Minneapolis grew up far enough away from Hollywood to be free of conventions: most of their movies, to some degree, contain elements of film noir and kooky comedy, with a postmodern, eclectic compositional style that always surprises.

While Joel gravitated to the film industry from the start, Ethan began by studying philosophy and went on to publish short stories. Even their first movie, however, the neo-noir *Blood Simple* (1984), was the result of a screenplay they wrote together. After the crazy fantasy comedy *Raising Arizona* (1987) and cynical gangster movie *Miller's Crossing* (1990), their breakthrough came with *Barton Fink* (1991): the surreal story with overtones of Kafka and Polanski about a screenwriter with writer's block won three top awards at the Cannes Film Festival. From the outset, they were artistically independent, their creative energies flourishing in the comedies that followed. The snow-set film *Fargo* (1996) was populated with blundering killers and inept insurance fraudsters, while in the splendid, 70s detective story *The Big Lebowski* (1998) – with Jeff Bridges in the classic hippie role, "The Dude" – mischief-making German nihilists complicate the action further. What was striking in these highly artificial films was also the meticulous eye for regional and temporal peculiarities: the assumption that the only reality the Coens know is their films is refuted at least on occasion by their elaborately crafted characters. Then again, the mythical American odyssey *O Brother, Where Art Thou?* (2000) consisted almost exclusively of films from the Depression and the comedies of Preston Sturges.

The noir homage shot in black and white, *The Man Who Wasn't There* (2001), revealed a minimalist side to their visual flamboyance. It was followed initially by an artistic low; only the Coens themselves are in a position to overplay their own excessive style. With the literary adaptation *No Country for Old Men* (2007), a crime movie set in the Texan desert that won four Oscars, they were back on top form, finding a new virtue in restraint – until their next madcap grifter movie, *Burn After Reading* (2008).

they tended to make their mark with comedies; there, too, the narrative they created of America primarily as myth is indicative of their supreme confidence.

The Oscars came far too late for fans of these visionary jesters. Maybe it was the joke that worked: the one about the Coens making a serious film just for a laugh, and it made it big! Even that venerable institution, the Academy of Motion Picture Arts and Science, must have noticed the underlying humor. Like all the other Coen movies, its almost obsessive craftsmanship and precision are compulsive. As is often the case, the focus is on physical activities: unscrewing the air vent, loading a gun or sweeping a crime scene for the tiniest traces. Yet what happened quickly and was filmed in slapstick style in films like *Fargo* (1996) is now tantalizingly slow and heavily laden with meaning – only those new to the Coens, and who are likely to stay that way, will fail to notice the irony in all this.

The fear factor lies precisely in the blend of comic and serious elements. In Chigurh's hands, life becomes a joke. He is the shadow in the back of a car, the assassin creeping around in his socks, his feet appearing at a crack in a door. Like death itself, no-one can escape him. With *No Country for Old Men*, the Coens have also established a metaphysical superstructure for the rest of their work that infuses their surreal observations about life with existential depth, with the exception perhaps of *Burn After Reading* (2008), their next and by far their wackiest movie. Traces soon disappear. PB

THE DIVING BELL AND THE BUTTERFLY

LE SCAPHANDRE ET LE PAPILLON

2007 – FRANCE / USA – 112 MIN. – MELODRAMA
DIRECTOR JULIAN SCHNABEL (*1951)
SCREENPLAY RONALD HARWOOD, from the novel by JEAN-DOMINIQUE BAUBY
DIRECTOR OF PHOTOGRAPHY JANUSZ KAMINSKI EDITING JULIETTE WELFLING MUSIC PAUL CANTELON
PRODUCTION KATHLEEN KENNEDY, JON KILIK for PATHÉ, CANAL+, CINÉCINÉMA.
STARRING MATHIEU AMALRIC (Jean-Do), EMMANUELLE SEIGNER (Céline), MARIE-JOSÉE CROZE (Henriette Roi), ANNE CONSIGNY (Claude), PATRICK CHESNAIS (Doctor Lepage), OLATZ LÓPEZ GARMENDIA (Marie Lopez), MAX VON SYDOW (Papinou), MARINA HANDS (Joséphine), NIELS ARESTRUP (Roussin), ISAACH DE BANKOLÉ (Laurent).
IFF CANNES 2007 SILVER PALM for BEST DIRECTION (Julian Schnabel) and PRIX VULCAIN (Janusz Kaminski).

"My first word is I. I am starting with myself."

For modern medicine, the so-called "locked-in syndrome" might be a mystery, but for patients it is a disaster. The film adaptation of Jean-Dominique Bauby's memoir of his illness, *The Diving Bell and the Butterfly*, became a piece of good fortune for cinema. The audience is reborn as an eye along with Bauby, who is locked inside what has become a useless body. This unusual perspective is sustained for over half an hour, pushing the art of film to new limits.

In the hospital in Berck-sur-Mer, Jean-Dominique (Mathieu Amalric) – who is known to his friends as "Jean-Do" – wakes from a coma that has lasted nearly three weeks. He is unable to move. His brain functions are still intact, however, as is his left eye. It registers what is going on around him, with a rising sense of panic. Doctors approach his bed; nurses care for him; and flowers are on the bedside table. Who are they from? He discovers that he has had a stroke, from which there is no hope of recovery. It is horrendous. The editor of "Elle" in France, a family man – and ladies' man – when times were good, he sees himself reduced to a lifeless lump of flesh. Who would put up with that? Jean-Do protests. He wants out of this diving suit. He wants to die, but no one can hear him.

Director and painter Julian Schnabel makes an artistic virtue of necessity. The subjective camerawork of Janusz Kaminski (Steven Spielberg's regular cameraman) transports us into the inner world of a person robbed of all their future prospects. Paradoxically, the restriction unlocks the vision: unbelievable paintings flit over the screen while, in constantly adjusting its focus, the blinking camera-eye never fully establishes the depicted area. Light and colors dance on Jean-Do's retina in ever-changing constellations, each washing into the next. To achieve effects like this, Schnabel occasionally put his own glasses over the camera lens – that is all.

Gradually the perspective broadens out to reveal the patient, who up till now has been present only in voice-over, in all his misery. Yet it is actually Jean-Do who leaves the prison of his body. In his despair, the gifted cynic learns to love life and gives flight to his fantasy. New images follow, with memories as beautiful as they are painful: his girlfriend's hair blowing in the wind, time spent with his children, and his frail father (Max von Sydow) with whom he suddenly has so much in common. But what is the point of wallowing in self pity? What's to stop him imagining eating oysters with the lovely publisher's assistant to whom, for days, he has been dictating his memoirs? Under the direction of speech therapist Henriette (Marie-Josée Croze), Jean-Do has actually discovered a language. It is a painstaking process, but he now thinks it is worth the effort: she reads letters of the alphabet to him, according to the

1

2

1 Rediscovering shapes and colors: a trip to the beach with Céline (Emmanuelle Seigner) turns into the visual feast of an unfettered camera.

2 Reborn as an eye: with the help of his speech therapist Henriette (Marie-Josée Croze) Jean-Do discovers the language within him. The French alphabet becomes the film's silent mantra.

3 Nurturing relations: his relationship with his father (Max von Sydow) takes on new meaning for high-flyer Jean-Do (Mathieu Amalric).

"A gloriously unlocked experience, with some of the freest and most creative uses of the camera and some of the most daring, cruel, and heartbreaking emotional explorations that have appeared in recent movies." *The New Yorker*

JULIAN SCHNABEL Julian Schnabel had already become famous as a painter before his second career as a film director. He is regarded as one of the main exponents of the "New Expressionism" of the early 1980s. Born in Brooklyn in 1951, but raised in Texas, he became well-known for his large-scale, highly expressive visual compositions, including "plate paintings" applied to broken plates. The boom years and his delight in acts of self-promotion were eminently well-suited: the financier Gordon Gekko in Oliver Stone's *Wall Street* (1987) was not the only yuppie whose office was decorated with a genuine Schnabel.

When interest in him quieted down in the 1990s, he exploited his considerable knowledge of the New York art scene for his first work as a director: *Basquiat* (1996) is the moving, if somewhat conventionally narrated, portrait of the penniless painter Jean-Michel Basquiat, played by Jeffrey Wright. David Bowie appeared in a supporting role as Andy Warhol, while Schnabel himself created Basquiat's images in the film. In *Before Night Falls* (2000) he devoted himself once again to a misunderstood artist. Spanish actor Javier Bardem won an Oscar nomination for his role as the gay Cuban writer, Reinaldo Arenas, while Schnabel himself won several awards at the Venice Film Festival. He exceeded all expectations, however, with *The Diving Bell and the Butterfly* (*Le scaphandre et le papillon*, 2007). Schnabel had a personal connection to the painful story of former "Elle" editor Jean-Dominique Bauby's illness, even though it was a commissioned work. The carer of a friend suffering from multiple sclerosis had passed on Bauby's book to him, to help him come to terms with his grief. Schnabel created an iridescent screen painting full of light and life out of the desperately sad theme. He won the director's award at the Cannes Film Festival for the movie and Ronald Harwood's screenplay won a BAFTA. In 2007 he also made the eponymous *Lou Reed Berlin*, a documentary about the concert performance by his friend Reed, whose music features throughout Schnabel's brilliant soundtracks.

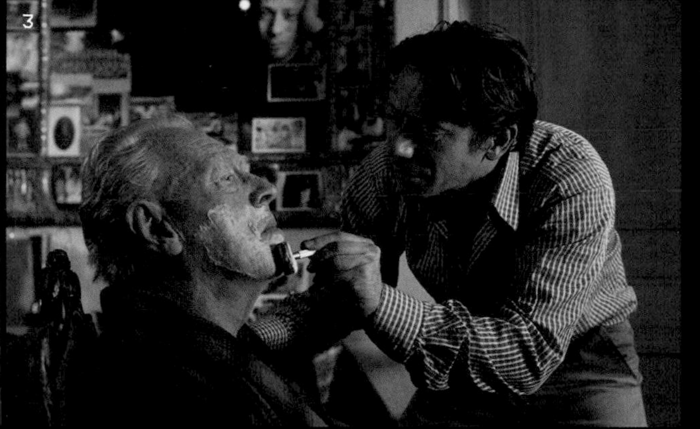

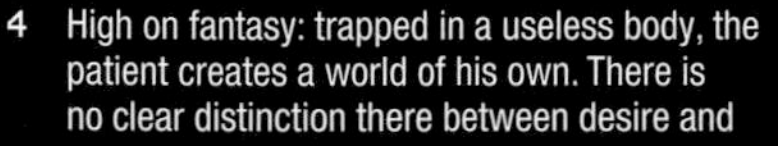

4 High on fantasy: trapped in a useless body, the patient creates a world of his own. There is no clear distinction there between desire and memory. He recognizes the value of life per se, thus finding inner freedom.

5 Jean-Do is pinned to a wheelchair by the bizarre “locked-in syndrome.” But meeting his lovers again revives his spirits. He writes his biography – a medical and human miracle.

frequency of their use in French; he creates content by blinking E-S-A-R-I-N-T-U, etc. – the movie’s mantra has a slow release symbolizing both the tragic hero’s rebirth and his demise. A few days after his book appeared, Jean-Dominique Bauby died of a lung infection, at 44 years of age.

In *The Diving Bell and the Butterfly* the viewer follows in delighted amazement both Bauby’s progress from failed high-flyer to artist and the stylistic liberation of the artist and biographer, Julian Schnabel. He also finds his own language; his own musicality of forms and colors. If heartrending pain and a late insight into the beauty of life do not descend into cliché, it is partly due to the fantastic performance of Mathieu Amalric, who can be funnier with just one eye than others with their whole body, and also to Bauby himself, whose account remains free from all sentimentalism. In his typically sarcastic tone, the “shipwrecked man on the shores of loneliness” had already given thought to the possibility that an uplifting film version of his suffering might be made. The fact that Schnabel made this film is a blessing. PB

SILENT LIGHT
STELLET LICHT

2007 – MEXICO / FRANCE / NETHERLANDS / GERMANY – 136 MIN. – ROMANTIC DRAMA
DIRECTOR CARLOS REYGADAS (*1971)
SCREENPLAY CARLOS REYGADAS DIRECTOR OF PHOTOGRAPHY ALEXIS ZABE EDITING NATALIA LÓPEZ
PRODUCTION CARLOS REYGADAS, JAIME ROMANDIA for MANTARRAYA PRODUCCIONES, NO DREAM CINEMA, FOPROCINE, INSTITUTO MEXICANO DE CINEMATOGRAFÍA, MOTEL FILMS, NEDERLANDS FONDS VOOR DE FILM, WORLD CINEMA FUND, ARTE FRANCE CINÉMA.
STARRING CORNELIO WALL (Johan), MARIA PANKRATZ (Marianne), MIRIAM TOEWS (Esther), PETER WALL (Father), ELIZABETH FEHR (Mother), JACOBO KLASSEN (Zacarias).
IFF CANNES 2007 GRAND JURY PRIZE for Carlos Reygadas (jointly with *Persepolis*).

"Peace is stronger than love."

With names like Alejandro González Iñárritu, Guillermo del Toro and Alfonso Cuarón, Mexican cinema has proved something of an eye-opener in recent years. Far removed from the old clichés, it is now an international, multicultural cinema that affords plenty of room for minorities. Exceptional director Carlos Reygadas came across the Mennonites (who number around 100,000 members) in the federal state of Chihuahua. They speak a virtually forgotten form of German dialect called "Plautdietsch." With their stern faces, strict religious rules and archaic behavioral norms, they remain on the fringes of Mexican society while still belonging to it. The tantalizing opening sequence of *Silent Light* locates them in an almost cosmic context: the sun rises, incredibly slowly despite daybreak being seasonally curtailed. The starry sky fades, and th voices of birds and beasts answer the dawning light – God's creation awakenin anew. The family sits in the cozy parlor at breakfast, praying in silence. Th father, Johan (Cornelio Wall), finally says "Amen." After the six children hav left the house, he and his wife Esther (Miriam Toews) confirm their mutua affection. But when he is alone, he sheds quiet tears – for the past two year he has loved another woman. Esther has known it for some time. No God an no faith can protect a person from such a test.

The word "Mennonite" does not feature at all in the film. Using non professional actors from the local community, Reygadas tells the simple stor

1

"Terse and sumptuous, filmed in endlessly long takes and using non-professional actors, the film seems to summon up the shadows of Carl Dreyer and Robert Bresson, only to irradiate them with the blinding light of the southern hemisphere or dissolve them in floods of torrential rain." *Le Monde*

2

1 Community of outsiders: director Carlos Reygadas cast mainly non-professional actors for his portrait of Mennonites of German origin.

2 Natural, and somewhat pantheistic: the images of family affection are permeated with a belief in humanity.

3 Farmer Johan (Cornelio Wall) is in love with another woman. His life of devotion to God is turned upside-down as a result.

of a man caught between two women, independent of time and place. Their religious devotion does not differentiate the protagonists significantly from other country folk. Their isolated rural life may not include television, but it is familiar with man's pain and suffering – and even modern milking machines. Esther drives the tractor: part of the machinery that sets the quiet rhythm in the movie, as seen in the long journeys across country by car and the carefully observed workings of a threshing machine. Unlike Peter Weir in *Witness* (1985), Reygadas does not portray this community of outsiders as an exotic ethnic group. The Mennonites represent something else. They are ciphers for modern man who, even in the 21st century, still believes that his individual action has meaning in the eyes of God, as well as for himself and the rest of creation. This strong belief is reflected in the camerawork. Its eye is not cold and impartial, but empathetic and not without faith. The family bathing in a lake, soaping each other amid reflections of light on the water, has a pantheistic naturalism about it. The married couple's despair emerges even more clearly in the occasional moments of apparent happiness. Esther was at one with the world through Johan, but now she feels nearer to death than life. He himself does not know the answer to the question as to whether his forbidden love is the will of the devil, or in fact of God. And neither does Marianne (Maria Pankratz), who is just as demure and serious as her rival Esther, submit lightly

CARLOS REYGADAS Carlos Reygadas was born in 1971 in Mexico City. Before taking up a career in film, he worked as a human rights lawyer for the United Nations. His flamboyant style is characterized by his work with non-professionals; long, contemplative shots; and a preoccupation with the existential questions of humanity, including guilt, forgiveness, religious faith and death. It is mostly his extreme sex scenes, however, which have provoked heated debate.
In his debut movie *Japan* (*Japón*, 2001) an Argentinian painter moves to a valley in Mexico with the intention of committing suicide. The high point of this film from the stable of Russian filmmaker Andrei Tarkovsky is his spiritual purification through sexual relations with an 80-year-old peasant woman. *Battle in Heaven* (*Batalla en el cielo*, 2005), the tragic aftermath of a botched kidnapping of a baby, begins with a dispassionately filmed blowjob and ends with the conscience-stricken sinner walking in penitence amidst a bustling Catholic procession.
It is debatable whether this is high art or scandal-mongering kitsch. The complex camera shots across the sierra landscape in *Japan*, however, are early indications of his later masterpiece *Silent Light* (2007). The film shot in the Mennonite community of northern Mexico was received to rapturous applause and a degree of relief by the festival-going public (all three films were presented at Cannes). The sincerity of this recent search for spiritual meaning has established Carlos Reygadas as an exciting and thought-provoking voice in New Mexican Cinema.

to her fate. "These are the saddest moments of my life," she says to Johan when they meet for what is to be the last time. "But the best, too."

The contradictions between godly living and real life can only be resolved by a miracle that is clearly modeled on Carl Theodor Dreyer's *Ordet* (1954). Reygadas' Mennonites are descendants of Dreyer's Protestant doubters – not in an ethnographic, but a metaphysical sense. As in the films of the Denmark-born director, the spiritual aura of images imbued with silence and achingly long shots are not manifestations of cowering before God's might, but of the struggle for human expression and authenticity. It is almost as if the miracle of resurrection gave us the great Mexican director Carlos Reygadas in the year that Bergman and Antonioni died. *Silent Light* is filled with the magic of real life and, as a result, real cinema. PB

"This is a deeply considered, formally accomplished, beautiful-looking and unexpectedly gripping film from a director making a giant leap into the first rank of world cinema." *The Guardian*

5

4 Anachronistic: the portrayal of the Mennonites reveals their conflict with modern life, without making them seem unusual or strange.

5 Spiritual mood: the director's uncompromising visual language is characterized by long, contemplative shots.

6 Esther (Miriam Toews) believes in the God-given nature of things, but nothing can protect a person from the ensuing despair.

"*Silent Light* has some sublime, meditative moments: moments of pure, unapologetic visual ecstasy that come close to repealing the cinematic laws of gravity." *The Guardian*

PERSEPOLIS

2007 – FRANCE – 96 MIN. – AUTOBIOGRAPHY, ANIMATION MOVIE
DIRECTORS VINCENT PARONNAUD (*1970), MARJANE SATRAPI (*1969)
SCREENPLAY VINCENT PARONNAUD from a comic strip by MARJANE SATRAPI
EDITING STÉPHANE ROCHE **MUSIC** OLIVIER BERNET **PRODUCTION** XAVIER RIGAULT, MARC-ANTOINE ROBERT for 2.4.7. FILMS, DIAPHANA FILMS, FRANCE 3 CINÉMA, THE KENNEDY/MARSHALL COMPANY, FRANCHE CONNECTION ANIMATION.
VOICES CHIARA MASTROIANNI (Marjane), CATHERINE DENEUVE (Marjane's Mother), DANIELLE DARRIEUX (Marjane's Grandmother), SIMON ABKARIAN (Marjane's Father), GABRIELLE LOPES BENITES (Young Marjane), FRANÇOIS JEROSME (Uncle Anouche), SOPHIE ARTHUYS, JEAN-FRANÇOIS GALLOTTE, ARIÉ ELMALEH, MATHIAS MLEKUZ.
IFF CANNES 2007 JURY PRIZE (Vincent Paronnaud and Marjane Satrapi), tied with *Silent Light* (Carlos Reygadas).

"Do not forget who you are and where you come from".

In an age when the animation business (and its public perception) is almost completely dominated by the expensive computer-animated productions of big American studios such as Pixar and DreamWorks, it is easy to forget that a whole series of works in this genre in the past few years has taken the art of animation in quite different, though just as new and exciting, directions.

Waltz with Bashir (*Vals Im Bashir*, 2008) is one such film, the personal and documentary odyssey of Israeli director Ari Folman about the Lebanon war in 1982, as of course is *Persepolis*, Marjane Satrapi's and Vincent Paronnaud's film adaptation of Satrapi's autobiographically-inspired comic book. In it, she shows the childhood and youth of a smart, rebellious girl in the Iran of the mullahs after the Islamic Revolution: the exile in Vienna chosen for her by her parents concerned for the 14-year-old's safety; her subsequent return to Iran; an unhappy marriage; and her emigration once again, this time to France. Satrapi and Paronnaud set this within a very personal story of a young woman's self-discovery against the turbulent political background of the times and in the process stick closely to the literary source material in terms of both style and content, despite the fact that Satrapi often reiterates that you cannot simply film a comic exactly as it is.

The only part designed in color is the filmic present – Marjane's flight from Tehran to France, which structures her memories of the various stages in her life. Everything else is black and white, done in a simple two-dimensional style with strong contrast effects and simplifications verging occasionally on caricature. The story of little Marjane unfolds at breakneck speed: it begins in 1978, shortly before the collapse of the Shah's regime when she is just nine years of age. Satrapi and Paronnaud have often declared their admiration for German Expressionism, which may well be an influence here; at times we are reminded of Lotte Reiniger's silhouette animations, for instance when the scenic construction is arranged in several layers without actually appearing in three dimensions.

Satrapi's style is characterized by powerful directness: the anger, rage, joy, sadness and depression of the characters is conveyed directly to the viewer, often in just a single image. This is also how the liberal sprinkling of wit operates in the film too: when Marjane describes the changes in her body during puberty, for example, she suddenly appears in flashed up images like a Cubist painting by Picasso.

Not one to shy away from conflict, Satrapi also addresses the political situation in Iran after the Islamic Revolution: after her family welcomed the fall of the Shah, expressing the hope that the situation certainly couldn't get any worse, this was rapidly disproved. The new regime persecuted and murdered its opponents, advocated martyrs' death in the war with Iraq, and tightened its grip on the private lives of its citizens with dubious religious laws. In *Persepolis*, however, Satrapi always deals with this on a personal level: a

1
PUNK IS NOT DED
2

3

communist uncle who had already been imprisoned under the Shah is murdered; and a friend is killed when he is followed by "revolutionary guards" after he attends a party with women, dancing and alcohol, and falls to his death.

Sometimes, however, the consequences of this supposed piety reach absurd levels: such as the time when Marjane has to draw a fully veiled woman as part of her anatomy class in art studies, and the lecturer tries to explain Botticelli's "Birth of Venus" though all nudity has been pre-censored on the picture; or when shadowy figures buy western pop music on the black market, as if it were an extremely dangerous drug.

Marjane – brought up to be an independent and self-assured young woman by her parents and her grandmother, who acts as the main moral compass – is a walking humbug detector: she spots nonsense and hypocrisy

1 Go your own way: Marjane is completely in tune with the rebellious spirit of Punk – though more intuitively than intellectually. For her, music – she loves heavy metal – and fashion are inextricably linked.

2 The female guardians of the revolution are threatening as well as stupid – and a superb example of Satrapi's stylized graphics. Marjane manages to get away by making lame excuses.

3 Uncle Anouche was imprisoned for being a communist back in the Shah's day, and after the revolution gets back in touch with a secret cell. He makes a swan out of breadcrumbs for Marjane.

4

4 Intellectual circles: Marjane eagerly absorbs the adults' political discussions and their accounts of torture.

5 Marjane is one smart cookie, brought up to be independent and in control of her own life.

a mile away, as in the fact that, more often than not, corrupt and bigoted macho men are behind the pretense of sublime morality on the part of the guardians of virtue. In the final analysis, she counters the danger of self-righteousness with dry self-irony and the realization that she will not always be able to do justice to her grandmother's strict code of personal integrity.

The only time Marjane's perceptive powers fail her is when it comes to matters of the heart, when her emotions hijack her time and again. And, as is always the case in *Persepolis*, even this subject juxtaposes both tragic and comic elements: her first boyfriend in Vienna comes out as gay after their first night in bed together, while the second summarily betrays her. Worse is yet to come, however. Upset and depressed when she realizes his betrayal, Marjane loses her lodgings in winter, and suffers a serious bout of bronchitis. But here, too, grim humor dominates: while she initially saw her boyfriend as a kind of blond angel with whom she floated on clouds, he now appears a complete moron when seen in the right light.

Persepolis is definitely more a film about the sense of always feeling like an outsider, rather than a political movie: this was true for Marjane in her own country as well as in exile, where she was faced with not only a culture baffling

MARJANE SATRAPI Born into a well-to-do family in Rasht in Iran in 1969, Marjane Satrapi experienced a more or less carefree childhood until the Islamic Revolution in 1979. Like many other intellectuals, her left-wing family at first welcomed the fall of the Shah's regime, but it soon became evident that the country's new leadership would pursue its opponents even more ruthlessly. When the family began to fear for the safety of their rebellious daughter Marjane, she was sent to Vienna in 1984 at the age of 14 where she attended the French high school. Four years later, Satrapi returned to Iran and studied visual communication at the Islamic Azad University in Tehran.
Satrapi's career as an artist began in earnest, however, after she went into exile in France in 1994. Between 2000 and 2003 she enjoyed international success with her autobiographical comic "Persepolis" (four-part in the French original): it was translated into around 25 languages and sold millions of copies. Apparently Hollywood wanted to make a film of the story starring Brad Pitt and Jennifer Lopez, but Satrapi decided on an animation feature, which she co-directed with comic artist Vincent Paronnaud (artist's name: Winshluss). *Persepolis* was co-winner of the Jury Prize at the Cannes Film Festival, and was nominated for an Oscar in the Best Animated Feature Film category. Satrapi stayed true to family stories in two more graphic novels: in "Embroideries" ("Broderies," 2003) her grandmother plays a central role, while in "Chicken with Plums" ("Poulet aux prunes," 2004) the focus is on one of her mother's uncles. Satrapi is currently collaborating with Vincent Paronnaud on a film version of *Chicken with Plums* starring Mathieu Amalric and Isabella Rossellini. She lives in Paris with her second husband, Mattias Ripa, who is Swedish.

"*Persepolis* is a beautifully crafted animated film, which handles the simplifications required of the genre with an elegant sure hand. Satrapi's graphic style removes depth from the space, emphasizing the two-dimensionality, simultaneously foregrounding the looming presence of the characters." *taz*

6

Young women in Tehran: they like the same things as every teenager, but their freedom is increasingly restricted.

7 Western pop music becomes coveted contraband for Iranian teenagers.

8 The war against Iraq also leaves its destructive mark on Tehran.

“Satrapi provides us with extra tuition in Iranian history that is both lively and instructive, and what she tells us can easily be applied to other dictatorships; after all, it’s not just Iran that has – and had – spies and traitors.” *Die Zeit*

her, but racism as well. She even feels alienated among social outcasts: for ime, she hangs out with a punk clique in Vienna, but eventually can stand eir trite, ineffective nihilism no longer. If your experience tells you that positional views can land you rapidly in front of a summary trial, then people bbling on in the West about revolution, as they light up another joint, are esumably quite hard to take.

Persepolis leaves open the question whether the Marjane who leaves n for France at the end of the film has finally truly found herself. In her own mitably frank way, Marjane Satrapi has consistently stressed the universal ture of her story in interviews: “The dividing line is not between East and est, or between the Orient and the Occident, or Muslims and Christians. It

THE BOURNE ULTIMATUM

2007 – USA / GERMANY – 115 MIN. – THRILLER
DIRECTOR PAUL GREENGRASS (*1955)
SCREENPLAY TONY GILROY, SCOTT Z. BURNS, GEORGE NOLFI from the novels by ROBERT LUDLUM DIRECTOR OF PHOTOGRAPHY OLIVER WOOD EDITING CHRISTOPHER ROUSE
MUSIC JOHN POWELL PRODUCTION PATRICK CROWLEY, FRANK MARSHALL, PAUL SANDBERG for UNIVERSAL.
STARRING MATT DAMON (Jason Bourne), JULIA STILES (Nicky Parsons), DAVID STRATHAIRN (Noah Vosen), SCOTT GLENN (Ezra Kramer), PADDY CONSIDINE (Simon Ross), ALBERT FINNEY (Dr. Albert Hirsch), JOAN ALLEN (Pam Landy), TOM GALLOP (Tom Cronin), DANIEL BRÜHL (Martin Kreutz), JOEY ANSAH (Desh).
ACADEMY AWARDS 2008 OSCARS for BEST FILM EDITING (Christopher Rouse), BEST SOUND MIXING (Scott Millan, David Parker, Kirk Francis), BEST SOUND EDITING (Karen M. Baker, Per Hallberg).

"Jesus Christ, that's Jason Bourne!"

Who is Jason Bourne? The question has plagued Matt Damon's character since he was pulled from the water at the start of the first part of the trilogy, with two bullets in his body and no memory. There is, however, simply no time to search for an answer: Bourne has been predestined by the CIA and Hollywood to the life of an all-action hero, so he must run. Part three, therefore, begins exactly where the second one ended: in Moscow, the top spy everyone is after manages to escape once again. Yet the name of the city is of less interest than that of his pursuers or, indeed, his own. Movement is king, tracked via the flexibility of a hand-held camera and furiously edited sequences. Flashbacks – snatched memories of being programmed into a conscienceless killer and of his murdered girlfriend, Marie, from the first part – are woven effortlessly into the seamless flow of images. The opening credits have barely rolled when the action and spirit of the series kick in with a vengeance. And the rest of *The Bourne Ultimatum* does not deviate from this concept of pure kinetic energy.

Bourne is still searching for those responsible for removing his identity as part of the CIA Treadstone program. Treadstone was closed down, and its successor is called Blackbriar – otherwise, nothing has changed. Both hunter and hunted, the man of many passports keeps changing location, moving from Moscow to London via Paris, in concentric circles closing in on his target: the CIA training center in New York. En route to this destination, director Paul Greengrass delivers what are without doubt the most spectacular sequence of the series. In the crowds of London's Waterloo Station, Bourne uses his cel phone to direct a journalist (who has information about Blackbriar) past snipers like a chess piece; the snipers are in turn controlled from New York by satellit technology. The same techniques are used to direct a crazy pursuit acros the roofs of the Moroccan city, Tangiers. Jason Bourne moves in a world o complete global surveillance. The only technical extension of his physica capabilities, an off-the-shelf cell phone, also means he can be located at an time. In this brave new world, the get-away is engineered by discarding th SIM card.

Jason Bourne is clearly *the* action hero of the new millennium. A superher like Spiderman, he also has his own trilogy. What sets the series based o Robert Ludlum's bestsellers apart, however – especially the third part – is th direction by Greengrass. Lightning-fast cuts in themselves would hardly b anything new. In the hypermodern whirlwind of images, however, there is a order that to some extent counteracts the usual tactics of surprise. Like Bourn Greengrass has everything under control, his eagle eye creating order fro chaos. And, in the same way that the agent in *The Bourne Identity* (2002) an *The Bourne Supremacy* (2004) gradually builds a picture of himself, the direct perfects the trademark elements of the series (a global network of actio documentary-style hand-held camera, and an almost total absence of hum

and cynicism) in this, his second film in the trilogy. The secret recipe of success of both the series and its characters is undoubtedly underpinned by this organic build-up. First of all, we had the litmus test of Doug Liman's *The Bourne Identity*: an opening sequence to a film that did not at first stir any great expectations but which ultimately took flight, turning the rather quiet actor Matt Damon into an action hero in the process. His Jason Bourne is the product of secret service machinations, as well as an interactive dialogue with an ever-growing audience. As if in the aftermath of a birth, everyone followed his steps, from feeling his way still tentatively into his new life to the cool strategist who plays cat-and-mouse with his creators, while apparently always remaining one step ahead of them. *The Bourne Ultimatum* becomes an intelligent mainstream thriller by avoiding any spurious psychological motivations, as witnessed by

1 Run, Jason, run: as ex-CIA agent Jason Bourne, Matt Damon is permanently on the move, the action hero for the new millennium.

2 Head of Blackbriar, Noah Vosen (David Strathairn), pursues Bourne across the globe. It's also about his own mind.

3 Moral core of the CIA: typically cast, Joan Allen plays Pam Landy, the only person Bourne can trust in the web of lies and betrayal.

4 Nicky Parsons (Julia Stiles) waits for Bourne in Tangiers. The question of their (unremembered) affair runs through the whole series.

5 Over the rooftops of Tangiers: the chase through an entire apartment block is one of the most spectacular movie action sequences of recent years.

"Their sights set far beyond the usual genre coordinates, the three *Bourne* movies drill into your psyche as well as into your body." *The New York Times*

PAUL GREENGRASS The background of Paul Greengrass in documentary making can be detected in his films. The trademark style of the British director includes a restless, hand-held camera that suggests authenticity and participation to the viewer. His first international hit, *Bloody Sunday* (2002), is the best example of this. This intense docudrama about the bloody events in Derry, Northern Ireland, in 1972 won this new talent the Golden Bear at the Berlin Film Festival, as well as attracting criticism for its form and content. His camera is never, after all, a neutral observer, but always in the thick of the action. The former investigative journalist had previously dealt with controversial political subjects. In his first TV movies, for example, he dissected the skills of a British special unit in the first Gulf War, as well as a historic betting scam in English football. The title of the documentary series made by British TV company, ITV (where he worked for ten years), is programmatic for Greengrass: "World in Action."

This long-haired eccentric became one of Hollywood's style-defining action directors through the adventures of the secret agent suffering from amnesia, Jason Bourne. Greengrass took over from the original director, Doug Liman, in making the two *Bourne* sequels. *The Bourne Ultimatum* (2007), the third part of the trilogy, grossed over 400 million US dollars worldwide. In the interim, Greengrass applied himself to the traumatic events of 9/11 with *United 93* (2006). Under his direction, the crash of United Airlines flight 93 hijacked by terrorists became a thrilling parallel montage of events on board the plane and the helpless actions of ground staff. In spite of audiences in tears, who felt that such an account of past events was "too soon," the film (produced in England as a precautionary measure) was nominated for an Oscar. His film about the Iraq war, *Green Zone* (2010), also met with some controversy.

6 CIA chief Ezra Kramer (Scott Glenn) authorized Operation Blackbriar, but lost control of it a long time ago.

7 In Tangiers, CIA assassin Desh (played by former martial arts practitioner Joey Ansah) engages in hair-raising stunts with Bourne.

8 In the chaos of Waterloo Station, Bourne keeps a firm rein on things. His inconspicuous appearance is the best camouflage.

"It's a fantasy we all have: of starting again from scratch and finding out that we're much more interesting than we and others think we are." *The Observer*

9 Complete global surveillance: the latest mobile technology means Bourne can be located anywhere.

10 Showdown at Waterloo: Bourne uses his cellphone to direct journalist Simon Ross (Paddy Considine) away from his pursuers.

"This is, simply put, some of the most accomplished filmmaking being done anywhere for any purpose." *Village Voice*

he extremely sparse dialogue. There is something unsettling about it. Our nodern-day star, as embodied by Matt Damon, is an empty cipher to some extent: a highly-skilled, average guy, but without an identity. The nightmare ınd utopia of an existence that begins at zero coincide in his character. Total lexibility is both a blessing and a curse for him. In a world shattered by economic crises and terrorism, marked by efficiency concepts and security nadness, he is simultaneously both part of the system and its enemy. This is precisely why the Bourne movies seemed far more in keeping with the times han the James Bond series, which responded immediately to the competition vith *Casino Royale* (2006). We all want to be like James Bond. But we are, in act, Jason Bourne – whoever he may be. PB

ATONEMENT

2007 – UK / FRANCE – 123 MIN. – DRAMA, LITERARY ADAPTATION
DIRECTOR JOE WRIGHT (*1972)
SCREENPLAY CHRISTOPHER HAMPTON from the novel of the same name by IAN McEWAN
DIRECTOR OF PHOTOGRAPHY SEAMUS MCGARVEY EDITING PAUL TOTHILL MUSIC DARIO MARIANELLI
PRODUCTION TIM BEVAN, ERIC FELLNER, PAUL WEBSTER, JANE FRAZER for UNIVERSAL, WORKING TITLE FILMS, RELATIVITY MEDIA, STUDIO CANAL.
STARRING KEIRA KNIGHTLEY (Cecilia Tallis), JAMES MCAVOY (Robbie Turner), ROMOLA GARAI (Briony Tallis, age 18), SAOIRSE RONAN (Briony Tallis, age 13), BRENDA BLETHYN (Grace Turner), VANESSA REDGRAVE (Older Briony), JUNO TEMPLE (Lola Quincey).
ACADEMY AWARDS 2008 OSCAR for BEST MUSIC, Original Score (Dario Marianelli).

"It's about a young girl, a young and foolish girl, who sees something from her bedroom window which she doesn't understand, but she thinks she does."

Click, click, click. It begins with the sound of a typewriter: the keys strike the paper and leave behind letters, words, a story ... and it ends with a gray-haired writer telling her own story – the same woman who was typing at the start of the film. In the meantime, this woman's life unfolds. It is the story of Briony Tallis and its subject matter is weighty: betrayal and the search for forgiveness, for the atonement that supplies the title for both the film and the novel by Ian McEwan.

The year is 1935, on the estate of the English Tallis family: 13-year-old Briony (Saoirse Ronan) is watching her older sister Cecilia (Keira Knightley) with her lover, Robbie (James McAvoy), the housekeeper's son. Briony is piqued by what she sees and she later reads – and misinterprets – a risqué but basically innocuous letter the young man has written to her sister. In the light of these and other events she wrongly accuses Robbie of a rape; and on the strength of her statement to the police, Robbie is arrested and imprisoned The action moves forward four years; Robbie is released from prison and sen to fight in World War 2. He is separated from his unit in northern France anc tries to make it to the coast with two fellow soldiers. Briony (Romola Garai) now a nurse in London, has realized her terrible mistake and tries desperatel to resume contact with her estranged sister.

With his film adaptation of Ian McEwan's novel, English director Jo Wright (*Pride & Prejudice*, 2005) has created a "literary" film in the most litera sense of the word: a sympathetic adaptation that is also a narrative abou writing stories and the power of words – while at the same time representin cinema at its best. The film is divided into two parts, the first of which is se in the Tallis house and grounds. It is shot by cameraman Seamus McGarve (*The Hours*, 2002) in a stunningly beautiful pictorial style influenced by th

1

1 Cecilia (Keira Knightley): an innocent romp in the fountain has tragic consequences.

2 Daughter from a good family: Cecilia only realizes she loves Robbie, the housekeeper's son, when a slightly risqué letter from him goes astray.

3 Dead, crazed and injured people, plus a ship run aground: Robbie (James McAvoy) experiences the full madness of war on the beach at Dunkirk.

"Christopher Hampton's screenplay is a real tour de force. He has managed to compress and tighten McEwan's elegant, sweeping prose in an intelligent way." *Neue Zürcher Zeitung*

ainter's art. In directorial terms, it unfolds with the lightness of a musical box vhirring along in time to the clacking rhythm of the typewriter. Part two is set luring the war, with Robbie in France and the two sisters in London; it is lominated by a highly aesthetic visual language that contrasts markedly with he somber mood. In a single tracking shot, Wright shows the madness of war, s if through a magnifying glass: soldiers are encamped on Dunkirk beach, vaiting to be evacuated; the dead, the wounded and the mad constitute a haotic mess; soldiers are singing, crying, looking for food; they shoot healthy orses to stop them being of use to the enemy; and, in the middle of it all, a assive wheel is turning. Duplications, pairs and reflections are a recurring motif in *Atonement*: the two parts of the film; the two sisters; two scenes in the first part that are narrated twice, from two different points of view; two key scenes set under water; and a number of visual tableaux symmetrically constructed from a central perspective. The fact that this meticulously detailed form does not degenerate into mere decoration is down to the exciting story that deals with the great issues of humanity: love and war, appearance and reality, blame and forgiveness. The result is a masterpiece that stands alongside great works of British film history made by directors such as James Ivory (*The Remains of the Day*, 1993), thanks to its supremely emotional power and incredibly beautiful visual composition. HJK

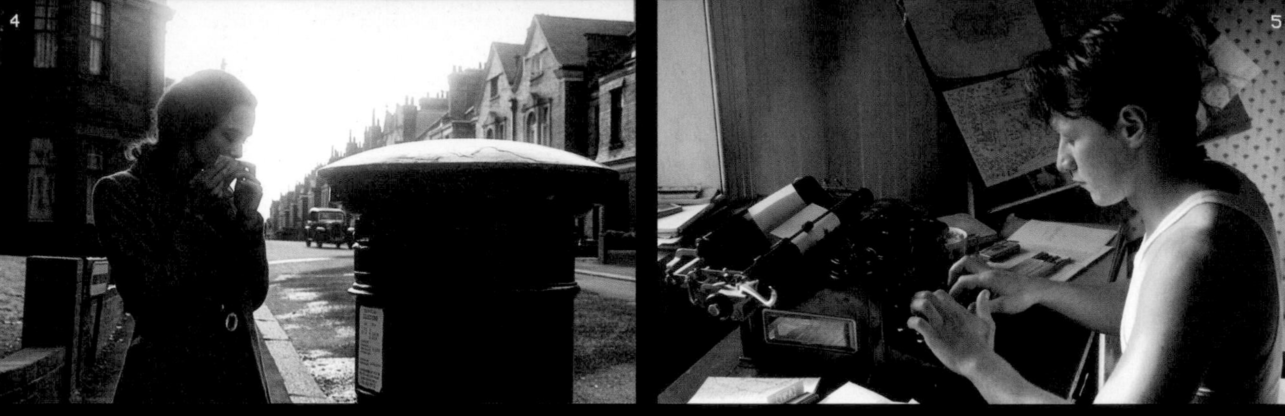

“The first sound we hear in *Atonement* is the tap of typewriter keys. Soon, the tapping becomes regular, like drumbeats. Later in the film, it rings out as loudly as gunshots. The implication is clear: words can stir us and set us dancing, but they can also kill.” *The New Yorker*

6

7

4 By forces' mail, with love: Cecilia sends Robbie letters to the French front.

5 The power of words: Robbie writes two letters to Cecilia, sends the wrong one, and his fate is sealed.

6 Robbie: guilty of a sex crime? Thirteen-year-old Briony (Saoirse Ronan, right) shares her suspicions with cousin Lola (Juno Temple).

7 Reunited in the turmoil of war: nurse Cecilia and frontline soldier, Robbie.

KEIRA KNIGHTLEY The daughter of actor Will Knightley and playwright Sharman Macdonald, Keira Knightley was as good as born into show business on March 26, 1985. She stood in front of the camera for the first time when she was seven, had her big break at the age of sixteen with *Bend It Like Beckham* (2002), and just a year later shot to superstardom alongside Johnny Depp in *Pirates of the Caribbean: The Curse of the Black Pearl* (2003). The second and third parts of *Pirates of the Caribbean* (2006 and 2007) made this English actress one of Hollywood's highest earners. She is not, however, involved in the fourth part (2011).
As well as swashbuckling pirate comedies, the costume drama also features regularly in Knightley's filmography. Her flawless face and sculptured beauty go extremely well with the sweeping decor of a bygone age, as witnessed for example in *Pride & Prejudice* (2005), which was adapted from the novel by Jane Austen, and *The Duchess* (2008). Knightley also had the opportunity to show her wilder, less refined side in her role as the eponymous bounty hunter in Tony Scott's action movie *Domino* (2005).

JUNO

2007 – USA / CANADA – 96 MIN. – COMEDY
DIRECTOR JASON REITMAN (*1977)
SCREENPLAY DIABLO CODY DIRECTOR OF PHOTOGRAPHY ERIC STEELBERG EDITING DANA E. GLAUBERMAN
MUSIC MATEO MESSINA PRODUCTION LIANNE HALFON, JOHN MALKOVICH, MASON NOVICK, RUSSELL SMITH for MANDATE PICTURES, MR. MUDD, DANCING ELK, FOX SEARCHLIGHT.
STARRING ELLEN PAGE (Juno MacGuff), MICHAEL CERA (Paulie Bleeker), JENNIFER GARNER (Vanessa Loring), JASON BATEMAN (Mark Loring), ALLISON JANNEY (Brenda MacGufff), J. K. SIMMONS (Mac MacGuff), OLIVIA THIRLBY (Leah), EILEEN PEDDE (Gerta Rauss), RAINN WILSON (Rollo), DANIEL CLARK (Steve Rendazo).
ACADEMY AWARDS 2008 OSCAR for BEST ORIGINAL SCREENPLAY (Diablo Cody).

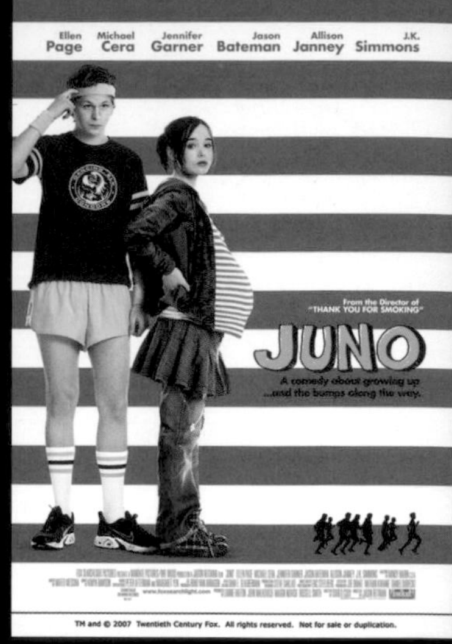

"I still have your underwear." (Paulie)
"I still have your virginity." (Juno)

She is 16, pretty, and pretty smart. And she wants to know about "it." Out of curiosity, Juno (Ellen Page) seduces her shy school friend Paulie Bleeker (Michael Cera) – an event that is not without consequences. Juno falls pregnant. Her best friend Leah (Olivia Thirlby) is the first to find out. Now the clueless lover has to be told. With a pipe in her mouth, she takes up position on an old sofa in front of Bleeker's house; when he appears in skimpy yellow shorts and a wine-colored top to go jogging, it makes for a ridiculously comic scene. Bleeker reacts like any 16-year-old who finds out he is about to be a father: he stumbles around and runs away.

At first, Juno is in no doubt that she wants an abortion. But then, whether it is the fruitcake-flavored condom pressed into her hand at the "Woman Now" abortion clinic, or the realization that embryos have fingernails even at that stage, her desire to just get rid of "the thing" begins to weaken. She has to come up with Plan B. How about making someone happy: someone who really longs for a child, but cannot have one?

She quickly finds the perfect couple in a newspaper: Vanessa (Jennifer Garner) and Mark (Jason Bateman) live in a rich suburb with a lifestyle straight out of Martha Stewart's *Living* magazine. Yet this apparently ideal solution turns out to be very different from what was promised in the ad. While Vanessa feels her calling as a mother, reading parenting books and kitting out the nursery, Mark would rather retreat to his den, strum his guitar and watch horror movies. This means, however, that he fits comfortably into the teenage world of Juno, whose room is crammed full of pictures and music. Posters on her wall include the painter David Choe, while Patti Smith records lie on the

1

Reserve your VIP Passes
while you can!
STAIRWAY to the Junior Prom

"It's not often that a film catches its viewers unawares like this. For Juno entertains too perfectly over long periods with its irreverent commentary on melodramatic clichés – pregnant, underage, penniless – for us to anticipate the well-placed emotional goal that comes later." *Der Spiegel*

floor. The film attaches great importance to set details in general, producing well-rounded, vibrant characters who are perfectly matched to the objects around them – somewhat ironically directed by Jason Reitman (*Thank You for Smoking*, 2005). When heavily pregnant Juno is watching the horror flick *The Wizard of Gore* with Mark, for example, we see (of all things) the scene where a woman's stomach is being drilled.

Mark and Juno love horror films and music, so it's no surprise that Juno enjoys spending time with the much older man. "Is that normal?" her friend Leah asks her at one point. "Probably not," replies Juno. But sticking to convention is not exactly her thing anyway. Mark's announcement that he wants to leave Vanessa drops into her life like a bombshell – as does his confession that he doesn't want to be a father either. Juno's world falls apart. She had, after all, believed she had found two people who were committed to each other and prepared to share the care of a baby. Juno learns her lesson about adults and realizes that Paulie Bleeker isn't quite so bad after all. And the baby? Vanessa gets the child, even though the bubble-like dream of the perfect family has burst. *Juno* is an unusual teen comedy, full of profound wit and lightly handled truths. Diablo Cody, an internet blogger and stripper, won an Oscar for her first screenplay, and with total justification. The way she juggles clichés is a joy to behold.

This is a movie about expectations denied: the perfect family isn't perfect; the annoying stepmother (Allison Janney) is both funny and pragmatic; a guitar-playing thirty-something who reads comics is not necessarily cool; and a burning desire lurks behind a prissy, yuppie facade. The style of the film is

2

3

1 Juno (Ellen Page) is sixteen and pregnant. This puts her way ahead of her fellow pupils in high school.

2 The baby arrives: at this stage we don't know if Juno will give it up for adoption.

3 Paulie Bleeker (Michael Cera), the father, is like a big kid. What he really wants to do is run a mile.

4 Juno tells her best friend Leah (Olivia Thirlby) everything. The film makes ironic reference to high school comedies.

"Nothing is as it seems in this subversive film, which takes wicked delight in constantly disappointing audience expectations in the most delicious way." *Neue Züricher Zeitung*

DIABLO CODY When she won the Oscar for her first screenplay, Juno, it caused a sensation. Overnight, Diablo Cody, born Brook Busey in Chicago in 1978, became famous. All the more so because she had previously worked in nightclubs as a stripper and published her autobiographical account of it in 2005, "Candy Girl: A Year in the Life of an Unlikely Stripper." Diablo Cody has always been passionate about writing: "I've told stories all my life," she comments on the German internet site Planetinterview.de. "I wake up every day and write stories, essays, and reviews of new records I have just bought."

Of course, she was lucky, as well as being talented. A film producer noticed her blog "The Pussy Ranch" and asked her to write a screenplay. It was her first, but the passionate author believes that anyone can write screenplays if he or she has seen enough films. At any rate, her script debut convinced director Jason Reitman: he made it into a marvelous tragicomedy with Canadian actress Ellen Page in the title role.

Since her surprising Oscar win, Diablo Cody has become a sought-after film writer and producer. Working with Steven Spielberg, she developed the TV series *United States of Tara* that was broadcast on the Showtime channel from 2009. She also penned the screenplay for the horror comedy *Jennifer's Body* (2009) by Karyn Kusama, as well as acting as the movie's executive producer. A horror movie fan herself, she is also scheduled to produce the romantic zombie comedy *Breathers: A Zombie's Lament* from the novel by S.G. Brownes, which will be released in cinemas in 2011.

Diablo Cody has been on screen as well: she made a brief appearance in *90210* (2008), the remake of the cult TV series "Beverly Hills, 90210." She was also a member of the Berlin Film Festival 2009 jury that awarded the prize for best first movie.

5 During the ultrasound examination: Juno's stepmother (Allison Janney) and best friend are there to support her.

6 Mark and Vanessa (Jason Bateman and Jennifer Garner) want to adopt Juno's baby. They seem the perfect couple.

7 Juno has a difficult relationship with her father (J.K. Simmons). Each has to learn to appreciate the other.

8 Juno's room is a mixture of art and quirky designer objects. The set is meticulously detailed.

traditional and uncomplicated. According to Reitman: "We wanted to make a film with a kind of hand-made look about it, like something that might well be on the walls of Juno's room." The result is a smart comedy about growing up and being a grown-up. It's about lifelong dreams and popular culture, about women who crave motherhood and men who deny fatherhood. But one thing Juno is not, and that is a film about teenage pregnancy. It is no coincidence that Juno's surname is MacGuff, with echoes of Hitchcock's "MacGuffin" – an object that advances the action, but is not the theme itself. The baby in Juno's belly can be seen as the MacGuffin, while Juno herself (played by the wonderful Canadian actress, Ellen Page) is a lively, lovably brash girl of 16 who is far more mature than most who are twice her age. KK

6

7

“Yet it isn’t a question of *Juno* being realistic, even though the movie has such a contemporary feel about it. For it is designed to be a mainstream didactic comedy that explores what is morally desirable and what isn’t.” *die tageszeitung*

8

I'M NOT THERE

2007 – USA / GERMANY – 135 MIN. – BIOPIC, MUSIC FILM
DIRECTOR TODD HAYNES (*1961)
SCREENPLAY TODD HAYNES, OREN MOVERMAN DIRECTOR OF PHOTOGRAPHY EDWARD LACHMAN
EDITING JAY RABINOWITZ MUSIC BOB DYLAN PRODUCTION JOHN GOLDWYN, JOHN SLOSS, JAMES D. STERN, CHRISTINE VACHON for KILLER FILMS, JOHN WELLS PRODUCTIONS, JOHN GOLDWYN PRODUCTIONS, ENDGAME ENTERTAINMENT, FILM & ENTERTAINMENT VIP MEDIENFONDS 4 GMBH & CO. KG, GREY WATER PARK PRODUCTIONS, RISING STAR.
STARRING CHRISTIAN BALE (Jack Rollins/Pastor John), CATE BLANCHETT (Jude Quinn), MARCUS CARL FRANKLIN (Woody/Chaplin Boy), RICHARD GERE (Billy the Kid), HEATH LEDGER (Robbie Clark), BEN WHISHAW (Arthur Rimbaud), CHARLOTTE GAINSBOURG (Claire), DAVID CROSS (Allen Ginsberg), BRUCE GREENWOOD (Keenan Jones/Pat Garrett), JULIANNE MOORE (Alice Fabian).
IFF VENICE 2007 BEST FILM (Todd Haynes), SPECIAL JURY PRIZE (joint winner with *Couscous*), BEST ACTRESS (Cate Blanchett).

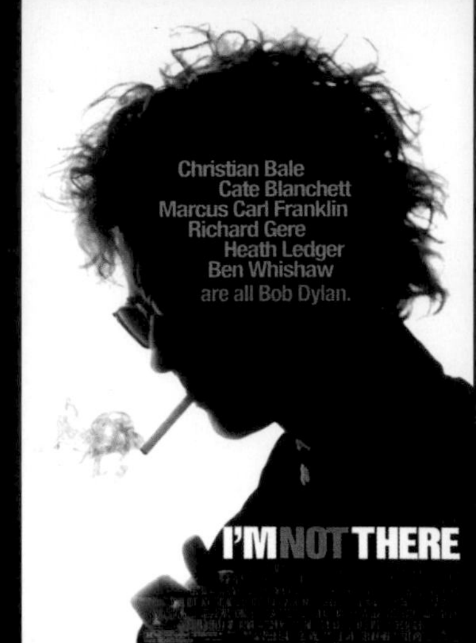

Christian Bale
Cate Blanchett
Marcus Carl Franklin
Richard Gere
Heath Ledger
Ben Whishaw
are all Bob Dylan.
I'M NOT THERE

"I'm glad I'm not me."

How do you portray a famous personality on film, cramming their life and work into the standard film format of 90 or 120 minutes? Many writers and directors often resort to no more than a traditional, chronological elaboration of the positive and negative high points in the life of the celebrity in question; a kind of "greatest hits" list that everyone instantly recognizes, but which is devoid of any element of surprise.

American writer and director Todd Haynes approached the issue differently. For, as we are told in the movie's opening credits, *I'm Not There* is certainly "inspired by the music and many lives of Bob Dylan," but it is anything but a standard biopic. In this film, five actors and one actress give us an interpretation (by association and without any claim to historical accuracy) of different stages in the life of the famous American musician who has always eluded conventional biographical formulae, thanks to his reclusiveness, the creation of various legends about himself and his own, single-handed shattering of these very legends: Bob Dylan seems more of an artistic synthesis than a real person.

Haynes' free interpretation of the subject is packed with allusion and relates mainly to the period in the 1960s and 70s, when Dylan's artistic direction and lifestyle were still undergoing rapid change. Many of the musician's actions may have sprung from either his desire to provoke or his off-beat sense of humor, but his main concern remained the same: to sabotage the expectations of both the public and media. He neither wanted to be the "mouthpiece of his generation" (as people were all too keen to label him) nor was he prepared

1

“Todd Haynes has held up to the mirror of his imagination the figure that served for 50 years as Dylan. He then smashed the mirror. His film is the attempt to put the broken mirror image back together.”

Berliner Zeitung

for his artistic scope to be restricted. As such, in covering a period of twenty years, the movie combines – albeit loosely – seven different stages of Dylan’s life that have pretty much equal weight: in *I’m Not There*, Marcus Carl Franklin plays an 11-year-old black folk musician who names himself for the famous folk singer and Dylan’s idol, Woody Guthrie; as he traverses the country by train, living the life of a hobo, he spreads crazy stories about his origins and artistic merits. As Jack Rollins, Christian Bale corresponds to the Dylan of early successes, a folk idol of the political protest culture in America. In these scenes, Haynes creates the style of a classical documentary: one of them involves Julianne Moore in mock interviews – a reference to the documentary by Martin Scorsese, *No Direction Home: Bob Dylan* (1995) – playing Alice Fabian, a beautiful parody of Dylan’s fellow artist and intermittent partner, Joan Baez.

In the role of Dylan lookalike and teen rebel poet Arthur Rimbaud, Ben Whishaw has to account for his influence before a kind of commission of inquiry, producing an interpretation of Dylan’s dealings with the media. On the other hand, Heath Ledger plays an actor called Robbie Clark who has just played Jack Rollins in a film: in this case, the background is America’s role in the Vietnam War, with the focus mainly on Dylan’s private life and his relationship with his partners, all of whom are rolled into one character, Claire (Charlotte Gainsbourg). A decade passes from first love to bitter separation, with a discussion in the interim of the accusations of sexism leveled against Dylan in the 1970s due to a few song lyrics and things he said in interviews. According to Haynes, he modeled the style of the Ledger and Gainsbourg scenes on Jean-Luc Godard’s films of the mid-1960s, because they successfully combined personal

3

1 Bob Dylan: more media invention than real person? Cate Blanchett as Dylan's alter ego, Jude Quinn.

2 Rock music, protest and drugs instead of folksy coziness and milk: Jude Quinn shocks his audience in the mid-1960s.

3 So, where's the art? Jude Quinn armors himself against all expectations with surreal farce.

"*I'm Not There* is far from being a conventional, formally structured biopic like *Walk The Line* or *Control*. Here, we do not get to know the person behind the pop-star shell. Instead we get a complex fictional character of pop culture." *Berliner Morgenpost*

TODD HAYNES Born in Los Angeles in 1961, director and screenwriter Todd Haynes started out studying art and semiotics at the eminent Brown University in Providence, Rhode Island. Haynes had been making amateur Super-8 movies since he was a child, but he first attracted the public's attention with the short film (just 45 minutes long) *Superstar: The Karen Carpenter Story* (1987). In it, using Barbie dolls but in a serious way and without any deliberate parody, he recreated the life story of the pop singer who died as a result of anorexia in the 1970s.

For his first full-length feature, *Poison* (1991), the openly gay artist and AIDS activist worked up three Jean Genet short stories, each in completely different styles. *Poison* won the Grand Jury Prize at the Sundance Film Festival and is now regarded as one of the key works of "New Queer Cinema." Haynes became familiar to mainstream audiences with the psycho-thriller *Safe* (1995), the story of a housewife played by Julianne Moore who becomes allergic to her environment. Haynes once again devoted himself to music with *Velvet Goldmine* (1998): loosely based on the careers of David Bowie and Iggy Pop, the director plunged into the colorful, crazy world of glam rock, telling the story of a reporter who is investigating the rise and fall of his one-time idol in the 1980s, the fictional rock star Brian Slade (Jonathan Rhys Meyers).

Far From Heaven was released in 2002, a stylistically confident homage to Douglas Sirk's colorful melodramas of the 1950s. Here, Haynes expands on the theme of the narrow-minded, small-town life that Haynes' characters often have to suffer, dealing with issues of race and homosexuality. Haynes' most recent film to date is the experimental Bob Dylan "biography" *I'm Not There* (2007), in which he returns to the theme of changing identities that has been a constant feature of his previous movies, interpreting the various stages of the musician's life through different actors.

4 “Country-livin’ Dylan” in a highly evocative scene: an ageing Billy the Kid (Richard Gere) has withdrawn from life.

5 The beginning of the legend(s): Woody (Marcus Carl Franklin) hitches across the country spreading fantastic tales about his background.

6 Icon of a politicized protest culture: Christian Bale as early Dylan incarnation, Jack Rollins.

7 Dylan, women and his private life: Heath Ledger as actor Robbie Clark, who is stuck in a difficult relationship with his partner Claire.

histories with political ideas. As Jude Quinn, Cate Blanchett represents the Dylan who became a Judas in the eyes of his fans when he picked up an electric guitar at the Newport Folk Festival in July 1965 and belted out a few loud, ill-rehearsed songs. Haynes underlines this radical change of direction and its consequences by making the band open fire on the shocked audience with submachine guns. The director then presents the following period of the exhausting British tours in 1965/6, the drug excesses and the constant justifications to the press as a grotesque nightmare; its inspiration alternates between D.A. Pennebaker’s tour movie *Don’t Look Back* (1967), Richard Lester’s antics with the Beatles (who make a brief appearance as characters) and Federico Fellini’s surreal and paranoid drama about artists, *8½* (1963).

Dylan retreated to become a country rancher after a motorbike accident in 1966; this corresponds to Richard Gere’s character (a reclusive Billy the Kid) complete with stylistic references to Dylan’s own part in Sam Peckinpah’s

"In the conflict between illusion and 'reality,' this film comes down forcefully on the side of art: it is a 135-minute commitment to experimentation that gloriously and deliberately gets out of hand, rising to the heights of great form precisely in its amorphousness." *Die Zeit*

late western *Pat Garrett & Billy the Kid* (1973). Christian Bale brings the story full circle as Jack Rollins, who converts to a preacher, a reminder that Dylan (who came from a middle-class Jewish family) suddenly appeared in the form of an evangelical Christ figure singing Gospel music in the late 1970s.

On the one hand, Haynes has arranged these different episodes into a rough chronological sequence, while on the other the skilful montage also interweaves them in terms of content, creating a stream of new reflections. Haynes' use of music, which involved access to Dylan's original recordings, is suitably associative; the original pieces serve to elucidate the words and actions of the different Dylan characters, while in the scenes where these figures appear in concert, for instance, cover versions of Dylan songs by younger artists are used exclusively.

While many of Haynes' interpretations are free, he is meticulous in the way he reproduces concerts, photos and interviews; and the recreation of the various film styles of the 1960s is never a rip-off, but an elaborate game that triggers further associations on the one hand and gives the viewer a temporal orientation point on the other. And you don't have to be a Dylan fan or film historian to enjoy *I'm Not There*, as the occasional recognition factor is just an added bonus. Todd Haynes does not explain the enigma of Bob Dylan; he has created an art movie instead, which takes an unusual form but is still entirely appropriate for the subject matter. It is about an artist we find difficult to fathom, who has always heeded the key features of his trade in order to remain creative: being open to all kinds of influences, constantly reinventing himself and refusing to live up to expectations. LP

THE DARJEELING LIMITED

2007 – USA – 91 MIN. – TRAGICOMEDY
DIRECTOR WES ANDERSON (* 1969)
SCREENPLAY WES ANDERSON, ROMAN COPPOLA, JASON SCHWARTZMAN
DIRECTOR OF PHOTOGRAPHY ROBERT D. YEOMAN EDITING ANDREW WEISBLUM
PRODUCTION WES ANDERSON, SCOTT RUDIN, ROMAN COPPOLA, LYDIA DEAN PILCHER, STEVEN RALES for FOX SEARCHLIGHT PICTURES, AMERICAN EMPIRICAL PICTURES, DUNE ENTERTAINMENT.
STARRING OWEN WILSON (Francis), ADRIEN BRODY (Peter), JASON SCHWARTZMAN (Jack), ANJELICA HUSTON (Patricia), AMARA KARAN (Rita), WALLACE WOLODARSKY (Brendan), CAMILLA RUTHERFORD (Alice), BILL MURRAY (The Businessman).

“We haven’t been able to locate ourselves yet.”

Wes Anderson turns to his favorite subject once again in his fifth feature film: a tragicomic family saga. The father has died the previous year and, since then, the mother has disappeared without trace. The three brothers Francis (Owen Wilson), Peter (Adrien Brody) and Jack (Jason Schwartzman) then try – with varying degrees of success – to stand on their own feet. Francis is the one who invites his brothers to go on a trip: it is to be a spiritual journey across India, in a brightly painted train. Francis only reveals the real reason for their trip several days later: they are on their way to see their mother, who has retreated to an Indian convent. It is supposed to be a chance for them to become closer again, and for the family to be reunited. Yet the prevailing mood is far from harmonious. They snitch on each other, blurt out secrets, and fight about mere trifles like little kids. Added to which, they are incapable of disengaging from their everyday problems, constantly trying to maintain phone contact with the outside world.

More than anything else, the face of Francis, heavily bandaged after a motor bike accident, represents the spiritual wounds and scars that are far from healed, while the painted box is an unmistakable reference to the family baggage that the brothers tote around with them. Any spiritual purification is out of the question. The journey follows a strict schedule that has been carefully worked out by Francis’s assistant, Brendan (Wallace Wolodarsky), details of which are set out in laminated notes each morning. Their impressions are limited verbally to “wow,” “great,” and “amazing,” irrespective of whatever the next “thing” is they are praying to, or how exactly the ritual with the peacock feathers is actually meant to be carried out. So they end up as mere tourists in a strange, colorful land they do not understand, in which the get-together with their mother signifies just a brief, disenchanting interlude.

By reducing it to three main characters, *The Darjeeling Limited* seems far more compact and clearer than its predecessors, *The Royal Tenenbaums*

(2001) and *The Life Aquatic with Steve Zissou* (2004). In the latter's case, it was mainly Anderson's compulsive control and obsession with detail that led many critics to accuse him of mannerism and superficiality. For this reason, the director decided not to shoot in a film studio on this occasion and instead to leave it more or less to chance. By way of preparation, Anderson traveled through India for several weeks with Roman Coppola and Jason Schwartzman, and went on to incorporate their respective impressions in a joint screenplay.

During filming itself, the director set great store on spontaneity, with the vibrantly colorful culture of India proving a perfect location for this. In the teeming cities, even a short pan or zoom is enough to find the next interesting cinematic image. This curious look at the foreign land is celebrated with gusto. The director, who had never been in India before himself other than the preparatory

"One of the rules we set for our film was that we would not change or try to control anything, that we would not build any sets and just take things as we found them. You don't need all that anyway, because there are thousands of interesting possibilities. All you have to do is keep your eyes open." *Wes Anderson*

1 Jack (Jason Schwartzman), Francis (Owen Wilson) and Peter (Adrien Brody) on their spiritual journey: the brothers are named for the new "Hollywood greats" – Nicholson, Coppola and Bogdanovich.

2 When a snake escapes from the brothers' compartment, the guard fails to see the joke and throws them off the train.

3 Deceptively idyllic moments in the Indian temple – yet, even when praying, the brothers cannot stop bickering.

4 "F*** the itinerary!" The laminated travel plans, scheduled down to the last minute, illustrate the idiotic nature of the whole venture.

trip, did draw plenty of inspiration from other films, however, especially Jean Renoir's film about India, *The River* (1951). For the film score, Anderson made repeated use of compositions from films by the famous Indian director Satyajit Ray, as well as several songs by the British rock band The Kinks. Yet, more than anything else, Anderson's film pays tribute to The Beatles. Their father-figure, manager Brian Epstein, died in 1967 of an accidental overdose of sleeping pills. The following year, The Beatles set out on their famous India tour. In the meantime, the musicians shot their mainly improvised TV film *Magical Mystery Tour* (1967), in which they plunged into the unknown with the same lack of planning as Anderson did with *The Darjeeling Limited.*

It is certainly no coincidence that the bright blue and yellow train colors hark back to The Beatles' bus, the three brothers run down a hill in the same slow motion as Paul McCartney did to the song "Fool on the Hill," and Jack looks like Ringo Starr with his handlebar moustache. In fact, in the same year Jason Schwartzman used the same look to play the drummer in the musical comedy *Walk Hard: The Dewey Cox Story* (2007). These references clearly indicate the ongoing influence of The Beatles' trip to India as a place of self-discovery. The Whitman brothers may not be enlightened at the end, but they do end up becoming a little closer to each other. "Let's go get a drink and smoke a cigarette." CZ

JASON SCHWARTZMAN was born in Los Angeles in 1980, son of film producer Jack Schwartzman and actress Talia Shire, sister of Francis Ford Coppola. At first, Jason wanted to be a musician, and in 1994 he founded the band Phantom Planet, continuing as its drummer until 2003. Schwartzman came to film more by chance and through family connections.

His cousin, Sofia Coppola, recommended him to Wes Anderson when he was looking for a lead actor for his film *Rushmore* (1998). Jason generated immediate sympathy as the eccentric schoolboy with the horn-rimmed glasses and beret. He turned up three years later in *CQ* (2001), the directorial debut of his cousin Roman Coppola. In *Spun* (2002) he played a dropout with a drug habit. Yet it was not until his third leading role in *I Heart Huckabees* (2004) that he decided to concentrate on his acting career, and left Phantom Planet. In nearly all of his movies, including *Shopgirl* (2005), Schwartzman plays a dithery but nice twenty-something.

Schwartzman co-wrote a screenplay for the first time with *The Darjeeling Limited* (2007). Since 2009 he has also starred as amateur sleuth Jonathan Ames in the TV comedy series *Bored to Death* (2009–2011). After a gap of many years, the actor is once again devoting himself to music: he has now released two albums from his solo project "Coconut Records."

EASTERN PROMISES

2007 – USA / CANADA / UK – 100 MIN. – GANGSTER MOVIE, DRAMA
DIRECTOR DAVID CRONENBERG (*1943)
SCREENPLAY STEVEN KNIGHT DIRECTOR OF PHOTOGRAPHY PETER SUSCHITZKY EDITING RONALD SANDERS
MUSIC HOWARD SHORE PRODUCTION ROBERT LANTOS, PAUL WEBSTER, TRACEY SEAWARD for SERENDIPITY POINT FILMS, FOCUS FEATURES, KUDOS FILM AND TV, SCION FILMS, BBC FILMS, ASTRAL MEDIA, CORUS ENTERTAINMENT, TÉLÉFILM CANADA.
STARRING VIGGO MORTENSEN (Nikolai), NAOMI WATTS (Anna), VINCENT CASSEL (Kirill), ARMIN MUELLER-STAHL (Semyon), SINÉAD CUSACK (Helen), JERZY SKOLIMOWSKI (Stepan), JOSEF ALTIN (Ekrem), MINA E. MINA (Azim), ALEKSANDAR MIKIC (Soyka).

FROM ACCLAIMED DIRECTOR
LEAVES A MARK.
VIGGO MORTENSEN NAOMI WATTS VINCENT CASSEL
EASTERN PROMISES

"If Papa says okay, I can start telling you about the serious stuff – import, export."

It gets off to a gory start. A man's throat is slashed with a razor in a barber's shop. A pregnant young woman collapses in a store. The child is born: a small body, covered in blood, but alive.

Anna (Naomi Watts), a midwife of Russian origin, looks after the newborn baby in her clinic. She takes home the diary (written in Cyrillic) of the mother, who died during the birth, hoping to find a hint of where she came from. In it, she discovers the business card for a Russian restaurant. She pays the restaurant a visit and meets the owner, Semyon (Armin Mueller-Stahl), his son Kirill (Vincent Cassel) and their driver Nikolai (Viggo Mortensen). Semyon shows an obvious interest in the diary and offers to translate it for Anna; as she can speak Russian, however – although she cannot read it – she has already given it to her uncle Stepan (Jerzy Skolimowski) to translate. And it turns out that Semyon and Kirill are mentioned in it. "In Russian prisons, it is customary to have your story written on your body," we are told in the film. "Without tattoos, you simply don't exist." The markings of the Mafia gang that Semyon, Kirill and Nikolai belong to is a star over the heart and one on the knee, showing that the wearer never kneels for anyone. The movie shows the initiation ritual when Nikolai is admitted to the gang: dressed only in shorts, he stands before the gang bosses. He declares the origin of the tattoos he already has, renounces his biological relatives and pledges himself to his Mafia family. This is the only scene in which a degree of fascination for criminals and their world filters through. Otherwise, thriller and horror movie director David Cronenberg (*Videodrome*, 1983; *A History of Violence*, 2005) portrays them as unpredictable, dangerous guys who deal in very nasty businesses using extremely brutal

1

methods. At the same time, family patriarch Semyon appears like an amiable grandfather – in reality, however, he is completely devoid of scruples. By comparison, his son Kirill comes over as a crazed psychopath, whose character flicks between that of chilling gangster and whining little boy. In the middle is Nikolai, a taciturn stoic who at least manages – occasionally – to restrain the mad Kirill. All three of them are violent. And, like a travesty of the western justice system, one of them is finally revealed to be working undercover for the police.

Cronenberg cast the parts of the Russian mobsters with non-Russians: German actor Armin Mueller-Stahl (*Angels & Demons*, 2009), Frenchman Vincent Cassel (*Black Swan*, 2010) and American-born Viggo Mortensen (Aragorn in *The Lord of the Rings*, 2001/2002/2003). They are perfect in the roles, with

“*Eastern Promises* is fundamentally about the moral scandal of slavery, the traffic in human bodies and human misery that persists, in secret and in the shadows, even in the modern, cosmopolitan West.” *The New York Times*

1 Nikolai (Viggo Mortensen): from henchman, “cleaner” and driver to a big noise in London’s Russian mafia.

2 Hood with a heart? Nikolai repairs Anna’s (Naomi Watts) broken-down vintage scooter.

3 Putting on a friendly face: Semyon (Armin Mueller-Stahl) makes borscht for Anna, calling her by her Russian name - Anna Ivanovna.

4

4 Viggo Mortensen as Nikolai: "With never a hair out of place and the deep dimple in his slightly bent chin, he reminds us of a young Kirk Douglas", according to the New York Times.

5 Weird initiation ritual: Nikolai (l.) explains the origins of his tattoos to Semyon (2nd f. l.) and the other mafia bosses.

6 Semyon threatens midwife Anna, demanding she hands over the diary of the dead young woman.

Mortensen's Nikolai in particular a figure of darkly morbid charm. Here there are no good cops and no chasing after felons. For Eastern Promises is a desperately melancholic elegy rather than a conventional gangster thriller. It is not about crime and its punishment, but about the description of an environment. Canadian director Cronenberg sets his movie in the side streets and back alleys of a dismal part of London, dominated by rain and darkness – though his favorite cinematographer, Peter Suschitzky (*A History of Violence*), still manages to make it visually compelling.

The only character we identify with is Anna (Naomi Watts; *The International*, 2009). She is concerned about the baby, yells at the gangsters and confronts them over the crimes they have committed – although she also briefly succumbs to Nikolai's charms. She has the final scene in the film: the only one that does not occur in the narrative period between Christmas and New Year, and one that is shot quite differently, in bright, warm tones – an ending that offers a glimmer of hope. HJK

5

6

“What the director and writer do here is not unfold a plot, but flay the skin from a hidden world.” *Chicago Sun-Times*

ARMIN MUELLER-STAHL Nazi war criminal in *Music Box* (1989), the relentlessly strict father of the gifted pianist in *Shine* (1996), and now Semyon: in his long career, Armin Mueller-Stahl has tended to play either strict or evil characters, though he always invests them with a little humanity. Mueller-Stahl, who turned 80 on December 17, 2010, managed to make it as an actor under three different political systems with completely different production conditions. In 1956 he had his first film role in the former East Germany.

After moving to West Germany in 1980, he also attracted international attention in films such as *Lola* (1981) by Rainer Werner Fassbinder. He then had his US breakthrough with *Music Box* and *Avalon* (1990): he was 60 years old by then and at first hardly spoke a word of English. One of his most attractive characterizations must be that of East German taxicab driver Helmut in Jim Jarmusch's *Night on Earth* (1991): in this role, he grapples with his car's automatic transmission and the turbulence of New York, while maintaining his dignity throughout. Armin Mueller-Stahl now belongs to the exclusive club of Germans who have made it in Hollywood. He was awarded the Honorary Golden Bear for Lifetime Achievement at the 2011 Berlin International Film Festival.

7 Nerves of steel: Nikolai prepares a body so that it cannot be identified.

8 Kirill (Vincent Cassel, l.) asserts his power, humiliating his driver Nikolai.

9 Kirill is a crazy gangster who can't resist alcohol and prostitutes.

10 "We don't kill babies!" Nikolai appeals to the vestiges of gangster honor in Kirill.

"I'm not interested in the mechanics of the mob, but criminality and people who live in a state of perpetual transgression – that is interesting to me." *David Cronenberg*

THERE WILL BE BLOOD

2007 – USA – 158 MIN. – HISTORY FILM, LITERARY ADAPTATION
DIRECTOR PAUL THOMAS ANDERSON (*1970)
SCREENPLAY PAUL THOMAS ANDERSON from the novel "OIL!" by UPTON SINCLAIR
DIRECTOR OF PHOTOGRAPHY ROBERT ELSWIT EDITING DYLAN TICHENOR MUSIC JONNY GREENWOOD
PRODUCTION JOANNE SELLAR, PAUL THOMAS ANDERSON, DANIEL LUPI for GHOULARDI FILM COMPANY, PARAMOUNT VANTAGE, MIRAMAX FILMS.
STARRING DANIEL DAY-LEWIS (Daniel Plainview), PAUL DANO (Paul Sunday/Eli Sunday), KEVIN J. O'CONNOR (Henry), CIARÁN HINDS (Fletcher), DILLON FREASIER (Young H.W.), RUSSELL HARVARD (Adult H.W.), SYDNEY MCCALLISTER (Young Mary Sunday), COLLEEN FOY (Adult Mary Sunday), DAVID WILLIS (Abel Sunday), CHRISTINE OLEJNICZAK (Mother Sunday).
ACADEMY AWARDS 2008 OSCARS for BEST LEADING ACTOR (Daniel Day-Lewis), BEST CINEMATOGRAPHY (Robert Elswit).
IFF BERLIN 2008 SILVER BEARS for BEST DIRECTOR (Paul Thomas Anderson) and OUTSTANDING ARTISTIC CONTRIBUTION (Jonny Greenwood, Music).

DANIEL DAY LEWIS
There Will Be Blood

"I have a competition in me. I want no one else to succeed."

Right from the very first scenes of *There Will Be Blood*, we see the main character totally at one with himself: the year is 1898 and Daniel Plainview (Daniel Day-Lewis) is prospecting in the darkness of his New Mexico mine. His efforts are met with fortune and misfortune in equal measure: he does find silver, but breaks his leg in an accident. Characteristically, however, he manages to get out of the mine on his own and drag himself to the nearest town, where he eventually sells his silver. Plainview is the quintessential self-made man: he is alone, and will stay that way, no matter how many people surround him over the years. He rises to become a multi-millionaire oil baron, yet the end of the movie shows him sitting forsaken in his huge stately home, an alcoholic touched by insanity.

In *There Will Be Blood* director Paul Thomas Anderson presents the epic study of a sociopath who, as he himself freely admits, hates most people and sees only the worst in them. Plainview has no dealings with others apart from to use and exploit them; his only vice and passion is making money – so much money, in fact, "that I don't have to see anyone any more." Daniel Day-Lewis, in an Oscar-winning performance, merges completely with the character of Plainview, managing to invest this pretty unappealing personality with such an immediacy of power and presence that we are held spellbound.

It is hardly surprising that Anderson shows his antisocial "hero" withou any family ties as well: the "son" H.W. (Dillon Freasier) is in fact just an adoptec orphan who is used as a kind of prop by Plainview in his negotiations for lanc and drilling rights, to build trust with the local communities. On the other hand a putative half-brother called Henry (Kevin J. O'Connor) is basically a harmless petty conman who is only hoping for a job and a little security from the rich Plainview. But Plainview kills him and buries the body in a scene that draws a clear parallel with the start of the film in its representation of a man digging alone in the dark desert, while also delivering for the first time on the "promise" of the movie title.

The religious community is not, of course, to Plainview's taste either: a man who has built his fortune mainly by buying the poor Sunday family's farmin land on the cheap (along with the oil situated under it), he is always at loggerhead with their son Eli (Paul Dano), a fanatical preacher. Yet it is not any moral oppositio that separates them, but sheer competitive spirit: a straight power struggle tha Anderson depicts as a series of humiliations on both sides. Capital and religio are by no means opponents here, but two sides of the same coin called greec Accordingly, cameraman Robert Elswit's images tell the systematic tale of

1

"As for Day-Lewis, he has become justifiably celebrated for disappearing into his characters with a completeness that is both terrifying and an ideal match for Anderson's filmmaking approach." *Los Angeles Times*

1 A film that is also about industrialization's destruction of the landscape: one of the first drilling towers in the American Southwest.

2 Black gold is more profitable than silver: Daniel Plainview (Daniel Day-Lewis) and his assistants discover the oil, a natural resource.

3 Their apparent closeness is deceptive: Daniel Plainview's relationship with his adopted son HW (Dillon Freasier) has its tensions.

4

4 The road to becoming a magnate worth millions: Plainview views his oil well with satisfaction.

5 Greed and wealth don't bring happiness: sociopath Plainview winds up paranoid and insane.

6 There is always more to be had somewhere: Plainview and HW set out on the road once more.

"What Anderson is saying is that we have travestied this nation's incalculable natural wealth, in the process surrendering its potential to finance a paradise on earth in favor of a purely selfish materialism, feebly justified by desperate religious fantasies."

Time Magazine

landscape being conquered and destroyed by the technical progress that capitalism entails. Plainview, originally digging alone at the start of the film, very soon owns a rough little oil well in which the crude oil is siphoned off with buckets. Ten years later, the first drilling tower stands on the desolate Sunday farm, in the middle of the wide, barren landscape; very soon afterward, there are three, followed by a pipeline that seems to divide nature completely in two.

There Will Be Blood is very loosely based on the novel "Oil!" written in 1927 by Upton Sinclair, an avowed socialist writer and denouncer of the capitalist system. Sinclair also tells the story of an oil baron and his relationship with his son, who sympathizes with the exploitation of the workers and the betrayal of the "small" landowners that are almost inevitably associated with the rise of his father's company. There is none of the writer and journalist's social romanticism

7 The most important prop in negotiations to buy land cheaply is adopted son HW, as Plainview can masquerade as a decent family man.

8 Religion and rampant capitalism as two sides of the same coin: both preacher Eli Sunday (Paul Dano) and Plainview are hypocrites and crooks.

in Anderson's film, however; instead, in concentrating on the individual case of the evil (and insane) capitalist, from which no wider inferences can be drawn, it appears at first glance to be relatively conformist and unthreatening. Yet it does provide a clear, if totally non-didactic, analysis of both unbridled capitalism and religious fanaticism. For Plainview and Eli Sunday are both rhetorically gifted and past masters in the lies and false promises that underpin all their apparent achievements. Eli ends up as a successful radio preacher, although he has backed the wrong financial horse. The capitalist Plainview promises schools, roads, water wells and fertile landscapes to the community of naïve individuals now in his thrall; preacher Eli, on the other hand, promises salvation in the hereafter to the people he deceives in wonderfully staged scenes. Furthermore, both men are always prepared to renounce their professed principles if they expect to gain some advantage from it. We can draw our own analogies from all this with ex-US president George W. Bush's term of office and his conservative administration. LP

UPTON SINCLAIR The famous American writer and journalist Upton Sinclair was born in 1878 in Baltimore. At the age of just 14 he was a student at New York's City College, paying his way with the royalties he received for the publication of his short stories in newspapers and magazines. In 1901, Sinclair published his first novel "Springtime and Harvest," at which time his style was mainly influenced by the American naturalist Frank Norris and his group.
Sinclair, who by then had begun to take an interest in social issues and socialist ideas, made a name for himself with his novel "The Jungle" (1906) in which he portrayed the unspeakable living conditions of immigrants working in Chicago's meat-packing industry. The novel was so successful that US President Theodore Roosevelt felt compelled to set up a commission to look into the grievances. Yet critics of Sinclair's literary works were already bemoaning his fairly obvious penchant for didacticism in "The Jungle." During his lifetime the writer, who had published around 90 books by the time he died in 1968, hoped that his oeuvre might contribute to social and political change. He finally won the Pulitzer Prize for his anti-Nazi novel "Dragon's Teeth" (1942). Sinclair joined the Socialist Party of America in 1904 and repeatedly ran as their candidate for political office, but without success.
The writer was also interested in cinema: as early as 1914 he collaborated in an eponymous adaptation of "The Jungle," but his most significant contribution to film history was without doubt the funding for Sergei M. Eisenstein's project *Que Viva Mexico!* (1930–1932/1979) in the early 1930s. But Sinclair eventually ran out of cash during the global economic crisis of 1932, and Eisenstein's film remained unfinished. Eisenstein no longer had the material in his possession by his death in 1948; recent research assumes that Sinclair did in fact try to send it to him in Moscow, but Soviet functionaries refused to accept it as the director had by that time fallen into disfavor. Paul Thomas Anderson's epic drama *There Will Be Blood* (2007) – a very loose reworking of the novel "Oil!" – is the most recent adaptation of Upton Sinclair's work for cinema.

AMERICAN GANGSTER

2007 – USA – 157 MIN. – GANGSTER MOVIE, DRAMA
DIRECTOR RIDLEY SCOTT (*1937)
SCREENPLAY STEVEN ZAILLIAN, from the article "The Return of Superfly" by MARK JACOBSON DIRECTOR OF PHOTOGRAPHY HARRIS SAVIDES EDITING PIETRO SCALIA MUSIC MARK STREITENFELD PRODUCTION BRIAN GRAZER, RIDLEY SCOTT for UNIVERSAL PICTURES, IMAGINE ENTERTAINMENT.
STARRING DENZEL WASHINGTON (Frank Lucas), RUSSELL CROWE (Richie Roberts), JOSH BROLIN (Detective Trupo), LYMARI NADAL (Eva), RUBY DEE (Mama Lucas), CHIWETEL EJIOFOR (Huey Lucas), CUBA GOODING JR. (Nick Barnes),TED LEVINE (Lou Toback), ARMAND ASSANTE (Dominic Cattano), JOHN ORTIZ (Javier J. Rivera), CARLA GUGINO (Laurie Roberts), JOHN HAWKES (Freddi Spearman), RZA (Moses Jones).

"You represent progress. The kind of progress that's going to see them lose a lot of money."

Financial success depends on a lot of factors, one of which is a flair for new ideas. Frank Lucas (Denzel Washington) has this flair. And he knows how to combine his extra-sensitive nose for business with sticking to principles and refusing to compromise. So it comes as no surprise that this man from a poor background moved rapidly through the ranks to become a millionaire. Ridley Scott's film is not set in the money markets of Wall Street, however, but in Harlem. And, as well as being a streetwise businessman, Frank Lucas is also a ruthless criminal. He gets his money from selling heroin – "Magic Blue" is his brand. It is pure, and cheaper than his competitors' merchandise, because Lucas circumvents all middle men and buys the drug direct from Vietnam. Set in the early 1970s, the movie is based on true events. The grainy, bleached-out shots and striking set design give the film a realistic feel, as does the archive TV footage used. News flickers constantly in the background across the screen, and frequently the historical events also impinge on the film's plot.

What is surprising is that we are faced with a black man in Frank Lucas. At the time, African-Americans were regarded as small fry who acted as

1

“If Frank Lucas was the man in the 1970s who dominated the drug market with the uncut heroin he imported himself, thus enabling him to eliminate the middle men, then it seems to be Ridley Scott today who has created similar success for himself, metaphorically speaking, in the *Dream Factory*.” *Schnitt*

4

1 Smart gangster Frank Lucas (Denzel Washington) looks unassuming. But he has built an undercover, multi-million-dollar drugs empire.

2 Frank Lucas is not just a successful drugs baron. He wins the heart of Eva (Lymari Nadal) and gives her an engagement ring.

3 After Richie Roberts (Russell Crowe) catches Frank, they work together to dry up the New York drugs supply.

4 The drug lab is right next door. The women, often prostitutes, work naked to prevent stealing. The personal supply is tested here first.

5 Roberts makes enemies when he confiscates a pile of money from a drugs deal and doesn't keep any for himself or his colleagues.

couriers for the Italian Mafia. Frank Lucas is proof that this image is based on racial prejudice rather than actual fact. His character is unsettling – capable of both forward planning and cold-blooded murder. He deals with important "jobs" himself – even killing – rather than entrusting them to someone else. So we see him coolly executing a competitor in broad daylight after a brief argument, yet soon afterward as a family man surrounded by relatives in his stately home. Church services and big family celebrations set the rhythm in his life. Frank Lucas combines tradition and innovation, realizing the American Dream between these extremes: this is what makes him an "American gangster." Denzel Washington's performance brings impressive complexity to the character, now reserved and watchful, now acting purposefully. Plumbing the darkest depths of this man remains a challenge for the viewer.

But the movie is not just about Frank Lucas; it is also the story of the man who brings him to justice – Richie Roberts. Russell Crowe plays the honest cop who is noticeable for being incorruptible. This makes his character far simpler than Frank's. Yet the screenplay manages to oppose the two protagonists in an interesting way: on the one hand Lucas' traditional family life and, on the other, Roberts' chaotic private life; the drug baron's modest

DENZEL WASHINGTON Denzel Washington has been a major-league Hollywood star for over 30 years. Born in 1954, the actor's career began in the late 1970s with several stage parts. He became widely known for his role as Dr. Philip Chandler in the hospital series *St. Elsewhere* (1982–1988), combining such TV appearances with film work. In 1990 he won his first Oscar, for Best Supporting Actor, as Private Trip in the Civil War drama *Glory* (1989); he had previously been nominated for an Oscar for his role as Steve Biko in *Cry Freedom* (1987). In the years that followed, he attained the rank of superstar. He played civil rights activist Malcolm X in the eponymous film (1992); reporter Gray Grantham in Grisham adaptation *The Pelican Brief* (1993); and lawyer Joe Miller in AIDS drama *Philadelphia* (1993). His performance as boxer Rubin Carter in *The Hurricane* (1999) stands out among the films that followed. He was awarded his second Oscar, for Best Leading Actor, for his role as the corrupt Detective Alonzo Harris in *Training Day* (2001). In recent years Washington has tried his hand at directing, with *Antwone Fisher* (2002) and *The Great Debaters* (2007). Most recently, he has starred in apocalyptic film *The Book of Eli* (2010) as well as two action movies: *The Taking of Pelham 1 2 3* (2009) and *Unstoppable* (2010).

6 They look happy, yet a serious battle is going on. Roberts argues with his ex-wife Laurie (Carla Gugino) over custody of his son.

7 Frank Lucas' empire has collapsed. Roberts waits for him after a church service. It will be the first meeting of these adversaries.

8 Eye to eye: Lucas and Roberts realize they have the same enemies, and decide to cooperate. Together, they set out to expose the corrupt police officers.

9 Eva, the beautiful wife of a drugs baron: Frank's present to her of an eye-catching fur coat inadvertently reveals his secret to the police.

"Call it the black *Scarface* or the *Harlem Godfather* or just one hell of an exciting movie." *Rolling Stone*

9

style, versus the policeman's scruffy appearance. In an intriguing directorial device, the two opponents only meet at the very end of the film. For a long time the plot develops, not just in two separate strands, but also in the two adversaries' mutual failure to "recognize" each other. Richie Roberts remains invisible to Lucas because he isn't on the take, unlike sleazy Detective Trupo (Josh Brolin). Lucas remains invisible to Roberts because he doesn't behave like other criminals. While the latter flaunt themselves as rich men-about-town, Lucas relies on being inconspicuous. His pursuer only notices him at a boxing match, where Lucas is wearing an expensive fur coat to please his wife. In this sense, the film is also a comment on prejudices about "blindness."

In the end the viewer realizes that, in spite of the differences between the two protagonists, they share some basic features. They stick rigidly to their principles, trusting only themselves and carefully chosen colleagues; and they are both creative, as well as relentlessly ambitious. This is precisely what makes them so successful, and also serves as the precondition for the lengthy closing dialogue in which they find common ground. Each can appreciate the other, recognizing himself in his opponent. Both are outsiders because of their principles, hated by the police and criminals in equal measure. In the end, they fight together – not against drugs or corruption, but against their phony environments, for terms on which they can see eye to eye. JDM

WELCOME TO THE STICKS
BIENVENUE CHEZ LES CH'TIS

2007 – FRANCE – 106 MIN. – COMEDY
DIRECTOR DANY BOON (*1966)
SCREENPLAY DANY BOON, ALEXANDRE CHARLOT, FRANCK MAGNIER
DIRECTOR OF PHOTOGRAPHY PIERRE AÏM EDITING LUC BARNIER, JULIE DELORD MUSIC PHILIPPE ROMBI
PRODUCTION CLAUDE BERRI, JÉRÔME SEYDOUX for PATHÉ RENN PRODUCTIONS, HIRSCH, LES PRODUCTIONS DU CHICON, TF1 FILMS PRODUCTION.
STARRING KAD MERAD (Philippe Abrams), DANY BOON (Antoine Bailleul), ZOÉ FÉLIX (Julie Abrams), LORENZO AUSILIA-FORET (Raphaël Abrams), ANNE MARIVIN (Annabelle Deconninck), PHILIPPE DUQUESNE (Fabrice Canoli), GUY LECLUYSE (Yann Vandernoout), PATRICK BOSSO (Gendarme), LINE RENAUD (Antoine's Mother).

"So, y'all from the south too, heeeh?"

A small family, a house, and a secure income to boot: but Philippe Abrams (Kad Merad), who works for the postal service in the south of France, wants more. Encouraged by his wife, Julie (Zoé Félix), he keeps applying for a job as branch manager on the Mediterranean coast. Without success. When he tries again, pretending to be a wheelchair user to increase his chances, it all ends in disaster: the scam is busted and Philippe's punishment is a transfer to the very north of the country – to Bergues in Nord-Pas-de-Calais, of all places! Philippe is pretty sure what to expect there: Siberian climate, dreary, gray houses and, worst of all, coarse hillbillies – nicknamed "Ch'tis" they are notorious throughout France for their unusual dialect, which is almost impossible for anyone outside the region to understand.

No surprise, then, that the husband is forced to make the trip minus wife and child. And, sure enough, Philippe's worst fears are confirmed when he arrives in Bergues on a rainy night and someone with apparently suicidal tendencies runs out in front of his car. Helping him up, Philippe has his first experience of the Ch'ti dialect, and thinks the guy is speaking with a broken jaw. He is Philippe's new colleague Antoine (Dany Boon) and, as becomes evident the next day, is not averse to a drop of alcohol, even at work. After getting over the initial shock, however, Philippe begins to realize that it's actually quite bearable in the supposedly harsh north.

For it turns out that the Ch'tis are extremely kind-hearted and that even their lingo can be quickly picked up. Furthermore, as Julie has started to make big efforts to spoil her poor, punished husband on his weekends in the south, to Philippe it suddenly begins to feel like heaven on earth. Naturally, however, there is a catch: for, in an attempt to gain her sympathy, Philippe has told his wife several horror stories about the Ch'tis. And now Julie wants to go up north, too, to stand by him in this alien territory. *Welcome to the Sticks* is a phenomenon. A gentle comedy about ordinary folk, it went on to become the

1

1 As Philippe Abrams, Kad Merad represents the typically average Frenchman with all his foibles and idiosyncrasies, including a phobia about the allegedly inhospitable North of France and its inhabitants.

2 Despite their good intentions, Philippe and Antoine (Dany Boon) cannot manage their postal deliveries without getting drunk: the invitations to partake of a fine drop are too friendly to resist.

3 Director and actor Dany Boon is a "ch'ti" himself: born and raised in the Nord-Pas-de-Calais region, he made *Welcome to the Sticks* as a declaration of love for his oft-derided homeland.

biggest home-grown feature film of all time in France – a film without big names, spectacular locations, or even a particularly crazy storyline, yet which sold over twenty million tickets, attracting one in three of the population into the cinema, statistically speaking. Only James Cameron's *Titanic* (1997) was more successful in the land of Amélie, Astérix and Jacques Tati. A key to the hype surrounding this film is probably its considerable scope for identification. As Philippe, Kad Merad portrays the almost perfectly average citizen, with professional and family troubles that must have seemed all too familiar to many people in France. The same applies to his resentment about the north, which is sketched by director Dany Boon (a born stand-up comedian) with the same affectionate eye he casts on the endearingly eccentric ways of the Ch'tis. Notwithstanding the genre-related exaggerations, there is a simple explanation

“A delightful story, full of well-worn clichés, and the not particularly attractive protagonists (apart, that is, from the village beauty, Anne Marivin) win over the audience’s hearts in the process.” *Frankfurter Rundschau*

4 At his mother’s side: the secret of the film’s success is in the tongue-in-cheek humor used by Dany Boon (seen here alongside his screen mother, Line Renaud) to portray his lovably quirky French compatriots, from both North and South.

5 Feel-good movie: the two leading actors have good reason to be cheerful, and not just in the film. *Welcome to the Sticks* went on to become a huge box-office hit in France, ranking among the highest grossing films ever, just behind *Titanic* (1997).

for Boon's obvious familiarity in portraying this world and for his totally credible performance as Antoine the quirky postal worker: he is Ch'ti by birth himself. This does not, however, make him the first regional director to find fame with a film about his homeland; furthermore, while Bruno Dumont painted a picture of provincial misery in his award-winning *The Life of Jesus* (*La vie de Jésus*, 1997) and *Humanity* (*L'humanité*, 1999), *Welcome to the Sticks* can be seen as a real declaration of love for the land and its people.

Above all, however, Dany Boon has made a feel-good movie that celebrates values such as friendship, solidarity and tolerance and the happiness that lies in the more mundane things of life such as a sociable lunch break with fries and beer at a mobile snack bar. Given the increasing fragmentation of society and progressive leveling of regional differences in the globalized world, this

"... filmed like a song with verses that occasionally gain tempo. And because the outstanding cast of actors' delivery of the punchlines is so spot-on, we hardly notice just how much we are taking the quirky characters from the North to our hearts – complete with their unique customs and habits." *kino-zeit.de*

7

6 Putting on a show for his other half: when Philippe's wife (Zoé Félix) pays a visit, his new friends pull out all the stops to confirm her preconceptions of the reputedly knuckle-dragging Ch'tis.

7 Life can be this beautiful: a sociable get-together over beer and fries is just to Philippe's liking. Having said which …

8 … to begin with, he was anything but sold on the idea of having to spend his lunch breaks with colleagues at the hot-dog stand. *Welcome to the Sticks* is an affectionate cinematic plea for mutual cooperation, free of prejudice.

film clearly taps into nostalgia for the good old days as well. More importantly, however, *Welcome to the Sticks* is a call for people to look beyond clichés and see for themselves, and with visible success: since the film's release, tourism in the Nord-Pas-de-Calais region has experienced a noticeable upturn.

On a final note, and in spite of its virtually untranslatable humor, *Welcome to the Sticks* was far from being a phenomenon only in French cinemas. In Germany, for instance, the dubbed version with a specially created, imaginary dialect was incredibly successful. In Italy, on the other hand, they produced a remake called *Welcome to the South* (*Benvenuti al sud*, 2010), transposing the storyline to the Campania region of the country. A remake is also planned for the USA – Ch'tis, it would appear, are ubiquitous. JH

CLAUDE BERRI In the French film sector he was known as "the boss:" indeed, Claude Berri (1934–2009) was universally acknowledged as one of the outstanding producers and directors of the last five decades in French cinema. Yet this son of eastern European Jewish immigrants was certainly not without controversy. In the course of his long career, he may have produced films for such legendary auteurs as Maurice Pialat, Philippe Garrel, Jacques Rivette and even Roman Polanski to name but a few, but critics of the film journal "Cahiers du Cinéma" constantly reproached him for making too many concessions to the kind of mass taste found in what they called "grandpa's cinema." Berri, in fact, had a sure feel for the wider public's taste, especially in France, as the box-office hits he produced demonstrate: *Asterix & Obelix: Mission Cleopatra* (2002) and various Claude Zidi comedies, but also successful films he directed himself, such as the two Pagnol adaptations *Jean de Florette* (1986) and *Manon of the Spring* (*Manon des sources*, 1986) and the film version of Zola's *Germinal* (1993).
Some of the criticism may be justified but Berri was certainly always prepared to back unusual film projects, for example Jean-Jacques Annaud's *The Bear* (*L'ours*, 1988). A passionate mover and shaker, he was also well known for his social conscience, which found expression in the first-rate gangster movie *Tchao pantin* (1983).
He also made a very personal film in *The Two of Us* (*Le vieil homme et l'enfant*, 1967), based on his childhood experiences during the war. This was, according to François Truffaut, the first French feature film to deal honestly with the German Occupation. Meanwhile, Berri – who also made frequent appearances as an actor – realized his biggest commercial success as a producer in the year before his death, with Dany Boon's comedy about cultural preconceptions *Welcome to the Sticks* (2007).

IN BRUGES

2007 / 2008 – UK / USA – 107 MIN. – COMEDY THRILLER
DIRECTOR MARTIN MCDONAGH (*1970)
SCREENPLAY MARTIN MCDONAGH DIRECTOR OF PHOTOGRAPHY EIGIL BRYLD EDITING JON GREGORY
MUSIC CARTER BURWELL PRODUCTION GRAHAM BROADBENT, PETER CZERNIN for BLUEPRINT PICTURES, FILM4, FOCUS FEATURES, SCION FILMS.
STARRING COLIN FARRELL (Ray Cranham), BRENDAN GLEESON (Ken Blakely), RALPH FIENNES (Harry Waters), CLÉMENCE POÉSY (Chloë Villette), JÉRÉMIE RENIER (Eirik), THEKLA REUTEN (Marie), JORDAN PRENTICE (Jimmy), ELIZABETH BERRINGTON (Natalie), ERIC GODON (Yuri), SACHI KIMURA (Imamoto).

"How's the movie going?"
– "It's a jumped-up Eurotrash piece of rip-off fucking bullshit."
– "Like, in a bad way?"

When irascible contract killer Colin Farrell asks the woman of his dreams how the filming of a "movie about midgets" set in Bruges, Belgium is going, we get yet another flash of the self-mocking tone of *In Bruges*. In his first feature film, British playwright Martin McDonagh parodies three clichés simultaneously: the Irish as hard drinkers, always up for a fight; the art movie sector as an arrogant, narcissistic microcosm; and Bruges as a pretty, but deathly boring, little town. The very fact that this extremely dry, brash comedy about two contract killers – sent on an enforced holiday as a punishment for their misdemeanors – is set in pictorial Bruges ensures one of the best "running gags" of recent years. Gangster Harry Waters (Ralph Fiennes) is treating his paid assassins Ray (Colin Farrell) and Ken (Brendan Gleeson) to a few nice days before one has to kill the other, in this idyllic little town of all places

1

COLIN FARRELL He has enjoyed the dubious reputation of a womanizer and heartbreaker, and for a long time was regarded as something of a hell raiser among international movie celebrities. Colin Farrell has done much to divest himself of this image, however, with films like Woody Allen's *Cassandra's Dream* (2007) and In Bruges, for which he won a Golden Globe in 2009, proving his talent as an actor. This followed a long period of being treated as just another pretty face, reinforced when he was named one of the "50 Most Beautiful People" and rated as the sixth "sexiest man" in various magazines.

Colin James Farrell was born in Ireland on May 31, 1976 in the Dublin suburb of Castleknock. His father Eamon and Uncle Tommy were professional footballers who played for Shamrock Rovers F.C., and Colin himself aspired to a sporting career up until the early 1990s, standing in goal for the Dublin team Castleknock Celtics. He auditioned for the Irish pop group "Boyzone" but was turned down; shortly afterward, he won a role in the British TV series "Ballykissangel" (1996–2001). After his movie breakthrough in Joel Schumacher's war drama *Tigerland* (2000) he successfully played the hero in action films and thrillers like *Phone Booth* (2002) and *S.W.A.T.* (2003) as well as the sinister adversary in *Minority Report* (2002) and *Daredevil* (2003). His most memorable roles to date include Alexander the Great in Oliver Stone's *Alexander* (2004), Sonny Crockett in Michael Mann's film version of *Miami Vice* (2006), and his critically acclaimed performance as Syracuse in *Ondine* (2009).

Colin Farrell's son James was born on September 12, 2003 from his relationship with model Kim Bordenave, from whom he has now separated. He was previously married to English actress Amelia Warner. His private life made the headlines once again in 2006 when a sex video of Farrell and his ex-girlfriend Nicole Narain was released on the internet without his consent.

3

1 Bejesus! Philistine and contract killer Ray (Colin Farrell) is forced to stick it out in the sleepy little Belgian town of Bruges.

2 Cursing, brawling and going to wild parties: Ray's way of killing time in Bruges.

3 By contrast Ken (Brendan Gleeson) – a gangster and a gentleman – positively flourishes in the capital of Flanders.

4 Ray flirts with the lovely Chloë (Clémence Poésy), not exactly endearing him to her ex boyfriend.

"... an endlessly surprising, very dark, human comedy, with a plot that cannot be foreseen but only relished."

Chicago Sun-Times

Blustering Irishman Ray, however, does not really appreciate the beauty of Bruges, which he repeatedly describes (at the top of his voice) as "a boring shit-hole."

With its hard-edged yet affectionate tone and quirky humor, McDonagh's comedy follows in the tradition of Tarantino's *Pulp Fiction* (1994) and makes open and quite explicit reference to Nicolas Roeg's *Don't Look Now* (1973) through the motif of the film-within-the-film and its protagonists (especially the presence of the vertically challenged leading actor). The long, brilliantly written passages of dialogue are indicative of McDonagh's stage background – as are the eruptions of violence that are also to be found in his plays *Beauty Queen of Leenane* and *The Pillowman*. Moreover, in *The Pillowman* one of the characters struggles with the fact that he has an innocent person's death on

4

5

6

"Ralph Fiennes is no *Sexy Beast* and writer/director Martin McDonagh is stronger on dialogue than story, but this is still a laugh-out-loud dark comedy, giving Colin Farrell his finest role in ages." *Total Film*

7

8

5 Medieval alleyways and picturesque squares: Bruges' beauty affects Ken and Ray quite differently.

6 Harry (Ralph Fiennes, l.) the gangster boss orders Ken to get rid of hothead Ray.

7 Dammit, nothing's going right! So Harry is forced to check everything's okay in the Flemish capital.

8 Not exactly keeping his head down: hard-drinking, and increasingly suicidal, Ray's behavior is far from discreet.

9 Can Ken and Harry finally restore calm in Bruges?

"*In Bruges* is a haunting and hypnotic movie, just the thing to get lost in." *Rolling Stone*

his conscience, another parallel with *In Bruges*. The debate about guilt and atonement between odd couple Ray and Ken takes up nearly as much space as the exaggerated argument about the beauty and dreariness of Bruges. In all other respects, the stage director and playwright adapts his "fish out of water" story in an eminently cinematic way: Eigil Bryld's camerawork is nothing less than sumptuous in celebrating the morbid beauty of this unusual location.

Before he began filming, McDonagh followed the pattern of his plays by rehearsing on location for three days in Bruges with his entire cast. This technique is one of the main ways in which he ensures that the tragic moments of his dark comedy thriller remain free of pathos, while the one-liners appear as casual asides. Moreover, he neither glorifies his main characters' lethal "business" as cool and glamorous, nor portrays them as cold-blooded monsters. Instead, Brendan Gleeson and Colin Farrell play complex individuals whose bottled up emotions are finally released, against the most scenic of backdrops as it happens. Even Bruges-hater Ray ends up falling in love with the town – a tiny bit, at least. ES

HAPPY-GO-LUCKY

2007 – UK – 118 MIN. – TRAGICOMEDY
DIRECTOR MIKE LEIGH (*1943)
SCREENPLAY MIKE LEIGH DIRECTOR OF PHOTOGRAPHY DICK POPE EDITING JIM CLARK MUSIC GARY YERSHON
PRODUCTION SIMON CHANNING WILLIAMS for FILM4, INGENIOUS FILM PARTNERS, SUMMIT ENTERTAINMENT, THIN MAN FILMS, UK FILM COUNCIL.
STARRING SALLY HAWKINS (Poppy), ALEXIS ZEGERMAN (Zoe), EDDIE MARSAN (Scott), JACK MACGEACHIN (Nick), KATE O'FLYNN (Suzy), ANDREA RISEBOROUGH (Dawn), SINEAD MATTHEWS (Alice), CAROLINE MARTIN (Helen), KARINA FERNANDEZ (Flamenco Teacher).
IFF BERLIN 2008 SILVER BEAR for BEST ACTRESS (Sally Hawkins).

"Oh! What-chu-ma-call-it ding dang dilly dilly da da hoo hoo!"

Like a cross between Mary Poppins and Pippi Longstocking, elementary school teacher Pauline, a.k.a. Poppy (Sally Hawkins), trips merrily through life – in the dreary world of north London, home to the poorer members of society.

Mike Leigh, the great improviser of British cinema, has repeatedly portrayed the English lower and middle classes in acute studies such as *Naked* (1993), *Secrets & Lies* (1996) and *All or Nothing* (2002). His characters experience problems in their relationships, but they try to cope with dignity. This Poppins/Pippi/Poppy is different, however: happy and carefree, she could quite easily be prescribed as an antidepressant by healthcare professionals – if she didn't somehow get on everyone's nerves, including the audience's, with her naïve cheerfulness, strange way of talking and gaudy clothes that look as if Jackson Pollock has splashed his paint pots over her.

She's a bird of paradise that wants to fly, like the boy from Paul Auster's "Mr. Vertigo," and yet can only make bird costumes with her pupils. Yet the surprising thing is that Poppy does not suffer in any way from the disparity between dreams and reality: she is content with her lifestyle, and at age 30 still hasn't quite grown up. She shares an apartment with her best friend, Zoe (Alexis Zegerman), doesn't have a boyfriend, goes dancing with friends at the weekend, and initially rides a bike instead of driving a car. Yet for all her silliness Poppy is a good, responsible teacher, who fascinates her pupils with her childlike charm, but also takes problems seriously and tries to help. We might well wonder why on earth Mike Leigh makes this ray of sunshine the central focus of his film: a character seemingly unaffected by depressing relationships, or one who at least faces them with a disarming sense of humor.

We are soon struck, though, by the contrast between her and her environment; one that gives a fresh edge to the social critique that defines Mike Leigh's movies. For, the happier Poppy is, the more disturbed seem the people around her. Her sister, Helen (Caroline Martin), for instance, appears to have the perfect middle-class life: she is pregnant, yet is always in a bad mood and worried about everything; or the aggressive boy in Poppy's class who hits other children because he is being beaten by his mother's new boyfriend.

The strangest character in this assortment is Poppy's driving instructor Scott (Eddie Marsan): short-tempered and grumpy, he directs his giggly pupil whose boots are ridiculously high-heeled, around London's suburbs while

1

SALLY HAWKINS Sally Hawkins is a cheerful person, which may be why Mike Leigh cast her in the role of Poppy in his movie *Happy-Go-Lucky* (2007). A stroke of luck, for the actress from London plays the eccentric elementary school teacher who is always upbeat with a degree of credibility that captivated the 2008 Berlin Film Festival jury and won her the Silver Bear. *Happy-Go-Lucky* is her third collaboration to date with the British director. He directed Sally Hawkins in her first major appearance in 2002 in *All or Nothing*, playing the difficult, lonely teenager, Samantha. In 2004 we saw her in Mike Leigh's drama *Vera Drake*, which looked back at social conditions in London in the 1950s. Born in 1976, the daughter of children's books' authors and illustrators, Sally Hawkins studied at the prestigious Royal Academy of Dramatic Arts. Before appearing in front of the camera, she gained stage experience in plays by Shakespeare and Chekhov. In 1999 she was cast in her first television role, in the BBC series "Casualty," and more TV work followed, including BBC productions "Tipping the Velvet" (2002) and "H.G. Wells: War with the World" (2006). In the ITV adaptation of Jane Austen's "Persuasion" (2007), her portrayal of Anne Elliot won her the Golden Nymph award at the Monte Carlo TV Festival.

In the cinema, she had parts in Matthew Vaughn's gangster thriller *Layer Cake* (2004) and the film version of W. Somerset Maugham's *The Painted Veil* (2006), and was Colin Farrell's fiancée in Woody Allen's *Cassandra's Dream* (2008). She appeared alongside Emma Thompson in Lone Scherfig's film *An Education* (2009), a drama for which Nick Hornby ("Fever Pitch") wrote the screenplay. In the film adaptation of Waris Dirie's bestseller, "Desert Flower," she took on the role of Marylin. One of her most recent projects is Nigel Cole's movie *Made in Dagenham*, which tells the story of women involved in the 1968 strike at the Ford Dagenham automobile plant.

1 Like a scene from a French film: Poppy (Sally Hawkins) is shown breezing through a deprived area of London, with a lightness of touch that is rare in British cinema.

2 Elementary schoolteacher Poppy gives "happy" lessons, reminiscent of Mary Poppins crossed with Pippi Longstocking.

3 Poppy's driving instructor, Scott (Eddie Marsan), lives in a dark world of his own making: one that is filled with prejudice, fear and paranoia.

4 Sour-faced Scott directs his pupil, who keeps giggling and telling corny jokes, around the outskirts of London.

"Movies sometimes seem made for misery, for rivers of tears, stormy skies and third-act woe. Happiness is for suckers and Disney Inc. But happiness is a complicated, difficult matter, and in *Happy-Go-Lucky* it's also a question of faith." *The New York Times*

insulting her with a theatrical "enraha," an expression that simply means the rearview mirror, but in Scott's world is also one of three elements in a comical yet alarming incantation. He has built a gloomy edifice around himself, filled with prejudices and paranoia. Poppy realizes that he is, deep down, a lonely little boy who is acting out his painful relationships through these negatively forceful methods in his job. Despite all their differences, Scott falls in love with Poppy. Incapable of expressing his feelings, he turns into a stalker, loitering in front of her house. She has to acknowledge, with some irritation, that she really cannot help in this case.

Poppy is a great teacher. Like her predecessor Mary Poppins she takes on the grown-up world, not with magic, but a spellbinding aura of happiness instead. She is in a transitional world, reluctant to cross the threshold into

"*Happy-Go-Lucky* is as funny, serious, life-affirming and beautifully performed as anything Leigh has done, but with a lightness of touch only previously found in his Gilbert and Sullivan movie, Topsy-Turvy." *The Guardian*

5 Poppy is a bird of paradise who wants to fly. Yet her permanent cheeriness can really get on your nerves sometimes.

6 Poppy finds love: In Nick (Jack MacGeachin) she has found a man she can laugh with.

7 Will Poppy make it in the grown-up world? We wouldn't wish that on her.

8 Poppy is like a fish out of water in the flamenco lesson. The discipline of dance is completely alien to her.

adulthood; a utopian character who does not embody an abstract idea, but is fresh and true-to-life – an unprecedented creation in movies of recent years.

Mike Leigh manages to achieve this impression of spontaneity through a particular working method: as in all of his films, he improvises for months with his cast before the film is given any structure. There hasn't been a script for a long time. So it is interesting to note that Happy-Go-Lucky was nominated in the 2008 Oscars for "Best Original Screenplay." Lead actor Sally Hawkins, who has now appeared in three of Mike Leigh's films, loves this method: in an interview with the German magazine, "KinoKino," she says: "Working with Mike Leigh is not a job, it's an intense togetherness, sharing visions and pushing creativity to the limits. An experiment that involves using your brain and mentally reaching places that you would never have imagined. After this filming I was a different person." KK

IRON MAN

2008 – USA – 121 MIN. – ACTION MOVIE, COMIC ADAPTATION
DIRECTOR JON FAVREAU (*1966)
SCREENPLAY MARK FERGUS, HAWK OSTBY, ART MARCUM, MAT HOLLOWAY from the "IRON MAN" comic by STAN LEE, DON HECK, LARRY LIEBER, JACK KIRBY
DIRECTOR OF PHOTOGRAPHY MATTHEW LIBATIQUE **EDITING** DAN LEBENTAL **MUSIC** RAMIN DJAWADI
PRODUCTION AVI ARAD, KEVIN FEIGE for MARVEL STUDIOS, FAIRVIEW ENTERTAINMENT.
STARRING ROBERT DOWNEY JR. (Tony Stark), GWYNETH PALTROW (Pepper Potts), JEFF BRIDGES (Obadiah Stane), TERRENCE HOWARD (Colonel James "Rhodey" Rhodes), SHAUN TOUB (Yinsen), LESLIE BIBB (Christine Everheart), FARAN TAHIR (Raza), SAYED BADREYA (Abu Bakaar), CLARK GREGG (Agent Coulson).

"Let's face it, this is not the worst thing you've caught me doing."

Good technology is invented by individuals. Whether in the caves of Afghanistan or the hi-tech computer lab of a luxury garage, the creative genius of a mastermind is always a step ahead of all other engineering innovations combined. Like Iron Man, alias Tony Stark (Robert Downey Jr.): child prodigy, M.I.T. graduate, arms dealer and cynical man-about-town with a super-brain, who gives his restricted body superhero powers using a metal suit with built-in flying and weapons technology. Of the comic heroes that have populated cinema screens post-2000, such as Spider-Man or X-Men, Iron Man is by far the most ironic, not least because of the superb performance of Robert Downey Jr., who is back to his brilliant screen form. This is the first time the media empire of Marvel Comics has made a film adaptation without a Hollywood studio.

Director Jon Favreau moves the story from 1963 to the present day; from Vietnam to Afghanistan, where Tony Stark sits in a sand-colored Humvee convoy, drinking whiskey as he rumbles across the desert. He has just finished presenting his latest rocket to the US army – or, rather, conducting its explosion like an orchestra. But then his vehicle is attacked. The last thing he sees is a grenade with the logo "Stark Industries." Lacerated by his own weapons, he wakes up in a Taliban cave. There is an electro-magnet in his chest that is designed to keep the grenade splinters from his heart, while at the same time act as an artificial heart. The arms manufacturer who is happy to be called the "dealer in death" discovers his feelings in these Afghan caves. Firstly for his fellow prisoner, engineer Yinsen (Shaun Toub) who built the life-saving device for him, and then for humanity itself, as befitting a future superhero.

Instead of building the rocket for the Taliban as he is supposed to, he uses ancient technology to forge a suit of armor in iron, the prototype of his later, sassy, gold-titanium outfit. In this way he escapes from the cave Rambos who are brutal and ridiculous in equal measure, and after a desperate flight crashes down in the desert sand. Back in America, he announces to stunned journalists at a press conference that he intends to give up arms manufacture. The stock value of his business takes a dive and his right-hand men – Obadiah Stane (Jeff Bridges), who co-manages the company, and Air Marshal James Rhodes (Terrence Howard) – turn their backs on him. The only one to stay loyal is his flame-haired assistant, Pepper Potts (Gwyneth Paltrow), who puts on a cool and super-sexy act: she watches with amusement – and irritation – as the techno-playboy occupies himself with strange gadgets instead of women.

"The gadgetry is absolutely dazzling, the action is mostly exhilarating, the comedy is scintillating and the whole enormous enterprise, spawned by Marvel comics, throbs with dramatic energy because the man inside the shiny red robotic rig is a daring choice for an action hero, and an inspired one." *Wall Street Journal*

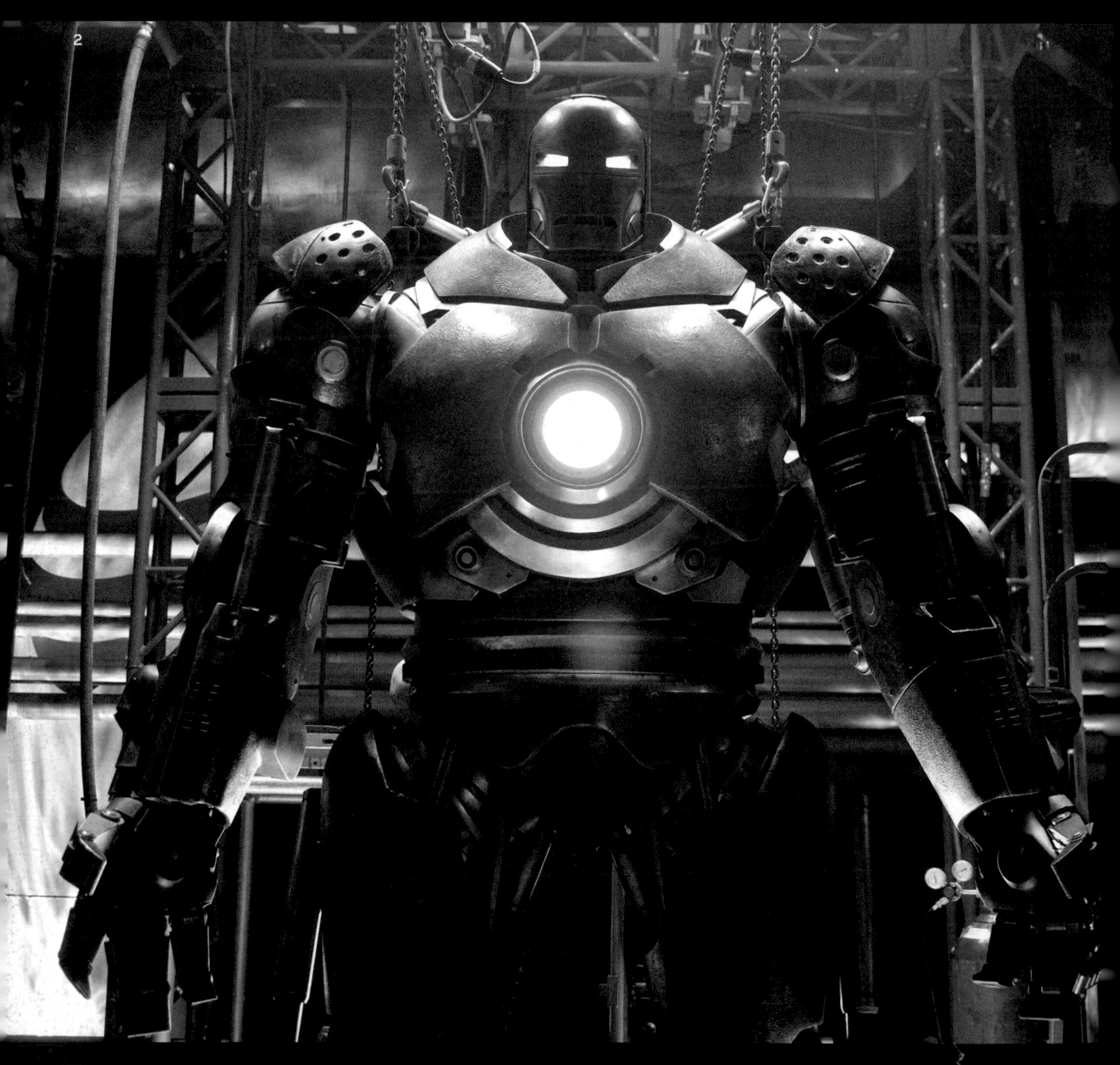

3

1 Hi-tech meets design: Tony Stark (Robert Downey Jr.) alias Iron Man has come to save the world – as stylishly as possible.

2 Stark's rival (Jeff Bridges as Obadiah Stane) has also built himself a suit of armor. They will face each other in the battle of the Titans.

3 Stark tinkers in his garage with a hi-tech suit that will give him superhuman powers.

4 When imprisoned in Afghanistan, Stark meets engineer Yinsen (Shaun Toub), who inserts an electromagnetic reactor in his chest.

5 Primitive images: Stark forges his first armored suit in an Afghan cave.

In the garage (where else?) that houses his vintage car collection, Tony Stark fiddles with the design of a superhero suit so that he can deal with the baddies and save the world from his own weapons. He builds a new electromagnet for his chest, which acts as both a mini power plant and the centerpiece of his exoskeleton. His first attempts at flying are turns of slapstick humor, but finally the red-gold, hi-tech armor is fully operational. Without further ado he flies off to Afghanistan, frees the prisoners of the Taliban, and narrowly avoids a fight with the US air force. The film hovers between visual appeal and a critique of militarism, though the current political implications of the Afghan war in the film remain hazy, acting merely as a foil for a story about the battle between two heavily armed individuals, following action comic-book rules. For his real opponent is also his closest friend: Obadiah Stane, who supplies weapons to the Taliban and is intent on destroying the now enlightened Tony Stark. He constructs his own battle suit from the remains of the first iron armor

7

6 Ethereal beauty Pepper Potts (Gwyneth Paltrow) is Stark's faithful assistant. She watches his flying skills in astonishment.

7 Adversary Obadiah Stane seeks to destroy Tony Stark by copying the brilliant inventor's technology.

8 Stark shows Stane the reactor in his chest. He is still unaware that Stane is planning to steal it.

MATTHEW LIBATIQUE Matthew Libatique once said that camerawork is like learning to play a musical instrument – and he is a virtuoso. He won many prizes and an Oscar nomination for his camerawork on Darren Aronofsky's *Black Swan* (2010). The images of ballet dancer Natalie Portman, shot on-stage using a lightweight, handheld camera, are some of the most impressive in recent years.

Born in New York in 1968 to immigrant parents from the Philippines, Libatique has forged a lifelong friendship and close working relationship with Darren Aronofsky. Back in the 1990s they made films together as students of the American Film Institute (AFI), continuing their collaboration with Aronofsky's first feature film, *Pi* (1998). For *Requiem for a Dream* (2000) they developed a quite unique, almost surrealist, film language characterized by extreme close-ups, color changes and rapid cuts. Libatique was also responsible for the cinematography in Aronofsky's spiritual film *The Fountain* (2006).

Matthew Libatique also works for other directors as a cameraman: for example, Joel Schumacher on *Tigerland* (2000); and Spike Lee, with whom he made *She Hate Me* (2004) and *Inside Man* (2006). The camerawork on *Iron Man* (2008) and *Iron Man 2* (2010) enables the viewer further to appreciate the highly rhythmic, musical quality of Libatique's visual language. Lately, he has perfected his skills by shooting music videos, for Tracy Chapman and rapper Jay-Z among others.

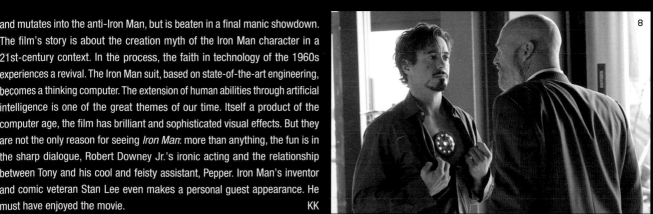

and mutates into the anti-Iron Man, but is beaten in a final manic showdown. The film's story is about the creation myth of the Iron Man character in a 21st-century context. In the process, the faith in technology of the 1960s experiences a revival. The Iron Man suit, based on state-of-the-art engineering, becomes a thinking computer. The extension of human abilities through artificial intelligence is one of the great themes of our time. Itself a product of the computer age, the film has brilliant and sophisticated visual effects. But they are not the only reason for seeing *Iron Man*: more than anything, the fun is in the sharp dialogue, Robert Downey Jr.'s ironic acting and the relationship between Tony and his cool and feisty assistant, Pepper. Iron Man's inventor and comic veteran Stan Lee even makes a personal guest appearance. He must have enjoyed the movie. KK

WALTZ WITH BASHIR
VALS IM BASHIR

2008 – ISRAEL / GERMANY / FRANCE – 90 MIN. – ANIMATION, WAR FILM
DIRECTOR ARI FOLMAN (*1963)
SCREENPLAY ARI FOLMAN ANIMATION DAVID POLONSKY, YONI GOODMAN EDITING NILI FELLER
MUSIC MAX RICHTER PRODUCTION ARI FOLMAN, SERGE LALOU, GERHARD MEIXNER, YAEL NAHLIELI, ROMAN PAUL for BRIDGIT FOLMAN FILM GANG, LES FILMS D'ICI, RAZOR FILM PRODUKTION GMBH.
CAST ARI FOLMAN, RON BEN-YISHAI, RONNY DAYAG, DROR HARAZI, ORI SIVAN, ZAHAVAN SOLOMON (as themselves), YEHEZKEL LAZAROV (Carmi Cna'an), MICKEY LEON (Boaz Rein-Buskila).

"This is not a love song!"

Images of war are illusions, fed by false perceptions and deceptive recollections. No film in the world is capable of showing what war is really like. In *Waltz with Bashir*, however, Israeli director Ari Folman stands the genre on its head: how would it be if a soldier on the battlefield experienced the madness around him no differently from a cinemagoer watching a war movie? What happens to those mental images afterward, when the film is over? Folman takes this direct cinematographic approach in dealing with his repressed memories of military service and its associated horrors. But because a radically new perspective requires a radically new form, *Waltz with Bashir* is the first animated documentary film, which makes it an unforgettable experience.

It all begins with the dogs – the panting demons of memory that pursue Ari's former comrades even while asleep. Over a beer in a bar his friend Boaz tells the filmmaker about this nightmare, which has its origins in the first Lebanese war. Ari, whose character looks just like the director, was also there at that time. But, to his own horror, he has completely forgotten the events of 1982. Where was he when the Christian Phalangists invaded the Palestinian refugee camp, with the tacit agreement of the Israeli military? What does he know about the Sabra and Shatila massacre in which it is estimated between 800 and 3,000 civilians were killed? Ari makes inquiries, interviewing old comrades and superiors, and even a few psychologists. He learns of the circumstances in which traumatic experiences are wiped from a person's consciousness and filed away in the dark recesses of the mind; and he learns how it feels when increasing shards of recollection begin to drill ever more deeply into one's memory.

This, then, is how the young soldier Ari, at just 19 years old and in the form of a comic character, comes to wander like a ghost through the battleground of his own memory. As in the great American Vietnam war epics, realism and poetry also have a role to play. A dream-like waltz of combat on the promenade in Beirut and a tank rolling across an idyllic olive grove to a gripping soundtrack confront the dangers of dealing with horror in an esthetic way. Of course, in this case, everything idyllic is deceptive. The background color of the movie, an artificial yellow light, emanates from the rocket flares used by the soldiers to illuminate their targets. Lasting longer and longer, these magical dream images become the stuff of nightmares: in a first encounter with Death, the viewer sees himself reflected in the lacerated eye of a horse that has been shot – an image that is ingenious and frightening in equal measure. How else could such nightmares be documented, if not by animation? In *Waltz with Bashir* it is not a question of it being an "overpainted" film, as

1 Down memory lane, using the comic strip format: the Beirut boardwalk glows under the shimmering light of flares.

2 Dreamlike poetry: the unique visual style is both magnetic and hallucinatory.

3 Man and machine: the style and subject matter of *Waltz with Bashir* are reminiscent of the classic war movies of the Vietnam era.

"Provocative, hallucinatory, incendiary, this devastating animated documentary is unlike any Israeli film you've seen. More than that, in its seamless mixing of the real and the surreal, the personal and the political, animation and live action, it's unlike any film you've seen, period." *Los Angeles Times*

4 Street scenes of Beirut: the images of war seem illusory, yet also frighteningly real.

5 Battlefield of memory: in Ari's mind, the boundaries between dream and nightmare, reality and fiction become blurred.

6 Panting demons of the past: the spirits of dead dogs pursue Ari's friend Boaz, even in his sleep.

with the rotoscoping process made famous by Richard Linklater's *Waking Life* (2000/2001). Instead, the animation crew used a very cheaply produced video tape as the basis for a complete redrawing. Interview scenes, dream sequences and flashbacks were recreated in this way, then animated using a mixture of classic and flash animation. The comedic effect combined with a unique style is astonishing: the fragility of the lines and slowness of movement exert an hypnotic attraction. What is suggested is a plunge into the dream, a painful journey into the darkest regions of the soul: an almost exact representation of the psychoanalytical processes to which Folman compared his four-year project. Only the ending brings frightening certainty. Documentary footage of Sabra and Shatila replaces the comic images, with corpses and weeping women showing the viewer the shocking reality. Does the artist distrust his own medium? That is precisely the issue in *Waltz with Bashir*. As in Laurent Cantet's *The Class* (*Entre les murs*, 2008), one of the things the hybrid format does is to document the unease of many modern filmmakers about the hyper-certain truths contained in the feature film and the documentary. Folman knows that the stylistically brilliant way he crosses borders only does justice to his own perspective, not that of the victims. He does not remove the boundaries between reality and fiction, but makes us aware of them. *Waltz with Bashir* is a cartoon for grown-ups: a stark reminder of the horrors of war, and a great artistic achievement.

PB

ARI FOLMAN Ari Folman was born in Haifa in 1963. He did his military service in the early 1980s, thus witnessing the massacre perpetrated by the Christian militia in Sabra and Shatila. After his period in the army, he graduated in film studies. His movie for his major thesis, *Comfortably Numb* (1991), a satirical documentary about the rocket fire on Tel Aviv during the first Gulf war, won a film award in Israel.
His first feature film, *Clara Hakedosha* (1996) – the adaptation of a novel about schoolchildren by the Czech author Pavel Kohout – was immediately recognized, winning seven awards. He also attracted international attention with *Made in Israel* (2001), a cliché-laden, fantasy drama about a Nazi criminal brought to Israel. After several TV documentaries about the Middle East conflict, Folman has since 2005 written a number of sequels to the Israeli TV series BeTipul, which worked up real psychological cases and has subsequently been remade by US broadcaster HBO, under the title *In Therapy* (since 2008).
Folman only realized the state of his own mind later on. With his work on *Waltz with Bashir* (*Vals im Bashir*, 2008), he dedicated himself to his extremely patchy memories of his own role during the war in Lebanon. He owed the idea of an animation (the film was always intended to be made in this way) to a successful experiment in his earlier TV series, *The Material That Love Is Made Of* (2004). The brilliantly made cartoon – a war movie as comic strip – caused a sensation at the 61st Cannes Film Festival. It won the Golden Globe for Best Foreign Language Film, as well as an Oscar nomination.

“His movie makes an acid-trip down memory lane, and Folman might have created his generation’s very own *Apocalypse Now*.” *The Guardian*

7 The young soldiers’ projected desires are constantly intermingled with their fear of war.

8 Submerged in dreams: even the helpless search for protection and security is expressed in powerful visual metaphors.

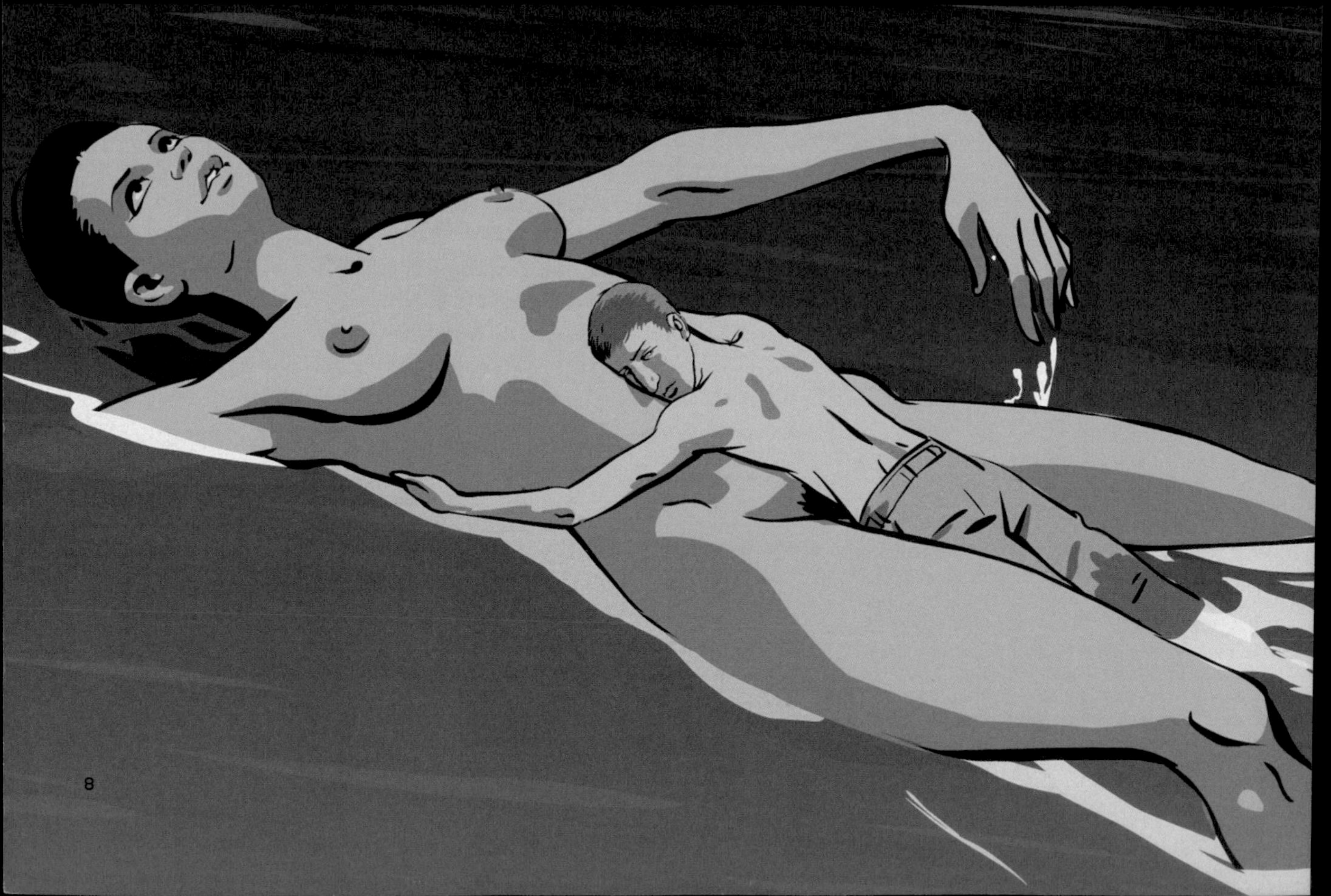

8

9 Portrait of the artist as a young soldier: director Ari Folman put himself at the center of his documentary.

10 Looking back at the past: the filmmaker observes his current situation through a complex flashback structure.

11 Boaz tells Ari about his dream. The interview scenes became just as animated as the dream sequences and flashbacks.

"*Waltz with Bashir* is a memoir, a history lesson, a combat picture, a piece of investigative journalism and an altogether amazing film." *The New York Times*

VICKY CRISTINA BARCELONA

2008 – USA / SPAIN – 96 MIN. – ROMANCE, COMEDY
DIRECTOR WOODY ALLEN (*1935)
SCREENPLAY WOODY ALLEN DIRECTOR OF PHOTOGRAPHY JAVIER AGUIRRESAROBE EDITING ALISA LEPSELTER
PRODUCTION LETTY ARONSON, STEPHEN TENENBAUM, GARETH WILEY, BERNAT ELIAS, EVA GARRIDO for MEDIAPRO, GRAVIER PRODUCTIONS, DUMAINE PRODUCTION.
STARRING REBECCA HALL (Vicky), SCARLETT JOHANSSON (Cristina), PATRICIA CLARKSON (Judy), KEVIN DUNN (Mark), JAVIER BARDEM (Juan Antonio), PENÉLOPE CRUZ (María Elena), CHRIS MESSINA (Doug).
ACADEMY AWARDS 2009 OSCAR for BEST SUPPORTING ACTRESS (Penélope Cruz).

"We'll live well, drink good wine and make love."

Two friends from New York spend their summer in Spain. Both women are stunningly beautiful, but their libidos could not be more different. Cristina (Scarlett Johansson) is the full-blooded extrovert who seeks fulfillment in unbridled passion. For Vicky (Rebecca Hall), a reserved and profound person, sex is above all the intimate extension of emotional trust. Her plan to explore her Catalan identity is the only indication that her life is not quite fulfilled – and also a sign of Woody Allen's trademark analytical approach. At an art preview the two women meet a Spanish painter called Juan (Javier Bardem), who combines all the masculine charms; barely have they been introduced, when he invites them in his deep, supremely languid voice to spend a weekend with him in Oviedo, a small town in Asturias. Cristina falls for him immediately and ends up in Juan's bed on the very first night, but she has to leave at the crucial moment as she feels unwell – too much alcohol combined with a long-standing, troublesome stomach ulcer. So, while Cristina is forced to stay in bed, Juan and Vicky (who is engaged to a New York banker and initially resists all Juan's advances) set out on a trip together. It's not long before Vicky, too, succumbs

1

to Juan's charm and sleeps with him. In *Vicky Cristina Barcelona* the mechanics of love and being in love are explored in Woody Allen's typically ironic style. He plays around with audience expectations, causing his protagonists to encounter each other in inauspicious circumstances. The film contains both comic and tragic elements, though to begin with we do not sense the latter as the camera shows us the gleaming surfaces of the city and people: the images exude the carefree mood of summer, as if Woody Allen had taken them straight from a tourist brochure. Yet the voice-over providing a distinctly non-erotic commentary on the action clearly indicates that the film is far from being romantic, while also letting the audience know that the plot is highly artificial.

A third woman then appears on-screen, in the shape of the even more beautiful María Elena (Penélope Cruz). She is Juan's ex-wife, who loves passionately to the point of self-destruction, and embodies the third model of impossible love. A *ménage à trois* develops between Cristina, Juan and María Elena. This temporary high point will be the beginning of the end, leading the viewer back to where it all began: the airport. The two friends look the same, but have been profoundly affected by their experiences. They will return to their old lives with their impressions of a sexually liberated Europe.

Is the film just an ironic look at the old continent? There can be no doubt that Woody Allen plays with the clichés of both worlds. The Spaniards in *Vicky Cristina Barcelona* seem permanently surrounded by color and sound, indulging

1 Penélope Cruz won an Oscar for Best Supporting Actress for her role as María Elena, a rare distinction for any European actor.

2 María Elena and Juan Antonio (Javier Bardem) can't live with, or without, each other. They went on to marry in real life.

3 The title's telegram style succinctly describes the beginning of the plot: two women, one city. At the same time, the city is given the significance of a third character.

4 Woody Allen doesn't just leave it at romantic ingredients. The story keeps changing, contrary to the viewer's expectations.

5 Two women with quite different ideas about love meet the same man. The ensuing reversal of the initial situation could be straight out of Shakespeare.

"The film belongs to Bardem and Cruz ... Their scenes are some of the funniest Allen has ever put on film, and the culmination of this love/hate tango is not to be missed." *The Hollywood Reporter*

6

6 Vicky (Rebecca Hall) and Juan Antonio: one of several possible pairings that develop in turn, before those involved realize that no combination will last forever.

7 Cristina (Scarlett Johansson) is looking for an outlet for her creative side and finds it in photography. The search for the right motifs, moments and configurations is also a reference to the filmmaking process per se.

8 Vicky's ideas about love begin to falter: a passionate life in Spain versus a neat and tidy one on the east coast of America.

PENÉLOPE CRUZ The obvious and undisputed attribute of this Spanish actress is her transcendental beauty. Born in Madrid in 1974, she began studying ballet before being discovered for the camera. Her face is, as it were, a physiognomic work of art, her eye-catching, sensuous features further accentuating her unmistakable appearance. She can be extremely funny and scathingly ironic, as well as wildly impulsive and lethargically sad, sides she has revealed in Pedro Almodóvar's films in particular. She has made four movies with him (*Live Flesh / Carne trémula*, 1997; *All About My Mother / Todo sobre mi madre*, 1999; *Volver*, 2006; and *Broken Embraces / Los abrazos rotos*, 2009) where she not only portrays sexy, wild, gutsy and tragic women but commands the films with her range of expressive talents. We are tempted to think of the output of brilliant movie teams such as von Sternberg / Dietrich and Cassavetes / Rowlands, where the approach of the actress in question perfectly complements that of the director. Penélope Cruz is the first Spanish actress to win an Oscar – for her impressive supporting role in *Vicky Cristina Barcelona* (2008) – as well as to receive a Star on the Walk of Fame, thereby opening the doors to this illustrious circle of Hollywood greats often closed to Europeans.

6

7

“The most impressive aspect of *Vicky Cristina Barcelona*, however, is its sensuality and sophistication: sun-drenched images in which ‘beautiful women do beautiful things’ and the city becomes another female star.” *epd Film*

in soft guitar chords and their creative impulses, and of course making love at every opportunity. In the evenings there is always a candle burning, giving off such a sensual light that the sinful behavior appears almost like a reflex. Vicky’s fiancé in Wall Street looks pale and shallow by comparison, as if his only duty is to his bank balance.

After filming mainly in his hometown of New York with the life of the city forming an integral part of his movies, Woody Allen chose locations in Europe on several occasions in the first decade of the millennium. Was it his intention, in opposing two very different lifestyles, to flag American prudishness and flatter his European fans? Whatever the motivation, Woody Allen simply creates a messy initial situation, from which a film unfolds that is worthy of no less than Shakespeare or Eric Rohmer. MM

GOMORRAH
GOMORRA

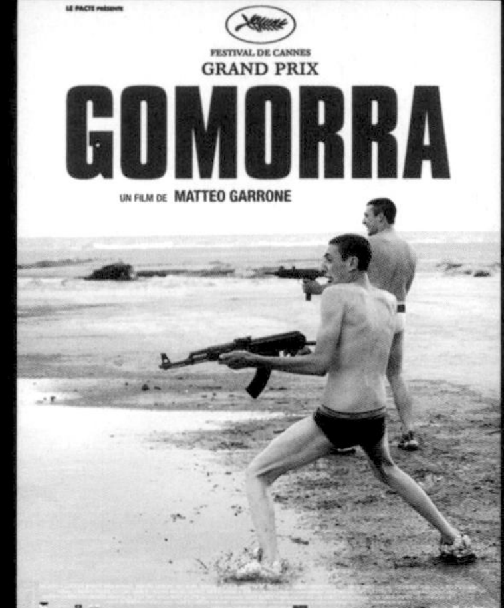

2008 – ITALY – 135 MIN. – GANGSTER MOVIE
DIRECTOR MATTEO GARRONE (*1968)
SCREENPLAY MAURIZIO BRAUCCI, UGO CHITI, GIANNI DI GREGORIO, MATTEO GARRONE, MASSIMO GAUDIOSO, ROBERTO SAVIANO, from the novel "GOMORRA" by ROBERTO SAVIANO DIRECTOR OF PHOTOGRAPHY MARCO ONORATO EDITING MARCO SPOLETINI
PRODUCTION DOMENICO PROCACCI for FANDANGO, RAI CINEMA, SKY.
STARRING SALVATORE ABRUZZESE (Totò), SIMONE SACCHETTINO (Simone), GIANFELICE IMPARATO (Don Ciro), TONI SERVILLO (Franco), CARMINE PATERNOSTER (Roberto), SALVATORE CANTALUPO (Pasquale), GIGIO MORRA (Iavarone), MARCO MACOR (Marco), CIRO PETRONE (Ciro), GIOVANNI VENOSA (Giovanni), MARIA NAZIONALE (Maria).
IFF CANNES 2008 GRAND JURY PRIZE (Matteo Garrone).

"I'm Tony Montana. You fuck with me, you fuckin' with the best!"

They dream big in Scampia, the suburb north of Naples. It's the world's biggest drug dealing area, yet the dreary apartment blocks and streets pitted with potholes give the impression of being in a ghost town. Tony Montana, the hero of Brian de Palma's gangster movie *Scarface* (1983), is idolized by teenagers Marco and Ciro (Marco Macor, Ciro Petrone). They talk big like Tony, tote big-bore guns around like Tony, and snort lines of coke like Tony. And they end up realizing that the world is not theirs after all. Like Tony. The southern Italian provinces of Naples and Caserta are in the grip of war, but for some time now

1

“The remorseless, glamourless scenes – their businesslike realism, their shrugging fatalism, their workaday brutality – come closer than most films to identifying and depicting the banality of evil.” *Financial Times*

4

1 Marco (Marco Macor) and Ciro (Ciro Petrone) see themselves as big gangsters – like Al Pacino as Tony in *Scarface* (1983).

2 Using children to transport toxic waste: as professional teamsters refuse to do it, contractor Franco hires stray boys in Rome, puts them behind the wheel and makes them drive the lethal cargo.

3 Contractor Franco (Toni Servillo) makes a killing through the illegal disposal of toxic waste.

4 Dangerous game: wannabe gangster Ciro takes aim and shoots like a sniper.

5 One man says "No:" university graduate Roberto (Carmine Paternoster) doesn't want anything more to do with the dumping, so he backs out of his arrangement with Franco.

the police have only made sporadic appearances, if at all. It is a world ruled by the criminal organization known as the *camorra*, a million miles from the nice family image portrayed by Francis Ford Coppola in *The Godfather* (1972) or Martin Scorsese in *Goodfellas* (1990). Based on Roberto Saviano's semi-fictional novel "Gomorra," Matteo Garrone paints an almost documentary picture of how children are caught up in the front line of a three-way gang war, how toxic waste is shunted around, and how poorly paid tailors make fake designer fashion items. In the process, Garrone takes a painfully critical look at his actors, his restless camera following their gazes and movements; on more than one occasion he takes shelter around the corner of buildings when violence breaks out.

There is no place for any romantic glorification of the Mafia and honor in this drama, which loosely connects five episodes and tells the story, not of

ROBERTO SAVIANO Perhaps he did not realize the extent of the storm he had unleashed. Since Roberto Saviano published his semi-documentary novel "Gomorra" in 2006, describing the involvement of the Naples branch of the Mafia, the *camorra*, in the global economy extending to China, South America and Germany, he has been living in fear of his life. Death threats from several *camorra* bosses in Naples followed the publication, and the Italian Interior Minister provided the writer with permanent police protection; since then Saviano has lived with the tightest security possible. But the storm has not abated: "Gomorrah" sold over 2 million copies in Italy alone, and has been translated into 43 languages across the world.
Roberto Saviano was born on September 22, 1979 in Naples. After completing his philosophy studies at Federico II University there, he went on to write for the famous Italian newspapers *l'Espresso* and *La Repubblica*, among others. After publishing articles in other journals, the freelance writer and journalist produced his first book, "Gomorra." After Saviano was forced by death threats to move away from his home in Naples, it was revealed in the fall of 2008 that the *camorra* wanted him dead by that Christmas. The authorities advised him to go abroad, and Saviano announced that he was leaving Italy. Six Nobel Prize winners, including Desmond Tutu, Orhan Pamuk, Günter Grass and Mikhail Gorbachov, expressed solidarity with the writer by signing an article in which they described the *camorra*'s wheeling and dealing as a "problem for democracy." In spite of everything, Roberto Saviano travels round the world, giving lectures and readings from "Gomorra." Thanks to his courage, the murky mechanisms of organized crime have become a little clearer. He is paying a high price, but there is no going back.

6

the big bosses, but the *camorra*'s foot soldiers and "tradesmen" – 13-year-old Totò (Salvatore Abruzzese), who has dreamt of becoming a godfather since he was a small child; "Sottomarino" Don Ciro (Gianfelice Imparato), an accountant who pays out a kind of pension to dependants of "family members" who have been killed or imprisoned; Roberto (Carmine Paternoster), who learns all the tricks about getting rid of toxic waste from Franco (Toni Servillo); tailor Pasquale (Salvatore Cantalupo), who is selling his knowledge to Chinese competitors; and finally, Marco and Ciro, who feel like gangsters but are no better than two stray dogs in the eyes of the real *camorristi*.

Gomorrah translates the raw, violent tone of Saviano's book into colorful images that have a documentary quality as well as a suggestive, compelling power. For this, *Gomorrah* won the Grand Jury Prize at the Cannes Film Festival in 2008. Saviano and Garrone are unequivocal in demonstrating the relentless growth and extent of the corruption, racketeering and power games that have long since gone global. In Naples alone, the *camorra*'s economic empire controls over half of all businesses. And in Hollywood the superstars wear clothes that have been made with the blood and sweat of Neapolitan tailors. ES

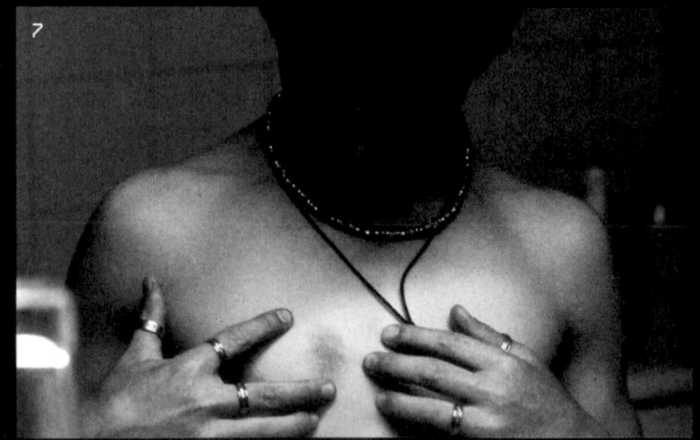
7

"*Gomorrah* is a powerful example of that thrilling current of energy which right now is lighting up Italian cinema." *The Guardian*

8

6 Marco and Ciro dream of being in charge. But when they get in the way of the real bosses, their lives aren't worth a dime.

7 Initiation ritual: the shot on his bulletproof vest has left its mark on Totò (Salvatore Abruzzese).

8 Maria (Maria Nazionale) receives monthly payments from the Di Lauro family – until her son Simone moves over to the Scissionisti.

9 The actress who plays Maria, Maria Nazionale (*1969), is a famous singer whose lyrics are about everyday life in Naples. This is her movie debut.

10 Corpses are the order of the day in Scampia, the crime-ridden northern suburb of Naples.

"More thoughtful than most gangland films, its attempt to show how organized crime has infiltrated every level of society is impressive." *Channel 4*

10

WALL•E

2008 – USA – 98 MIN. – ANIMATION, SCIENCE FICTION
DIRECTOR ANDREW STANTON (*1965)
SCREENPLAY ANDREW STANTON, JIM REARDON, from a story by ANDREW STANTON and PETE DOCTER EDITING STEPHEN SCHAFFER MUSIC THOMAS NEWMAN
PRODUCTION JIM MORRIS for PIXAR ANIMATION STUDIOS, WALT DISNEY PICTURES.
VOICES BEN BURTT (Wall•E/M-O), JEFF GARLIN (Captain McCrea), ELISSA KNIGHT (Eve), FRED WILLARD (Shelby Forthright), JOHN RATZENBERGER (John), SIGOURNEY WEAVER (Ship's Computer), KATHY NAJIMY (Mary).
ACADEMY AWARDS 2009 OSCAR for BEST ANIMATED FEATURE (Andrew Stanton).

"Humans would put seeds in the ground, pour water on them, and they grow food. Like pizza!"

Humans do not come off very well in this splendid mixture of sci-fi adventure and larger-than-life romance. It is no surprise really for, after totally mismanaging the Earth's resources and making it uninhabitable, they have been traveling through outer space for 700 years in a gigantic spaceship. They have mutated into fatty blobs hovering on chairs, feeding on fast food and pleased that even the drinks have an artificial pizza flavoring.

It would be presumptuous, of course, to describe *Wall•E* – the ninth computer animated feature of production company Pixar Animation Studios – as no more than a socio-political case against the ecological sell-out of the planet and the boundless consumerism of humanity. Overall, *Wall•E* is a flawless piece of popcorn cinema with all its benefits, which have taken Pixar to a level way beyond its competitors in the computer animation sector: from the engaging, exceptionally charming story to the superbly rounded characters and incredible technical prowess.

In terms of this last point, Pixar is constantly breaking the barriers that have already been set by its own films. For *Monsters, Inc.* (2001), programmers invented software that allowed hair and fur to be represented at a standard that had never been seen before; and, in *Finding Nemo* (2003), it was the digitally animated underwater world that had never seemed so lifelike. Likewise, the opening sequence of *Wall•E* – in which the "Waste Allocation Load Lifter: Earth class," to give the little metal hero of the title his full technical name, tirelessly crushes and stacks the garbage on post-apocalyptic Earth – is animated with such photographic realism that it is hardly possible to distinguish from a live-action movie.

2

As the British film magazine "Empire" states: "To any other animation studio – and this is why Pixar can make a fair claim to being the greatest in cinema history – *Wall•E* would not make sense as a mass market movie. It's an idea that can only have come from passion and inspiration ..." The hero is a rusty little pile of tin, capable of formulating only a few words; his best friend is a cockroach; and his favorite movie (or rather the *only* film he knows) is *Hello, Dolly!* (1969), a musical starring Barbra Streisand and Walter Matthau that could not be any less interesting for young cinemagoers. The philosophy of the Pixar filmmakers around creative boss John Lasseter dictates that such considerations should act as a deterrent. Wall•E falls in love with female reconnaissance robot EVE (Extra-terrestrial Vegetation Evaluator) who is searching for signs of organic life on Earth: the fact that a love story between two machines

"The paradox at the heart of *Wall-E* is that the drive to invent new things and improve the old ones – to buy and sell and make and collect – creates the potential for disaster and also the possible path away from it. Or, put another way, some of the same impulses that fill the world of "Wall-E" – our world – with junk can also fill it with art." *The New York Times*

3

1 Garbage robot Wall•E has developed a personality. He is alone on Earth, now devoid of humans, and is looking for company in the vastness of space.

2 Wall•E's best – and only – friend: his pet roach, HAL. It is named after the computer in *2001: A Space Odyssey* (1968).

3 Wall•E follows his companion EVE, who has to return to the humans on their sophisticated spaceship after her successful mission on Earth.

4 EVE is not too keen on relationships between robots, and gives Wall•E the brush-off.

is not at first glance something the audiences might find an affinity with did not prevent the screenwriter and director Andrew Stanton from developing the film, which began to evolve even before the production of the first Pixar movie, *Toy Story* (1995). *Wall•E* is certainly the most technically advanced cartoon film to come from Pixar Animation Studios. But the fact that some critics' groups voted *Wall•E* the best movie of the year (the first time ever for an animation film) is also proof of the touchingly emotional nature of the film, which is due not least to the wonderful main characters: the loneliness and longing, curiosity and excitement that are reflected in Wall•E's metal face could not be expressed more convincingly by a Robert de Niro. ES

BEN BURTT Science fiction fans are very familiar with his "voice" and, if you look closely, you can also spot his face on-screen. Sound technician and designer Ben Burtt has been an extra on the other side of the camera on two occasions: in *Star Wars: Episode VI – Return of the Jedi* (1983) and *Star Wars: Episode I – The Phantom Menace* (1999). But it was the sound design for the *Star Wars* movies (1977, 1980, 1983, 1999, 2002, 2005) that forever immortalized Burtt in his own lifetime. Among other things, he created the noise of the lightsaber, the rasping breath of Darth Vader, the peeping whistling sounds that the R2-D2 robot uses to communicate, and the noises of the "speeder bikes" in *Return of the Jedi.*

Benjamin Burtt Jr., born July 12, 1948 in Jamesville, New York, started out studying physics. Even during his student days he was experimenting with film as a medium, winning the top award at the National Student Film Festival in 1970 for his war movie, *Yankee Squadron.* Also around this time he developed the special effects for the amateur flick *Genesis.* On the basis of this film, he won a grant for the University of Southern California, where he graduated in film production.

In his first years as a sound engineer, Burtt revolutionized the sound design for fantasy and sci-fi movies by replacing the noises that had, until then, mainly been created electronically with natural or mechanical ones. To produce the legendary humming of the lightsaber in *Star Wars* (1977) he combined the sound of an old film projector with the feedback from a faulty TV set. For *E.T. – The Extra-Terrestrial* (1982) he recorded the noises made by his wife while she was asleep in bed suffering from a heavy cold. To date, Ben Burtt has won four Academy Awards for sound effects: for *Star Wars: Episode IV – A New Hope* (1977); *Raiders of the Lost Ark* (1981); *E.T.: The Extra-Terrestrial* (1982); and *Indiana Jones and the Last Crusade* (1989). He was not responsible for the sound effects for *WALL•E* (2008); instead he voiced, among others, the title role.

THE DARK KNIGHT

2008 – USA / UK – 152 MIN. – ACTION MOVIE, COMIC BOOK ADAPTATION
DIRECTOR CHRISTOPHER NOLAN (*1970)
SCREENPLAY JONATHAN NOLAN, CHRISTOPHER NOLAN, from a story by CHRISTOPHER NOLAN and DAVID S. GOYER, based on characters by BOB KANE
DIRECTOR OF PHOTOGRAPHY WALLY PFISTER EDITING LEE SMITH MUSIC JAMES NEWTON HOWARD, HANS ZIMMER PRODUCTION CHRISTOPHER NOLAN, CHARLES ROVEN, EMMA THOMAS, LORNE ORLEANS for LEGENDARY PICTURES, DC COMICS, SYNCOPY, WARNER BROS.
STARRING CHRISTIAN BALE (Bruce Wayne/Batman), HEATH LEDGER (The Joker), AARON ECKHART (Harvey Dent/Two-Face), MICHAEL CAINE (Alfred Pennyworth), MAGGIE GYLLENHAAL (Rachel Dawes), GARY OLDMAN (Jim Gordon), MORGAN FREEMAN (Lucius Fox), MONIQUE GABRIELA CURNEN (Detective Anna Ramirez), ERIC ROBERTS (Maroni), CHIN HAN (Lau), CILLIAN MURPHY (The Scarecrow).
ACADEMY AWARDS 2009 OSCARS for BEST SUPPORTING ACTOR (Heath Ledger, posthumous award) and BEST SOUND EDITING (Richard King).

"Why so serious?"

Batman – or "the bat man" as his opponent the Joker disparagingly refers to him – is one of the most enduring of comic superheroes. Like the citizens of Gotham City, each generation of cinemagoers has been given their own Batman. The darkest, most pessimistic and morally complex Batman movie of all time was, however, the most welcome. After months of anticipation, the release of *The Dark Knight* broke all box office records. It took over a billion dollars worldwide, making Christopher Nolan's most sinister action spectacle one of the most successful movies in cinema history.

Bruce Wayne (Christian Bale), the playboy billionaire behind the dark knight's mask, is also a superhero – although one without superpowers. This noble character for a post-heroic age is, to put it simply, very rich and highly traumatized. In fact, Nolan's *Batman Begins* (2005) had already covered precisely the same psychological background in impressive style, but in *The Dark Knight* – the sequel to the re-start of the series, following several flops – the perspective is instead turned toward the outside world. The avenger, armed with some heavy duty technology, is no longer fighting his own demons but a society gone crazy. The old standards of good and evil appear null and void. Thus Batman himself is suddenly less a part of the solution and more of the problem.

This new situation is down to the demonic actions of the Joker (Heath Ledger). After a series of brutal bank robberies, he terrorizes Gotham City with death threats communicated via video. With the local mob involved, he demands that Batman be handed over; if not, each day that goes by will see some people being murdered. Fundamentally for the Joker, however, it is neither about money nor his attempts to kill the man fighting for justice and order. The anarchic clown with the smile slashed into his face is having too much fun with his opponent. He enjoys watching the powerless reactions of Batman and responds to them with ever more innovative and horrific mindgames. As well as police lieutenant Jim Gordon (Gary Oldman), Batman has allied himself with district attorney Harvey Dent (Aaron Eckhart), whose desire for a new sense of justice is not hidden behind a mask. The dilemma is who to save first: Dent, wired with dynamite, or his fiancée Rachel (Maggie Gyllenhaal), Bruce Wayne's former love. Batman falls right into the Joker's trap. Rachel dies, and a horribly disfigured Dent turns into the crazed vigilante "Two-Face." As Wayne's butler (Michael Caine) tries to explain: "Some men just want to watch the world burn." More importantly, however, the Joker wants to be the one holding the match.

Heath Ledger immortalized himself in this role shortly before his tragic death. The feverish expectation of the public was informed by the shock of his loss, but his masterly acting performance will endure for much longer. His Joker – seedy, teeth-licking, and sardonically slurping – harks back to punk culture, but more than anything it is his own, one-off creation. His enjoyment of everything immoral, including other people's suffering, exudes literally from every pore and has an infectious effect on the viewer as well, who no doubt secretly applauds his perversely lethal pencil trick. Posh Batman is bound to look stale by comparison.

Otherwise, *The Dark Knight* has little in common with a classic comic book adaptation. In times of uncertainty, when great subjects were viewed with suspicion, superhero movies were the life assurance of the big studios.

1

2

3

X-Men (2000), *Spider-Man* (2002), *Hulk* (2003), *Fantastic Four* (2005) and *Iron Man* (2008) together with their various sequels offered lightweight blockbuster entertainment. Even Tim Burton's excellent *Batman* (1988/89) was still completely in thrall to the world of comics, with the playful treatment of color and Gothic elements that characterized the series. Its pleasurable frisson is dissipated in Nolan's version by a brighter, more realistic setting. The new Gotham City (shot in Chicago) is a cold world of glass and uninhabited tower block structures; the frozen corpse of failed investors' dreams. This is our world, whose darkness is not a matter of light, but one of moral ambivalence.

Dent and Batman, the white and black knights, are unable to conquer evil using legitimate means. Batman assumes the guilt for the collateral damage caused by his vigilantism, and is outlawed. Yet the serious way in which their

1 Christian Bale slips on the Batman gear for the second time. He also has the wheels to match his status, with his new Batpod.

2 Action fans are indulged too, thanks to a successful blend of special effects and real stunts.

3 "Some people just want to see the world burn:" the Joker (Heath Ledger) takes positive pleasure out of chaos and destruction.

"Heath Ledger is not a straightforward bad guy. He is a monster, Mephisto and punk, Marlon Brando and Sid Vicious, an animal and force of nature, everyone's worst nightmare. If Jack Nicholson's Joker in the 1989 Batman movie was an artist of death, then Heath Ledger is the God of Chaos." *Der Tagesspiegel*

4

5

1 Heath Ledger excels in his disturbing portrayal of clown, devil and punk combined. He was awarded a posthumous Oscar for his performance, the best in his short career.

5 Terrorizing Gotham City: the Joker is the fantasy element in a largely realistic setting.

6 A cold world of steel and glass: IMAX technology is also used to good effect in filming Batman's struggle against evil.

7 Dictated by the series: Rachel Dawes (Maggie Gyllenhaal) still doesn't suspect the secret identity of playboy millionaire Bruce Wayne (Christian Bale).

8 Batman's world lies in ruins – the reference to 9/11 is obvious.

9 The delightful grimace of violence: Heath Ledger epitomizes the anarchic spirit of the Joker in every scene.

"Ledger seems to make the film grow larger whenever he's onscreen."

The Village Voice

HEATH LEDGER His death at the age of just 28 aligned Heath Ledger with other Hollywood idols who have died young, such as James Dean and River Phoenix, although he has also been compared to Errol Flynn and Gene Kelly, his favorite actor. A melancholic, vulnerable quality, reckless love of fun and a smile to melt your heart – the Australian actor's short but impressive career revealed the enormous potential that still remained to be explored. He was awarded the Oscar posthumously for his role as the Joker in the Batman adventure *The Dark Knight* (2008).

Born in Perth, Australia, Ledger set off in a car for Sydney at the age of 16 to start a career in acting – despite his lack of training. After a few TV series and two feature films, the route to Hollywood was open to him. His first movie there, the high school romance *10 Things I Hate About You* (1999), made him a teenage heartthrob – an image he found it difficult to cast off. He appeared in the two quite different costume dramas, *The Patriot* (2000) and *A Knight's Tale* (2001), before finally proving his true abilities, playing the desperate hangman's son in the Southern drama *Monster's Ball* (2001). Yet Hollywood continued to cast him in rather inconsequential adventure movies such as *The Four Feathers* (2002), *The Brothers Grimm* (2005) and *Casanova* (2005).

Even after his artistic breakthrough in Ang Lee's western melodrama *Brokeback Mountain* (2005), this passionate actor still thought of himself as a wasted talent. In saying that, he had moved audiences everywhere to tears in the Oscar-nominated role of gay cowboy Ennis Del Mar. On January 22, 2008 the actor, who was undoubtedly the most promising of his generation, was found dead in his bed; the cause was established as an accidental overdose of a prescription drug. The fact that the part of the Joker in Christopher Nolan's *The Dark Knight* (2008) became his legacy led to much speculation, though all proved unfounded. It was not a self-destructive delusion that produced this masterly performance in the footsteps of Jack Nicholson, but the highly professional attitude that was typical of Ledger. For Terry Gilliam's *The Imaginarium of Doctor Parnassus* (2009), which Ledger was shooting at the time of his death, his role was split three ways, between Johnny Depp, Jude Law and Colin Farrell: a moving and fitting testament to the respect of his friends.

6
7

8

9

10

10 All hopes are now pinned on Harvey Dent (Aaron Eckhart). But an encounter with the Joker turns him into a crazed vigilante.

11 James Gordon (Gary Oldman) is one of Batman's few allies in the corrupt police force of Gotham City.

12 The smile is wiped off the Joker's face. But his stay in police custody is short-lived.

"Dark as night and nearly as long, Christopher Nolan's new Batman movie feels like a beginning and something of an end. Pitched at the divide between art and industry, poetry and entertainment, it goes darker and deeper than any Hollywood movie of its comic-book kind." *The New York Times*

11

moral dilemma is debated appears somewhat theoretical. *The Dark Knight* is not so much an authentic testimony to the paranoid mood of the "war against terror" as a carefully controlled movie about controversial issues. Fortunately, we have the Joker, who turns the pained attempts at explanation around – including on himself – with the ludicrous question: "Why so serious?"

This comic movie for grown-ups is entirely convincing, mainly because of its wonderful special effects. Six action sequences filmed with IMAX cameras, including a somersaulting heavy goods transporter and powerful explosions, are given scope to develop to their full effect. And Batman has a new motorcycle: the Batpod. This, at least, continues to provide him and his faithful audiences with fun – in trumps. PB

SLUMDOG MILLIONAIRE

2008 – UK – 120 MIN. – SOCIAL DRAMA
DIRECTOR DANNY BOYLE (*1956)
SCREENPLAY SIMON BEAUFOY, from the novel "Q & A" by VIKAS SWARUP
DIRECTOR OF PHOTOGRAPHY ANTHONY DOD MANTLE EDITING CHRIS DICKENS MUSIC A. R. RAHMAN
PRODUCTION CHRISTIAN COLSON for CELADOR FILMS, PATHÉ, FILM4.
STARRING DEV PATEL (Jamal), ANIL KAPOOR (Prem Kumar), IRRFAN KHAN (Police Inspector), SAURABH SHUKLA (Sergeant Srinivas), MADHUR MITTAL (Salim), FREIDA PINTO (Latika), AYUSH MAHESH KHEDEKAR (Jamal as a Child), AZHARUDDIN MOHAMMED ISMAIL (Salim as a Child), RUBINA ALI (Latika as a Child), MAHESH MANJREKAR (Javed), ANKUR VIKAL (Maman).
ACADEMY AWARDS 2009 OSCARS for BEST PICTURE (Christian Colson), BEST DIRECTOR (Danny Boyle), BEST ADAPTED SCREENPLAY (Simon Beaufoy), BEST CINEMATOGRAPHY (Anthony Dod Mantle), BEST MUSIC, Original Score (A.R. Rahman), BEST SOUND MIXING (Ian Tapp, Richard Pryke, Resul Pookutty), BEST FILM EDITING (Chris Dickens) and BEST MUSIC, Original Song (A.R. Rahman, Gulzar).

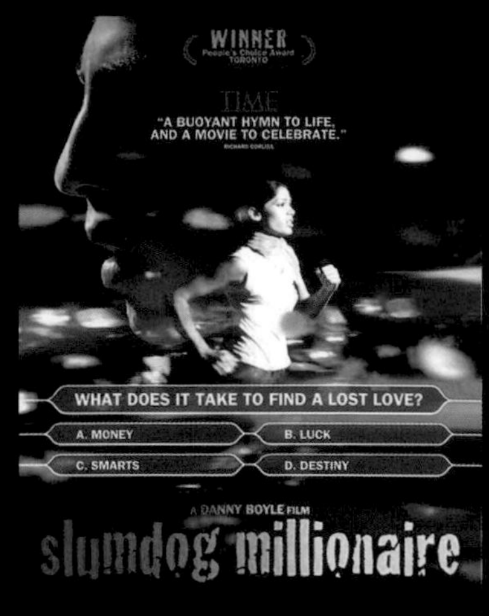

"What can a slumdog possibly know?"

This film is a hybrid in every respect: while modern India is conjured onto the screen in a fairytale rush of exotic color and movement, its central theme is the secular expression of desire for Western consumerism. What is more, the subcontinent has its own version of "Who Wants to be a Millionaire?" A young man, Jamal (Dev Patel), is led into the pristine studio, to the fanfare that is familiar worldwide. He tackles the questions put to him by quizmaster Prem Kumar (Anil Kapoor). At the same time we begin to see, in parallel, a montage of what is to come, which reveals the contradictions with startling clarity: Jamal also has to answer questions in the filthy interrogation room of a Mumbai police station. Applying the usual methods of torture, the inspector (Irrfan Khan) tries to extract what Prem also finds puzzling: how can a "slumdog," a tea-boy in a call center, know all this without cheating? Jamal is just about to face the final question, and a win of 20 million rupees is in sight.

How, indeed? Jamal knows the answers precisely *because* he comes from the slums. He tells the bitter story of his life in flashbacks, with every chapter providing him with the decisive experience that helps him win more lucrative points in the game. The movie plunges us into the unbearable living conditions in the Indian slums, its images whirling around in Jamal's memory like the studio spotlights. We find out how he became a street kid after losing his mother in the religious conflict between Hindus and Muslims; and how he then had to beg with his brother, Salim (Madhur Mittal), before finally landing a job in a call center. Ultimately, however, there is something else that has brought him into the studio: the search for his childhood sweetheart Latika (Freida Pinto), a street kid like him, who was sold to a pimp at a premium price because she was a virgin. Everyone watches "Who Wants to be a Millionaire?" The quiz is his last throw of the dice.

British director Danny Boyle tells a simple, heart-warming love story in *Slumdog Millionaire*, and in the process becomes immersed in the ubiquitous contradictions of India – wealth and poverty, tradition and modernity, suffering and hope. Like many Europeans before him, such as Jean Renoir in *The*

1

3

1 Leaving the slums behind: the train ride to the Taj Mahal is a charming, poetic montage of light, color and movement.

2 The harsh life in the Mumbai slums is not glossed over, but dynamic direction makes it seem exciting.

3 The filthiest toilet in India: little Jamal (Ayush Mahesh Khedekar) knows how to get out of a tricky situation.

4 Who wants to be a millionaire? The world-famous TV show, a symbol of capitalist wish fulfillment, becomes the game of his life for the older Jamal (Dev Patel).

"*Slumdog Millionaire* is just a piece of riveting cinema, meant to be savoured as a Cinderella-like fairy tale, with the edge of a thriller and the vision of an artist." *The Times of India*

River (1951) and Louis Malle in *Calcutta* (1969), he cannot, and does not want to, abandon the western view, but at the same time is clearly fascinated and inspired by the narrative patterns of classic Bollywood cinema. The resulting hybrid is a "masala movie:" a bit of everything, with a fantastic international cast – newcomer Dev Patel is from North London, while Irrfan Khan and Anil Kapoor are two megastars of Indian cinema – and an upbeat dance routine to close the action. Chris Dickens' fast-paced editing, Anthony Dod Mantle's exhilarating tracking shots and tantalizing play of colors, and the rhythmic energy of A.R. Rahman's music make the film a feast for the eyes and ears alike. Together, they won a total of eight Oscars for their outstanding work. Just as love triumphs in the film (of course), this relatively low-budget production knocked out all its competitors. The movie did not, however, defuse the arguments of Indian nationalists and intellectuals, who accused it of slum tourism and even "poverty porn." Boyle is like the tourists who are taken in by little Jamal's glossy deceptions when acting as a guide at the Taj Mahal. He allows himself to be all too easily dazzled, caught up by the incomprehensible zest for life of the very poorest people. But none of us will ever forget the scene in which a child is blinded so that he will collect more cash when begging. Boyle also stays true to his artistic tradition: as far back as *Trainspotting* (1996), his movie about Scottish drug addicts,

5

ANTHONY DOD MANTLE An impressive filmography that includes cult movies like *The Celebration* (*Festen*, 1998), 28 Days Later (2002) and the Oscar-winning *The Last King of Scotland* (2006) reveals Anthony Dod Mantle as one of the style-defining cameramen of his generation. His shots have an excitingly modern and vibrant quality that translates the artistic visions of directors such as Lars von Trier and Danny Boyle to perfection. He personally won the Oscar for his work on the latter's *Slumdog Millionaire* (2008). It has the classic trademarks of this British cinematographer: meticulous use of the hand-held camera, combined with a masterful blend of digital and analog recording techniques. To allow them to plunge directly into the chaos of the Indian slums, the crew developed an ingenious backpack system: ice-chilled laptops acting as separate data storage units, thus giving the tiny digital camera a terrific degree of mobility.

Yet Dod Mantle (born Oxford, 1955) was 25 before he picked up a camera for the first time. Following his instincts, he moved to Copenhagen, where he completed a camera course at the famous Danish film school in 1989. He was soon a core member of Denmark's Dogma95 movement. He shot three of the most important films in this controversial project by purists: Thomas Vinterberg's Festen, Søren Kragh-Jacobsen's *Mifune's Last Song* (*Mifunes sidste sang*, 1999) and Harmony Korine's *Julien Donkey-Boy* (1999). They were characterized by the use of Mini DV hand-held cameras with integral swish pan and the facility for a disturbing proximity to the characters. Dod Mantle also used this camera for *It's All About Love* (2003), *Dogville* (2003), *Dear Wendy* (2005) and *Antichrist* (2009).

The technical advances in HD and working with British *enfant terrible* Danny Boyle opened up completely new artistic possibilities. After the zombie shocker *28 Days Later*, which was again shot with Mini DV, they developed a symbiotic association with *Millions* (2004) and *Slumdog Millionaire* that is similar to the legendary collaboration between director Wong Kar-wai and his cameraman Christopher Doyle. Anthony Dod Mantle is taking his medium into the digital age.

his "exotic realism" created a wildly colorful spectacle out of misery. When he has Jamal jump into the dirtiest lavatory in India so that he can snatch the autograph of Bollywood superstar Amitabh Bachchan, he is even quoting himself. When he was filming in the Indian slums, thoughts of the bleak social conditions in his native land were also on his mind.

Who wants to be a millionaire? The game show symbolizes all the madness of the global economy that reduces millions of people's dreams of a better life to an image fit for television. The poor and hungry in front of their TVs naturally wish the boy in the hot seat the best of luck. And, of course, for Jamal it is not about money, but about happiness. The way *Slumdog Millionaire* conjures genuine feelings from this artifice says more about the modern world than any report on poverty. PB

"The best old-fashioned audience picture of the year, a Hollywood-style romantic melodrama that delivers major studio satisfactions in an ultra-modern way." *Los Angeles Times*

5 Fateful encounter: like leading man Dev Patel, fellow actor Freida Pinto made it to Hollywood as well, in the role of the older Latika.

6 Looking to the future: modern, developed India is nowadays replacing the former slums. The poverty has only been displaced, however.

7 Jamal's brother Salim (Madhur Mittal) goes off the rails and becomes a gangster. He dies in his dream of big money.

7

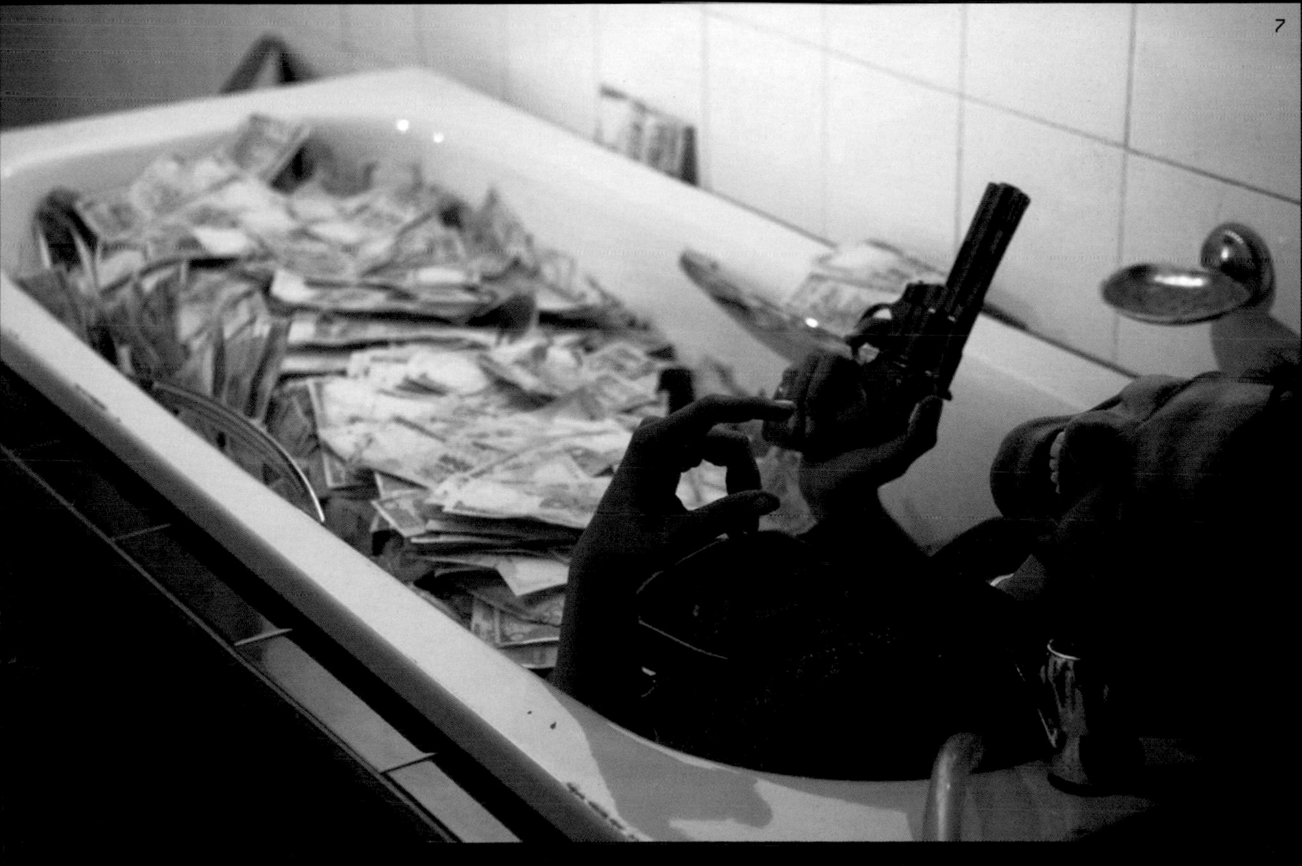

THE HURT LOCKER

2008 – USA – 131 MIN. – WAR MOVIE
DIRECTOR KATHRYN BIGELOW (*1951)
SCREENPLAY MARK BOAL DIRECTOR OF PHOTOGRAPHY BARRY ACKROYD EDITING CHRIS INNIS, BOB MURAWSKI MUSIC MARCO BELTRAMI, BUCK SANDERS PRODUCTION KATHRYN BIGELOW, MARK BOAL, NICOLAS CHARTIER, GREG SHAPIRO for VOLTAGE PICTURES, GROSVENOR PARK MEDIA, FIRST LIGHT PRODUCTION, KINGSGATE FILMS, SUMMIT ENTERTAINMENT.
STARRING JEREMY RENNER (Sergeant First Class William James), ANTHONY MACKIE (Sergeant JT Sanborn), BRIAN GERAGHTY (Specialist Owen Eldridge), GUY PEARCE (Staff Sergeant Matt Thompson), RALPH FIENNES (Contractor), DAVID MORSE (Colonel Reed), CHRISTIAN CAMARGO (Colonel John Cambridge), EVANGELINE LILLY (Connie James).
ACADEMY AWARDS 2010 OSCARS for BEST PICTURE (Kathryn Bigelow, Mark Boal, Nicolas Chartier, Greg Shapiro), BEST DIRECTOR (Kathryn Bigelow), BEST ORIGINAL SCREENPLAY (Mark Boal), BEST FILM EDITING (Chris Innis, Bob Murawski), BEST SOUND MIXING (Paul N.J. Ottosson, Ray Beckett), BEST SOUND EDITING (Paul N.J. Ottosson).

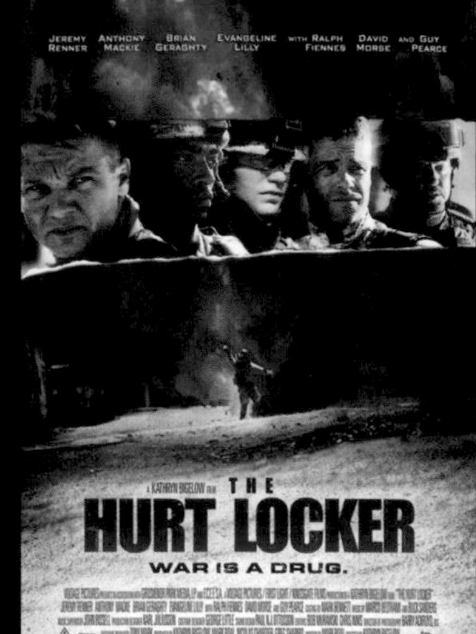

"That's just hot shit. You're a wild man, you know that?"

Danger lurks everywhere: in unremarkable piles of rubble, or the trunks of parked cars. The seemingly harmless passers-by, mobile phone in hand, who give a friendly wave before detonating a booby trap, are the enemy. What sounds like paranoid fantasy is everyday reality in Iraq for US soldiers Sanborn, Eldridge and Thompson (Anthony Mackie, Brian Geraghty and Guy Pearce). The job of the three men from Bravo Company is to defuse roadside bombs in Baghdad. A suicide squad, in which every member of the team must rely lock, stock and barrel on the others; and where even the slightest lapse in concentration or wrong call can have fatal consequences. When Thompson is killed in an attack, roughneck Sergeant William James (Jeremy Renner) takes over command of the unit: a daredevil with a tendency to go it alone. So Sanborn and Eldridge worry that they, too, will die before their tour of duty ends. Kathryn Bigelow scooped the biggest sensation of the Academy Awards ceremony in 2010 with *The Hurt Locker* (2008). It was not just the fact that she was the first woman in over 80 years of Oscars history to win the award for Best Directing. With a total of six wins, including the Oscar for Best Motion Picture, her grim war movie that cost just 11 million dollars to make stole the show from the favorite, *Avatar* (2009) – the 3D spectacle directed by her ex-husband, James Cameron. The decision was all the more astonishing as *The Hurt Locker* does not sit easily alongside the long list of Oscar nominated, so-called "anti-war" movies. Bigelow certainly doesn't spare the horror, but she refrains from any explicit judgment. Her critical view of the Iraq war is

1

2

1 Seven bombs at one go: Kathryn Bigelow depicts the specialist's job as a labor of Sisyphus, which is deadly and absurd in equal measure.

2 War does not stick to filmic conventions: Staff Sergeant Matt Thompson (Guy Pearce) – ostensibly the star of the movie – exits explosively after just a few minutes.

3 "Relaxing" in the desert: the controlled explosion of bombs is one of the unit's less spectacular tasks.

4 No "Ride of the Valkyries:" the image is deceptive – Bigelow's film is modeled less on war classics like *Apocalypse Now* (1979) than the cinema of John Ford.

5 Man on the moon: in Iraq, it's not just during ops that US soldiers move around in weird suits as if on some strange planet.

instead expressed indirectly: in images like those of the bomb disposal expert in weird protective garb, who trudges across the broken landscape under the gaze of curious locals like an astronaut on a remote planet. A bizarre sight that inevitably questions the sense of the operation: what on earth are the Americans doing here?

Bigelow's real interest lies more in the psychological state of the soldiers. It is not just the question: "What is the war doing to the men?" but also "Why are men so attracted to it?" She prefaces the movie with a quote from US war correspondent Chris Hedges: "The rush of battle is often a potent and lethal addiction. For war is a drug." And just a moment later the audience is subjected

3

4

“Mr. Renner’s performance – feverish, witty, headlong and precise – is as thrilling as anything else in the movie. In each scene a different facet of James’s personality emerges.” *The New York Times*

to an adrenalin-driven war scenario, which follows the three-man team on an operation in the dusty, searing heat of Baghdad's streets. The constantly moving camera, hand-held in documentary style with its abrupt changes in perspective, leaves us in no doubt of the illusion of safety. Bigelow presents the chaos of war in visual terms, the effect of which is heightened acoustically by frantic exchanges of information via headsets. Control can be totally lost, at any given moment in time. In proof of which the ostensible star of the movie, Guy Pearce, meets his on-screen death after just a few minutes.

Right from the start, it is clear that *The Hurt Locker* is not a film that invites the viewer to sit back and relax. In saying this, the story does not merely move from one action sequence to the next; on the contrary, Bigelow is sparing with the thrills. Sticking rigidly to the tradition of American warhorse directors like John Ford or Sam Peckinpah, she focuses on the relationships between the men; on what holds the team together psychologically. Hence, she leaves plenty of room for everyday life in the hermetically sealed US base and expeditions in the Humvee: the often dull conversations of the soldiers, as well as their macho rituals off-duty; the three men indulging in fist fights and drunken sprees to prove how tough they are. More importantly, however, this behavior is proof of their inner emptiness and fears. For they are all frightened – even William, who seems to have nerves of steel, though the fear is less of the dangers of war than of their daily lives back home. At one point, he says that his marriage nearly killed him. To feel alive, he seems to need the drug of war. Unlike his two comrades, who long for normality, William knows that he is not cut out for civilian life, and here too he is like the restless heroes of many westerns. The film begs the question whether he was always like this, or whether war has made him so. One scene shows the soldiers on home leave. As he is shopping in a supermarket, William walks absent-mindedly past monotonous rows of shelves. He seems completely alienated. It ends with him back in his element again. He walks into action in his protective suit, towards an uncertain future. It is another 365 days until his relief. JH

BARRY ACKROYD His career is inextricably linked to the work of veteran British director Ken Loach with whom he has made 12 movies in the past two decades, including taut social dramas such as *Riff-Raff* (1991) and *My Name Is Joe* (1998). If nothing else, the realism of these films about the British working class have earned cameraman Barry Ackroyd (born in Manchester, England in 1954) a reputation as one of the most accomplished artists in his field. His ability to capture original locations in an authentic way is not, however, restricted to his native country, as he proved when filming abroad with Loach – for example, in *Carla's Song* (1996), much of which was made in Nicaragua. Ackroyd's photography was just as impressive for the historical films he and Loach made together: *Land and Freedom* (1995) and *The Wind That Shakes the Barley* (2006). The latter won Ackroyd the European Film Award for Best Cinematographer (tied with José Luis Alcaine for *Volver*, 2006).
Ackroyd, who has also made several documentaries, is especially expert in the use of hand-held cameras. He began developing his hectic documentary style, which has increasingly become his trademark, in *Sweet Sixteen* (2002). He perfected it in a few films for other directors such as Paul Greengrass in the thrilling 9/11 drama *United 93*

6 A wild man: Jeremy Renner was nominated for an Oscar for his role as fearless Sergeant James.

7 Like a scene from a Western: Sanborn (Anthony Mackie) and James lie in wait for hours to take out invisible assailants.

8 Tilted horizon: hand-held camera shots convey a powerful impression of the deadly chaos of war.

9 Heat, dust, explosions: the documentary style in some action sequences creates a strong sense of proximity to what is happening.

"Taking moviegoers by the collar and throwing them headlong into one horrifying life-and-death situation after another, Bigelow and her collaborators remind us that cinema, like war, is a drug." *TAZ*

THE WRESTLER

2008 – USA / FRANCE – 111 MIN. – DRAMA, SPORTS FILM
DIRECTOR DARREN ARONOFSKY (*1969)
SCREENPLAY ROBERT D. SIEGEL DIRECTOR OF PHOTOGRAPHY MARYSE ALBERTI EDITING ANDREW WEISBLUM
MUSIC CLINT MANSELL PRODUCTION DARREN ARONOFSKY, SCOTT FRANKLIN for WILD BUNCH, PROTOZOA PICTURES, SATURN FILMS, SESSIONS PAYROLL MANAGEMENT.
STARRING MICKEY ROURKE (Randy "The Ram" Robinson), MARISA TOMEI (Cassidy), EVAN RACHEL WOOD (Stephanie), MARK MARGOLIS (Lenny), TODD BARRY (Wayne), WASS STEVENS (Nick Volpe), ERNEST MILLER ("The Ayatollah"), DYLAN KEITH SUMMERS (Necro Butcher), TOMMY FARRA (Tommy Rotten), MIKE MILLER (Lex Lethal).
IFF VENICE 2008 GOLDEN LION (Darren Aronofsky).

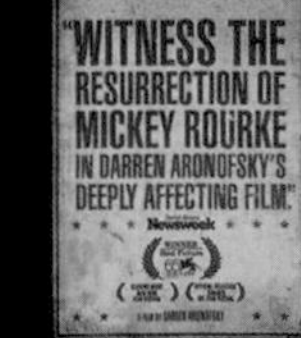

"I'm an old broken down piece of meat, and I deserve to be all alone."

Randy Robinson is past his prime. Puffing, he squeezes himself into clothes that are far too tight and just as out of fashion as he is. Randy is a relic of the 1980s, when his fight name "The Ram" filled wrestling arenas and the whole nation cheered him. He is now living in a lousy trailer, with barely enough money for renting the pitch, and still uses a coin-operated payphone. If he's lucky he'll get a fight in a small ring in the provinces. His body is all the capital he has, but it is falling apart: a mass of muscles and fat that are pumped full of steroids. His face looks like a mask of molded plastic, while his stringy, bottle-blond hair barely covers his hearing aid. With the exception, perhaps, of Heath Ledger's performance in Christopher Nolan's *The Dark Knight* (2008), audiences have never seen such grotesque makeup. Hold on a minute, though, this ain't makeup – it's Mickey Rourke!

In retrospect, it is hard to believe that the role of Randy "The Ram" was originally intended for Nicolas Cage. For *The Wrestler* ostensibly tells the story of none other than this fallen sex symbol of the 80s, the once good-looking *Johnny Handsome* (1989), who went back to his original career of boxing after a few bad decisions and drug excesses. His face became so disfigured after endless cosmetic surgery that the only story it could tell was its own. In the

1
2
rohwrestling.com

3

1 Grotesque body-cult cinema: as has-been wrestler Randy "The Ram" Robinson, Mickey Rourke goes the whole hog again.

2 Randy, now grown old, no longer sees wrestling as a performance but as a life-and-death struggle, mainly with himself.

3 Gritty realism: outside the ring, Randy leads a sad life on the fringes of society.

4 Aren't you ...? In his casual job in the supermarket, the flopped ex-star shows occasional flashes of his rough charm.

5 Damaged family relationships: Randy's daughter Stephanie (Evan Rachel Wood) stopped believing in her father a long time ago.

"Aronofsky finally gives schmaltz the forearm smash and puts the smackdown on sentimentality with a heavy-duty chokeslam – as it were." *The Guardian*

meantime, Mickey Rourke may well have fared the same as Randy, who takes a job at the meat counter of a supermarket. He radiates his youthful charm between egg salad and cold cuts, and the old Mickey Rourke smile still sparkles under the ridiculous hygiene cap; yet one question fazes him: "Aren't you ...?" Actors are allowed to age, not wrestlers. Mickey Rourke is a wrestler.

Director Darren Aronofsky tells the story of this macho sport with surprising sensitivity: a sport that, for Randy's age and fighting category at least, is brutal enough to have nothing in common with theater any more. Of course, the friendly agreements before each fight define its choreography: squashing the opponent with a jump from the ropes and breaking his bones are all as feigned as the mutual hatred. But the physical exertion is not. We feel every splinter and shard that Randy has to dig out of his skin afterward. When he cuts himself

5

DARREN ARONOFSKY Darren Aronofsky's career gives his critics and fans headaches similar to those suffered by the protagonists in his films. Born in Brooklyn in 1969, he studied film at Harvard and became an early prodigy with his major thesis movie *Supermarket Sweep* (1991). With *Pi* (1997/1998), an avant-garde black-and-white film about a schizophrenic mathematician crazy about numbers, he became internationally famous.
The combination of hallucinatory editing techniques and trance-inducing sounds made him the David Lynch of the impending cyber age. The sequel, *Requiem for a Dream* (2000), still enjoys cult status. This film adaptation of a novel by Hubert Selby Jr. is one of the most visually impressive depictions of drug addiction and the false dreams that make people's lives hell. With unusual camera angles, truly explosive editing and exhausting time-lapse montage sequences, Aronofsky was once again leading the way. Then, however, time overtook him as well, and ambitious avant-garde work was seen as no more than pretentious art house cinema.
A creative break that was far too lengthy, not to mention artistic turkey *The Fountain* (2006), were to blame. Following the approach of Tarkovski and Kubrick, the techno-ascetic had embarked on an esoteric search for meaning that only a few wanted to follow. In the meantime, successors with a similar outlook but who were more compatible with mainstream cinema, such as Christopher Nolan, had appeared on the scene: the latter realized one of Aronofsky's dream projects with *Batman Begins* (2005).
It was only the independent film *The Wrestler* (2008) – produced with minimal resources – that brought Aronofsky back into the ring. Directed with restraint and with Mickey Rourke brilliantly cast as the has-been ex-champion, this wrestling drama won the Golden Lion in Venice followed by two Oscar nominations, for Rourke and his co-star Marisa Tomei. Aronofsky's comeback seems to be long term: his lavish thriller set in the world of ballet, *Black Swan* (2010), was received with equal enthusiasm two years later at the Venice Film Festival, and won the Oscar for its leading actress, Natalie Portman.

with a razor blade he has smuggled into the ring, he really bleeds. The hardcore fight is part of preparations for a fight against "The Ayatollah" (Ernest Miller), a rematch of his famous encounter over 20 years ago. Maybe it will be his big comeback. But, like an aging porn star, he is forced to do things for it that he would never have done before.

Yet the actual fight is not that of the comeback, but for his self-respect. He is trying to get closer to his daughter Stephanie (Evan Rachel Wood) to whom he has never been a father, while his growing love for stripper Cassidy (Marisa Tomei) – who, like him, sells her body – holds the promise of the one true relationship in his lonely life. Yet a wrecked life story cannot simply be fixed like a bust eyebrow. And so, after a heart attack that has been threatening for a long time, he stumbles into what is likely to be his last, fatal fight.

Aronofsky, despite his reputation for eccentricity, does not make the mistake of approaching a straightforward subject in an intellectual way. Characters and action could not be simpler. Without completely dispensing with the tragicomic theatricality of the wrestling business, he creates a brilliant style merely through the exercise of restraint. Shot using grainy film and a hand-held camera, and with minimal editing, *The Wrestler* looks more in parts like the making of a documentary about a real wrestling match. The director draws back and leaves the field open to the actors. In this way, he can show all the brutal intensity of those things other films prefer to omit: the blood, the filth, the shame. This is definitely not the film that Randy would have made. It just looks like it, or like Mickey Rourke, who failed to win the Oscar in spite of being nominated. That would not have fit his personal story either. PB

THE BAADER MEINHOF COMPLEX

DER BAADER MEINHOF KOMPLEX

2008 – GERMANY – 144 MIN. – POLITICAL THRILLER, HISTORICAL FILM
DIRECTOR ULI EDEL (* 1947)
SCREENPLAY ULI EDEL, BERND EICHINGER from the non-fiction book of the same name by STEFAN AUST **DIRECTOR OF PHOTOGRAPHY** RAINER KLAUSMANN **EDITING** ALEXANDER BERNER **MUSIC** PETER HINDERTHÜR, FLORIAN TESSLOFF **PRODUCTION** BERND EICHINGER, TOMAS GABRIS, MANUEL CUOTEMOC MALLE, MARTIN MOSZKOWICZ, ALESSANDRO PASSADORE for CONSTANTIN FILM PRODUKTION, BAYERISCHER RUNDFUNK (BR), DEGETO FILM, DEUTSCHER FILMFÖRDERFONDS (DFFF), NORDDEUTSCHER RUNDFUNK (NDR), WESTDEUTSCHER RUNDFUNK (WDR).
STARRING MARTINA GEDECK (Ulrike Meinhof), MORITZ BLEIBTREU (Andreas Baader), JOHANNA WOKALEK (Gudrun Ensslin), NADJA UHL (Brigitte Mohnhaupt), BRUNO GANZ (Horst Herold), HANNAH HERZSPRUNG (Susanne Albrecht), ALEXANDRA MARIA LARA (Petra Schelm), DANIEL LOMMATZSCH (Christian Klar), STIPE ERCEG (Holger Meins), JAN JOSEF LIEFERS (Peter Homann).

"Stop seeing them the way they never were."

Germany in the 1960s. Young people are discovering naturist holidays on the North Sea island of Sylt. Among them is the future terrorist Ulrike Meinhof (Martina Gedeck) – a smart, beautiful woman – and her family. On seeing the movie's opening images, we could easily believe it to be about the escape of such people from bourgeois conventions: a fresh start after the self-deception of their parents' generation, who first served the Nazis, then retreated to the comfort of their own homes and kept their mouths shut.

Right from the outset, however, the film makes it clear that nudity is no guarantee of innocence: the young woman's husband is cheating on her, for a brief moment making her no different from many of the other women to whom she used to feel superior. Her ensuing disappointment constitutes a step toward the political commitment that will make her one of the most famous figures in the terrorist group known as the Red Army Faction (RAF).

At this point she is already a well established journalist, her brilliantly clear prose written during the student protests serving as a catalyst for action. Protests follow her calls to mobilize and her demands for retaliatory violence are met. Her fury is directed against the tabloid press, capitalist America and the Vietnam War. When a young student, Benno Ohnesorg, is shot dead by a policeman during a demonstration in West Berlin against the Shah of Iran's state visit, the violence escalates, although unlike many others Ulrike Meinhof does not throw any stones at first.

During the trials relating to the department store fires in Frankfurt, she gets to know Gudrun Ensslin (Johanna Wokalek) and Andreas Baader (Moritz Bleibtreu), who have already resorted to more radical methods to express their rage. Their approach is hard-line, and their love seems no more than the product of unbridled sexual attraction. Stage actress Johanna Wokalek gives

1

“They were horribly mistaken. They were the enemies of the state and in their obsessed universe they themselves became narrow-minded, jealous opponents addicted to love. And, in due course, the sexual dependence that connected Baader and Ensslin in particular escaped neither the tabloid press nor the federal police. Only now, however, do we realize, through the objective eye of art and the relentless logic of the narrative, the extent to which the second, Stammheim phase of this terrorism was also nothing other than a bourgeois battle for house and home.” *Frankfurter Allgemeine Zeitung*

her character the insensitivity of someone who speaks faster than she can think, while Moritz Bleibtreu personifies the directness of a narcissistic hothead. This interpretation makes it clear that Andreas Baader was neither a visionary nor even especially intelligent – at best he was a domineering show-off.

Yet Ulrike Meinhof admires the couple for their audacity. Compared to their actions, her writings – though certainly perceptive – also appear ineffective, even cowardly. The film's strength lies in its unsentimental, straightforward portrayal of these three characters, while still harvesting their potential for psychological depth. An emotional struggle for power and morality develops between Ensslin and Meinhof, in particular, asking not least what price a mother must pay for leaving her children. While Ensslin's reaction is ostensibly cold-hearted, Meinhof seems to have constant doubts, and ends up having a breakdown. The transition from civil disobedience to violent resistance occurs almost instantaneously for her, and simultaneously represents an abdication of responsibility for her children. She never comes close, however, to Ensslin and Baader's level of ruthlessness.

The psychological dimension of the dialogue – coming into its own in the second half of the film when the protagonists, worn down by solitary confinement, debate questions about steadfastness and betrayal – is combined with the fast cuts of an action movie. The events of the 1970s are presented in a staccatoesque sequence, with Ensslin and Baader resembling in some shots a latter-day Bonnie and Clyde. When the second RAF generation around Brigitte Mohnhaupt (Nadja Uhl) and Christian Klar (Daniel Lommatzsch) appear on screen – murdering several individuals they describe as agents of the system they despise – the pace of the film assumes an even greater intensity. The montage style emphasizes the demoralization of the perpetrators.

Co-screenwriters Bernd Eichinger and Uli Edel devote their attention here to a controversial topic in postwar German history that has been made into a number of films. The footage from that period has been firmly imprinted in the collective memory for a long time now: the body of the shot student, his head supported by a young woman; the car stopped at the curb, doors open, after Federal Prosecutor Siegfried Buback was shot dead in a hail of bullets along with his driver and bodyguard. The RAF's assassinations in the 1970s had a profound impact on a German society unprepared for the threat of being plunged into another unstable period following the Cold War. Terrorism seemed to be jeopardizing the liberalist state, culminating in emergency laws; the

1 Martina Gedeck as Ulrike Meinhof: when the protests begin, the smart, articulate journalist hesitates in the battle between words and deeds.

2 Andreas Baader, played by Moritz Bleibtreu, was famous in his time as the most reckless person in West Germany.

3 Students from mostly middle-class families became radicalized against the state and power structures: their motivation was to some extent unclear (Alexandra Maria Lara as Petra Schelm).

3

4 Solitary confinement wore down the Red Army Faction (RAF) members: the film specifically uses this section to develop psychological depth.

MARTINA GEDECK She pauses for a moment, blinking and pursing her lips: it could herald a self-important or thoughtful expression, simultaneously diffident yet arrogant. Martina Gedeck nails it in the role of Ulrike Meinhof, bringing an increased depth of character to the woman that everyone thought they knew everything about already. Born in Munich in 1961, she started out in German studies, subsequently changing to drama at the Max-Reinhardt-Seminar at the Berlin University of the Arts. She won on-stage acting roles in Frankfurt, Berlin and Hamburg before appearing on the big screen in two movies by Dominik Graf. She went on to work with all the famous German directors in film and television, including Sönke Wortmann, Helmut Dietl and Oskar Roehler, and was initially popular for her talents as a comic actor. But Martina Gedeck has really made her name in films such as *Mostly Martha* (*Bella Martha*, 2001), *The Lives of Others* (*Das Leben der Anderen*, 2005/2006) and *The Good Shepherd* (2006), playing clever women who are in inner turmoil or suffering from depression. She is now internationally acclaimed for her acting abilities in complex roles.

5 Holger Meins (Stipe Erceg) later died in prison following a hunger strike. The casting and props sought to be as faithful as possible to the images from that time.

6 The violence caught Germany off guard, at a time when bodyguards and surveillance were not yet standard. It created a sense of insecurity that is still tangible today.

7 Re-enacted down to the last detail: Rudi Dutschke (Sebastian Blomberg), here leading a Congress of the Socialist German Student Organization (SDS), became the symbolic representative of left-wing groups.

consequences of this social hiatus remain tangible to this day. What continues to provoke debate, however, is how this violence could arise from the bourgeois center and be perpetrated by the children of a prosperous elite. Their identity as a group has also led to a blurring of individual motivation, with the result that many of the murders are still unsolved.

Edel and Eichinger did not set out to provide a comprehensive explanation of the origins of radicalization in Germany. Notwithstanding the authenticity of set design and historical accuracy, they do not follow the rules of a history movie or costume drama, but instead give the film the pace of an action film through fast cuts and superb music. At the same time, they sketch a clever psychological profile of people whose identities have become totally merged in a group and whose rage has been exacerbated in and through the collective. The ensemble cast, comprising some of Germany's best actors, gives an impressive portrait of the fatal mistakes of this generation. MM

FROST / NIXON

2008 – USA / UK / FRANCE – 122 MIN. – POLITICAL DRAMA, HISTORICAL FILM
DIRECTOR RON HOWARD (* 1954)
SCREENPLAY PETER MORGAN DIRECTOR OF PHOTOGRAPHY SALVATORE TOTINO EDITING MIKE HILL, DANIEL P. HANLEY MUSIC HANS ZIMMER PRODUCTION BRIAN GRAZER, RON HOWARD, TIM BEVAN and ERIC FELLNER for UNIVERSAL PICTURES, IMAGINE ENTERTAINMENT, WORKING TITLE FILMS
STARRING FRANK LANGELLA (Richard Nixon), MICHAEL SHEEN (David Frost), REBECCA HALL (Caroline Cushing), KEVIN BACON (Jack Brennan), SAM ROCKWELL (James Reston Jr.), OLIVER PLATT (Bob Zelnick), TOBY JONES (Swifty Lazar).

FRANK LANGELLA MICHAEL SHEEN
FROST/NIXON
400 million people were waiting for the truth.

"Television and the close-up, they create their own sets of meaning."

Richard Nixon fell from power in 1974 over the Watergate affair, when he was found guilty of the illegal bugging of premises, burglary and lying. Though forced to resign, he was subsequently pardoned by his successor Gerald Ford in a controversial speech, and thus pensioned off without prosecution. The American people were furious, and disenchanted with the amnesty given to its former president. For three years, Nixon entrenched himself in his Californian villa, until a young TV presenter had a brilliant idea for upping his ratings. British TV personality David Frost, who was already a well-known satirical talk-show host, saw a Nixon interview as his golden opportunity to write himself into history. At the same time, to Nixon it was a chance to win back the goodwill of his fellow Americans.

The film's narrative begins with the tension in the run-up to the interview. Versatile actor Michael Sheen plays Frost as a vain, ambitious and occasionally cocky little man. He fights obsessively to secure financing for the media spectacle, at the same time struggling against his own image. Frank Langella as Richard Nixon portrays a smart, media-savvy, but emotionally isolated man. Both are driven by the same goal. They need to beat their opponent, because it is the only way their career can survive. In the process, they initially underestimate each other. The scenes in which Frost and Nixon clash are filmed like a boxing match. While the two protagonists face up to each other in the spotlight, the advisory teams on both sides are the ones determining tactics behind the scenes, timing the attacks and analyzing the opponent's weaknesses. The verbal exchanges are visualized as assaults, using the shot/countershot technique. And, to begin with, everything points to a clear points win for Nixon, as he neatly dodges the questions round after round, playing with Frost. The resources used by Nixon to win power rapidly become obvious. He is adept at appraising an opponent and manipulating him, unobtrusively moving away from a given direction and exploiting a topic for his own ends. On the last day, however the interview takes a decisive turn. When asked about the Watergate affair Nixon lets slip the key sentence: "When the president does it that means it is not illegal." This carelessness is enough – the lucky punch Frost needs to bring his apparently superior opponent to his knees. The anti-democratic

1

1 Michael Sheen had already played talk-show host, David Frost, in the play of the same name in London and New York. The part must have been second nature to him by the time he took it on again for the movie.

2 From a poor background, Richard Nixon (Frank Langella) tried his hardest to be part of the elite. In the end, however, he failed.

3 Are there actually still a few Cubans with CIA training? Even his advisor and most loyal aide Jack Brennan (Kevin Bacon) cannot bring himself to laugh at such jokes.

4 David Frost made TV history, though he had to arrange the production himself as well as meeting most of the costs.

5 It was well known that Nixon sometimes could not remember phone calls. This was his only weakness as President he was prepared to admit to.

"A film version of a play about two talking heads. Please. It shouldn't work at all. But it does work, spectacularly, as a matter of fact." *Rolling Stone*

attitude revealed by the ex-president in this sentence signals Frost's triumph. Nixon throws in the towel. At the time, the interview was watched by 45 million people, a figure that has never been reached to this day in terms of political debates. As a colleague of David Frost, James Reston Jr. (Sam Rockwell), says in the film, the close-up is both simplification and concentration, because it throws a complex idea to sharp relief. In this way *Frost/Nixon* deals with the film medium itself and the power of images. They can divert their viewers' attention, arousing their feelings and persuading them with exactly the rhetoric required of a skillful politician. The film by screenwriter Peter Morgan and director Ron Howard draws parallels between film techniques and political rhetoric. For the close-up is used like a slogan to clarify a complex situation: it can involve motives, feelings and even personality structures that people can then grasp in a kind of eureka moment. Based on the Nixon interview in 1977, Peter Morgan initially developed a play that enjoyed success in London's West End and on Broadway. For the film adaptation, they found a director who knew what was needed for mainstream cinema – Ron Howard. *Frost/Nixon* is not only a tense psychological drama but a self-referential movie about the power of images – how they are made, who makes them and how they are received. What is more, it becomes clear that images can assume public functions in society, as the TV interview was actually seen as an appropriate alternative to the trial many Americans had wanted, thereby reconciling them to this chapter in the politics of their nation. At the same time it also becomes evident that the Watergate affair changed the people's attitude to their politicians on a permanent basis. MM

PETER MORGAN was born in London in 1963. The playwright and screenwriter, who lives in Vienna, focuses on people who are generally regarded as powerful, popular and remote. He puts them into relationships with others, exploring their motivations through dialogue. Morgan's screenplays are based on in-depth research about the person in question and characterized by an excellent understanding of the finer points of a complex personality. In this way, not every single detail has to be derived from an historical event, but rather as a result of established psychological studies. This is reflected in subtle jokes, elegant dialogue and a pertinent point to the story.

Following these principles, he has produced works that focus on Tony Blair, who was UK Prime Minister from 1997 through 2007: TV movie *The Deal* (2003), where he is confronted by Gordon Brown, Chancellor of the Exchequer and PM-in-waiting; *The Queen* (2006); and *The Special Relationship* (2010), which dramatizes Blair's interactions with President Clinton.

In the process, Peter Morgan has developed the art of using historical facts, not as the basis for large-scale costume dramas but as the starting point for themes such as power, the media and friendship. This has won him, among other things, two Oscar nominations and he is now regarded as one of the UK's most important screenwriters.

GRAN TORINO

2008 – USA – 116 MIN. – DRAMA
DIRECTOR CLINT EASTWOOD (*1930)
SCREENPLAY NICK SCHENK, from a story by DAVE JOHANNSON and NICK SCHENK
DIRECTOR OF PHOTOGRAPHY TOM STERN EDITING JOEL COX, GARY ROACH MUSIC KYLE EASTWOOD, MICHAEL STEVENS PRODUCTION CLINT EASTWOOD, BILL GERBER, ROBERT LORENZ for WARNER BROS., GERBER PICTURES, MALPASO PRODUCTIONS, MEDIA MAGIK ENTERTAINMENT, VILLAGE ROADSHOW PICTURES.
STARRING CLINT EASTWOOD (Walt Kowalski), BEE VANG (Thao), AHNEY HER (Sue), CHRISTOPHER CARLEY (Pater Janovich), BRIAN HALEY (Mitch Kowalski), GERALDINE HUGHES (Karen Kowalski), DREAMA WALKER (Ashley Kowalski), BRIAN HOWE (Steve Kowalski), JOHN CARROLL LYNCH (Barber Martin), BROOKE CHIA THAO (Vu), CHEE THAO (Grandma).

"Get off my lawn!"

The world of Walt Kowalski (Clint Eastwood) is out of kilter: he has just buried his wife, but that is not the reason. He fought in the Korean War, so death cannot touch him any more. It is his street, his immediate environment, which has changed. When he looks from the veranda of his little suburban house in Detroit, he sees Asian and Hispanic gangs involved in turf wars. A Hmong family has moved in next door, where old Polarski used to live. Strange cooking smells waft over him; there are a lot of these people, having fun and not bothering about a lonely old man who once worked in the Ford plant and helped to build the good old US-of-A that is now going to the dogs. At moments like this he pinches his eyes together, spits on the ground and hisses "Barbarians."

But the very look we know so well is also directed at his own, good-for-nothing family. One of his two sons, now grown fat, sells Japanese cars. When they call, he is sure they are only doing it for their inheritance. Perhaps they do mean well, but they should not have suggested the old folks' home. Never in his long career has Clint Eastwood appeared so fierce. Eastwood was the original American, the man with the hat, and it is logical that he should have directed himself in *Gran Torino* as the last man standing – but there has never been so much self-irony. Eastwood, whose characters never had another home, and his Kowalski, whose name betrays his Polish origin, are related to each other in a highly idiosyncratic way. When Kowalski points his index finger like a pistol to chase the foreigners – much to their amusement – from his property, he caricatures the eponymous cop in *Dirty Harry* (1971) and the short work he made of hippies. Harry Callahan, who always seemed to come out on top, has turned into an embittered old man; a miserable racist with psychopathic tendencies, who no longer has a place in his transformed country. The way Eastwood plays him, with an implacability bordering on slapstick, renders him

1

a sympathetic figure yet again; Kowalski's racist abuse, which he spits out incessantly, becomes almost an art form in the movie. All things considered, this man is in fact like his pride and joy, the polished Ford Gran Torino 1972 model in his garage: his heyday is past; he uses up too much energy; and he pollutes the environment.

Kowalski's evolution is predictable, given Eastwood's most recent work as a director: very reluctantly he reaches a kind of truce with the new neighbors, takes a shine to feisty Sue (Ahney Her), and tries to make a man of her shy brother Thao (Bee Vang). He finds out about the Hmong culture, a people who once fought alongside the Americans in Vietnam, and finds American values in their modesty and love of family, which he misses so much in his own brood. This ostensible transformation, however, has little to do with a liberal approach

"The film's prosaic look is spot-on: photographed by Tom Stern, this sleepy suburban backwater, with its dried-up front lawns, has the look of an abandoned war zone, faded khaki tones suggesting that combat could erupt at any moment." *The Independent*

3

1 Directing himself, Clint Eastwood plays the lead role of Walt Kowalski as a pig-headed racist. The man of few words has never seemed fiercer.

2 Cheeky Sue (Ahney Her) introduces Walt to a foreign culture. He might not show it, but the food tastes mighty fine.

3 The last American: Walt doesn't like what he sees from his verandah. His distrust verges on the pathological.

4 As a champion of law and order, actor Clint Eastwood is naturally back in his element – and creates a powerful exit for himself.

or a straightforward education process. Initially, Nick Schenk's sublime screenplay and Tom Stern's usual, elegant camerawork are the only aspects of the film that work in harmony, but the dramatic developments that slowly unfold reveal a highly political reflection on the relationship between word and deed. Not surprisingly, Clint Eastwood is a man of action. The tirades of racist abuse that Kowalski engages in with the barber of Italian descent are in this sense ritual turns of phrase without any deeper meaning. They bear no relationship to the character of a person. This is why Kowalski can engage with Sue and her cheeky repartee while showing the door to the priest (Christopher Carley), the man of words concerned with saving his soul. This very loose relationship with language could well be seen as utopian or dangerous nonsense; more than anything, though, it is pure Eastwood. In the end, his hero shows what he is prepared to do to preserve this freedom. It is a great moment of melodrama, in which individual willingness to make sacrifices, mulish obstinacy, saving the American dream and forgiveness for sins all coincide as a matter of course. There can be no doubt: in *Gran Torino* – his last movie in an acting role – the 78-year-old Eastwood set out his inheritance, leaving a legacy for generations to come. If we do not act on it, his holy wrath will descend on us all. PB

TOM STERN Clint Eastwood owes his late directorial style essentially to Tom Stern, his main cinematographer since *Blood Work* (2002). Their first encounter, however, dates as far back as 1982, when Stern was lighting technician on *Honkytonk Man* under Eastwood's long-standing cameraman, Bruce Surtees. This is where the Californian (born in Palo Alto in 1946) who had meantime beautifully lit the suburbs of *American Beauty* (1999) recognized his vocation.
Eastwood's radical change was heralded by Stern's cool lighting design in *Mystic River* (2003): saturated colors, the emphasis on black surfaces and high-contrast facial lighting have subsequently been as characteristic of Eastwood's style as the gentle movements in Stern's visual compositions. Since then, the director has relied on him exclusively: they have also worked together on *Million Dollar Baby* (2004), *Flags of Our Fathers* (2006), *Gran Torino* (2008) and *Hereafter* (2010). Stern also received his first Oscar nomination for *Changeling* (2008). His camerawork without Eastwood includes the grim horror movie *The Exorcism of Emily Rose* (2005), John Turturro's romantic comedy *Romance & Cigarettes* (2005) and *Things We Lost in the Fire* (2007), a challenging drama by exceptional Danish director Susanne Bier.

THE READER

2008 – USA / GERMANY – 124 MIN. – DRAMA, LITERARY ADAPTATION
DIRECTOR STEPHEN DALDRY (*1961)
SCREENPLAY DAVID HARE, from the novel of the same name by BERNHARD SCHLINK
DIRECTOR OF PHOTOGRAPHY ROGER DEAKINS, CHRIS MENGES EDITING CLAIRE SIMPSON
MUSIC NICO MUHLY PRODUCTION DONNA GIGLIOTTI, ANTHONY MINGHELLA, REDMOND MORRIS, SYDNEY POLLACK for THE WEINSTEIN COMPANY, MIRAGE ENTERPRISES, NEUNTE BABELSBERG FILM.
STARRING KATE WINSLET (Hanna Schmitz), RALPH FIENNES (Michael Berg), DAVID KROSS (Young Michael Berg), BRUNO GANZ (Professor Rohl), MATTHIAS HABICH (Peter Berg), LENA OLIN (Ilana Mather/Rose Mather), ALEXANDRA MARIA LARA (Young Ilana Mather), HANNAH HERZSPRUNG (Julia), VIJESSNA FERKIC (Sophie), KAROLINE HERFURTH (Marthe).
ACADEMY AWARDS 2009 OSCAR for BEST LEADING ACTRESS (Kate Winslet).

"It doesn't matter what I feel. It doesn't matter what I think. The dead are still dead."

A small town in post-World War II Germany; it is raining. Fifteen-year-old schoolboy Michael Berg (David Kross) stumbles through the streets, ill and soaked through. A woman helps him. When he goes to thank her later, something more develops between him and tram conductor Hanna Schmitz (Kate Winslet), who is almost 20 years his senior. It is a passionate affair characterized by a special ritual: before their lovemaking, Michael is supposed to read aloud to her from the classics of world literature. For the boy, however, the erotic adventure ends as suddenly as it began, when Hanna vanishes without a trace one day.

Years later, they unexpectedly see each other again. In 1966, Michael is a law student sitting in on a war criminals trial, where Hanna is one of six accused former concentration camp guards alleged to have been responsible for the deaths of 300 Jewish women and children. Hanna had also made young prisoners read books to her in the camp. Michael realizes that she is illiterate and that she is taking the blame now only because she is ashamed to admit it. Although he could prevent Hanna from getting a life sentence, he keeps what he knows to himself. Michael tentatively re-establishes contact with her some time later. During Hanna's 20-year sentence he sends her cassettes with recordings of him reading out classics of literary history to her as he did before.

Bernhard Schlink's novel "Der Vorleser" was published in 1995 and became an international success: translated into over 40 languages, it became the first German book to make it to the top of the *New York Times* bestseller list. The author was personally involved in the German-American co-production and even appears briefly, in a small, walk-on part. The major difference between the film and book is in the role of Hanna Schmitz, whose story provides the focus for the film. This is mainly down to the outstanding performance by Kate Winslet, who has created a disturbingly complex character: from seductive

1

2

"Without so much as a single mention of the moral 'moral,' this film poses more probing questions about moral standards than has any other in a long time. Hanna is morally illiterate, and Michael – who belongs to the next generation – spends his whole life resetting his moral compass." *Welt online*

3

4

1, 2 Affair with an unusual ritual: as foreplay, Hanna (Kate Winslet) makes the younger Michael (David Kross) read out classics of world literature, from Homer to Lessing.

3 Hanna's relationship to her "little boy" oscillates between maternal care and sexual dominance. At this stage, Michael still has no idea about her Nazi past.

4 Hanna remains an enigma, and not just to Michael. Kate Winslet's Oscar-winning performance presents the viewer with a fascinating mystery.

young woman to callous SS criminal and finally gray-haired prisoner, she remains as inexplicable and alien to the viewer as she is to Michael Berg. Adding his memories and pangs of conscience in the form of a voice-over to the film was never an option for Schlink, director Stephen Daldry or screenwriter David Hare. Instead, they went for an approach in which 50-year-old Michael Berg (Ralph Fiennes) looks back on his life story in a series of flashbacks. This narrative framing in the film may have worked, but Ralph Fiennes' one-dimensional portrayal of an embittered, sad man falls well short of Winslet's performance. His choice for the part was also somewhat unfortunate, since he had played SS camp commander Amon Goeth in *Schindler's List* (1993).

Even though it may have been perceived as such by many viewers, *The Reader* was not intended as a Holocaust film; the filmmakers quite deliberately avoided showing war crimes directly on screen. This actually makes sense in so far as both the film and the book are narrated from Michael's perspective. Consequently, the inner conflict that he experiences as a student in the 1960s forms the core of the film. The clash between generations that his fellow students and their parents engage in is not represented in abstract form for Michael, but in a far more concrete, personal way. On the one hand, questions are raised, not about his affection for his parents, but rather about his intimate relationship with his first and only great love. On the other hand, Hanna is

KATE WINSLET When Kate Winslet was offered the part of Hanna Schmitz in *The Reader* (2008) she initially had to turn it down, as she was already in the middle of filming *Revolutionary Road* (2008) under the direction of her then husband Sam Mendes. Only after Cate Blanchett and Nicole Kidman also gave it the thumbs down because they were both pregnant did it come back to the English actress – fortunately for the movie and for Winslet, as she finally won her first Oscar after five previous nominations. Kate Elizabeth Winslet was born in 1975 in Reading, England and grew up in an acting family. She began her acting career with film and TV roles in the early 1990s. She made her movie debut in Peter Jackson's *Heavenly Creatures* (1994) and received the first of six Oscar nominations for her role in the Jane Austen adaptation *Sense and Sensibility* (1995). Her big breakthrough finally came when she teamed up with Leonardo DiCaprio in *Titanic* (1997). She then proved her talents as a comic actress in *Eternal Sunshine of the Spotless Mind* (2004) and *Romance & Cigarettes* (2005). Her image continued to be characterized by strong female roles, however, as in Little *Children* (2006). She was equally convincing in 2011 in Todd Haynes' five-part mini-series *Mildred Pierce*, a remake of Michael Curtiz' film noir melodrama of the same name (1945) in which Joan Crawford played one of her best roles.

5 Suddenly seeing her again leaves Michael reeling. At a war crimes trial, Michael spots his former lover on the defendants' bench.

6 Michael's conscience is bothering him. He knows that Hanna has made a false plea to hide her illiteracy.

7 A trip out gives a first indication of Hanna's problem: she cannot read the map.

8 Going into a little chapel brings back terrible memories for Hanna. She was guilty of causing the deaths of 300 women and children in a church fire.

uilty of war crimes in a way that goes far beyond mere knowledge of them. his coming to terms with the past remains first and foremost a personal story about guilt and silence. The main issue is that either the wrong decisions are nade or the right actions are not carried out, through fear of breaking social aboos. For illiterate Hanna is not the only one who is ashamed; Michael is oo. He keeps quiet about the sins of his youth; about his affair not only with an older woman but, more importantly, a member of the SS, even though he was unaware of her past at that point. Hanna gets life, but Michael feels it is the morally right decision not to do anything, even though it will haunt him fo the rest of his days. He eventually gets back in contact with Hanna, rathe hesitantly, with the cassettes, but even then he cannot forgive her. CZ

“The crucial decision in *The Reader* is made by a 24-year-old youth, who has information that might help a woman about to be sentenced to life in prison, but withholds it. He is ashamed to reveal his affair with this woman. By making this decision, he shifts the film’s focus from the subject of German guilt about the Holocaust and turns it on the human race in general.” *Chicago Sun-Times*

THE CURIOUS CASE OF BENJAMIN BUTTON 🏆🏆🏆

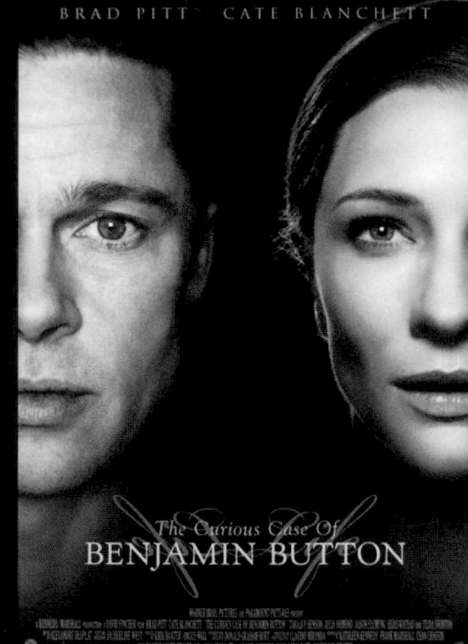

2008 – USA – 166 MIN. – DRAMA, LITERARY ADAPTATION
DIRECTOR DAVID FINCHER (*1962)
SCREENPLAY ERIC ROTH, ROBIN SWICORD from the short story by F. SCOTT FITZGERALD
DIRECTOR OF PHOTOGRAPHY CLAUDIO MIRANDA EDITING KIRK BAXTER, ANGUS WALL
MUSIC ALEXANDRE DESPLAT PRODUCTION CEÁN CHAFFIN, KATHLEEN KENNEDY, FRANK MARSHALL for WARNER BROS. PICTURES, PARAMOUNT PICTURES, THE KENNEDY/MARSHALL COMPANY.
STARRING BRAD PITT (Benjamin Button), CATE BLANCHETT (Daisy), TARAJI P. HENSON (Queenie), JULIA ORMOND (Caroline), JASON FLEMYNG (Thomas Button), ELIAS KOTEAS (Monsieur Gateau), TILDA SWINTON (Elizabeth Abbott), JARED HARRIS (Captain Mike), PETER DONALD BADALAMENTI II ("Young" Benjamin), ELLE FANNING (Young Daisy), MAHERSHALALHASHBAZ ALI (Tizzy).
ACADEMY AWARDS 2009 OSCARS for BEST ART DIRECTION (Donald Graham Burt, Victor J. Zolfo), BEST VISUAL EFFECTS (Eric Barba, Craig Barron, Burt Dalton, Steve Preeg), BEST MAKEUP (Greg Cannom).

"I was born under unusual circumstances."

"Life would be infinitely happier if we could only be born at the age of eighty and gradually approach eighteen." Writer Mark Twain's famous aphorism inspired his fellow novelist, F. Scott Fitzgerald, to write "The Curious Case of Benjamin Button," a short story first published in 1922. Director David Fincher in turn used it as the basis for his film. All he borrowed from it, however, were the names and basic idea of a life running backward.

Thus Benjamin Button comes into the world in New Orleans in 1918 as an old man. He is the size of a baby, but deaf, arthritic and wrinkled. After his mother dies in childbirth, his father leaves the strange-looking child on the steps of a seniors' home. There, housekeeper Queenie (Taraji P. Henson) adopts him as her own, and Benjamin grows up among people who are frail like him. At the age of 11, and still looking like an old man, Benjamin (Peter Donald Badalamenti II) meets young Daisy (Elle Fanning) in the home. She becomes the great love of his life. They meet up again years later and, now that Daisy (Cate Blanchett) is growing older and Benjamin (Brad Pitt) is getting younger, they can experience a brief period of happiness as a couple. Until, that is, Benjamin's strange fate tears them apart again ... This is all related within the framework of a narrative set in 2005, when Daisy's daughter Caroline (Julia

1

“There are plenty of ‘aha!’ moments, when the characters turn up, as if by magic, in places where the collective memory has snapped its iconographic souvenir pictures of the 20th century.” *Film-Dienst*

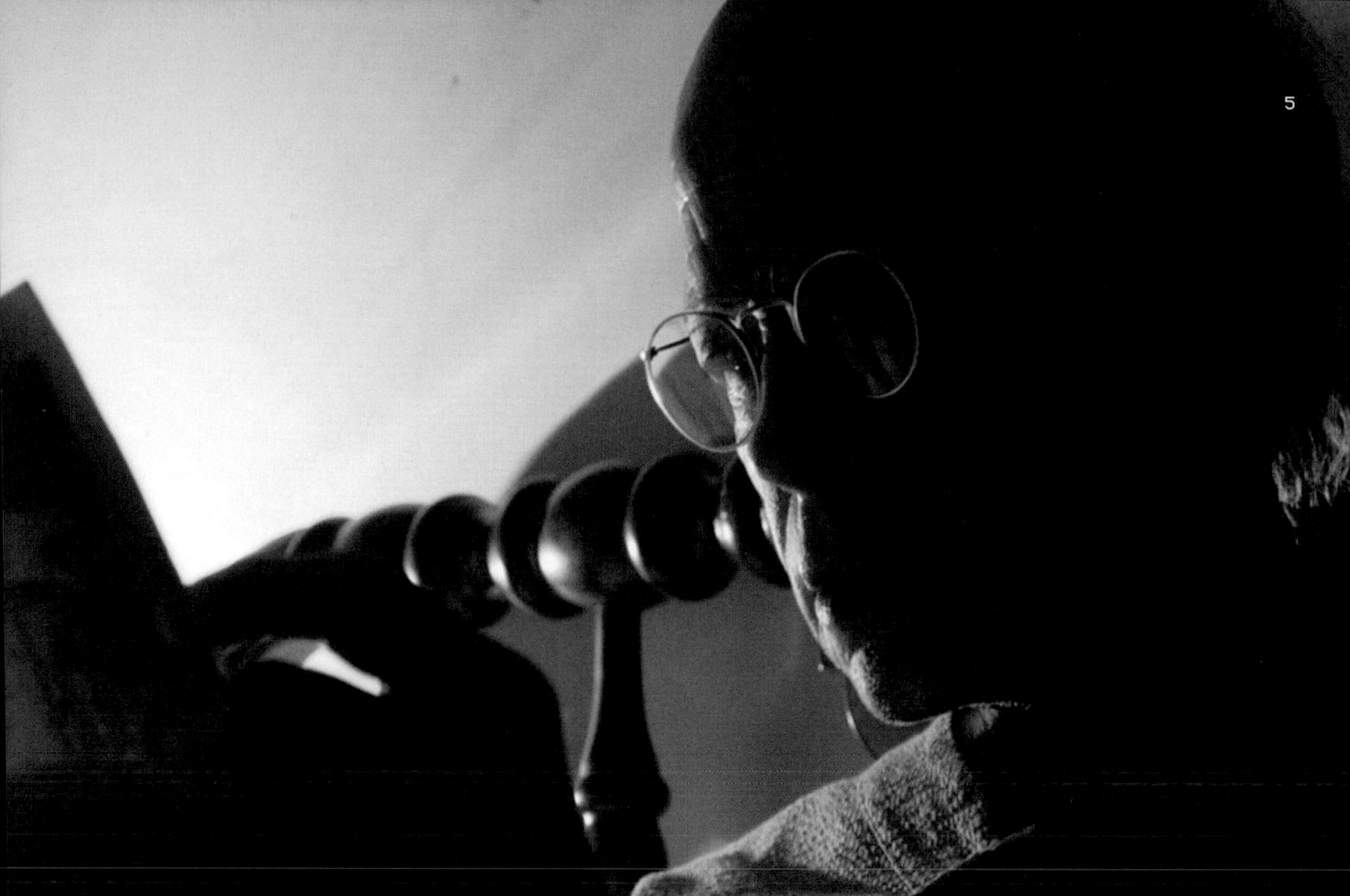

1 A few gray hairs and age spots: Brad Pitt plays Benjamin himself, as far as the capabilities of makeup will allow.

2 Working as a sailor on a barge, adolescent Benjamin becomes a man.

3 Benjamin inherits a button factory where he discovers a motor cycle in an old shed that allows him to drive again.

4 As a child, Benjamin (Peter Donald Badalamenti II) grows up in a seniors' home with housekeeper Queenie (Taraji P. Henson).

5 The body of an old man, holding a boy's book: Benjamin (Brad Pitt) is reading "Ivanhoe."

Ormond) reads aloud to her dying mother from Benjamin's diary. *The Curious Case of Benjamin Button* is a film that enchants, captivates and moves its audience, overwhelming us with its wonderful ideas, plays on form and joy in storytelling. First and foremost, the film provides a superb pictorial experience. Cameraman Claudio Miranda creates outstanding visual worlds. In the sepia-toned shots of New Orleans in the 1930s and 40s in particular he produces a seductively nostalgic mood of the South. The Oscar-winning visual effects and makeup show the process of aging and getting younger in the protagonists in a believable way. But the film is far more than just a technical achievement.

The director, David Fincher, and screenwriter Eric Roth develop a powerful – and melancholically beautiful – love story about two people finding and losing one another, which evolves through time and chance. The former is indicated in various ways. There is linear time, which makes one grain of sand after another disappear irrevocably in the hourglass of our life. The misery of Benjamin's existence lies in the fact that his hourglass is running in the opposite direction to Daisy's. Herein lie the great melodramatic moments of the story of two lovers who are prevented from spending their lives together. Then, there is cyclical time, revealing many things in the finite nature of life to be recurring events. This becomes apparent in various aspects of the movie, such as the story told by one of the home's residents, who tells Benjamin about an accident he had when he was hit by lightning. This light, playful touch in *Benjamin Button* is occasionally reminiscent of the French comedy *Amelie* (*Le fabuleux destin d'Amélie Poulain*, 2001). Added to which, the film links Benjamin's story with the great events of world history – a reference to *Forrest Gump* (1994),

ERIC ROTH As screenwriter Eric Roth (*1945) said about *Benjamin Button*: "It's simply about a person's life – both the ordinary and the very unusual aspects of it." He had already demonstrated his impressive ability to combine these two extremes in his script for Robert Zemeckis' *Forrest Gump* (1994), for which he won an Oscar.
Roth began his career in 1974 with the screenplay for Robert Mulligan's *The Nickel Ride*. In his long working life he has proved to be not only prolific but also a writer who has worked with the really big names in directing: for example, Michael Mann (*The Insider*, 1999) and Steven Spielberg (*Munich*, 2005). His trademark has become the panoramic life story of an unusual character, whether it is someone in real life such as boxer Muhammad Ali (*Ali*, 2001), *The Horse Whisperer* (1998), or fictional figures such as Forrest Gump and Benjamin Button.

CHAMBRES MEUBLEES
PIAGGIO
3H5
AZ 75

8

6 A key scene in their love story: Benjamin (Brad Pitt) visits …

7 … Daisy (Cate Blanchett) in Paris, and tells her all the things he has always wanted to – but it's the wrong time and place.

8 The Beatles release "Twist and Shout" in 1963 as Benjamin and Daisy fix up their first apartment together.

"A great deal of exquisite dying goes on in this astonishing *ars moriendi* film from Hollywood, which has rarely paid as much attention to human decay." *Die Zeit*

9

10

9 After the Second World War ends in 1945, Benjamin and Daisy meet up again; she dances for him, and …

10 … they become closer – but Benjamin is afraid to get involved with her.

11 Benjamin and Daisy share only a brief period of happiness with each other.

also from the pen of screenwriter Roth, in which Tom Hanks as the slightly backward, long-distance runner straddles the twentieth century. Benjamin Button is born at the end of the First World War. After the attack on Pearl Harbor in 1941, he serves in the Marines. When he goes sailing with Daisy in 1969, the launch vehicle for the Apollo 11 lunar module can be seen ascending in the background. And Hurricane Katrina, which devastated New Orleans in 2005, rages as Daisy lies on her deathbed in the framing narrative. Ultimately, *Benjamin Button* is also about the coincidences that determine the course of a person's life. The film illustrates this powerfully in the scene showing the accident that finishes Daisy's dancing career: if various events had not happened at exactly that moment and a taxi driver had not ended up screeching past the stage door at the decisive moment, he would not have knocked Daisy down. This beautifully played "What If?" sequence is also a great example of the way *Benjamin Button* combines the dramatic with the whimsical – a captivating chiaroscuro that pervades the whole film. HJK

REVOLUTIONARY ROAD

2008 – USA / UK – 119 MIN. – DRAMA, LITERARY ADAPTATION
DIRECTOR SAM MENDES (*1965)
SCREENPLAY JUSTIN HAYTHE, from the novel by RICHARD YATES
DIRECTOR OF PHOTOGRAPHY ROGER DEAKINS EDITING TARIQ ANWAR MUSIC THOMAS NEWMAN
PRODUCTION BOBBY COHEN, JOHN N. HART, SAM MENDES, SCOTT RUDIN for DREAMWORKS PICTURES, BBC FILMS.
STARRING KATE WINSLET (April Wheeler), LEONARDO DICAPRIO (Frank Wheeler), DAVID HARBOUR (Shep Campbell), KATHY BATES (Helen Givings), MICHAEL SHANNON (John Givings), KATHRYN HAHN (Milly Campbell), ZOE KAZAN (Maureen Grube), RICHARD EASTON (Howard Givings), JAY O. SANDERS (Bart Pollock), DYLAN BAKER (Jack Ordway).

"It takes backbone to lead the life you want"

It all gets off to a fairly smart start: brief eye contact at a party, some small talk, a slow dance together. As the music drones on, seven years pass by. April (Kate Winslet) and Frank Wheeler (Leonardo DiCaprio) have long since married, had two children and are living in a Connecticut suburb in the 1950s. The premiere of a play by the local amateur dramatic society has been a disaster, with former drama student April flopping in the lead role. On the way home, we find ourselves in the middle of a humiliating marital hell, fed by mutual misunderstanding and thwarted ambition.

"The suburbs were our parents' dream, and they became our nightmare," as Legs McNeil – co-founder of the legendary New York "Punk" magazine in the mid-1970s – once remarked about the flight of a whole generation from the inner cities and the desire for neat houses surrounded by manicured lawns, where people could, or had to, bury all thoughts of a more exciting life. Richard Yates, the author and contemporary critic on whose novel "Revolutionary Road" the movie was based, always slightly resisted the reading of his book as anti-suburbia. Instead, he saw the story of April and Frank, whose marriage fails on account of the mistaken and slowly festering idea they are something special, as a general attack on American society's tendency to conform.

In his film adaptation, however, Sam Mendes shows the extent to which this is all mutually dependent: just how much the standardized suburbs are ultimately the expression of a uniform state of mind of uniform people pursuing uniform jobs. Even at the railroad station, where commuters take the suburban

1

1 When all was right in the world: April (Kate Winslet) and Frank (Leonardo DiCaprio) meet and are captivated by each other.

2 The 1950s' idyll of home ownership in the suburbs, complete with immaculate lawn. But cracks begin to appear in the façade.

3 Neighbors Shep (David Harbour) and Milly Campbell (Kathryn Hahn) see the Wheelers as the ideal couple.

"*Revolutionary Road* is a disaster film, with the disasters reflected in the facial expressions: Leonardo DiCaprio's cute baby face and Kate Winslet's flawless beauty – a single look replaces much of the dialogue that Mendes dispenses with." *Süddeutsche Zeitung*

4 Realtor Helen Givings (Kathy Bates) fights tooth and nail against this allegedly perfect world: she long ago ceased to believe in it, partly because of her son's psychological problems.

5 The gloss in their relationship has worn off: Frank has settled for mediocrity, no longer able to understand what his wife wants. Disaster takes its course.

train to work, they stand in countless rows: the men in gray suits, wearing hats and carrying newspapers; and, in amongst them, Frank. Walking practically in step, they leave Grand Central Station in New York City, hurrying to their ugly, open-plan offices: we immediately think of Orson Welles' Kafka adaptation *The Trial* (*Le procès*, 1962) or King Vidor's *The Crowd* (1928), in which the main character has been reduced to a number in the office, while his father still believes his son is destined for great things. Yet this applies to him as little as it does to Frank, who doesn't really have a proper answer to April's question of what actually interests him in their first conversation together. He will never find it out. A man who never wanted to become like his father (who grafted for 20 frustrated years for the same firm), he has long since resigned himself to his own mediocrity and the presumed security of a job that does not interest him, including an affair with the secretary.

Revolutionary Road is an actor's film: a domestic drama filmed with cool detachment; a tortuous pas de deux for Winslet and DiCaprio, in which the dynamic is determined among other things by the fact that the viewer – unlike

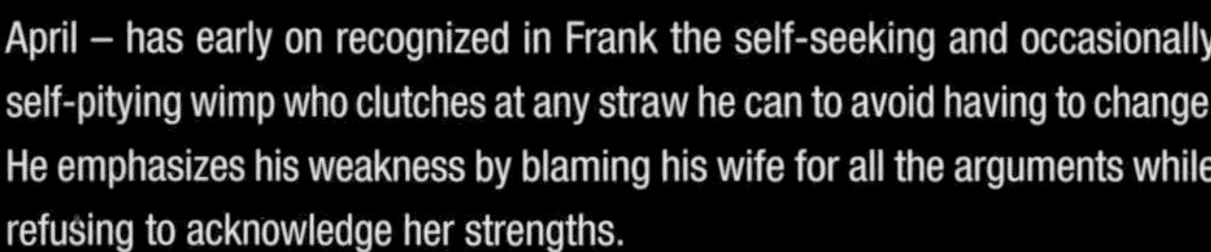

April – has early on recognized in Frank the self-seeking and occasionally self-pitying wimp who clutches at any straw he can to avoid having to change. He emphasizes his weakness by blaming his wife for all the arguments while refusing to acknowledge her strengths.

So April's planned move to Paris, where she wants to work as a secretary in order to give her husband time to find his "true calling," is inevitably no more than a dream either. Her unplanned pregnancy and a ridiculous promotion for Frank (told in the film with wicked humor) are ultimately all the excuses he needs to stay exactly where he is – in the process of which the film also clearly reveals the sexual hierarchy still prevalent in the 1950s. On another level, the film tells the story of the reaction of neighbors and work colleagues to the Wheelers' emigration plans: on the one hand, there is the mentally ill son of the conservative realtor Helen (Kathy Bates), John Givings (Michael Shannon), who can utter precisely those truths no one wants to hear, regardless of any social conventions, rather like a court jester; and, on the other hand, friends like the Campbells, a couple who are almost relieved at the collapse of the Paris plan because this means they don't have to think about their own boring existence – after all, up until that point they had had no misgivings about it whatsoever.

"You wanted out?" Shep Campbell (David Harbour) asks April rather incredulously at one point, to which she replies: "I wanted in. I wanted us to live again." LP

8

9

6 Secretary Maureen (Zoe Kazan) is fascinated by Frank and starts an affair with him.

7 April is the stronger partner in the relationship: she makes plans for the family, and Frank applies the brakes whenever he can.

8 After April and Frank announce their plans to emigrate to Paris, the Campbells are relieved, reassuring themselves that nothing is lacking in their stuffy existence.

9 For a long time, April has believed her husband capable of achieving great things. But as what? A writer? An artist? Frank goes on selling office equipment.

"DiCaprio is in peak form, bringing layers of buried emotion to a defeated man. And the glorious Winslet defines what makes an actress great, blazing commitment to a character and the range to make every nuance felt. Winslet's last scene, as April prepares breakfast for a husband who can't see the torment behind her smile, is emotionally devastating."

Rolling Stone

SAM MENDES Born in Reading, England in 1965, Sam Mendes began his artistic career as a stage director, after completing his studies at Cambridge University. In the years that followed, Mendes' jobs in British theater included working as director for the Royal Shakespeare Company and as artistic director of the Donmar Warehouse in London. In 1999 Mendes directed his first movie, the satire *American Beauty* with Kevin Spacey, which boldly takes a cynical and cool look at the dark side of American suburbia. At the Academy Awards in 2000 the film won the top five Oscars, including Best Film and Best Director. Since then, Mendes has proved to be a versatile director: *Road to Perdition* (2002) features Tom Hanks as a contract killer on the run with his son, while in *Jarhead* (2005) Jake Gyllenhaal plays a soldier for whom the events of the first Gulf War take on increasingly disturbing dimensions. After working with his wife Kate Winslet (from whom he is now separated) on the film adaptation of the novel "Revolutionary Road," Mendes made the comedy *Away We Go* (2009) about a young couple expecting their first child and looking for the perfect home. He is currently in pre-production for the next James Bond movie. Between film commitments, Mendes continues to work in theater, dividing his time between London and New York.

PRECIOUS

2008 – USA – 109 MIN. – SOCIAL DRAMA, LITERARY ADAPTATION
DIRECTOR LEE DANIELS (*1959)
SCREENPLAY GEOFFREY FLETCHER, from the novel "Push" by Sapphire
DIRECTOR OF PHOTOGRAPHY ANDREW DUNN EDITING JOE KLOTZ MUSIC MARIO GRIGOROV
PRODUCTION LEE DANIELS, GARY MAGNESS, SARAH SIEGEL-MAGNESS for LIONSGATE, LEE DANIELS ENTERTAINMENT, SMOKEWOOD ENTERTAINMENT GROUP.
STARRING GABOUREY SIDIBE (Precious), MO'NIQUE (Mary), PAULA PATTON (Ms. Rain), NEALLA GORDON (Mrs. Lichtenstein), MARIAH CAREY (Mrs. Weiss), LENNY KRAVITZ (Nurse John), XOSHA ROQUEMORE (Joann), CHYNA LAYNE (Rhonda), AMINA ROBINSON (Jermaine), ANGELIC ZAMBRANA (Consuelo), STEPHANIE ANDUJAR (Rita), BILL SAGE (Mr Wicher).
ACADEMY AWARDS 2010 OSCARS for BEST ADAPTED SCREENPLAY (Geoffrey Fletcher) and BEST SUPPORTING ACTRESS (Mo'Nique).

"I'll be okay, I guess, 'cause I'm lookin' up."

Gabourey Sidibe often said later "I'm not Precious," and without this personal distance she would arguably never have been able to play the role. The beautiful name sounds like a bad joke. For nothing in black teenager Claireece's life seems particularly "precious," despite her nickname. She is poor, seriously overweight and pregnant for the second time by her father, who has raped her on a regular basis since childhood. In the Harlem of 1987, self-confidence is rare to find, but it is quite shocking to see her: eyes fixed on the ground, she trudges along the streets as if she wants them to swallow her up. Shame also affects her speech; added to which she is illiterate, and all life has taught her is a sense of her own worthlessness.

When Precious gets home, she is met by Hell in the form of her mother (Mo'Nique). This woman's hateful tirades – she says her daughter has "stolen" her husband from her – would break far stronger spirits. She spends the days behind lowered blinds, smoking in front of the TV and devouring the meals prepared by Precious; she dismisses any thought of a better life as stupid talk. She regards state handouts as her income. Sometimes she appears to be a loving, selfless mother – when the social workers visit and she pretends that Precious' baby, born with Down's syndrome, is her own.

Need we also add that Precious – abused her whole life mentally, physically and sexually – has been infected with HIV by her father? Precious (based on the novel "Push" by Sapphire) ticks all the boxes of a gloomy social drama. But art follows its own rules. It is a film that is starkly realistic and harrowing, but also moving and full of hope. Above all, it is astonishingly well made.

The fleeting dream sequences, showing Precious as a successful showbiz star on the red carpet or a voluptuous top model amid a frenzy of flashing cameras, are just one part of a flawless visual concept. Director Lee Daniels'

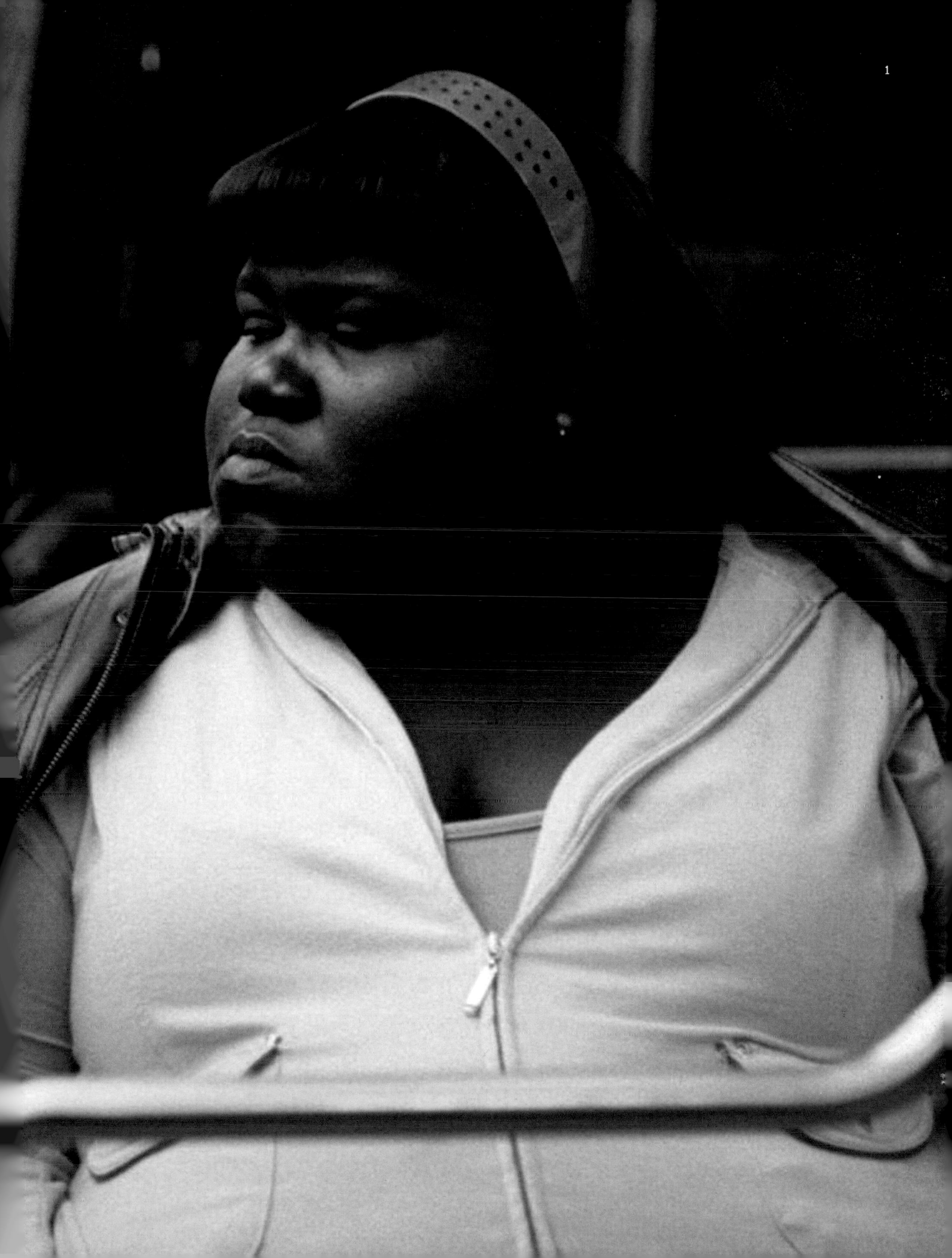

1 Plenty of weight, but no self-confidence: things are tough for 16-year-old Precious. Gabourey Sidibe won an Oscar nomination for her first role.

2 The pride of Harlem: Precious finds her way back into life, helped by a gang of faithful ghetto queens (Chyna Layne, Angelic Zambrana, Stephanie Andujar).

3 It hurts to run the gauntlet: in bad times, everyone feels like Precious. But there are no good times for her either.

4 No makeup: pop star Mariah Carey also gives a convincing performance, as the tenacious social worker who keeps asking questions.

5 Alternative learning: teacher Ms. Rain (Paula Patton) helps the girl to believe in herself.

"*Precious* is a stand-in for anyone – black, white, male, female – who has ever been devalued or underestimated."

The New York Times

intention is to avoid any gloss, but his personal sensibility allows him to find beauty where others see only misery, heartache, and corruption – even in the life of a desperate 16-year-old who is discriminated against because of her extreme obesity. Dreams make us what we are; and not all of them are nightmares, even if large sections of the film seem that way.

Added to which, the first signs of hope appear at a very early stage: in an alternative school (there is such a thing as a welfare system) Precious gets extra tuition from dedicated teacher Ms. Rain (Paula Patton). The austere classroom full of delinquent ghetto queens her own age is where she first experiences success. Gradually, Precious becomes more self-assured, and eventually even finds her own language. As in "Push," Sapphire's book on which the movie is based, the letters slowly begin to flow together on the paper, and sentences become structured. At one point she says about her teacher and her partner as they play, of all things, Scrabble®: "They talk like TV channels I don't watch." The film is not without humor, either.

In a cast that is all fantastic – including the amazing guest appearances by pop stars Mariah Carey as a helpful social worker and Lenny Kravitz as a male nurse – Sidibe and Mo'Nique are, quite simply, outstanding. Sidibe, actually ten years older than the character she plays in this, her first movie, was nominated for an Oscar. Mo'Nique, a star of popular black TV programs,

3

4

"On the page, we as readers can pretty Precious up, pretend we wouldn't ignore or judge her if she passed us on the street. But Daniels and Sidibe give us a Precious we can't deny, who earns our respect even more than our pity. Dignity is her victory." *Time Magazine*

5

LEE DANIELS Lee Daniels first attracted attention as director of *Monster's Ball* (2001). Born in 1959 in Philadelphia, he had previously worked as a casting director and actor's agent. The drama set in the southern states not only earned Halle Berry a sensational Oscar, it also secured a place in film history for Daniels as the first African-American solo producer of an Oscar-winning film.

Yet his subsequent projects initially met with less success, and for good reason: as both producer and director, the openly gay, all-round artist is a man who tackles controversial material. He is not averse to the mainstream, but approaches it consistently from the outsider's perspective.

In *The Woodsman* (2004), Kevin Bacon plays a convicted pedophile given a second chance on his release. Daniels' directorial debut, *Shadowboxer* (2005), brought together Helen Mirren and Cuba Gooding Jr. as an odd couple of killers. He then put Mariah Carey in front of the camera for the first time, in 2008, in *Tennessee*. Working with famous stars from the world of hip-hop and R&B is part and parcel of his stressful production role, always having to secure new sources of financing for difficult projects. This has also led to acting appearances for Mos Def and rapper P. Diddy.

The financing and distribution of *Precious* (2009) proved a grueling process as well. Without the moral support of Oprah Winfrey and Tyler Perry, two megastars of the black showbiz world, the film would have been pushed to find a mass audience. On a wave of enthusiasm, the tragic story of an overweight black girl from Harlem managed to win a total of six Oscar nominations, including the first for Daniels himself.

won the award for a breathtakingly malevolent performance that almost borders on comedy – horrific and painfully real comedy.

Accusations of racism were not long in coming, as Daniels feared. It was said that the film was too vague historically, negating the progress made in Harlem in particular since 1987 and showing black people in a bad light. Precious does indeed venture into the realm of African-American suffering that even "Black Cinema" tends to sidestep. Daniels is less interested in the politically correct representation of discriminated groups, however, than in the damaged self-image of their outsiders and their right to dignity. Celebrated as the first film of the Obama era its emphasis is, in fact, on hope and the famous anticipated "change" – albeit in an unconventional and highly unusual way.

PB

"When is the last time we saw a movie with this level of hardship and gravity? More to the point, a film brimming with comedy and joie de vivre that features such hardship?" *Der Tagesspiegel*

6 Shockingly malicious: her mother makes Precious' life hell. Comedienne Mo'Nique won an Oscar for her virtuoso performance.

7 Nicotine-stained nightmare: the family lives in a cramped community housing apartment. Precious' daughter "Mongo" has Down's Syndrome.

8 Musician Lenny Kravitz even makes an appearance, as a sexy male nurse. Director Lee Daniels worked for a long time in a nursing agency.

SIN NOMBRE

2008/09 – MEXICO / USA – 96 MIN. – DRAMA
DIRECTOR CARY FUKUNAGA (*1977)
SCREENPLAY CARY FUKUNAGA DIRECTOR OF PHOTOGRAPHY ADRIANO GOLDMAN EDITING LUIS CARBALLAR, CRAIG MCKAY MUSIC MARCELO ZARVOS PRODUCTION AMY KAUFMAN for SCION FILMS, CANANA FILMS, CREANDO FILMS, PRIMARY PRODUCTIONS.
STARRING EDGAR FLORES (Willy "El Casper"), PAULINA GAITAN (Sayra), KRISTIAN FERRER (El Smiley), GERARDO TARACENA (Horacio, Sayra's Father), GUILLERMO VILLEGAS (Orlando, Sayra's Uncle), DIANA GARCÍA (Martha Marlene), TENOCH HUERTA (Lil' Mago), LUIS FERNANDO PEÑA (El Sol), GABINO RODRÍGUEZ (El Scarface), DAVID SERRANO (El Smokey).

"Mara forever, homie."

Sin Nombre tells two stories that only gradually become connected, though they belong together from the start. One is about Sayra (Paulina Gaitan), a young refugee from Honduras, who is traveling with her father and uncle to the land of milk and honey. The map they are using shows only the area south of the USA. En route, they have to hold tight to the roof of the gently rattling freight train that is tortuously transporting its human cargo northward. The refugees are silent. They are some of the tens of thousands of illegal migrants who take control of their destiny every year, without knowing how they will get across the border. Half of them never arrive.

El Casper (Edgar Flores) is sitting at the end of the wagon, on his own and avoided by the others. Casper, the subject of the second story in the movie, is a member of the hated Mara Salvatrucha, the most vicious gang in Central America. As they were on the point of taking the refugees' last worldly possessions, Casper killed the gang leader Lil' Mago (Tenoch Huerta), saving Sayra's life. At this point, we know enough about the Mara to guess the consequences: Casper, who has gone from hunter to prey, is as good as dead. The road to "The North" is still a long one, but not as long as the vengeful arm of the Mara. The train and the Mara; the Mara and the train – these are the visual elements of a thrilling drama that follows the trajectory of its relentless tale straight to its disastrous conclusion. Every image is permeated by this dire outcome; every false move is punished. The film begins with the Mara's gruesome initiation ceremony, to which Casper's little friend El Smiley (Kristian Ferrer) unquestioningly submits himself. After being brutally beaten up by the gang for a whole 13 seconds, he emerges with a broad grin on his blood-smeared face. Thereafter, it is a question of killing a defenseless enemy, whose flesh is then fed to the dogs. The shocking images are no exaggeration. The initiation, standard procedure for all gang members, had already been shown in *La vida loca* (2008), a documentary by the Spanish-French photojournalist Christian Poveda. A few months after the film was completed, Poveda was murdered.

Director Cary Joji Fukunaga might address the issue of the fascination with power in a less explicit way than the Brazilian slum drama *City of God* (*Cidade de Deus*, 2002), but the images still speak for themselves. The Mara's

1

2

"*Sin Nombre* is pure filmmaking: a great story told in beautiful images."

The Washington Post

striking appearance seems to be a hypertext version linked to American gang culture: black body tattoos up to the face; a comprehensive set of rules governing well-practiced hand gestures; visual codes; and nauseating punishment rituals. They are fiendishly cool Hell's Angels, beyond all social norms. Their attraction is crystallized in the charismatic figure of Lil' Mago, who is holding a baby in, of all things, the worst scenes in the film: in a life characterized by poverty and desperation, the organization offers not just security and protection, but also meaning and structure – you are never too young to become a member. This is how the octopus-like tentacles of the real life Mara, originally set up by refugees in the USA, now control the drugs, weapons and people trade throughout Central America. There is an inherent logic in the fact that Sayra and Casper's paths meet: escape and criminality are not merely caused by the same things, they also use the same smuggling routes. So the boy with tears tattooed under his eye, who is making a trip he has done before, proves to be a valuable scout. In an action-packed, cat-and-mouse drama, dodging customs and the tentacles of the Mara, elements of the western, thrillers and classic Hollywood romance are intermingled. The actors (inexperienced for the most part) and Fukunaga's confident direction give the film a documentary-style authenticity, while the precisely tuned rhythm of editing, images and lyrical score make it a perfect cinematic experience. In what is a rare occurrence in the history of committed filmmaking, sober realism and esthetic brilliance work in harmony. In a quietly oppressive and heart-stopping tale, *Sin Nombre* tells the gripping story of those with no name whose suffering knows no borders. PB

1 Hunter becomes hunted: El Casper (Edgar Flores), a member of the Mara Salvatrucha, flees from his own people. His life isn't worth much any more.

2 Sayra (Paulina Gaitan) boards the North-bound train as well. Their stories combine both visually and emotionally, in a powerful portrait of the fate of refugees today.

3 Quiet prayer: the Mara follows a strict code of well-rehearsed rules and rituals. Disobeying them in any way means punishment.

4 Search for meaning and structure: Casper's friend El Smiley (Kristian Ferrer) submits to the Mara. Their second-in-command, El Sol (Luis Fernando Peña), gives him a dreadful order.

5 The boy with the tear: after his girlfriend is murdered, Casper turns against the gang. Fear, despair and rage are mirrored in his face.

"A big new talent arrives on the scene with *Sin Nombre*. Writer-director Cary Joji Fukunaga's enthralling feature debut takes viewers into a shadow world inhabited by many but noticed by very few." *Variety*

CARY FUKUNAGA Young directorial talent Cary Joji Fukunaga is a child of the globalized age. Born in Oakland, California in 1977 to a Japanese father and Swedish mother, he is fluent in several languages after spending time in France, Japan and Mexico City. His multi-award-winning short film *Victoria para chino* (2004) dealt with the tragedy of 19 illegal refugees who died in 2003 while trying to cross the Texas border in an overcrowded and overheated truck.
His interest in the theme of migration also led to his first feature film: *Sin Nombre* (2008/2009) gives a face to the tens of thousands of Central American refugees who undertake the dangerous journey to the USA every year. Fukunaga carried out extensive research in the southern Mexican state of Chiapas in the making of the film. It was filmed around Mexico City, slotting this international production easily into the ranks of the enormously successful New Mexican cinema. The movie – with Gael García Bernal as one of its producers – took the Sundance Festival by storm, winning awards for Best Direction and Best Cinematography. The simply narrated love story in *Sin Nombre* is, however, an early indication of Fukunaga's penchant for classic movie themes.
An American citizen living in New York, he has recently made a film version of the tragic story of governess *Jane Eyre* (2011) from the 1847 novel by Charlotte Brontë. The film has a stellar cast that includes Michael Fassbender, Judi Dench, Sally Hawkins and Mia Wasikowska.

THE MESSENGER

2008 – USA – 113 MIN. – DRAMA, WAR, ROMANCE
DIRECTOR OREN MOVERMAN (*1966)
SCREENPLAY ALESSANDRO CAMON, OREN MOVERMAN DIRECTOR OF PHOTOGRAPHY BOBBY BUKOWSKI
EDITING ALEXANDER HALL MUSIC NATHAN LARSON PRODUCTION MARK GORDON, LAWRENCE INGLEE, ZACH MILLER for OSCILLOSCOPE LABORATORIES, OMNILAB MEDIA.
STARRING BEN FOSTER (Staff Sergeant Will Montgomery), JENA MALONE (Kelly), WOODY HARRELSON (Captain Tony Stone), SAMANTHA MORTON (Olivia Pitterson), STEVE BUSCEMI (Dale Martin).
IFF BERLIN 2008 SILVER BEAR for BEST SCREENPLAY (Alessandro Camon, Oren Moverman) and PEACE FILM AWARD (Oren Moverman).

"We walk into these people's lives. We don't know shit."

The scene, a few moments before the end of the film: a soldier in uniform, an unprepossessing woman in jeans, restrained expressions, silence, children playing in the background beside a modest suburban house – "Will you give me your address? Can I write you a letter?" It doesn't really sound like famous last words, does it? But it is precisely the last question – apparently so mundane – that takes on a subtle resonance during the long, frozen and contemplative final shot. It is the end of a long road. Yet this end is a beginning: a rather quiet, modest and decent beginning, completely devoid of pretense. The film does not reveal where the road leads; instead, it indicates what must be done: "start from scratch." This is the motto, after all the pain the Iraq war has brought to these ordinary people. Staff Sergeant William Montgomery, played in an outstanding performance by Ben Foster, has survived by the skin of his teeth, but was wounded when he unwittingly dragged a badly injured colleague onto a mine, while trying to save his life.

Oren Moverman, a relatively unknown director till now, has made one of the most searching movies about the consequences of the Iraq War, and one that has also met with the highest critical acclaim. Its photography faithfully follows the tradition of recent war films, which dispense with the extravagant mise-en-scène of shocking images: war movies without war imagery, like *Jarhead* (2005). Yet seldom has it been as radical as in *The Messenger*. Though an anti-war film in the literal sense, it yet makes the ravages of war felt all the more deeply, by projecting onto the fallen soldiers' family members all the suffering that war entails.

Montgomery, who has come back from the fighting, and veteran Stone (Woody Harrelson) are representatives of a unit that informs families about the death of their sons, daughters, mothers, fathers, husbands and wives. The war with weapons "over there" reverberates on the home front; not just in the conflict faced by the messengers of death with their buried, unsaid and suppressed emotions and feelings, but also in the entirely natural reactions of those affected: screaming, weeping, despair and helplessness – just like the experiences of the wounded soldiers in the war. These reactions are shocking, not least in their immediacy. The film conveys this directness using simple but effective visual strategies. For instance, we see the darkened, half-shaded interiors where the two messengers of death live alone – as Stone says at one point i

is also a form of self-preservation from the demands of the job. Later Stone – the ostensibly hardened ex-soldier – breaks down in tears himself under the weight of the task. When they visit the family members in their simple homes, the images become fragile and brittle. They are filmed with a restless, hand-held camera, which itself seems burdened by the superhuman task, squirming around in the truly awful situations when the messengers meet the war victims at home.

The camera loses its composure in a visual sense, unlike Montgomery and Stone, who go to great lengths to preserve the correct protocol and proper behavior. They are soldiers turned social workers by necessity, mostly successful at what they do, but only at the expense of neglecting their own emotions. Montgomery listens to aggressive music, gets drunk, and takes medication

"A glorious moment: the performances of Ben Foster and Samantha Morton in *The Messenger*, as the Iraq war widow and the soldier who has to give her the sad news, take our breath away." *Neue Zürcher Zeitung*

4

1 Caught between dreadful memories and a glimmer of hope: Staff Sergeant Will Montgomery (Ben Foster) faces the bitter reality of the man who brings news of death.

2 Clinging resignedly to protocol as a way of coping with the daily battle on the home front.

3 Bewilderment in the silence of pain: a deathly calm after the storm.

4 Woody Harrelson brings fragile depth to the seemingly callous Captain Tony Stone.

to numb the pain. He can't get it on with women any more. Unlike Stone, who pretends to be a real womanizer, as a way of reassuring himself and carving out an identity he no longer has. The carefully crafted narrative follows the two men on their bitter mission, which also deals *en passant* with issues of sex and race, and the states of mind and living conditions of ordinary people who have lost their loved ones in this conflict.

Yet the film dispenses with emotionalism, even the pathos of mourning, so that all seems candid and true to life. Grief work is uncomfortable and dispiriting. At one point Dale Martin, the father of a dead soldier, appears from the shadows, asks forgiveness for his behavior and then silently disappears again. When they met before, he spat on Montgomery in the heat of the moment. Steve Buscemi needs only minimal gestures to bring a harrowingly profound sadness to this character. *The Messenger* has outstanding actors and dialogue, carried mainly by the film's great discovery, Ben Foster, and Woody Harrelson in impressive form. The characters they play will somehow manage to make it through; it's just how they do it that is left open in the film.

And just as the end is a beginning, the beginning also takes the form of an ending – a homecoming scenario: flowers, sex with his old girlfriend who has found someone else, dinner with her in a restaurant, talking about marriage and jobs – a last kiss – and that is where the homecoming grinds to a halt, without reintegration. Going back to a tolerable life requires other ways and means, as the end of the story tells us: minimalist and sublime. BR

WOODY HARRELSON Born Woodrow Tracy Harrelson in 1961, the actor came to fame as the naive bartender Woody Boyd in the TV sitcom *Cheers* (1982–1993). Harrelson had his first major role alongside Wesley Snipes in the basketball comedy *White Men Can't Jump* (1992).
He finally achieved international recognition with Oliver Stone's controversial drama about a couple of serial murderers, *Natural Born Killers* (1994), in which Harrelson plays cynical and violent Mickey Knox opposite Juliette Lewis as the other half of the ruthless duo. By the time he starred in Stone's film, Harrelson had made a very direct, muscular acting style his trademark. He received an Oscar nomination for Best Leading Actor for his role in the less controversial *The People vs. Larry Flint* (1996), the biopic about the founder and publisher of the male magazine "Hustler;" and for his portrayal of the traumatized ex-soldier in *The Messenger*, which won him numerous awards, Harrelson again received an Oscar nomination, for Best Supporting Actor.

STATE OF PLAY

2009 – USA / UK – 127 MIN. – POLITICAL THRILLER
DIRECTOR KEVIN MACDONALD (*1967)
SCREENPLAY MATTHEW MICHAEL CARNAHAN, TONY GILROY, BILLY RAY, from the mini-series of the same name by PAUL ABBOTT DIRECTOR OF PHOTOGRAPHY RODRIGO PRIETO
EDITING JUSTINE WRIGHT MUSIC ALEX HEFFES PRODUCTION TIM BEVAN, ERIC FELLNER, ANDREW HAUPTMAN for ANDELL ENTERTAINMENT, STUDIO CANAL, RELATIVITY MEDIA, WORKING TITLE FILMS, UNIVERSAL PICTURES.
STARRING RUSSELL CROWE (Cal McAffrey), BEN AFFLECK (Stephen Collins), RACHEL MCADAMS (Della Frye), HELEN MIRREN (Cameron Lynne), ROBIN WRIGHT PENN (Anne Collins), JASON BATEMAN (Dominic Foy), JEFF DANIELS (George Fergus), MICHAEL BERRESSE (Robert Bingham), HARRY LENNIX (Detective Donald Bell), VIOLA DAVIS (Dr. Judith Franklin).

"Do you have a pen?"

It will end with a story. Over a dozen rotary presses and conveyor belts take the freshly printed article into the hands of the delivery men; from there it will reach the newsstands and shake the world. Director Kevin Macdonald's wonderful final credits summarize his love of the newspaper medium in these expressive images and, with them, the spirit and purpose of his film. Newspapers have been produced like this for a hundred years. You can almost smell the printing ink. Anyone else would have *begun* his film with this seductive imagery. But Scottish-born Macdonald is serious about good old-fashioned journalism. The medium is not the message: in the beginning are the facts.

A drug addict is murdered and a pizza courier shot. Shortly afterward, a young woman falls in front of a subway train, and it turns out she is the assistant and lover of Congressman Stephen Collins (Ben Affleck). We are all familiar with conspiracy thrillers, so we know these events are connected. Collins asks his old friend Cal McAffrey (Russell Crowe), who happens to be an old-school investigative reporter, for help. When he hears the word "story," he instinctively reaches for his breast pocket, where his pen has lived for decades. While his rivals are busy writing the headlines, only to write disclaimers the next day, he is gathering facts. He drives a rusty Saab that never fails him, despite its neglected condition. Cal believes the real story is far bigger than everyone imagines.

His steely boss, Cameron Lynne (Helen Mirren), says the real story is the impending ruin of her paper. *The Washington Globe* has just been taken over by a media corporation with a name as lacking in charm as PointCorp, the evil concern behind it all. And this, in fact, is the real story: the demise of independent journalism, while the government's dark plans to transfer the high-value commodity of internal security to a private mercenary army are likewise dictated by a secret agenda. Everything really is interconnected, with even Cal becoming embroiled in the machinations of personal and political interest. As if that

1

1 Likeable relic of the 1970s: Cal (Russell Crowe), the man with the ballpoint pen, is an old-school investigative reporter.

2 Editor-in-chief Cameron Lynne (Helen Mirren) introduces draconian cuts. A businesswoman, she wants to sell headlines rather than win awards for journalism.

3 Collapse of a co-conspirator: sleazy PR man Dominic Foy (Jason Bateman) falls into Cal's trap and provides crucial information.

wasn't bad enough, he is forced to cooperate with the mortal enemy: Cameron assigns him a young blogger from the online editorial team to give him a hand with all his painstaking research. Della Frye (Rachel McAdams) is "cheap and hungry." The gruff, dyed-in-the-wool journalist and smart network operative embody the most diametrically opposed concepts of the same profession imaginable. She doesn't even own a pencil.

The truth about *State of Play* is that a medium often considered dead in the water has once again wielded its full strength. The British mini-series on which it is based, *State of Play* (2003), has all the advantages that TV can muster over the cinema: long periods of suspense filled with well developed characters and a formidable wealth of detail. Yet the film stands up well to its direct competition. Director Kevin Macdonald does not imitate, but instead heightens the tension in a brilliantly edited sequence of exciting moments, condensing a long report into a headline. This still leaves room for informative insights into everyday journalism. Piles of paper accumulate even on modern news desks, as seen in the impressive set design. It is a film that knows its

“*State of Play* is, at heart, a tribute to the virtues of old-fashioned newspaper reporting, but it embodies old-fashioned movie-making virtues, too.” *The Independent*

4 Enemy in my office: pushy online blogger Della Frye (Rachel McAdams) forces the pace of Cal's all-too-painstaking research.

5 Damaged goods: politician Stephen Collins (Ben Affleck) carries the hopes of his party, but is caught in a quagmire of lies and intrigue.

5

6 Checks and balances at the heart of power: even in Washington's official world, independent journalist Cal moves around pretty much as he likes.

KEVIN MACDONALD Born in Glasgow in 1967, Kevin Macdonald originally worked in the documentary sector of the industry. He began his career with biographical film essays about personalities as diverse as Charlie Chaplin, Howard Hawks, Mick Jagger and his famous grandfather, the director and screenwriter Emeric Pressburger. Early in his career he won an Oscar, jointly with producer Arthur Cohn, for *One Day in September* (1999), a documentary about the terrorist attack on the 1972 Olympic Games in Munich. Even more sensational was *Touching the Void* (2003): the re-enacted scenes of a disastrous mountaineering expedition in 1985 made Macdonald a leading exponent of the now popular genre of docufiction.

He also picked a real-life subject for his first feature film proper: *The Last King of Scotland* (2006) shows the Ugandan dictator Idi Amin through the eyes of his Scottish physician. Forest Whitaker won an Oscar for his terrifying incarnation of the psychopathic butcher with a lust for life, while Macdonald, his writers and producers shared the BAFTA for Best British Film. The conspiracy thriller *State of Play* (2009) was well received even by British critics, who were naturally skeptical about the American remake of a British TV series. In 2010 he wrapped *The Eagle*, a sword-and-sandals movie about the disappearance of a Roman legion in the wild expanses of the Scottish highlands.

7 Even Cameron begins to worry about Cal. English actress Helen Mirren has a star role as the Iron Lady in this all-American remake of a British TV series.

8 Cal's friendship with the politician leads to a clash of personal and political interests. At the same time, Stephen's role in the scandal is far more extensive than he is prepared to admit.

9 Declaration of love for the newspaper business: paper remains piled high in the movie's impressive set design. But the advance of computerization is inexorable.

trade as well as the city in which it is set. Washington's day-to-day life has seldom been presented as realistically as here, where Cal pursues his research on one street corner and orders a greasy chili burger on another. Journalists have to eat, too – a thought we should always bear in mind.

Russell Crowe, as a long-haired, thoughtful guy who has put on a few pounds over the years, plays this dinosaur with quiet intensity. Cal is how we might imagine those amiable eccentrics who went to ground on the internet after the great age of investigative journalism. But he is still there. *State of Play* brings the 1970s conspiracy thriller into the present day, confirming its current relevance in the process. The clean, astute and even humorous mise-en-scène – devoid of technical gimmickry and superfluous sub-plots – may seem nostalgic, but then so too does the belief in the press as the indispensable fourth estate. The editorial team releases the story with a click of the mouse. Cinema is also evolving, but Macdonald sticks unshakeably to fundamental principles with his "requiem to the newspaper." PB

UP

2009 – USA – 96 MIN. – ANIMATION, ADVENTURE MOVIE
DIRECTOR PETE DOCTER (*1968)
SCREENPLAY BOB PETERSON, PETE DOCTER, from a story by THOMAS MCCARTHY, BOB PETERSON and PETE DOCTER EDITING KEVIN NOLTING MUSIC MICHAEL GIACCHINO
PRODUCTION JONAS RIVERA for PIXAR ANIMATION STUDIOS, WALT DISNEY PICTURES.
VOICES EDWARD ASNER (Carl Fredricksen), CHRISTOPHER PLUMMER (Charles Muntz), JORDAN NAGAI (Russell), BOB PETERSON (Dug/Alpha), DELROY LINDO (Beta), JEROME RANFT (Gamma), JOHN RATZENBERGER (Construction Foreman Tom), DAVID KAYE (Newsreel Announcer), ELIE DOCTER (Young Ellie), JEREMY LEARY (Young Carl).
ACADEMY AWARDS 2010 OSCARS for BEST ANIMATED FEATURE FILM (Pete Docter), and BEST MUSIC, Original Score (Michael Giacchino).

"Tell your boss he can have my house ... When I'm dead!"

Carl Fredricksen's face is made for the big screen. With his squat, square head and permanently miserable expression, he is just the man for large-format film projection – but also the kind of "grumpy old man" little seen in movies nowadays. Yet Carl, voiced with superb peevishness by veteran American TV actor Edward Asner, was not always like this. In a touching, silent sequence at the beginning, *Up* runs through the years of an entire life: while still a young man, Carl woos the love of his life, Ellie, marries her and experiences a life filled with happiness, but their big dreams are finally shattered by illness and death. Well into their retirement, Carl and Ellie have shared a common love of exploration, with plans to travel to South America, but the millstones of life have always thwarted them: moving into their dream house, a leaky roof, a car repair ... It is an emotive montage of existence and its transitory nature, in a style made familiar to us by the silent movie masters. Director Pete Docter has also introduced his young audience to a main character armed with just a walking stick and hearing aid. You'll be old yourselves some day, kids, is the message! But it's not necessarily the end.

For this generation-bridging spectacle has yet to begin. When Carl is due to be shunted off into a "retirement home," he takes off: lifted high into the sky by thousands of brightly colored balloons, his cozy little house makes a beeline for South America. This old man wants to live again! His strange airship has an unintentional stowaway, however: a chubby and awkward little Scout called Russell (Jordan Nagai), who has plenty of time for chocolate and old folks and will be Carl's companion on the envisaged journey to Paradise Falls.

What awaits the adventurers proves once more the Pixar team's boundless creativity: a Venezuelan jungle beneath a misty high plateau; a crazy ostrich called Kevin, in colors brighter than Carl's balloons; a pack of trained dogs that are unable to talk (unlike those in rival animations) but instead convey their thoughts to humans via a microphone on their collars; and an unexpected adversary, whom Carl knows from the old days of cinema. References to film history give the movie added theatrical value, but the supremely original basic idea of the flying house stands easily on its own merits. In saying that, for long periods in the film it is just excess baggage, as Carl is forced to pull his home through the jungle by the garden hose, in the same way that the eponymous hero drags his opera-houseboat in Werner Herzog's *Fitzcarraldo* (1978–1981). It has yet to make its big entrance, just like pesky Russell, whom the grumpy old man actually grows fond of through all their trials and tribulations.

Up was the first animation film (and the first 3-D movie) to have the privilege of opening the Cannes Film Festival in 2009. By then, the financial ventures of Wall Street had long since seen the share price of Disney, Pixar's parent company, tumble: who on earth would want to see a movie about an old man? As it turned out, *Up* effortlessly surpassed the success of the equally quirky pioneering movies *Ratatouille* (2007) and *WALL•E* (2008), exceeding their box-office returns in the

Municiberg Herald

EDWARD ASNER With no fewer than seven Emmy Awards and five Golden Globes, Edward Asner is one of the most outstanding and, above all, best loved personalities of US television. This 80-year-old character actor was made for the voice part of grumpy and stubborn Carl Fredricksen in *Up* (2009). Everyone knows his real face from his role as a TV news director in the *Mary Tyler Moore Show* (1970–1977), which spawned a spin-off series *Lou Grant* (1977–1982) tailor-made especially for him. As Lou Grant, he played the permanently bad-tempered boss who is always clashing with his female manager. He also became well-known through appearances in the outstanding miniseries *Rich Man, Poor Man* (1975–1976) and *Roots* (1977).

Born in Kansas City in 1929, Asner's political commitment has left him little time to undertake big screen roles, although he has appeared in movies such as Oliver Stone's conspiracy thriller *JFK* (1991) as well as a number of Christmas movies, including *Elf* (2003). He was not only heavily involved in a strike in 1980 by the Screen Actor's Guild (the presidency of which he then assumed for a four-year period), he fought for years as a human rights activist against racism, the death penalty and war, as well as for stricter gun laws. As far back as 1982, a dispute with gun fanatic Charlton Heston reputedly led to Lou Grant being dropped. In 2002, Edward Asner followed in the footsteps of colleagues including Elizabeth Taylor, Kirk Douglas and Sidney Poitier in receiving a Life Achievement Award from the Screen Actors Guild.

US market as well as abroad. The ongoing success of Pixar's original and witty stories (which are made to appeal to adults as well as children) must certainly give the industry food for thought in the foreseeable future.

Yet again, the use of 3-D technology shows how little the team around producer John Lasseter is guided by preconceived models. Could Carl's huge square glasses be their way of caricaturing Hollywood's latest attempt to gain advantage over its media competitors? The 3-D effect in some daredevil flying sequences is not to be missed but, like everything else in *Up*, is secondary to the plot, which leaps from treetop to treetop, speeding along from one high point to the next. The message is this: if you free yourself from life's baggage, you will rise to the top. *Up*, however, is one of the few memories it is safe to retain. PB

1 Flying high! Pixar's unusual animation masterpiece soared effortlessly above competitors.

2 Generation-spanning spectacle in 3-D: with his square head, grumpy old Carl Fredricksen (voiced by Edward Asner) won over even younger viewers.

3 Pixar has never been interested in given forms – bird of paradise Kevin is the most colorful example.

4 The old man and the boy: together with anxious lad Russell (voiced by Jordan Nagai), Carl rises above it all again in his old age.

"The greater the adventure, the more the images acquire depth. And Carl's grumpy old man's face would certainly be less effective without 3D." *die tageszeitung*

A PROPHET
UN PROPHÈTE

2009 – FRANCE / ITALY – 150 MIN. – PRISON DRAMA, GANGSTER MOVIE
DIRECTOR JACQUES AUDIARD (*1952)
SCREENPLAY THOMAS BIDEGAIN, JACQUES AUDIARD, ABDEL RAOUF DAFRI, NICOLAS PEUFAILLIT DIRECTOR OF PHOTOGRAPHY STÉPHANE FONTAINE EDITING JULIETTE WELFLING MUSIC ALEXANDRE DESPLAT PRODUCTION LAURANNE BOURRACHOT, MARTINE CASSINELLI, MARCO CHERQUI for WHY NOT PRODUCTIONS, CHIC FILMS, PAGE 114, FRANCE 2 CINÉMA, UGC, CELLULOID DREAMS, BIM DISTRIBUZIONE.
STARRING TAHAR RAHIM (Malik El Djebena), NIELS ARESTRUP (César Luciani), ADEL BENCHERIF (Ryad), HICHEM YACOUBI (Reyeb), REDA KATEB (Jordi), SLIMANE DAZI (Lattrache), JEAN-PHILIPPE RICCI (Vettori), GILLES COHEN (Prof).

Jordi: "What will you do outside?"
Malik: "I don't know. What about you?"
Jordi: "The same as here, only bigger."

Even before we see the first image, we know that this is a prison movie. The soundtrack gives us the metallic echo of iron bars and rattling bowls, mixed with the voices of criminals and law enforcers. This far from life-affirming environment is characterized by coarse conversation. Details begin to filter through the darkness, slowly at first: cuffed hands appear, then the anxious face of a young man. Malik (Tahar Rahim) is only just of legal age, but his past seems as alien to him as it does to the viewer. He has no one on the outside, and doesn't know anyone inside: illiterate, he has no training, religion or cultural roots. His life is actually just beginning, in prison. He has been sentenced to six years, though we never really find out why.

Corsicans call the shots inside the prison walls. Their leader is César Luciani (Niels Arestrup), who has several corrupt warders in his pocket. He sees the Arab prisoners, whom he refers to in derogatory terms as "the beards," as the enemy. Malik finds himself once again caught in the middle; the first lesson he learns is: kill or be killed. The Corsicans force him to murder the Arab Reyeb (Hichem Yacoubi), who is about to testify as a key witness in a trial. His death does in fact ensure César's trust and protection, but the deed haunts Malik from that point on. The dead man's spirit becomes his constant companion. Malik's rise is rapid and steep, until he ends up as César's eyes and ears. This "career" is narrated episodically, with the occasional subtitle

1

1 Tahar Rahim won two French César awards for his role as Malik El Djebena: Best Actor and Most Promising Actor.

2 For Malik, there is little difference between prison and freedom. At a routine airport check, he automatically opens his arms wide, from his experience of prison inspections.

3 The symbiotic relationship between Malik and César (Niels Arestrup) is changing. Malik learns to stand on his own feet, gradually cutting the cords with his foster father.

interspersed to mark his progress and name the important people he meets en route, both friends and foes. *A Prophet* transposes the *Bildungsroman* principle to an unusual setting. Malik learns to read and write only once he is in prison; he also teaches himself Corsican to add to his mother tongues, Arabic and French, and acquires the basic business skills to allow him to manage his drug deals more effectively. Malik's assimilation opens more and more doors to him, inside the prison walls to start with and later on outside them as well.

Unlike classic prison movies, with Audiard it is most definitely not about a break-out or revolt behind bars. Malik does his time patiently, goes along with things, and winds up with a TV, fridge and the services of prostitutes. Besides, any clear boundary between inside and outside is dissolved by visits, cell phones and day passes. Where you conduct your business is immaterial. Prison is not portrayed as an institution for punishment and reform, but as an environment where contacts can be made and education pursued; it can even act as a springboard for a criminal career.

“*A Prophet* allows us to watch the way power arises and then crumbles again, creating new victims, perpetrators and silent sufferers in the process. The most disturbing thing about it is that, somewhere along the way to Malik becoming top dog in the joint, we become his accomplices.” *Zeit-online*

Jacques Audiard Jacques Audiard was born in Paris in 1952, the son of the famous French screenwriter Michel Audiard (1920–1985), with whom he had an uneasy relationship. He said his father always saw film work as just a job; however, he always regretted that he had no real passion for cinema. This personal story also left its mark on Jacques Audiard's own screenplays. Thus in both *The Beat That My Heart Skipped* (*De battre mon cœur s'est arrête*, 2005) and *A Prophet* (*Un Prophète*, 2009) the main character is a young rebel who has to stand up to an omnipotent father figure (played by Niels Arestrup in both films) but wins through in the end.

At first, Audiard had no intention of following in his father's footsteps. Instead, he studied literature and philosophy at the Sorbonne in Paris with the aim of becoming a teacher. Through an internship as a film editor, however, he ended up in the movies, working, among other things, as an assistant editor on Roman Polanski's *The Tenant* (*Le locataire*, 1976). A few years later Audiard also collaborated with his father, co-writing his first screenplay for the psychological thriller *Deadly Circuit* (*Mortelle randonnée*, 1983). Once he had established himself as a screenwriter, he made his directorial debut with *See How They Fall* (*Regarde les hommes tomber*, 1994), in which a sales rep sets out to solve the murder of a policeman friend. He received the award for Best Screenplay at Cannes for *A Self-Made Hero* (*Un héros très discret*, 1996), jointly with Alain Le Henry; then, with *Read My Lips* (*Sur mes lèvres*, 2001), Audiard turned his attention once more to the gangster genre. Vincent Cassel plays an ex-con who does a number on his enemies with the help of a secretary with a hearing impairment. On the basis of his genre movies, as dark as they are realistic, Jacques Audiard is often regarded as the successor of French thriller maestros such as Jean-Pierre Melville (1917–1973) and Henri-Georges Clouzot (1907–1977).

New Hollywood cinema has been just as significant an influence on his directorial style: his *The Beat That My Heart Skipped* is a loose remake of James Toback's *Fingers* (1978). His five feature films to date have brought Audiard countless French film awards, making him one of the most important French directors today.

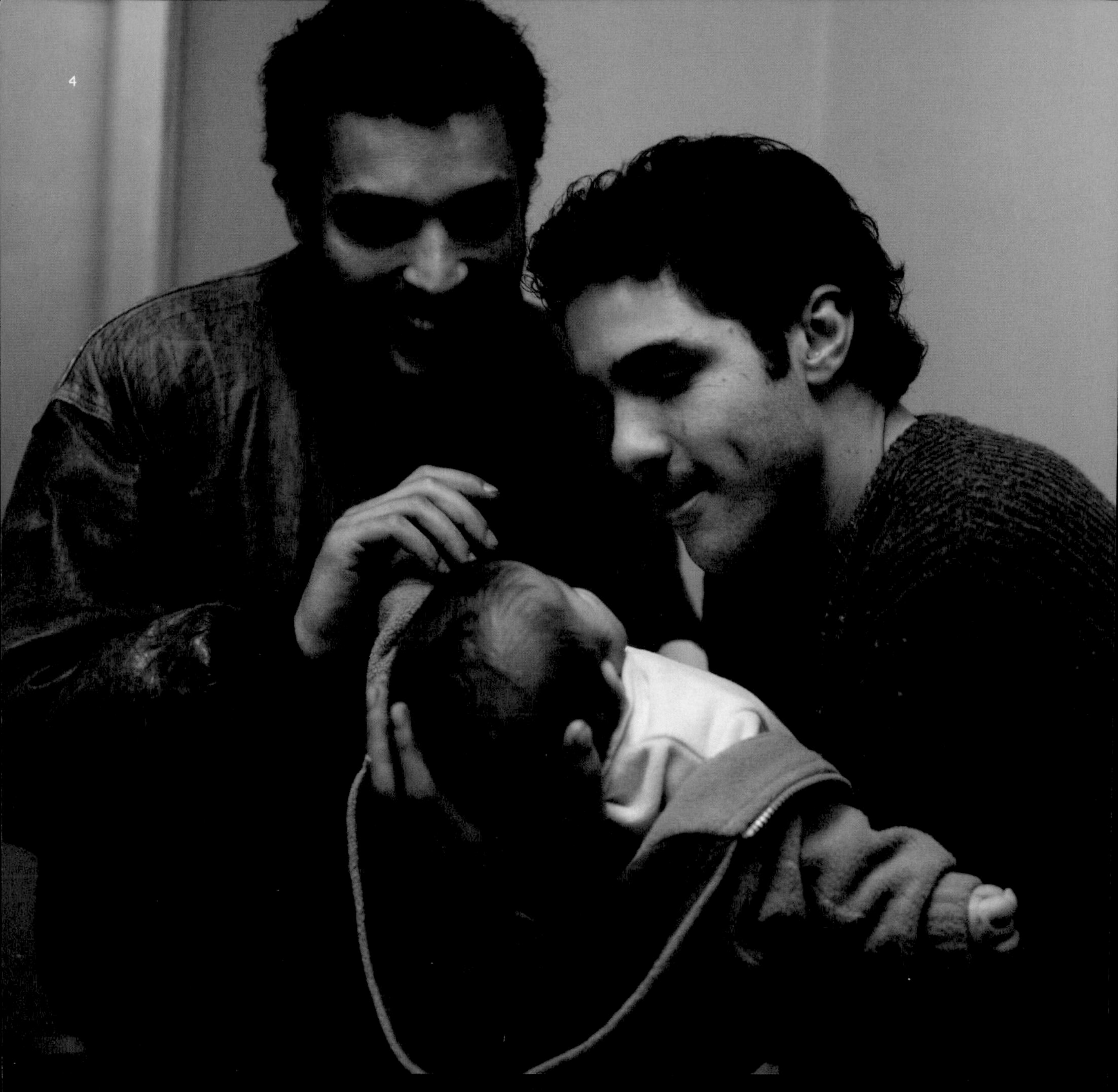

The remarkable thing about this film, however, is the extent to which we as viewers empathize with Malik: we admire this self-made hero without begrudging him what he has built up for himself. When Malik's drug deals are filmed in a montage of time-lapse and fast cuts to a rap and rock soundtrack, we are understandably reminded of the film language in Danny Boyle's *Trainspotting* (1996) in which heroin addiction is portrayed as a lifestyle that is as normal as incarceration in *A Prophet*.

The film's title can be understood initially in its original sense: in ancient Greek, it means "emissary" or "spokesman," an apt description of Malik's services for the Corsicans. Malik only gradually develops prophetic abilities when he uses his knowledge about fellow felons to predict their actions, exploiting it for his own ends. Similarly, he is also able to anticipate the shift in power relations. Audiard deliberately changed the title of the original screenplay "The Prophet," which could easily be seen to reference Muhammad, to the weaker version with the indefinite article. For Malik is just one prophet among many; whether he is a true or false one remains open to question. By the end he has built up his own disciples, who follow him around faithfully in a kind of motorcade. When Malik is released and goes out into the world, the soundtrack to this final scene is, significantly enough, an English version of the "Mack the Knife" song. The little fish thrown into the shark pool has become a predator himself; and he is smart as well, for he knows when to hide his razor-sharp teeth. CZ

4 Ryad (Adel Bencherif) doesn't have it easy after his release. Malik agrees to be godfather to his son, Issam.

5 *A Prophet* can also be seen as a swansong to the traditional mobster. Helpless and embittered, César is forced to accept the new power relations.

6 His own business brings Malik into contact with drug dealer Jordi (Reda Kateb), a gypsy who is as free from family ties as he is.

7 Peaceful moments. When out on parole, Malik dreams of a better world. He falls into a blissful sleep with his godson in his arms.

“The 155-minute running time may suggest excess and periods when nothing happens; but *A Prophet* is told with a high degree of concentration.” *Spex*

6

7

INGLOURIOUS BASTERDS

2009 – USA / GERMANY – 153 MIN. – WAR MOVIE
DIRECTOR QUENTIN TARANTINO (*1963)
SCREENPLAY QUENTIN TARANTINO DIRECTOR OF PHOTOGRAPHY ROBERT RICHARDSON
EDITING SALLY MENKE PRODUCTION LAWRENCE BENDER for THE WEINSTEIN COMPANY, A BAND APART, STUDIO BABELSBERG GMBH, UNIVERSAL PICTURES.
STARRING BRAD PITT (Lt. Aldo Raine), MÉLANIE LAURENT (Shosanna Dreyfus), CHRISTOPH WALTZ (Col. Hans Landa), ELI ROTH (Sgt. Donny Donowitz), SAMM LEVINE (Gerold Hirschberg), MICHAEL FASSBENDER (Lt. Archie Hicox), DIANE KRUGER (Bridget von Hammersmark), DANIEL BRÜHL (Pvt. Fredrick Zoller), AUGUST DIEHL (Major Dieter Hellstrom), TIL SCHWEIGER (Sgt. Hugo Stiglitz), DENIS MENOCHET (Perrier LaPadite), SYLVESTER GROTH (Joseph Goebbels), MARTIN WUTTKE (Adolf Hitler), ROD TAYLOR (Winston Churchill), SAMM LEVINE (Gerold Hirschberg).
ACADEMY AWARDS 2010 OSCAR for BEST SUPPORTING ACTOR (Christoph Waltz).
IFF CANNES 2009 SILVER PALM for BEST ACTOR (Christoph Waltz).

"We're in the Nazi-killing business."

In the movies, as in real life, those acting in the name of the Third Reich have got off too lightly. Nazis in films have died as honorable opponents, naive enforcers or, at most, repulsive baddies on the battlefield – they have been spared the fate they deserved. In *Downfall* (*Der Untergang*, 2004) Adolf Hitler takes his own life off-screen in a quiet and dignified manner. In *Inglourious Basterds*, Quentin Tarantino takes a baseball bat to this injustice, rewriting history while staying within the boundaries of cinematic reality. In fact, it is hard to say whether he was ever seriously concerned about National Socialism at all. The opening title immediately defines the crazy story as a fairy tale: "Once upon a time in Nazi-occupied France ..."

The infamous Basterds, a Jewish-American special unit led by Lt. Aldo Raine (Brad Pitt), have the most extreme (yet at the same time least convincing) scenes in this overlong, half-baked and yet brilliant bastard of a film. They hunt down Nazis behind enemy lines. This means they smash their heads with baseball bats, scalp the corpses and, on one occasion, brand a survivor by carving a swastika on his forehead. This they do without any kind of analysis. The Basterds are the loose cannons of a Jewish revenge fantasy; cartoon cut-outs without any visible connection to anything as terribly real as the Holocaust. Their role models are the dubious heroes of Italian B-movies such as Enzo G. Castellari's *Quel maledetto treno blindato* (1977/78) – its international distribution title is *The Inglorious Bastards* – and dozens of war movies like *The Dirty Dozen* (1967).

The only world Tarantino knows is that of film, but he inhabits it like no-one else. The terrific introductory sequence smacks of a Sergio Leone

1

2

“Detractors and proponents alike will see what they want to see in this two-and-a-half-hour World War II fable, which hits all the beats of a retribution-laden genre piece without ever entirely satiating character or audience bloodlust.”

Time Out New York

1 Elegant butcher: Christoph Waltz won the Oscar for his role as fiendish "Jew hunter" Hans Landa.

2 Loose cannons of revenge: Inglourious Basterds Hirschberg, Stiglitz and Donowitz (Samm Levine, Til Schweiger and Eli Roth) hunt the Nazis.

3 Farmer LaPadite (Denis Menochet) has been hiding Jews. SS Officer Landa knows this – and savors every moment of the interrogation.

4 Who are these Basterds?! Leading Nazis – including Adolf Hitler (Martin Wuttke) – get their just deserts in the movie.

5 See Paris and die: decent German soldier Fredrick Zoller (Daniel Brühl) has fallen in love with a French woman.

spaghetti western. "Jew Hunter" Hans Landa (Christoph Waltz) approaches from the far horizon. A French farmer (Denis Menochet) has been hiding Jews. SS Officer Landa knows this, and savors every minute of the torturous interrogation. He is a man who brutalizes his victims with well-chosen words until they capitulate. The movie's true qualities lie in these kinds of dialogic sequences, in which Tarantino once again proves himself master of the spoken word. Not only does he convey the bloody activities of "Naziploitation" but also, and equally, the classic melodrama, the Ernst Lubitsch-style of comedy and, as becomes evident in extensive quotations, the wider canon of German and French film history as well. The only person to survive the inevitable massacre is a Jewish girl, Shosanna (Mélanie Laurent). Not long afterward, she is running a cinema in Paris, showing films by G.W. Pabst and Henri-Georges Clouzot. It

6 The elegant world of art in gloom: like cinema owner Shosanna (Mélanie Laurent), many of the protagonists work in the film industry.

7 Jewish avenger with a southern drawl: Lt. Aldo Raine (Brad Pitt) pulls out all the stops.

8 Jolly game of "guess the famous person:" Tarantino's knowledge of ancient German customs and traditions is remarkable.

9 Playing with fire: Shosanna brings a premature end to World War 2 with an unprecedented inferno – thus taking her own revenge.

"Quentin Tarantino's *Inglourious Basterds* is a big, bold, audacious war movie that will annoy some, startle others and demonstrate once again that he's the real thing, a director of quixotic delights." *Chicago Sun-Times*

is a gloomily elegant, artistic world with echoes of Edward Hopper paintings and François Truffaut's *The Last Metro* (*Le dernier métro*, 1980) – a film that Tarantino does not even like. In this cinema – where else? – the threads of the plot, divided into chapters, are brought together: practically the entire German leadership, including Hitler, Goebbels and Bormann, are expected to attend the premiere of a new propaganda film. The Basterds know about it, while Shosanna is also planning to exploit this unique, historical moment. An unprecedented inferno is meant to bring an early end to World War 2, acting as the harbinger of her revenge. The Nazis deserve it, and a stock of nitrate film will burn three times faster than paper. A British film critic slips into Nazi uniform and becomes a spy; a German actress collaborates with the enemy; Lieutenant Raine swaps his southern drawl for Italian, failing as dismally as the elegant butcher Landa is spectacular as the cosmopolitan who speaks four languages. *Inglourious Basterds* is a subtitled farce at the highest linguistic level, devoid of any moral depth, breathtaking in detail and unsustainable as an overall concept – a real Tarantino movie. It is an assault on good taste and at the same time, an intellectual risk we would not have imagined the erstwhile wunderkind taking. Without Christoph Waltz (who won Oscar for Best Supporting Actor for his mad portrayal of Landa) the whole edifice would have probably collapsed like Shosanna's cinema. As it is, the quarter-pounder with cheese has become strudel – and *Inglourious Basterds* his best movie since *Pulp Fiction* (1994). PE

HARVEY AND BOB WEINSTEIN Without the creative and commercial input of brothers Harvey and Bob Weinstein, Hollywood as it is today would be inconceivable. Names like Quentin Tarantino, Peter Greenaway, Steven Soderbergh and Martin Scorsese are intertwined with this powerful production team. For decades their company Miramax – founded in 1979 and named after their parents Miriam and Max – has virtually single-handedly occupied the unexpectedly profitable niche between independent and mainstream cinema.

Born in New York in 1952 and 1954 respectively, Harvey and his younger brother Bob proved their Midas touch after a slow start with the distribution of sometimes controversial art house films such as *Sex, Lies and Videotape* (1989) and *The Crying Game* (1992). They achieved legendary status with the global success of Tarantino's *Pulp Fiction* (1994). In the interim they mainly acted (as was mostly the case later on) as executive producers. Their biggest hits include *The English Patient* (1996), *Good Will Hunting* (1997), *Shakespeare in Love* (1998), *Chicago* (2002) and *The Aviator* (2004). Harvey in particular (notorious for his often gruff manner) has the reputation of an old-style studio head: a friend to his directors and actors on the one hand, while being a creative nightmare on the other.

"Harvey Scissorhands" made Martin Scorsese's life difficult with his editing specifications for *Gangs of New York* (2002), though it was all the better for it – the film received ten Oscar nominations. In 2005, the political stance of Michael Moore's documentary *Fahrenheit 9/11* (2004) caused a split with the conservative parent company, Disney; the Weinsteins left Miramax and founded The Weinstein Company.

The financial crisis, and presumably dwindling involvement on the brothers' part, soon led however to a struggle for survival. Until the phenomenal success of *Inglourious Basterds* (2009), a quarter of the 70 films produced by the Weinsteins grossed under a million dollars. If nothing else, their own business model caught up with them: following their example, every reasonable size Hollywood studio now has its own art house subsidiary.

THE WHITE RIBBON
DAS WEISSE BAND

2009 – GERMANY / AUSTRIA / FRANCE / ITALY – 145 MIN. – DRAMA, HISTORICAL MOVIE
DIRECTOR MICHAEL HANEKE (*1942)
SCREENPLAY MICHAEL HANEKE DIRECTOR OF PHOTOGRAPHY CHRISTIAN BERGER EDITING MONIKA WILLI
PRODUCTION STEFAN ARNDT, VEIT HEIDUSCHKA, MICHAEL KATZ, MARGARET MÉNÉGOZ, ANDREA OCCHIPINTI for X FILME CREATIVE POOL GMBH, WEGA FILM, LES FILMS DU LOSANGE, LUCKY RED.
STARRING CHRISTIAN FRIEDEL (The School Teacher), BURGHART KLAUSSNER (The Pastor), ULRICH TUKUR (The Baron), RAINER BOCK (The Doctor), JOSEF BIERBICHLER (The Steward), LEONIE BENESCH (Eva), SUSANNE LOTHAR (The Midwife), URSINA LARDI (Marie-Luise, the Baroness), BIRGIT MINICHMAYR (Frieda), DETLEV BUCK (Eva's Father), ERNST JACOBI (Narrator).
IFF CANNES 2009 GOLDEN PALM (Michael Haneke).

"I get the feeling you are hiding something from me."

Eichwald – a village in the Protestant north of Germany, a year before the outbreak of World War One. At first glance, everything seems to be the way it always was, and people's lives follow the same predefined paths as they have since time immemorial. The old hierarchies survive undiminished: the landowner (Ulrich Tukur) autocratically determines the fate of the village, while the strict pastor (Burghart Klaußner) urges the inhabitants to be industrious, humble and well behaved. The only brief excitement occurs when the village doctor is thrown from his horse by a wire. It was just an accident – or was it?

For these sinister events become more frequent: a farmer's wife dies in an accident at work; the baron's young son is abused; and one night a barn is burned down. Then the midwife's disabled child disappears and is found the next day battered in the woods. No one seems to have any idea as to who is behind these incidents. The young teacher (Christian Friedel) is the only one who harbors a monstrous suspicion: could it be the village children who are responsible for these deeds? *The White Ribbon* is a film of glacial beauty; a cross-section of an apparently idyllic microcosm, filmed with a searing precision that gradually exposes horrific goings-on beneath the surface. The camera captures the carefully reconstructed historical setting in razor-sharp black-and-white images, showing people who seem to be taken straight from early 20th-century photographs: physiognomies shaped by ancient rural life; faces that tell stories. It goes without saying that these stories are also deeply disturbing in a film by Michael Haneke, the director of such controversial masterpieces as *Hidden* (*Caché*, 2005) and *Funny Games* (1997).

If the story were taken at face value, it could be read as a crime drama in some distant, self-contained past. But the narrator who introduces the plot makes a connection to the present day from the start: it is the voice of the

1 The girls walking so peacefully along the village street in this image belong to the generation that would support the Nazi terror state two decades later. Michael Haneke's film dips, in a sense, into the kindergarten of German fascism.

2 In its strict symmetry, the image of the gathered community is reminiscent of a military formation. *The White Ribbon* shows the church as a pillar of the old authoritarian order.

3 Haneke shows a whole range of paternal violence: while the pastor (Burghart Klaußner) torments his children with torturous educational measures "for their own good"…

former village schoolteacher, who conveys his memories to us because he believes they could be useful for a better understanding of what subsequently happened in Germany. It is a vague formulation that gives room for conjecture; in his "children's story" Haneke focuses on the prehistory of National Socialism, i.e. on the childhood years of later fascists. To begin with, it is not actually the puzzling "accidents" that give Haneke's film such an oppressive atmosphere. It is the family relationships, which are marked by a chilly absence of joy and, above all, the ubiquitous, everyday paternal violence. Whether farmer, pastor, doctor or landowner, these patriarchs block their children's individual development with a level of strictness that reveals just how much the subtle social transformation has already undermined their authority. In saying that, the beatings administered by the peasant farmer to his son seem almost harmless compared to the

4 … the village doctor (Rainer Bock) abuses his daughter at night.

5 A symbolic image: the pastor's youngest son gives his father a present of the sparrow he has raised himself – in a cage.

6 Eva, the nanny who is barely an adult herself, is one of the few positive characters in the film. Significantly, she is an "outsider."

7 The scenes in which the young schoolteacher (Christian Friedel) reveals his love for Eva (Leonie Benesch) are the antithesis of the cold, joyless atmosphere in the village.

"This film is the greatest, the most immense and beautiful thing that has happened in German cinema in a long time; it is a thrilling detective story, an analytical look at society, and a horrific psychological study rolled into one." *Berliner Zeitung*

perfidious educational methods of the "caring" pastor, who punishes his offspring with a stick "for their own good," ties his pubescent son to his bed at night and even marks his children with a white armband, so that their wickedness is always visible to them.

The Austrian director unflinchingly records these cruel family scenes in a pointedly matter-of-fact way, making them appear all the more distressing through dispensing with any form of soundtrack. Against the background of this oppressive atmosphere, the mysterious "accidents" seem increasingly like the logical consequence of the unbearable relationships; compensatory acts carried out by perpetrators who resort to terrorist tactics instead of open rebellion. Whether it is actually the children who are committing the crimes remains an unanswered question. Haneke does, however, create incredibly

8 Marked out: the purpose of the white armband is to remind the pubescent pastor's son of his sinfulness.

9 The children are particularly haunting, their faces a harrowing reflection of the violence they have suffered.

BURGHART KLAUSSNER He is the most distinctive actor playing paternal roles in recent German cinema: born in 1949 in Berlin, Burghart Klaußner had his first screen debut in 1983 after a successful 10 year career on stage. Although Klaußner appeared in countless German film and TV productions in the 1980s and 90s, including Hans-Christian Schmid's *23* (1998) and *Crazy* (2000), it took almost two decades for him to attract the attention of an international audience playing the father who escaped to the West in Wolfgang Becker's reunification comedy *Good Bye Lenin!* (2002). Following on from this, he gave an inspired performance in Hans Weingartner's *The Edukators* (*Die fetten Jahre sind vorbei*, 2004) as the industrialist kidnapped by young urban revolutionaries – a role that won him the German Film Award for best supporting actor.
His melancholic performance as a presumed pedophile in *Der Mann von der Botschaft* (2006; directed by Dito Tsintsadze), one of his few lead roles, won Klaußner the Silver Leopard at the Locarno International Film Festival. His outstanding portrayal of a devout father in Hans-Christian Schmid's exorcism drama *Requiem* (2005/2006) was good enough to put him in competition in the Berlinale, and equally in the years that followed with *Yella* (2006/2007; directed by Christian Petzold) and *The Reader* (2008; directed by Stephen Daldry). Most recently Klaußner (who has a career as a singer as well as in acting) was in excellent form as the strict pastor in Michael Haneke's acclaimed masterpiece originally entitled *Das weiße Band – Eine deutsche Kindergeschichte* (*The White Ribbon – A German Children's Story*, 2009).

11

10 The children's frustration vents itself in an eruption of violence that also suggests a social element: the baron's son is thrown into the lake for no good reason.

11 Haneke never fails to find disturbing images for the adolescents' potential for violence – like the peasant's son who "shaves" the baron's cabbage field, beside himself with rage …

12 … or even the barn burning at night, almost like a beacon. The First World War comes shortly afterward in the film – and, along with it, the beginning of the end of the old order.

"At the end, we are left not so much moved as anxious. We certainly want to reflect further on this extraordinary film. But, before that, we feel like breathing in the air that is lacking in its imagery." *Frankfurter Rundschau*

powerful images of the adolescents' potential for violence, such as when the pastor's daughter arranges a canary crucified with scissors on her father's writing desk like a macabre still life.

Yet *The White Ribbon* owes its extraordinary intensity not only to such horrifying images but above all to its outstanding cast, which brings together the best actors that German-language cinema has presently to offer. Another potent factor is the facial expressions of the unknown young actors that are indelibly imprinted in our minds: the faces of the humiliated and maltreated children. The disturbing realization that they could go on some day to become war criminals or concentration camp guards renders Haneke's film a haunting cinematic experience. JH

12

THE HANGOVER

2009 – USA – 100 MIN. – COMEDY
DIRECTOR TODD PHILLIPS (*1970)
SCREENPLAY JON LUCAS, SCOTT MOORE DIRECTOR OF PHOTOGRAPHY LAWRENCE SHER
EDITING DEBRA NEIL-FISHER MUSIC CHRISTOPHE BECK PRODUCTION DANIEL GOLDBERG, TODD PHILLIPS for GREEN HAT FILMS, LEGENDARY PICTURES, WARNER BROS.
STARRING BRADLEY COOPER (Phil Wenneck), ED HELMS (Stu Price), ZACH GALIFIANAKIS (Alan Garner), JUSTIN BARTHA (Doug Billings), HEATHER GRAHAM (Jade), SASHA BARRESE (Tracy Garner), JEFFREY TAMBOR (Sid Garner), KEN JEONG (Mr. Chow), RACHAEL HARRIS (Melissa), MIKE TYSON (as himself).

"Some guys just can't handle Vegas."

We only see moving images of that disastrous night on a surveillance camera – which, incidentally, belongs to Mike Tyson. Nothing less than criminally liable, the shots in question comprise: mindless drunkenness, urinating in a former boxing champion's pool, and kidnapping a big cat. By this late stage, far worse things have already come to light, but the fuzzy quality of the grainy, gray images is itself indicative of the main blank space in the movie: we don't know what on earth Phil (Bradley Cooper), Stu (Ed Helms), Doug (Justin Bartha) and his future brother-in-law, Alan (Zach Galifianakis), have been up to that night. We don't know, because they don't know themselves. When three of them wake up the next morning after much clinking of glasses during a debauched bachelor party (shown in a daringly edited sequence) they cannot remember a thing.

Their luxury suite in Caesars Palace looks like a battle zone. The dentist, Stu (of all people) is missing a tooth; a baby is crying in the closet; and what's the tiger doing in the bathroom, for goodness' sake? All of this can be sorted out, of course. Gambling debts can be settled, the hellish hangover will stop – eventually – and, when all's said and done, why else would people go to Vegas? As the four friends swore to each other, what happens in Vegas, stays in Vegas. But after a classic bachelor party, there is no way that some things *can* stay in Vegas. The groom, for instance: a few hours before Doug's wedding, the boozy buddies are feverishly searching for their missing companion.

The process of reconstructing the lost night through pounding heads and with the help of minute clues may seem in parts like the detection patterns of a *film noir*, but the ensuing developments are more fanciful, as might be expected. Alan, Phil, Stu and Doug have apparently blown it with none other than ex-boxer Mike Tyson, played by himself, but have also managed to antagonize a small but incredibly mean Chinese gangster (Ken Jeong); plus a trip to Vegas would naturally not be complete without paying a visit to the fast-track wedding chapel – along with the almost immediate, cringe-making annulment of said wedding.

This seemingly endless cascade of embarrassments places *The Hangover* in a long line of smutty comedies in the world of guys, numerous in the years between 2000 and 2010. The shamelessly adolescent humor of Judd Apatow in *Knocked Up* (2007) was a big success in relation to its minimal production

1

2

1 Caesar doesn't live here any more. When the four men check into the grandiose Caesars Palace hotel, everything is still under control.

2 "What happens in Vegas, stays in Vegas!" From left, Alan, Stu, Doug and Phil (Zach Galifianakis, Ed Helms, Justin Bartha and Bradley Cooper) salute the glorious night to come.

3 Three men and a baby: Alan is quite laid back about what the "morning after" brings.

costs. And Todd Phillips not only started it all, but his masterpiece is both the apotheosis and catharsis of the genre. It is a film about guilty conscience, and the remorse that follows intoxication. The four friends pay a bitter price for what happened that night – the lost "film-within-the-film," as structured by its young director. It makes the humor less obscene, but all the more relevant. Put more simply, *The Hangover* is incredibly funny.

This is down to a screenplay with imaginative gags and twists in the plot, coupled with a brilliantly chosen cast. Stand-up comic Zach Galifianakis (who was spotted for the movie and most obviously embodies the retrograde aspect of the whole operation) deserves special mention. The point of the trip, namely temporarily relapsing into puberty, is apparently yet to come for chubby big baby Alan, who sometimes wears his baggy underpants like diapers. At the same time, he is artful enough to ask the receptionist at Caesars Palace, in all apparent innocence, whether Caesar really lived there. His riposte to the put-down answer: "That's what I thought."

What is amazing is that all those involved in this craziness maintain a vestige of dignity. What is more, they have completely different ideas about fun, so it was a stroke of genius in terms of screenplay to remove the boring groom-to-be, Doug, from the game at the outset. PB

TODD PHILLIPS Born in Brooklyn in 1970, Todd Phillips began his career as a documentary filmmaker. This may sound serious, but on closer inspection it confirms his status as a trailblazer of bad taste. His debut *Hated* (1994) was a portrait of hardcore punk rocker GG Allin, famous for his excessively obscene stage shows. Phillips broke off his film studies to work on the documentary, which was released in cinemas against all expectations. He then went on to devote himself to the goings-on of American brotherhoods in *Frat House* (1997/1998).

From an early stage his obsessions included crude male rituals, drunken orgies and a form of humor indebted to the shameful and disgusting.

Albeit in a watered-down form, he then began to explore his proclivities in Hollywood. Producer Ivan Reitman hired him as screenwriter and director for the college comedy *Road Trip* (2000). The concept was repeated in *Old School* (2002/2003), this time with actors well-known as members of the so-called "frat pack"– Luke Wilson, Will Ferrell and Vince Vaughn. He at least found commercial success with the series parody *Starsky & Hutch* (2003/2004). Without Phillips' trademark frat-boy humor, but wearing outrageous retro gear, Ben Stiller and Owen Wilson played the 1970s TV idols in the movie.

Treated as a potential sleeper hit, *The Hangover* (2009) wound up exceeding all expectations. Taking well over 400 million dollars at the box office, this guys' lifestyle comedy became the most successful R-rated movie – the second highest age rating – ousting *Beverly Hills Cop* (1984) and Eddie Murphy after 25 years in the top spot.

4 Stu has found his ideal woman in stripper Jade (Heather Graham). But should he marry her straight away?

5 A chain of unfortunate circumstances: before long, Phil and the others wind up at the police department.

6 No car, no money, no wedding: back home, the miserable threesome dare not show their faces.

"*The Hangover* is a funny movie, flat out, all the way through. Its setup is funny. Every situation is funny. Most of the dialogue is funny almost line by line."

Chicago Sun-Times

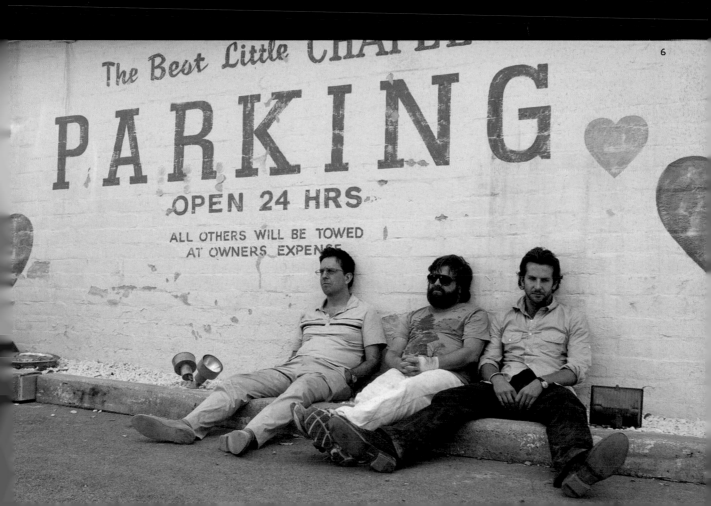

PUBLIC ENEMIES

2009 – USA – 140 MIN. – GANGSTER MOVIE, CRIME DRAMA
DIRECTOR MICHAEL MANN (*1943)
SCREENPLAY RONAN BENNETT, MICHAEL MANN, ANN BIDERMAN from the book "PUBLIC ENEMIES: AMERICA'S GREATEST CRIME WAVE AND THE BIRTH OF THE FBI, 1933–34" by Bryan Burrough DIRECTOR OF PHOTOGRAPHY DANTE SPINOTTI EDITING JEFFREY FORD, PAUL RUBELL MUSIC ELLIOT GOLDENTHAL PRODUCTION MICHAEL MANN, KEVIN MISHER for FORWARD PASS, MISHER FILMS, UNIVERSAL PICTURES.
STARRING JOHNNY DEPP (John Dillinger), MARION COTILLARD (Billie Frechette), CHRISTIAN BALE (Melvin Purvis), BILLY CRUDUP (J. Edgar Hoover), STEPHEN GRAHAM (Baby Face Nelson), CHANNING TATUM (Pretty Boy Floyd), STEPHEN DORFF (Homer Van Meter), CHRISTIAN STOLTE (Charles Makley), STEPHEN LANG (Charles Winstead), BILL CAMP (Frank Nitti), GIOVANNI RIBISI (Alvin Karpis), LILI TAYLOR (Sheriff Lillian Holley), BRANKA KATIC (Anna Sage).

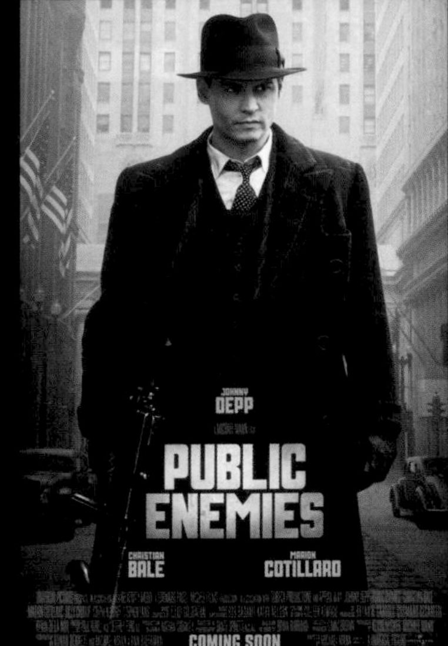

"Bye-bye, blackbird."

On the evening of July 22, 1934 John Dillinger was riddled with police bullets as he left a cinema. It was the very same Biograph Theater in Chicago where Michael Mann spent a large part of his youth. Like Mann, Dillinger was also fond of the movies. In the final scenes of *Public Enemies* he mirrors real life by watching the gangster movie that was then showing in the Biograph, *Manhattan Melodrama* (1934) with Clark Gable and Myrna Loy. Gable's moustache and hard talk resemble his own performance, and he even seems to recognize himself in the tragic love story. All gangster films end the same way and, like Clark Gable, Dillinger has known for a long time that his life is forfeit. Although the ending is clear, however, *Public Enemies* is quite different from any other gangster film to date.

John Dillinger (Johnny Depp) is the most wanted bank robber in the United States, yet at the same time a folk hero – during a global economic crisis, bank robbers have more credit with the masses than bankers. Director Michael Mann cannot show this popularity openly, so it is suggested through Johnny Depp's overwhelming charisma. When his Dillinger raids one of the classically palatial banks of that era, it is with the chivalrous panache of a pirate boarding a ship. He uses the same charm to win over little hat-check girl Billie Frechette (Marion Cotillard), whisking her away from her counter like a beautiful coat. She becomes the great love of a man who does not waste any time thinking about the past, or the future: "I'm having far too much fun to think about tomorrow." What other attitude to life is left for a jail breaker who runs around with notorious career criminals like Pretty Boy Floyd (Channing Tatum) and Baby Face Nelson (Stephen Graham)?

On the other side of the law is J. Edgar Hoover (Billy Crudup), head of the state investigating authority, and the extension of his long arm, Melvin Purvis (Christian Bale). Gangsters can evade arrest just by fleeing to a different state, something their small outfit finds difficult to prevent. By combining all their forces, however, Hoover is able to declare the "war against crime" and John Dillinger as "Public Enemy Number One" – and the FBI is born.

The methods of the law enforcers and outlaws are pretty much the same; and we see not only topical references in Mann's script, but also the trusted signature of the director. Depp and Bale engage in a duel between two men, similar to Robert De Niro and Al Pacino in *Heat* (1995). In the shootouts, which are choreographed like a ballet, automatic handguns are swapped for heavy submachine guns. But overall, the differences outweigh the similarities.

In *Public Enemies* Michael Mann confirmed, as he had before in *Collateral* (2004) and *Miami Vice* (2006), his position at the forefront of modern digital

1

filmmaking. In parts, the film looks like the abstract form of a gangster movie, with its seemingly pared-down aesthetic and use of high-resolution digital cameras. In the daylight shots, in particular, the razor sharp HD images produce a hyper-realistic effect. They convey John Dillinger's view: for him, reality is reduced to buildings, cars and escape routes. The strangely empty banking halls look like film sets, while long shots interspersed with close-ups of tense faces somehow free the action from its context. Dillinger's world is that of the self-contained male, in which there is no desire to encourage nostalgic empathy through psychoanalysis and fake sepia tones. The strange, ghostly quality of these images tends rather to remind us of the black-and-white movies that inspired John Dillinger back in his day. It is only on closer observation that this cool stylization becomes more transparent, with the emotional heart of

"Where digital methods have gradually become the industry standard by simulating the dense, luxuriant textures of film, Mann embraces video precisely for the ways in which it is unlike film: for the hyper-real clarity of its images, for the way the lightweight cameras move through space, and for its ability to see sharper and more deeply into his beloved night. At every turn, Mann rejects classical notions of cinematic 'beauty' and formulates new ones." *The Village Voice*

1 Gangsters and film myth: action expert Michael Mann dedicates a portrait with an assured sense of style to John Dillinger (Johnny Depp).

2 Billie Frechette (Marion Cotillard) falls for Dillinger's charms, but doesn't conform to the usual cliché of the gangster's moll.

3 Michael Mann makes cool movies that admit only as much emotion as necessary and rely entirely on the magnetism of his actors.

4 Captured gangster as media star: intelligent thought is also given to the popularity of this smart criminal.

the story revealed in Mann's love of detail. The love story (and Cotillard as Billie may just have a look of Myrna Loy about her) is beautifully crafted, with the members of the huge cast perfectly complementing one another. The briefest time-lapse effects or the reflection of a wooded area in a car door create precious, unforgettable moments that consciously pierce the deliberately formal style. John Dillinger is no pioneer himself, but yesterday's man – like a character from a western who accidentally winds up in a thriller. These new gangster syndicates do not rob banks; they sort out their gambling frauds by phone, in exactly the same way that the FBI carries out its surveillance operations, drawing the noose ever tighter around Dillinger's neck. In his last big heist, this last criminal anarchist goes into the Chicago Police Department and, with the faraway look of the living dead, looks at his mug shots. It is the moment when the myth of this man, who recognizes himself as such, is realized. John Dillinger can make his last exit.

PB

CHRISTIAN BALE Much to the surprise of many, the independent actor whose performances were always somewhat morose has turned into an all-action hero. Christian Bale was not particularly renowned for his physique until his first, well publicized method acting stunt when he lost over 66 lb / 30 kg for *The Machinist* (2003). Bale plays men on the edge of a nervous breakdown, his trademark being his painstaking control of every muscle in his body. Only on one occasion did he use this obsession with control to humorous effect, in what, of all things, was his best known role for a time: the perverse murderer of women in Mary Harron's film adaptation *American Psycho* (1999).

Born in Wales in 1974, the actor comes from an artistic family, whose travels took him as a child to places like Portugal and the USA. At the age of 13, he had his first lead role, in Steven Spielberg's *Empire of the Sun* (1987). Minor movies like *Swing Kids* (1993), *Little Women* (1994) and *Velvet Goldmine* (1998) only raised his profile slightly. Since *American Psycho*, however, Bale has been regarded as an outstanding character actor who brings credibility to big-budget productions and star appeal to indie films. For *Batman Begins* (2005) and later *The Dark Knight* (2008) he slipped into the costume of the famous superhero.

At the same time, he was committed to ambitious art house films. In Werner Herzog's *Rescue Dawn* (2006) he played German-American navy pilot Dieter Dengler, shot down over Laos in 1965, while in *I'm Not There* (2007) by Todd Haynes he was one of the six Bob Dylans. In 2008, he unfortunately gained another type of fame for an outburst of rage on the set of *Terminator Salvation* (2009) that was widely distributed over the internet. After his thrilling appearance in Michael Mann's gangster epic *Public Enemies* (2009) Christian Bale – who is very serious about his work – won the Oscar for Best Supporting Actor in the realistic boxing drama *The Fighter* (2010).

UP IN THE AIR

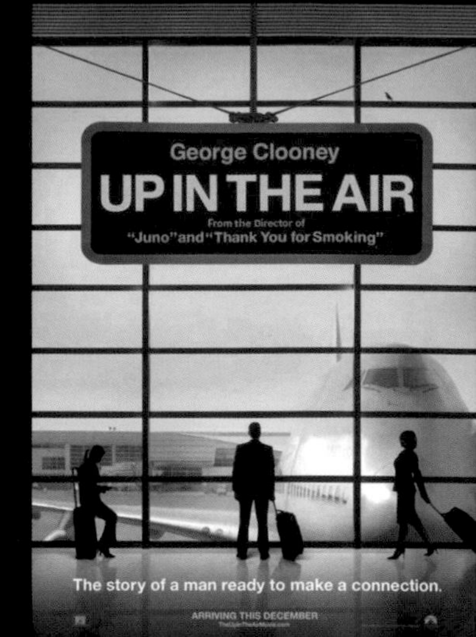

2009 – USA – 110 MIN. – TRAGICOMEDY
DIRECTOR JASON REITMAN (*1977)
SCREENPLAY JASON REITMAN, SHELDON TURNER, from the novel of the same name by WALTER KIRN DIRECTOR OF PHOTOGRAPHY ERIC STEELBERG EDITING DANA E. GLAUBERMAN MUSIC ROLFE KENT PRODUCTION IVAN REITMAN, JASON REITMAN, JEFFREY CLIFFORD, DANIEL DUBIECKI for DW FILMS, THE MONTECITO PICTURE COMPANY, PARAMOUNT PICTURES.
STARRING GEORGE CLOONEY (Ryan Bingham), VERA FARMIGA (Alex Goran), ANNA KENDRICK (Natalie Keener), JASON BATEMAN (Craig Gregory), AMY MORTON (Kara Bingham), MELANIE LYNSKEY (Julie Bingham), J. K. SIMMONS (Bob), SAM ELLIOTT (Maynard Finch), ZACH GALIFIANAKIS (Steve), DANNY MCBRIDE (Jim Miller).

"All the things you probably hate about travelling – the recycled air, the artificial lighting, the digital juice dispensers, the cheap sushi – are warm reminders that I'm home."

Wife, children, own home, an office job with desk and colleagues … these things don't do anything for Ryan Bingham (George Clooney). For him, commitments are excess baggage. He prefers to travel light: an easily maneuvered cabin case and platinum credit card are quite sufficient. Airports and business-class hotels are his home, while his professed goal is a number: the "sound barrier" of 10 million air miles, which only a handful of people have broken through. Bingham is convinced he will very soon belong to this exclusive club; after all, he travels almost constantly for his job. He jets about all over the country for his consulting firm based in Omaha. His area of expertise: redundancy talks. Wherever someone is being fired, be it L.A. or New York, Detroit or Houston, and the bosses don't want to get their hands dirty, Bingham is right there. The economic crisis represents a boom time for him.

Bingham is a smart hit man. With a reassuring expression and conviction in his voice, he sells the job loss as an opportunity to the person getting the boot. Curbing negative feelings is the name of the game – potential suicides, killing sprees and law suits must be prevented. Bingham is a past master at this. Just as he smoothly and efficiently negotiates the impersonal and standardized world of the frequent flyer, he confidently manipulates his opponents in redundancy discussions. He is a professional, through and through. And, as immoral as it may sound, it is highly entertaining to watch this steely hatchet man giving his flawless performance; the more so because he is played by George Clooney.

Since hitting the big time in the mid-1990s, Clooney has been regarded as the legitimate successor to Cary Grant. Never before, however, has he come quite as close to the great charmer from the good old dream factory days as in his role as *Up in the Air*'s messenger of misfortune, unscrupulous and appealing in equal measures. This can also be attributed to the fact that co-author and director Jason Reitman cast Vera Farmiga and Anna Kendrick as the female leads opposite his star. They are more than equal to the task, with the verbal skirmishes between them and Clooney being on a par with the best screwball comedies of Howard Hawks. First, we have Alex (Vera Farmiga), the attractive businesswoman with plenty of air miles. "I am the woman that you don't have to worry about," she says straight to Bingham's face. "Just think of me as you with a vagina." The perfect lover, it would seem.

On the other hand, his new colleague Natalie (Anna Kendrick), a tight-lipped college graduate, challenges Bingham in a completely different way. For her debut she promptly presents a radical proposal for rationalization:

"It's tough to capture an era while it's still happening, yet *Up in the Air* does so brilliantly, with wit and humanity." *USA TODAY*

1 Ryan Bingham (George Clooney) specializes in redundancy talks. As a sideline, he enthusiastically collects frequent-flyer miles. Clooney finally inherits Cary Grant's crown in his role as a cynical business traveler.

2 Clooney delivered such a fine performance not least because director Jason Reitman cast two worthy "opponents" alongside him: the wonderful Vera Farmiga as seductive and capable businesswoman Alex …

3 … and Anna Kendrick as sharp and careerist college graduate Natalie Keener, who nearly makes Bingham a victim of rationalization as well.

2

instead of taking care of the redundancies on site, the people could just be fired by video conference, saving time and, above all, the cost of flights. This is, of course, a potential nightmare for Bingham. So, on a redundancy trip through the States, he puts everything into convincing the tiresome newcomer that a personal talk, face-to-face, is indispensable.

As in his feature film debut *Thank You for Smoking* (2005), a satire about a tobacco lobbyist, Reitman once again proves his unerring sense of the *Zeitgeist*. One of the main reasons his comedy sizzles is because his gags are mostly drawn from experiences and observations shared by both the director and his audience. But the more crucial factor is that this rising star of American independent cinema is not only brilliant at doing the fun stuff, he is a filmmaker with an excellent sense of timing and an exuberant imagination that seems to run really wild in a few fast-cut sequences. In this way, Bingham's eloquence always finds a formal equivalent in the film.

Reitman is also a moralist, however. There is never any doubt that Bingham is stepping over bodies and that behind his attractive exterior lurks the ugly

4 Reitman tells his hero's tale in the best screwball tradition: as an entertaining war of the sexes that is fought out on the battlefield of feelings …

5 … as well as on a professional level. In both spheres, Bingham initially finds himself on the winning side.

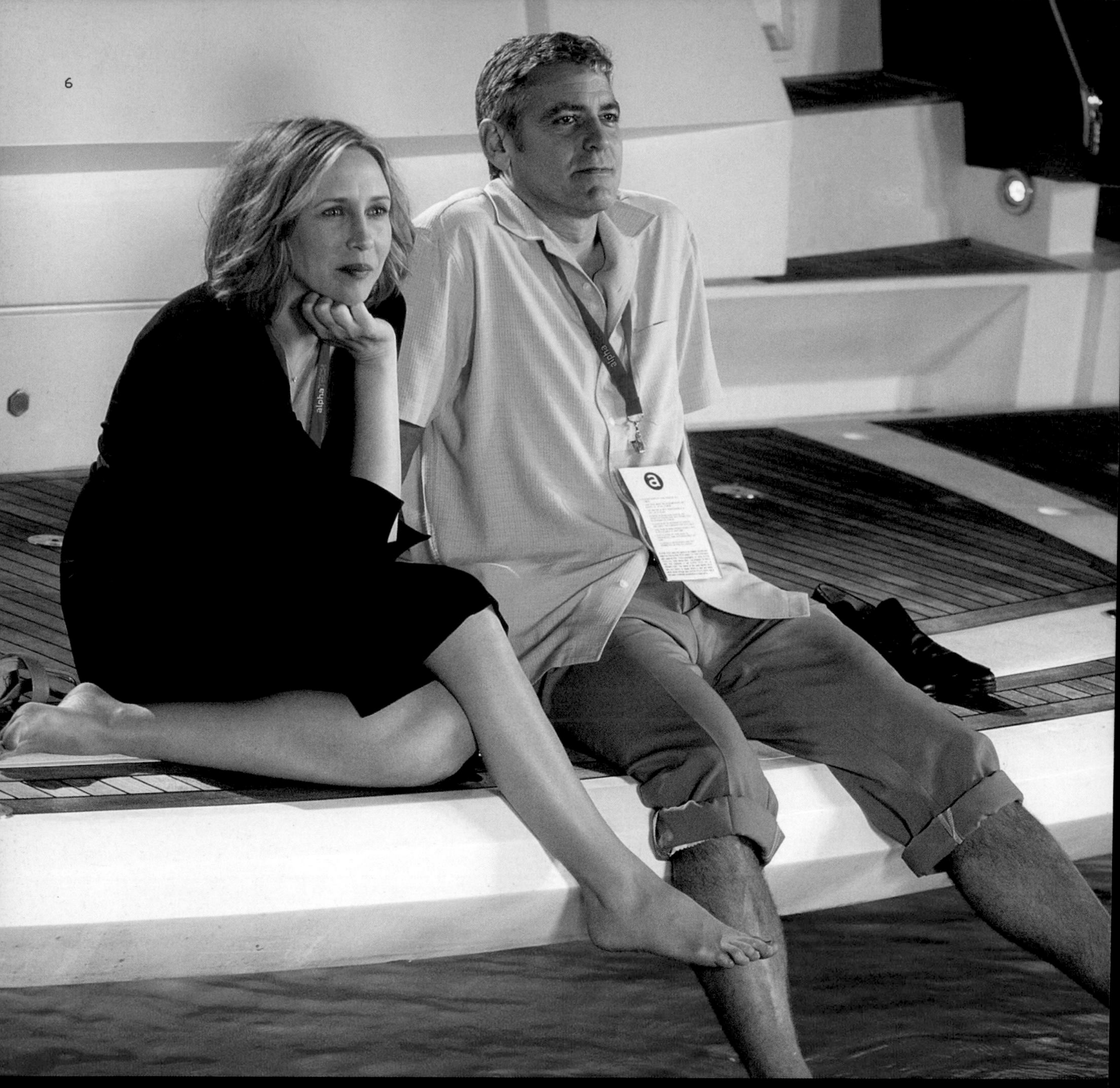

VERA FARMIGA Some actors never fail to bring both charm and substance to even minor roles, and give convincing performances as leads in relatively small independent productions. Years can pass without us becoming really aware of just how good they are. Then suddenly, like a revelation, a certain film comes along and we ask ourselves: "Why on earth is he or she not already a major star?" In the case of Vera Farmiga, this may well be explained by her self-professed lack of interest in a big career. Maybe also because the daughter of Ukrainian immigrants (born in New Jersey in 1973) for all her elegance does not correspond to Hollywood's current ideal of beauty, but also exudes a kind of ambiguity and irony that is perhaps a little unusual today.

Farmiga began her film career in the late 1990s and was soon acting in the shadow of top stars like Richard Gere, *Autumn in New York* (2000), and Robert De Niro, *15 Minutes* (2001). She achieved greater recognition from US film critics for the first time for her role as the drug-addicted mother in *Down to the Bone* (2003/04). A wider audience discovered her qualities in Martin Scorsese's Mafia thriller *The Departed* (2006) in which she played the police psychologist and lover to tough guys Leonardo DiCaprio and Matt Damon. After once again appearing in unusual mother roles in the controversial Holocaust film *The Boy in the Striped Pyjamas* (2008) and horror flick *Orphan* (2009), Farmiga took a quantum leap with Jason Reitman's *Up in the Air* (2009). The fact that her performance as both quick-witted and sexy businesswoman Alex Goran was "only" enough to earn an Oscar nomination doesn't change anything: anyone who so casually befuddles the senses of such a hard-boiled Casanova as George Clooney is quite simply in the premier league.

6 Frequent-flyer heaven: Bingham thinks he has found his alter ego in Alex – a woman who, like him, rejects the unnecessary baggage of permanent relationships.

7 Some critics accuse *Up in the Air* of moral conservatism. Not totally without cause: while Bingham is at first mildly scornful about the marriage plans of his niece Julie (Melanie Lynskey) and …

8 … Reitman films the wedding preparations with an ironic eye, the smart businessman is reformed in the course of the movie …

9 … but, instead of wedded bliss, all that awaits our hero in the end is the cold impersonality of airports and business hotels.

face of capitalism. To connect his cold actions with the harsh basis of reality, Reitman even lets "real" unemployed people have their say: ordinary people who paint a moving picture of their feelings when faced with unemployment. Yet Bingham, too, is brought down to earth in the course of the film and, thanks to the women, finally discovers family values. Looking at this wonderful transformation in true Hollywood style one might accuse Reitman of being a closet conservative. The fact that he denies his enlightened protagonist a happy ending, however – by not allowing him to enter the now sought-after haven of marriage but virtually condemning him to eternal frequent-flying – is a brilliant point on which to finish. A movie hero is not often doomed to an unbearable lightness of being.

JH

A SINGLE MAN

2009 – USA – 99 MIN. – DRAMA, LITERARY ADAPTATION
DIRECTOR TOM FORD (*1961)
SCREENPLAY TOM FORD, DAVID SCEARCE from the novel of the same name by CHRISTOPHER ISHERWOOD **DIRECTOR OF PHOTOGRAPHY** EDUARD GRAU **EDITING** JOAN SOBEL **MUSIC** ABEL KORZENIOWSKI, SHIGERU UMEBAYASHI **PRODUCTION** TOM FORD, CHRIS WEITZ, ANDREW MIANO,
ROBERT SALERNO for ARTINA FILMS, DEPTH OF FIELD, FADE TO BLACK PRODUCTIONS.
STARRING COLIN FIRTH (George Falconer), JULIANNE MOORE (Charley), NICHOLAS HOULT (Kenny Potter), MATTHEW GOODE (Jim), JON KORTAJARENA (Carlos), PAULETTE LAMORI (Alva), RYAN SIMPKINS (Jennifer Strunk), GINNIFER GOODWIN (Mrs. Strunk).

"Looking in the mirror, staring back at me isn't so much a face as the expression of a predicament. Just get through the goddamn day."

The tragicomic story of this single man takes place over the course of just one day in 1962, in a smart area of Los Angeles. Just eight months earlier, English professor George Falconer (Colin Firth) has lost his long-term lover Jim (Matthew Goode) in a car crash. Since then, the daily routines of getting dressed in the morning, having coffee and going to work, shot in pallid sequences, seem no more than the repetition of empty processes. Contrasting with the emptiness of everyday life are his memories and daydreams, creating a place he longs for in flashbacks of saturated color.

George has decided to kill himself: he will commit suicide with a shot from his revolver, in the same minimalist way in which he talks, controls his facial expressions, dresses himself, and decorates his house. But while he is preparing to die, life goes on around him. He is surrounded by people who keep diverting him from his plan. His old friend and ex-lover Charley (Julianne Moore), who like him has moved from London to Los Angeles, just manages to keep her own head above the empty waters of daily life through an insatiable lust for life and copious quantities of gin. She needs George to escape from loneliness. And a boyishly handsome student thwarts his plan as well. Kenny (Nicholas Hoult) has fallen in love with him, making advances that are definitely ambiguous without ever explicitly expressing his intentions or putting them into action. But the searching looks, the tentative, apparently casual physical contact and the mere possibility of a sexual adventure arouse feelings in George he thought were gone forever. Thus George lives through a normal day, at the end of which he does seem to be enjoying himself a bit more. Tom Ford put his money on Colin Firth's acting abilities, his faith in a man who can represent a wide range of feelings with minimal movements. Apart from which the film – occasionally criticized for being superficial – is

1
2

3

1 Colin Firth as impeccably dressed Professor George Falconer: but, behind the immaculate façade, he hides mourning and longing.

2 A young student, Kenny (Nicholas Hoult) pursues his professor, unexpectedly spoiling his suicide plans.

3 Julianne Moore as Charley, an aging drama queen, and Colin Firth as ostensibly perfect husband material. The film traces the cracks in surface appearances.

"*A Single Man* is an impressive film debut that sometimes gets lost in the details. But its visual flair and masterful lead performance make it a rare film of equal parts style and poignancy." *USA Today*

4

5

4 Janet Leigh's wildly staring eyes from Hitchcock's *Psycho* make the connection to the great cinema of the 1960s.

5 Spanish male model Jon Kortajarena appears as the epitome of superficial beauty: the worlds of cinema and fashion converge.

6 An extrovert with a lust for life – Julianne Moore wearing classic 60s makeup.

brought to life by its stunning images. Tom Ford worked with the Catalan cameraman Eduard Grau, then 28 years old, filming on Kodak 5279 500 ASA, a rather old film stock that is no longer manufactured. Its specific grain gives the movie the look of films, magazine covers, and advertising posters of the 1960s, which Ford matches in the set design while avoiding a costume drama effect.

For George's impressions, thoughts and the memories that play before his eyes like an inner newsreel, Ford uses techniques such as slow motion, jump cuts and fluid contrast changes. These stylish effects give the film an aesthetic rhythm that has great visual appeal for the viewer. In addition to the score proper by Abel Korzeniowski, the scenes are also given emphasis by the music of Shigeru Umebayashi, a Japanese film composer who has mainly worked with Wong Kar Wai, one of the great contemporary masters of highly colorful, other-worldly film imagery.

When George brings his car to a halt in a parking lot, he places it directly between the wide eyes of Janet Leigh, who gazes on the viewer from an outsize film poster advertising Alfred Hitchcock's *Psycho* (1960). The aim is not just to make a link to the great cinema of the 1960s; as the poster gleams

TOM FORD Fashion sees itself as substance rather than just an outer shell, and if film and fashion are quite similar in this respect, who would know better than a movie-making fashion designer?

By way of various detours, Tom Ford (born 1961) first became involved in fashion design before moving on to film. In the course of which he seems to have gradually approached his goal, working his way through every artistic discipline. He started out studying art history at New York University, then architecture at the famous Parsons New School for Design in New York, and later at its annex in Paris. After graduating, he was hired by various fashion companies, before finally being discovered by Gucci in 1990. Taken on to steer the dusty fashion house, which was facing a crisis at the time, toward a successful future with new collections, he took the business to the top of its sector within a few years, going on to become internationally famous in the fashion world as its creative director.

After his departure from Gucci in 2005 and a brief hiatus, he developed his own label, mainly concentrating on menswear. Since then, on an annual basis, his designs have been presented by androgynous males springing rhythmically along the catwalks of top fashion shows. Jon Kortajarena – who plays Carlos in Ford's directorial debut *A Single Man* (2009) – comes from this world as well. He is like a male muse, or rather a projection surface, whose way of slightly narrowing his eyes against the setting sun, while dragging on a cigarette, constitutes the high art of looking beautiful. It is certainly eye candy for both the male and female observer, and is again down to the wonderful combination of fashion and fluid imagery in this film.

crimson in the sunlight, the scene is also a reminder of the power of seduction and the fact that images act as independent signifiers.

As well as being based on the famous novel of the same name by Christopher Isherwood, written in 1964, the movie is also about how society deals with homosexuality. When George gives his last lecture on Aldous Huxley's novel "After Many a Summer Dies the Swan," he digresses into a speech about minorities and society's fear of them. In the process, it becomes clear that George is also speaking as a gay man. In this sense, the film is also a critique of an earlier time, when minorities did not enjoy the same protection and respect they do today. The flawless images do not, then, gloss over the film's social relevance. MM

7 Colin Firth's powerful performance as George Falconer was nominated for both an Oscar and a Golden Globe, and won him the 2010 BAFTA for Best Leading Actor.

8 Beauty in sadness: life seems empty and lackluster to George after Jim's death.

9 Remembering happier days: the flashbacks are disconnected and surreal, like stills from a black-and-white movie.

"The film belongs to Firth. Uncanny at showing the heart crumbling under George's elegant exterior, he gives the performance of his career. Ford is a true visionary, but it's his humanity that gives the love story a ravishing, bruised grandeur." *Rolling Stone*

9

A SERIOUS MAN

2009 – USA – 106 MIN. – TRAGICOMEDY
DIRECTORS ETHAN COEN, JOEL COEN (*1954, *1957)
SCREENPLAY ETHAN COEN, JOEL COEN DIRECTOR OF PHOTOGRAPHY ROGER DEAKINS
EDITING RODERICK JAYNES (PSEUDONYM for JOEL AND ETHAN COEN)
MUSIC CARTER BURWELL PRODUCTION ETHAN COEN, JOEL COEN for FOCUS FEATURES, STUDIO CANAL, RELATIVITY MEDIA, MIKE ZOSS PRODUCTIONS, WORKING TITLE FILMS.
STARRING MICHAEL STUHLBARG (Prof. Lawrence "Larry" Gopnik), RICHARD KIND (Uncle Arthur), FRED MELAMED (Sy Ableman), SARI LENNICK (Judith Gopnik), AARON WOLFF (Danny Gopnik), JESSICA MCMANUS (Sarah Gopnik), SIMON HELBERG (Rabbi Scott), GEORGE WYNER (Rabbi Nachtner), ALAN MANDELL (Rabbi Marshak), AMY LANDECKER (Mrs. Samsky).

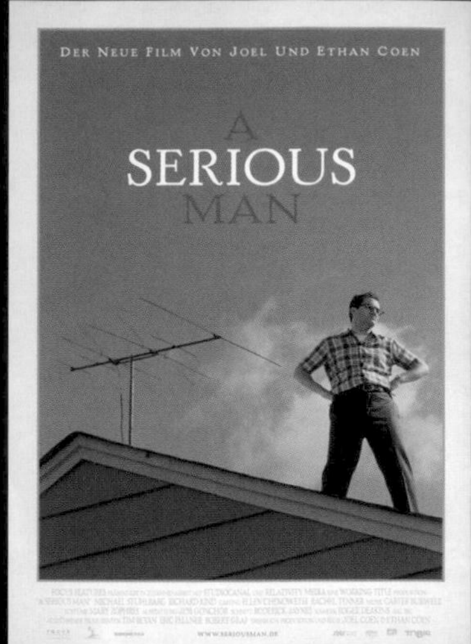

"Please. Accept the mystery."

The year is 1967, and life is nicely balanced for Larry Gopnik (Michael Stuhlbarg) – a university physics professor, he lives with his Jewish family in an idyllic suburb of Minnesota. His full academic tenure and son's bar mitzvah are imminent. But suddenly, everything starts to fall apart. Out of the blue, his wife Judith (Sari Lennick) asks for a divorce because she has fallen in love with Sy Ableman (Fred Melamed). Larry is forced to move into a motel with his brother Arthur (Richard Kind), who is later arrested because of his gambling. Larry's career is suddenly under threat, too, as a Korean student is trying to bribe him for a better grade. On top of all this, he is involved in a car accident. And then there are the results of the medical tests he has been awaiting for some time. What the Coen brothers expect this poor man to put up with is pretty mean; and they do not even offer any explanation for these blows of fate. As he is an orthodox Jew, they have Larry seeking advice from several rabbis, but without success. He finds no satisfactory answer to his situation in any of the pearls of wisdom or parables offered him. Everything remains shadowy and mysterious to him. As a scientist, he finds himself faced with equally weighty problems. Even physics – the infallible explanatory model of all earthly things – has been tainted with uncertainty since the advent of quantum mechanics. Prof. Gopnik writes impressively long derivations of the Heisenberg uncertainty principle on the board, it's true, and explains the conceptual model of Schrödinger's cat, which is meant to illustrate the paradox of a particle's simultaneously different properties. Yet he cannot really understand it himself. Larry Gopnik's real problem is that he is not capable of comprehending the world, either as a practicing Jew or as a physics professor. Rabbi Marshak puts this dilemma in a nutshell at the end of the film with a quote based loosely on Jefferson Airplane, formulating it characteristically in the form of a question: "When the truth is found to be lies and all the hope within you dies … then what?" Or, to quote the father of the Korean student: "Please. Accept the mystery."

1

"A tart, brilliantly acted fable of life's little cosmic difficulties, a Coen brothers comedy with a darker philosophical outlook than *No Country for Old Men* but with a script rich in verbal wit." *Chicago Tribune*

2

1 It only appears as though Larry Gopnik (Michael Stuhlbarg) has an overview: in reality, he cannot understand the things that are going on around him.

2 Helplessly, Larry puts up with the duplicitous embrace of Sy Ableman (Fred Melamed). The man has just made off with his wife.

3 Uncle Arthur (Richard Kind) creates his own explanatory model, "Mentaculus," though it means he falls foul of the law.

4 "The Rabbi is busy." Though it might not seem so, Rabbi Marshak (Alan Mandell) has more important things to do than bother with Larry's problems.

"We didn't want any stars in *A Serious Man*. The film was meant to be no-frills, realistic." *Coen brothers*

The theme of ambiguity runs as a common thread through *A Serious Man*. It starts from the outset with the Jewish prologue used by the Coens as a preface to the movie: is Treitle Groshkover actually still alive? Didn't the old man die three years earlier? Or is he really a dybbuk, a demon that has assumed the form of the dead man? At any rate, the housewife plays it safe, and sticks an ice pick into the poor man's chest. Apparently, the Coens just wanted to get the audience attuned to the film's main, Jewish setting with this macabre little story. But the dybbuk motif crops up again later, if indirectly. It is implied in the hugs inflicted on helpless Larry by Sy Ableman, for the term "dybbuk" comes from the Jewish word for clutching or attachment.

Sy dies not long afterward in a car crash. Larry also has an accident around that time, and asks himself whether *HaSchem* (*The Name*), as the

5 You can never know what is really going on. Larry clings to his work. But even physics has run its course as an explanatory model.

6 Do not covet your neighbor's wife. Mrs. Samsky (Amy Landecker) symbolizes the promises of the flower-power age that practicing Jew Larry finds hard to resist. But it goes no further than a joint, as the sex scene is just a dream.

Jews refer to God, wants to tell him something: perhaps that he and Sy might just be one and the same person? And which of them is actually the "serious man"? Larry says occasionally that he is trying to be one. Sy, on the other hand, is described twice as a serious person. Did Sy Ableman transfer into Larry Gopnik as a dybbuk? At any rate, he pursues him even in his dreams, hugging him tight. According to the legend, a dybbuk induces the person possessed into behaving irrationally – and Larry Gopnik does come to some remarkable decisions following Sy's death. He pays his seductive neighbor Mrs. Samsky (Amy Landecker) a visit after smoking a joint, and ends up succumbing to the bribery. He takes the money and changes the grade, even though he has stated emphatically from the beginning that every action in his office has consequences, not just physical but moral too. Immediately, and ominously, the telephone starts to ring, in a directorial reaping of the whirlwind.

Ultimately, it is up to the viewer to choose whether to rationalize this story or simply be entertained by it. The Coen brothers have made their most Jewish film to date with *A Serious Man*. It might also be seen as their most personal work, as so many memories of their childhood in Minnesota are woven into it. In any event, they have made an ensemble movie that is perfectly cast, right down to the most minor role; and even without any well-known actors, it definitely ranks alongside their comedy classics. CZ

CARTER BURWELL Born in New York in 1955, Carter Burwell is the other key player in the Coen brothers' team alongside cameraman Roger Deakins. The film composer came on board for their directorial debut *Blood Simple* (1984): at this point, he was using a stop watch to "synchronize" the simple, powerfully dark piano melody with the film. For *Miller's Crossing* (1990) the Coens left him to compose his first orchestral score without any prior knowledge of the movie. Burwell then produced a charming score for the provincial thriller *Fargo* (1996), adapting a Scandinavian folk song meant for a solo instrument such as the Hardanger fiddle with its delicate, melodic sound and contrasting it with a powerful film-noir orchestration.
Carter Burwell believes that far too much music is used in cinema today. He showed that mood can also be created without music in *No Country for Old Men* (2007) by dispensing with any background music and simply mixing single notes into the sound design. By contrast, in *A Serious Man* (2009) he composed a polyrhythmic harp movement that seems perpetually to repeat itself, with slight variations. According to Burwell, such a serial sound pattern produces a kind of monotone that becomes entirely distinct from the plot, suggesting to the viewer that something rather different – and far more significant – is actually going on, apart from what is happening onscreen. As well as working for the Coen brothers, Burwell has also been responsible for the soundtracks of all Spike Jonze's feature films. His biggest commercial success to date is the soundtrack for *Twilight* (2008).

MAO'S LAST DANCER

2009 – AUSTRALIA – 117 MIN. / 121 MIN. – BIOPIC, DANCE FILM
DIRECTOR BRUCE BERESFORD (*1940)
SCREENPLAY JAN SARDI, from the autobiography of the same name by LI CUNXIN
DIRECTOR OF PHOTOGRAPHY PETER JAMES EDITING MARK WARNER MUSIC CHRISTOPHER GORDON
PRODUCTION JANE SCOTT, GENG LING for GREAT SCOTT PRODUCTIONS.
STARRING CHI CAO (Li Cunxin as an Adult), CHENGWU GUO (Li Cunxin as a Teenager), WEN BIN HUANG (Li Cunxin as a Child), BRUCE GREENWOOD (Ben Stevenson), KYLE MACLACHLAN (Charles Foster), AMANDA SCHULL (Elizabeth Mackey), XIUQING YUE (Jiang Qing), JOAN CHEN (Niang), SHUANGBAO WANG (Dia), SU ZHANG (Chang), ADEN YOUNG (Dilworth), MADELEINE EASTOE (Lori), CAMILLA VERGOTIS (Mary McKendry), PENNE HACKFORTH-JONES (Cynthia Dodds).

"You know, I must dance political ballet in China. But I dance better here, because I feel more ... free."

Craggy cliffs, bare trees, and low stone houses with no electricity or running water. Little Li Cunxin (Wen Bin Huang) lives in a rural part of Shandong province on the east coast of China with his parents and six brothers and sisters. In 1972 when he is 11 years old, party functionaries are scouring classrooms in the search for talented children who can be trained as ballet dancers. They choose Li because he is so agile and send him to the Dance Academy in Beijing. He ends up as a world famous principal dancer for ballet companies in America and Australia.

Producer Jane Scott and writer Jan Sardi, who were responsible for the Oscar-winning film about a pianist, *Shine* (1996), joined up with director Bruce Beresford to adapt the memoirs of Chinese-born dancer Li Cunxin. The result is emotional cinema on a grand scale; a moving biographical tapestry spanning

Little Li Cunxin is subjected to a harsh regime at ballet school. Painful and exhausting exercises in the rehearsal room, for hours on end, alternate with tedious propaganda lessons on the teachings of Mao. At first, Li Cunxin doesn't seem strong enough to become a good dancer. But he is relentless, pushing his body to its physical limits and improving all the time. Eventually, he is even allowed to dance before Mao's wife Jiang Qing (Xiuqing Yue). And when they are looking for a pupil for an exchange program with America, once again the choice falls on Li. He travels to the USA to continue his training with the Houston Ballet. Getting to know the world beyond Mao's Cultural Revolution transforms his life.

Beresford's story covers different areas which his regular Australian cameraman Peter James (*Meet the Parents*, 2000) brings to life using a range

2

BRUCE BERESFORD When Bruce Beresford became internationally famous in 1989 with *Driving Miss Daisy*, which won four Oscars, the Australian director had already made 18 movies. Along with Baz Luhrmann (*Moulin Rouge!*, 2001) Beresford is the best-known filmmaker from Down Under: his 30 feature films in a career spanning 40 years to date make him one of the most prolific in the world. And he has traveled far in his career: after growing up in a Sydney suburb, Beresford first tried to find employment in the British film industry in his early twenties. When that did not work out, he went to Nigeria for three years to work as a film editor. He returned to England in 1967 and found a job as a producer for the British Film Institute. In 1970 he returned to Australia to work in its emergent film industry, which ten years later took him to Hollywood. Beresford has not committed himself to one genre in his considerable body of work, which includes family dramas like *Crimes of the Heart* (1986), thrillers such as *Double Jeopardy* (1999), a war movie (*Paradise Road*, 1997) and even a Biblical epic (*King David*, 1985). He has also worked with stars including Richard Gere, Sean Connery, Glenn Close and Sharon Stone. In 2007, Beresford published his memoirs: "Josh Hartnett Definitely Wants to Do This." This odd title alludes to a meeting with the Hollywood star who, allegedly, definitely wanted to be in a biopic of the jazz trumpeter Chet Baker. Beresford said in an interview: "That always happens, producers calling and claiming that some star or other definitely wants to do this movie. Just wishful thinking! Usually these stars have never heard of the project in question."

3

and the glittering world of the ballet stage. Li's Chinese village is depicted in atmospheric grainy images, dominated by shades of gray and brown. Those who live there must work hard, but it is a warm, close-knit community; they are also, however, governed by the strict rules of behavior that Mao's communist regime imposes on them. Bruce Beresford's crew reconstructed a run-down village about 60 miles from Beijing following a real historical model.

America in the 1980s – garish and noisy, with its individual freedoms, overflowing shelves and loud discos – gives Li a real culture shock. This is tempered, however, by the warmth and sense of shared identity he experiences as a member of the ballet company. Li finally finds his true calling on the stage, where the film also has its most visually electric moments. The artistic climax is the final dance scene from Igor Stravinsky's "The Rite of Spring,"

"Beresford uses full-framed shots and keeps editing to a minimum in service to the excellent dance sequences choreographed by Aussie top gun Graeme Murphy." *Variety*

1 Teacher Chang (Su Zhang, r.) bids farewell to his star pupil Li Cunxin (Chengwu Guo). Soon after, Chang is arrested for counter-revolutionary behavior.

2 Mao's wife Jiang Qing (Xiuqing Yue) takes a close personal interest in the ballet academy pupils.

3 Li Cunxin's parents, Dia (Shuangbao Wang) and Niang (Joan Chen) receive a call from their son in Beijing.

4 At first, little Li Cunxin (Wen Bin Huang) is very lonely at the ballet academy. Is he strong enough for the harsh regime?

5 In Houston, Li Cunxin (Chi Cao) falls in love with Elizabeth Mackey (Amanda Schull), also a dancer.

6 As a teenager at the ballet academy Li (Chengwu Guo) keeps training long after his fellow pupils have gone.

7 On Madame Mao's orders, the pupils of the academy rehearse a revolutionary dance piece.

8 The film's artistic high point is the dance scenes from Igor Stravinsky's "The Rite of Spring."

9 Soloist Mary McKendry (Camilla Vergotis) in "Swan Lake." Li appears in Houston for the second time alongside her.

as designed by Australian choreographer Graeme Murphy. As stylishly as the film comes across, not least in its richly varied visual language, the real stroke of genius in *Mao's Last Dancer* lies in the casting of the main part. Li as an adult is played by Chi Cao, not only a brilliant dancer but also a very good actor who brings passionate ballet dancing to the screen with as much power as the emotive acting scenes. Like Li Cunxin, Chi Cao trained in Beijing and then moved to the West, where he danced with the Birmingham Royal Ballet in England. Chi Cao's father was, incidentally, a teacher at the Beijing Dance Academy, where he taught Li Cunxin.

The film traces the story of Li's life up to 1989, sticking very closely to what actually happened to Li Cunxin, who was born in 1961. This includes the real-life dramatic incident at the Chinese Embassy in Houston, when Li refused to return to China but the embassy staff almost managed to drag him back there. Li married a fellow dancer, the Australian Mary McKendry (played by Camilla Vergotis) in America in 1987. He continued to dance in the USA and then Australia until 1995. He retired from dancing in 1998 at age 37, and since then has worked in Melbourne as a stockbroker. HJK

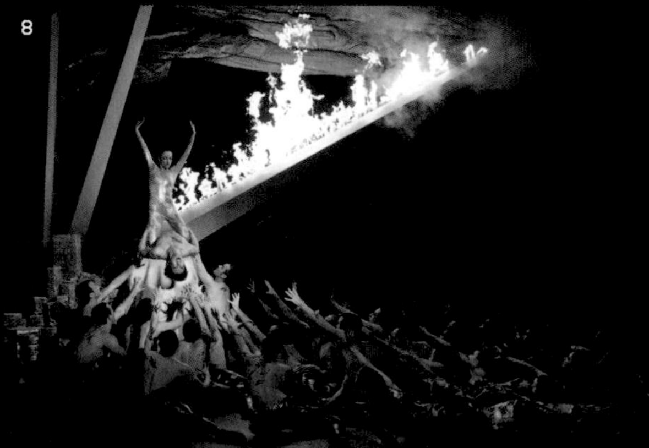

10 With grim determination, Li (Chengwu Guo) exercises his body, allegedly too weak, so that he can become a good dancer.

11 Attorney Charles Foster (Kyle MacLachlan) negotiates with the Chinese ambassador so that Li can stay in the USA.

12 Originally as an exchange student in Houston, Li Cunxin (Chi Cao) takes over in "Die Fledermaus" when the soloist is injured.

"It was obvious to me that only a dancer could play the part. You can't cheat with a ballet film, you have to show the dancing." *Bruce Beresford*

12

AVATAR 🏆🏆🏆

2009 – USA / UK – 162 MIN. – FANTASY
DIRECTOR JAMES CAMERON (*1954)
SCREENPLAY JAMES CAMERON **DIRECTOR OF PHOTOGRAPHY** MAURO FIORE **EDITING** JAMES CAMERON, JOHN REFOUA, STEPHEN E. RIVKIN **MUSIC** JAMES HORNER **PRODUCTION** JAMES CAMERON, JON LANDAU for 20TH CENTURY FOX, DUNE ENTERTAINMENT, GIANT STUDIOS, INGENIOUS FILM PARTNERS, LIGHTSTORM ENTERTAINMENT.
STARRING SAM WORTHINGTON (Jake Sully), ZOE SALDANA (Neytiri), SIGOURNEY WEAVER (Doctor Grace Augustine), STEPHEN LANG (Colonel Miles Quaritch), JOEL MOORE (Norm Spellman), GIOVANNI RIBISI (Parker Selfridge), MICHELLE RODRIGUEZ (Trudy Chacon), LAZ ALONSO (Tsu'tey), WES STUDI (Eytukan), CCH POUNDER (Moat).
ACADEMY AWARDS 2010 OSCARS for BEST CINEMATOGRAPHY (Mauro Fiore), BEST ART DIRECTION (Rick Carter, Robert Stromberg, Kim Sinclair), BEST VISUAL EFFECTS (Joe Letteri, Stephen Rosenbaum, Richard Baneham, Andy Jones).

"I see you."

There must be a fourth dimension, inhabited by no-one else but James Cameron, in which the ecological message of his film makes sense: at the very moment the old world is facing destruction, he simply creates a new one on his computer. Welcome to the alternative reality of Pandora! As if not just the development of 3-D but evolution in its entirety has taken a completely different direction, the trees, bushes and creatures of this distant world resemble those in the known universe, but in their archetypal forms. As if in an enchanted rainforest, everything – even down to the fluorescent leaf tips – is flooded with a surreal light, evoking the magic of a sunken, underwater kingdom. It is a subtropical aquarium, inhabited by weird flying lizards, dinosaur-like predators, and birds in the most iridescent colors imaginable. The blue-skinned humanoid creatures live in total harmony in this psychedelic world, in which the viewer, too, immediately feels at home.

Just like the old world, however, this new one is also under threat. Unfortunately for the Na'vi, a forest people resembling American Indians, Pandora has a raw material that is valuable to the human race. In order to extract it, a heavily armed space company approves a plan to destroy their civilization. In preparation, paraplegic US marine Jake Sully (Sam Worthington) is hot-wired to a body shell constructed from Na'vi DNA in order to study their way of life. Controlled by Sully in his sleep, this avatar is able not only to run and fight like a Na'vi, but also to overcome the justified suspicions of these people. Yet this electronic merger with an artificial body runs far more smoothly than his bosses would like: captivated by the virtual harmony with nature, the mercenary falls in love with the beautiful daughter of the Na'vi chieftain (Zoe Saldana, animated in similar fashion) and ends up leading the revolt of the Pandora people against the brutal invaders.

The simple storyline of *Avatar* is one of the movie's many contradictions – just as Cameron intended. Not only does he combine a pantheistic belief in nature with the latest technology, thus feeding the appetites of New Age hippies and restless computer games fans alike, he also fills his science fiction tale

1

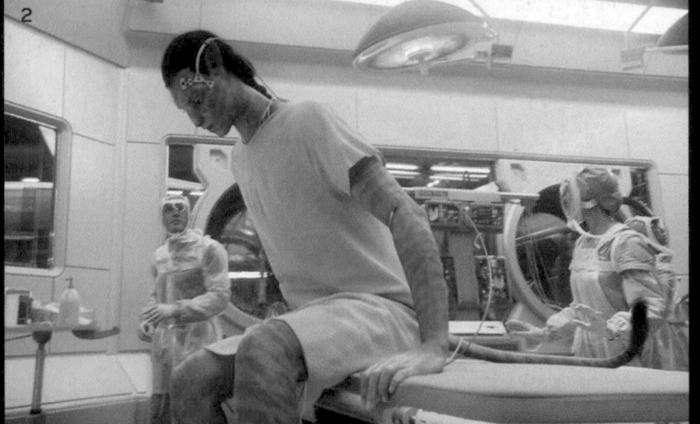

1 The blue princess: "virtual camera" motion capture creates unexpected emotional depth in fantasy figures such as Neytiri (Zoe Saldana).

2 Wonders of technology: an artificially constructed body shell allows US marine Jake Sully (Sam Worthington) to walk again.

3 Man and body: Jake experiences the symbiosis of these two separate entities as a rebirth.

4 Pocahontas myth for the new Millennium: Jake lets Princess Neytiri introduce him to the world of the Na'vi.

"*Avatar* is not simply a sensational entertainment, although it is that. It's a technical breakthrough." *Chicago Sun-Times*

5 Fluorescent rain forest: the magical world of Pandora bears an archetypal similarity to the universe as we know it.

6 Man and machine: the head of the research project, Grace Augustine (Sigourney Weaver), has long since been disempowered.

7 New Age rhapsody in blue: Grace also ventures into the world of the suspicious Na'vi in her avatar body.

with well known themes, in a way that is quite unprecedented for him. It is no coincidence that the much-slated recourse to the Pocahontas myth (an American Indian princess teaches the white invader respect for nature) forms the core of the plot; the viewer joins Jake Sully as he enters the 3-D world of Pandora, brimming with unfamiliar sensations as if setting foot on a new continent. Pure reason alone can protect it. In this way, criticism of civilization and an equally clearly articulated pacifism sit side by side with a narrative consensus based on the highest common denominator, which was essential to the success of this risky megaproject. Cameron's tried-and-tested blockbuster concept was to prevail: *Avatar* ousted his own movie *Titanic* (1997) from its position as the most successful film of all time, being the first to break the 2-billion-dollar barrier at the box office. It was hardly surprising, however, that this commercial hit bombed at the Oscars. *Avatar* has little in common with film in the traditional sense. Cameron estimates that around 80 percent of the material filmed was created on computer. The "fusion camera system," which was over ten years in development, worked wonders in giving even blue-skinned fantasy figures an incredible depth of character, but it reduces actors (who constitute a substantial part of the Oscar jury) to mere appendages of

6

7

“What *Avatar* does mark is a new breed. A new breed of action film, a new hero in Sam Worthington (who delivers a much more believable, and compelling performance than previous outings) and a new cinematic experience.” *The Independent*

10

8 The face of civilization: Colonel Miles Quaritch (Stephen Lang) leads the military against the Na'vi.

9 Threatened world: home to whole civilizations, the trees in Pandora also act as a spiritual reference point.

10 Critical message: the war against the Na'vi is also a powerful metaphor for man's exploitation of nature.

11 Proud warrior: betrothed to Neytiri, the chief's son Tsu'tey (Laz Alonso) is suspicious of Jake.

12 At the same time, the leader of his tribe is Jake's most crucial ally in the battle against the superior invaders.

13 New-look flora and fauna: for Pandora, James Cameron created a panoply of mythical avatar creatures.

technology. One of the movie's key strengths, however, lies in the way the film itself is a self-referential route to the technical nature of the fantasy. The stereoscopic 3-D effect is just another artificial prop and, in the same way that the viewer needs his special eyeglasses, Sully needs his avatar to meet the challenges of the film – seeing things in a new way. Yet what is achieved in the Na'vi kingdom through a quasi-metaphysical linking of tail ends is not so easy for a human being. Another disturbing message of the film is that he threatens to become just one among many potentially dispensable special effects within this sensational three-dimensional space, in which every leaf point and pendant blossom is subsumed in a lavish, undifferentiated spectacle. As we might expect, it is a point that is completely in accord with the movie's undeniably humanistic and even Utopian themes. PB

JAMES CAMERON The most commercially successful director in the world, James Cameron is also one of the technological pioneers in modern cinema history, using new developments to translate his creative ideas onto the big screen, and vice versa. Even as a child, Cameron (who was born in Canada in 1954) avidly explored all kinds of special effects. He gained his first experiences in Roger Corman's studios and, shortly afterward, made his feature debut *The Terminator* (1984), starring Arnold Schwarzenegger as the soulless robot from the future. This cool and gloomy sci-fi adventure, which brought Cameron to the forefront of filmmaking, also proved his skills in stylistically combining funny and serious elements. It also revealed his penchant for strong female characters: he made the sequel *Aliens* (1986) – with Sigourney Weaver playing the hard-bitten monster hunter Ellen Ripley – into one of the best follow-ups of all time. However, it was in the less successful underwater spine-chiller *The Abyss* (1989) that Cameron pushed innovative visual effects to the limits. His experimentation with computer morphing, blue screen filming and motion control photography came to fruition with *Terminator 2: Judgment Day* (1991) but, while other filmmakers were copying his ideas, Cameron was already planning his biggest project to date. The disaster movie *Titanic* (1997), filmed with miniature models in huge water tanks and digitally edited at enormous expense, was predicted to be the flop of the century because of the huge budget and the constant negative reports concerning his alleged dictatorial behavior on set. In the end, the film won 11 Oscars, with the tragic love story between new stars Leonardo DiCaprio and Kate Winslet aboard a sinking luxury liner meeting with wild enthusiasm worldwide.

The fact that Cameron himself also writes the screenplays for his visual extravaganzas is certainly one of the major reasons for his success. In the meantime, he collaborated with ex-wife Kathryn Bigelow in co-writing the excellent feminist cyberpunk thriller *Strange Days* (1995). It was, of all things, her war movie *The Hurt Locker* (2008) that denied him his next great Oscar coup: the 3-D spectacle *Avatar* (2009) netted just three gongs after winning nine nominations. His futuristic project proved the most commercially successful movie of all time, however, knocking *Titanic* off this spot.

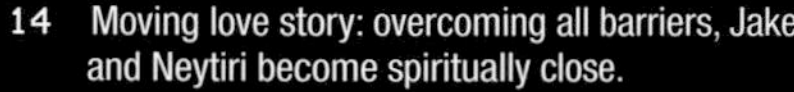

14 Moving love story: overcoming all barriers, Jake and Neytiri become spiritually close.

15 Psychedelic pixel matrix: every blossom becomes a lavish spectacle through Cameron's eyes.

16 Pacifist warriors: an attractive combination of grace with strength.

17 Eternal harmony: if nothing else, western ideals find expression in the bond the Na'vi have with nature.

"Whatever way you choose to look at it, *Avatar's* shock and awe demand to be seen. You've never experienced anything like it, and neither has anyone else." *Los Angeles Times*

17

WINTER'S BONE

★★★★
"A riveting thriller"
"One of the year's best films"
JENNIFER LAWRENCE JOHN HAWKES
WINTER'S BONE

2009 – USA – 100 MIN. – DRAMA, THRILLER
DIRECTOR DEBRA GRANIK (*1963)
SCREENPLAY DEBRA GRANIK, ANNE ROSELLINI from the novel by DANIEL WOODRELL
DIRECTOR OF PHOTOGRAPHY MICHAEL MCDONOUGH EDITING AFFONSO GONÇALVES
MUSIC DICKON HINCHLIFFE PRODUCTION ALIX MADIGAN, ANNE ROSELLINI for ANONYMOUS CONTENT, WINTER'S BONE PRODUCTION.
STARRING JENNIFER LAWRENCE (Ree), JOHN HAWKES (Teardrop), DALE DICKEY (Merab), CASEY MACLAREN (Megan), KEVIN BREZNAHAN (Little Arthur), RONNIE HALL (Thump Milton), WILLIAM WHITE (Blond Milton), LAUREN SWEETSER (Gail), SHELLEY WAGGENER (Sonya), GARRET DILLAHUNT (Sheriff Baskin).

"Never ask for what oughta be offered."

The Ozark Mountain chain is wild and rugged, as are the faces of the people who live there. This landscape and its people are like no other. If you knock on their door, assuming you even get that far, you will be met with inexplicable hostility. It is no different for 17-year-old Ree (Jennifer Lawrence). She has grown up here and is related to just about everyone, but her questions are not wanted. Ree is looking for her father, Jessup. In advance of court proceedings he has put up as bail their squalid wooden house, where Ree single-handedly looks after her brother and sister and her mentally ill mother. If he fails to turn up, the house will be seized by the court. The charge is producing and dealing crystal meth, and herein lies the secret – everyone here makes a living from, or lives with, the drug; it has taken hold of them mentally and physically, weighing on them like an evil curse. They all know that anyone asking questions is taking a life-threatening risk.

Ree won't be intimidated, though, and courageously sets off through the lumbered forests, from hut to hut past trampled wire fences, piles of trash and rusty car wrecks, seeking information about her missing father. She has not managed to break free from this environment, but she knows its unwritten laws. She knows you cannot enter a house without permission, what you have to use as a threat and when you have to be silent in order to learn something. She also suspects that her father is dead, and that this would probably be best for everyone. But she needs the body in order to keep the house. Proof of his death is the only thing that will secure their survival.

The hard-headed anger and resolution embodied by Jennifer Lawrence in this role make *Winter's Bone* an extraordinary experience. The first decade of the 2000s belonged to strong young women, but the unswerving courage of Lawrence's character is almost frightening. At one point, someone asks "Ain't you got no man to do this?" – but she doesn't need one. We see her chopping wood, and hunting and gutting animals; she takes a beating and gets up again. Her only chance is to show no fear under the woolly hat that she wears as a soldier does his helmet. She actually plucks up the courage

2

1 Quiet fighter: Ree Dolly (Jennifer Lawrence) faces a hostile environment with courage and determination. It's her only hope of survival.

2 The end of the American Dream: in the wild of the Ozark Mountains in Missouri, the people live in archaic conditions. The film combines images of "white trash" lifestyle with the iconography of the Western.

to enter a US Army recruitment office at one stage, in order to collect the 40,000 dollar bonus. She is turned away from this, her only way out of a dead-end situation, though sometimes her bare-knuckle survival instinct is almost comical. To her little brother's question whether they have to eat the insides of the small squirrel she has caught, she replies: "Not yet."

Ree is the tragic female figure of myth in a film in which the uniquely oppressive mood of hopelessness should not necessarily be confused with social realism. Dealing meth in the Ozarks is the sad reality, described in the powerful introduction to Daniel Woodrell's book. Yet the wintery light – the sun never seems to shine here – is entirely down to Michael McDonough's wonderful digital photography and the aesthetic flair of director Debra Granik. Some of the night sequences were actually filmed during daytime, using the "day-for-night" technique. What we see are mental landscapes where even the soil seems poisoned – literally, in the case of the burned-down meth lab – and we are struck to the core by a sense of the post-apocalyptic decomposition of life.

3

4

"There are moments in the harshly beautiful *Winter's Bone* in which the characters are so deeply, unfathomably mean in response to a 17-year-old girl's pleas to find her father (or at least his body) that we search their faces for a glimmer of sympathy, kinship—anything human." *New York Magazine*

3 Family secrets: Ree's relatives don't like her questions. Her cousin Blond Milton (William White) even sets her on the wrong track.

4 Female solidarity: Gail (Lauren Sweetser) is the only one who is prepared to help her friend Ree.

5 Independent cinema's new hope: Jennifer Lawrence received an Oscar nomination for the role. At first, she was considered "too pretty" to play Ree.

5

6

6 Wild and rugged: character actor John Hawkes is great as Ree's dangerous Uncle Teardrop. A soft center hides behind a menacing exterior.

7 A kind of rural film noir: the heroine keeps hitting a dead end in the form of surly Merab (Dale Dickey). The atmosphere is chilly.

8 Seeking a better life: substitute mother Ree teaches her little brother and sister how to shoot as well.

JENNIFER LAWRENCE The independence that Jennifer Lawrence brings to her roles has also been applied to her Hollywood career. Born in Kentucky in 1990, she moved to New York when she was 14 to get closer to her goal. Her first interviews went so well that it wasn't long before TV parts began to roll in. At the age of 16 Lawrence completed her first TV movie and subsequently appeared in 24 episodes of the TBS series "The Bill Engvall Show" (2007–2009). During this time she showed the first signs of a feel for more serious roles in *The Burning Plain* (2008), the directorial debut of Mexican scriptwriting prodigy Guillermo Arriaga. This intricate women's drama received a muted response but Lawrence in particular had excellent reviews, alongside Kim Basinger and Charlize Theron.

Her role in *Winter's Bone* (2010) made her the new star of independent cinema. Director Debra Granik had already met with similar success with her debut movie *Down to the Bone* (2004) starring Vera Farmiga. As the hard-fighting substitute mother Ree who quietly accepts archaic blood ties in the rural drug environment while still maintaining her independence, this new kid on the block received rave reviews and ended up with an Oscar nomination. We then saw her directed by Jodie Foster in *The Beaver* (2011), a quirky psychodrama with Mel Gibson. Her appearance as the blue-skinned mutant Mystique in *X-Men: First Class* (2011) has also taken Lawrence – who by her own admission has never been to acting school – into the blockbuster sector.

This nightmare thriller from the American hinterland really comes alive through the subtle addition of country sounds, the local cast of non-professionals and the equally plausible character actors such as Dale Dickey and John Hawkes. Their gaunt faces and rotten teeth put the fear of God into us, yet if we look long enough we can also detect a sense of some kind of community behind their blanket distrust. The harsh structure of this film depends on more than just surface appearances, however: the characters are deeply rooted in the whole three-dimensional space of this landscape, which is captured beautifully by *Winter's Bone*. In the end, they have no option but to help Ree. The gruesome title ends in a dénouement that is even grislier than we would have expected. Films like this are a real treat. PB

"It is the scene in which we realize why it is called *Winter's Bone*: a moment from a horror movie. But here it has a tragic dignity that separates true cinema from genre films, and great stories from industry-dictated ones." *Frankfurter Allgemeine Zeitung*

8

BLUE VALENTINE

2009 – USA – 112 MIN. GENRE DRAMA, ROMANTIC DRAMA
DIRECTOR DEREK CIANFRANCE (*1974)
SCREENPLAY DEREK CIANFRANCE, CAMI DELAVIGNE, JOEY CURTIS
DIRECTOR OF PHOTOGRAPHY ANDRIJ PAREKH EDITING JIM HELTON, RON PATANE MUSIC GRIZZLY BEAR
PRODUCTION JAMIE PATRICOF, LYNETTE HOWELL, ALEX ORLOVSKY for SILVERWOOD FILMS, HUNTING LANE FILMS.
STARRING RYAN GOSLING (Dean), MICHELLE WILLIAMS (Cindy), FAITH WLADYKA (Frankie), JOHN DOMAN (Jerry), MIKE VOGEL (Bobby), MARSHALL JOHNSON (Marshall), JEN JONES (Gramma), MARYANN PLUNKETT (Glenda), JAMES BENATTI (Jamie), BARBARA TROY (Jo), CAREY WESTBROOK (Charley), BEN SHENKMAN (Dr. Feinberg), EILEEN ROSEN (Mimi), ENID GRAHAM (Professor), ASHLEY GURNARI (Checker), JACK PARSHUTICH (Billy), SAMII RYAN (Amanda).

"You always hurt the ones you love."

The soundtrack over the opening credits does not bode well. Viewers are left wondering whether they are hearing strange electronic noises or just crickets chirping. Gradually, children's cries blend in with these sounds and a green field comes into view: Frankie (Faith Wladyka) and her father Dean (Ryan Gosling) are apparently searching for a dog in the knee-high grass. The worst is yet to come – like finding a severed ear in David Lynch's *Blue Velvet* (1986). But the horror in *Blue Valentine* is understated, making it far more gruesome. Dean and his wife Cindy (Michelle Williams) have outgrown each other, and the plot painstakingly dissects this unbearable situation. In the process, carefully composed sequences using documentary-style dialogue and improvised scenes are edited together in such a way that we feel we are witnessing at first hand the everyday life of this family in rural Pennsylvania.

Dean is 30-ish, smokes, drinks and does casual work as a house painter, the tattoo on his upper arm showing the cover image of Shel Silverstein's classic children's book "The Giving Tree" (1964). He takes good care of his small daughter though, when Cindy is out at her nursing work. To save their marriage, they check into a run-down motel. Instead of "Cupid's Cave" they choose the "Future Room" – and in this windowless dystopia with a revolving bed the two attempt to revive their love under the pitiless blue neon light. It's not so much about the future – without it being particularly noticeable at first, the action moves between the immediate present and flashbacks to the time when Cindy and Dean met in Brooklyn. Flirting and passionate infatuation intermingle with coldness and repulsion, until marriage and possible separation become almost conflated. So it becomes obvious in retrospect why Dean overreacts when Cindy meets her ex-boyfriend Bobby (Mike Vogel) in a supermarket: the pair had loveless, unprotected sex and Frankie is the outcome of this relationship.

To the film's credit, it introduces the audience to the fragile emotional state of both protagonists on an equal footing, without taking sides. Dean is lacking in ambition, sometimes seeming like a big kid, but is extremely empathetic, both sexually and emotionally. Cindy seems more mature, and has a better job, but it's not often that she can adequately express her feelings. When Cindy is called in to work unexpectedly, Dean follows her in the car, drunk; a scuffle ensues. She ends up being fired and they have a fierce argument. Whether it really ends in divorce, however, is left open. Dean simply decides to give his wife some space to think. The only certainty is that this relationship is following its own unique logic, creating a power to sustain it that is difficult for outsiders to understand.

Blue Valentine is a lesson in human complexity. Like the gender roles, everything is in a state of flux: love and hate, past and present are indistinguishable, merging into an endless gray area. It is not the ambiguous feelings, the sexual rejection represented in detail, or an abortion scene that are difficult to bear;

1
2

1 Nominated for the Oscar: Michelle Williams as Cindy. The movie title refers, incidentally, to Tom Waits' album of the same name.

2 As Dean, Ryan Gosling's aging appearance – his clothes and incipient baldness – was modeled on the director, Derek Cianfrance.

3 Michelle Williams and Ryan Gosling lived together for a month in preparation for their roles as an old married couple.

MICHELLE WILLIAMS Michelle Williams (born 1980) is one of Hollywood's famous up-and-coming young actresses. She left the parental home to develop her career at the tender age of 15. She became known mainly for playing bad girl Jen Lindley in the TV series *Dawson's Creek* (1998–2003). From 1993, Williams also had minor roles in *Baywatch* (1989–2001) and *Home Improvement* (1991–1999).

In 1994, however, she landed a bigger role in the remake of the film classic *Lassie*; appearances then followed in a few independent productions such as Wim Wenders' *Land of Plenty* (2004) and the TV movie *If These Walls Could Talk 2* (2000). Williams achieved fame as well as her first Oscar nomination for her role as the wife of a gay cowboy in Ang Lee's drama *Brokeback Mountain* (2005); in 2010, we saw her on screen in Martin Scorsese's literary adaptation *Shutter Island*. The actress won her second Oscar nomination for her leading role in *Blue Valentine*. Williams has a daughter by the late actor Heath Ledger.

what weighs more heavily by far is the fact that they have the deep, historical bond of a once passionate romance – despite its leading to an unfulfilled, mundane married life. Yet they have something important in common: Dean and Cindy both come from dysfunctional families and want to avoid making the same mistakes as their parents. Equally, it could well be that we are being shown, as if through a magnifying glass, not the dramatic end of a relationship, but simply the routine moods of a couple married for many years; the embraces and some of the conversations come across as rather too intimate. Ultimately, the film illustrates that successful relationships are the result of hard work. Romantic, everlasting love that springs from nowhere only happens in fairytales – or mainstream Hollywood cinema. PLB

"*Blue Valentine* is that rare creation: a love story that doesn't shy away from sex, ignore its consequences, or droop into pointless fantasy." *The New Yorker*

4 The scenes from the past were created using Super-16mm film stock, while those of the present day used digital technology.

5 Dean was beaten up by Cindy's ex-boyfriend Bobby but still stands by his feelings.

BAL
HONEY

2009/10 – TURKEY / GERMANY – 103 MIN. – DRAMA
DIRECTOR SEMIH KAPLANOĞLU (*1963)
SCREENPLAY SEMIH KAPLANOĞLU, ORÇUN KÖKSAL DIRECTOR OF PHOTOGRAPHY BARIŞ ÖZBIÇER
EDITING AYHAN ERGÜRSEL, SEMIH KAPLANOĞLU, SUZAN HANDE GÜNERI
PRODUCTION SEMIH KAPLANOĞLU for KAPLAN FILM PRODUCTION, HEIMATFILM, ZDF/ARTE.
STARRING BORA ALTAŞ (Yusuf), ERDAL BEŞIKÇIOĞLU (Yakup), TÜLIN ÖZEN (Zehra), AYŞE ALTAY, ALEV UÇARER, ÖZKAN AKÇAY, SELAMI GÖKÇE, KAMIL YILMAZ, ADEM KURKUT, ERHAN KESKIN.
IFF BERLIN 2010 GOLDEN BEAR for BEST FILM (Semih Kaplanoğlu).

"Do you know when you'll be coming home?"

Seven-year-old Yusuf (Bora Altaş) is very close to his father, Yakup (Erdal Beşikçioğlu). A quiet boy, he often accompanies the honey gatherer as he walks through the lonely Anatolian mountain forests. As he does so, Yusuf listens to his father's words, which let him into the secrets of nature and his work. The latter is arduous and dangerous, for often Yakup has first to climb to the tops of ancient trees in order to hang his beehives and harvest the honey. One day, because the bees are dying, he is forced to move on to remoter valleys, but his son cannot go with him as he must attend school. Yusuf waits for days for his father to come back, but in vain. Yakup does not return from the forests.

Bal, winner of the Golden Bear at the 2010 Berlin International Film Festival, is the third part of Semih Kaplanoğlu's retrospectively narrated "Yusuf" trilogy, a work that can in many respects be seen as a cinematic journey in time: on the one hand, because the Turkish director wants to shed light on his own roots through the figure of Yusuf, as well as rekindling general interest in rural life and its traditions; and also because Kaplanoğlu has chosen to use what appears to be an outmoded form at a time when cinema's use of digital technology produces unprecedented visual stimulation, making it seem like a radical alternative in terms of style. For, like the films of his avowed "guru" Robert Bresson, Kaplanoğlu also challenges the audience through what comes

"In images that sensually conjure up the primitive world of the protagonists while equally filling them with poetic meaning, a haunting, existential drama about the end of childhood unfolds quietly and with little dialogue." *film-dienst*

1 Living with and in nature: the honey gatherer climbs to the top of huge trees to harvest the "essence of the forest."

2 Father as teacher: Yusuf (Bora Altaş) listens carefully to Yakup (Erdal Beşikçioğlu), as he introduces him to nature's secrets.

3 Yusuf is a quiet boy; an outsider in school who stutters hopelessly when reading aloud. The third film in Kaplanoğlu's autobiographically-inspired Yusuf trilogy tells the story of a poet's childhood.

2

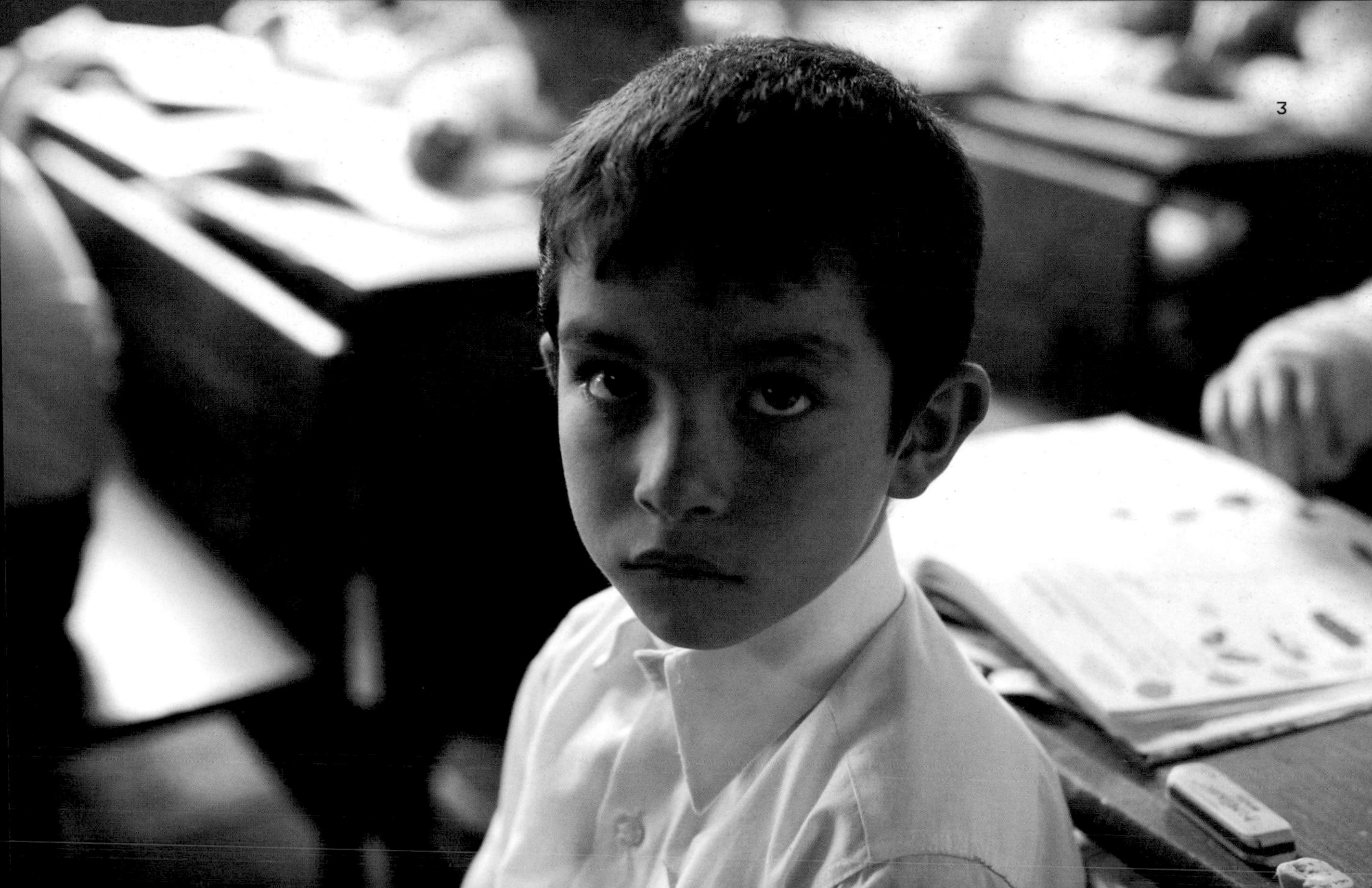

3

over as ascetic simplicity and an utterly serene sense of peace. *Bal* is "slow cinema" in its purest form.

The plot unfolds in Kaplanoğlu's film without any background music of any kind, in a long series of carefully composed images that have an almost documentary quality about them. They show the boy in a magically primitive environment. His native village seems to have dropped right out of another era, set in an elemental landscape with wood and stone houses devoid of any modern comforts, and residents who go about their daily work the way they have done since time immemorial. So Yusuf grows up in a world that has not yet divulged its secrets, in which knowledge is passed on from one generation to the next and people live on and in harmony with nature. And just as Yakup acts as a mediator in opening his son's eyes and ears to this enchanted world, Kaplanoğlu makes the audience aware of its beauty. The crackle of trees and the steam of the forest; this terrific film enables us to experience these details with the intensity of a child. And when Yusuf sticks his finger in the honey they have just gathered and licks it, we can almost taste the golden nectar or, as Kaplanoğlu calls it, "the essence of the forest."

Yumurta (*Egg*, 2007) and *Süt* (2008), the first two "Yusuf" films, show the protagonist when he is older as a budding and eventually successful writer. In fact, *Bal* gives no direct indication that Yusuf will one day become a writer. Acquiring language, however, and the ability to express what has been experienced, felt or imagined, plays a central role in the film. Thus the boy is evidently fascinated by the power of words, even though he is exceptionally quiet himself. His repeated attempts to read aloud in school always end, however, in terrible stuttering. In the meantime, his father is the only one who understands that this inability to convey thoughts aloud to others lies in Yusuf's receptiveness

SEMIH KAPLANO LU Semih Kaplanoğlu is one of the biggest names in contemporary Turkish cinema, which has been experiencing a renaissance since the turn of the millennium. Born in Izmir in 1963, he gained his first experience as a director when he was an art student at the university in his home town. After years working as a journalist and advertising copywriter among other things, as well as doing minor film jobs, he became known to a wider general public through the TV series *Şehnaz Tango* (1994/1996), which he co-wrote and directed. The filmmaker had his international breakthrough with his second feature film *Meleğin Düşüşü* (*Angel's Fall*, 2004), made by Kaplanoğlu's own company, Kaplan Film Production: it is a dark drama about incest, reminding some critics of Tarkovski's work. But the highpoint of his career to date is without doubt the autobiographically inspired "Yusuf" trilogy, in which Kaplanoğlu tracks the life of a writer in three stages back to his childhood and promotes the rediscovery of provincial life. In *Yumurta* (*Egg*, 2007) the 40-year-old protagonist, now an established writer, returns to his little native village from the big city after the death of his mother. *Süt* (2008) tells of the young man's growing ambitions to be a writer at least 20 years earlier, leading to conflict with his mother, who is a simple dairy farmer. Finally, *Bal* (*Honey*, 2009/2010) deals with the child's formative experiences at the side of his father, a honey gatherer. This last film in the trilogy earned Kaplanoğlu the Golden Bear at the 2010 Berlin International Film Festival and was nominated for an Oscar for Best Foreign Language Film.

4 Kaplanoğlu wanted to show traditional provincial life through the eyes of a curious child. Some critics accused the Turkish filmmaker of idealizing primitive rural conditions.

5 Yakup the honey gatherer is a man of few words, but very empathetic; Yusuf is very close to him …

6 … making the son's futile wait for his father all the more painful, when one day he doesn't return from his dangerous job in the forest.

7 The magic of words: Yusuf is fascinated by the poetry of language – but it would seem this is precisely what makes reading aloud so hard for him.

to the poetry of language. The scene in which he succeeds in persuading the boy to whisper his dreams into his ear is filled with a tenderness, the like of which is rarely found in cinema.

Overall, *Bal* generates an unexpectedly forceful quality, directly through the portrayal of the father–son relationship. This can be attributed not just to Kaplanoğlu's supreme control of the filmic medium but also to the young lead actor, Bora Altaş, whose serious and profound expression carries the film; his child's face is invested with emotional responses, yet without a trace of mawkishness. This makes the boy's grief over his gentle father's absence – a father who thus avoids the cliché of the strict Turkish patriarch – seem all the more painful. Yakup's death, heralded as early as the prologue, is for Yusuf synonymous with the end of his childhood in paradise. JH

“Bora Altas as Yusuf is definitely a minor miracle, who brings a profoundly melancholic richness to *Bal* – a film that is practically a documentary and has little action – without relying on any kind of musical support.” *Frankfurter Rundschau*

MY NAME IS KHAN

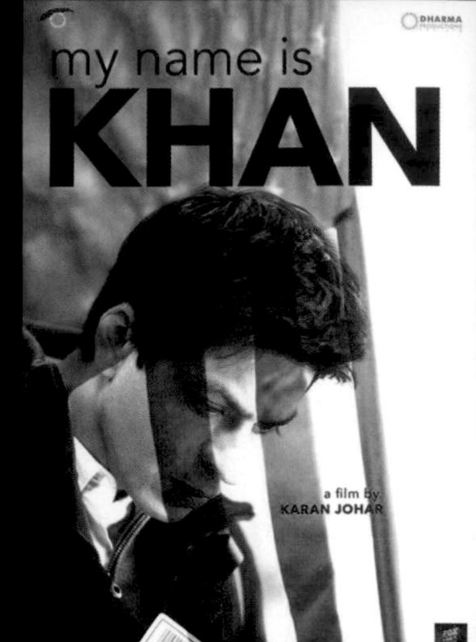

2009/10 – INDIA – INTERNATIONAL VERSION 128 MIN. / LONG VERSION 165 MIN. – SOCIAL DRAMA
DIRECTOR KARAN JOHAR (*1972)
SCREENPLAY SHIBANI BATHIJA, NIRANJAN IYENGAR DIRECTOR OF PHOTOGRAPHY RAVI K. CHANDRAN
EDITING DEEPA BHATIA MUSIC SHANKAR MAHADEVAN, LOY MENDONSA, EHSAAN NOORANI
PRODUCTION GAURI KHAN, HIROO JOHAR for DHARMA PRODUCTIONS, RED CHILLIES ENTERTAINMENT.
STARRING SHAH RUKH KHAN (Rizwan Khan), KAJOL (Mandira Khan), KATIE A. KEANE (Sarah Garrick), KENTON DUTY (Reese Garrick), BENNY NIEVES (Detective Garcia), CHRISTOPHER B. DUNCAN (President Obama), JIMMY SHERGILL (Zakir Khan), SONYA JEHAN (Hasina Khan), SHANE HARPER (Tim).

"My name is Khan and I am not a terrorist!"

Rizwan Khan (Shah Rukh Khan) seems rather odd to people who do not know him. For he is autistic, and virtually incapable of conveying his own feelings or understanding those of others. A good-natured man from India, he is also disarmingly honest and will always take what his fellow human beings say literally. Above all else, however, he is always true to his word. As a result, he moves to San Francisco to live with his brother and seek his fortune, because this is what he promised his mother before she died. In his work as a sales rep for beauty products he meets divorcée Mandira (Kajol), a hairdresser, and persists until this beautiful Hindu woman truly falls in love with and marries him. But then the USA is hit by the events of 9/11 and the Khan family is made painfully aware of the consequences of the attacks. When Mandira's son is beaten up by racists who assume he is a Muslim, everything changes. In a state of unimaginable anguish, Mandira sends her husband away, telling Rizwan that he is only allowed to come back when he has said face-to-face to the US President: "My name is Khan and I am not a terrorist." So Rizwan sets out on what will prove a long journey. It is a well known fact that India produces more movies than Hollywood, yet outside the Indian community Hindi cinema has gone virtually unnoticed on the international scene for many years. Now, all that has changed. For some time now the films of the Indian dream factory have enjoyed a steadily growing global fan base (overwhelmingly female, understandably) not in spite of, but because of, their unfettered romanticism and the obligatory music and dance sequences. This hype is inextricably linked with one name: Shah Rukh Khan.

My Name is Khan – distributed in Europe and the US mainly by Fox Studios and filmed for the most part in California – is regarded as the most ambitious attempt to date by the King of Bollywood to win over a mass audience in the West. So the smoldering-eyed hero of the title is a bit like a cross between the protagonists in *Rain Man* (1988) and *Forrest Gump* (1994). In other ways too, though, the film makes it easy for a cinemagoer who has not been smitten by Bollywood: for one thing, the subject of 9/11 is an eminently universal one, but even more importantly the storyline itself is far more robustly detailed than would normally be the case in Indian cinema, with even the musical elements remaining discreetly in the background. The fact that the movie was released in many locations in versions that were shorter than the original 165 minutes can safely be taken as a further concession – after all, Hindi films can easily last three hours or more.

1

1 A man who doesn't really need chocolates: Shah Rukh Khan is the most popular movie star in the world, thanks to his female fan base. *My Name is Khan* was the most ambitious film to date from the "King of Bollywood."

2 In this US–Indian co-production, Khan plays an autistic man who falls in love with an Indian hairdresser (Kajol) in his new home of California. Love's bliss is shattered, however, by the anti-Muslim violence following 9/11.

3 Mumbai goes L.A.: *My Name is Khan* is a convincing combination of Hindi cinema's colorful sentimentality and Hollywood's narrative style. The musical elements are thinly spread, however.

"A complete intoxication of a film – when western standards cannot be applied, it's difficult to decide whether the result is a stroke of genius or simply a piece of kitsch. At any rate, it is a bit chaotic; such a wild mixture of styles that it presents as a new variant, even to fans of Bollywood cinema." *Süddeutsche Zeitung*

Having said which, the tone of the movie is clearly set by Indian cinema's emotional force and musicality. With a sure sense of rhythm and timing, director Karan Johar alternates between sentimental and humorous moments, while not shying away from the occasional lurid touch. We can just about overlook the fact that there are no elaborate dance sequences, given the beautifully matched visual choreography and spirited film score that is clearly of Indian provenance. Most important of all, however, are the sparks clearly flying between Khan and Kajol: they epitomize the Bollywood dream couple, appearing the most natural thing in the world even under a Californian sun.

Yet *My Name is Khan* is more than just romantic entertainment cinema, of course; it also carries a message, calling for tolerance and united action in an age of global terror. It is, in fact, remarkable that this message comes across so clearly, as it is presented in an extremely impartial way that avoids any overdone reflection. Yet neither does it sink into the mawkish or kitsch; the genuine pathos of this movie makes it incredibly powerful, not least because Shah Rukh Khan faultlessly fulfills the dual role of protagonist and narrator. Playing the lovable autistic man, he is an incorruptible moral authority who subtly transforms chaotic reality into a clear-cut world of good and evil for the viewer. Furthermore, thanks to his star qualities he also projects the ideal role model and screen presence even when playing an outsider. When the film was premiered at the 2010 Berlin International Film Festival, Karan Johar aptly described *My Name Is Khan* as the story of a superhero whose only power is his humanity. In saying this, however, the director failed to mention this character's most effective weapon – his charm. JH

SHAH RUKH KHAN It is hard to say whether he is the most popular actor in the world, but the title "King of Bollywood" definitely belongs to him. Shah Rukh Khan, born in New Delhi in 1965 to Muslim parents, is the first truly international star to emerge from the Indian film capital Mumbai. In saying that, the screen charmer – who once described himself as a heartthrob – was not always the automatic choice to play the romantic hero.

Following his early success in films in the early 1990s, he was cast as an obsessive villain in various movies including the hit *Baazigar* (1993). In this revenge drama, he appeared for the first time alongside Kajol, and they went on to become India's most popular screen couple in five other films. One movie they made together, *Dilwale Dulhania Le Jayenge* (1995), achieved special cult status. Filmed partly in Switzerland, this film is seen as a pioneer of modern Bollywood cinema, which in the years that followed was gradually discovered by a niche audience in the West. Khan's more recent appearances have clearly revealed his ambition to create an even wider international audience for "Made in Mumbai" cinema. The star, who comes over as likeable and self-deprecating, recognized the main obstacles to this when he admitted "our films are too long" at the Berlin Film Festival press conference for his film *Om Shanti Om* (2007). In addition, according to Khan, the musical elements should be integrated more intelligently into the plot. *My Name is Khan* (2009/10) is proof his approach works.

4 Dream couple of Indian cinema: *My Name is Khan* is proof that the chemistry between Khan and his favorite movie partner, Kajol, also works perfectly in a movie with a message designed for the international market.

5 Repairs almost anything: for director Karan Johar, Shah Rukh Khan as Rizwan represents a superhero with a single power – his humanity.

BIUTIFUL

2010 – MEXICO / SPAIN – 148 MIN. – SOCIAL DRAMA
DIRECTOR ALEJANDRO GONZÁLEZ IÑÁRRITU (*1963)
SCREENPLAY ALEJANDRO GONZÁLEZ IÑÁRRITU, ARMANDO BO, NICOLÁS GIACOBONE
DIRECTOR OF PHOTOGRAPHY RODRIGO PRIETO EDITING STEPHEN MIRRIONE
MUSIC GUSTAVO SANTAOLALLA PRODUCTION FERNANDO BOVAIRA, ALEJANDRO GONZÁLEZ IÑÁRRITU, JON KILIK for MENAGEATROZ, MOD PRODUCCIONES, IKIRU FILMS, FOCUS FEATURES, TELEVISIÓ DE CATALUNYA (TV3), TELEVISÓN ESPAÑOLA (TVE), UNIVERSAL PICTURES.
STARRING JAVIER BARDEM (Uxbal), MARICEL ÁLVAREZ (Marambra), HANAA BOUCHAIB (Ana), GUILLERMO ESTRELLA (Mateo), EDUARD FERNÁNDEZ (Tito), CHEIKH NDIAYE (Ekweme), ANA WAGENER (Bea), DIARYATOU DAFF (Ige), CHENG TAI SHEN (Hai), LUO JIN (Liwei).
IFF CANNES 2010 SILVER PALM for BEST ACTOR (Javier Bardem, jointly with Elio Germano for *La nostra vita*).

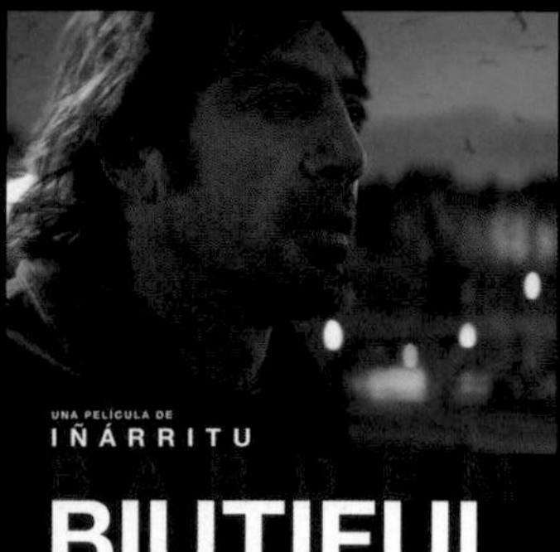

"The dead suffer, if they leave debts behind."

When Ana asks her father Uxbal how to write "beautiful," he replies that it is written as it sounds. Of course, this is untrue. So if you believe it, you'll write it incorrectly. But does it really matter?

Uxbal (Javier Bardem) is a man plagued by bad luck. It is clear from the beginning, when his distrust of the nurse makes him demand a new needle, that civilization and its standards have no place in his world. It is somewhere you can inject yourself, and occasionally have to. At the same time, however, we are in Barcelona. Alejandro González Iñárritu is showing us an alternative city: one that is not a seaside resort, has no wonderful beach, and is not famed for its beauty. Instead, it is a harsh, terrible place where you can feel the tense atmosphere and smell the damp walls. Only once do we see the shoreline – littered with the bodies of desperate Chinese immigrants. We are given the impression that here, people live in poverty; illegally, with no place in society.

Uxbal has the spiritual gift of being able to hear the voices of the dead, and earns himself a dubious income by conveying their last thoughts to those left behind. He also acts as a go-between for illegal workers: the Chinese who produce the goods and the Africans who sell them on the street, in a criminal enterprise that has no further questions of morality. As his wife Marambra (Maricel Álvarez) is mentally ill, Uxbal has to stay home to take care of his two children, Ana (Hanaa Bouchaib) and Mateo (Guillermo Estrella), by himself. A loving father, he tries his best to give them a better future: he takes them to school each morning and is strict about their behavior. And while he doesn't exactly rise to the role of hero, we identify with him, seeing through his eyes and experiencing the same sensations and feelings as he does.

1 Anger, yet gentleness, reflected in his eyes: Uxbal (Javier Bardem) tries to find a dignified way out of a hard life.

2 A street seller runs for his life. Through the eye of the camera, the violence in Barcelona's slum district is unadorned and brutal.

3 Uxbal takes his kids to school. It is touching, the way he assumes his paternal duties and tries to distance his children from all the cruelty.

4 Out of very little, Uxbal creates a safe home for his children. Ritual and duty are meant to make a path to a better future.

5 The relationship between Marambra (Maricel Álvarez) and Uxbal is by no means perfect, but we catch glimpses of their love very occasionally in their gentle encounters.

"In characteristic style, González Iñárritu creates a sense of raw, all pervasive intimacy in every scene." *The New York Times*

5

"It's a gorgeous, melancholy tone poem about love, fatherhood and guilt." *The Hollywood Reporter*

As if things were not already difficult enough for Uxbal, he finds out at the start of the film that he is seriously ill, with not long to live. In the time remaining to him, he has to put his affairs in order, but all his efforts seem doomed to failure. Many hopes are dashed and, worse still, Uxbal lets down the very people who have relied on him. The African street sellers are picked up in a raid, while the Chinese workers die from the effects of the cheap gas heaters he has supplied them with. A final attempt to live with his wife and children together ends in disaster.

Yet, in spite of the depressing plot and many blows of fate Uxbal has to face, it is a deeply moving film, uniquely intimate and beautiful. Credit for this must go to Javier Bardem, who plays the part of Uxbal with absolute credibility and thereby dignifies him. For this is basically the story of a man who, even at the critical point of death, continues to oscillate between rebellion and humility, redemption and resignation, as if there was still a chance to turn things around.

The images, too, are breathtakingly beautiful, created by the same cameraman responsible for Ang Lee's *Brokeback Mountain* (2005). The light alternates between harsh brightness and hazy, glittering or warmly vibrant tones, the sequences sometimes strident, sometimes muted. When Uxbal is in the grip of delirium, seeing the souls of the dead stuck to the ceiling as if

JAVIER BARDEM The assassin in Joel and Ethan Coen's *No Country for Old Men* (2007), quadriplegic Ramón Sampedro in Alejandro Amenábar's Oscar-winning *The Sea Inside* (*Mar adentro*, 2004), the writer in Julian Schnabel's *Before Night Falls* (2000) or the heartthrob in Woody Allen's *Vicky Cristina Barcelona* (2008) – Javier Bardem can play all kinds of roles and never look miscast. So it comes as no surprise that he is one of the few European actors to make it in Hollywood – and the first Spaniard ever to win an Oscar, for his supporting role in *No Country for Old Men*.
Born in Las Palmas, Gran Canaria in 1969, Bardem comes from a family that has worked in Spanish cinema since its early stages, either as actors, directors or screenwriters. So it is almost as if he inherited a certain physiological expressiveness and stage presence. He studied art in Madrid, rather than taking acting classes. From a young age he had parts in films by Pedro Almodóvar – *High Heels* (*Tacones lejanos*, 1991), and *Live Flesh* (*Carne trémula*, 1997). His choice of directors shows that he is more interested in art and narrative technique than commercialism. This is far from saying, however, that Bardem hasn't also made some brilliant movies for sheer entertainment.

6 Uninhibited and out of control – Marambra is crazy, her exaggerated gestures beautifully expressed by Maricel Álvarez.

7 Temptation lurks everywhere, but there's no fooling conscience: Uxbal bathed in the exotic colors of a disco.

8 Coldness, distrust, betrayal – Uxbal helplessly looks for a way to make amends.

9 Javier Bardem won a Best Actor award at Cannes for his portrayal of Uxbal.

the concrete jungle is preventing them from reaching heaven, the imagery does not appear ridiculous, but deeply alarming. The viewer is carried along on a tide of sadness and horror that is felt almost viscerally. There is, however, a counter-current: in returning to the same image at the end, the prevailing sense created by this film is one of hope and reassurance.

Biutiful is both typical and atypical of Mexican director Alejandro González Iñárritu. It is another story about death, but this time he sticks to one central character in the development of a coherent plot. In each of his previous films – *Amores perros* (2000), *21 Grams* (2003) and *Babel* (2006) – he telescoped and interwove three episodes, as if this fragmented approach would contribute in some way to the force of the plot. The structure in Biutiful is closed, however, corresponding to the human notion of growing and passing – a calm, self-contained cycle as a symbol of divine providence. MM

"From one scene to the next, as is his custom, Mr. González Iñárritu creates a feeling of raw, sprawling intimacy. The coarse-grained, lyrical naturalism of his shooting style can seem more tactile than visual, and every shot is full of emotional and social detail, bringing Barcelona to itchy, sweaty life." *The New York Times*

CARLOS THE JACKAL
CARLOS

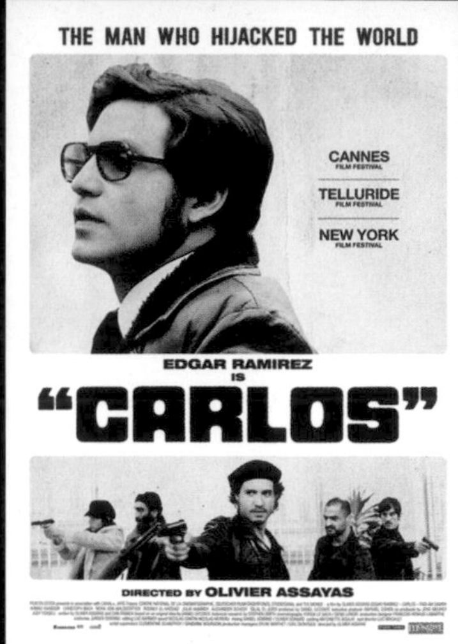

2010 – FRANCE / GERMANY – 330 MIN. (TV VERSION) / 190 MIN. (CINEMA RELEASE) – BIOPIC, POLITICAL THRILLER
DIRECTOR OLIVIER ASSAYAS (*1955)
SCREENPLAY OLIVIER ASSAYAS, DAN FRANCK DIRECTOR OF PHOTOGRAPHY YORICK LE SAUX, DENIS LENOIR EDITING LUC BARNIER, MARION MONNIER PRODUCTION DANIEL LECONTE, JENS MEURER, JUDY TOSSELL for FILMS EN STOCK, EGOLI TOSSELL FILM, CANAL+, ARTE FRANCE, MEDIENBOARD BERLIN-BRANDENBURG, GERMAN FEDERAL FILM BOARD.
STARRING EDGAR RAMIREZ (Ilich Ramírez Sánchez aka "Carlos"), NORA VON WALDSTÄTTEN (Magdalena Kopp), ALEXANDER SCHEER (Johannes Weinrich aka "Steve"), CHRISTOPH BACH (Hans-Joachim Klein aka "Angie"), JULIA HUMMER (Gabriele Kröcher-Tiedemann aka "Nada"), ALJOSCHA STADELMANN (Wilfred Böse aka "Boni"), JULE BÖWE (Christa Margot Fröhlich aka "Heidi"), KATHARINA SCHÜTTLER (Brigitte Kuhlmann), JOHANNES WEINRICH (Alexander Scheer), RODNEY EL HADDAD (Khalid).

"My name is Carlos. You may have heard of me."

A few hours before, he killed some innocent people with a bomb. Now this young man (Édgar Ramírez) is standing in a Paris hotel room, freshly bathed and naked. Looking at his athletic body in the mirror, he complacently takes hold of his genitals – terrorist as narcissist. His name is Ilich Ramírez Sánchez, better known as "Carlos the Jackal." A Venezuelan by birth, he rose in the mid-1970s to become a key player on the stage of international terrorism. After the turn of the millennium, many films dealt with the theme of left-wing terrorism in the 1970s and '80s. None deconstructed the myth of the terrorist as idealistic fighter as painstakingly as *Carlos*.

This brilliant biopic spanning two decades was the most expensive and ambitious work to date by French auteur Olivier Assayas – a substantial feat involving 92 shooting days, a 120-strong international cast and sets in 8 countries: only manageable as a co-production with television. The film was therefore designed from the very outset for both cinema and as a TV mini-series. The result is a masterpiece that even in its running time of 330 minutes, or a good 190 minutes in the shorter version, blows apart the usual dimensions – proof that exciting political cinema does not necessarily have to abandon complexity and individual hallmarks.

In terms of structure, *Carlos* is similar to the classic rise-and-fall story of the gangster genre. We start out seeing the protagonist as a charismatically macho figure, a womanizer who styles himself as a Marxist freedom fighter. His convictions are initially not negated by the fact that Carlos is obviously also driven by his own vanity. His charisma and cold-bloodedness are what mainly differentiate him from his comrades-in-arms. Tracked down in his hideout, he unhesitatingly shoots dead two police officers. He ceremoniously executes the traitor. Thereafter, everyone talks about him as "the Jackal." And for the "Popular Front for the Liberation of Palestine," he is the perfect choice for a special mission: an attack on the OPEC conference in Vienna.

This bloody hostage-taking incident in 1975 forms the climax of the film. Assayas films it brilliantly as a mixture of action-packed, high octane cinema and didactic political film. The mission ends with Carlos missing his real target, although he manages to negotiate a lucrative deal that saves his own skin. He justifies himself to his men by claiming he is a soldier, not a martyr. Yet even when he poses Che Guevara-style with revolutionary beard and beret, the moment marks the birth of a ruthless entrepreneurial terrorist rather than a new Che.

Carlos went on to become the godfather of terrorism. He had close links with the KGB and Stasi, as well as terrorist organizations and dictators worldwide. He moved into a villa in Budapest with his German colleague Johannes Weinrich (Alexander Scheer) and his lover Magdalena Kopp (Nora von Waldstätten), indulging in a hedonistic lifestyle behind the protection of the Iron Curtain. But then the tables were turned. When Magdalena Kopp was arrested during an

1

"How good is Olivier Assayas' *Carlos*? Think of *The Bourne Identity* with more substance, or *Munich* with more of a pulse, and you begin to have a sense of what the French filmmaker accomplished." *Los Angeles Times*

1 Terrorist as narcissist: Ilich Ramírez Sánchez, alias "Carlos" (Édgar Ramírez), poses Che Guevara-style with beret and cigar.

2 Revolutionary fighter or chilling assassin? In the early days, his sangfroid sets Carlos apart from his comrades-in-arms …

3 … which is why the uncontrolled fanaticism of Gabriele Kröcher-Tiedemann (Julia Hummer) is completely alien to him.

4 A revolutionary pause: director Olivier Assayas takes time to show the tedious side of a terrorist's life – the hanging around and almost interminable waiting between operations.

5 Phantom as media star: Carlos' ego is evidently flattered by the coverage of his assassinations. For a time, the Venezuelan was seen as the world's most wanted terrorist.

assassination attempt in Paris, Carlos became obsessed with a bloody private vendetta. The end of the Cold War eventually signaled his downfall. Dropped by his clients, he went into hiding in the Sudan and was handed over to France in 1994. Unlike other films about terrorists, Assayas is never in danger of stylizing its protagonist as a hero. One reason for this lies in the way he always counters the action with scenes that run contrary to the notion of a manic, dangerous life, by exposing the banality and dreariness of the terrorist's everyday existence. Added to which, Assayas' view of Carlos is never anything but cold. The handheld camera and staccato editing do not encourage the sense of closeness needed for us to identify with him; instead they stress even more the character's volatile, elusive nature, as do the constant changes in location. The phantom Carlos has many faces, but apparently no solid inner core or

6

6 No pop star: Assayas exposes the cool fighter for the global revolution as his protagonist's own projected image. In actual fact, Carlos proved increasingly to be an unscrupulous, entrepreneurial terrorist.

7 To give the film greater authenticity, Assayas used an international cast with several Arab actors, including Rodney El Haddad as Khalid, one of the terrorists in the OPEC attack in Vienna.

8 Carlos exploits his charisma to manipulate women. Magdalena Kopp (Nora von Waldstätten) seems pretty amendable to him.

"Directed by Olivier Assayas, the movie crawls hypnotically into the skin of this global assassin and astonishes you with its brazenly violent and sexual audacity. It's a dynamite movie (...) It'll knock you sideways." *Rolling Stone*

7

identity. While his skillfully created self-image manages to hide this at the beginning, the blank space where a convincing projection of Carlos the man should be becomes more prominent in the course of the film.

Persecuted in equal measure by his enemies and his own impulses, Carlos ends up as nothing more than a bloated wreck, stripped of home, future and ideals. When he is exiled in Africa and uses hard cash to buy himself a Sudanese lover, the self-proclaimed revolutionary hardly differs in the final analysis from a common sex tourist. This transformation was a veritable tour de force on the part of the lead actor, Édgar Ramírez, a native Venezuelan like Carlos. His performance, on a par with Robert De Niro's legendary appearance in *Raging Bull* (1980), is one of the exceptional acting achievements of the decade. JH

OLIVIER ASSAYAS Olivier Assayas is one of the key filmmakers of the new French auteur cinema. Born in Paris in 1955, the son of a screenwriter, he found himself in the late 1970s on the editorial team of the film journal "Cahiers du Cinema," once the beating heart of the New Wave. After a few short films and screenplays, he made his directorial debut with *Disorder* (*Désordre*, 1986), which like his next movie *Winter's Child* (*L'enfant de l'hiver*, 1989) painted a very realistic portrait of aimless young people in Paris and made Assayas the dark horse among cinéphiles.

He attracted wider attention with *Irma Vep* (1996) – his first collaboration with his future wife Maggie Cheung – in homage to the pioneer of French cinema, Louis Feuillade, which also expressed his admiration for Asian action cinema and reflected the position of French auteurist filmmakers. After *Late August, Early September* (*Fin août, début septembre*, 1998), another empathetic portrait of generations, and the historical drama (an unusual genre for him) *Les destinées sentimentales* (2000), he caused a sensation with the neo-noir *Demonlover* (2002). This aesthetically fascinating examination of pornography and digital technology once more revealed Assayas' soft spot for rock music and Asian pop culture; in the eyes of some American intellectuals, it brought him closer to "New French Extremism," which was apparently confirmed by his radical erotic thriller *Boarding Gate* (2007) with Asia Argento. Assayas cannot be understood in terms of such labels, however, as demonstrated by his sensitive family drama *Summer Hours* (*L'heure d'été*, 2008) and the highly emotional portrayal of a woman, *Clean* (2004), with Maggie Cheung as a drug-addicted musician with a child, as well as his extremely influential biography of a terrorist, *Carlos the Jackal* (2010).

UNCLE BOONMEE WHO CAN RECALL HIS PAST LIVES

LUNG BOONMEE RALEUK CHAT

2010 – THAILAND / UK / FRANCE / GERMANY / SPAIN – 113 MIN. – DRAMA
DIRECTOR APICHATPONG WEERASETHAKUL (*1970)
SCREENPLAY APICHATPONG WEERASETHAKUL DIRECTOR OF PHOTOGRAPHY YUKONTORN MINGMONGKON, SAYOMBHU MUKDEEPROM EDITING LEE CHATAMETIKOOL PRODUCTION SIMON FIELD, KEITH GRIFFITHS, APICHATPONG WEERASETHAKUL for ILLUMINATIONS FILMS, KICK THE MACHINE.
STARRING THANAPAT SAISAYMAR (Uncle Boonmee), SAKDA KAEWBUADEE (Tong), JENJIRA PONGPAS (Jen), NATTHAKARN APHAIWONK (Huay), GEERASAK KULHONG (Boonsong), KANOKPORN THONGARAM (Roong), SAMUD KUGASANG (Jaai), MONGKOLPRASERT (Princess Wallapa), SUMIT SUEBSEE (Soldier), VIEN PIMDEE (Farmer).
IFF CANNES 2010 GOLDEN PALM (Apichatpong Weerasethakul).

"Heaven is overrated."

It is nighttime in the jungle; the sounds of plants and animals are all around. Although you cannot see them, they are there. Uncle Boonmee (Thanapat Saisaymar) finds comfort in the thought that there is something waiting in the darkness. Suffering from kidney failure, he has returned to his native village to die. He is sitting with his sister-in-law Jen (Jenjira Pongpas) and nephew Tong (Sakda Kaewbuadee) in the pale glow of a lamp on the veranda, dining on roasted ginger and chili. But they are not alone. As if a place had been kept for her, the figure of a woman appears on their left: it is Boonmee's deceased wife, Huay (Natthakarn Aphaiwonk). She seems like a reflection – which she actually is, from a purely technical point of view. Her spirit wishes to accompany Boonmee on his journey to the next world. Later on, his son, Boonsong, who went missing in action, joins them: a shaggy, ape-like figure with glowing, red eyes that penetrate the jungle like searchlights until daybreak puts them out.

In *Uncle Boonmee Who Can Recall His Past Lives*, winner of the Palme d'Or (Golden Palm) at Cannes, the boundaries become blurred between the dead and the living, man and beast, as much as between past and present,

2

3

"Weerasethakul's thinking is tropical. In his life, as in his movies, he is constantly drawn to the jungle. His school of perception is the untouched rainforest. It is a world in which all boundaries disappear into the impenetrable, reality always runs rampantly into the surreal, and the cycles of growth and decay, and life and death, intertwine to the extent that meaning and the supernatural become indistinguishable." *Le Monde*

4

1 Previous life as a princess: Uncle Boonmee imagines himself in the most diverse incarnations in the cycle of transmigration and rebirth.

2 Thai paradise: man and nature reach an harmonious co-existence in the jungle, the director's spiritual home and main theme.

3 Ordinary Buddhism: monk Tong (Sakda Kaewbuadee) changes into western clothes without any problem.

4 Sick bodies, healthy minds: Uncle Boonmee (Thanapat Saisaymar) finds comfort in the bosom of his family, where he lived as a child.

5 Friendly spirit: dead woman Huay (Natthakarn Aphaiwonk) comes for supper, as if it's quite natural.

"It all has something sublime and visionary about it, with a spiritual quality I can't remember seeing in any film recently. *Uncle Boonmee* offers pleasure and heartbreak in equal measure." *The Guardian*

memory and dream. Yet coming face-to-face with the animistic tradition of South-East Asia is less strange and unusual than the matter-of-fact way that people deal with the spirits around them. They solicitously enquire of Huay whether she has enough to eat in the afterlife. She is more concerned about the living and mentions in passing that heaven is overrated. The spiritual nature of all things is a constant feature in the work of Apichatpong Weerasethakul, who has become a favorite with the critics through his enigmatic films. The inscrutably hypnotic yet essentially simple nature of his work finds expression in the serene image of a water buffalo, or the cave that Boonmee seeks out as a source of life for his final resting place. Whether he recalls his previous lives or not in this film is as vague as everything else; for Weerasethakul, recollection is primarily a cinematic experience linked directly to his belief in reincarnation and the transmigration of souls. In his film, he deals with Thai TV series and comics as well as personal experiences and memories: its six film cycles are stylistically coherent, yet connected to each other in a highly associative way, constantly alternating between magical realism and documentary fiction. In one of his remembered lives, Boonmee is an aging princess who sees the reflection of her younger self in a lagoon and experiences the joys of physical love with a talking catfish – one of the strangest and most charming sex scenes in cinema history. The ape-like creature, Boonsong, may well represent his dead son, but it also symbolizes the guilty conscience of his father who "killed many communists" during the war. A rather strange

6 Apichatpong Weerasethakul locates the unreal in everyday existence. Mosquito nets break up the light, giving it a magical quality, and spirits are a natural part of life.

7 Source of life: Uncle Boonmee finally finds peace in a cave that symbolizes the womb.

8 Jen (Jenjira Pongpas) likes to sit on the veranda – the threshold between man and nature, but also between life and death.

9 Playing with the visual traditions of South-East Asia: the princess finds her younger reflection in the lagoon, and sexual fulfillment – with a fish.

photographic sequence shows the figure cheerfully posing among other soldiers, a visual reminder of a hollow victory.

Notwithstanding its surreal atmosphere, Weerasethakul's cinema would be inconceivable without such social and political contexts. A filmmaker censored in his native land, he lives completely in the present, as demonstrated by the last scene. Boonmee has just been buried. Tong then appears in a hotel room as a Buddhist monk, removes his traditional robes, takes a shower and gets dressed again, this time in western clothes. After what is already a singular act, he goes with Aunt Jen to a restaurant, while their souls – or is it the other way round? – remain sitting in front of the TV in the hotel. Weerasethakul's advice is to experience the film like a dream. This meditative process will open us up to the universal meaning of the movie, beyond the occasional, deceptive glimmers of understanding. PB

7 8

APICHATPONG WEERASETHAKUL This Thai director has emerged as one of the leading *auteurs* in world cinema, due to his use of aesthetic imagery that is simultaneously cumbersome and sensuous. His theme is the jungle of his native land with its alien sounds, shapes and colors, which he mythologizes in long shots. Elements of European surrealist cinema are also interwoven into his style, which he deliberately presents as exotic and technically primitive to western eyes. Born in Bangkok in 1970, Apichatpong Weerasethakul formed his own production company Kick the Machine in 1999, and first attracted attention with *Blissfully Yours* (*Sud sanaeha*, 2002). A love story filmed in real time about an illegal immigrant with a rare skin disorder won the top award in the "Un Certain Regard" category at the Cannes Film Festival in 2002. Two years later in Cannes, *Tropical Malady* (*Sud pralad*, 2004) was awarded the Jury Prize. (By this time, festival critics had begun to take note of his complicated name; he actually calls himself "Joe" to keep things simple.)

The story of homosexual love reveals its animalistic side in the film, when one of the men – or so it seems at least – transforms into a tiger. As the screen bursts into flames, the movie splits literally into two parts. Today, however, fewer people are voicing the opinion, as they did then, of Weerasethakul being no more than a canny festival director. The Palme d'Or for *Uncle Boonmee Who Can Recall His Past Lives* (*Lung Boonmee raleuk chat*, 2010), in which the great film shaman showed restraint, if anything, met with widespread approval. Even the Thai censorship board that had made substantial cuts to his previous movie *Syndromes and a Century* (*Sang sattawat*, 2006) relented. Through his free representation of homosexuality, Buddhism and political conflicts, Weerasethakul attracts constant criticism in his native land.

BLACK SWAN

2010 – USA – 108 MIN. – COMING-OF-AGE DRAMA, PSYCHOLOGICAL THRILLER
DIRECTOR DARREN ARONOFSKY (*1969)
SCREENPLAY MARK HEYMAN, ANDRES HEINZ, JOHN J. MCLAUGHLIN
DIRECTOR OF PHOTOGRAPHY MATTHEW LIBATIQUE **EDITING** ANDREW WEISBLUM **MUSIC** CLINT MANSELL
PRODUCTION SCOTT FRANKLIN, MIKE MEDAVOY, ARNOLD MESSER, BRIAN OLIVER, JOSEPH P. REIDY, JERRY FRUCHTMAN for 20TH CENTURY FOX, PROTOZOA PICTURES, PHOENIX PICTURES, CROSS CREEK PICTURES.
STARRING NATALIE PORTMAN (Nina Sayers), VINCENT CASSEL (Thomas Leroy), MILA KUNIS (Lily), BARBARA HERSHEY (Erica Sayers), WINONA RYDER (Beth MacIntyre), BENJAMIN MILLEPIED (David), KSENIA SOLO (Veronica), KRISTINA ANAPAU (Galina).
ACADEMY AWARDS 2011 OSCAR for BEST LEADING ACTRESS (Natalie Portman).

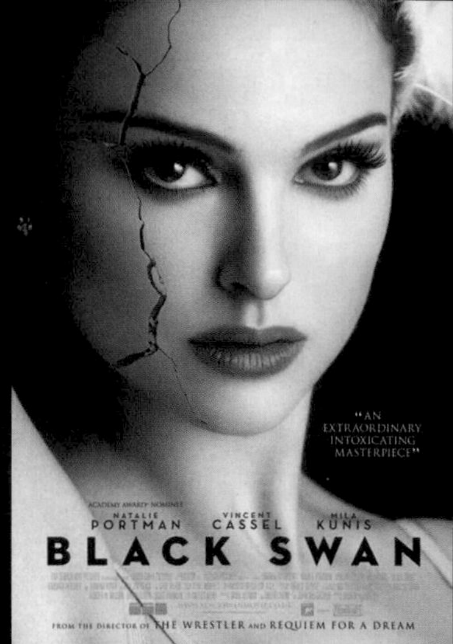

"I just want to be perfect."

It begins with a dream. A ballerina is dancing the White Swan from Tchaikovsky's Swan Lake in a beam of bright light – the lifelong wish of Nina Sayers (Natalie Portman), a dancer in the world-famous New York City Ballet. The new production of this classic is to be the highlight of the season. Whoever wants to dance the coveted role must, however, be able to play the Black Swan as well. Star choreographer Thomas (Vincent Cassel) indeed sees innocent Nina as the perfect casting for the White Swan, but he cannot find the dark, seductive side in her that constitutes the essence of the Black Swan. When he tries to kiss Nina, however, and she bites his lip, Thomas knows that she does in fact have this dark side deep inside her. To her own astonishment, she gets the challenging dual role. Yet the price she has to pay for it is high. The harder and harder she strives to transform herself into the Black Swan, the more she loses grip on reality and ends up being the victim of her own schizophrenia. Her dream did come true, however: "I was perfect." Aronofsky's films are about lone individuals, and in *Black Swan* this is presented through the world of ballet. Each ballerina is driven by the enormously competitive pressure to be better than all the rest – simply the best. Surrounded on all sides by mirrors, Nina is constantly confronted with her own image, forcing her to continually examine and control herself, becoming a critic of her own body. This mixture of vanity and self-hatred leads almost inevitably to schizophrenia. We clearly see the consequences in her mother (Barbara Hershey), who was once an ordinary ballet dancer and now has countless self-portraits hanging on her mirror, their harrowing features sad testament to her own failure. Yet even a prima ballerina like Beth MacIntyre (Winona Ryder) cannot cope with the end of her career, resorting to the destructive act of self-mutilation.

As a result, *Black Swan* is anything but a standard ballet movie. Here, it is not about the effortlessly light qualities of dance, but about the extreme physical and psychological burdens of professional ballet. The film focuses

1

1 The transformation is complete: Nina (Natalie Portman) has become Odile, the black swan from Tchaikovsky's "Swan Lake."

2 Vincent Cassel plays top choreographer Thomas Leroy. He alone decides who is to dance the coveted lead role.

3 Rival and role model: Lily (Mila Kunis) represents the dark side lacking in Nina, and not just physically.

"Part tortured-artist drama, *Black Swan* looks like a tony art-house entertainment. [...] But what gives it a jolt is its giddy, sometimes sleazy exploitation-cinema savvy." *The New York Times*

4

5

4 The methods of the top choreographer Thomas Leroy are immoral and effective in equal measure. He challenges Nina to discover her own sexuality.

5 The masterpiece is complete. The premiere of the new "Swan Lake" is the high point of the film. In the threatening red light of the stage, it will become clear whether Nina is up to the demanding dual role. She has finally left her pink, girlish bedroom behind.

sharply on the fragility of the human body: cracking joints, broken toenails, scratched and bleeding skin. Close-ups of small, everyday injuries (which make them all the more intimate) produce a feeling of deep unease in the viewer. These self-destructive aspects of the pursuit of perfection are translated by Aronofsky into metamorphoses that can only be explained in terms of Nina's warped perception. But instead of a transformation from ugly duckling to beautiful swan, we see a lovely young woman assuming increasingly inhuman features as she almost literally tears herself apart, bends and breaks. These brief, though fiercely intense, sequences are at times torturous for the viewer. In the process, Black Swan comes very close to "body horror" David Cronenberg-style, while also reminding us of Charles Burns' comic-book classic "Black Hole" and its exaggerated depiction of the corporeal experiences of American teenagers.

It is easy to read *Black Swan* as a coming-of-age movie as well. Although Nina is already on the wrong side of twenty, her life at the beginning is like that of a twelve-year-old, mainly because her mother is a control freak. Erica

6

6 Her rival eliminated, the mirror broken: Nina may have won, but she ends up paying a high price.

7 Erica (Barbara Hershey) sees the opportunity in her daughter that she missed herself.

8 Machiavelli of the ballet: Thomas Leroy accepts there will be casualties in the realization of his ideas.

9 The ballet world is characterized by the ubiquitous mirror mazes, which also serve as a metaphor for Nina's inner turmoil.

NATALIE PORTMAN Born Natalie Hershlag on June 9, 1981 in Israel, the actress grew up in various cities including Washington D.C. and New York and took her grandmother's maiden name at the start of her career. She enjoyed her first success at the tender age of 13 in *Leon* (*Léon*, 1994), playing a girl who has lost her family and is cared for by the eponymous hit man (Jean Reno). Her breakthrough came, however, with the part of Padmé in Episode III of the second *Star Wars* trilogy (1999, 2002 and 2005). She won the Golden Globe for her role as a stripper, Alice, in Mike Nichols' relationship drama *Closer* (2004), as well as an Oscar nomination for Best Supporting Actress. Although her career to date has involved a broad range of parts and different types of movie – from indie film *Garden State* (2004) through action movie *V for Vendetta* (2006) to historical drama *The Other Boleyn Girl* (2008) – her youthful beauty has sustained her reputation as Hollywood's good girl, and she has had few opportunities to play more complex characters. Thus the role of Nina Sayers in *Black Swan* (2010) has unlocked a door for Natalie Portman. She prepared for the part over a ten-month period with intensive ballet training. Through this she met ballet dancer and choreographer Benjamin Millepied, now her fiancé.

8

Sayers wants to protect her daughter from the mistakes she made, keeping her safe in a pink-tinged world of innocence and youth. Nina's escape from this naive, musical-box world is inevitable. She has her rival Lily (Mila Kunis), of all people, to thank for her sexual awakening; in her uncomplicated zest for life, Lily is the polar opposite of the driven perfectionist, lightening the heavy atmosphere of the film to some extent.

Ultimately, however, *Black Swan* is about women who fail. The film challenges the images of femininity in popular culture and, in so doing, exposes the problems of not only the obsession with youth to which Beth and Erica fall victim, but also the conflicting roles demanded of women. The perfect synthesis of Madonna and whore will never work. According to Aronofsky, *Black Swan* and its predecessor *The Wrestler* (2008) form a diptych. Both films feature artists who use and exploit their physical beings for others' entertainment; they are about people whose only capital is their own bodies. Losing their mind, however, goes hand in hand with this extreme obsession with physicality. With her role in *Black Swan*, Natalie Portman takes her place in a long line of cinematic doppelgangers, conveyed by one film reference in particular: the movie's ending is very like the fatal conclusion of the silent classic *The Student of Prague* (*Der Student von Prag*, 1913 and 1926; a.k.a. *A Bargain with Satan*, 1913 and *The Man Who Cheated Life*, 1926). Just as the student Balduin is forced to acknowledge that, in shooting at the mirror, he has killed not just his double but himself as well, Nina also realizes that she has inflicted a fatal wound on herself. Her ambition has triumphed, but she has lost her life. CZ

9

MIRAL

2010 – FRANCE / ISRAEL / ITALY / INDIA – 112 MIN. – DRAMA, LITERARY ADAPTATION
DIRECTOR JULIAN SCHNABEL (*1951)
SCREENPLAY RULA JEBREAL, from her novel of the same name DIRECTOR OF PHOTOGRAPHY ERIC GAUTIER
EDITING JULIETTE WELFLING MUSIC LAURIE ANDERSON PRODUCTION JON KILIK for PATHÉ, ER PRODUCTIONS, EAGLE PICTURES, INDIA TAKE ONE PRODUCTIONS.
STARRING FREIDA PINTO (Miral), HIAM ABBASS (Hind Husseini), YASMINE AL MASSRI (Nadia), ALEXANDER SIDDIG (Jamal, Mirals Father), RUBA BLAL (Fatima), OMAR METWALLY (Hani), WILLEM DAFOE (Eddie), VANESSA REDGRAVE (Bertha), STELLA SCHNABEL (Lisa), MAKRAM KHOURY (Khatib).

"This school is the difference between you and the children in the refugee camp."

A yellowish-brown map: cities, desert, rivers, and the Mediterranean. In the opening credits, the camera pans across a map of the Middle East. *Miral* is a story about the conflict in this region: the movie covers a time-span of five decades, focusing on four women, to which its four sections are dedicated. In 1948 – the year the state of Israel was founded – Palestinian woman Hind Husseini (Hiam Abbass) opens the Dar-Al-Tifl Institute, a school for orphan children in East Jerusalem. The initial 55 children soon become hundreds. Hind uses her own money to finance the institution and tries to accommodate both Palestinians and Israelis equally. Thirty years after the school's foundation, seven-year-old Miral, a semi orphan, comes to live and learn with Hind.
Nine years on, during the Palestinian intifada in 1987, Miral (Freida Pinto) is now 16 and has been appointed as a teaching assistant. She is sent into a camp to teach refugee children; there she experiences the hardship and misery suffered by the Palestinians and falls in love with PLO activist Hani (Omar Metwally). Through him, she comes into contact with the militant anti-Israeli movement. She takes part in actions herself and is arrested, interrogated and tortured, but eventually released. In 1994, a year after the signing of the Oslo Peace Accord between Israel and the Palestinians, Miral has to bury her teacher and friend, Hind. The film also focuses on the fates of Nadia (Yasmine Al Massri) and Fatima (Ruba Blal) as well as Hind and Miral. Nadia, Miral's mother, takes her own life after being sexually abused, while Fatima, who is a nurse, joins a militant group. Miral's own story takes up most of the film, while Hind's narrative is woven through the whole movie.

This is the basic outline of the story that is told in the fourth feature film by American painter and film director Julian Schnabel (*The Diving Bell and the Butterfly*, 2007). Yet this synopsis comes nowhere near conveying the impression of what Schnabel "paints" (the word that comes to mind) onscreen.

New York director Schnabel and his French cameraman Eric Gautier (*Into the Wild*, 2007) create a stunning visual language that is both highly artificial and impressionistic; it seems to breathe life into the glaring light and heat of

1

"Instead of rejecting the film, Israelis should ask that it be shown in the Knesset. Yes, the Knesset. Because then maybe – someday – they might show *Schindler's List* or *The Diary of Anne Frank* in the Palestinian parliament and schools." *The Jerusalem Post*

1 Miral (Freida Pinto) dreams of a world in which Israelis and Palestinians can live peacefully side by side, in their own states.

2 A moving portrayal: Palestinian Hind Husseini (Hiam Abbass) cares for children, hungry for food and knowledge, in her orphanage.

3 The police arrest Miral: she is suspected of working for the PLO.

4 After she has been led away for interrogation, she is beaten, but doesn't give up the names of other activists.

5 Miral's mother Nadia (Yasmine Al Massri) commits suicide after being raped.

he Middle East through the use of warm tones, color filters and extreme ighting to the point of overexposing whole areas of the image. The camera is xtremely mobile, freely approaching the protagonists and often shooting in lose-up. Black-and-white archive footage is edited repeatedly into *Miral*. The isual composition is nicely supported by Laurie Anderson's hypnotic musical ieces that shift between Western and Arab elements.

Miral deals with a political subject through highly poetic visual language the conflict between the Israelis and Palestinians that remains unresolved t this day. The narrative is completely apolitical and highly emotional withou being judgmental. Schnabel does not look for people to blame, but insteac gives space and a voice to the victims. The Jewish-American director attractec some criticism for being on the Palestinian side. This is his choice as a narrator

6 7

"It is remarkable how Schnabel avoids all the high dramatic moments – warfare, exploding bombs, dead children, hospital gore – that are the bread and butter of many movies set in the Middle East." *The Hollywood Reporter*

however, which should be respected; and he has never denied that there have been, and still are, victims on the Israeli side. Added to which, he tells the story of the friendship between Miral and the young Jewish girl, Lisa (played by Schnabel's daughter, Stella) – thus working through the reservations and prejudices on both sides. Julian Schnabel's narrative perspective is the result of his choice of subject matter as well as his personal proximity to it. *Miral* is the film version of the autobiographical novel "Miral: one country. Three women. A shared dream." Hind Husseini lived from 1916 through 1994 and was actually the director of the orphanage. The Palestinian novelist Rula Jebreal (*1973), who wrote the screenplay, spent her youth in the home; she has a daughter called Miral, and is Julian Schnabel's long-term partner. HJK

8

6 After Nadia takes her own life, her husband Jamal (Alexander Siddig) finds himself unable to cope with bringing up little Miral.

7 The American colonel, Eddie (Willem Dafoe), helps Hind Husseini in her orphanage.

8 Hind Husseini tries to find sponsors for her privately funded orphanage.

9 Miral has fallen in love with PLO activist Hani (Omar Metwally).

FREIDA PINTO "Just imagine Angelina Jolie tapping you on the shoulder – and your mouth is full of turkey paste." The story goes that this is what happened to Indian actress Freida Pinto (*1984) at a buffet in Los Angeles. Her role in the 8-Oscars triumph *Slumdog Millionaire* (2008) catapulted the young woman from Mumbai abruptly into the top rank of Hollywood darlings. The daughter of a head teacher and bank manager had a few modeling jobs and was presenting a largely unnoticed TV program when director Danny Boyle discovered her for his movie. And Hollywood loved her exotic looks and flawless beauty. Her next parts were in Woody Allen's *You Will Meet a Tall Dark Stranger* (2010) alongside Antonio Banderas and Anthony Hopkins, followed by *Miral* (2010). She is now being talked about as the next potential candidate for the role of Bond girl. Some critics of *Miral* complained that Pinto was too beautiful for this story. Why did Schnabel cast an Indian model for his story about Palestine? "There's a simple explanation," wrote the news magazine *Der Spiegel*. "Freida Pinto and Rula Jebreal could pass for sisters."

THE KING'S SPEECH

2010 – UK / USA / AUSTRALIA – 118 MIN. – HISTORICAL FILM, DRAMA
DIRECTOR TOM HOOPER (*1972)
SCREENPLAY DAVID SEIDLER DIRECTOR OF PHOTOGRAPHY DANNY COHEN EDITING TARIQ ANWAR
MUSIC ALEXANDRE DESPLAT PRODUCTION IAIN CANNING, GARETH UNWIN, EMILE SHERMAN for BEDLAM PRODUCTIONS, SEE-SAW FILMS.
STARRING COLIN FIRTH (King George VI), GEOFFREY RUSH (Lionel Logue), HELENA BONHAM CARTER (Queen Elizabeth), GUY PEARCE (Edward), MICHAEL GAMBON (King George V), CLAIRE BLOOM (Mary), DEREK JACOBI (Archbishop Cosmo Lang), TIMOTHY SPALL (Winston Churchill), JENNIFER EHLE (Myrtle Logue), ROGER PARROTT (Neville Chamberlain), EVE BEST (Wallis Simpson).
ACADEMY AWARDS 2011 OSCARS for BEST PICTURE (Iain Canning, Gareth Unwin, Emile Sherman), BEST DIRECTOR (Tom Hooper), BEST LEADING ACTOR (Colin Firth), and BEST ORIGINAL SCREENPLAY (David Seidler).

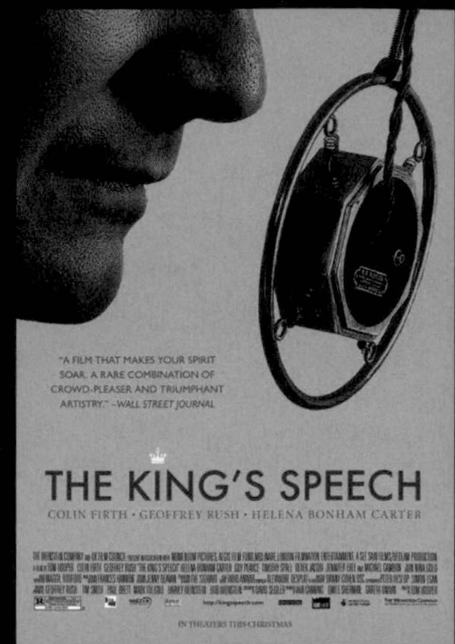

"We've become actors."

The film opens with a public execution: an unusual beginning, but one that befits the imposing subject matter. Composed, Prince Albert (Colin Firth) takes the last few steps and looks out into the huge, gaping crowd. And then – a deathly silence. It is time for the closing speech, but all that comes out is a strangled stutter, like the rattle of a dying man. This painful situation is almost unbearable, for everyone concerned. His wife (Helena Bonham Carter) casts another sympathetic glance at Albert, and then a merciful edit releases the viewer from the discomfiting exhibition of another's humiliation. For poor Albert, Duke of York and later King George VI, ruler of the British Empire, this torture endured for a whole lifetime. *The King's Speech* shows the monarch, not as the highest representative of an empire, but as a prisoner of his office. He had never wanted to become king, precisely on account of public appearances like the infamous speech at London's Wembley Stadium in 1925. The personal drama of the stuttering king, a mere footnote in history, makes the ideal historical film: it is tragic, funny and moving at the same time. Yet it also rises to the level of outstanding artistic triumph through direction that never fails to surprise, unusual camera angles, razor-sharp dialogue and a magnificent cast – a complete work of art.

The sessions with Lionel Logue (Geoffrey Rush), a self-styled speech therapist from Australia, form the core of the movie. It is an often adversarial encounter between completely opposing characters: citizen and nobleman, colonized and colonizer, vociferous self-promoter and speechless victim. Logue's

1

2

1 Representing an empire – and a prisoner of his office: Colin Firth in his Oscar-winning role as stuttering King George VI.

2 His worst enemy: Bertie has terrible fear of microphones. The boom in radio and TV was his historical bad luck.

3 Sympathetic look: Bertie's wife Elizabeth (Helena Bonham Carter), who went on to become the popular Queen Mum, insists on professional help.

"It's a prizewinning combination, terribly English and totally Hollywood, and Firth is, once more, uncanny: He evokes, in mid-stammer, existential dread." *New York Magazine*

3

4

picturesque but neglected practice rooms reveal the soul of an artist; a man who already has a failed career as an actor behind him. Curiously enough – more specifically through the use of wide-angle lenses – the rooms seem far bigger and more inviting than the royal palaces. This is where Logue manages to free the king-in-waiting, stiff as a poker, from his inner paralysis. Swearing, in its crudest form, proves in prominent fashion to be the best medicine. In a hilarious reversal of the Pygmalion motif, the proletarian teacher loosens the tongue of the eminently refined pupil.

And it is urgently needed, for the events unfolding in Buckingham Palace will have huge political significance, perhaps for the last time in history. A conventional movie might well have focused on the abdication crisis surrounding Albert's dandyish brother Edward (Guy Pearce) that actually led to second-born son "Bertie" becoming king. With much wit and irony, though less satire than Stephen Frears' *The Queen* (2006), director Tom Hooper instead unfolds the internal drama of the British royal family: authoritarian and imperious George V (Michael Gambon) – the psychological causes of Albert's stutter are all too obvious – has two sons, one of whom is incapable of ruling and the other incapable of speaking. And this comes at a time when a frightful demagogue is threatening to plunge the Empire into a second world war. Albert watches the weekly newsreels with a mixture of fascination and dismay: he's not a nice chap, this Adolf Hitler, but what a speaker!

His own announcement of the country's entry into war becomes a greatly improved repeat of the introductory scene under Logue's direction and, with his considerable input as well as Beethoven's 7th symphony, the new king manages to produce a speech imbued with patriotic pathos. These (in every sense) moving images tell us that whoever wins their own personal war will

GEOFFREY RUSH Geoffrey Rush gives his public something that modern cinema with its visual excesses and special effects usually promises, but rarely delivers: a rush of exhilaration, enjoyment of a real treat, and method in madness. His characters are often narcissistic, sometimes devious or cowardly, but always interesting. Associating him with the theatricality of Grand Guignol isn't far off the mark: until his Oscar-winning role in the Australian production *Shine* (1995/1996) Rush – born 1951 in a small town near Brisbane – was mainly known to theater audiences in his native country. By then he was 44 years old, and had only been involved in a couple of films. The biopic of schizophrenic piano virtuoso David Helfgott naturally showed us that sensitive side without which his performances as an actor would be inconceivable.
For whether playing the sinister police inspector Javert in *Les Misérables* (1998), the wily court advisor in *Elizabeth* (1998) or the sarcastic theater producer in *Shakespeare in Love* (1998), Rush never upstages his colleagues but rather holds up a mirror to their talents. One-off escapist efforts like the starring role as the Marquis de Sade in *Quills* (2000) are more the exception than the rule. Before proving the immense breadth of his emotional range once again in the melancholic biopic *The Life and Death of Peter Sellers* (2004), he also introduced himself to a young audience as the scheming ghost pirate Barbossa in *Pirates of the Caribbean – The Curse of the Black Pearl* (2003), forever sealing his popularity. Most recently he was nominated for an Oscar for the fourth time for his role as the voluble (though, more importantly, effective) Australian speech therapist in *The King's Speech* (2010).

6

“A picnic for Anglophiles, not to mention a prospective Oscar bonanza for the brothers Weinstein, *The King’s Speech* is a well-wrought, enjoyably amusing inspirational drama that successfully humanizes, even as it pokes fun at, the House of Windsor.” *The Village Voice*

7 8

4 The bohemian life: Bertie's only hardship is therapy with Logue.

5 Linguistic genius and self-promoter: speech therapist Lionel Logue (Geoffrey Rush) uses unusual methods to teach his king how to speak.

6 Public execution: Bertie's speech turns into one of the most humiliating displays of human shame. The audience is silently horrified.

7 The monarch would have been sunk without Logue, a starring role for Geoffrey Rush. As in the Windsor hit, *The Queen*, a commoner saves the royal House.

8 Historical footnote: Timothy Spall's grumpy portrayal of Winston Churchill reminds us more of Alfred Hitchcock.

9 "God Save The Queen:" Elizabeth stands by her man through all the humiliation and embarrassment. There was also a happy ending at the Oscars.

also conquer the external enemy. Yet *The King's Speech* is a sophisticated and thoroughly modern movie that never loses sight of the way the media stages history. This process was responsible during those very years for throwing all rules of representation into disarray, reducing even the highest office bearers to state actors. Thanks to radio and television, Albert's real enemy, the microphone, is suddenly everywhere. In a palace side room doing service as a makeshift studio, he of all people, this Job of the media age who was abundantly blessed with historical misfortune, becomes the prototype of the modern politician. In cases where the office and the person are so obviously mismatched, caricature is never far away. But Colin Firth's brilliant portrait of a shy man leaves us in no doubt: Albert became a good king and Firth himself an Oscar winner. PB

BARNEY'S VERSION

2010 – CANADA / ITALY – 134 MIN. – DRAMA, LITERARY ADAPTATION
DIRECTOR RICHARD J. LEWIS
SCREENPLAY MICHAEL KONYVES, from the novel of the same name by MORDECAI RICHLER
DIRECTOR OF PHOTOGRAPHY GUY DUFAUX **EDITING** SUSAN SHIPTON **MUSIC** PASQUALE CATALANO
PRODUCTION ROBERT LANTOS for SERENDIPITY POINT FILMS, THE HAROLD GREENBERG FUND, LYLA FILMS.
STARRING PAUL GIAMATTI (Barney Panofsky), ROSAMUND PIKE (Miriam Grant-Panofsky), MINNIE DRIVER (The 2nd Mrs. P.), RACHELLE LEFEVRE (Clara Charnofsky), ANNA HOPKINS (Kate Panofsky), JAKE HOFFMAN (Michael Panofsky), SCOTT SPEEDMAN (Boogie), BRUCE GREENWOOD (Blair), DUSTIN HOFFMAN (Izzy Panofsky), SAUL RUBINEK (Charnofsky), MARK ADDY (Detective O'Hearne).

"Don't be ridiculous. We just met. At your wedding."

The story of Barney Panofsky (Paul Giamatti) could be told in many versions, but it is doubtful whether he could possibly come off any better than in his own. There were three women in his life: the first, who committed suicide; the second, whom he married for money; and the third, the love of his life, whom he betrayed nevertheless, driving her to the verge of despair with his foibles. Barney, the owner of a TV production company in Montreal (the aptly named Totally Unnecessary Productions), is a heartless cynic who smokes and drinks far too much as a way of numbing his self-pity. The old friends he once shared whiskey and cigars with are long gone. It gets worse: since the disappearance years ago of his best buddy Boogie (Scott Speedman), Barney has been under suspicion of murder. So it is high time he told his own version of events – especially as his arch enemy has just published a book that carries further scathing criticism of him.

In *Barney's Version*, a confession about his life spanning four decades, we also get to know another Barney. In Rome during the 1970s he showed promise among a group of artists, but his life was thrown off course by a bohemian woman with suicidal tendencies called Clara (Rachelle Lefevre). Could he have done anything about her death? How do you put into words the bad luck of a man who meets the love of his life at his own wedding? Before getting together with the wonderful Miriam (Rosamund Pike), he goes through

marital hell with an anonymous Jewish heiress (Minnie Driver). At around the same time, Boogie disappears while they are on vacation together. There was an argument, and a pistol was involved; but Barney can't remember precisely what happened – he was simply too drunk.

Anyone who has seen Paul Giamatti in *Sideways* (2004) can imagine how this rather uptight, not exactly muscular man might lead such a wild life at the side of three extremely attractive women. In fact, Barney has it both better and worse than his earlier incarnation, Miles, though the two have much in common – such as the tendency to make drunken phone calls in the middle of the night. Before long, we grow fond of him, for beneath the hard exterior of this rampant misanthropist beats the heart of a hopeless romantic. Based on the Canadian bestselling book of the same name by Mordecai Richler, the

"Selecting Dustin Hoffman to play Mr Giamatti's father is a stroke of genius, since it throws into relief the blend of intense seriousness and wry self-mockery that they have in common as screen performers." *The New York Times*

1 Ballad of the unhappy drunk: Barney (Paul Giamatti) has aged – whiskey and cigars are the only things that keep him going.

2 Marriage to "the 2nd Mrs P." doesn't live up to the sparkling wedding. Minnie Driver is brilliant in a thankless role.

3 Like father, like son: widowed philanderer Izzy (Dustin Hoffman) is Barney's closest confidante through all his troubles.

ROSAMUND PIKE She would have been stuck with the "coolly elegant" image even without her role as Bond girl Miranda Frost, though her early appearance in *Die Another Day* (2002) revealed only half the picture: Rosamund Pike is always elegant, but the flawless façade hides a capacity for anything. This is best illustrated in the sensitive part of Miriam in *Barney's Version* (2010), in which she remains true to her husband, a floundering cynic, almost to the point of self-sacrifice.

That said, with her education she could sign up with MI6 anytime: born to musician parents in London in 1979, she has traveled the world, mastering several instruments and languages, and is also a university graduate. After the Bond movie and ambitious historical dramas including *The Libertine* (2004) and *Pride and Prejudice* (2005), she was not above genre nonsense such as the computer games adaptation *Doom* (2005). Meanwhile, the British actress has also established herself in Hollywood with the sci-fi thriller *Surrogates* (2009) alongside Bruce Willis. Yet her sophisticated British demeanor still works best on home territory: in the much-praised teen drama *An Education* (2009) all eyes are drawn to Pike as the chic socialite in early 60s London; and in the women's lib story *Made in Dagenham* (2010) she plays the boss's frustrated wife who supports the strike of female Ford workers for the right to equal pay. Ever since her student days, Rosamund Pike – who by her own admission will "never ever play a junkie" – has also been active on the British stage.

film would be utterly inconceivable without Giamatti. The adaptation was soon criticized for painting a rather too sentimental portrait of its antihero. But then this is Barney's version, who to make matters worse is also suffering from Alzheimer's disease. He is an unreliable narrator, who may well put a gloss on things, but we also trust him to be hard on himself given his feelings of self-doubt and guilt. Quite apart from which, the flashback format is structured in such a way that we expect disaster to strike any time. At what point did everything go wrong? What will be the next blow of fate? The action probably corresponds more to Barney's outlook on life than to the facts. His greatest failing is not to recognize happiness, which in turn makes him unable to hold

Director Richard J. Lewis brings these psychological agonies to the screen using a large dose of situation comedy and a form of black humor that does not flinch from the ultimate questions. The film is also a glorious visual foray into the life of the Jewish middle class in French-speaking Canada; not to mention an example of the particularly Canadian style of effortlessly combining Hollywood cinematography and French *auteur* cinema. The outstanding cast includes not only Paul Giamatti, Rosamund Pike and Dustin Hoffman, but also cameos from revered Canadian directors David Cronenberg, Atom Egoyan and Denys Arcand. Veteran star Hoffman pulls out all the stops as Barney's similarly disposed, if distinctly less pessimistic, father: Mr Panofsky, Sr dies in a brothel.

4 An American in Rome: the young man about town gets his fingers burnt by Clara (Rachelle Lefevre). Paul Giamatti won a Golden Globe for the role.

5 Marital bliss: Miriam (Rosamund Pike) is intelligent, and gives Barney the stability he has longed for in his life. But he ends up losing her too.

6 A waste of time: Barney's second wife has trouble arousing his interest. He has only married her for her money.

7 Murder suspect: Boogie (Scott Speedman), Barney's best friend and witness on more than one occasion, mysteriously disappears.

8 Love at first sight: Miriam can't understand Barney's sudden appearance. The man has come straight from his own wedding.

"Giamatti's Barney is not especially smart or talented or good-looking, but he is especially there – a presence with a great depth of need that apparently appeals to the lovely Miriam." *Chicago Sun-Times*

THE SOCIAL NETWORK

2010 – USA – 120 MINS DRAMA, BIOPIC
DIRECTOR DAVID FINCHER (*1962)
SCREENPLAY AARON SORKIN from Ben Mezrich's book "THE ACCIDENTAL BILLIONAIRES"
DIRECTOR OF PHOTOGRAPHY JEFF CRONENWETH EDITING KIRK BAXTER, ANGUS WALL
MUSIC TRENT REZNOR, ATTICUS ROSS PRODUCTION DANA BRUNETTI, CEÁN CHAFFIN, MICHAEL DE LUCA, SCOTT RUDIN for COLUMBIA PICTURES, RELATIVITY MEDIA, SCOTT RUDIN PRODUCTIONS, MICHAEL DE LUCA PRODUCTIONS, TRIGGER STREET PRODUCTIONS.
STARRING JESSE EISENBERG (Mark Zuckerberg), ANDREW GARFIELD (Eduardo Saverin), ROONEY MARA (Erica Albright), JUSTIN TIMBERLAKE (Sean Parker), ARMIE HAMMER (Cameron Winklevoss/Tyler Winklevoss), MAX MINGHELLA (Divya Narendra), JOSEPH MAZZELLO (Dustin Moskovitz), DENISE GRAYSON (Gretchen), BRENDA SONG (Christy).
ACADEMY AWARDS 2011 OSCARS for BEST ADAPTED SCREENPLAY (Aaron Sorkin), BEST FILM EDITING (Kirk Baxter, Angus Wall), BEST MUSIC, Original Score (Trent Reznor, Atticus Ross).

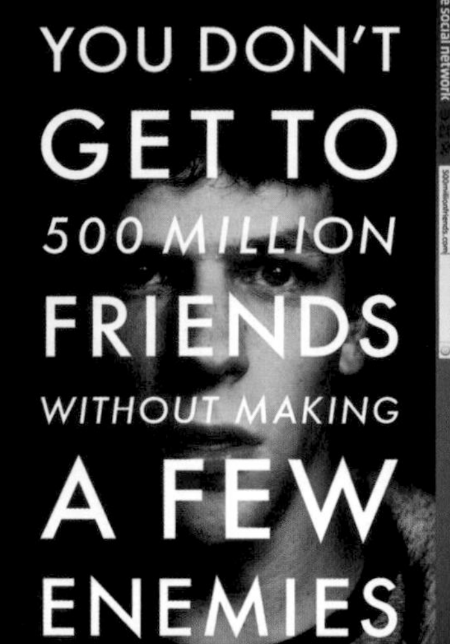
YOU DON'T
GET TO
500 MILLION
FRIENDS
WITHOUT MAKING
A FEW
ENEMIES
the social network

"Creation myths need a devil."

Mark Zuckerberg (Jesse Eisenberg) is a Harvard undergraduate and computer software genius, though more laid-back than career driven. He thinks his chances of being accepted into one of the famous "final clubs" are slim. After his girlfriend Erica (Rooney Mara) breaks up with him, he vilifies her in a blog and vents his frustration by writing the program for the Facemash website, which is an unexpected hit. From this basic idea and with the financial support of his best friend, Eduardo Saverin (Andrew Garfield), Mark develops an online network for Harvard students: The Facebook. They soon have to extend it to other universities and schools thanks to its growing popularity. In searching for financial backers, they meet Napster founder Sean Parker (Justin Timberlake), who persuades Mark that more profit could be squeezed from Facebook with the help of investors rather than through advertising revenue. Parker is also responsible for reducing Eduardo's share of the business to a minimum under some clause, leading not only to a split but a legal battle between Mark and Eduardo as well. In addition to which, twin brothers Cameron and Tyler Winklevoss (Armie Hammer) accuse the Facebook founder of stealing their idea. We all know what happened next: Mark Zuckerberg became the youngest billionaire on the planet.

It was predictable yet inconceivable that Hollywood would pick up the success story of Facebook, the biggest online network in the world. How does one make a movie about a virtual community now comprising over 750 million users? David Fincher and screenwriter Aaron Sorkin do not even attempt the impossible; for the film is actually not about the Facebook phenomenon itself, but rather about the associated transformation in communication modes. The film hits the ground running, demanding the viewer's undivided attention from the word "go." We see Mark and Erica talking in the noisy student bar in the classic shot/reverse shot format. Fincher apparently filmed 99 takes for this five-minute opening scene. He wants to show not only every nuance of a lively dialogue, but also how the way in which something is said determines the thrust of a conversation. Mark's facial expressions and intonation make him seem vain and arrogant: the slight squint of his eyes, the twitch at the corners of his mouth, a raised eyebrow – his face speaks volumes. By contrast, Erica

1

"Erica: 'Okay, you are probably going to be a very successful computer person. But you're gonna go through life thinking that girls don't like you because you're a nerd. And I want you to know from the bottom of my heart that that won't be true. It'll be because you're an asshole.'" *faz.net*

AARON SORKIN Aaron Sorkin was born of Jewish parents in New York in 1961 and grew up in the suburb of Scarsdale. As a child they often took him along to the theater and, perhaps because he did not understand much of the content, he became fascinated all the more by the sound of the dialogue, which was like music to his ears. This feel for language was later to become his trademark: clever, quick-fire exchanges, and plenty of them. After trying for some years without success to make it as an actor, Sorkin finally began to write his own plays. His first big success came in 1989 with a military court drama that he adapted himself a couple of years later for the feature film *A Few Good Men* (1992).

Based on his research for *The American President* (1995) he developed the concept for the TV series *The West Wing* (1999–2006) about the everyday life and decisions of the US president (Martin Sheen) and his advisory staff. More than anything else, the realistic depiction and adaptation of current political events (Sorkin wrote the scripts just a few weeks in advance) contributed to the success of the TV series. One of Sorkin's favorite narrative techniques is the "walk and talk:" the camera follows a character through several rooms and corridors as he or she talks to various other people who join the scene. Although his two other TV series, *Sports Night* (1998–2000) and *Studio 60 on the Sunset Strip* (2006–07), operated on the same principle (set, however, in fictitious TV studios rather than the White House) they were only short-lived. After a 12-year absence he returned to cinema with *Charlie Wilson's War* (2007).

Sorkin sometimes appears as himself in a minor role in his films – for instance, as a bored New York ad executive in *The Social Network*.

1 From computer nerd to billionaire: who is this Mark Zuckerberg (Jesse Eisenberg), whose influence on Web 2.0 is second to none?

2 Jesse Eisenberg's facial expressions invite interpretations. Is Mark self-confident or arrogant, sincere or devious, a genius or a pain in the ass?

3 Erica (Rooney Mara) leaves Mark because she cannot take any more of his arrogant, hurtful ways.

4 Mark also puts his friendship with Eduardo (Andrew Garfield) on the line.

5 Eduardo develops an algorithm for Facemash, the forerunner of Facebook.

always seems sincere and open. Fincher and Sorkin celebrate dialogue as an art form in an almost analytical way; they understand interpersonal communication as a cultural commodity that is both complex and important, one that cannot be replaced by merely exchanging short text messages, photos and videos.

The screenplay for *The Social Network* is based on the bestseller "The Accidental Billionaires" by Ben Mezrich, who fictionalized the founding of Facebook as a story about "sex, money, genius and betrayal." Sorkin transposes its chronological narrative into an asynchronous parallel montage in which the success story is elaborately interwoven with the two court cases. Smooth transitions between the two narrative levels are created through the constant interplay of direct and indirect speech.

Mark Zuckerberg's meteoric rise to become the youngest billionaire in the world is reminiscent of *Citizen Kane* (1941), which also uses flashbacks to reconstruct the life story of a media mogul who is both successful and

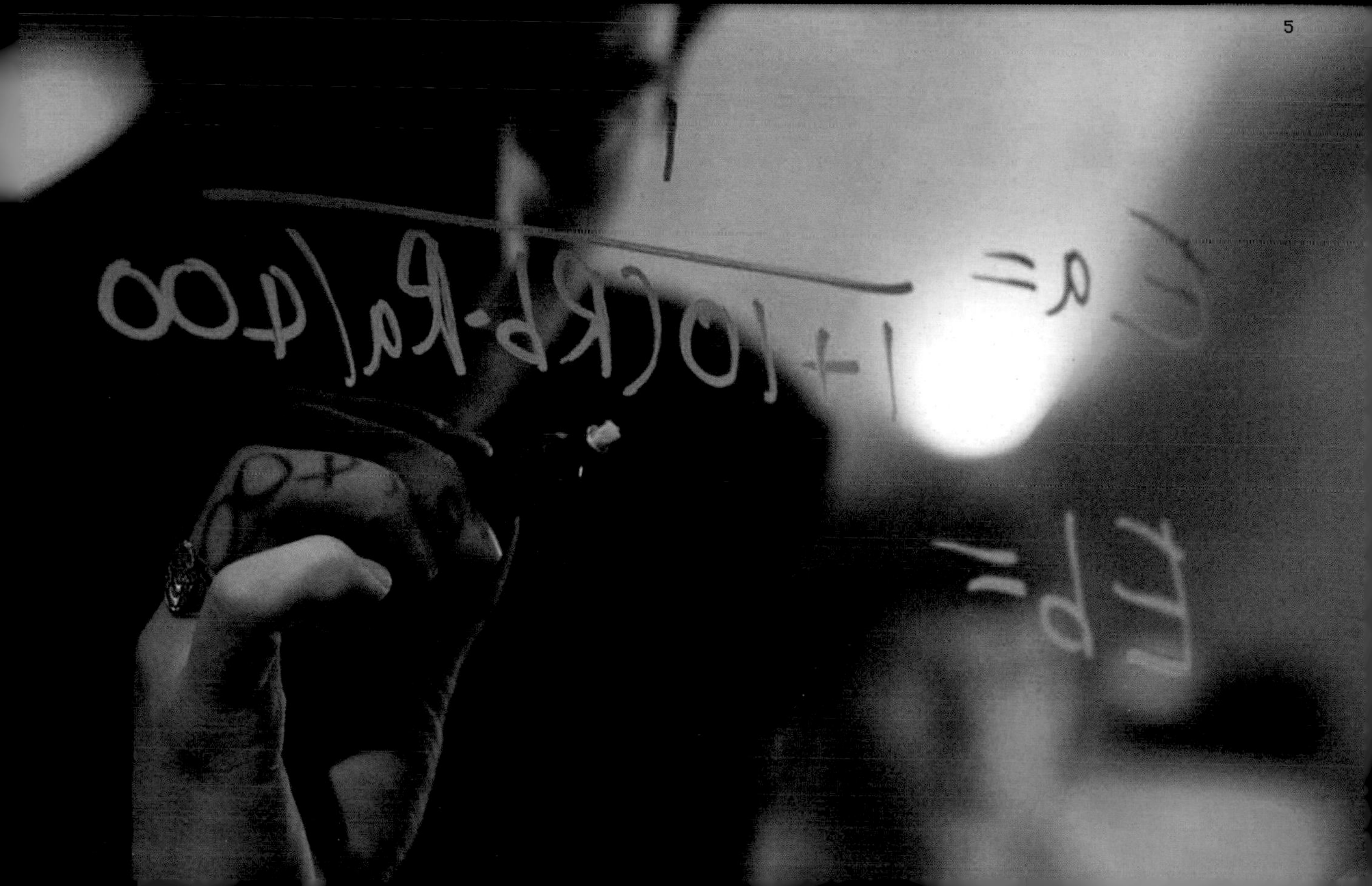

6

7

6 The twin brothers Cameron and Tyler Winklevoss (both played by Armie Hammer, l.) and Divya Narendra (Max Minghella, r.) accuse Mark Zuckerberg of stealing their basic concept for an exclusive network.

7 Christy (Brenda Song) can take a joke, but her boyfriend Eduardo has just forgotten to change his relationship status on Facebook.

8 Flip flops and dressing gown: Mark makes it clear it's not money he cares about, in his personal appearance too.

9 With his charming, winning ways, Sean Parker (Justin Timberlake) quickly wins over the Facebook founder. Mark brings him on board, in spite of Eduardo's reservations.

"The drama of domination and betrayal is played out in eyes, eyebrows, mouths, mutual gazes, and the like as much as it is in the dialogue and incidents." *davidbordwell.net*

8

alone, in equal measure. This film classic drew its inspiration from another real-life figure, William Randolph Hearst, who revolutionized the newspaper industry to the same extent that Zuckerberg did with Web 2.0. In contrast to Orson Welles' expressive imagery, however, the cinematic language in *The Social Network* seems positively sober and restrained, with Fincher's direction yielding at times to Sorkin's verbal duels.

The Erica Albright character is particularly significant for the structure of the film; for Mark, she embodies the same idea as Charles Foster Kane's famous "Rosebud." She is actually a purely filmic concept of Sorkin's own invention, which does not feature in either Zuckerberg's life or Bezrich's book. She is the peg on which the movie is hung; the starting point and driving force behind Mark's actions. It is only when he notices that Erica still thinks of Facebook as a computer game that he decides to expand it further. When Sean Parker tells him that he only founded Napster to impress his high school sweetheart, Mark seems to remember Erica. He can't get her out of his head. Facebook may have made him rich and famous, but Erica's friendship is the only thing he could never have; something he lost forever a long time ago. When Mark is sitting alone at the end in front of his Facebook profile – hesitantly clicking on the "friends" button, refreshing the page every few seconds looking for some sign from her – only at this point do we feel some pity for the man who made his mark, possibly more than anyone, on the meaning of "friendship" on the internet.

CZ

DUE DATE

2010 – USA – 95 MIN. – COMEDY
DIRECTOR TODD PHILLIPS (*1970)
SCREENPLAY ALAN R. COHEN, ALAN FREEDLAND, ADAM SZTYKIEL, TODD PHILLIPS
DIRECTOR OF PHOTOGRAPHY LAWRENCE SHER EDITING DEBRA NEIL-FISHER MUSIC CHRISTOPHE BECK
PRODUCTION DANIEL GOLDBERG, TODD PHILLIPS for WARNER BROS., LEGENDARY PICTURES, GREEN HAT FILMS.
STARRING ROBERT DOWNEY JR. (Peter Highman), ZACH GALIFIANAKIS (Ethan Tremblay), MICHELLE MONAGHAN (Sarah Highman), JAMIE FOXX (Darryl), JULIETTE LEWIS (Heidi), DANNY MCBRIDE (Lonnie), JAKOB ULRICH (Patrick), NAIIA ULRICH (Alex), BOBBY TISDALE (Carl), TODD PHILLIPS (Barry).

"My father loved coffee, and now we loved him as coffee."

In the life of modern *Homo sapiens*, endlessly mobile and sexually tamed, only one seriously incalculable event remains: a baby – the final mystery. It starts with the birth. And architect Peter Highman (Robert Downey Jr.), who has just traveled to Atlanta on business, has only five days to get to Los Angeles in order to be there for the happy event. Impending fatherhood foreshadows sleepless nights for this cool high-flier, but it should be doable. What he hasn't foreseen, though, is a traveling companion who will put his paternal patience and empathy to the test a little too soon: chaotic big kid Ethan Tremblay (Zach Galifianakis) enters his life like a kind of trial infant and, from that point on, Highman doesn't have a moment's peace.

Thanks to Ethan, Peter ends up on the "no-fly" lists as a terrorist suspect, loses his wallet, and has to tackle the onerous journey in the rental car of his worst enemy, of all people. Yet the problems are only just beginning. For, like a childlike force of nature both sensitive and truculent, Ethan leads them both into every disaster imaginable: he blows the travel money on soft drugs, smokes a joint and falls asleep at the wheel; then, instead of filling up with

1

"Galifianakis and Downey Jr. are deft comic performers, and Phillips has displayed genuine talent at staging comedic episodes, both in *Old School* and *The Hangover*. (...) But the undercurrents of the film suggest darker themes about the realities of parenthood than one might have guessed from the outset." *filmcritic.com*

gas at Texaco™, he drives to Mexico. Given these and even worse mishaps, Peter finds it increasingly hard to come to terms with his role as a father – this quick-tempered guy is really losing it. In a typical scene he even punches a kid he doesn't know, as a substitute outlet for his frustration. Even the fact that Ethan is carrying the mortal remains of his own father around in a coffee tin is not enough to soften his heart. Yet all his attempts to shake off this pain in the butt, or even bump him off, backfire.

Todd Phillips' films show male stereotypes in crisis, with the adolescent humor of his protagonists only a symptom of this. For the first time, however, *Due Date* tackles the comedy with a character from outside the boundaries of this filmic universe. The bachelor party of *The Hangover* (2009) is over for good. Peter would never want to see a film by Phillips, nor would he have someone like Ethan as his friend. But there is no getting away from it. As the two finally head toward a type of reconciliation, Peter takes the last steps to maturity, even if from the outside it looks more like capitulation.

Even more so than Steve Martin and John Candy in the obvious model *Planes, Trains & Automobiles* (1987), Robert Downey Jr. and Zach Galifianakis are actors from opposite ends of the spectrum; Downey Jr. was always funny

2

3

1 Two men in the same boat: successful guy Peter (Robert Downey Jr.) and wacky Ethan (Zach Galifianakis) make a really odd couple.

2 Disastrous road trip: Peter doesn't fancy the idea of relying on the rather disorganized Ethan's help. The tense atmosphere is also noticed by fellow travelers.

3 High at the wheel: the sensitive big kid steers the pair unerringly from one disaster to the next. The comedic timing is perfect.

"In fact, so infuriating is Ethan that *Due Date* very nearly loses us, too, at the outset, but over time, the bearded boor manages to win everyone over, audience included." *Variety*

ROBERT DOWNEY JR. Robert Downey Junior's off-screen antics have been a significant contributory factor to his image as the last rock star of the movie business. His career, however, which nearly always features brilliant performances, has clearly been hampered by his frequent spells in prison. Born in New York, the son of an artist family, he began to make a name for himself in teen flicks like *Weird Science* (1985) and *The Pick-up Artist* (1987). The breakthrough came with *Less Than Zero* (1987) from the novel by Bret Easton Ellis. Unfortunately, the part of drug addict Julian was already dangerously close to reality.

No one then expected his Oscar-nominated portrayal of a film legend in *Chaplin* (1992). Downey Jr. successfully combined his own inimitable style with the famous histrionic mannerisms of the little tramp. He also gave a convincing performance in Robert Altman's *Short Cuts* (1993) with his well-orchestrated repertoire of erratic gestures; he is without peer in his realistic portrayal of wryly dispirited characters. Perhaps he simply arrived too late for the New Hollywood. In the squeaky clean reality of contemporary Tinsel Town, he was fired after a Golden Globe-winning part in the TV series *Ally McBeal* (1997–2002) and, until a kind of rebirth in the thriller *Gothika* (2003), was regarded as a production risk.

That said, the reformed Robert Downey Jr. has long since been seen as a safe bet for blockbusters. After films like *Wonder Boys* (2000), *Kiss Kiss Bang Bang* (2005) and *Zodiac* (2007) – dream movies for actors – he finally made it as a highly paid superhero and action star in *Iron Man* (2008). His exceptionally inspired performances have even benefited slick entertainment movies such as *Sherlock Holmes* (2009), for which he won another Golden Globe. His controversial role as a "blacked-up" white actor in the war movie parody *Tropic Thunder* (2008) is proof that one of the funniest actors of his generation is nobody's fool in the comedy genre.

4 Stopover at good friends: once again, Juliette Lewis is magnificent in her guest appearance as hash dealer Heidi.

5 Peter makes it to the hospital, battered and bruised both mentally and physically. He has failed miserably so far in his role as a father.

"The best scenes in *Due Date* are their arguments and make-up moments, one staged at the Grand Canyon, when the movie feels closer to a Wenders-like relationship drama than anything else." *Time Out New York*

6 Women tend to have passive roles in Todd Phillips films: Peter's pregnant wife, Sarah (Michelle Monaghan), is no exception.

7 Touchy-feely buddy movie: Galifianakis and Downey Jr., from different planets as actors as well, are simply wonderful together.

in serious roles, while Galifianakis – *The Hangover*'s big, new-found talent – delivers his brand of humor in all seriousness. Some of his madcap actions (for example, Ethan has a masturbating contest with his dog and steals Peter's wallet) are deliberate performances, to provoke a reaction. It is not surprising that his big dream is to become a Hollywood actor. As for the rest of his mistakes, however, he appears to have no sense of responsibility about them, which regularly infuriates his traveling companion. This in turn affects Ethan's sensitive side, with the lack of self-consciousness in one exceeded only by the vulnerability of the other. Ultimately, the suffering on both sides is boundless.

As in his previous movie, *The Hangover*, Phillips's brilliance derives more from his comedic timing than profundity. Even the old gag with the ashes of a loved one gets an unexpected twist – no matter how obvious it might be to confuse the father's cremated remains with ground coffee. Whether the squabbling pair is fleeing the Mexican border police or being beaten up by a crippled war veteran, the buddy movie operates as inexorably as the rules of Homeland Security. With a superb cast of two, abysmal dialogue and his surefire handling of primal male fears, Phillips' most "grown-up" film to date is a disastrous delight. PB

THE FIGHTER

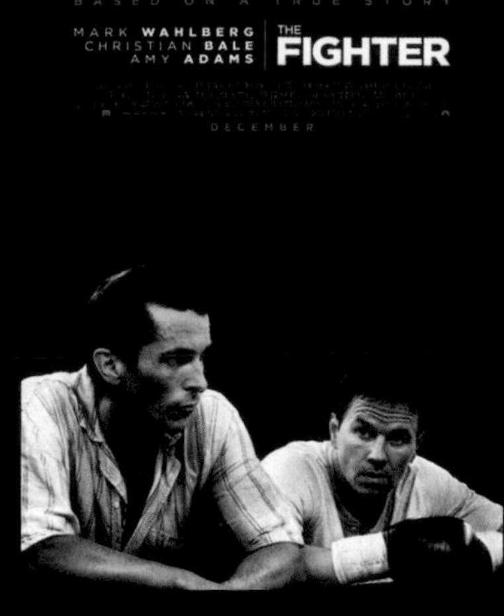

2010 – USA – 115 MIN. – BIOPIC, DRAMA, BOXING MOVIE
DIRECTOR DAVID O. RUSSELL (*1958)
SCREENPLAY SCOTT SILVER, PAUL TAMASY, ERIC JOHNSON, KEITH DORRINGTON
DIRECTOR OF PHOTOGRAPHY HOYTE VAN HOYTEMA EDITING PAMELA MARTIN MUSIC MICHAEL BROOK
PRODUCTION DOROTHY AUFIERO, MARK WAHLBERG, JEFF G. WAXMAN, KEN HALSBAND, DAVID HOBERMAN, RYAN KAVANAUGH, TODD LIEBERMAN, PAUL TAMASY for CLOSEST TO THE HOLE PRODUCTIONS, FIGHTER, MANDEVILLE FILMS, RELATIVITY MEDIA, THE WEINSTEIN COMPANY.
STARRING MARK WAHLBERG (Micky Ward), CHRISTIAN BALE (Dicky Eklund), MELISSA LEO (Alice Ward), AMY ADAMS (Charlene Fleming), JACK MCGEE (George Ward), JENNA LAMIA (Sherri Ward), MICKEY O'KEEFE (as himself), SUGAR RAY LEONARD (as himself).
ACADEMY AWARDS 2011 OSCARS for BEST SUPPORTING ACTOR (Christian Bale) and BEST SUPPORTING ACTRESS (Melissa Leo).

"You were my hero, Dicky." – "I was. I was."

Micky and Dicky are half-brothers; two boxers from Lowell, Massachusetts. While Dicky Eklund (Christian Bale) is famous for winning a fight against Sugar Ray Leonard and was town hero for a time, success has so far eluded his younger brother, Micky Ward (Mark Wahlberg), who has always been more of a stepping stone for other boxers' careers. All that is about to change, however. With his big brother as trainer and mother Alice (Melissa Leo) as manager, Micky is to be molded into the new "pride of Lowell." The film is based on a true story, portraying the career of "Irish" Micky Ward from the mid-1990s to the turn of the millennium, when he became the WBU Light Welterweight Champion. Lowell – once a boom town of the American textile industry – is now small and desolate, its residents struggling with poverty and unemployment. Between occasional, lucrative fights, Micky earns his living as a road worker. His ex-wife is with someone else, and he rarely sees their daughter. He meets a waitress, Charlene (Amy Adams), who makes it clear to him that he has to stand on his own two feet to be a successful boxer. It leads to a split between Micky and his family.

Mark Wahlberg trained for several years for the part, and we can admire the results in the strikingly realistic fight scenes. *The Fighter* clearly operates within the conventions of the genre. From the initial, painful defeats, through rejection of (and then reconciliation with) his family and trainer, to the winning pose for much acclaimed World Championship title in freeze frame – Micky's rise from road worker to champ uses all the standard clichés of the boxing movie. What also makes it an interesting film is the tragicomic portrayal of Micky Ward's social milieu, the representational style of which almost makes the sporting success a secondary issue. First and foremost, we have the high-pitched family, comprising Dicky, Alice, helpless father George (Jack McGee) and no less than seven sisters, whose characterizations substantially mine the worst white-trash clichés. And yet, no matter how overwrought and crazy this awfully nice lower-class family seems, David O. Russell never holds the characters up to ridicule. Micky, quiet and introverted, seems like an alien being in this social melee. Mark Wahlberg's performance in the leading role is deliberately restrained and low-key for, alongside Micky's rise to fame, the

EVERLAST
EVERLAST

1 The winning pose signals a happy ending. The rise of Micky Ward (Mark Wahlberg) is merely the framework for a far more compelling family drama.

2 Boxing as a family business: but Micky's career has been rather disappointing with his mother Alice (Melissa Leo) as manager and brother Dicky (Christian Bale) as trainer.

3 Micky's girlfriend Charlene (Amy Adams) persuades him to take control of his own career.

film also tells the far more tragic story of Dicky Eklund. Christian Bale's performance is the one that stays in the viewer's mind: the way he raves about his big fight, gesticulating and staring wildly, or re-enacts it later, stoned in some bar. "The Pride of Lowell is back," he says cockily to the cameras of a TV station that ostensibly wants to make a documentary about the boxer's comeback. But 45 minutes later we learn in passing that the TV crew is not, in fact, filming Dicky on account of his sporting achievements; they have instead chosen him as the pathetic main figure for a documentary about crack addicts. This film-within-a-film actually exists: it was made by DCTV and HBO as *High on Crack Street: Lost Lives in Lowell* (1995). Several scenes from it were remade with Christian Bale for *The Fighter*, using TV cameras from the 1990s to give it a particularly authentic look. The TV broadcast of the documentary in the middle of the film actually forms the highpoint – as well as turning point – of *The Fighter*. In a parallel montage we see the various characters, in various

"If you think *Rocky* and *Raging Bull* define the alpha and omega of boxing movies, think again. David O. Russell's *The Fighter* proves there's still punch in the genre, especially when a filmmaker tells a familiar story in a brand-new way." *The Washington Post*

MARK WAHLBERG *The Fighter* (2010) was a movie project dear to the heart of actor and producer Mark Wahlberg. There are clear parallels to his own life story: he was born in Boston in 1971, the youngest of nine siblings, and grew up in the working-class district of Dorchester. His parents split up when he was 11 years old, and two years later he left school and started dealing and taking drugs. At 16, he was jailed for 45 days for assault and resisting arrest. To begin with, Mark was also in the shadow of his older brother, Donnie, who became famous as a member of the boy band "New Kids on the Block." It was Donnie, however, who helped him to his first successes as rapper "Marky Mark." After being hired as an underwear model for Calvin Klein, Wahlberg also started to get offers of minor film roles. His breakthrough as an actor came as porn star Dirk Diggler in *Boogie Nights* (1997). Two years later, he worked for the first time with director David O. Russell in the Iraq War satire *Three Kings* (1999), playing alongside George Clooney and Ice Cube. Wahlberg followed up with appearances in a series of gangster movies including *The Yards* (1999), *The Italian Job* (2003) and *We Own the Night* (2007), sharing the billing with Joaquin Phoenix in the first and third of these; apparently they were also offered the main leads in *Brokeback Mountain* (2005) that were then filled by Jake Gyllenhaal and Heath Ledger. Mark Wahlberg won his first Oscar nomination for his supporting role in Martin Scorsese's *The Departed* (2006) followed by a second for Best Film (*The Fighter*, 2010). As well as feature films, Wahlberg also produces several American TV series.

4 The family sticks together. After his release, Dicky is given a warm welcome by his sisters.

5 Two very different brothers: while Micky is heading toward champion status, Dicky's best years are behind him.

5

6

6 Dicky was once the "pride of Lowell." Then he descended into crack addiction. He even ends up behind bars, after fighting with the police.

7 The road to the title: after Dicky has come to grips with his issues, he leads his brother on to a series of wins.

8 Her influence on Micky means more friends for Charlene than just the Ward family.

9 Mark Wahlberg struggled for years on his own to realize a project that was so dear to his heart. And all the while he was training hard, to be convincing in the title role.

"Dicky is a constant let-down, but try as he might, Micky can't break free from Dicky, his mother or his family. He's the glue that holds them all together." *Orlando Sentinel*

7

8

stages of preparation, facing the reality of Dicky's crack addiction. This is the point at which the family is torn furthest apart, both emotionally and physically. Dicky is in jail after a brawl. At first he enjoys being hailed as a TV star by the inmates but, when he sees himself as a washed-up mess on screen, he cannot stand it any more and turns the program off. Alice is sitting at home with her daughters; they shake their heads with tears in their eyes as they, too, see on screen what they had all been trying to ignore until then. Micky is the only one who is not overcome by these events; alone in his apartment, he searches out information on his brother's affliction. This mirror held up to reality naturally leaves its mark on the protagonists; they are reformed and reunited as a boxing family by the end of the movie, and rewarded with Micky's World Championship title. *The Fighter* marked an unexpected comeback for director David O. Russell, who had been pretty much written off after several arguments on film sets and the flop of his quirky movie *I Heart Huckabees* (2004). It was only when the original choice for director, Darren Aronofsky, pulled out in order to realize his long-held dream *Black Swan* (2010) that Wahlberg gave his friend a break (he had worked with him twice before). Russell repaid him with an entertaining mixture of sports movie, family drama and real-life satire. He also considerably enriched the boxing movie genre, which is usually characterized by loners, with a glittering cast of players in this ensemble movie.

CZ

TRUE GRIT

2010 – USA – 110 MIN. – WESTERN, LITERARY ADAPTATION
DIRECTORS ETHAN COEN, JOEL COEN (*1954, *1957)
SCREENPLAY ETHAN COEN, JOEL COEN, from the novel of the same name by CHARLES PORTIS DIRECTOR OF PHOTOGRAPHY ROGER DEAKINS EDITING RODERICK JAYNES (PSEUDONYM for JOEL AND ETHAN COEN) MUSIC CARTER BURWELL
PRODUCTION ETHAN COEN, JOEL COEN, SCOTT RUDIN for PARAMOUNT PICTURES, SKYDANCE PRODUCTIONS, SCOTT RUDIN PRODUCTIONS, MIKE ZOSS PRODUCTIONS.
STARRING JEFF BRIDGES (Rooster Cogburn), HAILEE STEINFELD (Mattie Ross), MATT DAMON (LaBœuf), JOSH BROLIN (Tom Chaney), BARRY PEPPER (Lucky Ned Pepper), DAKIN MATTHEWS (Colonel Stonehill), JARLATH CONROY (Undertaker), PAUL RAE (Emmett Quincy).

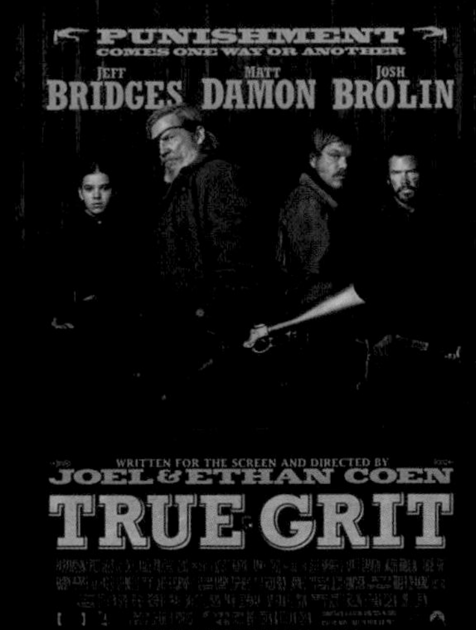

"Punishment comes one way or another."

Arkansas 1878. Fourteen-year-old Mattie Ross (Hailee Steinfeld) has a very close relationship with her father. When he is shot dead by hired hand, Tom Chaney (Josh Brolin), the girl sets out to ensure that the murderer gets his comeuppance. She hires US Marshal Rooster Cogburn (Jeff Bridges) and meets Texas Ranger LaBœuf (Matt Damon), who is also pursuing the wanted man for another crime. The three of them set off for American Indian territory in the search for Chaney.

Just a year after the story "True Grit" was serialized in the Saturday Evening Post in 1968, John Wayne appeared on the big screen as the US Marshal in the eponymous movie *True Grit* (1969). He received his first and only Oscar for his role as Rooster Cogburn. As the Coens have repeatedly stressed, however, their film should not be read as a remake of the late Henry Hathaway's western, but as an adaptation of the novel in its own right. Nonetheless, there are a few extra scenes that are intended as tongue-in-cheek cross-references within the Coen universe. We are unavoidably reminded of the lavatory scene at the start of *The Big Lebowski* (1998), when Mattie disturbs Jeff Bridges as he sits on the toilet in his first appearance onscreen. And the strange dentist in the bearskin (Ed Corbin) is an obvious reference to Dr. Sussman, the Jew from Big Bear in *A Serious Man* (2009).

The film's title refers to Marshal Cogburn's reputation for toughness and reliability: he is said to be a man of sterling qualities, or "true grit." Initially, however, he fails to live up to this reputation, behaving more like a drunken, washed-up western-hero who has seen better days. LaBœuf is not much of an improvement: he constantly talks up the honor of Texas Rangers, yet the fact that he has been after Chaney for months without success hardly speaks in his favor. Mattie instead is the one who shows real courage, capable of standing her ground against these two warhorses; her fearless sense of purpose knows no bounds.

1 The Dude playing the Duke: Jeff Bridges as aging US Marshal "Rooster" Cogburn. John Wayne won his only Oscar for the same role in 1969.

2 Mattie Ross (Hailee Steinfeld) seeks out the best man to help. She hires the notorious Marshal to ensure that her father's killer gets the punishment he deserves.

3 Mattie offers the Marshal a lucrative bonus. But he thinks it's a bad idea for her to take part in the search for the killer.

Mattie knows her Bible, and believes her revenge to be legitimized by the Old Testament: no one can escape the just wrath of God. This pervasive religious dimension is reflected in Carter Burwell's choice of 19th-century Protestant hymns for his soundtrack. At the Coens' request, there is also a version of "Leaning on the Everlasting Arms" at the end of the film – a song known to film buffs mainly from Charles Laughton's *The Night of the Hunter* (1955). The brothers frequently incorporate references to this classic into their movies.

Only a few of the many Bible quotations find their way into the film. One is inserted at the beginning as a kind of motto: "The wicked flee when no man pursues" (Proverbs 28: 1). Only the first half of the proverb is given in both the film and Portis' book; the second part, however, tells us: "but the righteous are bold as a lion." Mattie is likewise absolute in her convictions, seeing herself as having the moral high ground. Later, though, she is forced to acknowledge that her actions have consequences as well, and that she is at God's mercy. When she achieves her goal, killing Tom Chaney with the shotgun, she has to pay a considerable price for her actions. The weight of the shot throws her backward into a ravine, where she is bitten by a poisonous snake. She does survive, thanks to Cogburn, but her arm has to be amputated.

The Coens film this rescue far more dramatically than is portrayed in the book. As in the poem "The Erlking" (Der Erlkoenig) by Goethe, the finale becomes a metaphysical horseback ride between sundown and pitch-black night, the back projection rendering the journey almost surreal. As the scene progresses, the colors become increasingly washed out and contrasts heightened, until

JEFF BRIDGES Son of actor Lloyd Bridges, Jeffrey Leon Bridges was born in Los Angeles in 1949. He and his older brother, Beau (who also became a famous movie star), learned the acting trade from their parents at an early age. Jeff received his first Oscar nomination as Best Supporting Actor in one of his first major roles, as Duane Jackson in Peter Bogdanovich's *The Last Picture Show* (1971). His languid style and mischievous charm became young Bridges' trademark in the early 1970s: he appeared as the ambitious boxer in John Huston's *Fat City* (1972), the wily outlaw in Robert Benton's revisionist western *Bad Company* (1972) and Clint Eastwood's young sidekick in *Thunderbolt and Lightfoot* (1974). Then, in the 1980s and '90s, he went on to play a wide range of different parts – from expressionless alien in *Starman* (1984) through eccentric radio presenter in *The Fisher King* (1991) – never tying himself to one specific image. This came to an abrupt end with the Coen brothers' *The Big Lebowski* (1998). In "The Dude," Bridges created one of the most memorable cult figures in cinema history – an image that has since stayed with the actor like an alter ego. After coming away empty-handed from his previous four Oscar nominations, he finally won the coveted Academy Award for his leading role as aging country-music star Bad Blake in *Crazy Heart* (2009). This must have sweetened the pill when an Oscar nomination for his leading role as Rooster Cogburn the following year failed to convert.

4 Josh Brolin only makes a brief appearance as the sly killer, Tom Chaney, who suddenly finds himself face-to-face with his victim's daughter, intent on vengeance.

5 After Mattie has crossed the fast-flowing river on her horse, Little Blackie, Cogburn and LaBœuf (Matt Damon) are forced to accept that the gutsy young girl won't be shaken off so easily.

6 Figure of fun with handlebar moustache and a stubborn streak: Texas Ranger LaBœuf is also pursuing Tom Chaney.

"As usual, the Coens pack the smaller roles – undertakers, horse traders, and assorted no-goodniks – with carefully chosen character actors whose faces look straight from an old tintype photograph." *Slate*

"In some ways, much like Charles Laughton's *Night of the Hunter*, which the Coens quote both musically and visually, *True Grit* is a parable about good and evil. Only here, the lines between the two are so blurred as to be indistinguishable, making this a true picture of how the West was won, or – depending on your view – lost." *The New York Times*

7 Mattie is surprised when she suddenly comes face-to-face with Tom Chaney. She tries to hold him at bay with her father's ancient revolver.

8 As in the book, Rooster Cogburn is a US Marshal, a man with true grit. But it ends with him playing in a Wild West show across the country, a parody of himself.

9 Rooster Cogburn lives up to his reputation: the Marshal keeps up his (high-proof) spirits in the lengthy pursuit of Tom Chaney.

the filmic image seems almost to have been shot in black-and-white. The clear, starry night sky and animal sounds calling from the wild are once again reminiscent of a famous scene from *The Night of the Hunter*, in which the two children escape from the priest in a boat. Delirious with fever, Mattie thinks she sees Chaney fleeing across the horizon. When the pony collapses and dies from exhaustion, Cogburn carries the girl onward. In what must be his greatest act of heroism, he saves Mattie's life. His energies almost spent, he finally spots a light in the darkness. After sinking to his knees, Mattie still in his arms, he fires a shot in the air to attract attention. Then, exhausted, he murmurs that he has gotten old.

The brilliant command of camera language coupled with a supreme awareness of cinematic potential is impressive. Plus, as well as being a thrilling story, it is also a clever reflection on the issue of justice: possibly the key theme in a western. The movie was nominated for numerous Oscars and, although it came away empty-handed, it is clear that the Coens have breathed fresh life into the western genre, previously and popularly written off. CZ

"That old-time American religion of vengeance runs like a river through *True Grit*, a comic-serious tale about some nasty, brutish times." *The New York Times*

ACADEMY AWARDS 2002–2011

2002 OSCARS

1 Denzel Washington was the second African-American actor to win an Oscar for Best Leading Actor, for his compelling performance as the corrupt cop in *Training Day*. Ethan Hawke (right) was nominated for Best Supporting Actor, but went away empty-handed.
2 Danis Tanovic's civil war farce *No Man's Land* (image shows Rene Bitorajac) was showered with awards from all over the world. Beating off the competition from *Amélie*, he won the Oscar for Best Foreign Language Film that year.

BEST PICTURE	A BEAUTIFUL MIND (Brian Grazer, Ron Howard)
BEST DIRECTOR	RON HOWARD for *A Beautiful Mind*
BEST LEADING ACTRESS	HALLE BERRY in *Monster's Ball*
BEST LEADING ACTOR	DENZEL WASHINGTON in *Training Day*
BEST SUPPORTING ACTRESS	JENNIFER CONNELLY in *A Beautiful Mind*
BEST SUPPORTING ACTOR	JIM BROADBENT in *Iris*
BEST ORIGINAL SCREENPLAY	JULIAN FELLOWES for *Gosford Park*
BEST ADAPTED SCREENPLAY	AKIVA GOLDSMAN for *A Beautiful Mind*
BEST FOREIGN LANGUAGE FILM	*No Man's Land* by DANIS TANOVIC (Bosnia)
BEST ANIMATED FEATURE	ARON WARNER for *Shrek*
BEST CINEMATOGRAPHY	ANDREW LESNIE for *The Lord of the Rings: The Fellowship of the Ring*
BEST ART DIRECTION	CATHERINE MARTIN, BRIGITTE BROCH for *Moulin Rouge!*
BEST FILM EDITING	PIETRO SCALIA for *Black Hawk Down*
BEST MUSIC	HOWARD SHORE for *The Lord of the Rings: The Fellowship of the Ring*
BEST SONG	RANDY NEWMAN for *"If I Didn't Have You"* in *Monsters Inc*
BEST MAKEUP	PETER OWEN, RICHARD TAYLOR for *The Lord of the Rings: The Fellowship of the Ring*
BEST COSTUME DESIGN	CATHERINE MARTIN, ANGUS STRATHIE for *Moulin Rouge!*
BEST VISUAL EFFECTS	JIM RYGIEL, RANDALL WILLIAM COOK, RICHARD TAYLOR, MARK STETSON for *The Lord of the Rings: The Fellowship of the Ring*
BEST SOUND MIXING	MICHAEL MINKLER, MYRON NETTINGA, CHRIS MUNRO for *Black Hawk Down*
BEST SOUND EDITING	CHRISTOPHER BOYES, GEORGE WATTERS II for *Pearl Harbor*

2003 OSCARS

3 Best Directing: Roman Polanski, who made *The Pianist* (2002), the moving story of Holocaust survivor Władysław Szpilman, had lived through the horrors of the Krakow ghetto himself.

4 *Chicago* (2002) triumphed at the Academy Awards ceremony, scooping six Oscars. Catherine Zeta-Jones cut an especially fine figure in the musical, winning her the award for Best Supporting Actress.

BEST PICTURE	CHICAGO (Martin Richards)
BEST DIRECTOR	ROMAN POLANSKI for *The Pianist*
BEST LEADING ACTRESS	NICOLE KIDMAN in *The Hours*
BEST LEADING ACTOR	ADRIEN BRODY in *The Pianist*
BEST SUPPORTING ACTRESS	CATHERINE ZETA-JONES in *Chicago*
BEST SUPPORTING ACTOR	CHRIS COOPER in *Adaptation*
BEST ORIGINAL SCREENPLAY	PEDRO ALMODÓVAR for *Talk to Her*
BEST ADAPTED SCREENPLAY	RONALD HARWOOD for *The Pianist*
BEST FOREIGN LANGUAGE FILM	*Nowhere in Africa* by CAROLINE LINK (Germany)
BEST ANIMATED FEATURE	HAYAO MIYAZAKI for *Spirited Away*
BEST CINEMATOGRAPHY	CONRAD L. HALL for *Road to Perdition*
BEST ART DIRECTION	JOHN MYHRE, GORDON SIM for *Chicago*
BEST FILM EDITING	MARTIN WALSH for *Chicago*
BEST MUSIC	ELLIOT GOLDENTHAL for *Frida*
BEST SONG	EMINEM (Music, Lyrics), JEFF BASS (Music), LUIS RESTO (Music) for *"Lose Yourself"* in *8 Mile*
BEST MAKEUP	JOHN E. JACKSON, BEATRICE DE ALBA for *Frida*
BEST COSTUME DESIGN	COLLEEN ATWOOD for *Chicago*
BEST VISUAL EFFECTS	JIM RYGIEL, JOE LETTERI, RANDALL WILLIAM COOK, ALEX FUNKE for *The Lord of the Rings: The Two Towers*
BEST SOUND MIXING	MICHAEL MINKLER, DOMINICK TAVELLA, DAVID LEE for *Chicago*
BEST SOUND EDITING	ETHAN VAN DER RYN, MIKE HOPKINS for *The Lord of the Rings: The Two Towers*

2004 OSCARS

1 Holding the record: Peter Jackson's *The Lord of the Rings: The Return of the King* (2003) won 11 Oscars, matching *Ben-Hur* (1959) and *Titanic* (1997).
2 Courage to be ugly: Hollywood beauty Charlize Theron won the gong for Best Leading Actress for her role as serial killer Aileen Wuornos.

BEST PICTURE	THE LORD OF THE RINGS: THE RETURN OF THE KING (Barrie M. Osborne, Peter Jackson, Fran Walsh)
BEST DIRECTOR	PETER JACKSON for *The Lord of the Rings: The Return of the King*
BEST LEADING ACTRESS	CHARLIZE THERON in *Monster*
BEST LEADING ACTOR	SEAN PENN in *Mystic River*
BEST SUPPORTING ACTRESS	RENÉE ZELLWEGER in *Cold Mountain*
BEST SUPPORTING ACTOR	TIM ROBBINS in *Mystic River*
BEST ORIGINAL SCREENPLAY	SOFIA COPPOLA in *Lost in Translation*
BEST ADAPTED SCREENPLAY	F. WALSH, PHILIPPA BOYENS, P. JACKSON for *The Lord of the Rings: The Return of the King*
BEST FOREIGN LANGUAGE FILM	*The Barbarian Invasions* by DENYS ARCAND (CANADA)
BEST ANIMATED FEATURE	ANDREW STANTON for *Finding Nemo*
BEST CINEMATOGRAPHY	RUSSELL BOYD for *Master and Commander*
BEST ART DIRECTION	GRANT MAJOR, DAN HENNAH, ALAN LEE for *The Lord of the Rings: The Return of the King*
BEST FILM EDITING	JAMIE SELKIRK for *The Lord of the Rings: The Return of the King*
BEST MUSIC	HOWARD SHORE for *The Lord of the Rings: The Return of the King*
BEST SONG	FRAN WALSH, HOWARD SHORE, ANNIE LENNOX for *"Into the West"* in *The Lord of the Rings: The Return of the King*
BEST MAKEUP	RICHARD TAYLOR, PETER KING for *The Lord of the Rings: The Return of the King*
BEST COSTUME DESIGN	NGILA DICKSON, RICHARD TAYLOR for *The Lord of the Rings: The Return of the King*
BEST VISUAL EFFECTS	JIM RYGIEL, JOE LETTERI, RANDALL WILLIAM COOK, ALEX FUNKE for *The Lord of the Rings: The Return of the King*
BEST SOUND MIXING	CHRISTOPHER BOYES, MICHAEL SEMANICK, MICHAEL HEDGES, HAMMOND PEEK for *The Lord of the Rings: The Return of the King*
BEST SOUND EDITING	RICHARD KING for *Master and Commander*

3 Best Picture, Best Directing: past master Clint Eastwood repeated his double win for *Unforgiven* (1992) with the boxing drama *Million Dollar Baby* (2004).

4 Jamie Foxx is more than just a talented comedian – he is a gifted musician as well. This proved an obvious advantage for his Oscar-winning role as blues legend Ray Charles.

BEST PICTURE	MILLION DOLLAR BABY (Clint Eastwood, Albert S. Ruddy, Tom Rosenberg)
BEST DIRECTOR	CLINT EASTWOOD for *Million Dollar Baby*
BEST LEADING ACTRESS	HILARY SWANK in *Million Dollar Baby*
BEST LEADING ACTOR	JAMIE FOXX in *Ray*
BEST SUPPORTING ACTRESS	CATE BLANCHETT in *Aviator*
BEST SUPPORTING ACTOR	MORGAN FREEMAN in *Million Dollar Baby*
BEST ORIGINAL SCREENPLAY	CHARLIE KAUFMAN, MICHEL GONDRY, PIERRE BISMUTH for *Eternal Sunshine of the Spotless Mind*
BEST ADAPTED SCREENPLAY	ALEXANDER PAYNE, JIM TAYLOR for *Sideways*
BEST FOREIGN LANGUAGE FILM	*The Sea Inside* by ALEJANDRO AMENÁBAR (Spain)
BEST ANIMATED FEATURE	BRAD BIRD for *The Incredibles*
BEST CINEMATOGRAPHY	ROBERT RICHARDSON for *Aviator*
BEST ART DIRECTION	DANTE FERRETTI, FRANCESCA LO SCHIAVO for *Aviator*
BEST FILM EDITING	THELMA SCHOONMAKER for *Aviator*
BEST MUSIC	JAN A.P. KACZMAREK for *Finding Neverland*
BEST SONG	JORGE DREXLER for *"Al Otro Lado Del Río"* in *The Motorcycle Diaries*
BEST MAKEUP	VALLI O'REILLY, BILL CORSO for *Lemony Snicket's A Series of Unfortunate Events*
BEST COSTUME DESIGN	SANDY POWELL for *Aviator*
BEST VISUAL EFFECTS	JOHN DYKSTRA, SCOTT STOKDYK, ANTHONY LAMOLINARA, JOHN FRAZIER for *Spider-Man 2*
BEST SOUND MIXING	SCOTT MILLAN, GREG ORLOFF, BOB BEEMER, STEVE CANTAMESSA for *Ray*
BEST SOUND EDITING	MICHAEL SILVERS, RANDY THOM for *The Incredibles*

2006 OSCARS

1 Taiwanese filmmaker Ang Lee can turn his hand to anything: martial arts movies, Westerns, comic adaptations, screen versions of classics ... He deservedly won the Oscar for Best Directing for *Brokeback Mountain* (2005), a moving drama about two gay cowboys.

2 The feisty femme at Johnny's side: Reese Witherspoon gave an inspired performance as country icon June Carter Cash in *Walk The Line* (2005) – and was rewarded with an Oscar.

BEST PICTURE	CRASH (Paul Haggis, Cathy Schulman)
BEST DIRECTOR	ANG LEE for *Brokeback Mountain*
BEST LEADING ACTRESS	REESE WITHERSPOON in *Walk the Line*
BEST LEADING ACTOR	PHILIP SEYMOUR HOFFMAN in *Capote*
BEST SUPPORTING ACTRESS	RACHEL WEISZ in *The Constant Gardener*
BEST SUPPORTING ACTOR	GEORGE CLOONEY in *Syriana*
BEST ORIGINAL SCREENPLAY	PAUL HAGGIS, ROBERT MORESCO for *Crash*
BEST ADAPTED SCREENPLAY	LARRY MCMURTRY, DIANA OSSANA for *Brokeback Mountain*
BEST FOREIGN LANGUAGE FILM	*Tsotsi* by GAVIN HOOD (South Africa)
BEST ANIMATED FEATURE	STEVE BOX, NICK PARK for *Wallace & Gromit in The Curse of the Were-Rabbit*
BEST CINEMATOGRAPHY	DION BEEBE for *Memoirs of a Geisha*
BEST ART DIRECTION	JOHN MYHRE, GRETCHEN RAU for *Memoirs of a Geisha*
BEST FILM EDITING	HUGHES WINBORNE for *Crash*
BEST MUSIC	GUSTAVO SANTAOLALLA for *Brokeback Mountain*
BEST SONG	JORDAN HOUSTON, CEDRIC COLEMAN, PAUL BEAUREGARD for *"It's Hard Out Here for a Pimp" in Hustle & Flow*
BEST MAKEUP	HOWARD BERGER, TAMI LANE for *The Chronicles of Narnia: The Lion, the Witch and the Wardrobe*
BEST COSTUME DESIGN	COLLEEN ATWOOD for *Memoirs of a Geisha*
BEST VISUAL EFFECTS	JOE LETTERI, BRIAN VAN'T HUL, CHRISTIAN RIVERS, RICHARD TAYLOR for *King Kong*
BEST SOUND MIXING	CHRISTOPHER BOYES, MICHAEL SEMANICK, MICHAEL HEDGES, HAMMOND PEEK for *King Kong*
BEST SOUND EDITING	MIKE HOPKINS, ETHAN VAN DER RYN for *King Kong*

2007 OSCARS

3 Martin Scorsese was nominated five times for Best Directing without winning the Oscar. Sixth time lucky: *The Departed* (2006) was also chosen as Best Picture that year.

4 Crowned head: Helen Mirren's brilliant portrait of the Queen was deemed worthy of an Oscar by the members of the Academy of Motion Picture Arts and Sciences, and rightly so.

BEST PICTURE THE DEPARTED (Graham King)
BEST DIRECTOR MARTIN SCORSESE for *The Departed*

BEST LEADING ACTRESS HELEN MIRREN in *The Queen*
BEST LEADING ACTOR FOREST WHITAKER in *The Last King of Scotland*
BEST SUPPORTING ACTRESS JENNIFER HUDSON in *Dreamgirls*
BEST SUPPORTING ACTOR ALAN ARKIN in *Little Miss Sunshine*

BEST ORIGINAL SCREENPLAY MICHAEL ARNDT for *Little Miss Sunshine*
BEST ADAPTED SCREENPLAY WILLIAM MONAHAN for *The Departed*
BEST FOREIGN LANGUAGE FILM *The Lives of Others* by FLORIAN HENCKEL VON DONNERSMARCK (Germany)
BEST ANIMATED FEATURE GEORGE MILLER for *Happy Feet*
BEST CINEMATOGRAPHY GUILLERMO NAVARRO for *Pans Labyrinth*
BEST ART DIRECTION EUGENIO CABALLERO, PILAR REVUELTA for *Pans Labyrinth*
BEST FILM EDITING THELMA SCHOONMAKER for *The Departed*
BEST MUSIC GUSTAVO SANTAOLALLA for *Babel*
BEST SONG MELISSA ETHERIDGE for *"I Need To Wake Up"* in *An Inconvenient Truth*

BEST MAKEUP DAVID MARTÍ, MONTSE RIBÉ for Pans Labyrinth
BEST COSTUME DESIGN MILENA CANONERO for *Marie Antoinette*
BEST VISUAL EFFECTS JOHN KNOLL, HAL T. HICKEL, CHARLES GIBSON, ALLEN HALL for *Pirates of the Caribbean: Dead Man's Chest*
BEST SOUND MIXING MICHAEL MINKLER, BOB BEEMER, WILLIE D. BURTON for *Dreamgirls*
BEST SOUND EDITING ALAN ROBERT MURRAY, BUB ASMAN for *Letters from Iwo Jima*

1

2

2008 OSCARS

1 Joel and Ethan Coen have been making movies together since the mid-1980s. 2008 was their big year: *No Country for Old Men* (2007) brought the brothers the Oscars for Best Picture, Best Directing and Best Adapted Screenplay.

2 Paul Thomas Anderson's *There Will Be Blood* (2007) was a disturbing, yet fascinating, American epic with a superb leading actor: as monstrous oil baron Daniel Plainview, Daniel Day-Lewis gave his second Oscar-winning performance.

BEST PICTURE	NO COUNTRY FOR OLD MEN (Scott Rudin, Ethan Coen, Joel Coen)
BEST DIRECTOR	ETHAN COEN, JOEL COEN for *No Country for Old Men*
BEST LEADING ACTRESS	MARION COTILLARD in *La vie en rose*
BEST LEADING ACTOR	DANIEL DAY-LEWIS in *There Will Be Blood*
BEST SUPPORTING ACTRESS	TILDA SWINTON in *Michael Clayton*
BEST SUPPORTING ACTOR	JAVIER BARDEM in *No Country for Old Men*
BEST ORIGINAL SCREENPLAY	DIABLO CODY for *Juno*
BEST ADAPTED SCREENPLAY	JOEL COEN, ETHAN COEN for *No Country for Old Men*
BEST FOREIGN LANGUAGE FILM	*The Counterfeiters* by STEFAN RUZOWITZKY (Austria)
BEST ANIMATED FEATURE	BRAD BIRD for *Ratatouille*
BEST CINEMATOGRAPHY	ROBERT ELSWIT for *There Will Be Blood*
BEST ART DIRECTION	DANTE FERRETTI, FRANCESCA LO SCHIAVO for *Sweeney Todd – The Demon Barber of Fleet Street*
BEST FILM EDITING	CHRISTOPHER ROUSE for *The Bourne Ultimatum*
BEST MUSIC	DARIO MARIANELLI for *Atonement*
BEST SONG	BRUCE SPRINGSTEEN for *"The Wrestler"* in *The Wrestler*
BEST MAKEUP	DIDIER LAVERGNE, JAN ARCHIBALD for *La vie en rose*
BEST COSTUME DESIGN	ALEXANDRA BYRNE for *Elizabeth – The Golden Age*
BEST VISUAL EFFECTS	MICHAEL L. FINK, BILL WESTENHOFER, BEN MORRIS, TREVOR WOOD for *The Golden Compass*
BEST SOUND MIXING	SCOTT MILLAN, DAVID PARKER, KIRK FRANCIS for *The Bourne Ultimatum*
BEST SOUND EDITING	KAREN M. BAKER, PER HALLBERG for *The Bourne Ultimatum*

2009 OSCARS

3 In a rather undistinguished Oscar year, Danny Boyle's Mumbai melodrama *Slumdog Millionaire* (2008) was the big winner, taking eight awards. Although a UK production, the movie added to the growing international interest in Bollywood films.

4 Award for a dead man: 28-year-old Heath Ledger was honored posthumously for his brilliant performance as The Joker in Christopher Nolan's Batman film *The Dark Knight* (2008).

BEST PICTURE	SLUMDOG MILLIONAIRE (Christian Colson)
BEST DIRECTOR	DANNY BOYLE for *Slumdog Millionaire*
BEST LEADING ACTRESS	KATE WINSLET in *The Reader*
BEST LEADING ACTOR	SEAN PENN in *Milk*
BEST SUPPORTING ACTRESS	PENÉLOPE CRUZ in *Vicky Cristina Barcelona*
BEST SUPPORTING ACTOR	HEATH LEDGER in *The Dark Knight*
BEST ORIGINAL SCREENPLAY	DUSTIN LANCE BLACK for *Milk*
BEST ADAPTED SCREENPLAY	SIMON BEAUFOY for *Slumdog Millionaire*
BEST FOREIGN LANGUAGE FILM	*Departures* by YÔJIRÔ TAKITA (Japan)
BEST ANIMATED FEATURE	ANDREW STANTON for *Wall·E*
BEST CINEMATOGRAPHY	ANTHONY DOD MANTLE for *Slumdog Millionaire*
BEST ART DIRECTION	DONALD GRAHAM BURT, VICTOR J. ZOLFO for *The Curious Case of Benjamin Button*
BEST FILM EDITING	CHRIS DICKENS for *Slumdog Millionaire*
BEST MUSIC	A.R. RAHMAN for *Slumdog Millionaire*
BEST SONG	A.R. RAHMAN (Musik), GULZAR (Texte) for *"Jai Ho"* in *Slumdog Millionaire*
BEST MAKEUP	GREG CANNOM for *The Curious Case of Benjamin Button*
BEST COSTUME DESIGN	MICHAEL O'CONNOR for *The Duchess*
BEST VISUAL EFFECTS	ERIC BARBA, STEVE PREEG, BURT DALTON, CRAIG BARRON for *The Curious Case of Benjamin Button*
BEST SOUND MIXING	IAN TAPP, RICHARD PRYKE, RESUL POOKUTTY for *Slumdog Millionaire*
BEST SOUND EDITING	RICHARD KING for *The Dark Knight*

2010 OSCARS

1 Kathryn Bigelow was not only the first woman to win an Oscar for Best Directing, which she did for her war movie *The Hurt Locker* (2009), she beat her ex-husband James Cameron as well, who had entered the running as favorite with *Avatar* (2009).

2 Jeff Bridges single-handedly made *Crazy Heart* (2009) a film to remember. His wonderful performance as a fading country music star earned the 60-year-old actor his first Oscar.

BEST PICTURE	THE HURT LOCKER (Kathryn Bigelow, Mark Boal, Nicolas Chartier, Greg Shapiro)
BEST DIRECTOR	KATHRYN BIGELOW for *The Hurt Locker*
BEST LEADING ACTRESS	SANDRA BULLOCK in *The Blind Side*
BEST LEADING ACTOR	JEFF BRIDGES in *Crazy Heart*
BEST SUPPORTING ACTRESS	MO'NIQUE in *Precious*
BEST SUPPORTING ACTOR	CHRISTOPH WALTZ in *Inglourious Basterds*
BEST ORIGINAL SCREENPLAY	MARK BOAL for *The Hurt Locker*
BEST ADAPTED SCREENPLAY	GEOFFREY FLETCHER for *Precious*
BEST FOREIGN LANGUAGE FILM	*In ihren Augen* by JUAN JOSÉ CAMPANELLA (Argentina)
BEST ANIMATED FEATURE	PETE DOCTER for *Up*
BEST CINEMATOGRAPHY	MAURO FIORE for *Avatar*
BEST ART DIRECTION	RICK CARTER, ROBERT STROMBERG, KIM SINCLAIR for *Avatar*
BEST FILM EDITING	BOB MURAWSKI, CHRIS INNIS for *The Hurt Locker*
BEST MUSIC	MICHAEL GIACCHINO for *Up*
BEST SONG	RYAN BINGHAM, T-BONE BURNETT for *"The Weary Kind"* in *Crazy Heart*
BEST MAKEUP	BARNEY BURMAN, MINDY HALL, JOEL HARLOW for *Star Trek*
BEST COSTUME DESIGN	SANDY POWELL for *Young Victoria*
BEST VISUAL EFFECTS	JOE LETTERI, STEPHEN ROSENBAUM, RICHARD BANEHAM, ANDY JONES for *Avatar*
BEST SOUND MIXING	PAUL N.J. OTTOSSON, RAY BECKETT, JUDAH GETZ for *The Hurt Locker*
BEST SOUND EDITING	PAUL N.J. OTTOSSON for *The Hurt Locker*

2011 OSCARS

3 Colin Firth's sensitive performance as the stuttering British monarch in *The King's Speech* (2010) ranks as one of the most outstanding acting achievements of the decade, and was fittingly rewarded with an Oscar.

4 Her flawless beauty sometimes masks the fact that Natalie Portman is a fantastic actress. This stood out a mile in her Oscar-winning role as prima ballerina in Darren Aronofsky's nightmarish thriller *Black Swan* (2010).

BEST PICTURE THE KING'S SPEECH (Iain Canning, Emile Sherman, Gareth Unwin)
BEST DIRECTOR TOM HOOPER for *The King's Speech*

BEST LEADING ACTRESS NATALIE PORTMAN in *Black Swan*
BEST LEADING ACTOR COLIN FIRTH in *The King's Speech*
BEST SUPPORTING ACTRESS MELISSA LEO in *The Fighter*
BEST SUPPORTING ACTOR CHRISTIAN BALE in *The Fighter*

BEST ORIGINAL SCREENPLAY DAVID SEIDLER for *The King's Speech*
BEST ADAPTED SCREENPLAY AARON SORKIN for *The Social Network*
BEST FOREIGN LANGUAGE FILM *In a Better World* by SUSANNE BIER (Denmark)
BEST ANIMATED FEATURE LEE UNKRICH for *Toy Story 3*
BEST CINEMATOGRAPHY WALLY PFISTER for *Inception*
BEST ART DIRECTION ROBERT STROMBERG, KAREN O'HARA for *Alice in Wonderland*
BEST FILM EDITING KIRK BAXTER, ANGUS WALL for *The Social Network*
BEST MUSIC TRENT REZNOR, ATTICUS ROSS for *The Social Network*
BEST SONG RANDY NEWMAN for *"We Belong Together"* in *Toy Story 3*

BEST MAKEUP RICK BAKER, DAVE ELSEY for *Wolfman*
BEST COSTUME DESIGN COLLEEN ATWOOD for *Alice in Wonderland*
BEST VISUAL EFFECTS CHRIS CORBOULD, ANDREW LOCKLEY, PETE BEBB, PAUL J. FRANKLIN for *Inception*
BEST SOUND MIXING LORA HIRSCHBERG, GARY RIZZO, ED NOVICK for *Inception*
BEST SOUND EDITING RICHARD KING for *Inception*

INDEX OF MOVIES

GENERAL INDEX

All those involved in a film's production are mentioned.
The production companies are indicated in italics, and the film genres are highlighted by dashes.
Numbers in semi-bold refer to a glossary text..

A

B

G

Qiu, Lin *380*

ABOUT THE AUTHORS

Philipp Bühler (PB), *1971, studied Political Science, History and English Studies. Film journalist; works for various daily newspapers, online media and educational media publications. Lives in Berlin.

Malte Hagener (MH), *1971, Professor of Media Studies, specializing in film history, theory and aesthetics, at the Philipps University of Marburg. Main research areas: film theory and history; media education. Author of an introduction to film theory (with Thomas Elsaesser) and "Moving Forward, Looking Back: The European Avant-garde and the Invention of Film Culture, 1919–1939," Amsterdam, 2007. Lives in Marburg.

Steffen Haubner (SH), *1965, studied Art History and Sociology. Many academic and press articles. Runs an editorial office in Hamburg. Lives in Hamburg.

Jörn Hetebrügge (JH), *1971, Studied German Literature. Author and journalist of many articles on film. Lives in Berlin.

Katja Kirste (KK), *1969, studied Literature and Film in Kiel; works for the The Independent State Board for Broadcasting (ULR) in Schleswig-Holstein and the broadcaster Premiere; project leader of a film research project; director of press and PR with Discovery Channel; lectures at the University of Kiel and Passau, and the Media College in Stuttgart; currently freelance journalist and communications consultant. Lives in Munich.

Heinz-Jürgen Köhler (HJK), *1963, Film & TV journalist; author of many academic and press articles. Lives in Hamburg.

Petra Lange-Berndt (PLB), *1973, Lecturer / Assistant Professor in History of Art department, University College London. Publications on art and science, animal studies, history and the history and theory of materiality and mediality. Writings include a book on animal art, and she has co-edited a book on the artist Sigmar Polke. Lives in London and Dresden. .

Jan-David Mentzel (JDM), *1982, studied Art History and Philosophy in Dresden and Florence. Research areas: North European art in the Early Modern Age and the development of genre painting. Currently works at collaborative research center "Transcendence and Public Spirit" at the TU Dresden. Lives in Dresden.

Mailena Rosa Mallach (MM), *1981, studied Art History and Romance Studies in Dresden and Bologna. Working visits in Berlin, Vienna and Salzburg. Works at "Overbeck-Gesellschaft" art association in Lübeck. Lives in Lübeck.

Eckhard Pabst (EP), *1965, PhD, lectures at Institute for Contemporary German Literature and Media in Kiel. Publications on film and television include a book on images of the city in two German TV series. Lives in Rendsburg, near Kiel.

Lars Penning (LP), *1962, studied Journalism, Theatre Studies and General and Comparative Literature. Freelance film journalist. Writes for, among others, "tip" and "taz." Author of books on Cameron Diaz and Julia Roberts, as well as many critical articles on film history for various publications. Lives in Berlin.

Stephan Reisner (SR), *1969, Literature and Philosophy. Many articles on film, photography, art and literature. Lives and works as a freelance writer in Berlin.

Burkhard Röwekamp (BR), *1965, PhD, media scholar and lecturer at the Institute for Media Studies at the Philipps University in Marburg. Author of books on film aesthetics, history and theory. Specialist areas: the militarization of perception in AV media; the aesthetics, theory and history of film; media pragmatics. His most recent work is on the anti-war film. Lives in Marburg.

Eric Stahl (ES), 1965 – 2009, German Studies graduate, specializing in communication science. Film journalist and cultural editor, wrote many articles in various journals.

Christoph Ziener (CZ), *1980, studied Art History and Medieval History. Main research areas: film history and North European art of the Early Modern Age. Lives in Dresden.

CREDITS

The publishers would like to thank the distributors, without whom many of these films would never have reached the big screen.

20TH CENTURY FOX, 3L FILMVERLEIH, ASCOT ELITE ENTERTAINMENT GROUP, BUENA VISTA, CAPELIGHT PICTURES, CELLULOID DREAMS, COLUMBIA, CONCORDE, CONSTANTIN FILM, FOCUS FEATURES, GHIBLI INTERNATIONAL, HIGHLIGHT FILM, KINOWELT, LES FILMS DU LOSANGE, LOOK NOW!, MADMAN ENTERTAINMENT, MITOSFILM, MOVIENET, NEUE VISIONEN, NFP DISTRIBUTION, PANDORA FILMPRODUKTION, PARAMOUNT PICTURES GERMANY, PIFFL MEDIEN, PROKINO, SENATOR FILM, SONY PICTURES, SUNFILM, TIMEBANDITS, TOBIS FILM, TOBIS STUDIO CANAL, UIP, UNIVERSAL PICTURES INTERNATIONAL, UNIVERSUM FILM, WALT DISNEY STUDIOS MOTION PICTURES, WARNER BROS., X VERLEIH.

Academy Award® and Oscar® are the registered trademark and service mark of the Academy of Motion Picture Arts and Sciences.

If, despite our concerted efforts, a distributor has been unintentionally omitted, we apologise and will amend any such errors brought to the attention of the publishers in the next edition.

ACKNOWLEDGEMENTS

As the editor of this volume, I would like to thank all those who invested so much of their time, knowledge and energy into the making of this book. My special thanks to Martin Holz and Florian Kobler from TASCHEN for their coordination work and truly amazing ability to keep track of everything. Thanks also to Birgit Eichwede and Andy Disl for their ingenious design concept that gives pride of place to the pictures, the true capital of any film book. My thanks to Thomas Dupont from ddp images and Paul Duncan for their help in accessing the original stills. Then, of course, I am hugely indebted to the authors, whose keen analyses form the backbone of this volume. I would also like to thank Jörn Hetebrügge, Christoph Ziener, Philipp Bühler and David Gaertner for their meticulous technical editing. And last but not least, Benedikt Taschen, who not only agreed to produce and publish the series, but enthusiastically followed each volume's progress from start to finish. My personal thanks to him and everyone else mentioned here.

ABOUT THIS BOOK

The 139 films selected for this book represent a decade of cinema. It goes without saying that this particular selection is based on a decision that could have turned out differently. Each film is presented by an essay, and additionally accompanied by a glossary entry devoted to one person or a cinematographic term. To ensure optimal access to all this information, an index for the films and a general index are provided at the back of the book. As in the preceding volumes, the films are dated according to the year of production, not the year of release.

IMPRINT

ENDPAPERS / PAGES 1–29, 832–833	NO COUNTRY FOR OLD MEN ETHAN & JOEL COEN / MIRAMAX FILMS / PARAMOUNT VANTAGE
PAGE 30	EDWARD SCISSORHANDS / Tim Burton / 20TH CENTURY FOX
PAGE 333–337	© LES FILMS DU LOSANGE–CACHÉ–2005
PAGES 628–633	THE BAADER MEINHOF COMPLEX © 2008 CONSTANTIN FILM, MUNICH
PAGES 698–703	© LES FILMS DU LOSANGE–LE RUBAN BLANC–2010

Hohenzollernring 53, D-50672 Köln

WWW.TASCHEN.COM

PHOTOGRAPHS	ddp images, Hamburg BRITISH FILM INSTITUTE Stills, Posters and Designs, London (pp. 50br, 55, 57b, 84b, 187, 189, 315b) THE KOBAL COLLECTION, London/New York (pp. 53, 56, 212t, 236b, 237, 267, 270tl, 270tr, 270b, 271, 272tl, 272tr, 272b, 273, 315t, 317t, 456t, 656 t, 666, 744t, 750t)
EDITORIAL COORDINATION	STILISTICO and MARTIN HOLZ, Cologne
DESIGN	SENSE/NET Art Direction, ANDY DISL und BIRGIT EICHWEDE, Cologne www.sense-net.net
TEXTS	PHILIPP BÜHLER (PB), MALTE HAGENER (MH), STEFFEN HAUBNER (SH), JÖRN HETEBRÜGGE (JH), KATJA KIRSTE (KK), HEINZ-JÜRGEN KÖHLER (HJK), PETRA LANGE-BERNDT (PLB), MAILENA ROSA MALLACH (MM), JAN-DAVID MENTZEL (JDM), ECKHARD PABST (EP), LARS PENNING (LP), STEPHAN REISNER (SR), BURKHARD RÖWEKAMP (BR), ERIC STAHL (ES), CHRISTOPH ZIENER (CZ)
TECHNICAL EDITING	JÖRN HETEBRÜGGE, PHILIPP BÜHLER and DAVID GAERTNER, Berlin CHRISTOPH ZIENER, Dresden
PRODUCTION	MARTINA CIBOROWIUS, Cologne
ENGLISH TRANSLATION	ANN DRUMMOND in association with FIRST EDITION TRANSLATIONS LTD, Cambridge, UK
EDITING	SALLY HEAVENS in association with FIRST EDITION TRANSLATIONS LTD, Cambridge, UK
TYPESETTING	THEWRITEIDEA in association with FIRST EDITION TRANSLATIONS LTD, Cambridge, UK
PROJECT MANAGEMENT	MELANIE FITZGERALD, FIRST EDITION TRANSLATIONS LTD, Cambridge, UK

PRINTED IN ITALY
ISBN 978-3-8365-0197-2